John Willis

WITH ASSOCIATE EDITOR **Barry Monush**

SCREEN WORLD

2006 FILM ANNUAL

VOLUME 57

APPLAUSE
THEATRE & CINEMA BOOKS

SCREEN WORLD
Volume 57

Copyright © 2006 by John Willis

Art Direction: Mark Lerner
Book design: Pearl Chang **Cover design**: Pearl Chang

ISBN-10: 1-55783-706-6 **ISBN-13:** 978-1-55783-706-6 **(hardcover)**
ISBN-10: 1-55783-707-4 **ISBN-13:** 978-1-55783-707-3 **(paperback)**
ISSN: 1545-9020

Applause Theatre & Cinema Books
19 West 21st Street, Suite 201
New York, NY 10010
Phone: (212) 575-9265
Fax: (212) 575-9270
Email: info@applausepub.com
Internet: www.applausepub.com

Applause books are available through your local bookstore, or you may order at www.applausepub.com or call Music Dispatch at 800-637-2852

Sales & Distribution
North America:
   Hal Leonard Corp.
   7777 West Bluemound Road
   P.O. Box 13819
   Milwaukee, WI 53213
   Phone: (414) 774-3630
   Fax: (414) 774-3259
   Email: halinfo@halleonard.com
   Internet: www.halleonard.com
Europe:
   Roundhouse Publishing Ltd.
   Millstone, Limers Lane
   Northam, North Devon EX 39 2RG
   Phone: (0) 1237-474-474
   Fax: (0) 1237-474-774
   Email: roundhouse.group@ukgateway.net

CONTENTS

EDITOR   John Willis

ASSOCIATE EDITOR   Barry Monush

ACKNOWLEDGEMENTS:

Anthology Film Archives, Bazan Entertainment, Brian Black,

Thomas Buxereau, Pearl Chang, The Cinema Guild, Columbia Pictures,

Consolidated Poster Service, Samantha Dean and Associates, DreamWorks,

Film Forum, First Look Pictures, First Run Features, Focus Features, Fox Searchlight,

IFC Films, Kino International, Leisure Time Features, Lions Gate Films, Tom Lynch,

MGM, Mike Maggiore, Magnolia Pictures, Michael Messina, Miramax Films,

Courtney Napoles, New Line Cinema/Fine Line Features, New Yorker Films,

Newmarket Films, Susan Norget, Palm Pictures, Paramount Pictures,

Paramount Classics, 7th Art Releasing, Samuel Goldwyn Films, Kallie Shimek,

Sony Classics, Sony Pictures Entertainment, Sheldon Stone, Strand Releasing,

TLA Entertainment, ThinkFilm, Twentieth Century Fox, Universal Pictures,

Walt Disney Pictures, Warner Independent Pictures, Wellspring

The Prime of Miss Jean Brodie

Death on the Nile

Lily in Love

The Secret Garden

To **MAGGIE SMITH**

whose gloriously full-bodied, heartfelt, and unique performances have made her one of the most admired ladies in her field and whose mere presence is an asset to any motion picture.

FILMS: 1958: Nowhere to Go; **1962:** Go to Blazes; **1963:** The V.I.P.s; **1964:** The Pumpkin Eater; **1965:** Young Cassidy; Othello (Academy Award nomination); **1967:** The Honey Pot; **1968:** Hot Millions; **1969:** The Prime of Miss Jean Brodie (Academy Award Winner); **1969:** Oh! What a Lovely War; **1972:** Travels with My Aunt (Academy Award nomination); **1973:** Love and Pain and the Whole Damn Thing; **1976:** Murder by Death; **1978:** Death on the Nile; California Suite (Academy Award Winner); **1981:** Clash of the Titans; Quartet; **1982:** Evil Under the Sun; The Missionary; **1983:** Better Late Than Never; **1985:** Lily in Love; A Private Function; **1986:** A Room with a View (Academy Award nomination); **1987:** The Lonely Passion of Judith Hearne; **1990:** Romeo-Juliet (voice); **1991:** Hook; **1992:** Sister Act; **1993:** The Secret Garden; Sister Act 2: Back in the Habit; **1995:** Richard III; **1996:** The First Wives Club; **1997:** Washington Square; **1999:** Tea with Mussolini; **2000:** The Last September; **2001:** Harry Potter and the Sorcerer's Stone; Gosford Park (Academy Award nomination); **2002:** Divine Secrets of the Ya-Ya Sisterhood; Harry Potter and the Chamber of Secrets; **2004:** Harry Potter and the Prisoner of Azkaban; **2005:** Ladies in Lavender; Harry Potter and the Goblet of Fire; **2006:** Keeping Mum.

SCREEN HIGHLIGHTS OF 2005

CRASH
Top: Thandie Newton, Matt Dillon
Bottom, left: Ryan Phillippe
Bottom Right: Michael Peña

BROKEBACK MOUNTAIN
Above: Jake Gyllenhaal, Heath Ledger
PHOTO COURTESY OF FOCUS FEATURES

TRANSAMERICA
Right: Kevin Zegers, Felicity Huffman
PHOTO COURTESY OF WEINSTEIN COMPANY

A HISTORY OF VIOLENCE
Top, left: Viggo Mortensen, Maria Bello

PHOTOS COURTESY OF NEW LINE CINEMA

THE CONSTANT GARDENER
Below: Ralph Fiennes

PHOTOS COURTESY OF FOCUS FEATURES

MATCH POINT
Bottom, left: Matthew Goode

PHOTOS COURTESY OF DREAMWORKS

HUSTLE & FLOW
Right: Terrence Howard
PHOTO COURTESY OF PARAMOUNT CLASSICS

SYRIANA
Below: George Clooney
PHOTO COURTESY OF WARNER BROS.

CAPOTE
Above: Philip Seymour Hoffman,
Catherine Keener
PHOTOS COURTESY OF SONY CLASSICS

MUNICH
Left: Eric Bana, Ayelet Zurer
PHOTOS COURTESY OF UNIVERSAL

PRIDE & PREJUDICE
Right: Keira Knightley, Matthew Macfadyen
PHOTO COURTESY OF FOCUS FEATURES

**THE CHRONICLES OF NARNIA:
THE LION, THE WITCH
AND THE WARDROBE**
Below: Tilda Swinton, Skandar Keynes
PHOTO COURTESY OF WALT DISNEY PICTURES

WAR OF THE WORLDS
Top, right: Tom Cruise, Dakota Fanning
PHOTO COURTESY OF PARAMOUNT

MEMOIRS OF A GEISHA
Below: Zhang Ziyi
PHOTO COURTESY OF COLUMBIA

MARCH OF THE PENGUINS
PHOTO COURTESY OF WARNER INDEPENDENT

FLIGHTPLAN
Top, left: Jodie Foster
PHOTO COURTESY OF TOUCHSTONE

MYSTERIOUS SKIN
Middle, left: Joseph Gordon-Levitt, Jeff Licon, Elisabeth Shue
PHOTO COURTESY OF TLA RELEASING

BATMAN BEGINS
Above: Christian Bale, Katie Holmes
PHOTO COURTESY OF WARNER BROS.

TIM BURTON'S CORPSE BRIDE
Bottom, left: Victor Van Dort, Corpse Bride
PHOTO COURTESY OF WARNER BROS.

WALK THE LINE
Above: Joaquin Phoenix (left)
PHOTO COURTESY OF 20TH CENTURY FOX

JUNEBUG
Left: Benjamin McKenzie
PHOTO COURTESY OF SONY CLASSICS

**HARRY POTTER AND THE
GOBLET OF FIRE**

Right: Stanislav Ianevski, Emma Watson

PHOTO COURTESY OF WARNER BROS.

KING KONG

Below: T. Rex, King Kong, Naomi Watts

PHOTO COURTESY OF UNIVERSAL

CHARLIE AND THE CHOCOLATE FACTORY
Above: (left to right) Freddie Highmore, Julia Winter, David Kelly, Franziska Troegner, James Fox, AnnaSophia Robb, Missi Pyle, Johnny Depp, Adam Godley, Jordan Fry
PHOTO COURTESY OF WARNER BROS.

CHICKEN LITTLE
Left: Chicken Little
PHOTO COURTESY OF WALT DISNEY PICTURES

RENT
Above: (left to right) Jesse L. Martin, Adam
Pascal, Anthony Rapp, Wilson Jermaine Heredia,
Rosario Dawson, Idina Menzel, Tracie Thoms
PHOTO COURTESY OF COLUMBIA

MRS. HENDERSON PRESENTS
Right: Kelly Reilly
PHOTO COURTESY OF WEINSTEIN COMPANY

THE SQUID AND THE WHALE
Left: Jesse Eisenberg, Owen Kline
PHOTO COURTESY OF SAMUEL GOLDWYN

SHOPGIRL
Below: Claire Danes, Steve Martin
PHOTO COURTESY OF TOUCHSTONE

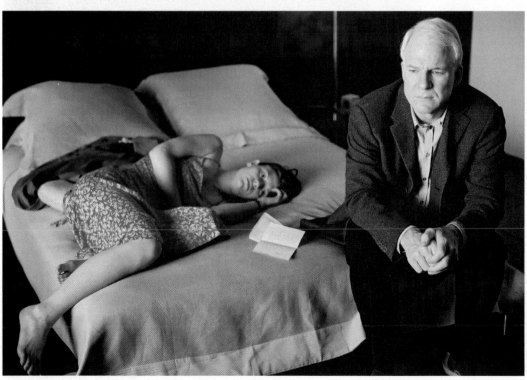

RED EYE
Above: Rachel McAdams, Cillian Murphy
PHOTO COURTESY OF DREAMWORKS

**WALLACE & GROMIT:
THE CURSE OF THE WERE-RABBIT**
Bottom: Gromit
PHOTO COURTESY OF DREAMWORKS

DOMESTIC FILMS
2005 RELEASES

RACING STRIPES

(WARNER BROS.) Producers, Andrew A. Kosove, Broderick Johnson, Ed McDonnell, Lloyd Phillips; Executive Producer, Steven P. Wegner; Director, Frederik Du Chau; Screenplay, David F. Schmidt; Story, David F. Schmidt, Steven P. Wegner, Kirk DeMicco, Frederik Du Chau; Photography, David Eggby; Designer, Wolf Kroeger; Costumes, Jo Katsaras; Music, Mark Isham; Music Supervisor, Deva Anderson; Editor, Tom Finan; Co-Producers, Philip A. Patterson, Kira Davis, Kirk DeMicco; Visual Effects Supervisors, Kent Houston, Dion Hatch, Eric Rosenfeld; Animation Supervisor, Alexander Williams; Animal Training Supervisor, Karl Lewis Miller; Casting, Amanda Mackey Johnson, Cathy Sandrich Gelfond; an Alcon Entertainment production; Dolby; Technicolor; Rated PG; 101 minutes; Release date: January 14, 2005

Buzz, Scuzz

Cast

Nolan Walsh **Bruce Greenwood**
Channing Walsh **Hayden Panettiere**
Woodzie **M. Emmet Walsh**
Clara Dalrymple **Wendie Malick**

Voice Cast

Stripes **Frankie Muniz**
Sandy **Mandy Moore**
Clydesdale **Michael Clarke Duncan**
Reggie **Jeff Foxworthy**
Trenton's Pride **Joshua Jackson**
Lightning **Snoop Dogg**
Goose **Joe Pantoliano**
Ruffshodd **Michael Rosenbaum**
Buzz **Steve Harvey**
Scuzz **David Spade**
Sir Trenton **Fred Dalton Thompson**
Tucker **Dustin Hoffman**
Franny **Whoopi Goldberg**
Young Stripes **Jansen Panettiere**
Young Ruffshodd **Frankie Manriquez**
Young Pride **Kyle Alcazar**

and Caspar Poyck (Mailan), Gary Bullock (John Cooper), Thandi Puren,

Hayden Panettiere, Stripes, Bruce Greenwood

Morne Visser, Dawn Matthews, Matt Stern (Reporters), John Lesley (Paddock Boss), Graeme Hawkins (Track Announcer), Tarryn Downes (Anthem Singer), David Busch, Nicholas Guest, Archie Hahn, Jess Harnell, Phil Proctor, Gail Thomas (Additional Voices)

A zebra, found and raised by a farmer and his daughter, develops a knack for racing, encouraging the family to train him for the Kentucky Open.

Franny, Tucker

Wendie Malick PHOTOS COURTESY OF WARNER BROS.

COACH CARTER

(PARAMOUNT) Producers, Brian Robbins, Mike Tollin, David Gale; Executive Producers, Van Toffler, Thomas Carter, Sharla Sumpter, Caitlin Scanlon; Director, Thomas Carter; Screenplay, Mark Schwahn, John Gatins; Inspired by the life of Ken Carter; Photography, Sharone Meir; Designer, Carlos Barbosa; Costumes, Debrae Little; Co-Producer, Nan Morales; Music, Trevor Rabin; Music Supervisor, Jennifer Hawks; Choreographer, Dave Scott; Editor, Peter Berger; Casting, Sarah Halley Finn, Randi Hiller; an MTV Films, Tollin/Robbins production; Dolby; Deluxe color; Rated PG-13; 137 minutes; Release date: January 14, 2005

Rob Brown, Ashanti

Channing Tatum, Rob Brown, Antwon Tanner

Cast

Coach Ken Carter **Samuel L. Jackson**
Kenyon Stone **Rob Brown**
Damien Carter **Robert Ri'chard**
Timo Cruz **Rick Gonzalez**
Junior Battle **Nana Gbewonyo**
Worm **Antwon Tanner**
Jason Lyle **Channing Tatum**
Kyra **Ashanti**
Maddux **Texas Battle**
Principal Garrison **Denise Dowse**
Tonya **Debbi Morgan**
Coach White **Mel Winkler**
Renny **Vincent Laresca**
Ty Crane **Sidney Faison**
Mrs. Battle **Octavia Spencer**
Worm's Mother **Sonya Eddy**
Kenyon's Mother **Gwen McGee**
Maddux's Mother **Ausanta**
Gruff Uncle **Adam Clark**
Guardian **Paul Rae**
Team Parent **Eugene Lee**
Dominique **Adrienne Eliza Bailon**
Peyton **Dana Davis**
Himself **Bob Costas**
St. Francis Coach **Ray Baker**
Susan **Lacey Beeman**
Susan's Dad **Marc McClure**
Amber **Kara Houston**

and Carl Gilliard (Store Clerk), Taryn Myers (Berkeley Girl), Carolina Garcia (Bella), Jenny Gago (President Martinez), Ben Weber (Mr. Gesek), Sylvia Kelegian (Office Assistant), Marcus Woodswelch (Teacher), Derrelle "Shortymack" Owens (Pinole Guy), Quiana Potts, Nina N. Onwubere (Cute Market Girls), Terrell Byrd (Shay), Tara Jett (Library Girl), Richard Vasquez (Deejay), Floyd Leivne (Taxi Driver), Rob Fukuzaki,

Rob Brown, Rick Gonzalez

Samuel L. Jackson

Channing Tatum, Antwon Tanner, Robert Ri'chard, Texas Battle, Rick Gonzalez, Rob Brown, Nana Gbewonyo

Gregory Storm (Reporters), Tracey Costello, Mark Jones, Deena Dill (Field Reporters), Greg McMullin (Bay Hill Coach), Andy Umberger (Bay Hill Athletic Director), Leonard L. Thomas (Pre-Season Game Referee), Darin Rossi (Bay Hill Referee), Deon Lewis (Hercules Game Referee), David Medrano (Shooter), Michael Jesse James (Passenger), Mario Garcia, Danny Kanamori, Mark McClanahan, Brandon Jerrard Pratt, Chris Young (Additional Richmond Players), Clyde Goins, Dustin Fuller (Team Managers), Maya Dennis, Felise Johnson, Rashaé Minor, Marae Onsgard, Twani Sua, Miranda White (Richmond Cheerleaders), Cindy Chiu, Jessica Church, Jessica Herrera, Nicole Oliveros, Kasie Sage, Nicole Volmer (Bay Hill Cheerleaders), Deanna Watkins, Lizzie Lander, Diana Shepard, Chauntal Lewis, Michelle Boehle, Anna Zielinski (St. Francis Cheerleaders), Tuere McCall, Allison Kyler, Kristi Crader, Diona Robinson, Nicole Neal, Kerry Wee, Brandon Phillips, Britta'ny Dixon, Roland Tabor, Robert Hoffman, Isaiah Vest, Marty Dew (Dancers)

Richmond High's new basketball coach, Ken Carter, rocks the boat by insisting that his team members give as much attention to their grades as to their capabilities on the court.

Nana Gbewonyo PHOTOS COURTESY OF PARAMOUNT

ASSAULT ON PRECINCT 13

(ROGUE) Producers, Pascal Caucheteux, Stephane Sperry, Jeffrey Silver; Executive Producers, Don Carmody, Sebastien Kurt Lemercier, Joseph Kaufman; Director, Jean-Francois Richet; Screenplay, James DeMonaco; Based on the film written by John Carpenter; Photography, Robert Gantz; Designer, Paul Denham Austerberry; Costumes, Vicki Graef, Georgina Yarhi; Music, Graeme Revell; Music Supervisor, John Houlihan; Visual Effects Supervisor, Dennis Berardi; Casting, Billy Hopkins, Suzanne Smith, Kerry Barden; a Why Not, Liaison Films, Biscayne Pictures production; Dolby; Super 35 Widescreen; Deluxe color; Rated R; 109 minutes; Release date: January 19, 2005

Jeffrey "Ja Rule" Atkins, Maria Bello

Cast

Jake Roenick	**Ethan Hawke**
Marlon Bishop	**Laurence Fishburne**
Beck	**John Legiuzamo**
Alex Sabian	**Maria Bello**
Smiley	**Jeffrey "Ja Rule" Atkins**
Iris Ferry	**Drea de Matteo**
Capra	**Matt Craven**
Jasper O'Shea	**Brian Dennehy**
Marcus Duvall	**Gabriel Byrne**
Anna	**Aisha Hinds**
Gil	**Dorian Harewood**
Lt. Ted Holloway	**Peter Bryant**
Ray Ray	**Fulvio Cecere**
Rosen	**Kim Coates**
Tony	**Hugh Dillon**
Danny Barbero	**Tig Fong**

and Jasmin Geljo (Marko), Currie Graham (Kahane), Jessica Greco (Coral), Robert Hayley (Sniper James), Ray Kahnert (Priest), Philip Marshall (Hagen), Arnold Pinnock (Carlyle), Ed Queffelec (Bronco Gunman), Sasha Roiz (Jason Elias), Alan Vrkljan (Sniper Sebastien), Titus Welliver (Milos), Courtney Cunningham, Roman Podhora (Cops), Darren Frost, Gilson Lubin (Movers), Jeff Ironi, Brian King (Firemen), J. C. Kenny (Reporter #1), Leford Lawes (P21 Cop #1), Dave Tommasini (Pilot), Melissa Thompson (Lawyer)

Laurence Fishburne, Drea de Matteo

On its last night of operation, the police officers of Precinct 13 agree to hold a bus load of prisoners including gangster Marlon Bishop, whose presence causes an undercover cop and his team to invade the station to kill Bishop and anyone who tries to stop them. Remake of the 1976 film that starred Austin Stoker and Darwin Joston.

Jeffrey "Ja Rule" Atkins, Maria Bello, Ethan Hawke

Gabriel Byrne PHOTOS COURTESY OF FOCUS FEATURES

ARE WE THERE YET?

(COLUMBIA) Producers, Ice Cube, Matt Alvarez, Dan Kolsrud; Executive Producers, Todd Garner, Derek Dauchy; Director, Brian Levant; Screenplay, Steven Gary Banks, Claudia Grazioso, J. David Stern, David N. Weiss; Story, Steven Gary Banks, Claudia Grazioso; Photography, Thomas Ackerman; Designer, Stephen Lineweaver; Costumes, Gersha Phillips; Music, David Newman; Editor, Lawrence Jordan; Casting, Juel Bestrop, Jeanne McCarthy; a Revolution Studios presentation of a Cube Vision production; Dolby; Deluxe color; Rated PG; 95 minutes; Release date: January 21, 2005

Cast

Nick Persons **Ice Cube**
Suzanne Kingston **Nia Long**
Lindsey Kingston **Aleisha Allen**
Kevin Kingston **Philip Daniel Bolden**
Marty **Jay Mohr**
Al **M. C. Gainey**
Voice of Satchel Paige **Tracy Morgan**
Carl **Henry Simmons**
Car Dealer **Ray Galletti**
Nick's Pal on the Street **Viv Leacock**
Shoplifters **Casey Dubois, JB McEown**
Basketball Players **Kenyan Lewis, Daniel Cudmore, Timothy Paul Perez, Adrian Holmes**
Lady Airport Cop **Nancy Robertson**
Airport Security Guard **Tony Ali, Deejay Jackson**
Airport Screener **Reynard Howard**
Train Conductor **Alistair Abell**

and Ann Warn Pegg (Woman in Bathroom), Frank C. Turner (Amish Man), Derek Lowe (Car Mechanic), Sean Millington (Frank Kingston), Shiraine Haas (Frank's Wife), David Mackay (Drugstore Clerk), Esme Lambert (Grandmother at Kid's Party), Jerry Hardin (Pharmacist/Clown), Curtis Butchart (Hungry Kid at Party), C. Ernst Harth (Ernst), Denalda Williams (Suzanne's Co-Worker), Robert Manitopyes (Cop at Party), Nichelle Nichols (Miss Mable)

In order to impress an attractive divorcee, Nick Persons offers to drive her two children from Portland to Vancouver to visit their mom.

Dakota Fanning, Robert De Niro PHOTO COURTESY OF 20TH CENTURY FOX

HIDE AND SEEK

(20TH CENTURY FOX) Producer, Barry Josephson; Executive Producer, Joe Caracciolo, Jr.; Director, John Polson; Screenplay, Ari Schlossberg; Photography, Dariusz Wolski; Designer, Steven Jordan; Costumes, Aude Bronson-Howard; Music, John Ottman; Editor, Jeffrey Ford; Co-Producers, Dana Robin, John Rogers; Casting, Amanda Mackey Johnson, Cathy Sandrich Gelfond; a Josephson Entertainment production; Dolby; Super 35 Widescreen; Deluxe color; Rated PG-13; 101 minutes; Release date: January 28, 2005

Cast

David Callaway **Robert De Niro**
Emily Callaway **Dakota Fanning**
Katherine **Famke Janssen**
Elizabeth **Elisabeth Shue**
Alison Callaway **Amy Irving**
Sheriff Hafferty **Dylan Baker**
Laura **Melisa Leo**
Steven **Robert John Burke**
Amy **Molly Grant Kallins**
Mr. Haskins **David Chandler**
Stephanie **Amber McDonald**
Little Boy **Josh Flitter**
Waitress **Alicia Harding**

After his wife commits suicide, a psychologist and his daughter move to the country where the traumatized little girl begins talking to an imaginary friend.

Philip Daniel Bolden, Nia Long, Ice Cube, Aleisha Allen PHOTO COURTESY OF COLUMBIA

BOOGEYMAN

(SCREEN GEMS) Producers, Sam Raimi, Rob Tapert; Executive Producers, Joe Drake, Nathan Kahane, Carsten Lorenz, Steve Hein, Gary Bryman; Director, Stephen Kay; Screenplay, Eric Kripke, Juliet Snowden, Stiles White; Story, Eric Kripke; Photography, Bobby Bukowski; Designer, Robert Gillies; Costumes, Jane Holland; Music, Joseph Loduca; Editor, John Axelrad; Casting, Lynn Kressel; a Ghost House Pictures production, presented in association with Senator International; Dolby; Color; Rated PG-13; 86 minutes; Release date: February 4, 2005

Skye McCole Bartusiak, Barry Watson PHOTO COURTESY OF SCREEN GEMS

Cast

Tim **Barry Watson**
Kate Houghton **Emily Deschanel**
Franny Roberts **Skye McCole Bartusiak**
Jessica **Tory Mussett**
Boogeyman **Andrew Glover**
Tim's Mother **Lucy Lawless**
Tim's Father **Charles Mesure**
Uncle Mike **Philip Gordon**
Young Tim **Aaron Murphy**
Pam **Jennifer Rucker**

and Scott Wills (Co-Worker), Michael Saccente (Jessica's Dad), Louise Wallace (Jessica's Mom), Brenda Simmons (Jessica's Grandma), Josie Tweed (Jessica's Sister), Ian Campbell (Franny's Father), Robyn Malcolm (Dr. Matheson), Olivia Tennet (Terrified Girl), Edward Campbell (Priest), Andrew Eggleton (Jessica's Brother-in-Law)

Fifteen years after Tim believes he saw his father dragged into oblivion by an evil creature, he decides to spend a night at his former home in an effort to confront his fears.

THE WEDDING DATE

(UNIVERSAL) Producers, Nathalie Marciano, Michelle Chydzik Sowa, Jessica Bendinger, Paul Brooks; Executive Producers, Norm Waitt, Scott Niemeyer, Steven Robbins, Jim Reeve; Director, Clare Kilner; Screenplay, Dana Fox; Based on the book *Asking for Trouble* by Elizabeth Young; Photography, Oliver Curtis; Designer, Tom Burton; Costumes, Louise Page; Music, Blake Neely; Music Supervisor, Randy Gerston; Editor, Mary Finaly; Co-Producer, Jeff Levine; Line Producer, Mairi Bett; Casting, Carl Proctor; a Gold Circle Films presentation of a 26 Films production in association with Visionview Ltd.; Dolby; Color; Rated PG-13; 88 minutes; Release date: February 4, 2005

Cast

Kat Ellis **Debra Messing**
Nick Mercer **Dermot Mulroney**
Amy **Amy Adams**
Edward Fletcher-Wooten **Jack Davenport**
TJ **Sarah Parish**
Jeffrey **Jeremy Sheffield**
Victor Ellis **Peter Egan**
Bunny **Holland Taylor**
Woody **Jolyon James**

and G. Gerod Harris (Bike Messenger), Martin Barrett (Teenager), Jay Simon (Flight Attendant), Danielle Lewis (Pretty Woman), Ivana Horvat (Smitten Girl), Linda Dobell (Sonja), Helen Lindsay (Aunt Bea), Lucy Bermingham (Posh American Woman), John Sackville (Phil), George Asprey (Pat), Alan Wills, Nick Miers (Limo Drivers), David Nobbs (Rolls Royce Driver), Steve Hall, Dave Brown, Colin Staplehurst, Peter Guihen, Michael McCarthy (Taxi Drivers), Anthony Blackman (Wedding Car Starter), Adrian Walker (Stag), Ivan Johnson (Organist), Anna Sands, Jens La Barre, Brian Lesseat, Alice Brickwood (Strippers)

In order to make her ex-boyfriend jealous, Kat Ellis hires a male escort to accompany her to her half-sister's London wedding and pretend that the two are actually a couple.

Dermot Mulroney, Debra Messing PHOTO COURTESY OF UNIVERSAL

HITCH

(COLUMBIA) formerly *The Last First Kiss*; Producers, James Lassiter, Will Smith, Teddy Zee; Executive Producers, Michael Tadross, Wink Mordaunt; Director, Andy Tennant; Screenplay, Kevin Bisch; Photography, Andrew Dunn; Designer, Jane Musky; Costumes, Marlene Stewart; Music, George Fenton; Editors, Troy Takaki, Tracey Wadmore-Smith; Casting, Kathleen Chopin; an Overbrook Entertainment production; Dolby; Panavision; Deluxe color; 117 minutes; Release date: February 11, 2005

Will Smith, Kevin James

Cast

Alex "Hitch" Hitchens **Will Smith**
Sara Melas **Eva Mendes**
Albert Brennaman **Kevin James**
Allegra Cole **Amber Valletta**
Casey **Julie Ann Emery**
Cressida **Robinne Lee**
Geoff **Nathan Lee Graham**
Max Trundle **Adam Arkin**
Ben **Michael Rappaport**
Vance **Jeffrey Donovan**
Mandy **Paula Patton**
Mr. O'Brien **Philip Bosco**
Neil **Kevin Sussman**
Mika **Navia Nguyen**

and Matt Malloy (Pete), Maria Thayer (Lisa), Ato Essandoh (Tanis), Nayokah Afflack (Stephanie), Jack Hartnett (Tom Reda), David Wike (Chip), Frederick B. Owens (Larry), Jenna Stem (Louise), Adam LeFevre (Speed Dating Host), Joe Lo Truglio (Personable Guy), Ptolemy Slocum (Ron), Kahan James (Guy Nearby), Matt Servitto (Eddie), Amy Hohn (Marla), Mimi Rogers Weddell (Grandma Wellington), Maulik Pancholy (Raoul), Caprice Benedetti (Gorgeous Wife), Tony Travis (Nebishy Husband), Mercedes Renard (Maria), Austin Lysy (Magnus), Jose Llana (Ross), Niels Koizumi (Sous Chef), Chris Santos (Cooking Teacher), Ryan Cross (Charles Wellington), Tobias Truvillion (Kurt), Jeffrey Carlson (Egon), Henry Binje (Zak), Rain Phoenix (Kate), Remy Selma (Newsguy),

Amber Valletta, Kevin James

Beau Sia (Duane Reade Clerk), Mika Nishida (Waxer), Trevor Oswalt (Messenger), Darrell Foster (Bartender)

While trying to help meek Albert Brennaman land the girl of his dreams, New York City "date doctor" and professional bachelor Alex Hitchens finds himself falling head over heels in love with reporter Sara Melas.

Eva Mendes, Will Smith

Will Smith, Eva Mendes PHOTOS COURTESY OF COLUMBIA PICTURES

Gerard Damiano

INSIDE DEEP THROAT

(UNIVERSAL) Producers, Brian Grazer, Fenton Bailey, Randy Barbato; Executive Producer, Kim Roth; Co-Producer, Mona Card; Directors/Screenplay, Fenton Bailey, Randy Barbato; Photography, David Kempner, Teodoro Maniaci; Music, David Steinberg; Editors, William Grayburn, Jeremy Simmons; Associate Producers, Ashley York, Sarah Brown; Narrator, Dennis Hopper; an Imagine Entertainment presentation in association with HBO Documentary Films of a Brian Grazer production in association with World of Wonder; Dolby; CFI Color; Rated R; 92 minutes; Release date: February 11, 2005. Documentary about the most notorious and influential of all X-rated films of the seventies, *Deep Throat*, and the controversy it invoked.

With

Peter Bart, Carl Bernstein, Tony Bill, Ralph Blumenthal, Barbara Boreman, Helen Gurley Brown, Susan Brownmiller, Lenny Camp, Patsy Carroll, Dick Cavett, Wes Craven, Gerard Damiano, Alan Dershowitz, Larry Flynt, Al Goldstein, John Goreman, Hugh Hefner, Xaviera Hollander, Erica Jong, Herb Krassner, Charles Keating, Bruce Kramer, Bill Maher, Norman Mailer, Peter Manouse, Lindsay Marchiano, Camille Paglia, Larry Parrish, William Purcell, Harry Reems, Ray Shipley, Arthur Sommer, Terry Sommer, Georgina Spelvin, Andrea True, Gore Vidal, Ron Wertheim, Dr. Ruth Westheimer, Linda Williams, David Winters, Erica Yong

Roo, Lumpy PHOTO COURTESY OF WALT DISNEY PICTURES

POOH'S HEFFALUMP MOVIE

(WALT DISNEY PICTURES) Producer, Jessica Koplos-Miller; Director, Frank Nissen; Screenplay, Brian Hohlfeld, Evan Spilotopoulos; Based on characters created by A. A. Milne; Songs, Carly Simon; Music, Joely McNeely; Voice Casting/Dialogue Director, Jamie Thomason; Art Director, Tony Pulham; Supervising Film Editor, Nancy Frazen; Animation Director, Don Mackinnon; Associate Producer, Clay Renfroe; Produced by DisneyToon Studios; Dolby; Color; Rated G; 67 minutes; Release date: February 11, 2005

Voice Cast
Winnie the Pooh/Tigger **Jim Cummings**
Piglet **John Fiedler**
Roo **Nikita Hopkins**
Kanga **Kath Soucie**
Rabbit **Ken Sansom**
Eeyore **Peter Cullen**
Mama Heffalump **Brenda Blethyn**
Lumpy **Kyle Stanger**

As the rest of the residents of the Hundred Acre Wood set out to trap the dreaded Heffalump, little Roo ventures on his own and discovers this illusive creature is not quite as harmful as perceived.

THE WILD PARROTS OF TELEGRAPH HILL

(SHADOW DISTRIBUTION) Producer/Director/Photography/Editor, Judy Irving; Music, Chris Michie; a Pelican Media production; Dolby; Color; 16mm; Rated G; 83 minutes; Release date: February 11, 2005. Documentary about San Francisco resident Mark Bittner, who decided to study and feed the wild parrots that converged around his home in his North Beach neighborhood.

Mark Bittner and the Parrots PHOTO COURTESY OF SHADOW DISTRIBUTION

CONSTANTINE

(WARNER BROS.) Producers, Lauren Shuler Donner, Benjamin Melniker, Michael E. Uslan, Erwin Stoff, Lorenzo di Bonaventura, Akiva Goldsman; Executive Producers, Gilbert Adler, Michael Aguilar; Director, Francis Lawrence; Screenplay, Kevin Brodbin, Frank Cappello; Story, Kevin Brodbin; Based on characters from the DC Comics/Vertigo *Hellblazer* graphic novels; Photography, Philippe Rousselot; Designer, Naomi Shohan; Costumes, Louise Frogley; Music, Brian Tyler, Klaus Badelt; Editor, Wayne Wahrman; Visual Effects Supervisor, Michael Fink; Stunts, R. A. Rondell; Casting, Denise Chamian; a Village Roadshow presentation of Donners' Co., Batfilm Prods.,Weed Road Pictures, 3 Arts Entertainment production; Dolby; Super 35 Widescreen; Technicolor; Rated R; 120 minutes; Release date: February 18, 2005

Keanu Reeves, Rachel Weisz

Cast

John Constantine **Keanu Reeves**
Angela Dodson/Isabel Dodson **Rachel Weisz**
Chas **Shia LaBeouf**
Midnite **Djimon Hounsou**
Beeman **Max Baker**
Father Hennessy **Pruitt Taylor Vince**
Balthazar **Gavin Rossdale**
Gabriel **Tilda Swinton**
Satan **Peter Stormare**

and Jesse Ramirez, Jose Molina (Scavengers), Jose Zuniga (Det. Weiss), Francis Guinan (Father Garret), Larry Cedar (Vermin Man), April Grace (Dr. Leslie Archer), Suzanne Whang (Mother), Jhoanna Trias (Possessed Girl), Alice Lo (Old Woman), Nicholas Downs (Church Attendant), Tanoai Reed (Midnite Bouncer), Quinn Buniel (10-Year-Old Constantine), Ann Ryerson (Old Woman on Bus), Stephanie Fabian (Molly's Server), Connor Dylan Wryn (Teenage Constantine), Laz Alonso (Morgue Security Guard), Jeremy Ray Valdez (Liquor Store Clerk Nico), Barbara Pilavin (Old Woman on Bus/Demon), C. W. Pryun (Korean Man), Sharon Omi, Abe Pagtama (Tenants), Edward J. Rosen (Liquor Store Clerk), John Gipson (Smoking Man), Roberto Kawata (Police Officer), Kevin Alejandro (Border Patrol), Doug Tochioka (Bowler)

An exorcist returned from the dead seeks redemption by fighting the demons who have invaded Earth's mortal sphere.

Keanu Reeves, Djimon Hounsou, Shia LaBeouf PHOTOS COURTESY OF WARNER BROS.

BECAUSE OF WINN-DIXIE

(20TH CENTURY FOX) Producers, Trevor Albert, Joan Singleton; Executive Producer, Ralph Singleton; Director, Wayne Wang; Screenplay, Joan Singleton; Based on the novel by Kate DiCamillo; Photography, Karl Walter Lindenlaub; Designer, Donald Graham Burt; Costumes, Hope Hanafin; Co-Producer, Becki Cross Trujillo; Music, Rachel Portman; Music Supervisor, Deva Anderson; Head Animal Trainer, Mark Forbes; Casting, Todd Thaler; a Walden Media presentation; Dolby; Deluxe color; Rated PG; 106 minutes; Release date: February 18, 2005

Cast

India Opal Buloni **AnnaSophia Robb**
Preacher **Jeff Daniels**
Gloria Dump **Cicely Tyson**
Otis **Dave Matthews**
Miss Franny **Eva Marie Saint**
Amanda Wilkinson **Courtney Jines**
Dunlap Dewberry **Nick Price**
Stevie Dewberry **Luke Benward**
Sweetie Pie Thomas **Elle Fanning**
Mrs. Dewberry **Marca Price**
Mrs. Detweller **Lenore Banks**
Mr. Alfred **B. J. Hopper**
Store Manager **John McConnell**
Policeman **Harland Williams**

Winn-Dixie, Elle Fanning, AnnaSophia Robb PHOTO COURTESY OF 20TH CENTURY FOX

and William Arthur Pitts, Enid Trotiner, Charles A. Daigle, Clarice H. Gauthereaux, Guy G. Gauthereaux (Churchgoers), Julia Lashae, Darrell Jupiter (SPCA Officers), Lara Grice (Opal's Mom), Becca Lish (Voice of Gertrude the Parrot)

A lonely little girl befriends an orphaned dog who helps bring together Opal and her distant dad, as well as the other inhabitants of a small Florida town.

Christina Ricci, Jesse Eisenberg PHOTO COURTESY OF DIMENSION/MIRAMAX

CURSED

(DIMENSION) Producers, Kevin Williamson, Marianne Maddalena; Executive Producers, Bob Weinstein, Harvey Weinstein, Andrew Rona, Brad Weston; Director, Wes Craven; Screenplay, Kevin Williamson; Photography, Robert McLachlan; Designer, Bruce Alan Miller; Costumes, Alix Fridberg; Music, Marco Beltrami; Music Supervisor, Ed Gerrard; Editor, Patrick Lussier; Special Makeup Effects, Rick Baker; Visual Effects Supervisor, Richard H. Hoover; Special Effects Supervisor, Ron Bolankowski; Co-Producers, Jennifer Breslow, Dan Arredondo, Julie Plec; Co-Executive Producer, Stuart Besser; Stunts, Charlie Croughwell; Casting, Lisa Beach, Sarah Katzman; an Outerbanks Entertainment production in association with Craven/Maddalena Films; Dolby; Clairmont-Scope; Deluxe color; Rated PG-13; 97 minutes; Release date: February 25, 2005

Cast

Ellie **Christina Ricci**
Jake **Joshua Jackson**
Jimmy **Jesse Eisenberg**
Joannie **Judy Greer**
Himself **Scott Baio**
Bo **Milo Ventimiglia**
Brooke **Kristina Anapau**
Zela **Portia de Rossi**
Becky **Shannon Elizabeth**

and Mya (Jenny), Daniel Mora (Jose), Jonny Acker (Earl), Eric Ladin (Louie), Derek Mears (Werewolf), Nick Offerman (Officer), Michael Rosenbaum (Kyle), Ken Rudolph (Newscaster), Michelle Krusiec (Nosebleed Co-Worker), Shashawnee Hall (Wrestling Coach), Craig Kilborn, Lance Bass (Themselves), Emily O'Deile (Co-Worker), Egan Friedlander (Bouncer), Randolph Le Roi (Randy), Brian Boone (Frantic Bouncer), Gary Dubin, Chris Johnson, Wilmer Calderon (Police Officers), Brett Rickaby (Animal Control Officer), Bowling for Soup (Carnival Band)

Ellie and her brother Jake find themselves possessing beastly instincts after being bitten by a werewolf.

DIARY OF A MAD BLACK WOMAN

(LIONS GATE) Producer, Reuben Cannon; Executive Producers, Michael Paseornek, John Dellaverson, Robert L. Johnson; Co-Producer, Mike Upton; Director, Darren Grant; Screenplay, Tyler Perry, based on his play; Photography, David Claessen; Designer, Ina Mayhew; Costumes, Keith Lewis; Music, Elvin D. Ross; Editor, Terilyn A. Shropshire; Casting, Reuben Cannon, Kim Williams; a Diary of a Woman, Inc. presentation in association with BET Pictures; Dolby; Technicolor; Rated PG-13; 116 minutes; Release date: February 25, 2005

Kimberly Elise, Tyler Perry

Tyler Perry, Kimberly Elise

Cast

Helen McCarter **Kimberly Elise**
Charles McCarter **Steve Harris**
Orlando **Shemar Moore**
Debrah **Tamara Taylor**
Brenda **Lisa Marcos**
Tiffany **Tiffany Evans**
Myrtle **Cicely Tyson**
Brian/Madea/Uncle Joe **Tyler Perry**
Reverend Carter **Terrell Carter**
Mildred **Carol Mitchell-Leon**
BJ **Avery Knight**
Christina **Vickie Eng**
Jamison **Gary Sturgis**
Chandra **Chandre Currelley-Young**
Cora **Tamela Mann**

and Bart Hansard (Guard), Sho Dixon (Child), Ric Reitz (D.A.), Lauren Leah Mitchell (Doctor), Mike Pniewski (Foreman), Wilbur Fitzgerald, L. Warren Young (Judge), Mablean Ephriam (Judge Ephriam), Tony Vaughn (Juror), E. Roger Mitchell (Kalvin), Cedric Pendleton (Max), Richard Reed (Bailiff), Joe Washington (Reporter), Kate Donadio (Secretary), Crystal Porter (Woman), Ryan Gentles (Bartender), Ronnie Garrett, Marcus Williams, Earl Fleming (Band Members), Christian Keyes (Man Proposing)

Cicely Tyson, Kimberly Elise

Tossed out by her philandering husband after 18 years of marriage, Helen McCarter moves in with her grandmother and tries to start life anew.

Steve Harris, Lisa Marcos PHOTOS COURTESY OF LIONS GATE

THE PACIFIER

(WALT DISNEY PICTURES) Producers, Roger Birnbaum, Gary Barber, Jonathan Glickman; Executive Producers, Adam Shankman, Jennifer Gibgot, Derek Evans, Garrett Grant, George Zakk; Director, Adam Shankman; Screenplay, Thomas Lennon, Robert Ben Garant; Photography, Peter James; Designer, Linda DeScenna; Costumes, Kirston Mann; Music, John Debney; Editor, Christopher Greenbury; Casting, Vickie Thomas; Presented in association with Spyglass Entertainment; Dolby; Panavision; Technicolor; Rated PG; 91 minutes; Release date: March 4, 2005

Cast

Shane Wolfe **Vin Diesel**
Principal Claire Fletcher **Lauren Graham**
Julie Plummer **Faith Ford**
Zoe **Brittany Snow**
Seth **Max Thieriot**
Capt. Bill Fawcett **Chris Potter**
Helga **Carol Kane**
Vice Principal Murney **Brad Garrett**
Lulu **Morgan York**
Peter **Keegan Hoover, Logan Hoover**
Baby Tyler **Bo Vink, Luke Vink**
Howard Plummer **Tate Donovan**

Vin Diesel, Lauren Graham

Director **Scott Thompson**
Mr. Chun **Denis Akiyama**
Mrs. Chun **Mung-Ling Tsui**

and Anne Fletcher (Liesel), Allison Lynn (Maria), Gabriel Antonacci (Capt. Von Trapp), Mary Pitt (Brigitta), Dan Sutcliffe (Friedrich), Vanessa Cobham (Gretl), Jordan Allison (Kurt), Rachael Dolan (Louisa), Charlotte Szivak (Maria), Toya Alexis (Mother Abbess), Valerie Boyel, Karla Jang, Silver Kim, Robert Yeretch (Nuns-Nazis), Scott Hurst (Nuns); Christie Allaire, Stephanie Allaire, Amy Allicock, Helena Chow, Joella Crichton, Laura Jeanes, Rebecca Priestley (Cheerleaders), Taryn Ash (Customer), Catherine Burdon, Shane Cardwell (Teachers), Tommy Chang (Showroom Cleaner), Alexander Conti (Little Boy), David Lipper (Cute Cop), Tip Fong (Cute Cop's Partner), Maria Georgas, Nikki Shah, Jordan Todosey, Emi Yaguchi-Chow (Fireflies), Demetrius Joyette, Christopher Lortie (Junior Grizzlies), Sotiri Georgas, Steven Georgas, Gannon Racki (Grizzlies), Seth Howard (Woody Woodchuck Manager), Marcus Hutchings, David Sparrow (FBI Agents), Evelyn Kaye (Piano Accompanist), Miriam Laurence, David Smukler (Dialect Coaches), Christian Laurin (Marcel), John MacDonald (Car Salesman), Bill Oliver (Customer), Curits Parker, Matt Purdy (Wrestlers), Jean Pearson (Swiss Banker), Kyle Schmid (Scott), Robert Thomas (Construction Worker), Cade Courtley (Wyatt, Navy S.E.A.L. #2), Michael Quintero, Cameron Hickox (Navy S.E.A.L.s), Cassius Clay (Boat Captain), Jeff Podgurski, Valentino Morales (Serbians), Hank Amos (Serbian Gunner), Charlie Haugk (Stagehand), Scott Reiff (Serbian Pilot)

A tough Navy S.E.A.L. is given the job of protecting the endangered children of an assassinated scientist who was working on a secret invention.

Vin Diesel, Max Thieriot, Morgan York, Brittany Snow

Brad Garrett, Vin Diesel

Faith Ford, Chris Potter PHOTOS COURTESY OF WALT DISNEY PICTURES

John Travolta, Uma Thurman, Steven Tyler

John Travolta, Danny DeVito, Anna Nicole Smith, Phil Jackson

BE COOL

(MGM) Producers, David Nicksay, Danny DeVito, Michael Shamberg, Stacey Sher; Executive Producers, F. Gary Gray, Elmore Leonard, Michael Siegel; Director, F. Gary Gray; Screenplay, Peter Steinfeld; Based on the novel by Elmore Leonard; Photography, Jeffrey L. Kimball; Designer, Micahel Corenblith; Costumes, Mark Bridges; Uma Thurman's Costumes, Betsy Heimann; Music, John Powell; Music Supervisor, Mary Ramos; Choreographer, Fatima Robinson; Editor, Sheldon Kahn; Associate Producers, Andy Gose, Linda Favila, Anson Downes; Casting, Sheila Jaffe, Georgianne Walken; a Jersey Films/Double Feature Films production; Dolby; Panavision; Deluxe color; Rated PG-13; 114 minutes; Release date: March 4, 2005

Cast

Chili Palmer **John Travolta**
Edie Athens **Uma Thurman**
Raji **Vince Vaughn**
Sin LaSalle **Cedric the Entertainer**
Dabu **André Benjamin**
Aerosmith **Steven Tyler, Joe Perry, Tom Hamilton, Brad Whitford, Joey Kramer**
Joe Loop **Robert Pastorelli**
Linda Moon **Christina Milian**
Hy Gordon **Paul Adelstein**
Marla **Debi Mazar**

Darryl **GregAlan Williams**
Nick Carr **Harvey Keitel**
Elliot Wilhelm **The Rock**
Martin Weir **Danny DeVito**
Tommy Athens **James Woods**

and Wyclef Jean, Fred Durst, Segio Mendes, Gene Simmons, The RZA, Anna Nicole Smith (Themselves), Anthony J. Ribustello (Fast Freddie), Steve Maye (Steve), Alex Kubik (Roman Bulkin), Darren Carter (Glenn), Carol Duboc (Pumpkin), Minae Noji (Miss Bangkok), Arielle Kebbel (Robin), Kimberly J. Brown (Tiffany), Jordan Moseley (Deshawn), Margaret Travolta (Marge), Scott Adsit (Program Director), Brian Christensen (Hairy Russian), Nick Loren, Craig Susser (Assistant Directors), George Fisher (Ivan), Frank Lloyd (A&R Guy), Sahar Simmons (Sin LaSalle's Wife), Serdar Kalsin (Bearded Russian), Dr. Frank Nyi (Coroner), Noelle Scaggs, Joyce Tolberty (Back-up Singers), Russ Irwin (Aerosmith Keyboardist), The Black Eyed Peas (Themselves), Steve Lucky, Carmen Getit (Rumba Bums), Chris Lewis, Daryl Jones, Alex-Andre Watkins, Floyd Tremmel, Quincy Taylor, Will Harris (Dub Mds), Kimberly Wyatt, Kasey Campbell, Ashley Roberts, Nicole Sherizinger (Pussycat Dolls), Leon C. Carswell, Jovan Clatyon, Corinthea Henderson, Micah Jenkins, Donyelle Denise Jones, Clifford McGhee, Rashad Miles, Oscar Orosco, Quinette Price, Jerry Randolph, Shellee Samuels, Roel Ruasin, Christopher Toler, Ceasare Willis, Shanelle Woodgett, Ivan Velez (Music Video Dancers), Lesa Maiava, Mervyn Lilo (Samoan Dancers)

Hoping to break into the music business, Chili Palmer becomes mentor to promising singer Linda Moon who is already under contract to ruthless mogul Nick Carr. Second in the Chili Palmer-Elmore Leonard films, following *Get Shorty* (MGM, 1995), which also starred John Travolta and Danny DeVito.

André Benjamin, Cedric the Entertainer

The Rock, Vince Vaughn, Harvey Keitel   PHOTOS COURTESY OF MGM

THE JACKET

(WARNER INDEPENDENT PICTURES) Producers, Peter Guber, George Clooney, Steven Soderbergh; Executive Producers, Ori Marumur, Peter E. Strauss, Ben Cosgrove, Jennifer Fox, Todd Wagner, Mark Cuban, Andy Grosch, Chris Roberts; Director, John Maybury; Screenplay, Massy Tadjedin; Story, Tom Bleecker, Marc Rocco; Photography, Peter Deming; Designer, Alan MacDonald; Costumes, Doug Hall; Music, Brian Eno; Music Supervisor, Andy Richards; Editor, Emma Hickox; Casting, Laray Mayfield; a Mandalay Pictures presentation in association with 2929 Entertainment of a Section Eight Ltd. production, co-produced with VIP Medienfonds 3,VIP Medienfonds 2,MP Pictures GmbH in association with Rising Star; U.S.-German; Dolby; Super 35 Widescreen; Deluxe color; Rated R; 102 minutes; Release date: March 4, 2005

Keira Knightley

Kris Kristofferson, Jennifer Jason Leigh

Cast

Jack Starks **Adrien Brody**
Jackie Price **Keira Knightley**
Dr. Thomas Becker **Kris Kristofferson**
Dr. Lorenson **Jennifer Jason Leigh**
Jean Price **Kelly Lynch**
The Stranger **Brad Renfro**
Rudy Mackenzie **Daniel Craig**
Dr. Hopkins **Steven Mackintosh**
Damon **Brendan Coyle**
Nurse Harding **Mackenzie Phillips**
Young Jackie **Laura Marano**
Officer Harrison **Jason Lewis**
Captain Medley **Richard Dillane**

and Jonah Lotan, Angel Coulby (Interns), Paul Birchard (Doctor), Nigel Whitney (Lieutenant), Ian Porter (Major), Antony Edridge (Dr. Morgan), Kerry Shale (Prosecutor), Richard Durden (Dr. Hale), Tristan Gemmill (Officer Nash), Colin Stinton (Jury Foreman), Tara Summers (Nurse Nina), Angelo Andreou (Babak/Iranian Boy), Teresa Gallagher (Nurse Sally), Anne Kidd (State Representative), Charneh Demir (Jamille/Iranian Mother), Frances Brady-Stewart (Woman with Dog), Lolly Susi (Nurse), Garrick Hagon (Defense Lawyer), Fish (Jimmy Fleischer)

After being declared dead following a head wound during the Gulf War, Jack Starks returns to consciousness a year later only to find himself on trial for a murder he can't remember committing.

Keira Knightley, Adrien Brody

Mackenzie Philips, Brendan Coyle

Adrien Brody PHOTOS COURTESY OF WARNER BROS.

Piper Pinwheel, Rodney Copperbottom, Fender

ROBOTS

(20TH CENTURY FOX) Producers, Jerry Davis, John C. Donkin, William Joyce; Executive Producer, Christopher Melendandri; Director, Chris Wedge; Co-Director, Carlos Saldanha; Screenplay, David Lindsay-Abaire, Lowell Ganz, Babaloo Mandel; Story, Ron Mita, Jim McClain, David Lindsay-Abaire; Designer, William Joyce; Supervising Animators, James Bresnahan, Michael Turmeier; Music, John Powell; Music Supervisor, Becky Mancuso-Winding; CG Supervisor, Michael J. Travers; Editor, John Carnochan; a Fox Animation presentation of a Blue Sky Studios production; Dolby; Deluxe color; Rated PG; 90 minutes; Release date: March 11, 2005

Voice Cast

Rodney Copperbottom **Ewan McGregor**
Cappy **Halle Berry**
Fender **Robin Williams**
Ratchet **Greg Kinnear**
Bigweld **Mel Brooks**
Crank Casey **Drew Carey**
Madame Gasket **Jim Broadbent**
Piper Pinwheeler **Amanda Bynes**
Aunt Fanny **Jennifer Coolidge**
Herb Copperbottom **Stanley Tucci**
Mrs. Copperbottom **Dianne Wiest**
Tim the Gate Guard **Paul Giamatti**
Loreatta Geargrinder **Natasha Leone**

Ratchet

and Paula Abdul (Watch), Lucille Bliss (Pigeon Lady), Terry Bradshaw (Broken Arm Bot), Dylan Denton (Youngest Rodney), Will Denton, Crawford Wilson (Young Rodney), Marshall Efron (Lamppost/Toilet Bot/Bass Drum/Microphone), Damien Fahey (Stage Announcer), Lowell Ganz (Mr. Gasket), Dan Hedaya (Mr. Gunk), Jackie Hoffman (Water Cooler), James Earl Jones (Voice Box at Hardware Store), Jay Leno (Fire Hydrant), Brian McFadden (Trashcan Bot), Tim Nordquist (Tin Man), Jansen Panettiere (Younger Rodney), Al Roker (Mailbox), Alan Rosenberg (Jack Hammer), Stephen Tobolowsky (Bigmouth Executive/Forge), Harland Williams (Lug)

Cappy

Herb Copperbottom, Mrs. Copperbottom, Rodney Copperbottom

Arriving in Robot City to find work at Bigweld Industries, Rodney Copperbottom is shocked to discover that the corporation's heartless CEO intends to stop manufacturing replacement parts, meaning those robots who cannot afford upgrades will be consigned to the scrap heap.

Rodney Copperbottom PHOTOS COURTESY OF 20TH CENTURY FOX

THE UPSIDE OF ANGER

(NEW LINE CINEMA) Producers, Alex Gartner, Jack Binder, Sammy Lee; Executive Producers, Mark Damon, Stewart Hall, Andreas Grosch, Andreas Schmid; Director/Screenplay, Mike Binder; Photography, Richard Greatrex; Designer, Chris Roope; Costumes, Deborah Scott; Music, Alexandre Desplat; Editors, Steve Edwards, Robin Sales; Associate Producer, Chris Curling; Line Producer, Peter Heslop; Casting, Danielle Rofe; a VIP Medienfonds 2,VIP Medienfonds 3, MDP Filmproduktion co-production of a Sunlight production, presented in association with Media 8 Entertainment; Dolby; Super 35 Widescreen; Technicolor; Rated R; 121 minutes; Release date: March 11, 2005

Joan Allen, Alicia Witt

Kevin Costner, Joan Allen

Dane Chistensen, Evan Rachel Wood

Cast

Terry Ann Wolfmeyer	**Joan Allen**
Denny Davies	**Kevin Costner**
Andy Wolfmeyer	**Erika Christensen**
Emily Wolfmeyer	**Keri Russell**

Keri Russell, Joan Allen, Erika Christensen

Erika Christensen, Evan Rachel Wood

Keri Russell, Kevin Costner

Dane Christensen, Evan Rachel Wood, Kevin Costner

Hadley Wolfmeyer **Alicia Witt**
Lavender "Popeye" Wolfmeyer **Evan Rachel Wood**
Adam "Shep" Goodman **Mike Binder**
David Junior **Tom Harper**
Gorden Reiner **Dane Christensen**
Grey Wolfmeyer **Danny Webb**
Darlene **Magdalena Manville**
Gina **Suzanne Bertish**
David Senior **David Firth**
Dean Reiner **Roderick P. Woodruff**

A Detroit housewife, Terry Wolfmeyer, deeply bitter about her husband's abrupt departure and having to raise her four daughters on her own, is wooed by neighbor Denny Davies, a former baseball player who bonds with Terry over their dependency on alcohol.

Erika Christensen, Mike Binder

Joan Allen, Erika Christensen, Evan Rachel Wood, Alicia Witt

and Stephen Greif (Emily's Doctor), Arthur Penhallow (Himself), Richard Mylan (Disc Jockey), Robert Perkins (Town Car Man), William Tapley (Dr. Lewis), Owen Oakshoot (Builder Foreman), Bella Sabbagh (Radio Station Receptionist), Kathryn Wade, Michelle Denholm, Natalie Domanski, Sophie Gorrod, Carolyn Logan, Alison McWhinney, Natasha O'Brien, Stina Quagebeur, Olivia Racliffe, Laura Suttle, Nicola Wallis, Miki Weatherford, Nao Yamazato (Ballet Dancers), Gavin Munn, Nicholas White, Peter Hajioff, Chris Banks, Roger Batting (Wedding Band)

Kevin Costner PHOTOS COURTESY OF NEW LINE CINEMA

HOSTAGE

(MIRAMAX) Producers, Bruce Willis, Arnold Rifkin, Mark Gordon, Bob Yari; Executive Producers, Hawk Koch, David Wally, Andreas Thiesmeyer, Josef Lautenschlager; Director, Florent Siri; Screenplay, Doug Richardson; Based on the novel by Robert Crais; Photography, Giovanni Fiore Coltellaci; Designer, Larry Fulton; Costumes, Elisabetta Beraldo; Music, Alexandre Desplat; Music Supervisor, Richard Glasser; Editors, Olivier Gajan, Richard J. P. Byard; Stunts, Billy Burton; Casting, Victoria Burrows, Scot Boland; a Straus Film Co. presentation of a Cheynne Enterprises, Equity Pictures Medienfonds GmbH & Co. KG II production in association with Syndicate Films International; U.S.-German; Dolby; Panavision; Deluxe color; Rated R; 113 minutes; Release date: March 11, 2005

Bruce Willis

Bruce Willis, Rumer Willis

Jimmy Bennett, Bruce Willis

Cast
Jeff Talley	**Bruce Willis**
Walter Smith	**Kevin Pollak**
Tommy Smith	**Jimmy Bennett**
Jennifer Smith	**Michelle Horn**
Mars Krupcheck	**Ben Foster**
Dennis Kelly	**Jonathan Tucker**

Kevin Kelly	**Marshall Allman**
Jane Talley	**Serena Scott Thomas**
Amanda Talley	**Rumer Willis**
The Watchman	**Kim Coates**
Wil Bechler	**Robert Knepper**
Laura Shoemaker	**Tina Lifford**
Mike Anders	**Ransford Doherty**
Carol Flores	**Marjean Holden**
Ridley	**Michael D. Roberts**
Bill Jorgenson	**Art LaFleur**

and Randy McPherson (Kovak), Hector Luis Bustamante (Officer Ruiz), Kathryn Joosten (Louise), Johnny Messner (Mr. Jones), John Ingle (Gray Hair Man), Jamie McShane (Joe Mack), Jimmy Pinchak (Sean Mack), Glenn Morshower (Lt. Leifitz), Chad Smith (Bobby Knox), Scott Allan Campbell (Police Psychologist), Jane McPherson (Nurse), Phil Shuman, Christina Cabot (News Reporters)

When three young men break into a mansion and take its owners hostage, former hostage negotiator Jeff Talley snaps back into action in an effort to stop the situation from getting any more dangerous.

Bruce Willis

OFF THE MAP

(MANHATTAN PICTURES) Producers, Campbell Scott, George Van Buskirk; Executive Producers, David Newman, Paul E. Cohen, Ron Gell, Jonathan Filley, Martin Garvey, Kesim Hason, Sezin Hason; Director, Campbell Scott; Screenplay, Joan Ackermann, based on her play; Photography, Juan Ruiz Anchia; Designer, Chris Shriver; Costumes, Amy Westcott; Music, Gary DeMichele; Editor, Andy Keir; Casting, Laylee Olfat; a Holedigger Films, New Films International production; Dolby; Color; Rated PG-13; 105 minutes; Release date: March 11, 2005

Valentina de Angelis

Cast
Arlene **Joan Allen**
Charley **Sam Elliott**
Young Bo **Valentina de Angelis**
George **J. K. Simmons**
William Gibbs **Jim True-Frost**
Adult Bo **Amy Brenneman**
Rusty **Boots Southern**
Romero **J. D. Garfield**
Store Clerk **Matthew E. Montoya**
Consuela **Kathy Griego**

Valentina de Angelis, Sam Elliott, Joan Allen

Sam Elliott

Interpreter **William Hart McNicholas**
Priest **Timothy Martinez**
Jack **J. D. Hawkins**
Don **Kevin Skousen**

While coping with a series of personal problems, a highly individualistic New Mexico family receives a visit from an agent from the Internal Revenue Service.

Joan Allen PHOTOS COURTESY OF HOLEDIGGER STUDIOS

THE RING TWO

(DREAMWORKS) Producers, Walter F. Parkes, Laurie MacDonald; Executive Producers, Mike Macari, Roy Lee, Neil Machlis, Michele Weisler; Director, Hideo Nakata; Screenplay, Ehren Kruger; Based upon the novel *The Ring* by Koji Suzuki and on the motion picture *The Ring* by the Spiral Production Group; Photography, Gabriel Beristain; Designer, Jim Bissell; Costumes, Wendy Chuck; Music, Henning Lohner, Martin Tillman; Themes, Hans Zimmer; Co-Executive Producers, Neal Edelstein, Chris Bender, JC Spink; Editor, Michael N. Knue; Special Makeup Effects, Rick Baker; Casting, Deborah Aquila, Tricia Wood; a Parkes/MacDonald production; Dolby; Technicolor; Rated PG-13; 111 minutes; Release date: March 18, 2005

Naomi Watts, Kelly Stables PHOTO COURTESY OF DREAMWORKS

Cast

Rachel Keller **Naomi Watts**
Max Rourke **Simon Baker**
Aidan Keller **David Dorfman**
Dr. Emma Temple **Elizabeth Perkins**
Martin Savide **Gary Cole**
Jake **Ryan Merriman**
Emily **Emily Vancamp**

and Kelly Overton (Betsy), James Lesure (Doctor), Daveigh Chase (Samara), Kelly Stables (Evil Samara), Cooper Thornton (Father of Emily), Marilyn McIntyre (Mother of Emily), Jesse Burch (Reporter), Michael Chieffo (Printing Staffer), Steven Petrarca (Young Detective), Michael Dempsey (Desk Sergeant), Kirk B. R. Woller (Detective), Jeffrey Hutchinson (Coroner Attendant), Chane't Johnson (Adoption Counselor), Mary Joy (Sister Elizabeth), Michelle Anne Johnson, Jill Farley (Nurses), Teri Bibb (Head Nurse), Aleksa Palladino (Young Nurse), Victor McCay (Desk Man), Brendan Quinlan (Rental Car Owner), Michael Tomlinson (Father of Jake), Phyllis Lyons (Mother of Jake), Mary Elizabeth Winstead (Young Evelyn), Ant Haffner (Young Sister Elizabeth), Ted Detwiler, Stephen Holland (Cops), Omer Stephens III (Game Attendant), Jonathan Coburn (Marble Man), Caitlin Mavromates (Baby Samara)

Despite moving to Oregon, Rachel and her son Aidan find that they are still being haunted by the vengeful Samara and her cursed videotape. Sequel to the 2002 DreamWorks film *The Ring*, with Watts, Dorfman, and Chase repeating their roles.

ICE PRINCESS

(WALT DISNEY PICTURES) Producer, Bridget Johnson; Executive Producer, William W. Wilson III; Director, Tim Fywell; Screenplay, Hadley Davis; Story, Meg Cabot, Hadley Davis; Photography, David Hennings; Designer, Lester Cohen; Costumes, Michael Dennison; Music, Christophe Beck; Music Supervisor, Lisa Brown; Editor, Janice Hampton; Choreographer, Anne Fletcher; Skating Consultant/Assistant Choreographer, Jamie Isley; Casting, Randi Hiller, Sarah Halley Finn; Distributed by Buena Vista Pictures; Dolby; Panavision; Technicolor; Rated G; 92 minutes; Release date: March 18, 2005

Cast

Joan Caryle **Joan Cusack**
Tina Harwood **Kim Cattrall**
Casey Carlyle **Michelle Trachtenberg**
Gen Harwood **Hayden Panettiere**
Teddy Harwood **Trevor Blumas**
Nikki's Mom **Connie Ray**
Nikki **Kirsten Olson**
Zoey Bloch **Juliana Cannarozzo**
Tiffany **Jocelyn Lai**
Themselves **Michelle Kwan, Brian Boitano**
Mr. Bast **Steve Ross**

and Paul Sun-Hyung Lee (Tiffany's Dad), Roy Bradshaw (Tiffany's Coach), Mark Hind (Nikki's Coach), Ben Gilbank (Brian), Thanh Nguyen (Hot Dog Kid), Cole Campbell, Brandon Lajko, Jesse Primosig (Rink Kids), Colleen Collins (Lily), Andrea Tou (Devon), Jordan Hockley (Jeremy), Charmaine Hamp (Jeremy's Mom), Laura Aloisio, Amanda Lella, Emma Nielsen, Melissa Shears, Kaci Brandt, Edrea Khong, Alexandra Najarro (Snowplow Sams), Chantal Desforge (Harvard Physics Student), Diego Klattenhoff (Kyle Dayton), Joey Racki (Zipline Guy), Courtney Hawkrigg, Handy Butcher, Martha MacIsaac (Mean Party Girls), Sean Persaud (DJ), Stephanie Hutchison (Ballet Teacher), Flo Umphrey (Piano Teacher), Debbi Wilkes (Zoey's Coach), Jennifer Gelfer (Skate Saleswoman), Erik King (Chip Healey), Shanique Ollivierre-Lake (Chantal Degroat), Michele Moore (Near-Miss Skater), Signe Ronka (Emma Flanders), Sean Croft (Joan's Student), Kevin Jubinbille (Reporter)

A brainy high schooler decides to do a report on the physics of figure skating and finds herself competing in the sport, much to the surprise of her single mom, who has hoped for a different career path for her daughter.

Kim Cattrall, Michelle Trachtenberg PHOTO COURTESY OF WALT DISNEY PICTURES

MELINDA AND MELINDA

(FOX SEARCHLIGHT) Producer, Letty Aronson; Executive Producers, Jack Rollins, Charles H. Joffe, Stpehen Tenenbaum; Co-Producer, Helen Robin; Director/ Screenplay, Woody Allen; Photography, Vilmos Zsigmond; Designer, Santo Loquasto; Costumes, Judy L. Ruskin; Editor, Alisa Lepselter; Casting, Juliet Taylor; Dolby; Color; Rated PG-13; 100 minutes; Release date: March 18, 2005

Chloë Sevigny, Radha Mitchell

Chiwetel Ejiofor, Radha Mitchell

Will Ferrell, Amanda Peet

Will Ferrell, Radha Mitchell

Cast

Melinda **Radha Mitchell**
Laurel **Chloë Sevigny**
Lee **Jonny Lee Miller**
Hobie **Will Ferrell**
Susan **Amanda Peet**
Ellis **Chiwetel Ejiofor**
Sy **Wallace Shawn**
Greg **Josh Brolin**
Stacey **Vinessa Shaw**
Walt **Steve Carell**
Jack **Matt Servitto**
Sally **Arija Bareikis**
Peter **Zak Orth**
Doug **Andy Borowitz**
Joan **Shalom Harlow**
Steve **David Aaron Baker**
Jennifer **Christina Kirk**

and Neil Pepe (Al), Stephanie Roth Haberle (Louise), Larry Pine (Max), Michael J. Farina (Man with Dog), Alyssa Pridham (Acting Student), Katie Kreisler (Director), Quincy Rose (2nd A.D.), Rick Vincent Holmes, Michele Durning (Party Guests), Geoffrey Nauffts (Bud), Yi-wen Jiang, Honggang Li, Weignang Li, Nick Tzavaras (Shanghai Quartet), Rob Buntzen (Antique Shop Owner), Daniel Sunjata (Billy)

The unexpected appearance of a bedraggled Melinda at a Manhattan dinner party is told from both comic and tragic points of view.

Will Ferrell, Radha Mitchell, Steve Carell PHOTOS COURTESY OF FOX SEARCHLIGHT

Ashton Kutcher, Bernie Mac

GUESS WHO

(COLUMBIA) Producers, Jenno Topping, Erwin Stoff, Jason Goldberg; Executive Producers, Betty Thomas, Steven Greener, Joseph M. Caracciolo; Director, Kevin Rodney Sullivan; Screenplay, David Ronn, Jay Scherick, Peter Tolan; Story, David Ronn, Jay Scherick; Photography, Karl Walter Lindenlaub; Designer, Paul J. Peters; Costumes, Judy Ruskin Howell; Music, John Murphy; Editor, Paul Seydor; Casting, Victoria Thomas; a Regency Enterprises presentation of a 3 Arts Entertainment, Tall Trees Productions, Katalyst Films production; Dolby; Deluxe color; Rated PG-13; 105 minutes; Release date: March 25, 2005

Cast

Percy Jones **Bernie Mac**
Simon Green **Ashton Kutcher**
Theresa Jones **Zoë Saldaña**
Marilyn Jones **Judith Scott**
Howard Jones **Hal Williams**
Keisha Jones **Kellee Stewart**
Dante **Robert Curtis Brown**
Reggie **RonReaco Lee**
Darlene **Paula Newsome**
Fred **Phil Reeves**
Sydney **Sherri Shepherd**
Liz Klein **Nicole Sullivan**
Polly **Jessica Cauffiel**
Winnie **JoNell Kennedy**
Naomi **Niecy Nash**
Kimbra **Kimberly Scott**
Lisa **Denise Dowse**

and J. Kenneth Campbell (Nathan Rogers), Chad Gabriel (Waiter), Alex Morris (Preacher), James Eckhouse, Angel Viera (Workmen), Amanda Tosch (Dante's Wife), Richard Lawson (Marcus), Andy Morrow (Go-Kart Worker), Archie Hahn

Percy Jones hopes to be pleasantly surprised upon meeting his daughter's new boyfriend, but finds himself put off by the fact that the young man is white.

Bernie Mac, Ashton Kutcher, Zoë Saldaña, Hal Williams

Judith Scott, Bernie Mac, Ashton Kutcher, Zoë Saldaña

Ashton Kutcher, Zoë Saldaña

THE BALLAD OF JACK AND ROSE

(IFC FILMS) Producer, Lemore Syvan; Executive Producers, Jonathan Sehring, Caroline Kaplan, Graham King; Co-Producer, Melissa Marr; Director/Screenplay, Rebecca Miller; Photography, Ellen Kuras; Designer, Mark Ricker; Costumes, Jennifer von Mayrhauser; Music, Michael Rohatyn; Editor, Sabine Hoffman; Casting, Cindy Tolan; an Initial Entertainment Group presentation of an Elevation Pictures production; Dolby; 16mm-to-35mm; Color; Rated R; 111 minutes; Release date: March 25, 2005

Paul Dano, Ryan McDonald, Catherine Keener

Daniel Day-Lewis, Camilla Belle

Daniel Day-Lewis, Camilla Belle

Cast

Jack Slavin **Daniel Day-Lewis**
Rose Slavin **Camilla Belle**
Kathleen **Catherine Keener**
Rodney **Ryan McDonald**
Thaddius **Paul Dano**
Gray **Jason Lee**
Red Berry **Jena Malone**
Marty Rance **Beau Bridges**
Miriam Rance **Susanna Thompson**
Young Rose **Anna Mae Clinton**

A counterculture idealist, the last founder of an island commune, disrupts the close relationship with his teenage daughter when he invites his girlfriend and her sons to come live with them.

Camilla Belle PHOTOS COURTESY OF IFC FILMS

BEAUTY SHOP

(MGM) Producers, Queen Latifah, Skakim Compere, Robert Teitel, George Tillman Jr., David Hoberman; Executive Producers, Ice Cube, Matt Alvarez, Todd Lieberman; Director, Bille Woodruff; Screenplay, Kate Lanier, Norman Vance Jr.; Story, Elizabeth Hunter; Photography, Theo Van de Sande; Art Director, Jon Gary Steele; Costumes, Sharen Davis; Music Supervisor, Barry Cole; Music, Christopher Young; Editor, Michael Jablow; Co-Producer, Louise Rosner; Associate Producer, Otis Best; Casting, Victoria Thomas, Kim Taylor Coleman; a State Street Pictures, Madeville Films, Flavor Unit Films production; Dolby; Panavision; Deluxe color; Rated PG-13; 105 minutes; Release date: March 30, 2005

Alicia Silverstone, Golden Brooks, Queen Latifah, Sherri Shepherd, Alfre Woodard

Queen Latifah, Kevin Bacon

Queen Latifah, Mena Suvari, Andie MacDowell PHOTOS COURTESY OF MGM

Cast

Gina Norris **Queen Latifah**
Lynn **Alicia Silverstone**
Terri **Andie MacDowell**
Ms. Josephine **Alfre Woodard**
Joanne **Mena Suvari**
Mrs. Towner **Della Reese**
Chanel **Golden Brooks**
Paulette **Miss Laura Hayes**
Vanessa **Paige Hurd**
Willie **L'il JJ**
Rochelle **LisaRaye McCoy**
Darnelle **Keshia Knight Pulliam**
Ida **Sherri Shepherd**
Denise **Kimora Lee Simmons**
Catfish Rita **Sheryl Underwood**
James **Bryce Wilson**
Jorge **Kevin Bacon**
Joe **Djimon Hounsou**

and Omari Hardwick (Byron), Adele Givens (DJ Helen), Jim Holmes (Inspector Crawford), Larissa Bordere (Client of Chanel), Baby (Himself), Nancy Lenehan (Mrs. Struggs), Reagan Gomez-Preston, Crystal Garret (Women), Suzanne Covington (Mrs. Dexter), Joyful M. Drake (Mercedes), Tawny Dahl (Porsche), Mary Wickliffe (Music Teacher), Andrew Levitas (Stacy), Octavia Spencer (Big Customer), Jamie McBride (Detective), Melissa Wyler (Client at Jorge's), Ki Toy Johnson (Neighborhood Girl), Otis Best (Neighborhood Rapper), Christopher Lane (Bag Diva)

Fed up with her egotistical boss, single mom Gina Norris buys a rundown Atlanta beauty shop and turns it into a profitable business of her own. Latifah repeats her role from the 2004 MGM film *Barbershop 2*.

Sherri Shepherd, Alicia Silverstone, Queen Latifah, Golden Brooks, Bryce Wilson, Keshia Knight Pulliam, Alfre Woodard

SIN CITY

(DIMENSION) Producers, Elizabeth Avellan, Frank Miller; Robert Rodriguez; Executive Producers, Bob Weinstein, Harvey Weinstein; Directors, Frank Miller, Robert Rodriguez; Special Guest Director, Quentin Tarantino; Screenplay, Robert Rodriguez, Frank Miller; Based on the Graphic Novels by Frank Miller; Photography/Editor, Robert Rodriguez; Art Director/Set Decorator, Jeanette Scott; Costumes, Nina Proctor; Music, Robert Rodriguez, John Debney, Graeme Revell; Visual Effects Supervisors, Robert Rodriguez, Daniel Leduc; Special Makeup Effects, K.N.B. EFX Group; Design/Previsualization, Troublemaker Digital Studios; Stunts, Jeff Dashnaw; Casting, Mary Vernieu; a Troublemaker Studios production; Distributed by Miramax; Dolby; Black and white/Deluxe color; Rated R; 124 minutes; Release date: April 1, 2005

Jessica Alba, Bruce Willis

Benicio Del Toro

Cast

Nancy	**Jessica Alba**
Miho	**Devon Aoki**
Becky	**Alexis Bledel**
Senator Roark	**Powers Boothe**
Gail	**Rosario Dawson**
Jackie Boy	**Benicio Del Toro**
Manute	**Michael Clarke Duncan**
Lucille	**Carla Gugino**
The Man	**Josh Hartnett**
Cardinal Roark	**Rutger Hauer**
Stuka	**Nicky Katt**
Goldie/Wendy	**Jaime King**
Bob	**Michael Madsen**
Shellie	**Brittany Murphy**
Dwight	**Clive Owen**
Marv	**Mickey Rourke**
The Customer	**Marley Shelton**
Roark Jr./Yellow Bastard	**Nick Stahl**
Hartigan	**Bruce Willis**

Kevin	**Elijah Wood**
Liebowitz	**Jude Ciccolella**
Brian	**Tommy Flanagan**
Klump	**Rick Gomez**
Ronnie	**Jason McDonald**
Schutz	**Clark Middleton**
Priest	**Frank Miller**
Lenny/Benny	**Scott Teeters**
Nancy, Age 11	**Makenzie Vega**

and Jeff Dashnaw (Motorcycle Cop), Jesse De Luna (Corporal Rivera), Jason Douglas (Hitman), Christina Frankenfield (Judge), Arie Verveen (Murphy), David Hickey (Juicer), Evelyn Hurley (Josie), Greg Ingram (Bouncer), Helen Kirk (Maeve), Nick Offerman (Shlubb), Ethan Maniquis, Ken Thomas, Chris Warner, Iman Nazemzadeh (Bozos), Lisa Marie Newmyer (Tammy), Tommy Nix (Weevil), Marco Perella (Skinny Dude), Sam Ray (Interrogator #1), Randal Reeder (man with Hitman), David Alex Ruiz (Thug #2), Rayan Rutledge (Painted Cop), Jeff Schwan (Louie), Korey Simeone (Priest #2), Paul T. Taylor (Assistant DA), Rico Torres (Cop #2), Patricia Vonne (Dallas), Shaun Wainwright-Branigan (Doctor), Cara Briggs (Hearing Panel Person), Danny Wynands (Big Mercenary), J. D. Young (Store Employee)

In the ferociously corrupt underworld of Basin City, hulking half-man, half-beast Marv avenges the death of a hooker he loved; a cop tries to prevent a senator's pedophile son from raping a young girl; and Dwight and Jackie Boy's rivalry over waitress Shellie sets off a gang war.

Rosario Dawson, Clive Owen PHOTOS COURTESY OF DIMENSION/MIRAMAX

WINTER SOLSTICE

(PARAMOUNT CLASSICS) Producers, Doug Bernheim, John Limotte; Executive Producers, Anthony LaPaglia, Jodi Peikoff; Associate Producer, Amanda Slater; Director/Screenplay, Josh Sternfeld; Photography, Harlan Bosmajian; Designer, Jody Asnes; Costumes, Paola Ruby Weintraub; Music, John Leventhal; Editor, Plummy Tucker; Casting, Amanda Harding, Amanda Koblin; a Sound Pictures production; Dolby; Color; Rated R; 93 minutes; Release date: April 8, 2005

Aaron Stanford, Michelle Monaghan

Ron Livingston

Anthony LaPaglia, Allison Janney

Cast

Jim Winters	**Anthony LaPaglia**
Gabe Winters	**Aaron Stanford**
Pete Winters	**Mark Webber**
Molly Ripkin	**Allison Janney**
Mr. Bricker	**Ron Livingston**
Stacey	**Michelle Monaghan**
Robbie	**Brendan Sexton III**
Steve	**Ebon Moss-Bacharach**
Andrew	**Lars Engstrom**
Bob	**Jason Fuchs**
Jr.	**Paul Iacono**
Math Teacher	**Dana Segal**
Friends	**Rocco Rosanio, Tim Dowlin**

Mark Webber, Aaron Stanford PHOTOS COURTESY OF PARAMOUNT

A widower must cope with his one son's decision to leave and join his girlfriend in Florida, while the other boy retreats into a private world of disappointment and anger.

FEVER PITCH

(20TH CENTURY FOX) Producers, Alan Greenspan, Amanda Posey, Gil Netter, Drew Barrymore, Nancy Juvonen, Bradley Thomas; Executive Producers, Nick Hornby, David Evans, Marc S. Fischer; Co-Producer, Gwenn Gage Stroman; Directors, Peter Farrelly, Bobby Farrelly; Screenplay, Lowell Ganz, Babaloo Mandel; Based on the book by Nick Hornby; Photography, Matthew F. Leonetti; Designer, Maher Ahmad; Costumes, Sophie de Rakoff; Music, Craig Armstrong; Music Supervisors, Tom Wolfe, Manish Raval; Editor, Alan Baumgarten; a Fox 2000 Pictures presentation of a Gil Netter, Flower Films, Wildgaze Films, Alan Greenspan production; Dolby; Super 35 Widescreen; Deluxe color; Rated PG-13; 103 minutes; Release date: April 8, 2005

Cast

Lindsey Meeks **Drew Barrymore**
Ben **Jimmy Fallon**
Doug Meeks **James B. Sikking**
Maureen Meeks **JoBeth Williams**
Kevin **Willie Garson**
Troy **Evan Helmuth**
Molly **Ione Skye**
Robin **KaDee Strickland**
Sarah **Melissa Jaret Winokur**

Drew Barrymore, Jimmy Fallon

and Jason Spevack (Ben in 1980), Jack Kehler (Al), Scott H. Severance (Artie), Jessamy R. Finet (Theresa), Maureen Keiller (Viv), Lenny Clarke (Uncle Carl), Brandon Craggs (Casey), Brett Murphy (Ryan), Isabella Fink (Audrey), Miranda Black (Carrie), Greta Onieogou (Tammy), Johnny Sneed (Chris), Michael Rubenfeld (Ian), Armando Riesco (Gerard), Zen Gesner (Steve), Siobhan Fallon Hogan (Lana), Mark Andrada (Ezra), Charlotte Sullivan (Spin Instructor), Scott Desano (Binocular Guy), Lizz Alexander (Charlene), Shary Guthrie (Christie), Don Gavin (Cop), Andrew Wilson (Grant Wade), Dan Darin-Zanco (Husband), Gina Clayton (Lady at Other Table), Wayne Flemming (Leon), Bobby Curcuro (Loiterer), Bart Bedford (Man at Other Table), Jason Varitek, Johnny Damon, Trot Nixon, Jim Rice,

Jimmy Fallon, Drew Barrymore

Dennis Eckersley, Keith Macwhorter, Peter Gammons, Tim McCarver, Don Orsillo, Harold Reynolds, Jordan Leandre (Themselves), George King (Mr. Munsell), Jackie Burroughs (Mrs. Warren), John Boylan (Myerson), J. C. Kenny, Paul McGuire (Reporters), Quancetia Hamilton (Rita), Ken Rogerson (Scalper), Howard Nickerson (Usher), Matt Watts (Valet), George Ghali (Vern, Gym Teacher), Andrea Davis (Wife), Darren Frost (Zach), Sharlene Yuen (Receptionist), Geoffrey Williamson, Matthew Peart, David Klar, Jermaine Plummer (High School Kids), Melinda Lopez (Sheri), Sam Dissanayake (Mr. Abdo), Steve Levy (Reporter at Spring Training), Carl Beane (Stadium Announcer), Erin Nanstad (Fan), Johnny Cicco (Obnoxious Fan), Brian Hayes Currie (Screaming Fan), Bob Weekes, John Ruggiero (Hot Dog Vendors), Danny Murphy, Dan Cummings (1980s Vendors), Daniel Greene (Waiter), Tommy Jordan (Kid in Cast), Preston Thomas, Scott Rosenberg, Mark Cardi (1980s Red Sox Player), Keegan O'Donnell (1980s Batboy), John Macleod-Follows (Lindsey's Co-Worker), Sam Caswell (World's Greatest Red Sox Fan), Ron "Puppy" Cavallo (Bleacher Bum)

An ambitious corporate executive falls in love with affable schoolteacher Ben, whose intense obsession with the Boston Red Sox puts their relationship to the test. Previous film adaptation of Nick Hornby's novel was released in the U.S. in 1999 and starred Colin Firth and Ruth Gemmell.

Drew Barrymore, Jimmy Fallon PHOTOS COURTESY OF 20TH CENTURY FOX

PALINDROMES

(WELLSPRING) Producers, Mike S. Ryan, Derrick Tseng; Director/Screenplay, Todd Solondz; Photography, Tom Richmond; Designer, Dave Doernberg; Costumes, Victoria Farrell; Music, Nathan Larson; Editors, Mollie Goldstein, Kevin Messman; Casting, Ann Goulder; an Extra Large Pictures production; Dolby; DuArt color; Rated R; 100 minutes; Release date: April 13, 2005

Matthew Faber

Twelve-year-old Aviva, impregnated by the son of a family friend, is subjected to an abortion after which she runs away from home in an effort to find understanding and intimacy.

Alexander Brickel, Sharon Wilkins

Ellen Barkin, Jennifer Jason Leigh

Cast

Joyce Victor **Ellen Barkin**
Steve Victor **Richard Masur**
Mark Wiener **Matthew Faber**
Mrs. Wiener **Angela Pietropinto**
Mr. Wiener **Bill Buell**
"Dawn" Aviva Victor **Emani Sledge**
"Judah" Aviva Victor **Valerie Shustreov**
"Henry" Aviva Victor **Hannah Freiman**
"Huckleberry" Aviva Victor **Will Denton**
"Henrietta" Aviva Victor **Rachel Corr**
"Mama Sunshine" Aviva Victor **Sharon Wilkins**
"Bob" Aviva Victor **Shayna Levine**
"Mark" Aviva Victor **Jennifer Jason Leigh**
Hillary B. Smith **Hillary Bailey Smith**
Bruce Wallace **Danton Stone**
First Judah Wallace **Robert Agri**
Second Judah "Otto" Wallace **John Gemberling**
Joe-Earl-Bob **Stephen Adly Guirgis**
Peter Paul **Alexander Brickel**
Mama Sunshine **Debra Monk**
Jiminy **Tyler Maynard**

and Ashleigh Hertzig (Barbara), Risa Jaz Rifkind (Trixie), Dontae Huey (Shazaam), Walter Bobbie (Bo Sunshine), Courtney Walcott (Crystal), Joshua Eber (Skippy), Khush Kirpalani (Ali), Sydney Matuszak (Eli), David Castro (Carlito), Richard Riehle (Dr. Dan), Ebrahim Jaffer (Motel Clerk), Andrea Demosthenes (Gwyneth's Mom)

Stephen Adly Guirgis, Shayna Levine PHOTOS COURTESY OF WELLSPRING

HOUSE OF D

(LIONS GATE) Producers, Richard B. Lewis, Bob Yari, Jane Rosenthal; Executive Producers, Zanne Devine, Adam Merims, Jeff Skoll; Co-Producers, Melanie Greene, David Gaines; Director/Screenplay, David Duchovny; Photography, Michael Chapman; Designer, Lester Cohen; Costumes, Ellen Luter; Music, Geoff Zanell; Editor, Suzy Elmiger; Casting, Avy Kaufman; a Bob Yari Productions, Jeff Skoll Productions presentation of a Southpaw Entertainment, Tribeca production; Dolby; Color; Rated PG-13; 97 minutes; Release date: April 15, 2005

Anton Yelchin, Robin Williams

Cast

Tommy Warshaw **Anton Yelchin**
Katherine Warshaw **Téa Leoni**
Tom Warshaw **David Duchovny**
Pappass **Robin Williams**
Lady Bernadette **Erykah Badu**
Coralie Warshaw **Magali Amadei**
Odell Warshaw **Harold Cartier**
Mr. Papass **Mark Margolis**
Melissa **Zelda Williams**
Gerard **Gideon Jacobs**
Pitcher **Mark Richard Keith**
Another Kid **James Ockimey**
Kid #2 **Jonah Meyerson**
Simone **Olga Sosnovska**
Sasha **Bernard Sheredy**
Superfly **Orlando Jones**

and Claire Lautier (Madam Chatquipet), Alice Drummond (Mrs. Brevoort), Stephen Spinella (Ticket Seller), Frank Langella (Rev. Duncan), Jill Shackner (Lead Girl in Gym), Lisby Larson (Mrs. Loggia), Michael Chapman (Doorman), Adam LeFevre (Monty), Leslie Lyles (Sondra), Willie Garson (Ticket Agent), Andrée Damant (French Woman in Window), Etienne Draber (French Man in Window), Chantal Garrigues (French Wife in Window), Mary A. Fortune (Nurse #1), Lester Cohen (Irate Trotskyite), Roxy Toporowych (Miss Johnson), Francesca Buccellato (Mrs. Robinson), Erica N. Tazel (Reader), Stacy Lynn Spierer (Dog Walker), Amber Gristak (Leon's Mistress), Janet Huege (Stewardess)

David Duchovny, Robin Williams

Erykah Badu

Tom Warshaw looks back on his troubled youth in New York City as the son of a widowed nurse and how he sought advice from a woman incarcerated in the Women's House of Detention.

Téa Leoni PHOTOS COURTESY OF LIONS GATE

THE AMITYVILLE HORROR

(MGM/DIMENSION) Producers, Michael Bay, Andrew Form, Brad Fuller; Executive Producers, Ted Field, David Crockett; Director, Andrew Douglas; Screenplay, Scott Kosar; Based upon the screenplay by Sandor Stern and upon the book by Jay Anson; Photography, Peter Lyons Collister; Designer, Jennifer Williams; Costumes, David Robinson; Editors, Christian Wagner, Roger Barton; Music, Steve Jablonsky; Co-Executive Producers, Steven Whitney, Paul Mason, Randall Emmett, George Furla; Special Makeup Effects Designers/Creators, Greg Nicotero, Howard Berger; Casting, Lisa Fields; a Platinum Dunes production in association with Radar Pictures, presented in association with Michael Bay; Dolby; Panavision; Deluxe color; Rated R; 89 minutes; Release date: April 15, 2005

Chloë Grace Moretz PHOTO COURTESY OF MGM/DIMENSION

Cast

George Lutz **Ryan Reynolds**
Kathy Lutz **Melissa George**
Billy Lutz **Jesse James**
Michael Lutz **Jimmy Bennett**
Chelsea Lutz **Chloë Grace Moretz**
Lisa **Rachel Nichols**
Father Callaway **Philip Baker Hall**
Jodie Defeo **Isabel Conner**
Ronald Defeo **Brendan Donaldson**
Realtor **Annabel Armour**
Chief of Police **Rich Komenich**
ER Doctor **David Gee**
Officer Greguski **Danny McCarthy**
Librarian **Nancy Lollar**
Stitch **José Taitano**

After moving into a Long Island home in which the previous tenants had been brutally murdered, the Lutz family finds themselves terrorized by supernatural forces. Remake of the 1979 Filmways release which starred James Brolin and Margot Kidder.

Jeff Skilling

ENRON: THE SMARTEST GUYS IN THE ROOM

(MAGNOLIA) Producers, Alex Gibney, Jason Kliot, Susan Motamed; Executive Producers, Mark Cuban, Todd Wagner, Joana Vicente; Director/Screenplay, Alex Gibney; Photography, Maryse Alberti; Editor/Co-Producer, Alison Ellwood; Music, Matt Hauser; Associate Producers, Jennie Amias, Kate McMahon, Christine O'Malley; Executive in Charge of Production, Gretchen McGowan; Research, Crystal Whelan; Research Coordinator, Elissa Birke; Narrator, Peter Coyote; an HDNet Film Production; HD Video; Color; Not rated; 113 minutes; Release date: April 22, 2005. Documentary on the rise and fall of the Houston-based Enron corporation.

With

John Beard, Jim Chanos, Carol Coale, Gray Davis, Joseph Dunn, Max Eberts, Peter Elkind, Andrew Fastow, David Freeman, Philip Hilder, Al Kaseweter, Ken Lay, Bill Lerach, Loretta Lynch, Amanda Martin-Brock, Bethany McLean, Mike Muckleroy, Rev. James Nutter, John Olson, Lou Lung Pai, Kevin Phillips, Nancy Rapoport, Nancy Rapoport, Harvey Rosenfield, Jeff Skilling, Mimi Swartz, Sherron Watkins, Colin Whitehead, Charles Wickman

Andrew Fastow PHOTOS COURTESY OF MAGNOLIA

Hope Davis, Campbell Scott, Alexander Michaletos

DUMA

(WARNER BROS.) Producers, John Wells, Hunt Lowry, E. K. Gaylord II, Kristin Harms, Stacy Cohen; Executive Producers, David Wicht, Vlokkie Gordon; Director, Carroll Ballard; Screenplay, Karen Janszen, Mark St. Germain; Story, Carol Flint, Karen Janszen; Based on the book *How It Was with Dooms* by Carol Cawthra Hopcraft and Xan Hopcraft; Photography, Werner Maritz; Designer, Johnny Breedt; Costumes, Jayne Forbes; Music, John Debney, George Acogny; Head Animal Trainer, Jules Sylvester; Casting, Junie Lowry Johnson, Scott Genkinger; a John Wells Productions, Gaylord Films production; Dolby; Technicolor; Rated PG; 100 minutes; Release date: April 22, 2005

Eamonn Walker PHOTOS COURTESY OF WARNER BROS.

Alexander Michaletos, Duma

Alexander Michaletos, Duma

Cast

Xan **Alexander Michaletos**
Peter **Campbell Scott**
Thandi **Mary Makhatho**
Lucille **Nthabiseng Kenoshi**
Kristin **Hope Davis**
Aunt Gwen **Jennifer Steyn**
Coach Nagy **Nicky Rebelo**
Hock Bender **Garth Renecle**
Xan's Teacher **Andre Stolz**
Poetry Student **Charlotte Savage**
Policeman **Ronald Shange**
Ripkuna **Eamonn Walker**

and Nadia Kretschmer, John Whiteley, Clive Scott, Catriona Andrew (Tourists), Errol Ballantine (White Haired Doctor), Michele Levin (Doctor's Wife), Sam Nagakane (Old Man in Village), Adelaide Shabalala (Medicine Woman, Suliwa), Thokozani Ndaba (Rip's Wife, Melika), Wright Ngubane (Rip's Son), Bernard Msimang (Rip's Father), Bernard Msimang (Rip's Father), Ivy Nkutha (Rip's Mother), Anthony, Azaro, Nikita, Sasha, Savannah (Duma), Sheba (Young Duma)

After having raised a cheetah as the family pet, young Xan realizes it is up to him to release the animal back into the wild.

A LOT LIKE LOVE

(TOUCHSTONE) Producers, Armyan Bernstein, Kevin Messick; Executive Producers, Charlie Lyons, Zanne Devine, Suzann Ellis; Co-Producer, Lisa Bruce; Director, Nigel Cole; Screenplay, Colin Patrick Lynch; Photography, John de Borman; Designer, Tom Meyer; Costumes, Alix Friedberg; Music, Alex Wurman; Editor, Susan Littenberg; Casting, Joseph Middleton; a Beacon Pictures presentation of a Beacon Production in association with Kevin Messick Productions; Dolby; Deluxe color; Rated PG-13; 107 minutes; Release date: April 22, 2005

Amanda Peet, Ashton Kutcher

Cast

Oliver Martin	**Ashton Kutcher**
Emily Friehl	**Amanda Peet**
Michelle	**Kathryn Kahn**
Jeeter	**Kal Penn**
Graham Martin	**Ty Giordano**
Ellen Martin	**Taryn Manning**
Carol Martin	**Melissa van der Schyff**
Brent Friehl	**James Read**
Christine	**Molly Cheek**
Peter	**Gabriel Mann**
Gina	**Ali Larter**

and Aimee Garcia (Nicole), Lee Garlington (Stewardess), Birdie M. Hale (Old Woman), Theresa Sprull (Street Vendor), Sarah Ann Morris (Bartender), Amy Aquino (Diane Martin), Constance Hsu (Chinese Waitress), Josh Stamberg (Michael), Misty Louwagie (Elegant Beauty),

Ashton Kutcher, Kal Penn

Kathryn Hahn, Ali Larter, Amanda Peet

Sam Pancake (Hipster at Party), Sarah Shahi (Starlet), Moon Bloodgood (Bridget), Jeremy Sisto (Ben Miller), Robert Peters (Roy Douglas), Addison Bouquet (Hailey), Katherine Herzer (Little Girl), Kevin Robert Kelly (Park Ranger), Ron Bottitta, Steven Guy (VC Guys), Sean Smith, T. R. Hopper (Lawyers), Linda Hunt (Airline Attendant), Meghan Markle (Hot Girl), Joeanna Sayler (Gallery Owner), Lindsay MacFarland (Gallery Patron), Herschel Bleefeld (Bill), Conrad Bluth (Chris), Colin Patrick Lynch (Upstairs Neighbor), Rick Overton (Tailor), Brendan P. Connor (Wedding Guest), William Stanford Davis (Priest), Daniele O'Loughlin (Wedding Planner), Nora Burns, Nealla Gordon, Steve Filice (Caterers), Holmes Osborne (Stephen Martin)

Following an impromptu tryst in an airline toilet, Oliver Martin and Emily Friehl continue to meet off and on for romantic liaisons at various intervals in their lives.

Amanda Peet, Ashton Kutcher, Ty Giordano PHOTOS COURTESY OF TOUCHSTONE

Nicole Kidman, Sean Penn

THE INTERPRETER

(UNIVERSAL) Producers, Tim Bevan, Eric Fellner, Kevin Misher; Executive Producers, Sydney Pollack, Anthony Minghella, G. Mac Brown; Director, Sydney Pollack; Screenplay, Charles Randolph, Scott Frank, Steven Zaillian; Story, Martin Stellman, Brian Ward; Photography, Darius Khondji; Designer, Jon Hutman; Costumes, Sarah Edwards; Music, James Newton Howard; Editor, William Steinkamp; Co-Producers, Liza Chasin, Debra Hayward; Casting, Juliet Taylor, Ellen Lewis; a Working Title production in association with Misher Films, Mirage Enterprises, presented in association with MP Jota productions; U.S.-German; Dolby; Technovision; Technicolor; Rated PG-13; 128 minutes; Release date: April 22, 2005

Sean Penn, Catherine Keener   PHOTOS COURTESY OF UNIVERSAL

Cast

Silvia Broome **Nicole Kidman**
Tobin Keller **Sean Penn**
Dot Woods **Catherine Keener**
Nils Lud **Jesper Christensen**
Philippe **Yvan Attal**
Zuwanie **Earl Cameron**
Kuman-Kuman **George Harris**
Marcus **Michael Wright**
Police Chief Lee Wu **Clyde Kusatsu**
Rory Robb **Eric Keenleyside**
Simon Broome **Hugo Speer**
Mo **Maz Jobrani**
Doug **Yusuf Gatewood**

and Curtiss I' Cook (Ajene Xola), Byron Utley (Jean Gamba), Robert Clohessy (FBI Agent King), Terry Serpico (FBI Agent Lewis), David Fonteno (Phillip Ostroff), John Knox (Fred Jameson), David Zayas (Charlie Russell), Lynne Deragon (American Ambassador Davis), Christopher Evan Welch (Jonathan Williams), Manuel Mawele, Dino Mulima, Litto (African Boys),

Nicole Kidman

Adrian Martinez (Roland), Tsai Chin (Luan), Francine Roussel (Isobel), Enid Graham (Jenny), Lou Ferguson (Matoban Ambassador), Okwui Okpokwasili (Tour Guide), Vladimir Bibic (G.A. President), Jacques Sebag (French Ambassador), Pietro Gonzalez (Chilean Ambassador), Patrick Ssenjovu (Jad Jamal), Michael Patrick McGrath (Jonathan Ferris), Paul De Sousa (Portuguese Janitor), Chris McKinney (Forensic Officer), Martha Elliott (Woman on Bus), Jim Ward, Trevor Archer, Ricardo Walker, Harry O'Reilly, Kirby Mitchell, Guy Fortt (U.N. Security Officers), Ramsey Faragallah (Polygraph Technician), John Di Benedetto (Mechanic), Bridget L. Doerksen, Ana Maria Lupo (Strippers), Nelson Landrieu (Spanish Speaking Interpreter), Satish Joshi (Secretary General), Sophie Traub (Young Silvia), Monty Ashton-Lewis (Young Simon), Pat Kiernan (Himself), Margot Staub, Harry Prichett, Ed Onipede Blunt (News Reporters), Diana Winter (British Airways Ticket Agent)

U.N. interpreter Silvia Broome finds her life endangered after overhearing a death threat spoken in a rare dialect against an African head of state.

Anna Chancellor, Jeltz

Martin Freeman, Warwick Davis

Mos Def, Martin Freeman, Sam Rockwell

THE HITCHHIKER'S GUIDE TO THE GALAXY

(TOUCHSTONE) Producers, Nick Goldsmith, Jay Roach, Jonathan Glickman, Gary Barber, Roger Birnbaum; Executive Producers, Douglas Adams, Robbie Stamp, Derek Evans; Director, Garth Jennings; Screenplay, Douglas Adams, Karey Kirkpatrick; Based on the book by Douglas Adams; Photography, Igor Jadue-Lillo; Desginer, Joel Collins; Costumes, Sammy Sheldon; Music, Jody Talbot; Editor, Niven Howie; Visual Effects Supervisor, Angus Bickerton; Creature Effects, Jim Henson's Creature Shop; Co-Producers, Todd Arnow, Caroline Hewitt, Rebekah Rudd; Casting, Susie Figgis; a Spyglass Entertainment presentation of a Barber/Birnbaum production, a Hammer and Tongs, Everyman Pictures production; Dolby; Panavision; Technicolor; Rated PG; 110 minutes; Release date: April 29, 2005

Zooey Deschanel

Cast

Zaphod Beeblebrox **Sam Rockwell**
Ford Prefect **Mos Def**
Trish McMillan/Trillian **Zooey Deschanel**
Arthur Dent **Martin Freeman**
Slartibartfast **Bill Nighy**
Marvin **Warwick Davis**
Questular **Anna Chancellor**
Voice of Marvin **Alan Rickman**
Voice of Deep Thought **Helen Mirren**
Narrator **Stephen Fry**
Voice of Shipboard Computer **Thomas Lennon**
Humma Kavula **John Malkovich**

Sam Rockwell, Mos Def

Martin Freeman, Sam Rockwell, Mos Def, Zooey Deschanel

In the middle of a bad day, Arthur Dent is forced to hitch a ride with a passing spacecraft after Earth is destroyed to make way for a hyperspace freeway.

John Malkovich

and Bill Bailey (Voice of the Whale), Su Elliott (Pub Customer), Richard Griffiths (Voice of Jeltz), Dominique Jackson (Fook), Simon Jones (Ghostly Image), Mark Longhurst (Reporter), Ian McNeice (Voice of Kwaltz), Steve Pemberton (Prosser), Jack Stanley (Lunkwill), The League of Gentlemen (Additional Vogon Voices), Mark Wilson (Voice of Vogon Interpreter), Albie Woodington (Barman)

Martin Freeman, Bill Nighy

Sam Rockwell, Zooey Deschanel, Warwick Davis, Mos Def

John Malkovich PHOTOS COURTESY OF TOUCHSTONE PICTURES

MYSTERIOUS SKIN

(TLA RELEASING) Producer, Mary Jane Skalski, Jeffrey Levy-Hinte, Gregg Araki; Executive Producers, Wouter Barendrecht, Michael J. Werner; Co-Producers, Joshua Zeman, Hans C. Ritter; Director/Screenplay/Editor, Gregg Araki; Based on the novel by Scott Heim; Photography, Steve Gainer; Designer, Devorah Herbert; Costumes, Alix Hester; Music, Harold Budd, Robin Guthrie; Music Supervisor, Howard Paar; Casting, Shannon Makhanian; a Fortissimo Films presentation of an Antidote Films, Desperate Pictures production; Dolby; Color; Rated R; 99 minutes; Release date: May 6, 2005

Brady Corbet, Mary Lynn Rajskub

Joseph Gordon-Levitt, Jeff Licon, Elisabeth Shue

Cast
Neil McCormick **Joseph Gordon-Levitt**
Brian Lackey **Brady Corbet**
Eileen McCormick **Elisabeth Shue**
Wendy Peterson **Michelle Trachtenberg**
Coach Heider **Bill Sage**
Eric Preston **Jeff Licon**
Mrs. Lackey **Lisa Long**

Joseph Gordon-Levitt, Brady Corbet

Bill Sage, Elisabeth Shue, Chase Ellison PHOTOS COURTESY OF TLA RELEASING

Mr. Lackey **Chris Mulkey**
Charlie **Richard Riehle**
Neil McCormick, Age 8 **Chase Ellison**
Brian Lackey, Age 8 **George Webster**
Deborah Lackey, Age 12 **Rachel Kraft**
Alfred **David Lee Smith**
Wendy Peterson, Age 11 **Riley McGuire**

and Ryan Stenzel (Stephen Zepherelli), Larry Marko (Old Man with Scar), Mary Lynn Rajskub (Avalyn Friesen), Bruno Alexander (Redneck Hick), Forrest Fountain (Jackson), Zane Huett (Jackson's Son), Reedy Gibbs (Receptionist), David Alan Graf (Gay Lumberjack), John Ganun (NYC John), Kelly Kruger (Deborah Lackey), Pete Kasper (Sedan Driver), Billy Drago (Zeke)

Two boys who were molested by their baseball coach take different paths in life, one becoming a self-assured hustler, the other a sexually repressed young man who believes he was abducted by aliens.

Wilson Castillo, Jatnna Toribo

MAD HOT BALLROOM

(PARAMOUNT CLASSICS) Producers, Amy Sewell, Marilyn Agrelo; Director, Marilyn Agrelo; Screenplay, Amy Sewell; Photography, Claudia Raschke; Music, Steven Lutvak; Music Supervisor, Mark Reynolds; Editor, Sabine Krayenbuhl; Associate Producer, W. Wilder Knight II; a Just One Productions presentation; Dolby; Color; DV; Rated PG; 115 minutes; Release date: May 13, 2005. Documentary on a New York City dance competition for 10- and 11-year-old boys and girls.

Yomaira Reynoso PHOTOS COURTESY OF PARAMOUNT CLASSICS

With

Yomaira Reynoso, Wilson Castillo, Alyssa Polack, Michell Rodriguez, Elsamelys Ulerio, Clarita Zeppie, Tara Devon Gallagher, Alex Tchassov, Victoria Malvagno, Emma Biegacki, Cyrus Hernstadt, Jonathan Rodriguez, Jatnna Toribo, Taha Natab, Louise Verdemare, Jia Wen Zhu, Jonathan, Allison Sheniak, Sidney Grant, Terry Mintzer

Allison Sheniak, Alex Tchassov

KICKING & SCREAMING

(UNIVERSAL) Producer, Jimmy Miller; Executive Producers, Charles Roven, Judd Apatow, Daniel Lupi; Director, Jesse Dylan; Screenplay, Leo Benvenuti, Steve Rudnick; Photography, Lloyd Ahern; Designer, Clayton R. Hartley; Costumes, Pamela Withers Chilton; Music, Mark Isham; Music Supervisor, Dave Jordan; Editors, Stuart Pappé, Peter Teschner; Associate Producer, Mia Apatow; Casting, Juel Bestrop, Jeanne McCarthy; a Mosaic Media Group production; Dolby; Panavision; Technicolor; Rated PG; 96 minutes; Release date: May 13, 2005

Robert Duvall, Will Ferrell

Cast

Phil Weston **Will Ferrell**
Buck Weston **Robert Duvall**
Himself **Mike Ditka**
Barbara Weston **Kate Walsh**
Janice Weston **Musetta Vander**
Sam Weston **Dylan McLaughlin**
Bucky Weston **Josh Hutcherson**
Mark Avery **Steven Anthony Lawrence**
Hunter **Jeremy Bergman**
Byong Sun **Elliot Cho**
Ambrose **Erik Walker**
Connor **Dallas McKinney**

Elliot Cho, Will Ferrell

Will Ferrell, Mike Ditka

Gian Piero **Francesco Liotti**
Massimo **Alessandro Ruggiero**
Jack **Sammy Fine**
Alex **Timmy Deters**

and Dave Herman (Referee), Rachael Harris (Ann Hogan), Laura Kightlinger (Donna Jones), Jim Turner (Jim Davidson, "The Captain"), Julia Campbell (Janet Davidson), Phill Lewis (John Ryan), Dave Bowe (Forest Avery), Matt Winston (Tom Hanna), Susan Barnes (Diana Ditka), Lu Elrod (Patty), Tom Virtue (Track & Field Coach), Karly Rothenberg (Jack's Mother), Joseph R. Sicari (Umberto), Timm Sharp, Stasi Glenn, Frank Cassavetes, Jose Vivanco (Butcher Shop Employees), Jarrad Paul, Robert Patrick Benedict (Beantown Employees), Martin Starr, Lisa Lackey, Brian Palermo (Beantown Customers), Scott Adsit (Stew), Peter Jason (Clark), Gus Buktenica (Caring Soccer Dad), Jeffrey Noah (Phil, Age 9 & 11), Kaitlyn Arens (Baby Phil), Harrison Doyle, Christopher Garcia-Reyes, Chase Klitzner, Brandon Vincent (Tigers), Zach Hendrickson, Logan Rouse, Daniel Barrera, Brett Berman, Richard G. Fray II, Jeffrey Koval, Kyle Nathanson, Jeffrey Thomas Nemit III, Jack Polson, Wesley Taylor, Michael Uyehara, Tyler Reid West (Gladiators), Willie Amakye (Cosmos Player)

Mild-mannered vitamin salesman Phil Weston agrees to coach his son Sam's last place little league soccer team, the Tigers, and ends up competing against his own overbearing dad who is coaching the rival team.

Will Ferrell, Kate Walsh PHOTOS COURTESY OF UNIVERSAL

Michael Vartan, Jennifer Lopez

Wanda Sykes, Jane Fonda

MONSTER-IN-LAW

(NEW LINE CINEMA) Producers, Paula Weinstein, Chris Bender, JC Spink; Executive Producers, Michael Flynn, Toby Emmerich, Richard Brener; Director, Robert Luketic; Screenplay, Anya Kochoff; Photography, Russell Carpenter; Designer, Missy Stewart; Costumes, Kym Barrett; Music, David Newman; Music Supervisor, Dana Sano; Editors, Scott Hill, Kevin Tent; Associate Producer, Magnus Kim; Casting, Ronna Kress; a Bender-Spink production; Dolby; Super 35 Widescreen; Deluxe color; Rated PG-13; 95 minutes; Release date: May 13, 2005

Cast

Charlotte "Charlie" Cantilini **Jennifer Lopez**
Viola Fields **Jane Fonda**
Kevin Fields **Michael Vartan**
Ruby **Wanda Sykes**
Remy **Adam Scott**
Fiona **Monet Mazur**
Morgan **Annie Parisse**
Kit **Will Arnett**
Gertrude **Elaine Stritch**
Dr. Chamberlain **Stephen Dunham**
Beverly Hills Dog Owner **Randee Heller**
Guy in Coffee Shop **Mark Moses**
Girl in Coffee Shop **Tomiko Fraser**
Nurse in Dr. Patel's Office **Rochelle Flexer**
George **Wayne Nickel**
Viola's Young Replacement **Jenny Wade**
TV Executive **Bruce Gray**

and Zach McLarty (Assistant Director), Stephanie Turner (Pop Star), Harriet Harris (Therapist), Jimmy Jean-Louis (Prince Amir), Christopher Scott (Prime Minister), Pamela Rowan (Woman Club Member), Monica R. Guiza (Rehearsal Dinner Guest), Amber Mead (Kit's Date), Christina Masterson (Young Girl at Wedding)

Monet Mazur, Will Arnett

Kevin's overbearing mother is so upset at his engagement to Charlie Cantilini that she sets out to drive his fiancée crazy and destroy any chance of their getting married.

Annie Parisse, Adam Scott PHOTOS COURTESY OF COLUMBIA

STAR WARS EPISODE III:
REVENGE OF THE SITH

(20TH CENTURY FOX) Producer, Rick McCallum; Executive Producer/Director/ Screenplay, George Lucas; Photography, David Tattersall; Designer, Gavin Bocquet; Costumes, Trisha Biggar; Music, John Williams; Editors, Roger Barton, Ben Burtt; Special Visual Effects/Animation, Industrial Light & Magic; Visual Effects Supervisors, John Knoll, Roger Guyett; Makeup Supervisor, Nikki Gooley; Stunts, Nick Gillard; Casting, Christine King; a Lucasfilm production; Dolby; Panavision; Color; Rated PG-13; 140 minutes; Release date: May 19, 2005

Bruce Spence

Wookies

Hayden Christensen

Cast

Obi-Wan Kenobi **Ewan McGregor**
Padmé **Natalie Portman**
Anakin Skywalker **Hayden Christensen**
Supreme Chancellor Palpatine **Ian McDiarmid**
Mace Windu **Samuel L. Jackson**
Senator Bail Organa **Jimmy Smits**
Voice of Yoda **Frank Oz**
C-3PO **Anthony Daniels**
Count Dooku **Christopher Lee**
Queen of Naboo **Keisha Castle-Hughes**
Ki-Adi-Mundi/Nute Gunray **Silas Carson**
Captain Typho **Jay Laga'aia**
Tion Medon **Bruce Spence**
Governor Tarkin **Wayne Pygram**
Commander Cody **Temuera Morrison**
Mas Amedda **David Bowers**
Sio Bibble **Oliver Ford Davies**
Jar Jar Binks **Ahmed Best**
Captain Antilles **Rohan Nichol**
Captain Colton **Jeremy Bulloch**
Terr Taneel **Amanda Lucas**
R2-D2 **Kenny Baker**
Plo Koon **Matt Sloan**
Chewbacca **Peter Mayhew**
Queen of Alderaan **Rebecca Jackson Mendoza**
Owen Lars **Joel Edgerton**
Beru **Bonnie Piesse**

Yoda

Samuel L. Jackson

Anthony Daniels, Kenny Baker, Natalie Portman, Hayden Christensen

and Jett Lucas (Zett Jukassa), Tux Akindoyeni (Agen Kolar), Matt Rowan (Senator Orn Free Taa), Kenji Oates (Saesee Tiin), Amy Allen (Aayla Secura), Bodie "Tihoi" Taylor (Clone Trooper), Graeme Blundell (Ruwee Naberrie), Trisha Noble (Jobal Naberrie), Claudia Karvan (Sola Naberrie), Neira Wingate (Ryoo Naberrie), Hayley Mooy (Pooja Naberrie), Sandi Finlay (Sly Moore), Katie Lucas (Chi Eekway), Genevieve O'Reilly (Mon Mothma), Warren Owens (Fang Zar), kee Chan (Malé-Dee), Rena Owen (Nee Alavar), Christopher Kirby (Giddean Danu), Matthew Wood (Voice of General Grievous), Kristy Wright (Moteé), Coinneach Alexander (Whie), Mousy McCallum (Bene), Michael Kingma (Tarfful, Wookie), Axel Dench, Steven Foy, Julian Khazzouh, James Rowland, David Stiff, Robert Cope (Wookies)

Hayden Christensen

Trained to be a Jedi, Anakin Skywalker is torn between accepting the Jedi Council's refusal to grant him master status and the offer by the Republic's Chancellor Palpatine to join the dark side, an act which he believes will save his wife from death in childbirth. Sixth and final film in the 20th Century Fox *Star Wars* series following *Star Wars* (1977), *The Empire Strikes Back* (1980), *Return of the Jedi* (1983), *Star Wars Episode I: The Phantom Menace* (1999), and *Star Wars II: Attack of the Clones* (2002).

Ewan McGregor, Natalie Portman

Yoda, Ewan McGregor, Jimmy Smits

Hayden Christensen PHOTOS COURTESY OF 20TH CENTURY FOX

MADAGASCAR

(DREAMWORKS) Producer, Mireille Sorla; Directors, Eric Darnell, Tom McGrath; Co-Producer, Teresa Cheng; Screenplay, Mark Burton, Billy Frolick, Eric Darnell, Tom McGrath; Designer, Kendal Cronkhite-Shaindlin; Music, Hans Zimmer; Editor, H. Lee Peterson; Visual Effects Supervisor, Philippe Gluckman; Head of Character Animation, Rex Grignon; Head of Layout, Ewan Johnson; Art Director, Shannon Jeffries; Casting, Leslee Feldman; a DreamWorks Animation presentation of a Pacific Data Images, DreamWorks production; Dolby; Technicolor; Rated PG; 86 minutes; Release date: May 27, 2005

Voice Cast
Alex **Ben Stiller**
Marty **Chris Rock**
Melman **David Schwimmer**
Gloria **Jada Pinkett Smith**
Julien **Sacha Baron Cohen**
Maurice **Cedric the Entertainer**
Mort **Andy Richter**

and Tom McGrath (Skipper/Fossa/Panicky Man on Subway), Christopher Knights (Private), Chris Miller (Kowalski), Conrad Vernon (Mason), Eric Darnell (Zoo Announcer/Lemur #1/Fossa/Subway Car Announcer), David Cowgill (Police Horse), Steve Apostolina (Police Officer), Elisa Gabrielli (Old Lady), Devika Parikh (News Reporter), David P. Smith (Spider/Lemur #2), Cody Cameron (Willie)

Marty, Alex, Gloria, Melman

Marty

Having spent his entire life in New York's Central Park Zoo, Alex the Lion lets his curiosity get the best of him and plans his escape in order to explore the world he's been missing, a decision that causes him and his fellow animals to end up on route to Africa.

Rico, Private, Skipper, Kowalski

King Julien, Mort, Maurice

Marty, Alex, Gloria, Melman PHOTOS COURTESY OF DREAMWORKS

SAVING FACE

(SONY CLASSICS) Producers, Teddy Zee, James Lassiter, Will Smith; Executive Producers, Robin O'Hara, Scott Macauley, John Penotti; Director/Screenplay, Alice Wu; Photography, Harlan Bosmajian; Designer, Dan Ouellette; Costumes, Jill Newell; Music, Anton Sanko; Editors, Sue Graef, Sabine Hoffman; Associate Producer, Jeff Morin; Casting, Heidi Griffiths, Jaclyn Brodsky; an Overbrook Entertainment production in association with Forensic Films, Greene-Street Films; Dolby; Color; Rated R; 91 minutes; Release date: May 27, 2005

Lynn Chen, Michelle Krusiec

Michelle Krusiec, Lynn Chen

Cast

Wilhelmina Pang **Michelle Krusiec**
Ma **Joan Chen**
Vivian Lu **Lynn Chen**
Wai Gun **Li Zhiyu**
Randi **Jessica Hecht**
Jay **Ato Essandoh**
Wai Po **Guang Lan Koh**
Norman **David Shih**
Little Yu **Brian Yang**
Stimson Cho **Nathanel Geng**
Old Yu **Mao Zhao**
Dr. Shing **Louyong Wong**
Mrs. Wong **Clare Sum**
Mrs. Shing **Qian Luo**
Stephen **Richard Chang**
Raymond Wong **Hoon Lee**

and Ruth Zhang (Mrs. Yao), Connie Hsia (Mrs. Chen), Jackson Ning (Mr. Chen), Jamie Guan (Mr. Yao), Paul Sum (Mr. Wong), Brittany Perrineau (Dara), Xiaofeng Zang (Mr. Fu), Lu Yu (Stoic Date), Fang Yulin (Wart Date), Pamela Payton-Wright (Dr. Morgan), Saidah Arrika Ekulona, Tina Johnson (Nurses), Twinkle Burke (Hospital Receptionist), Phillip Meng (Mambo Date), Chloe Tsang (8-Year-Old Chinese Girl), Rosa Luo (Cho Sister #1), Christy Qin (Nurse at Clinic), Nan Meng (Mother at Clinic)

Joan Chen

A woman who has never accepted her daughter's lesbian lifestyle is forced to seek her aid when she herself is cast out by her father for being pregnant.

Joan Chen, Ato Essandoh, Michelle Krusiec PHOTOS COURTESY OF SONY CLASSICS

THE LONGEST YARD

(PARAMOUNT/COLUMBIA) Producer, Jack Giarraputo; Executive Producers, Adam Sandler, Van Toffler, David Gale, Barry Bernardi, Allen Covert, Tim Herlihy, Michael Ewing, Albert S. Ruddy; Director, Peter Segal; Screenplay, Sheldon Turner; Based on the screenplay by Tracy Keenan Wynn, from a story by Albert S. Ruddy; Photography, Dean Semler; Designer, Perry Andelin Blake; Costumes, Ellen Lutter; Music, Teddy Castellucci; Music Supervisor, Michael Dilbeck; Co-Producer, Heather Parry; Editor, Jeff Gourson; a Happy Madison, MTV Films production in association with Callahan Filmworks; Dolby; Deluxe color; Rated PG-13; 113 minutes; Release date: May 27, 2005

Steve Austin, William Fitchner, Brian Bosworth

Chris Rock, Burt Reynolds, Adam Sandler

Cast

Paul Crewe **Adam Sandler**
Caretaker **Chris Rock**
Coach Nate Scarborough **Burt Reynolds**
Megget **Nelly**
Warden Hazen **James Cromwell**
Lynette **Cloris Leachman**
Deacon Moss **Michael Irvin**
Errol Dandridge **Walter Williamson**
Battle **Bill Goldberg**
Cheeseburger Eddy **Terry Crews**
Switowski **Bob Sapp**
Brucie **Nicholas Turturro**
Turley **Dalip Singh**
Torres **Lobo Sebastian**
Big Tony **Joey "Coco" Diaz**
Baby Face Bob **Steve Reevis**
Unger **David Patrick Kelly**

and Tracy Morgan (Ms. Tucker), Edward Bunker (Skitchy Rivers), William Fichtner (Captain Knauer), Bill Romanowski (Guard Lambert), Kevin Nash (Guard Engleheart), Steve Austin (Guard Dunham), Brian Bosworth (Guard

Garner), Michael Papajohn (Guard Papajohn), Conrad Goode (Guard Webster), Brandon Molale (Guard Malloy), Todd Holland (Guard Holland), Allen Covert (Referee), Rob Schneider (Punky), Chris Berman (Announcer), Jim Rome, Lauren Sanchez (Themselves), Patrick Bristow (Walt), Dan Patrick (Officer Jack Pugh), Christopher Neiman (Big Ear Cop), Ed Lauter (Duane), Sean Salisbury (Vic), Rob "Revolution" Moore (Gavin), Big Boy (Jesse), Michael H. Goodwin, Ray Stoney, Michael Silas, Andre Fuentes, Lonnie Henderson, Asiel Hardison, Colin Kim (Con Transvestites), Mark Ellis (Stretcher Guy), Tim Crowley (Umpire), Kon Artist, Bizarre, Proof, Kuniva, Swift (Basketball Convicts), Bryan Burwell, Sam Farmer, Jay Glazer, Peter King, John McClain, Adam Schefter, Larry Weisman (Sportswriters), Marc S. Ganis (Lorenzo), Shane Ralston (Bradlee), Jenae Altschwager, Candace Juleff, Bryan Ross (Party Guests), Ricardo J. King (Press Box Technician), Stink Fisher, Jasper Pendergrass, Sean McNamara (Cafeteria Prisoners), Robert Harvey (Cafeteria Guard), Eric Chmielecki (Guard Sniper), Denise Marie Jerome, Jaayda McClanahan, Tara Wilson, Rachel Saydak, Cara-Lee Knodel, Nora Hassan (Guard Cheerleaders), John Hockridge (Guard Hock), Courtney Cox Arquette (Lena)

Nelly, Michael Irvin PHOTOS COURTESY OF PARAMOUNT

After disgraced former quarterback Paul Crewe ends up in prison, he helps recruit a team of inmates to play a game against the guards. Remake of the 1974 Paramount film which starred Burt Reynolds and Eddie Albert. Reynolds plays the role of the coach played in the original film by Michael Conrad; Ed Lauter from the original film also has a bit role here.

America Ferrera, Blake Lively, Alexis Bledel, Amber Tamblyn

THE SISTERHOOD OF THE TRAVELING PANTS

(WARNER BROS.) Producers, Debra Martin Chase, Denise Di Novi; Executive Producers, Leslie Morgenstein, Kira Davis, Alison Greenspan; Co-Producers, Christine Sacani, Steven P. Wegner, Melissa Wiechmann; Director, Ken Kwapis; Screenplay, Delia Ephron, Elizabeth Chandler; Based on the novel by Ann Brashares; Photography, John Bailey; Designer, Gae Buckley; Costumes, Lisa Jensen; Music, Cliff Eidelman; Music Supervisor, Dawn Soler; Editor, Kathryn Himoff; Casting, Shani Ginsberg, Jakki Fink; an Alcon Entertainment presentation of a Di Novi Pictures, Debra Martin Chase production; Dolby; Panavision; Color; Rated PG; 120 minutes; Release date: June 1, 2005

Mike Vogel, Blake Lively

Amber Tamblyn, Jenna Boyd PHOTOS COURTESY OF WARNER BROS.

Cast
Tibby **Amber Tamblyn**
Lena **Alexis Bledel**
Carmen **America Ferrera**
Bridget **Blake Lively**
Bailey **Jenna Boyd**
Al **Bradley Whitford**
Lydia Rodman **Nancy Travis**
Carmen's Mother **Rachel Ticotin**
Eric **Mike Vogel**
Kostos **Michael Rady**
Brian McBrian **Leonard Nam**
Yia Yia **Maria Konstadarou**
Papou **George Touliatos**

America Ferrera, Amber Tamblyn

and Kyle Schmid (Paul Rodman), Erica Hubbard (Soccer Pal Diana), Emily Tennant (Krista Rodman), Jacqueline Stewart (Lena's Mother), Sarah-Jane Redmond (Tibby's Mother), Ernie Lively (Bridget's Father), Kendall Cross (Bridget's Mother), Kristie Marsden (Soccer Pal Olivia), Patricia Mayan Salazar (Camp Director Donna), Patrick Drake (Coach Karen), Katie Stuart (Bunkmate Jo), Diana Artuso (Mail Call Coach), Jonathon Young (Duncan), Beverley Elliot (Roberta), Victoria Tennant (Young Tibby), Allanna Dawn Ekkert (Young Lena), Tiara Santana (Young Carmen), Ashley Hale (Young Bridget), J. B. McEown (Jeering Boy), Charles Payne (Soccer Dad), Marek Wiedman (Funeral Minister), Georgia Craig (Saleslady), Mary Black, Chic Gibson (Bailey's Neighbors), Nicole Potvin, Lauren Jarrar (Catty Teens), Kathryn Kirkpatrick (Waitress Brenda), Valerie Tian (Interview Girl #1), Alisha Penev (Krista's Friend), Brenda James (Barbar the Tailor), Keith Dallas (Cab Driver), Terence Kelly (Wedding Minister), Kirsten Williamson (Aerobics Instructor), Cannon Smith (Soccer Kid), Efi Papatheodorou (Elderly Greek Woman), Olga Archontoy, Mariana Arvanitou, Despina Alefragi (Greek Cousins), Giorgos Zarkostas (Greek Fedex Man), Alan Belton (Seamstress), Anoop Virk, Rebecca William (Lemonade Stand Girls), Angela Hodgson, Clayton Al Leung, Genevieve Mac Kay, Sarah Tippett (Wedding Quartet), Michaelis Feroussis, Jorgos Makrakis, Chronis Mandas (Greek Band Members)

Four close friends, spending their first summer apart, vow to stay in touch by swapping a pair of blue jeans that magically fit each one of the girls.

LORDS OF DOGTOWN

(COLUMBIA) Producer, John Linson; Executive Producers, Art Linson, David Fincher, Joe Drake; Director, Catherine Hardwicke; Screenplay, Stacy Peralta; Co-Producer, Ginger Sledge; Photography, Elliot Davis; Designer, Chris Gorak; Costumes, Cindy Evans; Music, Mark Mothersbaugh; Music Supervisor, Liza Richardson; Editor, Nancy Richardson; Casting, Victoria Thomas; Stunts, Thomas Robinson Harper; Skate Coach, Tony Alva; a Linson Films production in association with Senator International; Dolby; Deluxe color; Rated PG-13; 106 minutes; Release date: June 3, 2005

Johnny Knoxville, Victor Rasuk

Cast

Jay Adams **Emile Hirsch**
Tony Alva **Victor Rasuk**
Stacy Peralta **John Robinson**
Sid **Michael Angarano**
Kathy Alva **Nikki Reed**
Philaine **Rebecca De Mornay**
Skip Engbloom **Heath Ledger**
Topper Burks **Johnny Knoxville**
Donnie **William Mapother**
Mr. Alva **Julio Oscar Mechoso**
Chino **Vincent Laresca**
Montoya **Brian Zarate**
Stecyk **Pablo Scheriber**
Billy Z **Elden Henson**

and Mitch Hedberg (Urethane Wheels Guy), Benjamin Nurick (Browser), Stepaheni Limb (Peggy Oki), Mike Ogas (Bob Biniak), Cheyene Magnusson (Jim "Red Dog" Muir), Don Nguyen (Shogo), Kristian Peterson (Wentzie Rumi), Melonie Diaz (Blanca), Mark Kubr (Donnie's Friend), René Rivera (Mr. Peralta), Chad Fernandez (Ryan Reef), Jim "Red Dog" Muir (Security Guard), Chris Chaput (Russ Howell), Matt Malloy (Contest Official), Jack Smith (Del Mar Announcer), Steve Badillo (Ty Page), Bill Cusack (Del Mar Judge), Kirk Ward (Bill Bahne), Eddie Cahill (Larry Gordon), Laura Ramsey (Gabrielle), Sarah Blakely-Cartwright (Vickie), Bob Biniak (Restaurant Manager), Eric "Tuma" Britton (Marty

Emile Hirsch, Victor Rasuk, Michael Angarano, Heath Ledger

Grimes), Chuck Hosak (Irate Husband), Chelsea Hobbs (Caroline), Reid Harper (Lookout Boy), Paulette Ivory (Magazine Reporter), America Ferrera (Thunder Monkey), Sofia Vergara (Amelia Burks), Raphael Verela (Topper's Bodyguard), Jay Adams (Party Guest), Ned Bellamy (Peter Darling), Tony Alva (Oregon Man at Party), Charles Napier (Nudie), Joe Virzi (Capitola Race Starter), Skip Engbloom (Seattle Race Starter), Stacy Peralta (TV Director), Daniel Venegas (Vato), Tony Hawak (Astronaut), Joel McHale (TV Reporter), Bai Ling (Punky Photographer), Shea Whigham (Drake Landon), Lucas Gasperik (Jay Clone), Ray Flores (Long Beach Announcer), Alexis Arquette (Tranny), Travis Peterson (Young Surfer), Rebeca Silva (Sid's Nurse)

The true story of how three California teens revitalized and revolutionized the sport of skateboarding.

Emile Hirsch, Victor Rasuk, John Robinson PHOTOS COURTESY OF COLUMBIA

CINDERELLA MAN

(UNIVERSAL/MIRAMAX) Producers, Brian Grazer, Ron Howard, Penny Marshall; Executive Producer, Todd Hallowell; Director, Ron Howard; Screenplay, Cliff Hollingsworth, Akiva Goldsman; Story, Cliff Hollingsworth; Photography, Salvatore Totino; Designer, Wynn Thomas; Costumes, Daniel Orlandi; Music, Thomas Newman; Editors, Mike Hill, Dan Hanley; Associate Producer, Louisa Velis; Co-Executive Producer, James Whitaker; Boxing Choreographer, Nick Powell; Boxing/Stunt Coordinator, Steve Lucescu; Casting, Jane Jenkins, Janet Hirshenson; a Brian Grazer production in association with Parkway Productions; Dolby; Technicolor; Rated PG-13; 147 minutes; Release date: June 3, 2005

Ariel Waller, Patrick Louis, Connor Price, Renée Zellweger

Russell Crowe, Paul Giamatti PHOTOS COURTESY OF UNIVERSAL

Cast

James Braddock **Russell Crowe**
Mae Braddock **Renée Zellweger**
Joe Gould **Paul Giamatti**
Max Baer **Craig Bierko**
Mike Wilson **Paddy Considine**
Jimmy Johnston **Bruce McGill**
Ford Bond **David Huband**
Jay Braddock **Connor Price**
Rosemarie Braddock **Ariel Waller**
Howard Braddock **Patrick Louis**
Sara **Rosemary DeWitt**
Lucille Gould **Linda Kash**
Sporty Lewis **Nicholas Campbell**
Jake **Gene Pyrz**
Father Rorick **Chuck Shamata**
Joe Jeanette **Ron Canada**
Alice **Alicia Johnston**
John Henry-Lewis **Troy Amos-Ross**
Art Lasky **Mark Simmons**
Corn Griffin **Art Binkowski**
Abe Feldman **David Litzinger**
Primo Carnera **Matthew G. Taylor**
Announcer Al Fazin **Rance Howard**

and James Ritz (Official, Griffin/Baer Fight), Fulvio Cecere (Referee McAvoy), Clint Howard, Gerry Ellison, Bill Mackie, Ray Marsh, Fernand Chretien, Dave Dunbar (Referees), Ken James (Ancil Hoffman), Rufus Crawford (Lewis Coach), Angelo Dundee (Angelo the Cornerman), Lou Eisen, Wayne Gordon (Braddock Cornermen), Wayne Flemming, Nick Alachiotis (Baer Cornermen), Christopher D. Amos, Nick Carusi (Lewis Cornermen), Keith Murphy, Everton McEwan, Johnny Kalbhenn (Lasky Cornermen), David Georgieff, Wayne Bourque, Paul Ryan (Griffin Countermen), Sean Gilroy, Michael McNamara (Feldman Cornermen), Billy Wine, Richard Sutton, Michael Chin (Carnera Cornermen), Stewart Lunn, Richard Lewis, Peter Wylie (Campbell Cornermen), Thomasz Kurzydlowski (Tuffy Griffith), Stuart Clark (Frankie Campbell), Nick Alachiotis, Julian Lewis (Undercard Boxers, Feldman), Eric Fink (Announcer, Lasky), Sergio Di Zio (Young Reporter), Gavin Grazer, Boyd Banks, Daniel Kash, Judah Katz, Angelo Tsarouchas, Robert Smith (Reporters), Craig Warnock, Aaron Abrams (1928 Fans), Duff MacDonald, Andrew Stelmack, Chris Crumb (1935 Fans), Gerry Quigley (Quincy), Peter MacNeill (Electric Man), Darrin Brown (Promoter), John Healy, Peter Didiano, James Kirchner, Mike Langlois (Dock Workers), Magdalena Alexander (Angry Woman), Nola Augustson (Relief Office Woman), Gino Marrocco (Waiter), Mark Taylor (George), Sharron Matthews (Lady), Alec Stockwell (Church Man), Chick Roberts (Church Old Man), Isabella Fink (Church Girl), Beau Starr (Sam), Philip Craig (Radio Commentator), Roman Podhora, R. D. Reid (Hooverville Cops), Michael Dyson (Hooverville Man), Sam Malkin (Gibson), Tony Munch (Sam Penny), Conrad Bergschneider (Limo Driver), Richard Binsley (Announcer, Griffith), Ramona Pringle, Katrina Matthews Swan (Flapper Girls), Cooper Bracken, Jacob Bracken (Jay Braddock, 4 yrs.), Alon Nashman (Deserting Father), Domenic Cuzzocrea (Junket), Neil Foster (Security Guard), Brian Jagersky (Cop), Ray Kerr, Tim Eddis (Fight Promoters), Dave Arkell (Mr. Mills), Debra Sherman (Mother), Joanne Ritcey, Alex Cairns (Baer Hotel Hotties), George Duff (Man on Street)

The true story of how washed-up boxer Jim Braddock received an unexpected second chance to revitalize his career and save his family from Depression Era poverty by returning to the ring to challenge heavyweight champion Max Baer.

This film received Oscar nominations for supporting actor (Paul Giamatti), editing, and makeup.

THE ADVENTURES OF SHARKBOY AND LAVAGIRL IN 3-D

(DIMENSION) Producers, Elizabeth Avellan, Robert Rodriguez; Executive Producers, Bob Weinstein, Harvey Weinstein; Director/Photography/Editor/Special Effects Supervisor, Robert Rodriguez; Screenplay, Robert Rodriguez, Marcel Rodriguez; Story, Robert Rodriguez, Racer Rodriguez; Art Director, Jeanette Scott; Costumes, Nina Proctor; Music, Robert Rodriguez, John Debney; Casting, Mary Vernieu; a Dimension Films, Columbia Pictures presentation of a Troublemaker Studios production; Dolby; Deluxe color; 3-Dimension; HD video; Rated PG; 92 minutes; Release date: June 10, 2005

Cast

Sharkboy **Taylor Lautner**
Lavagirl **Taylor Dooley**
Max **Cayden Boyd**
Mr. Electric/Tobor/Ice/Guardian/Mr. Electricidad **George Lopez**
Max's Dad **David Arquette**
Max's Mom **Kristin Davis**
Linus/Minus **Jacob Davich**
Marissa/Ice Princess **Sasha Pieterse**
Sharkboy's Dad **Rico Torres**

and Marc Musso, Shane Graham, Tiger Darrow (Classroom Kids), Rocket Rodriguez (Lug), Racer Rodriguez (Sharkboy, Age 7), Rebel Rodriguez (Sharkboy, Age 5), Peyton Hayslip (Teacher)

Taylor Dooley

Young Max conjures up the superhero characters he has created, Sharkboy and Lavagirl, to help him stop Planet Drool from being overwhelmed by evil forces.

Taylor Dooley, Taylor Lautner

Cayden Boyd, Taylor Lautner

Taylor Lautner PHOTOS COURTESY OF DIMENSION/MIRAMAX

MR. & MRS. SMITH

(20TH CENTURY FOX) Producers, Arnon Milchan, Akiva Goldsman, Lucas Foster, Patrick Wachsberger, Eric McLeod; Executive Producer, Erik Feig; Co-Producer, Kim Winther; Director, Doug Liman; Screenplay, Simon Kinberg; Photography, Bojan Bazelli; Designer, Jeff Mann; Costumes, Michael Kaplan; Music, John Powell; Music Supervisor, Julianne Jordan; Editor, Michael Tronick; Visual Effects Supervisor, Kevin Elam; Stunts, Simon Crane; Casting, Joseph Middleton, Michelle Morris Gertz; a Regency Enterprises presentation of a New Regency, Summit Entertainment, Weed Road Pictures production; Dolby; Clairmont-Scope; Deluxe color; Rated PG-13; 120 minutes; Release date: June 10, 2005

Cast

John Smith **Brad Pitt**
Jane Smith **Angelina Jolie**
Eddie **Vince Vaughn**
Benjamin Danz **Adam Brody**
Jasmine **Kerry Washington**
Father **Keith David**
Martin Coleman **Chris Weitz**
Suzy Coleman **Rachael Huntley**
Gwen **Michelle Monaghan**

and Stephanie March (Julie—Associate #1), Jennifer Morrison (Jade—Associate #2), Therea Barrera (Janet—Associate #3), Perrey Reeves (Jessie—Associate #4), Melanie Tolbert (Jamie—Associate #5), Jerry T. Adams (Guard—Bull), Elijah Alexander (Marco Racin), Hans F. Alexander (Louis), Noah Dahl, Lauryn Alvarez (Coleman Kids), Burke Armstrong (Restaurant Patron), Ron Bottitta (P. J.—Dive Bar Patron #2), Miguel Caballero (Bellboy—Bogota), Victor A. Chapa (American Hotel Manager), Maree Cheatham (Father's Secretary), Laine Collins (Eddie's Waitress), Ali Marsh, Merrilee A. Dale, Abigail Rose Solomon (Moms), Chris Daniels (Mailman Assassin), Patrika Darbo (50's Woman), Jennifer DeMille (Breakfast Diner Waitress), Liz Ramos, Keith Diorio (Salsa Dancers), Patricia Donaldson (Louise), Sam Sabbah, Sabi Dorr (Bodyguards), Greg Ellis (Mickey—Dive Bar Patron #1), David Escobedo (Americana Hotel Bartender), Kaela Freeman (Neighborhood Girl), Megan Gallagher (40's Woman), Amy Hathaway (Beauty), Katherine Herzer, Jessica Hedden, Hannah Von Kanel (Hopscotch Girls), Nigel Hudson (Boxing Sparring Partner), Ravil Isyanov (Curtis—Dive Bar Patron #4), Stephanie Ittleson (Party Guest), Mark Ivanir (Patron—Dive Bar), Benton Jennings (Matire'D), Chris Jensen (Restaurant Waiter), Simon Kinberg, Michael Winther (Investment Bankers), Peter Lavin (Leroy—Dive Bar Patron #3), Deren LeRoy (Doorman), Sean Mahon (Lucky—Dive Bar Patron #5), Kevin Makely, Mike McCaul (Hotel Doormen), Joel Munoz, Derek Medina, Luis Racer, Richie Ornelas (Policia), Will Moore, Jordan Osher (House Assassins), Mark Newsom (Guard #1), Edward Padilla (Colombian Military Officer), Eugene Palmer (Judge), Leonard Robinson (Watchguard), Felix A. Ruiz (Vocalist), Kim Schioldan (Bartender—Dive Bar), Ty Sharp (Towncar Driver), Jimmy Shubert (Ancient Barker), Kim H. Winther (Mr. Smith's Father), Michael-John Wolfe (Bartender—Coleman House), Jeff Yagher (40's Man), Bryan Anthony, Douglas Caldwell, R. J. Durell, Melissa Hurley, Jacqui Landrum, Carol Mack, Michael Morris,

Brad Pitt, Angelina Jolie, Adam Brody

Brad Pitt, Vince Vaughn

Gloria Rodriguez, Linda Kathleen Taylor, Anne Vardanian, Ara Vardanian, Luis Vasquez, John Woodruff (Dancers), Angela Bassett (Voice of Mr. Smith's Boss), William Fitchner (Voice of Marriage Counselor)

Husband and wife John and Jane Smith, each unaware that the other is a trained assassin, face a dilemma when each is assigned to dispose of the other.

Angelina Jolie, Brad Pitt PHOTOS COURTESY OF 20TH CENTURY FOX

Liam Neeson

Rutger Hauer, Michael Caine, Gus Lewis

Christian Bale

BATMAN BEGINS

(WARNER BROS.) Producers, Charles Roven, Emma Thomas, Larry Franco; Executive Producers, Benjamin Melniker, Michael E. Uslan; Director, Christopher Nolan; Screenplay, Christopher Nolan, David S. Goyer; Story, David S. Goyer; Based upon characters appearing in comic books published by DC Comics; Batman created by Bob Kane; Photography, Wally Pfister; Designer, Nathan Crowley; Costumes, Lindy Hemmings; Music, Hans Zimmer, James Newton Howard; Editor, Lee Smith; Visual Effects Supervisors, Janek Sirrs, Dan Glass; Casting, John Papsidera, Lucinda Syson; Stunts, Sy Hollande; a Syncopy production; Dolby; Panavision; Technicolor; Rated PG-13; 140 minutes; Release date: June 15, 2005

Cast

Bruce Wayne/Batman **Christian Bale**
Alfred **Michael Caine**
Ducard **Liam Neeson**
Rachel Dawes **Katie Holmes**
Jim Gordon **Gary Oldman**
Dr. Jonathan Crane **Cillian Murphy**
Carmine Falcone **Tom Wilkinson**
Earle **Rutger Hauer**
Ra's Al Ghul **Ken Watanabe**
Flass **Mark Boone Junior**
Thomas Wayne **Linus Roache**
Lucius Fox **Morgan Freeman**
Finch **Larry Holden**
Judge Faden **Gerard Murphy**
Loeb **Colin McFarlane**
Martha Wayne **Sara Stewart**
Bruce Wayne (age 8) **Gus Lewis**
Joe Chill **Richard Brake**
Homeless Man **Rade Sherbedgia**
Rachel Dawes (age 8) **Emma Lockhart**
Jessica **Christine Adams**

and Catherine Porter (Blonde Reporter/Assassin), John Nolan

Gus Lewis, Linus Roache, Sara Stewart

Gary Oldman, Christian Bale

Ken Watanabe

Teenagers), Mel Taylor (Narrows Resident), Ilyssa Fradin (Barbara Gordon), Andrew Pleavin (Uniformed Policeman #2), Jeff Christian (Driving Cop), John Burke (Arkham Lunatic Cell Mate), Earlene Bentley (Arkham Asylum Nurse), Alex Moggridge (Arkham Asylum Orderly), Jay Buozzi (Asian Man/Ra's Al Ghul), Jordan Shaw (African Boy in Rags), Omar Mostafa (Falafel Stand Vendor), Patrick Pond (Opera Performer #1, Faust, Bass), Poppy Tierney (Opera Performer #2, Margaret, Soprano), Rory Campbell (Opera Performer #3, Mefistofele, Tenor), Fabio Cardascia (Caterer), Spencer Wilding, Mark Smith, Khan Bonfils, Dave Legeno, Ruben Halse, Rodney Ryan (League of Shadows Warriors), Dominic Burgess (Narrows Cop), Nadia Cameron-Blakey (Additional Restaurant Guest #1), Mark Straker (Restaurant Guest #2), TJ Ramini, Kiernan Huley (Crane Thugs), Jeff Tanner (Bridge Cop)

The story of how billionaire Bruce Wayne, orphaned as a child after his parents were senselessly murdered, turned away from his frivolous lifestyle and decided to fight crime in Gotham City. Previous WB Batman films were *Batman* (1989) and *Batman Returns* (1992) starring Michael Keaton; *Batman Forever* (1995, Val Kilmer); and *Batman and Robin* (1997, George Clooney).

This film received an Oscar nomination for cinematography.

Morgan Freeman, Christian Bale

(Fredericks), Karen David, Jonathan D. Ellis (Courthouse Reporters), Tamer Hassan (Faden's Limo Driver), Ronan Leahy (Old Asian Prisoner), Tom Wu, Mark Chiu (Bhutanese Prison Guards), Turbo Kong (Enormous Prisoner), Stuart Ong, Chike Chan (Chinese Police Officers), Tenzin Clive Ball (Himalayan Child), Tenzin Gyurme (Old Himalayan Man), Jamie Cho (Stocky Chinese Man), David Murray (Jumpy Thug), John Kazek, Darragh Kelly (Dock Thugs), Patrick Nolan, Joseph Rye, Kwaku Ankomah (Dock Cops), Jo Martin (Police Prison Official), Charles Edwards (Wayne Enterprises Executive), Lucy Russell, Tim Deenihan (Restaurant Guests), David Bedella (Maitre D'), Flavia Masetto, Emily Steven-Daly (Restaurant Blondes), Martin McDougall (Gotham Dock Employee), Noah Lee Margetts, Joe Hanley, Karl Shiels (Arkham Thugs), Roger Griffiths (Arkham Uniformed Policeman), Stephen Walters (Arkham Lunatic), Richard Laing (Arkham Chase Cop), Matt Miller (Gotham Car Cop #3), Risteard Cooper (Captain Simonson), Shane Rimmer (Older Gotham Water Board Technician), Jeremy Theobald (Younger Gotham Water Board Technician), Alexandra Bastedo (Gotham Society Dame), Soo Hee Ding (Farmer), Con Horgan (Monorail Driver), Phill Curr (Transit Cop), Jack Gleeson (Little Boy), John Judd (Narrows Bridge Cop), Sarah Wateridge (Mrs. Dawes), Charlie Kranz (Basement Club Manager), Terry McMahon (Bad Swat Cop #1), Cedric Young (Liquor Store Owner), Tim Booth (Victor Zsaz), Tom Nolan (Valet), Leon Delroy Williams (Pedestrian), Roger Yuan (Hazmat Technician), Joe Sargent, Emmanuel Idowu (Narrows

Katie Holmes, Cillian Murphy PHOTOS COURTESY OF WARNER BROS.

HEIGHTS

(SONY CLASSICS) Producers, Ismail Merchant, Richard Hawley; Executive Producer, Paul Bradley; Director, Chris Terrio; Screenplay, Amy Fox, based on her play; Additional Material, Chris Terrio; Photography, Jim Denault; Designer, Marla Weinhoff; Costumes, Marina Draghici; Music, Martin Eskine, Ben Butler; Editor, Sloane Kelvin; Casting, James Calleri; a Merchant Ivory Productions presentation; Dolby; Color; Rated R; 96 minutes; Release date: June 17, 2005

Eric Bogosian, Glenn Close

Cast

Diana Lee **Glenn Close**
Isabel **Elizabeth Banks**
Jonathan **James Marsden**
Alec **Jesse Bradford**
Peter **John Light**
Liz **Isabella Rossellini**
Henry **Eric Bogosian**
Rabbi Mendel **George Segal**
Julliard Macbeth **Chandler Williams**
Julliard Lady Macbeth **Bess Wohl**
Wedding Rabbi **Daniel Neiden**
Marshall **Tom Lennon**
Mark **Matt Davis**
Rachel **Susan Malick**
Jesse **Michael Murphy**

and Rachel Siegel (Autograph Seeker), Katie Kreisler (Helen), Phil Tabor (Paul), Jordi Vilasuso (Benjamin's Exes), Joel de la Fuente (Nat DeWolf), Melanie R. Orr (Scorned Woman), Denis O'Hare (Andrew), Rufus Wainright (Jeremy), Angel Desai (Laura), Jonathan Walker (Michael), Regina McMahon (Amanda), Jane Nichols, Steven Glenn, Alexander Lange (Guests), Andrew Howard (Ian), Don Fitzgerald (Built Guy), Meghan Glennon (Party Girl), Winsome Brown, Michael Goldstrom (SNL Writers), Jim Parsons (Oliver), Alice Tan Ridley (Subway Singer), Caroline Clay (Subway Woman), Cindy Adams (Herself), Manny Siverio (Subway Mugger), Frank Shattuck (EMT), D'Vorah Bailey (Police Officer), Jan Ellis (Hospital Receptionist), Liza Colon-Zayas (Ana)

Matthew Davis

A series of intersecting storylines follow photographer Isabel; her fiancé Jonathan; Isabel's famous actress mother, Diana; and an aspiring young actor auditioning for a play Diana is directing.

Elizabeth Banks

Jesse Bradford PHOTOS COURTESY OF SONY CLASSICS

Najarra Townsend, Natasha Slayton

Miles Thompson, Brandon Radcliff

ME AND YOU AND EVERYONE WE KNOW

A shoe salesman who is suffering after having been dumped by his wife is courted by a lonely video artist.

(IFC FILMS) Producer, Gina Kwon; Executive Producers, Jonathan Sehring, Carolyn Kaplan, Holly Becker, Peter Carlton; Director/Screenplay, Miranda July; Photography, Chuy Chavez; Designer, Aran Mann; Costumes, Christie Wittenborn; Music, Mike Andrews; Editor, Andrew Dickler; Casting, Meg Morman; an IFC Productions, FilmFour presentation of a Gina Kwon production; Dolby; Deluxe color; Rated R; 90 minutes; Release date: June 17, 2005

John Hawkes, Miranda July

Cast

Richard Swersey **John Hawkes**
Christine Jesperson **Miranda July**
Peter Swersey **Miles Thompson**
Robby Swersey **Brandon Ratcliff**
Sylvie **Carlie Westerman**
Michael **Hector Elias**
Andrew **Brad William Henke**
Heather **Natasha Slayton**
Rebecca **Najarra Townsend**
Nancy Herrington **Tracy Wright**
Pam **JoNell Kennedy**
Ellen **Ellen Geer**

and Colette Kiroy (Sylvie's Mom), James Kayten (Sylvie's Dad), Amy French (Museum Assistant), Sven Holmberg (Artist), James Mathers (Teacher), Kelsey Chapman, Tiana Marie Nelms (Sylvie's Friends), Jordan Potter (Shamus), Cheryl Phillips (Shoe Customer), Patricia Skeriotis (Housewares Saleswoman), E. J. Callahn (Man Tapping Quarter), James Symington (Goldfish Dad), Giavanna Whited (Goldfish Girl), Erlinda Bugayong (Middle Car Passenger), Amber Binford, Kelli Greaney, Dina Kriger, Caitlin Reza, Devin Rockwell, Jesse Saenz, Michael Swinfard, Zachary Hackbarth (Peep Peep Kids), David Serfozo (Bus Stop Man), Candi Herbert (Talking Picture Frame Woman), Anthony Binford, Kelci Griffith-Young, Kwinci Griffith-Young, Lance Norling, Paige Norling, Brendan Reza, Kevin Montgomery, Ashi Toledano (Classroom Kids), Timmy Nilsson (Robby Look-a-Like), Richard Goodman (T'ai Chi Man)

Miranda July PHOTOS COURTESY OF IFC FILMS

HERBIE FULLY LOADED

(WALT DISNEY PICTURES) Producer, Robert Simonds; Executive Producers, Tracey Trench, Michael Fottrell, Charles Hirschhorn; Co-Producer, Lisa Stewart; Director, Amy Robinson; Screenplay, Thomas Lennon, Robert Ben Garant, Alfred Gough, Miles Millar; Screen Story, Thomas Lennon, Robert Ben Garant; Based on characters created by Gordon Buford; Photography, Greg Gardiner; Music, Mark Mothersbaugh; Designer, Daniel Bradford; Costumes, Frank Helmer; Editor, Wendy Greene Bricmont; Casting, Rick Montgomery; Stunts, Spiro Razatos, Steve Kelso; a Walt Disney Pictures presentation of a Robert Simonds production; Distributed by Buena Vista; Dolby; Color; Rated G; 100 minutes; Release date: June 19, 2005

Herbie, Justin Long, Lindsay Lohan

Lindsay Lohan

Matt Dillon

Cast

Maggie Peyton **Lindsay Lohan**
Ray Peyton, Sr. **Michael Keaton**
Trip Murphy **Matt Dillon**
Ray Peyton, Jr. **Breckin Meyer**
Kevin **Justin Long**
Sally **Cheryl Hines**
Crash **Jimmi Simpson**
Charisma **Jill Ritchie**
Larry Murphy **Thomas Lennon**
Crazy Dave **Jeremy Roberts**
Beeman **E.E. Bell**
Juan Hernandez **Peter Pasco**
Miguel Hernandez **Mario Larraza**
Jimmy D. **Patrick Cranshaw**

and Scoot McNairy (Augie), Amy Hill (Doctor), Jim Cody Williams (Monster Truck Driver), Allen Bestwick, Benny Parsons, Jeff Gordon, Jimmie Johnson, Dale Jarrett, Tony Stewart, Stuart Scott (Themselves), Bob Dillner (Speed Channel Reporter), Robert Ben Garant (Director), Tim

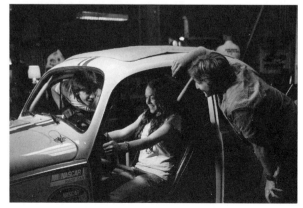

Justin Long, Lindsay Lohan, Breckin Meyer, Herbie

Michael Keaton, Cheryl Hines, Breckin Meyer

Sitarz (Security Guard), Bruno Gioiello (Bald Trip Fan), Andy Hillenburg (Crew Chief), Edmund L. Shaff (Dean), Caroline Limata, Mary Bonner Baker (Fans), Mark Deklin (ESPN Reporter), Rocky Soto (Trip Murphy Fan), Scott Martin Gershin (Herbie Vocalizations)

Maggie Peyton takes a broken down Volkswagen with a mind of its own and turns it into a champion NASCAR competitor. Fifth theatrical Herbie feature from the Disney Company and Buena Vista releasing, following *The Love Bug* (1969), *Herbie Rides Again* (1974), *Herbie Goes to Monte Carlo* (1977), and *Herbie Goes Bananas* (1980).

Herbie, Lindsay Lohan, Breckin Meyer, Justin Long

Lindsay Lohan, Justin Long

Justin Long, Lindsay Lohan, Herbie

Jeff Gordon, Jimmie Johnson, Breckin Meyer, Herbie PHOTOS COURTESY OF WALT DISNEY PICTURES

BEWITCHED

(COLUMBIA) Producers, Penny Marshall, Nora Ephron, Douglas Wick, Lucy Fisher; Executive Producers, James W. Skotchdopole, Steven H. Berman, Bobby Cohen; Director, Nora Ephron; Screenplay, Nora Ephron, Delia Ephron; Based on the television series created by Sol Saks; Photography, John Lindley; Designer, Neil Spisak; Costumes, Mary Zophres; Music, George Fenton; Music Supervisor, Nick Meyers; Editor, Tia Nolan; Casting, Francine Meisler, Kathy Driscoll-Mohler; a Lucy Fisher, Douglas Wick/Penny Marshall production; Dolby; Deluxe color; Rated PG-13; 98 minutes; Release date: June 24, 2005

Michael Caine, Nicole Kidman

Nicole Kidman, Shirley MacLaine, Will Ferrell

Cast

Isabel Bigelow/Samantha **Nicole Kidman**
Jack Wyatt/Darren **Will Ferrell**
Iris Smythson/Endora **Shirley MacLaine**
Nigel Bigelow **Michael Caine**
Richie **Jason Schwartzman**
Maria Kelly **Kristin Chenoweth**
Nina **Heather Burns**
Larry **Jim Turner**
Stu Robison **Stephen Colbert**

and David Alan Grier (Jim Fields), Michael Badalucco (Joey Props), Carole Shelley (Aunt Clara), Steve Carell (Uncle Arthur), Katie Finneran (Sheila Wyatt), James Lipton, Conan O'Brien, Ed McMahon (Themselves), Amy Sedaris (Gladys Kravitz), Richard Kind (Abner Kravitz), Ken Campbell, P. J. Byne (Writers), Carol Androsky (Realtor), Annie Mumolo, Andrew Friedman (Bed, Bath and Beyond Shoppers), Clay Bravo (Coffee Shop Waitress), Heather Freedman (Beverly Hills Hotel Hostess), Jonathan Floyd (Cable Man), Alison MacInnis, Bridget Brno, Dana Daurey, Dorie Barton, Katharine Carroll, Jennifer Elise Cox, Laura Sorenson, Brittany Paige, Dawn Ashley Cook, Julia Schuler, Abbey McBride (Auditioning Actresses), Jennifer Hall (Book Soup Cafe Waitress), Roxanne Beckford (Francine), Hugh Davidson (Network Executive), Joe Zymblosky (Randall), JJ Sacha (Voice-Over Announcer), Susan Chuang (Press Conference Reporter), Jordan Black (Press Conference Photographer), Mo Rocca (E! Reporter), Jason George, Wendi McLendon-Covey (E! Anchors), Julie Claire (Hilary), Terry Savage (Dinner Party Guests), Dianne Dreyer

Will Ferrell, Steve Carell

(Production Staff Assistant), Kate Walsh (Sexy Waitress), Valerie Azlynn (Gorgeous Model), Jarrad Paul (Valet), Victor Williams (Police Officer), Liesel Staubitz, Ruby Rose Skotchdopole, Molly Gordon (Trick-or-Treaters), Nick Lachey (Vietnam Soldier)

Jack Wyatt, hoping to get his acting career back on track, agrees to appear in an updated version of the 1960s sitcom *Bewitched* and encourages Isabel Bigelow to audition for the roll of his spell-casting wife Samantha, unaware that Isabel is, in fact, a real witch. Based on the series that ran on ABC (1964–72) and starred Elizabeth Montgomery, Dick York (and later Dick Sargent), and Agnes Moorehead.

Heather Burns, Nicole Kidman, Kristin Chenoweth PHOTOS COURTESY OF COLUMBIA

Simon Baker, Dennis Hopper

LAND OF THE DEAD

(UNIVERSAL) Producers, Mark Canton, Peter Grunwald, Bernie Goldmann; Executive Producers, Steve Barnett, Dennis E. Jones, Ryan Kavanaugh; Director/Screenplay, George A. Romero; Photography, Miroslaw Baszak; Designer, Arv Greywal; Costumes, Alex Kavanaugh; Music, Reinhold Heil, Johnny Klimek; Editor, Michael Doherty; Special Makeup Effects, Greg Nicotero, Howard Berger; Co-Producer, Neil Canton; Casting, Marci Liroff; an Atmosphere Entertainment MM presentation of a Mark Canton-Bernie Goldmann, Romero-Grunwald production in association with Wild Bunch; Dolby; Rated R; Release date: June 24, 2005

Cast

Riley **Simon Baker**
Cholo **John Leguizamo**
Kaufman **Dennis Hopper**
Slack **Asia Argento**
Charlie **Robert Joy**
Big Daddy **Eugene Clark**
Pretty Boy **Joanne Boland**
Foxy **Tony Nappo**
Number 9 **Jennifer Baxter**
Butcher **Boyd Banks**

and Jasmin Geljo (Tambourine Man), Maxwell McCabe-Lokos (Mouse), Tony Munch (Anchor), Shawn Roberts (Mike), Pedro Miguel Arce (Pillsbury), Sasha Roiz (Manolete), Krista Bridges (Motown), Alan Van Sprang (Brubaker), Phil Fondacaro (Chihuahua), Bruce McFee (Mulligan), Earl Pastko (Roach), Jonathan Whittaker (Sutherland), Jonathan Walker (Cliff Woods), Peter Outerbridge (Styles), Lara Amersey (Dead Teenage Girl), Michael Belisario (Dead Teenage Boy), Gene Mack (Knipp), Matt Birman (Kaufman's Security Guard), Devon Bostick (Brian), Jason Gautreau (Gus), Christopher Russell (Barrett), Christopher Allen Nelson (Veteran Soldier), Debra Felstead (Soldier), Tina Romero ("High Noon" Soldier), Colm Magner, Scott Wickware (Guards at the "Throat"), Ron Payne (Hobo), Richard Clarkin (Steele), Darrin Brown (Bettor), Eldridge

Hyndman (Deke), Ted Ludzik (Weapons Storage Guard), David Sparrow (Arena Policeman), Brian Renfro (Number 9's Victim), James Binkley (Grenade Soldier), Robin Ward (Fiddler's Green Promo Announcer), Dawne Furey (Topless Dancer), Sandy Kellerman, Donna Croce (Kissing Women), Wilbert Headley (Dead Tuba Player), Ross Sferrazza (Dead Trombone Player), Erica Olsen (Cheerleader Zombie), Liise Keeling (Zombie Mother), Sonia Belley (Zombie Daughter), Chad Cammelleri (Refrigerator Zombie), Gino Crognale (Policeman Zombie), Shane Cardwell (Fence Fry Zombie), Simon Pegg, Edgar Wright (Photo Booth Zombies), Kevin Rushton, Nick Alachiotis (Arena Fight Zombies), James Canton (Child Zombie), Ermes Blarasin (Clown Zombie), Jake McKinnon (Hillside Zombie), Greg Nicotero (Bridgekeeper Zombie), Susan Wloszczyna (Temperance Street Zombie), David Campbell (Legless Zombie), Tom Svaini (Machete Zombie)

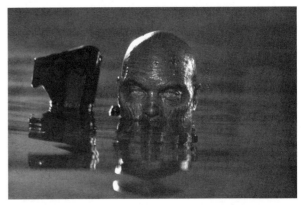

Eugene A. Clark

In the not-so-distant future a fortified city, cordoned off behind walls to keep the walking dead out, is run by the powerful Kaufman, who seems unaware that there is unrest among the city's disenfranchised as well as evolving zombies outside its weakening perimeters.

Asia Argento, Simon Baker PHOTOS COURTESY OF UNIVERSAL

Justin Chatwin, Dakota Fanning, Tom Cruise

WAR OF THE WORLDS

(PARAMOUNT/DREAMWORKS) Producers, Kathleen Kennedy, Colin Wilson; Executive Producer, Paula Wagner; Director, Steven Spielberg; Screenplay, Josh Friedman, David Koepp; Based on the novel by H. G. Wells; Photography, Janusz Kaminski; Designer, Rick Carter; Costumes, Joanna Johnston; Music, John Williams; Editor, Michael Kahn; Senior Visual Effects Supervisor, Dennis Muren; Visual Effects Supervisor, Pablo Helman; Stunts, Vic Armstrong; an Amblin Entertainment/Cruise-Wagner production; Dolby; Deluxe color; Rated PG-13; 117 minutes; Release date: June 29, 2005

Cast

Ray Ferrier **Tom Cruise**
Rachel Ferrier **Dakota Fanning**
Mary Ann **Miranda Otto**
Robbie Ferrier **Justin Chatwin**
Harlan Ogilvy **Tim Robbins**
Vincent **Rick Gonzalez**
Julio **Yul Vázquez**
Manny the Mechanic **Lenny Venito**
Bartender **Lisa Ann Walter**
Grandmother **Ann Robinson**
Grandfather **Gene Barry**
Tim **David Alan Basche**
Herself **Roz Abrams**
TV Reporter—Osaka **Michael Brownlee**
News Producer **Camillia Sanes**
News Cameraman **Marlon Young**
News Van Driver **John Eddings**
Narrator **Morgan Freeman**

and Peter Gerety (Hatch Boss/Load Manager), David Harbour (Dock Worker), Miguel Antonio Ferrer (Brazilian Neighbor), January Lavoy (Brazilian Neighbor's Wife), Stephen Gevedon (Neighbor with Lawnmower), Julie White (Woman), Marianni Ebert (Hysterical Woman), Rafael Sardina (Mechanic's Assistant), Amy Ryan (Neighbor with Toddler), Ed Vassallo, Michael Arthur (Intersection Guys), Danny Hoch (Intersection Guy Cop), Sharrieff Pugh (Man Studying Street), Erika

Tom Cruise

Tim Robbins, Tom Cruise

Justin Chatwin, Tom Cruise, Dakota Fanning

Dakota Fanning, Justin Chatwin, Miranda Otto, Tom Cruise

Divorced dad Ray Ferrier tries to save his shattered family during a devastating world-wide assault by hostile and relentless aliens. Remake of the 1953 Paramount film *The War of the Worlds* which starred Gene Barry and Ann Robinson, both of whom make cameo appearances here.

This film received Oscar nominations for visual effects, sound, and sound editing.

Rick Gonzalez, Tom Cruise, Yul Vázquez

Tom Cruise, Dakota Fanning

LaVonn, Christopher Evan Welch (Photographers), John Michael Bolger, Omar Jermaine (Men Holding Women), Robert Cicchini (Guy in Suit), Jim Hanna (Bus Driver), Tracy Howe, Adam Lazarre-White, Vito D'Ambrosio, Laura Zoe Quist, Ana Maria Quintana, Lorelei Llee (Crowd Onlookers), Mark Manley (Ferry Worker), John Scurti (Ferry Captain), Becky Ann Baker (Disaster Relief Volunteer), Mariann Mayberry (Mother), Ty Simpkins (3-Year-Old Boy), Jerry Walsh (Smart Guy), Tommy Guiffre, Daniel Franzese (National Guardsmen), Ed Schiff (Old Man), Ellen Barry (Woman from Upstate), Amy Hohn (Panicky Woman), Daniel Ziskie (Informative Guy), David Conley (Ill-Informed Guy), Daniel Eric Gold (Conspiracy Buff), Booker T. Washington (Conspiracy Debunker), Maggie Lacey (Upset Mother), Eric Zuckerman (Doomsday Guy), Daniel A. Jacobs (Younger Man), Asha R. Nanavati (Woman in Crowd), Joaquin Perez-Campbell (Young Soldier in Tank), Dendrie Taylor (Well-Meaning Mother), James DuMont (Well-Meaning Father), Travis Aaron Wade, Benny Ciaramello, Ricky Luna, Columbus Short, Kent Faulcon (War of the Worlds Soldiers), Kevin Collins, Terry Thomas (Marine Majors), Clay Bringhurst (Airforce Pilot), Jorge-Luis Pallo (Army Private), Suanne Spoke, Kirsten Nelson (Businesswoman), Melody Garrett, Lauri Johnson, Takayo Fischer (Older Women), Shanna Collins, Elizabeth Kayne Jong (Teenagers), Art Chudabala, Jeffrey Hutchinson, Dempsey Pappion, Chris Todd (Men in Baskets), Johnny Kastl, Juan Carlos Hernandez, Bruce W. Derdoski Jr., John N. Morales (Boston Soldiers)

Tim Robbins, Tom Cruise, Dakota Fanning PHOTOS COURTESY OF PARAMOUNT

MURDERBALL

(THINKFILM) Producers, Jeffrey Mande, Dana Adam Shapiro; Executive Producers, Randy Manis, Jeff Sackman, Mark Urman; Co-Producer, Christian Ettinger; Directors, Henry Alex Rubin, Dana Adam Shapiro; Based on an article by Dana Adam Shapiro; Photography, Henry Alex Rubin; Music, Jamie Saft; Editor, Geoffrey Richman; Animation, Damon Clarelli, David Egan; a ThinkFilm presentation in association with A&E Indie Films of an Eat Film production; Dolby; Color; DV; Rated R; 85 minutes; Release date: July 8, 2005. Documentary on members of the U.S. Paralympics quadriplegic rugby team.

Mark Zupan

Mark Zupan (right)

With

Keith Cavill, Andy Cohn, Scott Hogsett, Christopher Igoe, Bob Lujano, Joe Soares, Mark Zupan

Mark Zupan PHOTOS COURTESY OF THINKFILM

DARK WATER

(TOUCHSTONE) Producers, Bill Mechanic, Roy Lee, Doug Davison; Executive Producer, Ashley Kramer; Director, Walter Salles; Screenplay, Rafael Yglesias; Based on the novel *Hongurai Mizuno Soko Kara* by Koji Suzuki and the Hideo Nakata film *Dark Water*, produced by Taka Ichise; Photography, Affonso Beato; Designer, Therese DePrez; Costumes, Michael Wilkinson; Co-Producer, Diana Pokorny; Associate Producer, Kerry Foster; Music, Angelo Badalamenti; Editor, Daniel Rezende; Special Visual Effects, Digital Domain, Flash Film Works; Casting, Mali Finn; a Pandemonium Productions, Vertigo Entertainment production; Dolby; Technicolor; Rated PG-13; 103 minutes; Release date: July 8, 2005

Ariel Gade, Jennifer Connelly

Cast

Dahlia Williams **Jennifer Connelly**
Mr. Murray **John C. Reilly**
Jeff Platzer **Tim Roth**
Kyle **Dougray Scott**
Veeck **Pete Postlethwaite**
Mrs. Finkle **Camryn Manheim**
Ceci **Ariel Gade**
Natasha/Young Dahlia **Perla Haney-Jardine**
Young Dahlia's Teacher **Debra Monk**
Mediators **Linda Emond, Bill Buell**
Man in Tram **J. R. Horne**
Dahlia's Mother **Elina Lowensohn**
UPS Man **Warren Belle**
Radiology Clinic Supervisor **Alison Sealy-Smith**
Man in Elevator **Simon Reynolds**
Teacher's Aide **Kate Hewlett**
Mary **Jennifer Baxter**
Night Doorman **Diego Fuentes**
Natasha's Mother **Zoe Heath**
Platzer's Backseat Client **MuMs**
Steve **Matt Lemche**
Billy **Edward Kennington**

Tim Roth, John C. Reilly

Single mother Dahlia Williams moves with her young daughter into a rundown apartment building on New York's Roosevelt Island, where a series of unnerving events lead her to suspect that the place might be haunted.

Camryn Manheim

Jennifer Connelly, Pete Postlethwaite PHOTOS COURTESY OF TOUCHSTONE

FANTASTIC FOUR

(20TH CENTURY FOX) Producers, Bernd Eichinger, Avi Arad, Ralph Winter; Executive Producers, Stan Lee, Kevin Feige, Chris Columbus, Mark Radcliffe, Michael Barnathan; Co-Producer, Ross Fanger; Director, Tim Story; Screenplay, Mark Frost, Michael France; Based on the Marvel comic book created by Stan Lee and Jack Kirby; Photography, Oliver Wood; Designer, Bill Boes; Costumes, Jose I. Fernandez; Music, John Ottman; Editor, William Hoy; Creature Effects Supervisor, Mike Elizalde; Creature and Makeup Effects, Spectral Motion; Stunts, John Branagan, Owen Walstrom, Jacob Rupp; Casting, Nancy Klopper; a Constantin Film, Marvel Enterprises presentation of a 1492 Pictures, Bernd Eichinger production; Dolby; Deluxe color; Rated PG-13; 106 minutes; Release date: July 8, 2005

Michael Chiklis

Jessica Alba, Ioan Gruffud

Cast

Reed Richards **Ioan Gruffud**
Sue Storm **Jessica Alba**
Johnny Storm **Chris Evans**
Ben Grimm **Michael Chiklis**
Victor Von Doom **Julian McMahon**
Leonard **Hamish Linklater**
Alicia Masters **Kerry Washington**
Debbie McIlvane **Laurie Holden**
Ernie **David Parker**
Jimmy O'Hoolihan **Kevin McNulty**
Willie Lumpkin **Stan Lee**

and Maria Menoumos (Sexy Nurse), Michael Kopsa (Ned Cecil), Andrew Airlie (Compound Doctor), Pascale Hutton (Nightclub Girlfriend), G. Michael Gray (Nightclub Boyfriend), David Richmond-Peck (Gallery Patron), Penelope Corrin, Aonika Laurent (Bohemian Girls), Jason Schombing (Bridge Business Man), Jason Diablo, Colin Lawrence, Paul Belsito (NYPD Bridge Cops), DeeJay Jackson (Chief Fireman), Gina Holden (LV Receptionist), Donavon Stinson (X Games Announcer), Douglas Weston (Victor's Doctor), Tony Alcantar, Brenda M. Crichlow, Bobby Bysouth (Compound Reporters), Peter Bryant (Lame Joke Businessman), Lorena Gale, Danielle Dunn-Morris (Old Ladies with Car), Nicole Muñoz (Little Girl), Daniel Bacon (Bridge Reporter), Kenny Bartram,

Ronnie Renner (Themselves), Brian Deegan (X Games Rider), Marlaina Man, Tre Verhoeven, Juanita Mirehouse, Stefanie Singer (Lusting Models), Jamie Little (X Games Reporter), Doug Abrahams (Truck Driver), Ron Chartier (Hotel Guest), Barbara Christabella, Sanja Banic (Girls in Park), Ed Hodsno, John Speredakos (Construction Workers), Jason Kaufman (Cop), Preston Peet (Goth Guy), Steven Fulani Hart, Bethann Schebece (Newsstand Pedestrians), Lou Torres (Cab Driver), Peggy Gormley (Homeless Woman), Maurice Tyson (Homeless Guy), Jaimie McVittie (Little Girl on Bridge), Jenni Squair, Lia Salmond, Ellen Ewusie, Ylenia Aurucci, Michelle Kulas, Kate Mullan, Georgia Dewson (Elevator Ladies), Sienna Rose (Storm's Fan), Hector A. Leguillow (Newsstand Vendor), Ben Mulroney, Terry David Mulligan, Lauren Sanchez, Mark S. Allen, Jon Brady, Taryn Winter Brill, Sara Edwards, Heidi Eng, Jim Ferguson, CB Hackworth, Sam Hallenbeck, Mike Waco, Marian Etoile Watson, Richard Ho, Dave Holmes, Andrew Hunsaker, Taylor Johnson, Bonnie Laufer-Krebs, Jennifer Lothrop, Lisa Fuller Magee, Bret Martin, Liam Mayclem, Scott Patrick, Shaheem Reid, Sam Rubin, Maria Salas, Devon Soltendieck, Patrick Stoner, Lee Thomas, Tony Toscano, David Moss (Reporters)

Having obtained superhuman powers after contact with cosmic radiation, a team of scientists set out to fight evil, including billionaire industrialist Victor Von Doom who has developed powers of his own.

Chris Evans PHOTOS COURTESY OF 20TH CENTURY FOX

Jesse Bradford, Lisa Kudrow

HAPPY ENDINGS

(LIONS GATE) Producers, Holly Wiersma, Michael Paseornek; Executive Producers, Tom Ortenberg, Nick Meyer, Mike Elliott; Line Producer, Jon Kuyper; Co-Producers, Ali Forman, Bobby Cohen, Marc Platt; Director/Screenplay, Don Roos; Photography, Clark Mathis; Designer, Richard Sherman; Costumes, Peggy Anita Schnitzer; Music Supervisor, Nicole Tocantins; Editor, David Codron; Associate Producers, Robert Melnik, Donna Sloan, Laura Smith; Casting, Linda Lowy, John Brace; a Holly Wiersma, Lions Gate Films production and presentation; Dolby; Panavision; Deluxe color; Rated R; 132 minutes; Release date: July 15, 2005

Cast
Mamie **Lisa Kudrow**
Charley **Steve Coogan**
Nicky **Jesse Bradford**
Javier **Bobby Cannavale**
Jude **Maggie Gyllenhaal**
Otis **Jason Ritter**
Frank **Tom Arnold**
Gil **David Sutcliffe**
Diane **Sarah Clarke**
Pam **Laura Dern**
Mamie at 17 **Halle Hirsh**
Charley at 16 **Eric Jungmann**
Connie Peppitone **Kim Morgan Greene**
Annette **Rayne Marcus**
Lauren **Caker Folley**
Lane **Amanda Foreman**
Tess **Nicole Tocantins**

and Mark Fite (Tess's Drunk Husband), Soledad St. Hilaire (Dignora), Ramón de Ocampo (Alvin), A. J. Trauth (Bill), Carol Androsky (Naked Woman), Tamara Davies (Shauna), Ashleigh Darkbloom (Rain), Emma Hunton (Becca), Eric Jungmann (Tom), T. R. Hopper (Chuck Peppitone), Rob Macie (Steve the Lawyer), Lisa Hoyle (Driver), Joe Milton, Dave Beyer, Randy Landas (Musicians), Scott Sener (Karaoke Guy)

A series of interlocking stories set in Southern California: a woman who had given up an unwanted child for adoption is approached by an aspiring filmmaker who claims to know her long-lost son; two gay couples become involved in a dispute over child custody rights; a mercenary drifter seduces a sexually troubled teen and then sets her sights on landing the boy's rich father.

Lisa Kudrow, Bobby Cannavale

Laura Dern, Steve Coogan

Jason Ritter, Maggie Gyllenhaal PHOTOS COURTESY OF LIONS GATE

Freddie Highmore

Johnny Depp, Freddie Highmore, David Kelly

Freddie Highmore, David Kelly, Adam Godley, Jordan Fry, Philip Weigratz, Franziska Troegner, AnnaSophia Robb, James Fox, Missi Pyle, Julia Winter

Jordan Fry, Adam Godley, Johnny Depp, Freddie Highmore, David Kelly

CHARLIE AND THE CHOCOLATE FACTORY

(WARNER BROS.) Producers, Richard D. Zanuck, Brad Grey; Executive Producers, Patrick McCormick, Felicity Dahl, Michael Siegel, Graham Burke, Bruce Berman; Director, Tim Burton; Screenplay, John August; Based on the book by Roald Dahl; Photography, Philippe Rousselot; Designer, Alex McDowell; Costumes, Gabriella Pescucci; Music/Oompa Loompa Vocals, Danny Elfman; Lyrics, Roald Dahl; Choreographer, Francesca Jaynes; Editor, Chris Lebenzon; Co-Producer, Katterli Frauenfelder; Visual Effects Supervisor, Nick Davis; Makeup/Hair Designer, Peter Owen; Animatronics/Prosthetics Creative Supervisor, Neal Scanlan; Casting, Susie Figgis; a Zanuck Company, Plan B production presented in association with Village Roadshow Pictures; Dolby; Technicolor; Rated PG; 115 minutes; Release date: July 15, 2005

Cast

Willy Wonka **Johnny Depp**
Charlie Bucket **Freddie Highmore**
Grandpa Joe **David Kelly**
Mrs. Bucket **Helena Bonham Carter**
Mr. Bucket **Noah Taylor**

Johnny Depp

AnnaSophia Robb

Mrs. Beauregarde **Missi Pyle**
Mr. Salt **James Fox**
Oompa Loompa **Deep Roy**
Dr. Wonka **Christopher Lee**
Mr. Teavee **Adam Godley**
Mrs. Gloop **Franziska Troegner**
Violet Beauregarde **AnnaSophia Robb**
Veruca Salt **Julia Winter**
Mike Teavee **Jordon Fry**
Augustus Gloop **Philip Wiegratz**
Little Willy Wonka **Blair Dunlop**
Grandma Georgina **Liz Smith**
Grandma Josephine **Eileen Essell**
Grandpa George **David Morris**
Prince Pondicherry **Nitin Ganatra**
Princess Pondicherry **Shelley Conn**
Prodnose **Chris Cresswell**
Slugworth **Phil Philmar**
Finckelgruber **Tony Kirkwood**

and Todd Boyce (TV Reporter), Nayef Rashed (Moroccan Market Vendor), Menis Yousry (Moroccan Market Trader), Harry Taylor (Mr. Gloop),

Freddie Highmore, Jordan Fry, David Kelly, Julia Winter, James Fox, Missi Pyle, Adam Godley, Johnny Depp

Hubertus Geller (German Reporter), Francesca Hunt (Mrs. Salt), Garrick Hagon (Denver Reporter), Kevin Eldon, Mark Heap (Men with Dogs), Roger Frost (Tall Man), Oscar James (Shopkeeper), Colette Appleby (Customer in Shop), Debora Weston (Woman in Shop), Annette Badland (Jolly Woman), Stephen Hope-Wynne (Museum Guard), Geoffrey Holder (Narrator)

An eccentric candy maker gives five lucky children the chance to visit his factory if they find a golden ticket hidden inside one of his candybars. Remake of the 1971 Paramount film *Willy Wonka and the Chocolate Factory*, which starred Gene Wilder (Wonka), Peter Ostrum (Charlie), and Jack Albertson (Grandpa Joe).

This film received an Oscar nomination for costume design.

Julia Winter

Jordan Fry

Deep Roy PHOTOS COURTESY OF WARNER BROS.

Isla Fisher, Vince Vaughn

Christopher Walken, Ellen Albertini Dow

WEDDING CRASHERS

(NEW LINE CINEMA) Producers, Peter Abrams, Robert L. Levy, Andrew Panay; Executive Producers, Guy Riedel, Toby Emmerich, Richard Brener, Cale Boyter; Director, David Dobkin; Screenplay, Steve Faber, Bob Fisher; Photography, Julio Macat; Designer, Barry Robison; Costumes, Denise Wingate; Music, Rolfe Kent; Editor, Mark Livolsi; Casting, Lisa Beach; a Tapestry Films production; Dolby; Technicolor; Rated R; 119 minutes; Release date: July 15, 2005

Vince Vaughn, Owen Wilson

Jane Seymour, Rachel McAdams

Owen Wilson, Rachel McAdams

Bradley Cooper, Rachel McAdams

Keir O'Donnell

Cast

John Beckwith **Owen Wilson**
Jeremy Grey **Vince Vaughn**
Secretary William Cleary **Christopher Walken**
Claire Cleary **Rachel McAdams**
Gloria Cleary **Isla Fisher**
Kathleen Cleary **Jane Seymour**
Grandma Mary Cleary **Ellen Albertini Dow**
Todd Cleary **Keir O'Donnell**
Sack Lodge **Bradley Cooper**
Randolph **Ron Canada**
Father O'Neil **Henry Gibson**
Mr. Kroeger **Dwight Yoakam**
Mrs. Kroeger **Rebecca De Mornay**
Trap **David Conrad**
Christina Cleary **Jenny Alden**
Craig **Geoff Stults**
Attorneys **James McDonnell, Jesse Henecke**
Old Jewish Man **Lou Cutell**

Old Jewish Woman **Sparkle**
Old Italian Man **Frankie Ray Perelli**
Old Italian Woman **Patricia Place**
Old Chinese Man **Chao-Li Chi**
Old Irish Woman **Norma Michaels**
Old Indian Man **Noel DeSouza**
Ivana **Ivana Bozilovic**
Camille **Camille Anderson**
Brunette **Rachel Sterling**
Vivian **Diora Baird**
Frank Meyers **Ned Schmidtke**
Chazz **Will Ferrell**

and Jennifer Massey (Woman), Dylan James Turner (Bratty Kid), Sophia Blouin (Flower Girl), Stephen J. Downs (Franklin), Larry Joe Campbell (Best Man), Mark Duane Anderson (Secret Service Agent), Irene Roseen (Elderly Woman), Jules Mande (Rabbi), Besty Ames (Betty), Carson Elrod (Flip), Josh Wheeler (Kip), John G. Pavelec (Ken), Charles Kahlenberg (Priest), Kathryn Joosten (Chazz's Mom), Karen Miller (Chazz's Girlfriend), Tanaya Nicole (Woman at Jewish Reception), Naureen Zaim (Hindu Woman), Cindy Elizabeth Taylor (Girl at Irish Wedding), Melanie Hawkins, Summer Altice (Girls Who Cry), Lisa Beach, Lovelynn Ann Vanderhorst Jensen (Wedding Planners), Phyllis Samhaber (Woman at Table), O. J. Watson (Man at Table)

Two counselors, who look for fast pick-ups by crashing weddings, end up as house guests of the U.S. Treasury Secretary where they fall in love with his daughters.

Henry Gibson PHOTOS COURTESY OF NEW LINE CINEMA

BAD NEWS BEARS

(PARAMOUNT) Producers, J. Geyer Kosinski, Richard Linklater; Executive Producer, Marcus Viscidi; Director, Richard Linklater; Screenplay, Bill Lancaster, Glenn Ficarra, John Requa; Based upon the film written by Bill Lancaster; Photography, Rogier Stoffers; Designer, Bruce Curtis; Costumes, Karen Patch; Music, Edward Shearmur; Music Supervisor, Randall Poster; Editor, Sandra Adair; Casting, Joseph Middleton; a Media Talent Group production in association with Detour Filmproduction; Dolby; Deluxe color; Rated PG-13; 111 minutes; Release date: July 22, 2005

Brandon Craggs, Jeffrey Tedmori, Ridge Canipe, Timmy Deters PHOTOS COURTESY OF FILMCOMPANY

Cast

Morris Buttermaker **Billy Bob Thornton**
Roy Bullock **Greg Kinnear**
Liz Whitewood **Marcia Gay Harden**
Amanda Whurlitzer **Sammi Kane Kraft**
Toby Whitewood **Ridge Canipe**
Mike Engelberg **Brandon Craggs**
Kelly Leak **Jeffrey Davies**
Tanner Boyle **Timmy Deters**
Miguel Agilar **Carlos Estrada**
Jose Agilar **Emmanuel Estrada**
Matthew Hooper **Troy Gentile**

and Kenneth "K.C." Harris (Ahmad Abdul Rahim), Aman Johal (Prem Lahiri), Tyler Patrick Jones (Timmy Lupus), Jeffrey Tedmori (Garo Daragebrigadian), Carter Jenkins (Joey Bullock), Seth Adkins (Jimmy), Chase Winton (Ms. Cleveland), Arabella Holzbog (Shari Bullock), Nectar Rose (Paradise), Lisa Arturo (Peaches), Elizabeth Carter (Chandalier), Monique Cooper (Lolita), Candace Kita (China), Kate Luyben (Daisy), Shamron Moore (Cherry Pie), Jeffrey Hutchinson (Baseball Official), Sonya Eddy, Karen Gordon (Salesladies), Maura Vincent (Shopper), Jennifer Carta (Softball Player Suzy), Dennis LaValle (Deaver Dad), Robert Peters, Kevin R. Kelly (Yankee Dads), Shannon O'Hurley (All American Mom), Hunter Cole, Wil Myer (All American Boys), Pancho Moler (Kevin), Jack Acampora, Bretton Bowman, Ryan Cruz, Nick Lovullo, Richard

Ridge Canipe, Marcia Gay Harden PHOTOS COURTESY OF FILMCOMPANY

Billy Bob Thornton, Emmanuel Estrada, Kenneth "K.C." Harris, Carlos Estrada

Martinez, Payton Milone, Ernesto Junior Prado, Kirby James Shaw, Toby Thompson, Hayden Tsutsui, Matthew Walker (Yankee Players), Darin Rossi, Gary A. Rodriguez, Scott Adsit, Kevin Makely, Robert Matthew Wagner, Ken Medlock, Josh M. Goldfield, Mike Paciorek (Umpires), Jeff Conrad, Sam Farrar, Alex Greenwald, Darren Robinson (Skate Band Members)

Morris Buttermaker, a down on his luck former professional ballplayer, is bribed by his lawyer to coach an inept little league team. Remake of the 1976 Paramount film which starred Walter Matthau, Tatum O'Neal, Vic Morrow, and Jackie Earle Haley.

Billy Bob Thornton, Greg Kinnear PHOTOS COURTESY OF PARAMOUNT

THE ISLAND

(DREAMWORKS/WARNER BROS.) Producers, Walter F. Parkes, Michael Bay, Ian Bryce; Executive Producer, Laurie MacDonald; Director, Michael Bay; Screenplay, Caspian Tredwell-Owen, Alex Kurtzman, Roberto Orci; Story, Caspiran Tredwell-Owen; Photography, Mauro Fiore; Designer, Nigel Phelps; Costumes, Deborah L. Scott; Music, Steve Jablonsky; Editors, Paul Rubell, Christian Wagner; Visual Effects Supervisor, Eric Brevig; Stunts, Kenny Bates; Casting, Denise Chamian; a Parkes, MacDonald production; Dolby; Panavision; Technicolor; Rated PG-13; 127 minutes; Release date: July 22, 2005

Djimon Hounsou, Ewan McGregor

Steve Buscemi, Ewan McGregor

Scarlett Johansson

Michael Clarke Duncan PHOTOS COURTESY OF DREAMWORKS

Cast

Lincoln Six Echo/Tom Lincoln **Ewan McGregor**
Jordan Two Delta/Sarah Jordan **Scarlett Johansson**
Albert Laurent **Djimon Hounsou**
Merrick **Sean Bean**
McCord **Steve Buscemi**
Starkweather **Michael Clarke Duncan**
Jones Three Echo **Ethan Phillips**
Gandu Three Alpha **Brian Stepanek**
Community Announcer **Noa Tishby**

and Siobhan Flynn (Lima One Alpha), Troy Blendell, Jamie McBride, Kevin McCorkle, Gary Nickens, Kathleen Rose Perkins, Richard Whiten (Laurent Team Members), Max Baker (Carnes), Phil Abrams (Harvest Doctor), Svetlana Efremova (Harvest Midwife), Katy Boyer, Randy Oglesby (Harvest Surgeons), Yvette Nicole Brown, Taylor Gilbert, Wendy Haines (Harvest Nurses), Tim Halligan (Institute Coroner), Glenn Morshower (Medical Courier), Michael Canavan (Extraction RooM Doctor), Jimmy Smagula, Ben Tolpin (Extraction Room Technicians), Robert Sherman (Agnate in Pod), Rich Hutchman (Dept. of Operations Supervisor), Gonzalo Menendez (Dept. of Operations Technician), Olivia Tracey (Dept. of Operations Agnate), Rax Xifo (Elevator Agnate), Mary Pat Gleason (Nutrition Clerk), Ashley Yegan (Strim Bar Bartender), Whitney Dylan (Client Services Operator), Mitzi Martin (Atrium Tour Guide), Lew Dauber (Tour Group Man), Shelby Leverington (Tour Group Woman), Don Creech (God-Like Man), Richard V. Licata (Board Member), Eamon Behrens, Alex Carter, Kevin Daniels, Grant Garrison, Kenneth Hughes, Brian Leckner, Dakota Mitchell, Maritn Papazian, Phil Somerville, Ryan Tasz, Kirk Ward, Kelvin Han Yee (Censors), Shawnee Smith (Suzie), Chris Ellis (Aces & Spades Bartender), Don Michael Paul (Bar Guy), Eric Stonestreet (Ed the Trucker), James Granoff (Sarah's Son), James Hart, Craig Reynolds (LAPD Officers), Trent Ford (Calvin Klein Model), Sage Thomas (Girl at Beach), Mark Christopher Lawrence (Construction Worker)

In a contained facility in the mid-21st century, where the inhabitants look forward to being selected to go to a supposedly utopian location known as "The Island," Lincoln Six Echo begins to question the restrictions placed upon his life and decides to escape.

HUSTLE & FLOW

(PARAMOUNT CLASSICS) Producers, John Singleton, Stephanie Allain; Executive Producer, Dwight Williams; Director/Screenplay, Craig Brewer; Photography, Amelia Vincent; Designer, Keith Brian Burns; Costumes, Paul Simmons; Music, Scott Bomar; Music Supervisor, Paul Stewart; Editor, Billy Fox; Associate Producer, Preston Holmes; Casting, Kimberly R. Hardin; an MTV Films, New Deal Entertainment presentation of a Crunk Pictures, Homegrown Pictures production; Dolby; 16mm-to-35mm; Fotokem Color; Rated R; 115 minutes; Release date: July 22, 2005

Terrence Howard, Ludacris PHOTOS COURTESY OF FILMCOMPANY

Cast
Djay **Terrence Howard**
Key **Anthony Anderson**
Nola **Taryn Manning**
Shug **Taraji P. Henson**
Shelby **D. J. Qualls**
Skinny Black **Ludacris**
Lexus **Paula Jai Parker**
Yevette **Elise Neal**
Arnel **Isaac Hayes**
Tigga **Juicy J**
Slobs **William "Poon" Engram**

and Bobby "I-20" Sandimanie (Yellow Jacket), Haystak (Mickey), Claude Phillips (Harold) Josey Scott (Elroy), John Still (Shop Owner), Jay Munn (Prison Guard), Michael Hooks, Jr. (Block Manager), Jerome Toles (Police Officer), DJ Paul (R. L.), Al Kapone (Kateezy), Jennifer Bynum Green (Choir Lead Singer), Kelvin Birrus, Tiran D. Boyland, H. Renee Cogar, Brandon Seiferth, Deborah Manning Thomas (Choir Singers), Terrence Brown (Piano Player), T. C. Sharpe (Arnel's Drunk), Lindsey Roberts (Harper), Free Sol (Bathroom Kid), Clarence Mabon (Police Officer #2), Mark Goodfellow (Pawn Shop Owner), Latasha Texas, Tracy Davis (Strippers), Erica Miller (God Bless America Girl), Helen Bowman (Defendant)

Taraji P. Henson, Paula Jai Parker, Terrence Howard, Taryn Manning

Djay, a short-tempered pimp and dope dealer, believes he has found the ticket out of his dead-end life by putting his rhymes to music with the intention of producing a hit recording.

2005 Academy Award winner for Best Song ("It's Hard Out Here for a Pimp"). This film received an additional Oscar nomination for actor (Terrence Howard).

Terrence Howard, D.J. Qualls, Anthony Anderson

Isaac Hayes, Taryn Manning PHOTOS COURTESY OF PARAMOUNT CLASSICS

Lukas Haas, Nicole Vicius

LAST DAYS

(FINE LINE FEATURES) Producer, Dany Wolf; Director/Screenplay/Editor, Gus Van Sant; Photography, Harris Savides; Art Director, Tim Grimes; Costumes, Michelle Matland; Music Consultant, Thurston Moore; Casting, Mali Finn; an HBO Films presentation of a Meno Film Company production; Dolby; Color; Rated R; 97 minutes; Release date: July 22, 2005

Cast

Blake **Michael Pitt**
Luke **Lukas Haas**
Asia **Asia Argento**
Scott **Scott Green**
Nicole **Nicole Vicius**
Detective **Ricky Jay**
Donovan **Ryan Orion**

and Harmony Korine (Guy in Club), The Hermit (Band in Club), Kim Gordon (Record Executive), Adam Friberg, Andy Friberg (Elder Fribergs), Thadeus A. Thomas (Yellow Book Salesman), Chip Marks (Tree Trimmer), Kurt Loder, Michael Azerrad (TV Voiceovers), Chris Monlux, Jack Gibson, Gus Van Sant, Shon Blotzer, Dawnn Pavlonnis (Phone Voices)

A look at the final hours of self-destructive rock star Blake.

Michael Pitt, Kim Gordon PHOTOS COURTESY OF FINE LINE FEATURES

THE DEVIL'S REJECTS

(LIONS GATE) Producers, Michael Ohoven, Marco Mehlitz, Andy Gould, Mike Elliott, Rob Zombie; Executive Producers, Peter Block, Michael Paseornek, Michael Burns, Guy Oseary; Co-Producer, Brent Morris; Director/Screenplay, Rob Zombie; Photography, Phil Parmet; Designer, Anthony Tremblay; Costumes, Yasmine Abraham; Music, Tyler Bates; Editor, Glenn Garland; Special Effect Makeup, Wayne Toth; Visual Effects Supervisor, Robert Kurtzman; Casting, Monika Mikkelsen; a Lions Gate Film, Cinerenta presentation of a Cinelamda production in association with Devil's Rejects Inc., Firm Films; Dolby; Color; Super-16; Rated R; 101 minutes; Release date: July 22, 2005

Bill Moseley, Sheri Moon Zombie

Cast

Captain Spaulding **Sid Haig**
Otis Driftwood **Bill Moseley**
Baby Firefly **Sheri Moon Zombie**
Charlie Altamont **Ken Foree**
Tiny **Matthew McGrory**
Mother Firefly **Leslie Easterbrook**
Roy Sullivan **Geoffrey Lewis**
Gloria Sullivan **Priscilla Barnes**
Sheriff Wydell **William Forsythe**

and Kate Norby (Wendy Banjo), Lew Temple (Adam Banjo), Dave Sheridan (Officer Ray Dobson), EG Daly (Candy), Danny Trejo (Rondo), Diamond Dallas Page (Billy Ray Snapper), Brian Posehn (Jimmy), Tom Towles (George Wydell), Michael Berryman (Clevon), P. J. Soles (Susan), Deborah Van Valkenburgh (Casey), Ginger Lynn Allen (Fanny), Jossara Jinaro (Maria), Chris Ellis (Coggs), Mary Woronov (Abbie), Daniel Roebuck (Morris Green), Duane Whitaker (Dr. Bankhead), Michael "Red Bone" Alcott (Darrell), Juanita Guzman (Ruth), Sean Murphy (Turk Murphy), Jordan Orr (Jamie), Kelvin Brown (Bubba), Glenn Taranto (Anchorman)

A psychopathic brother and sister are pursued by a vengeful sheriff whose brother they had slain.

SKY HIGH

(WALT DISNEY PICTURES) Producer, Andrew Gunn; Executive Producers, Mario Iscovich, Ann Marie Sanderlin; Director, Mike Mitchell; Screenplay, Paul Hernandez, Bob Schooley, Mark McCorkle; Photography, Shelly Johnson; Designer, Bruce Robert Hill; Costumes, Michael Wilkinson; Music, Michael Giacchino; Music Supervisor, Lisa Brown; Editor, Peter Amundson; Casting, Allison Jones; Stunts, Scott Rogers; a Gunn Films production; Dolby; Technicolor; Rated PG; 99 minutes; Release date: July 29, 2005

Cast

Will Stronghold **Michael Angarano**
Steve Stronghold/The Commander **Kurt Russell**
Josie Stronghold/Jetstream **Kelly Preston**
Layla **Danielle Panabaker**
News Anchor **Chris Wynne**
Ron Wilson, Bus Driver **Kevin Heffernan**
Ethan **Dee-Jay Daniels**
Magneta **Kelly Vitz**
Little Larry **Loren Berman**
Zach **Nicholas Braun**
Penny **Malika**
Penny **Khadijah**
Lash **Jake Sandvig**
Speed **Will Harris**

Kelly Preston, Kurt Russell

Lynda Carter

Danielle Panabaker, Dee-Jay Daniels, Michael Angarano, Steven Strait

and Mary Elizabeth Winstead (Gwen/Royal Pain), Lynda Carter (Principal Powers), Bruce Campbell (Coach Boomer), Dustin Ingram (Carbon Copy Kid), Steven Strait (Warren Peace), Cloris Leachman (Nurse Spex), Jim Rash (Mr. Grayson/Stitches), Dave Foley (Mr. Boy), Kevin McDonald (Mr. Medulla), Amy Brown (Twin), Kimmy Brown (Evil Twin), Lucille Soong (Cook), Zachry Rogers (Young Commander), Tom Kenny (Mr. Timmerman), Jill Talley (Mrs. Timmerman), Patrick Warburton (Voice of Royal Pain)

The son of two legendary superheroes is sent to Sky High where they hope he will follow in their footsteps and live up to the family name.

Kurt Russell, Michael Angarano PHOTOS COURTESY OF WALT DISNEY PICTURES

Fred Willard PHOTO COURTESY OF THINKFILM

THE ARISTOCRATS

(THINKFILM) Producer, Peter Adam Golden; Executive Producers, Penn Jillette, Paul Provenza; Supervising Producer, Farley Ziegler; Director, Paul Provenza; Editors, Emery Emery, Paul Provenza; Music, Gary Stockdale; a Mighty Cheese production; Dolby; Color; Not rated; 89 minutes; Release date: July 29, 2005. Documentary in which several top comedians in show business give their interpretations of the world's dirtiest joke.

With

Chris Albrecht, Jason Alexander, Hank Azaria, Billy The Mime, Shelley Berman, Lewis Black, David Brenner, Mario Cantone, Drew Carey, George Carlin, Mark Cohen, Billy Connolly, Tim Conway, Pat Cooper, Wayne Cotter, Andy Dick, Frank DiGiacomo, Phyllis Diller, Susie Essman, Carrie Fisher, Joe Franklin, Joe Garden, Mike George, Todd Glass, Whoopi Goldberg, Judy Gold, Eddie Gorodetsky, Gilbert Gottfried, Dana Gould, Todd Hanson, Tim Harrod, Allan Havey, Eric Idle, Dom Irrera, Eddie Izzard, Richard Jeni, Penn Jillette, Jake Johannsen, Chris Karwowski, Kelly Kirkle, Alan Kirschenbaum, Jay Kogen, Carol Kolb, Sue Kolinsky, Paul Krassner, Cathy Ladman, Lisa Lampanelli, Richard Lewis, Wendy Liebman, Bill Maher, Howie Mandel, Merrill Markoe, Jay Marshall, Jackie "The Joke Man" Martling, Chuck McCann, Michael McKean, Eric Mead, Larry Miller, Owen Morse, Martin Mull, Kevin Nealon, Taylor Negron, Rick Overton, Gary Owens, Trey Parker, Otto Peterson, Emo Philips, Peter Pitofsky, Kevin Pollak, Paul Reiser, Andy Richter, Don Rickles, Chris Rock, Gregg Rogell, Jeffrey Ross, Jon Ross, Rita Rudner, Bob Saget, T. Sean Shannon, Harry Shearer, Sarah Silverman, Bobby Slayton, Dick Smothers, Tom Smothers, Carrie Snow, Doug Stanhope, David Steinberg, Jon Stewart, Matt Stone, Larry Storch, Rip Taylor, Teller, The Amazing Jonathan, Dave Thomas, Johnny Thompson, Carrot Top, Peter Tilden, Bruce Vilanch, Jonathan Wee, Fred Willard, Robin Williams, Steven Wright

STEALTH

(COLUMBIA) Producers, Laura Ziskin, Mike Medavoy, Neal H. Moritz; Executive Producers, E. Bennett Walsh, Arnold W. Messer; Director, Rob Cohen; Screenplay, W. D. Richter; Photography, Dean Semler; Designers, J. Michael Riva, Jonathan Lee; Costumes, Lizzy Gardiner; Music, BT; Music Supervisor, Bob Badami; Editor, Stephen Rivkin; Visual Effects, Digital Domain; an Original Film, Phoenix Pictures, Laura Ziskin production; Dolby; Panavision; Deluxe color; Rated PG-13; 120 minutes; Release date: July 29, 2005

Cast

Lt. Ben Gannon **Josh Lucas**
Kara Wade **Jessica Biel**
Henry Purcell **Jamie Foxx**
Capt. George Cummings **Sam Shepard**
Keith Orbit **Richard Roxburgh**
Capt. Dick Marshfield **Joe Morton**
Lt. Aaron Shaftsbury **Ian Bliss**
Josh Hudson **Ebon Moss-Bacharach**
Naval Controller **Michael Denkha**

and Rocky Helton (Master at Arms, USS Abraham), Clayton Adams, Maurice Morgan, Christopher Naismith, Charles Ndibe (Lincoln Sailors), Nicholas Hammond (Executive Officer), Joel Tobeck (Civilian), John Waters (Civilian Doctor), Sara Saliba (Korean Girl), Jim Diamond, Jaffar Hussain, Gary Quay (Rangoon Terrorists), Jason Lee (Yune), Rowan Schlosberg, Jason Chan, Mathew Wilkinson, Johann Walraven (EDI Technicians), Randall Mettam, Lucia Mastrantone, Dorion Nkono, Miles Paras, Ali Ammouchi, Adriano Capeltetta, Blazey Best, Paul Pantano (Naval Controllers), Alexandra Davies (Ben's Date), Caroline De Sounza Correa (Henry's Date), Ilya Morelle, Nikolai Nikolaeff, Warwick Young, Paul Donazzan (Russian Pilots), Vanessa Trezise (Newsreader), Matthew Jorgensen (Barricade Officer), Colby Sanders (Aviation Plane Captain), Diego Corral (Ships Safety Officer), Jaipetch Toonchalong (Henry's Thai Girlfriend), Wentworth Miller (Voice of EDI), CDR Robert L. Keane, CMC, USN (Air Craft Carrier Chaplain)

A team of test pilots must stop an artificial intelligence-based unmanned combat aerial vehicle that has lost control after being hit by lightning.

Josh Lucas, Jamie Foxx, Jessica Biel PHOTO COURTESY OF COLUMBIA

MUST LOVE DOGS

(WARNER BROS.) Producers, Suzanne Todd, Jennifer Todd, Gary David Goldberg; Executive Producers, Brad Hall, Ronald G. Smith; Director/Screenplay, Gary David Goldberg; Based on the novel by Claire Cook; Photography, John Bailey; Designer, Naomi Shohan; Costumes, Florence-Isabelle Megginson; Music, Craig Armstrong; Editors, Eric Sears, Roger Bondelli; Casting, Joanna Colbert; an Ubu Productions, Team Todd production; Dolby; Panavision; Color; Rated PG-13; 98 minutes; Release date: July 29, 2005

John Cusack, Diane Lane

Bobby Coleman, Dermot Mulroney

Cast
Sarah **Diane Lane**
Jake **John Cusack**
Carol **Elizabeth Perkins**
Bill **Christopher Plummer**
Bob **Dermot Mulroney**
Dolly **Stockard Channing**
Christine **Ali Hillis**
Leo **Brad William Henke**
June **Julie Gonzalo**
Michael **Glenn Howerton**
Charlie **Ben Shenkman**
Sherry **Jordana Spiro**
Deli Guy **Kirk Trutner**
Eric **Victor Webster**
Marc **Michael Spound**

and Will McCormack (Jason), Ted Griffin (Bill Jr.), Marylouise Burke (Aunt Eileen), Brad Hall (Stanley), Bobby Coleman (Austin), Emma Prescott (Molly), Jaden Sorensen (Justin), Will Rothhaar (Jeremy), Tony Bill (Walter), Patrick St. Espirit (Marshall), Josh Stamberg (Lennie), Anoush Nevart (Mrs. Parseghian), Krikor Satamian (Mr. Parseghian), Jon Lindstrom (Peter), Patrick Fabian (Donald), Steven R. Schirripa (Vinnie), Bess Wohl (Rebecca), Laura Kightlinger (Marcia), Rubria Martins-Negrao (Sonia), Colin Egglesfield (David), Suzy Nakamura (Mai), Jamie Denbo (Bertha), Miles Hull (Timmy), Amy Kidd (Jennifer), Ted Detwiler (Boat Guy), Kate McClafferty (Coxswain), Shana Hiatt (Hostess)

Christopher Plummer

Following her divorce, Sarah is pressured by her family into dating, ending up having to chose between a newly separated dad and an eccentric race boat builder.

Diane Lane, Elizabeth Perkins, Ali Hillis PHOTOS COURTESY OF WARNER BROS.

Scott Wilson, Celia Weston

Benjamin McKenzie, Embeth Davidtz

Amy Adams

Embeth Davidtz, Alessandro Nivola PHOTOS COURTESY OF SONY CLASSICS

JUNEBUG

(SONY CLASSICS) Producers, Mindy Goldberg, Mike S. Ryan; Executive Producers, Mark P. Clein, Ethan D. Leder, Daniel Rappaport, Dany Wolf; Director, Phil Morrison; Screenplay, Angus MacLachlan; Designer, David Doernberg; Costumes, Danielle Kays; Music, Yo La Tengo; Editor, Joe Klotz; Casting, Mark Bennett; an Epoch Films production; Dolby; Color; 16mm-to-HD; Rated R; 106 minutes; Release date: August 3, 2005

Cast
Ashley **Amy Adams**
Madeline **Embeth Davidtz**
Johnny **Benjamin McKenzie**
George **Alessandro Nivola**
David Wark **Frank Hoyt Taylor**
Peg **Celia Weston**
Eugene **Scott Wilson**

John Eddie McGee, Alessandro Nivola, Gregory Wagoner

and Amy Barefoot (Kitty), Annette Beatty (Dr. Beatty), Matt Besser (Scout Who Goes In), Beth Bostic (Lucille the Neighbor), Jamie Castlebury (Woman at Shower), Carrie Daniel (Bonnie), Jeffrey Dean Foster (Gallery Assistant), Katherine Foster (Pregnant Patient), Teresa Fowler (Nurse #1), Keith Harris (Bud, Young Pastor), Robert Harris (Art Gallery Patron), Kevin Harlow Hasper (Hollerin' Man), Tarra Jolly (Tarra at Replacements, Ltd.), David Kuhn (Auctioneer), Laura Lashley (Gallery Assistant), John Eddie McGee (Older Singer at Church), John McGee (Singer at Church), Dan McLamb (Hollerin' Man), Jerry Minor (Scout Who Stays Outside), Will Oldham (Bill Mooney), Joanne Pankow (Sissy), Adrian Roberts (Hollerer), Chuck Russell (Chuck at Replacements, Ltd.), Bobby Tisdale (Norman at Replacements, Ltd.), Alicia Van Couvering (Bernadette), John A. Van Couvering (Meerkat Expert), Caitlin Van Hecke (Emily, Pastor's Wife), Jill Wagner (Millicent), Gregory Wagoner (Young Singer at Church), Daniel Williard (George's Friend in Church)

While visiting the South to track down a reclusive artist, Madeline and George reluctantly visit his estranged, troubled family.

This film received an Oscar nomination for supporting actress (Amy Adams).

BROKEN FLOWERS

(FOCUS) Producers, Jon Kilik, Stacey Smith; Co-Producer, Ann Ruark; Director/Screenplay, Jim Jarmusch; Inspired by an idea from Bill Raden, Sara Driver; Photography, Frederick Elmes; Designer, Mark Friedberg; Costumes, John Dunn; Music, Mulatu Astatke; Editor, Jay Rabinowitz; Casting, Ellen Lewis; a Five Roses production; Dolby; Deluxe color; Rated R; 107 minutes; Release date: August 5, 2005

Cast

Don Johnston **Bill Murray**
Winston **Jeffrey Wright**
Laura Daniels Miller **Sharon Stone**
Dora Anderson **Frances Conroy**
Dr. Carmen Markowski **Jessica Lange**
Penny **Tilda Swinton**
Sherry **Julie Delpy**
The Kid **Mark Webber**
Carmen's Assistant **Chloë Sevigny**
Ron **Christopher McDonald**
Lolita **Alexis Dziena**
Will **Larry Fessenden**
Dan **Chris Bauer**
Sun Green **Pell James**
Mona **Heather Alicia Simms**
Rita **Brea Frazier**

Bill Murray, Julie Delpy

Jeffrey Wright, Bill Murray

Alexis Dziena, Sharon Stone, Bill Murray PHOTOS COURTESY OF FOCUS FEATURES

Bill Murray, Jessica Lange

Bill Murray, Tilda Swinton

and Jarry Fall, Korka Fall, Saul Holland, Zakira Holland, Niles Lee Wilson (Winston and Mona's Kids), Meredith Patterson (Flight Attendant), Jennifer Rapp, Nicole Abisinio (Girls on Bus), Ryan Donowho (Young Man on Bus), Dared Wright (Man with Rabbit), Suzanne Hevner (Mrs. Dorston), Brian F. McPeck, Matthew McAuley (Guys in SUV), Homer Murray (Kid in Car)

After receiving an anonymous note informing him that he has a 19-year-old son, Don Johnston decides to track down his ex-lovers to find out which of them is the mother of the boy.

THE DUKES OF HAZZARD

(WARNER BROS.) Producer, Bill Gerber; Executive Producers, Eric McLeod, Dana Goldberg, Bruce Berman; Director, Jay Chandrasekhar; Screenplay, John O'Brien; Story, John O'Brien, Jonathan L. Davis; Based on characters created by Gy Waldron; Photography, Lawrence Sher; Designer, Jon Gary Steele; Costumes, Genevieve Tyrrell; Music, Nathan Barr; Music Supervisor, Nic Harcourt; Editors, Lee Haxall, Myron Kerstein; Casting, Mary Vernieu; Stunts, Darrin Prescott, Scott A. Rogers; a Bill Gerber production, presented in association with Village Roadshow Pictures; Dolby; Technicolor; Rated PG-13; 105 minutes; Release date: August 5, 2005

Seann William Scott, Johnny Knoxville, Burt Reynolds

Cast

Luke Duke **Johnny Knoxville**
Bo Duke **Seann William Scott**
Daisy Duke **Jessica Simpson**
Boss Hogg **Burt Reynolds**
Gov. Jim Applewhite **Joe Don Baker**
Uncle Jessie **Willie Nelson**
Pauline **Lynda Carter**
Rosco P. Coltrane **M. C. Gainey**
Cooter **David Koechner**
Deputy Cletus **Jack Polick**
Deputy Enos Strate **Michael Weston**
Laurie Pullman **Alice Greczyn**
Jimmy **Steve Lemme**
Puncher **David Leitch**
The Balladeer **Junior Brown**

and Mitch Braswell (Out of Towner #1), Michael Roof (Dil Driscoll), Rusty Tennant, Dolan Wilson (Locals), James Roady (Billy Prickett), Heather Hemmens (Girl #1), A. J. Foyt IV (Race Car Driver #1), Jim Cody Williams (Security Guard Chip), Kevin Heffernan (Sheev), Tammi Arender (Local Reporter #1), Artist Robinson (18 Wheeler Driver), Tenia Taylor (Pretty Girl), Bruce McKinnon (Van Driver), Lara Grice (Passenger), Kristen Laird, Brittany Pourciau, Erica Lee, Crystal Barrett, Jillian Batherson, Kristen

Jessica Simpson, Michael Weston

Broussard, Christina DaRe, Amber Duke, Hana Dupre, Jenifer Rebecca Foster, Alexis Hebert, Tracey Mills (Sorority Girls), Nikki Griffin (Katie Johnson), Jacqui Maxwell (Annette), Jay Chandrasekhar, Erik Stolhanske (Campus Cops), Charlie Finn (Royce), Thomas Elliott, Dremaceo Giles (Tough Guys), Thomas Hyde, Wayne Douglas Morgan (Prisoners), Danny Hanemann (Older Cop), Tobi Gadison Brown (Younger Cop), Chris Richard (Lexus Driver), Dan Montgomery, Jr. (Spectator), Therial "Houseman" deClouet (Judge), Emily Smith, Stacy Brown (Reporters), Alicen Holden (Governor's Aide), Paul Soter (Rick Shakely), Ritchie Montgomery (Trooper), Kim Wall (State Trooper), Andrew Prine (Angry Man), Grace C. Gerber (Little Girl), Rip Taylor (Himself)

Jessica Simpson, Willie Nelson, Lynda Carter PHOTOS COURTESY OF WARNER BROS.

Cousins Bo and Luke Duke try to stop corrupt Boss Hogg from strip mining Hazzard County. Based on the CBS television series that ran from 1979 to 1985 and starred John Schneider, Tom Wopat, and Catherine Bach.

Terrence Howard, Josh Charles

Andre Benjamin, Garrett Hedlund, Mark Wahlberg, Tyrese Gibson

Tyrese Gibson, Sofia Vergara

FOUR BROTHERS

(PARAMOUNT) Producer, Lorenzo Di Bonaventura; Executive Producers, Ric Kidney, Erik Howsam; Director, John Singleton; Screenplay, David Elliot, Paul Lovett; Photography, Peter Menzies, Jr.; Designer, Keith Brian Burns; Costumes, Ruth Carter; Music, David Arnold; Music Supervisor, Paul Stewart; Editors, Bruce Cannon, Billy Fox; Casting, Kimberly R. Hardin; a Di Bonaventura Pictures production; Dolby; Deluxe color; Rated R; 109 minutes; Release date: August 12, 2005

Cast

Bobby Mercer **Mark Wahlberg**
Angel Mercer **Tyrese Gibson**
Jeremiah Mercer **André Benjamin**
Jack Mercer **Garrett Hedlund**
Lt. Green **Terrence Howard**
Detective Fowler **Josh Charles**
Sofi **Sofia Vergara**
Evelyn Mercer **Fionnula Flanagan**
Victor Sweet **Chiwetel Ejiofor**
Camille Mercer **Taraji P. Henson**
Council Douglas **Barry Shabaka Henley**
Efan **Jernard Burks**
Robert Bradford **Kenneth Welsh**
Charlie **Tony Nappo**

and Shawn Singleton (Victor Hoodlum), Reiya West Downs (Daniela Mercer), Riele West Downs (Amelia Mercer), Lyriq Bent (Damian), Richard Chevolleau, Awaovieyi Agie (El Camino Guys), Shomari Downer (Gangbanger), Mpho Koaho (Gang Leader), Costin Manu (Maschur), Kevin Duhaney (Keenon), Brad Borbridge, Timothy E. Brummond, Robert Thomas (Interrogating Cops), Benz Antoine, Dave Sparrow (Police Sergeants), Kathryn Haggis (Airline Attendant), Michael Brown (Huge Player), Victor A. Young (Father Lamont), Greg Ellwand (Insurance Man), Conrad Bergschneider (Johnny the Bartender), Eric Fink (Landlord), Pablo Silveira (Samir), Frank Spadone, Kevin Hanchard, Carlos Diaz (Baffled Cops), Dax Ravina (Young Tech), Billy Oliver (Prankster), Michelle Moffatt (Secretary), Derwin Phillips (Ref), Quincy Nanatakyi (Twelve Year Old), Evelynking Nanatakyi (Nine Year Old), Stefanie Samuels (Evan's Wife), Wes Williams (Victor's Driver), Kofi Payton, Travis Smith, Angel Weathered, Kiara Taylor (Kids Playing Cards), Matthew Peart (Kid Selling Chocolate), Odeen Eccleston (Gang Member), Tahliel Hawthorne (Darnell), Jeff Authors (Bitter Drunk Guy), Jennfier Doane (Casino Employee), Jamal Weathers (Detective)

The Mercer brothers reunite to track down the person responsible for killing their adoptive mother during a grocery store holdup.

Pablo Silveira, Tahliel Hawthorne, Fionnula Flanagan PHOTOS COURTESY OF PARAMOUNT

GRIZZLY MAN

(LIONS GATE) Producer, Erik Nelson; Executive Producers, Erik Nelson, Billy Campbell, Tom Ortenberg, Kevin Beggs, Phil Fairclough, Andrea Meditch; Co-Executive Producer, Jewel Palovak; Executive in Charge of Production, Dave Harding; Director/Narrator, Werner Herzog; Photography, Peter Zeitlinger; Music, Richard Thompson; Editor, Joe Bini; Associate Producer, Alana Berry; a Discovery Docs presentation of a Real Big Productions production; U.S.-Canadian; HD Video; Color; Rated R; 103 minutes; Release date: August 12, 2005. Documentary on Timothy Treadwell who chose to live in the Alaskan wilderness among the grizzly bears each summer starting in 1990 and leading up to his death 13 years later.

With

Timothy Treadwell, Amie Huguenard, Warren Queeney, Willy Fulton, Sam Egil, Marnie Gaede, Marc Gaede, Larry Van Daele, Franc Falico, Jewel Palovak, Val Dexter, Carol Dexter, Kathleen Parker

Kate Hudson, John Hurt, Gena Rowlands

THE SKELETON KEY

(UNIVERSAL) Producers, Daniel Bobker, Iain Softley, Michael Shamberg, Stacey Sher; Executive Producer, Clayton Townsend; Director, Iain Softley; Screenplay, Ehren Kruger; Photography; Dan Mindel; Designer, John Beard; Costumes, Louise Frogley; Music, Edward Shearmur; Editor, Joe Hutshing; Casting, Ronna Kress; a Shadowcatcher Entertainment, Double Feature Films production; Dolby; Panavision; Technicolor; Rated PG-13; 104 minutes; Release date: August 12, 2005

Cast

Caroline Ellis **Kate Hudson**
Violet Devereaux **Gena Rowlands**
Ben Devereaux **John Hurt**
Luke **Peter Sarsgaard**
Jill **Joy Bryant**
Mama Cynthia **Maxine Barnett**
Hallie **Fahnlohnee Harris**

Timothy Treadwell PHOTO COURTESY OF LIONS GATE

Bayou Woman **Marion Zinser**
Desk Nurse **Deneen Tyler**
C.N.A. **Ann Dalrymple**
Nurse Trula **Trula Marcus**
Nurse Audrey **Tonya Staten**

and Tom Uskali (Robertson Thorpe), Jen Apgar (Madeleine Thorpe), Forrest Landis (Martin Thorpe), Jamie Lee Redmon (Grace Thorpe), Ronald McCall (Papa Justify), Jeryl Prescott Sales (Mama Cecile), Isaach De Bankole (Creole Gas Station Owner), Christa Thorne (Creole Mother), Lakrishi Kindred (Frail Customer), Lawrence "King" Harvey (Bar Man), Mark Krasnoff (Pickup Driver), Sabah (Luke's Secretary), Susannah Thorarinsson (Waitress in Bar), Bill H. McKenzie (Mr. Talcott), Joe Chrest (Paramedic), David Curtis, Tiffany Helland, Bryan Ruppert (Party Guests), Philip Frazier, Derek Shezbie, Glen Andrews, Stafford Agee, Keith Frazier, Derrick Tabb, Shamar Allen, Byron Bernard, Herbert Stevens (Rebirth Brass Band), George Harper, Howard McCary, Kevin O'Neal, Ryan Porter, Rudy Regalado, Nolan Shaheed (Jazz Band), Dustin Fleetwood, Roderick Harrison, Torrey McKinley (3rd Infantry Band Members)

Hospice worker Caroline Ellis takes a job at a decrepit mansion in the Louisiana bayou where an unexplainable series of supernatural events leads her to uncover the secret tormenting its surviving occupants.

Peter Sarsgaard, Kate Hudson PHOTOS COURTESY OF UNIVERSAL

RED EYE

(DREAMWORKS) Producers, Chris Bender, Marianne Maddalena; Executive Producers, Bonnie Curtis, Jim Lemley, JC Spink; Director, Wes Craven; Screenplay, Carl Ellsworth; Story, Chris Bender; Photography, Robert Yeoman; Designer, Bruce Alan Miller; Costumes, Mary Claire Hannan; Music, Marco Beltrami; Editors, Patrick Lussier, Stuart Levy; Casting, Lisa Beach; a Benderspink production; Dolby; Panavision; Technicolor; Rated PG-13; 85 minutes; Release date: August 19, 2005

Cast

Lisa Reisert **Rachel McAdams**
Jackson Rippner **Cillian Murphy**
Lisa's Dad **Brian Cox**
Blonde Woman **Laura Johnson**
Headphone Kid **Max Kasch**
Cynthia **Jayma Mays**
Nice Lady **Angela Paton**
Senior Flight Attendant **Suzie Plakson**
Charles Keefe **Jack Scalia**
Marianne Taylor **Teresa Press-Marx**
Bob Taylor **Robert Pine**
Taxi Driver **Carl Gilliard**

Cillian Murphy, Rachel McAdams

Lisa Reisert is terrified to learn that the passenger sitting next to her on an airplane flight is part of a plan to kill the Deputy Secretary of Homeland Security and that Lisa is a key to the plan's success.

Rachel McAdams

Brian Cox PHOTOS COURTESY OF DREAMWORKS

and Mary-Kathleen Gordon (Airline Representative), Loren Lester (Irate Passenger), Philip Pavel, Amber Mead (Dallas Ticket Agents), Dey Young (Dallas Gate Agent), Brittany Oaks (Rebecca), Tina Anderson (Rebecca's Mom), Jeanine Jackson (Passenger with Iced Mocha), Joey Nader (Tex-Mex Bartender), Kyle Gallner (Headphone Kid's Brother), Dilva Henry (Newscaster), Monica McSwain (Junior Flight Attendant), Tom Elkins (Pilot), Amanda Young (Flight Attendant), Dane Farwell (Hit Man at Dad's House), Jennie Baek (Keefe's Assistant), Colby Donaldson (Keefe's Head Bodyguard), Beth Toussaint Coleman (Lydia Keefe), Adam Gobble (Keefe's Son), Megan Crawford (Keefe's Daughter), C. C. Taylor, Scott Leva (Keefe's Bodyguards), Marc Macaulay (Coast Guard Officer), Skip Crank, Mark Cotone, Jim Lemley (Men on Fishing Boat), Martin Trees (Male Flight Attendant), Noelle Drake, Jenny Wade (Coffee Shop Girls)

Jack Scalia, Colby Donaldson, Megan Crawford, Beth Toussaint Coleman

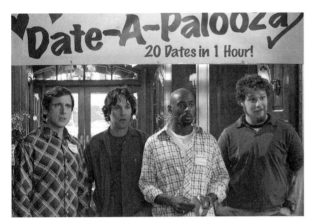
Steve Carell, Paul Rudd, Romany Malco, Seth Rogen

THE 40 YEAR OLD VIRGIN

(UNIVERSAL) Producers, Judd Apatow, Clayton Townsend, Shauna Robertson; Executive Producers, Steve Carell, Jon Poll; Director, Judd Apatow; Screenplay, Judd Apatow, Steve Carell; Photography, Jack Green; Designer, Jackson DeGovia; Costumes, Debra McGuire; Music, Lyle Workman; Editor, Brent White; Co-Producer, Seth Rogen; Casting, Allison Jones, Marla Garlin; an Apatow production; Dolby; Fotokem color; Rated R; 116 minutes; Release date: August 19, 2005

Cast

Andy Stitzer **Steve Carell**
Trish **Catherine Keener**
David **Paul Rudd**
Jay **Romany Malco**
Cal **Seth Rogen**
Beth **Elizabeth Banks**
Nicky **Leslie Mann**
Paula **Jane Lynch**
Mooj **Gerry Bednob**
Haziz **Shelley Malil**
Marla **Kat Dennings**
Mark **Jordan Masterson**
Julia **Chelsea Smith**
eBay Customer **Jonah Hill**
Jill **Erica Vittina Phillips**
Bernadette **Marika Dominczyk**
Amy **Mindy Kaling**
Gina **Mo Collins**

and Gillian Vigman, Kimberly Page, Siena Goines (Women at Speed Dating), Charlie Hartsock (Speed Dating MC), Nancy Walls (Health Clinic Counselor), Cedric Yarbrough, David Koechner, Jeff Kahn (Dads at Health Clinic), Nick Lashaway, Loren Berman, Julian Foster (Boys at Health Clinic), Loudon Wainright (Priest), Lee Weaver (Joe), Gloria Helena Jones (Sara), Jazzmun (Prostitute), Miki Mia (Waxing Lady), Denise Meyerson (Robin), Shannon Bradley, Brianna Lynn Brown, Elizabeth Carey, Elizabeth DeCicco, Hilary Shepard, Barret Swatek (Bar Girls), Carla Gallo (Toe-Sucking Girl), Michael Bierman (16-Year-Old Andy), Marisa Guterman (Girl with Braces), Stormy Daniels (Porn Star), Kevin Hart, Wayne Federman, Ron Marasco, Joseph T. Mastrolia (Smart Tech Customers), Kate Luyben (Woman Buying Videotapes), Joseph A. Nuñez (Man Buffing Floor), Matthew McKane (Motorist), Rose Abdoo (Mother at Restaurant), Steve Bannos (Father at Restaurant), Brooke Hamlin (Daughter at Restaurant), Miyoko Shimosawa (Waitress at Restaurant), Marilyn Dodds Frank (Woman Who Bought Television)

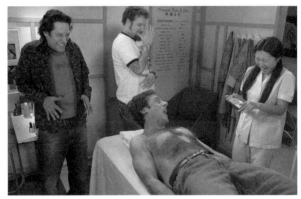
Paul Rudd, Seth Rogen, Steve Carell, Miki Mia

When his co-workers discover that timid Andy Stitzer is still a virgin at the age of 40, they make it their mission to ensure that he changes his image and has sex as soon as possible.

Steve Carell, Catherine Keener PHOTOS COURTESY OF UNIVERSAL

Robert Redford, Morgan Freeman

AN UNFINISHED LIFE

(MIRAMAX) Producers, Leslie Holleran, Kellian Ladd, Alan Ladd Jr.; Executive Producers, Michelle Raimo, Meryl Poster, Harvey Weinstein, Bob Weinstein, Matthew Rhodes, Mark Rydell, Graham King, Joe Roth; Co-Producer, Su Armstrong; Director, Lasse Hallström; Screenplay, Mark Spragg, Virginia Korus Spragg; Based on the novel by Mark Spragg; Photography, Oliver Stapleton; Designer, David Gropman; Costumes, Tish Monaghan; Music, Christopher Young; Editor, Andrew Mondshein; Casting, Kerry Barden, Suzanne Smith, Billy Hopkins; a Revolution Studios presentation, in association with Initial Entertainment Group, of a Ladd Company production; Dolby; Widescreen; Color; Rated PG-13; 107 minutes; Release date: September 9, 2005

Cast

Einar Gilkyson **Robert Redford**
Jean Gilkyson **Jennifer Lopez**
Mitch Bradley **Morgan Freeman**
Sheriff Crane Curtis **Josh Lucas**

Robert Redford, Jennifer Lopez, Morgan Freeman PHOTOS COURTESY OF MIRAMAX

Gary Watson **Damian Lewis**
Nina **Camryn Manheim**
Griff Gilkyson **Becca Gardner**
Kitty **Lunda Boyd**
Rancher Kent **R. Nelson Brown**
Drunk Cowboy **Sean J. Dory**
Deputy Bob **Rob Hayter**
Shelter Supervisor **P. Lynn Johnson**
Bear **Bart the Bear**

Fleeing from her abusive boyfriend, Jean Gilkyson and her daughter arrive at the farm of her estranged father-in-law, who blames her for his son's death.

Becca Gardner, Jennifer Lopez, Robert Redford in *An Unfinished Life*

KEANE

(MAGNOLIA) Producer, Andrew Fierberg; Executive Producer, Steven Soderbergh; Co-Producers, Brian Bell, Jenny Schweitzer; Director/Screenplay, Lodge Kerrigan; Photography, John Foster; Designer, Petra Barchi; Costumes, Catherine George; Editor, Andrew Hafitz; Casting, Heidi Levitt, Bernard Telsey, David Vaccari; a Populist Pictures presentation of a Studio Fierberg production; Dolby; Color; Rated R; 93 minutes; Release date: September 9, 2005

Cast

William Keane **Damian Lewis**
Kyra Bedik **Abigail Breslin**
Lynn Bedik **Amy Ryan**
Michelle **Tina Holmes**
Commuter **Brenda Denmark**
Motel Clerk **Christopher Evan Welch**
Bartender **Chris Bauer**
Drug Dealer **Lev Gorn**

and Liza Colon-Zayas, John Tormey, Sharon Wilkins (Ticket Agents), Ed Wheeler, Ray Fitzgerald (Bus Drivers/Ticket Takers), Yvette Mercedes (Woman in Department Store), Frank Wood (Assaulted Commuter),

Alexander Robert Scott, Phil McGlaston (Cab Drivers), Ted Sod (Gas Station Attendant), Stephen Henderson (Garage Employee), Omar Rodriguez (Garage Manager), Sean Modica (Ice Rink Employee), Mellini Kantayya (Newsstand Cashier)

A father frantically searches New York for his missing daughter, slowly unraveling from the stress of the ordeal.

Elijah Wood

Damian Lewis in *Keane*

Cast

Matt Buckner   **Elijah Wood**
Pete Dunham   **Charlie Hunnam**
Shannon Dunham   **Claire Forlani**
Steve Dunham   **Marc Warren**
Bovver   **Leo Gregory**
Carl Buckner   **Henry Goodman**
Tommy Hatcher   **Geoff Bell**
Swill   **Rafe Spall**
Ike   **Kieran Bew**

and Ross McCall (Dave), Francis Pope (Ned), Christopher Hehir (Keith), Terence Jay (Jeremy Van Holden), David Alexander (Nigel), Joel Beckett (Terry), Andrew Blair (Announcer), David Carr (Clive), Brendan Charleson (John Morris), Scott Christie (Millwall Lad, Ricky), Jacob Gaffney (Todd), Jon House (Commanding Officer), Jamie Kenna (Big Marc), Joshua Kennedy (Lad), Frank McAvennie (Himself), Johnny Palmiero (Garry), Martin T. Sherman (Mitch), Mhairi Steenbock (Young Girl), Steve Benham, Roy Borret, Mark Brighton, Alan Clarke, Barry Dowden, James S. Fisher, Elliott Hill, Nic Main, John Perkins, Kingsley Pilgrim, Peter Rinc, Wayne Saunders, Keven Schwarz, Ben Trow (Firm Members)

In London to visit his sister, journalist student Matt Buckner is befriended by his brother-in-law's brother Pete who is part of the Green Street Elite, a gang of football fans who indulge in violent confrontations with opposing "firms."

Abigail Breslin in *Keane* PHOTOS COURTESY OF MAGNOLIA

GREEN STREET HOOLIGANS

(ODD LOT ENTERTAINMENT) a.k.a. *Hooligans*; Producers, Gigi Pritzker, Deborah Del Prete, Donald Zuckman; Executive Producers, Lexi Alexander Bill Allen, Patrick Aluise, Paul Schiff; Director, Lexi Alexander; Screenplay, Lexi Alexander, Dougie Brimson, Josh Shelov; Photography, Alexander Buono; Designer, Tom Brown; Music, Christopher Franke; Editor, Paul Trejo; a Baker Street production; Dolby; Deluxe color; Rated R; 106 minutes; Release date: September 9, 2005

(center) Elijah Wood, Charlie Hunnam PHOTOS COURTESY OF ODD LOT ENTERTAINMENT

THE EXORCISM OF EMILY ROSE

(SCREEN GEMS) Producers, Tom Rosenberg, Gary Lucchesi; Executive Producers, Andre Lamal, Terry McKay, David McIlvain, Julie Yorn; Co-Producers, Paul Harris Boardman, Tripp Vinson, Beau Flynn; Director, Scott Derrickson; Screenplay, Paul Harris Boardman, Scott Derickson; Photography, Tom Stern; Designer, David Brisbin; Costumes, Tish Monaghan; Music, Christopher Young; Editor, Jeff Betancourt; Casting, Nancy Nayor Battino; a Lakeshore Entertainment production of a Firm Films production; Dolby; Widescreen; Color; Rated PG-13; 118 minutes; Release date: September 9, 2005

Cast

Erin Bruner **Laura Linney**
Father Richard Moore **Tom Wilkinson**
Ethan Thomas **Campbell Scott**
Emily Rose **Jennifer Carpenter**
Karl Gunderson **Colm Feore**
Jason **Joshua Close**
Dr. Mueller **Ken Welsh**
Dr. Cartwright **Duncan Fraser**
Ray **JR Bourne**
Judge Brewster **Mary Beth Hurt**
Dr. Briggs **Henry Czerny**
Dr. Adani **Shohreh Aghdashloo**

Laura Linney, Tom Wilkinson

Laura Linney, Colm Feore

Attorney Erin Bruner defends a Catholic priest accused of negligent homicide during the attempted exorcism of a young woman.

Jennifer Carpenter PHOTOS COURTESY OF FILMCOMPANY

and Steve Archer (Guy in Bar), Liduina Vanderspek, Arlene Belcastro (Praying Women), David Berner, George Gordon (Karl's Cronies), Mary Black (Dr. Vogel), Julian Christopher (District Attorney), Aaron Douglas, Marsha Regis, Chelah Horsdal (Asst. DA's), Lorena Gale (Jury Foreman), Iris Graham, Taylor Hill (Emily's Sisters), John Innes (University Professor), Jeff Johnson (Umbrella Guy), Michael Jonsson (Deputy #1), Katie Keating (Alice), Terence Kelly (Medical Examiner), Darrin Maharaj (On-the-Scene Reporter), Ryan McDonald (Student in Classroom), Marilyn Norry (Maria Rose), Joanna Piros (News Anchorperson), Bobby Stewart (Bailiff), Clay St. Thomas (Reporter on TV), Cory Lee Urhahn (Umbrella Girl), Andrew Wheeler (Nathaniel Rose)

Campbell Scott PHOTOS COURTESY OF SCREEN GEMS

Victor Van Dort, Corpse Bride

Paul the Head Waiter

TIM BURTON'S CORPSE BRIDE

(WARNER BROS.) Producers, Tim Burton, Allison Abbate; Executive Producers, Jeffrey Auerbach, Joe Ranft; Directors, Mike Johnson, Tim Burton; Screenplay, John August, Caroline Thompson, Pamela Pettler; Based on original characters created by Tim Burton, Carlos Grangel; Photography/Visual Effects Supervisor, Pete Kozachik; Designer, Alex McDowell; Animation Supervisor, Anthony Scott; Character Designers, Jordi Grangel, Carles Burges, Huy Vu; Music and Songs, Danny Elfman; Editors, Jonathan Lucas, Chris Lebenzon; Casting, Michelle Guish; a Tim Burton Animation, Laika Entertainment production; Dolby; Technicolor; Rated PG; 76 minutes; Release date: September 16, 2005

William Van Dort, Nell Van Dort, Victor Van Dort

Victoria Everglot, Barkis Bittern

Voice Cast

Victor Van Dort **Johnny Depp**
Corpse Bride **Helena Bonham Carter**
Victoria Everglot **Emily Watson**
Nell Van Dort/Hildegarde **Tracey Ullman**
William Van Dort/Mayhew/Paul, the Head Waiter **Paul Whitehouse**
Maudeline Everglot **Joanne Lumley**
Finis Everglot **Albert Finney**
Barkis Bittern **Richard E. Grant**
Pastor Galswells **Christopher Lee**
Elder Gutknecht **Michael Gough**
Black Widow Spider/Mrs. Plum **Jane Horrocks**
Maggot/Town Crier **Enn Reitel**
General Bonesapart **Deep Roy**
Bonejangles **Danny Elfman**
Emil **Stephen Ballantyne**
Solemn Village Boy **Lisa Kay**

On the eve of his wedding, a timid young man finds himself accidentally wed to a walking corpse.

This film received an Oscar nomination for animated feature.

Maudeline Everglot, Finis Everglot

Lou Pucci PHOTOS COURTESY OF FILMCOMPANY

THUMBSUCKER

(SONY CLASSICS) Producers, Anthony Bregman, Bob Stephenson; Executive Producers, Anne Carey, Ted Hope, Bob Yari, Cathy Schulman; Co-Executive Producers, Tilda Swinton, Jay Shapiro; Director/Screenplay, Mike Mills; Based on the novel by Walter Kirn; Line Producer, Callum Greene; Photography, Joaquin Baca-Asay; Designer, Judy Becker; Music, Tim DeLaughter; Music Supervisor, Brian Reitzell; a Bob Yari Productions presentation of a This Is That Cinema Go-Go production in association with Bullseye Entertainment; Dolby; Panavision; Color; Rated R; 95 minutes; Release date: September 16, 2005

Keanu Reeves, Lou Pucci PHOTOS COURTESY OF FILMCOMPANY

Cast

Justin Cobb **Lou Pucci**
Audrey Cobb **Tilda Swinton**
Mike Cobb **Vincent D'Onofrio**
Mr. Geary **Vince Vaughn**
Perry Lyman **Keanu Reeves**
Matt Schramm **Benjamin Bratt**
Rebecca **Kelli Garner**
Joel Cobb **Chase Offerle**

The Debaters:
Sasha—"I only drink beer" **Sarah Bing**
Elise—"TV violence kills morality" **Echo Brooks**
Ashley—"The stone-faced killer" **Olivia Brown**
Kevin—"You're missing my point" **Patrick Chu**
"Anybody want any Peach Schnapps" **Sarah Iverson**
"Countability needs to be enforced" **Lin Lu**
Lisa—"You're right. TV's not real" **Maura McNamara**
Mark—"Whatever, Speedfreak" **Mahdad Rezaujan**

and Ted Beckman (Stoner Guy), Arvin V. Entena (Perry Lyman's Assistant), Tyler Ganno (Stoner Chick), Allen Go (Biology Teacher), Dakota Goldhor (Girl on Plane), Walter Kirn (Debate Judge), Kit Koenig (Principal), Sarah Lucht (English Teacher), Eric Normington (Hotel Desk Clerk), Nancy O'Dell (Herself), Lanette Prazeau (School Nurse), Bob Stephenson (Debate Official), Colton Tanner (Ten-Year-Old Justin)

Chase Offerle, Vincent D'Onofrio, Tilda Swinton PHOTOS COURTESY OF FILMCOMPANY

A maladjusted, shy teen is diagnosed with Attention Deficit Disorder and put on medication that appears at first to help him develop a degree of self-confidence.

Vince Vaughn PHOTOS COURTESY OF SONY CLASSICS

LORD OF WAR

(LIONS GATE) Producers, Philippe Rousselet, Andrew Niccol, Nicolas Cage, Norman Golightly, Andy Grosch, Chris Roberts; Executive Producers, Fabrice Gianfermi, Bradley Cramp, Gary Hamilton, Christopher Eberts, Andreas Schmid, Michael Mendelsohn, James D. Stern; Director/Screenplay, Andrew Niccol; Photography, Amir Mokri; Designer, Jean Vincent Puzos; Costumes, Elisabetta Beraldo; Music, Antonio Pinto; Music Supervisor, John Bissell; Editor, Zach Staenberg; Co-Producer, Douglas E. Hansen; Executive Line Producer, Ronaldo Vasconcellos; Casting, Mindy Marin; an Entertainment Manufacturing Company presentation of a VIP Medienfonds 3, Ascendant Pictures, Saturn Films production in association with Rising Star, Copag V, Endgame Entertainment; Dolby; Super 35 Widescreen; Technicolor; Rated R; 122 minutes; Release date: September 16, 2005

Nicolas Cage, Eamonn Walker

Nicolas Cage, Jared Leto

Cast

Yuri Orlov **Nicolas Cage**
Ava Fontaine **Bridget Moynahan**
Vitali Orlov **Jared Leto**
Simeon Weisz **Ian Holm**
Jack Valentine **Ethan Hawke**
Andre Baptiste Senior **Eamonn Walker**
Andre Baptiste Junior **Sami Rotibi**
Irina Orlov **Shake Toukhmanian**
Anatoly Orlov **Jean-Pierre Nashanian**

and Jared Burke, Eric Uys, David Shumbris, Stewart Morgan (Ukranian Mobsters), Jasper Lenz (Gregor), Stephen Gregor (Eli Kurtzman), Kobus Marx (Boris), Stephan De Abreu (Liev), Jeremy Crutchley (Arms Fair Salesman), Tanya Finch (Ingird), Lize Jooste (Natasha), Yaseen Abdullah (Lebanese Customer), Donald Sutherland (Voice of Colonel Oliver Southern), David Harman, Neil Tweddle (Col. Oliver Southern), Prosper Hakiziman (Somalian Freedom Fighter), Yi Chi Zhang (Borneo Officer), Sajad Khan (Mujahadeen Leader), John Sferopoulos (Freighter Captain), Gamiet Petersen ("Kono" Painter), Danie Struwig (Interpol Agent Ryan), Toni Caprari (Raoul), Jack Niccol (Young Nicolai), Annelene Terblanche (Angel), Stanislav Majer (Ukranian Guard), Eugene Lazarev (Uncle Dmitri),

Zdenek Pechacek (Ukraine Major), Weston Cage (Vladimir), Larissa Bond (Alena), Gugulethu "Gugu" Zulu (Andre's Driver), Debbie Jones (Cheerleader Mariama), Mirriam Ngomani (Cheerleader Asura), Tayo Oyekoya (Liberian Lieutenant), Dexter Nwanya, Jr. (Hotel Africa Porter), Yule Masiteng (Head Porter), Liya Kebede (Faith), Jasmine Burgess (Gloria), Siyamthanda Ndlangalavu (Boy Lieutenant), Tani Phoenix (Candy), Kutcha (Interpol Agent Maxwell), Konstantine Egorov (Aleksei), Vadim Dobrin (Leonid), Hlomla Dandala (Interpol Pilot), Tony Kgoroge (Mbizi), Young Bakubas (Hotel Africa Band), Jerry Mofokeng (Ernest), Mzwanele Jafta (General "No Living Thing"), Carlin April (Jewel), Masisi Ndlumbini (Sadio), Bupe Chanda (Saran), Sonni Genius Chidierbere, Sydney Hall (Monrovian Militamen), Nalu Tripician (Older Nicolai), Jonathan Ave (Interpol Agent James), Akin Omotoso (General Solomon), Steven Ruge (A.T.F. Agent Callahan), Alik Mk, Mohamed Omar (Sudan Border Guards)

Yuri Orlov looks back on how becoming involved in the international arms trade turned him into a very wealthy man who has turned a blind eye to repercussions of his business.

Ethan Hawke, Nicolas Cage PHOTOS COURTESY OF LIONS GATE

JUST LIKE HEAVEN

(DREAMWORKS) Producers, Laurie MacDonald, Walter F. Parkes; Executive Producer, David Householter; Director, Mark Waters; Screenplay, Peter Tolan, Leslie Dixon; Based on the novel *If Only It Were True* by Marc Levy; Photography, Daryn Okada; Designer, Cary White; Costumes, Sophie de Rakoff; Music, Rolfe Kent; Executive Music Producer, Ralph Sall; Editor, Bruce Green; Co-Producer, Marc Levy; Visual Effects Supervisor, John Sullivan; Casting, Marci Liroff; a Parkes/MacDonald production; Dolby; Technicolor; Rated PG-13; 95 minutes; Release date: September 16, 2005

Reese Witherspoon

Jon Heder, Reese Witherspoon, Mark Ruffalo

Cast

Elizabeth	**Reese Witherspoon**
David	**Mark Ruffalo**
Jack	**Donal Logue**
Abby	**Dina Waters**
Brett	**Ben Shenkman**
Darryl	**Jon Heder**
Katrina	**Ivana Milicevic**
Grace	**Caroline Aaron**
Fran	**Rosalind Chao**
Dr. Walsh	**Ron Canada**

and Willie Garson (Maitre D'), Gabrielle Madé (Nurse Maria), William Caploe (Nurse Bill), Shulie Cowen (Nurse Jenny), Billy Beck (Mr. Clarke), Diego Sebastian (Bandage Guy), Cristian Cruz (Orderly Luis), Benjamin Hughes (Peroxide Rocker), Cara Vivien Rosenberg (Balloon Girl), Catherine Taber (Intern Karen), Chris Pflueger (Abby's Husband), Kerris Dorsey (Zoe), Alyssa Shafer (Lily), Paul Cassell (Brett's Friend), Drew Letchworth (UFO Guy), Raymond O'Connor (Catholic Priest), Lucille Soong (Chinese Exorcist), Joel McKinnon Miller (Lead Ghostbuster), Victor Yerrid, Roebrt Benjamin (Ghostbusters), Ron Hacker (Blues Guy), Kara Hamilton (Valerie), Nicole Wilder (Kim), Lorna Scott (Hippie Neighbor), Jeffrey Marcus (Uptight Neighbor), Ken Takemoto (Chinese Neighbor), Chaim Jeraffi (Dry Cleaner), Doug Krizner (Donald), Zoe Waters (Park Girl), Jacob Chambers (Kenny), Karen Harrison (Kenny's Friend), Ingrid Coree (Waitress), Lee Burns (Ivan), Amita Balla (Receptionist), Tim Connolly, Tony Brubaker, Tim Sitarz, Jimmy Ortega, Ken Clark (Security Guards)

Donal Logue

Convinced that she is a ghost, Elizabeth returns to her San Francisco apartment which has already been taken over by a new resident, who vows to help her find out whether or not Elizabeth has indeed passed into the next world.

Dina Waters   PHOTOS COURTESY OF DREAMWORKS

PROOF

(MIRAMAX) Producers, Jeffrey Sharp, John N. Hart Jr., Robert Kessel, Alison Owen; Executive Producers, Bob Weinstein, Harvey Weinstein, Julie Goldstein, James D. Stern; Co-Producer, Mark Cooper; Co-Executive Producer, Michael Hogan; Director, John Madden; Screenplay, David Auburn, Rebecca Miller; Based on the play by David Auburn; Photography, Alwin Kuchler; Designer, Alice Normington; Costumes, Jill Taylor; Music, Stephen Warbeck; Editor, Mick Audsley; Casting, Billy Hopkins, Suzanne Smith, Kerry Barden, Michelle Guish; a Hart Sharp Entertainment production presented in association with Endgame Entertainment; Dolby; Widescreen; Color; Rated PG-13; 100 minutes; Release date: September 19, 2005

Gwyneth Paltrow, Anthony Hopkins

Hope Davis, Gwyneth Paltrow

and Anne Wittman, Leigh Zimmerna (Friends at Party), Colin Stinton (Theoretical Physicist), Leland Burnett (Band Vocalist), John Keefe, Chipo Chung, C. Gerod Harris (University Friend), Lolly Susi (Airport Check-In Lady)

Following the death of her father, a brilliant mathematician, Catherine is approached by one of his former students who wishes to look through his notebooks in hopes that they contain the proof of a breakthrough mathematical theorem.

Gwyneth Paltrow, Jake Gyllenhaal PHOTOS COURTESY OF FILMCOMPANY

Cast

Catherine **Gwyneth Paltrow**
Robert **Anthony Hopkins**
Hal **Jake Gyllenhaal**
Claire **Hope Davis**
Prof. Jay Barrow **Gary Houston**
Prof. Bhandari **Roshan Seth**
Cop **Danny McCarthy**
Limo Driver **Tobiasz Daszkiewicz**

Gwyneth Paltrow, Jake Gyllenhaal PHOTOS COURTESY OF MIRAMAX

THE THING ABOUT MY FOLKS

(PICTUREHOUSE) Producers, Paul Reiser, Bobby Newmyer, Jeffrey Silver; Co-Producer, Jamie Zelermyer; Director, Raymond De Felitta; Screenplay, Paul Reiser; Photography, Dan Gillham; Designer, Timothy Whidbee; Costumes, Kathryn Nixon; Music, Steven Argila; Editors, David Leonard, Sheila Amos; Casting, Sheila Jaffe, Georgianne Walken; a Nuance production in association with Outlaw Productions; Dolby; Color; Rated PG-13; 97 minutes; Release date: September 19, 2005

Paul Reiser, Peter Falk

Peter Falk, Paul Reiser

Cast

Sam Kleinman **Peter Falk**
Ben Kleinman **Paul Reiser**
Muriel Kleinman **Olympia Dukakis**
Rachel Kleinman **Elizabeth Perkins**
Lily Kleinman **Mackenzie Connolly**
Mia Kleinman **Lydia Jordan**
Linda **Ann Dowd**
Hillary **Claire Beckman**
Bonnie **Mimi Lieber**
Mr. Harrison **Bernie McInerney**
Young Muriel **Catherine Taormina**

and Rachel Robinson (Voice of Young Muriel), Rich Duva (Young Sam), Marshall Efron (Tow Truck Driver), Dennis Sheehan (Tackle Shop Owner), Timothy Hsu (Drugstore Cashier), Michael Duvert (Ramone Asquincella), Lauren Bittner (Baseball Cutie), Alison Fraser (Cutie's Mom), Adam Mucci (Pool Hall Bully), Craig Pattison (Bully's Friend), Tonye Patano (Nurse), Kevin Cahoon (Perky Waiter)

Paul Reiser, Peter Falk

Disturbed that his mother has walked out on his dad, Ben Kleinman takes his devastated father on a road trip in hopes of taking his mind off the event.

Peter Falk, Paul Reiser PHOTOS COURTESY OF PICTUREHOUSE

EVERYTHING IS ILLUMINATED

(WARNER INDEPENDENT PICTURES) Producers, Marc Turtletaub, Peter Saraf; Executive Producer, Matthew Stillman; Director/Screenplay, Liev Schreiber; Based on the novel by Jonathan Safran Foer; Photography, Matthew Libatique; Designer, Mark Geraghty; Costumes, Michael Claney; Music, Paul Canteloni; Editors, Craig McKay, Andrew Marcus; a Big Beach production; Dolby; Technicolor; Rated R; 106 minutes; Release date: September 16, 2005

Cast

Jonathan Safran Foer **Elijah Wood**
Alex **Eugene Hutz**
Grandfather **Boris Leskin**
Lista **Laryssa Lauret**
Jonathan's Grandmother **Jana Hrabetová**
Jonathan's Grandfather Safran **Stepán Samudovsky**
Young Jonathan **Ljubomir Dezera**
Alexander Perchov (Father) **Oleksandr Choroshko**
Igor **Gil Kazimirov**
Alex's Mother **Zuzana Hodková**
Leaf Blower **Jonathan Safran Foer**
Breakdancer **Robert Chytil**
Woman on Train **Jarovslava Sochová**
Sammy Davis Jr. Jr. **Mikki & Mouse**

Eugene Hutz, Elijah Wood, Boris Leskin

Elijah Wood, Eugene Hutz

New York writer Jonathan Safran Foer treks to former Soviet territory in an effort to find the woman who may have saved his grandfather from the Nazis.

Laryssa Lauret, Elijah Wood

and Sergej Rjabcev, Jurij Lemeshev, Pamela Racine, Oleksandr Houtz (Ukranian Band), Ludmila Kartouská (Hotel Waitress), Igor Latta (Old Man at Fair), Eugenin Marandic, Orest Tkachyk (Fairgoers), Eliás Bauer (Goatherder Boy), Jurij Kokyrc, Sergej Kapitan, Jaroslav Jurichkanc, Igor Savivskij, Jan Filipensky (Well Diggers), Bert Schneider (Nazi Officer), Terez Veselková (Augustine), Lukás Král (Young Grandfather, Baruch), Vera Sindelárova (Young Lista)

Eugene Hutz (left) PHOTOS COURTESY OF WARNER INDEPENDENT

Heidi Hayes, Maria Bello, Viggo Mortensen, Ashton Holmes

A HISTORY OF VIOLENCE

(NEW LINE CINEMA) Producers, Chris Bender, JC Spink; Executive Producers, Roger E. Kass, Josh Braun, Justis Greene; Co-Producer, Jake Weiner; Director, David Cronenberg; Screenplay, Josh Olson; Based on the graphic novel by John Wagner, Vince Locke; Photography, Peter Suschitzky; Designer, Carol Spier; Costumes, Denise Cronenberg; Music, Howard Shore; Editor, Ronald Sanders; Casting, Deirdre Bowen; a Benderspink production; U.S.-Canadian; Dolby; Deluxe color; Rated R; 96 minutes; Release date: September 23, 2005

Cast

Tom Stall **Viggo Mortensen**
Edie Stall **Maria Bello**
Carl Fogarty **Ed Harris**
Richie Cusack **William Hurt**
Jack Stall **Ashton Holmes**
Leland Jones **Stephen McHattie**
Sheriff Sam Carney **Peter MacNeill**
Sarah Stall **Heidi Hayes**
William "Billy" Orser **Greg Bryk**
Judy Danvers **Sumela Kay**
Bobby Jordan **Kyle Schmid**
Charlotte **Deborah Drakeford**
Mick **Gerry Quigley**
Charlie Roarke **Aidan Devine**
Frank Mulligan **Bill MacDonald**
Jenny Wyeth **Michelle McCreee**
Ruben **Ian Matthews**
Pat **R. D. Reid**

and Morgan Kelly (Bobby's Buddy), Martha Reilly (Shoe Saleswoman), Jason Barbeck, Bruce Beaton, Neven Pajkic (Richie's Thugs), Brendan Connor, Nick Antonacci (Local TV Reporters), John Watson (Baseball Coach), Don Allison (TV Broadcaster), Brittany Payer (Motel Girl), Mitch Boughs, April Mullen (Kids in Diner), George King (Hospital Well-Wisher), Shawn Campbell (Orderly), Steve Arbuckle (Jared), Connor Price (Kid), Evan Rose ("Hulk" Boy), Michael Stevens (Guy on the Street)

William Hurt

Viggo Mortensen, Maria Bello

After he shows unexpected skill in shooting dead some thugs terrorizing his diner, Tom Stall is declared a small town hero, the attention bringing forth a mysterious visitor who claims to know all about Tom's shady past.

This film received an Oscar nomination for supporting actor (William Hurt).

Ed Harris PHOTOS COURTESY OF NEW LINE CINEMA

Tina Au, Wesley Jonathan, Tammy Fey, Tai'isha Davis

ROLL BOUNCE

(FOX SEARCHLIGHT) Producers, Robert Teitel, George Tillman Jr.; Executive Producers, Adam Robinson, Dana J. Reid, Jeremiah Samuels; Director, Malcolm D. Lee; Screenplay, Norman Vance Jr.; Photography, J. Michael Muro; Designer, William Elliott; Costumes, Danielle Hollowell; Music, Stanley Clarke; Editors, George Bowers, Paul Millspaugh; Choreographer, Kishaya Dudley; Casting, Monica Swann; a Fox 2000 Pictures presentation of a State Street Pictures production; Dolby; Panavision; Deluxe color; Rated PG-13; 107 minutes; Release date: September 23, 2005

Cast

Xavier "X" Smith	**Bow Wow**
Junior	**Brandon T. Jackson**
Boo	**Marcus T. Paulk**
Naps	**Rick Gonzalez**
Mixed Mike	**Khleo Thomas**
Curtis Smith	**Chi McBride**
Sonya	**Busisiwe Irvin**
Tori	**Jurnee Smollett**
Vivian	**Kellita Smith**
Byron	**Mike Epps**
Victor	**Charlie Murphy**
Naomi Phillips	**Meagan Good**
Bernard	**Nick Cannon**
Sweetness	**Wesley Jonathan**
Troy	**Paul Wesley**
Roy	**Daniel Yabut**
D. J. Johnny Feelgood	**Wayne Brady**
Garden D. J. Smooth Dee	**Darryl "DMC" McDaniels**
Meryvn Rosenfeld	**Joseph Hansa**
Donna	**Kat Tuohy**
Rhonda King	**Marcia Wright**

and Cassandra Lewis, Deanna K. Reed (Party Women), Mark Simmons (Guest #1), Ernest Perry, Jr. (Donald Robinson), Tim Kazurinsky (Car Salesman), Heather O'Brien (Receptionist #1), Kelly Jenkins (Cute Girl), Samirah Garnett (Girl Skater), Damon Williams, Norman Vance III (Ambush Kids), Tammy Fey, Tai'isha Davis, Tina Au (Candy Girls), Todd Donoho (Voice of Baseball Announcer), Booker T. Mattison (DJ Background Voice, Sweetwater)

Busisiwe Irvin, Chi McBride, Kellita Smith, Jurnee Smollett

In 1978 Chicago, young Xavier and his friends, all of whom excel at the art of jam skating, decide to enter the Sweetwater rink's skate-off in order to beat an arrogant dancer named Sweetness.

Meagan Good, Bow Wow PHOTOS COURTESY OF FOX SEARCHLIGHT

Bow Wow, Marcus T. Paulk, Brandon T. Jackson, Rick Gonzalez, Khelo Thomas

FLIGHTPLAN

(TOUCHSTONE) Producer, Brian Grazer; Executive Producers, James Whitaker, Charles J. D. Schlissel, Robert Dinozzi, Erica Huggins; Director, Robert Schwentke; Screenplay, Peter A. Dowling, Billy Ray; Photography, Florian Ballhaus; Designer, Alexander Hammon; Costumes, Susan Lyall; Music, James Horner; Editor, Thom Noble; Casting, Deborah Aquila, Tricia Wood, Jennifer Smith; Visual Effects Supervisor, Rob Hodgson; an Imagine Entertainment presentation; Dolby; Technicolor; Rated PG-13; 93 minutes; Release date: September 23, 2005

Erika Christensen, Judith Scott, Kate Beahan, Jodie Foster

Sean Bean, Peter Sarsgaard

Cast

Kyle Pratt **Jodie Foster**
Gene Carson **Peter Sarsgaard**
Captain Rich **Sean Bean**
Stephanie **Kate Beahan**
Obaid **Michael Irby**
Ahmed **Assaf Cohen**
Fiona **Erika Christensen**
Mr. Loud **Shane Edelman**
Mrs. Loud **Mary Gallagher**
Brittany Loud **Haley Ramm**
Rhett Loud **Forrest Landis**
Claudia **Jana Kolesarova**
Elias **Brent Sexton**
Julia Pratt **Marlene Lawston**
Estella **Judith Scott**
David Pratt **John Benjamin Hickey**
Eric **Matthew Bomer**
FBI Agent **Gavin Grazer**
Mike **Christopher Gartin**
Katerina **Bess Wohl**
Grunick **Kirk B. R. Woller**
Anna **Stephanie Faracy**
Mortuary Director **Christian Berkel**
West **Cooper Thornton**
Metal Detector Guard #1 **Klaus Schindler**
Iron Tracker Guard #1 **Eva Plackner**
Irene **Amanda Brooks**
Row 19 Male Passenger **Jesse Burch**
Therapist **Greta Scacchi**
Main Deck Kid **Drake Johnston**
Main Deck Grandma **Lois Hall**

On a flight from Berlin to New York to bring her husband's body home, Kyle Pratt becomes frantic when her daughter disappears and nobody on board will believe that the child ever existed.

Marlene Lawston, Jodie Foster PHOTOS COURTESY OF TOUCHSTONE

INTO THE BLUE

(MGM/COLUMBIA) Producer, David A. Zelon; Executive Producers, Peter Guber, Louis G. Friedman, Ori Marmur, Matt Luber; Director, John Stockwell; Screenplay, Matt Johnson; Photography, Shane Hurlbut; Designer, Maia Javan; Costumes, Leesa Evans; Music, Paul Haslinger; Music Supervisor, Dana Sano; Co-Producers, Rick Dallago, Brandon Birtell; Editors, Nicolas De Toth, Dennis Virkler; Casting, Randi Hiller, Sarah Halley Finn; a Mandalay Pictures production; Dolby; Color; Rated PG-13; 110 minutes; Release date: September 30, 2005

Tyson Beckford, Paul Walker

Jessica Alba, Paul Walker PHOTOS COURTESY OF MGM

Jessica Alba, Josh Brolin

Scott Caan, Ashley Scott, Paul Walker, Jessica Alba

Cast
Jared Cole **Paul Walker**
Samantha "Sam" Nicholson **Jessica Alba**
Bryce Dunn **Scott Caan**
Amanda Collins **Ashley Scott**
Derek Bates **Josh Brolin**
Reyes **James Frain**
Primo **Tyson Beckford**
Roy **Dwayne Adway**
Danny **Javon Frazer**
Quinn **Chris Taloa**

and Peter R. V. Bowleg, Jr. (Jake), Clifford McIntosh (Kash), Adam Collins (Raolo), Gill Montie (Big Dave), Dan Ballard (Scuba Bob), Samantha Lamb (Brazilian Bikini Girl), Arthur Thompson, Jr. (Jo-Jo), Ramon Saunders (Tec-9), Stephen Bellot (Pilot), Leo Quant (Co-Pilot), John Willinger (Pasty Diver), Mike Steven Powell (Large Diver), Vonetta Nicola Darling Flowers, Sean Owen Gordon (Immigration Officers), Lesli Barlett-Roker (Teacher), Donna Mackey (Officer), Jay Lance Gottlieb (Benoit), Billy Johnson (Rapper), Mike Roberts (Grungy Worker), Gina-Marie Knowles (Woman in Car Crash)

Part-time treasure hunter Jared Cole finds himself and his friends in danger after they stumble upon an ancient shipwreck and hope to claim it for themselves.

Philip Seymour Hoffman

Clifton Collins, Jr., Mark Pellegrino

Philip Seymour Hoffman, Catherine Keener

Chris Cooper, Clifton Collins, Jr.

CAPOTE

(SONY CLASSICS/UNITED ARTISTS) Producers, Caroline Baron, William Vince, Michael Ohoven; Executive Producers, Dan Futterman, Philip Seymour Hoffman, Kerry Rock, Danny Rosett; Director, Bennett Miller; Screenplay, Dan Futterman; Based on the book *Capote* by Gerald Clarke; Photography, Adam Kimmel; Designer, Jess Gonchor; Costumes, Kasia Walicka-Maimone; Music, Mychael Danna; Editor, Christopher Tellefsen; Associate Producers, Kyle Mann, Dave Valleau, Emily Ziff, Kyle Irving; Casting, Avy Kaufman; an A-Line Pictures, Cooper's Town Productions, Infinity Media production; Dolby; Panavision; Color; Rated R; 115 minutes; Release date: September 30, 2005

Cast
Truman Capote **Philip Seymour Hoffman**
Nelle Harper Lee **Catherine Keener**
Perry Smith **Clifton Collins, Jr.**
Alvin Dewey **Chris Cooper**
Jack Dunphy **Bruce Greenwood**
William Shawn **Bob Balaban**
Marie Dewey **Amy Ryan**
Richard Hickock **Mark Pellegrino**
Laura Kinney **Allie Mickelson**
Warden Marshall Krutch **Marshall Bell**
Dorothy Sanderson **Araby Lockhart**
New York Reporter **Rober Hoculak**
Roy Church **R. D. Reid**
Harold Nye **Rob McLaughlin**
Sheriff Walter Sanderson **Harry Nelken**
Danny Burke **Kerr Hewitt**
Judge Roland Tate **John Maclaren**
Jury Foreman **Jeremy Dangerfield**
Porters **Kwesi Ameyaw, Ernesto Griffith**
Chaplain **Jim Shepard**
Pete Holt **John B. Destry**
Lewel Lee Andrews **C. Ernst Harth**
Richard Avedon **Adam Kimmel**

and Olie Alto (Franklin Weeks), Craig Archibald (Christopher Isherwood), Norman Armour (Literary Enthusiast), Mia Faircloth, Ainsley Balcewich (Girls), Anne Baragar (Laura Kinney's Mother), Jon Ted Wynne, Jonathan Barrett, Christopher Read, Jerome Greencorn (Journalists), Michael J. Burg (Williams), Bronwen Coleman (Barbara), Nazariy Demkowicz (Paul Dewey), James Durham (Young Prison Guard), Frank Filbert, Boyd Johnson (ND Prison Guards), Michal Grajewski (Young Assistant), Michelle Harrison (Babe Paley), James Hanssens (Man in Courtroom), Tiffany Lyndall-Knight (Gloria Guiness), Ken Krotowich (Courthouse Guard), Wayne Niklas, Jason Love, Don Malboeuf (Row Guards), Manfred Maretzki (Herbert Clutter), Bess Meyer (Linda Murchak), Jason Mitchell (Kenyon Clutter), David Rakoff (Ben Baron), Kate Shindle (Rose), Miriam Smith (Bonnie Clutter), Kelci Stephenson (Nancy Clutter), Marina Stephenson (Operator), Edward Sutton (Old Man), Avery Tiplady (Alvin Dewey, Jr.), John Warkentin (Warren Hotel Desk Clerk), Will Woytowich (Cruiser)

Catherine Keener, Philip Seymour Hoffman

Author Truman Capote arrives in western Kansas to write about the brutal murders of a farming family and finds himself more emotionally involved with the crime and one of the killers responsible than he had anticipated.

Catherine Keener

Mark Pellegrino, Clifton Collins, Jr.

Bob Balaban

2005 Academy Award winner for Best Actor (Philip Seymour Hoffman).

This film received Oscar nominations for picture, director, actor, adapted screenplay, and supporting actress (Catherine Keener).

Philip Seymour Hoffman, Bruce Greenwood

Philip Seymour Hoffman PHOTOS COURTESY OF SONY CLASSICS

THE PRIZE WINNER OF DEFIANCE, OHIO

(DREAMWORKS) Producers, Jack Rapke, Steve Starkey, Robert Zemeckis; Executive Producer, Marty Ewing; Director/Screenplay, Jane Anderson; Based upon the memoir *The Prize Winner of Defiance, Ohio: How My Mother Raised 10 Kids on 25 Words or Less* by Terry Ryan; Photography, Jonathan Freeman; Designer, Edward T. McAvoy; Costumes, Hala Bahmet; Music, John Frizzell; Editor, Robert Dalva; Casting, Linda Lowy, John Brace; a Revolution Studios presentation of an ImageMovers production; Dolby; Technicolor; Rated PG-13; 99 minutes; Release date: September 30, 2005

Woody Harrelson   PHOTOS COURTESY OF DREAMWORKS

Cast

Evelyn Ryan **Julianne Moore**
Kelly Ryan **Woody Harrelson**
Dortha Schaefer **Laura Dern**
Bruce Ryan at 16 yrs. **Trevor Morgan**
Tuff Ryan at 13, 16 & 18 yrs. **Ellary Porterfield**
Ray the Milkman **Simon Reynolds**
Lea Anne Ryan at 17 yrs. **Monté Gagné**
Dick Ryan at 16 yrs. **Robert Clark**
Bub Ryan at 15 yrs. **Michael Seater**
Rog Ryan at 13 yrs. **Erik Knudsen**
Bruce Ryan at 11 yrs. **Jake Scott**
Tuff Ryan at 9 yrs. **Jordan Todosey**
Mike Ryan at 6 yrs. **Ryan Price**
Barb Ryan at 4 yrs. **Shae Norris**
Betsy Ryan at 2 yrs. **Abigail Falle**
Baby Dave **Luca Barbaro, Brando Barbaro**
Rog Ryan at 17 yrs. **Jack Murray**
Mike Ryan at 10 yrs. **Evan Rose**
Barb Ryan at 8 yrs. **Jessica Pollock**
Betsy Ryan at 6 yrs. **Emily Perisch**
Dave Ryan at 4 yrs. **Maxwell Uretsky**
Mike Ryan at 13 yrs. **Brendan Price**
Barb Ryan at 11 yrs. **Melanie Tonello**
Betsy Ryan at 9 yrs. **Julia Megan Thompson**
Dave Ryan at 7 yrs. **Connor Sharp**

Julianne Moore, Laura Dern

and Tuff Ryan, Betsy Ryan (Themselves as Adults), David Gardner (Father McCague), Martin Doyle (Cutter Murphy), Susan Merson (Mrs. Bidlack), Catherine Fitch (Emma Hartzler), Carolyn Scott (Gladys Tierney), Lindsay Leese (Betty Yearling), Tracey Hoyt (Betty White), Kathryn Haggis (Checkout Lady Marge), Noni White (Checkout Lady Pauline), Gerry Quigley (Vernon the Mailman), Brad Borbridge, Dan Willmott, Tim Dorsch (Detective Feeney), Lee Smart (Band Show Host), Frank Chiesurin (Rock 'n' Roll Singer), Nora Dunn, Erin Gooderman, Juliann Kuchocki (Girl Group Members), Jim York (Seabrook Executive), Timm Zemanek (Harvey the Manager), Paul Brogren (Joe the Mechanic), Eric Fink, Derek Keurvorst (Bike Contest Men), Scott Wickware (Neighbor Man), Conrad Bergschneider (Officer Dobbs), Bruce McFee (Officer Finney)

Kathryn Haggis, Noni White, Julianne Moore (center), Jim York, Timm Zemanek

The true story of how '50s housewife Evelyn Ryan used her knack for writing catchy jingles to enter various contests in order to help her struggling family.

SERENITY

(UNIVERSAL) Producer, Barry Mendel; Executive Producers, Christopher Buchanan, David Lester, Alisa Tager; Director/Screenplay, Joss Whedon; Photography, Jack Green; Designer, Barry Chusid; Costumes, Ruth Carter; Music, David Newman; Editor, Lisa Lassek; Visual Effects Producer, Juliette Yager; Special Effects Coordinator, Dan Sudick; Casting, Amy McIntyre Britt, Anya Colloff; a Barry Mendel production; Dolby; Panavision; Fotokem color; Rated PG-13; 119 minutes; Release date: September 30, 2005

Chiwetel Ejiofor

Adam Baldwin, Nathan Fillion

Cast

Mal **Nathan Fillion**
Zoe **Gina Torres**
Wash **Alan Tudyk**
Inara **Morena Bacarin**
Jayne **Adam Baldwin**
Kaylee **Jewel Staite**
Simon **Sean Maher**
River **Summer Glau**
Shepard Book **Ron Glass**
The Operative **Chiwetel Ejiofor**
Mr. Universe **David Krumholtz**
Dr. Mathias **Michael Hitchcock**
Dr. Caron **Sarah Paulson**
Mingo **Yan Feldman**
Fanty **Rafael Feldman**
Lenore **Nectar Rose**

and Tamara Taylor (Teacher), Glenn Howerton (Lilac Young Tough), Hunter Ansley Wryn (Young River), Logan Craig O'Brien, Erik Erotas (Boy Students), Demetra Raven, Jessica Huang, Marley McClean (Girl Students), Scott Kinworthy (Ensign), Erik Weiner (Helmsman), Conor O'Brien, Peter James Smith (Lab Technicians), Weston I. Nathanson (Trade Agent), CeCe Cline (Young Intern), Chuck O'Neil (Vault Guard), Amy Wieczorek (Lilac Mom), Tristan Jarred (Lilac Son), Elaine Lee (Fan Dancer), Terrence Hardy (Mining Camp Boy), Brian O'Hare (Alliance Pilot), Ryan Tasz, Colin Patrick Lynch (Black Room Soldiers), Terrell Tilford (News Anchor), Joshua Kwiat (Slovenly Beaumonde Man)

Sean Maher, Summer Glau PHOTOS COURTESY OF UNIVERSAL

Nathan Fillion, Alan Tudyk, Gina Torres, Adam Baldwin, Morena Bacarin, Sean Maher

The rebel crew of the spaceship *Serenity* hides a telepathic girl from the totalitarian alliance that will stop at nothing to find her. Based on the 2002–04 Fox series with all of the cast regulars repeating their roles.

THE GREATEST GAME EVER PLAYED

(WALT DISNEY PICTURES) Producers, Larry Brezner, Mark Frost, David Blocker; Executive Producer, David Steinberg; Director, Bill Paxton; Screenplay, Mark Frost, based on his book; Photography, Shane Hurlbut; Designer, François Ségun; Costumes, Renée April; Music, Brian Tyler; Editor, Elliot Graham; Casting, Mary Gail Artz, Barbara Cohen; a Morra Brezner Steinberg Tenenbaum production; Dolby; Technicolor; Rated PG; 115 minutes; Release date: September 30, 2005

Shia LaBeouf, Josh Flitter

Cast

Francis Ouimet **Shia LaBeouf**
Harry Vardon **Stephen Dillane**
Arthur Ouimet **Elias Koteas**
Eddie Lowery **Josh Flitter**
Sarah Wallis **Peyton List**
Mary Ouimet **Marnie McPhail**
Ted Ray **Stephen Marcus**
Lord Northcliffe **Peter Firth**
Wilfred Reid **George Asprey**
Freddie Wallis **Max Kasch**
John McDermott **Michael Weaver**
Alec Campbell **Luke Askew**
Young Francis **Matthew Knight**

and Luke Kirby (Frank Hoyt), James Paxton (Young Harry Vardon), Tom Rack, Armand LaRoche, Peter Hurley, Gregory Terlecki (Black Top-Hatted Men), Jonathan Higgins (Embry Wallis), Amanda Tilson (Young Sarah Wallis), Jamie Merling (Young Louise Ouimet), Eugenio Esposito (Young Raymond Ouimet), Robin Wilcock (Bernard Darwin), Michael Sinelnikoff (Lord Bullock), Justin Ashforth (Ted Hastings), Arthur Holden (Club Secretary), Len Cariou (Stedman Comstock), Nicolas Wright (Phillip Wainwright), Danette MacKay (Mrs. Wallis), Scott Faulconbridge (Billy), Joe Jackson (Club Pianist), Timothy W. Peper (Walter Gibbs), Mike "Nug" Nahrgang (Baritone), Dawn Upshaw (Soprano), James Bradford (Robert Watson), Marc James Beauchamp (Assistant Pro), Pierre Boudreau (Northcliffe's Valet), Johnny Griffin (Jack Lowery), Dennis St-John (Wallis' Butler), Terry Reid (Vernon's Caddy), Stephen Spreekmeester (Ted's Caddy), Philip Pretten (Comstock's Assistant), Patrick Whitebean

Peter Firth, Stephen Dillane, Stephen Marcus

(McDermott's Caddy), Walter Massey (President Taft), Melissa Carter, Melanie Beauline (Reid's Escorts), Jeremy Thibodeau (Raymond Ouimet), Alexina Ouimet (Louise Ouimet), Frank Fontaine (Wallis' Chauffeur), Marcel Jeannin (Irish Crew Boss), Brian Wrench (Know-It-All Gallery Member), Nicole Braber (Know-It-All Girlfriend), Kyle MacDougall (Vardon's Assistant), Jesse Rath (Runner), Domenico Salvaggio (Bartender), Howard Ryshpan (Gallery Member), James Scavone (Copy Boy), Pual Cagelet (Man Passing By), Stephen Wallace Lowe (Reporter)

The true story of how caddy Francis Ouimet ended up participating in the 1913 U.S. Open.

Shia LaBeouf, Elias Koteas

Max Kasch, Peyton List, Shia LaBeouf

LITTLE MANHATTAN

(20TH CENTURY FOX) Producer, Gavin Polone; Executive Producers, Ezra Swerdlow, Kara Francis, Vivian Cannon; Director, Mark Levin; Screenplay, Jennifer Flackett; Photography, Tim Orr; Designer, Stuart Wurtzel; Costumes, Kasia Walicka-Maimone; Music, Chad Fisher; Editor, Alan Edward Bell; Casting, Douglas Aibel; a Regency Enterprises presentation of a Pariah, New Regency Pictures production; Dolby; Color; Rated PG; 84 minutes; Release date: September 30, 2005

Josh Pais, Cynthia Nixon, Charlie Ray, Josh Hutcherson

Jacob **Brian W. Aguiar**
Daryl Kitzens **Nick Cubbler**
Tim Staples **Anthony Laflamme**
David Betanahu **Neil Jay Shastri**

and Leigha Nicoloro, Juliette Nicoloro (Mae-Li), Mike Chat, Loston Harris, Alex Trebek (Themselves), Doug Wright (Isaac), Olga Pavlova (Lina), Shane Rhoades (Young Adam), Caitlin McColl (Young Leslie), Robert Belk (Young Gabe), Franny Flackett-Levin (Young Rosemary), Aaron Grady Shaw (Second Grade Boy), Jacob Levine (Another Boy), Ray Robertson (Street Vendor), Christopher Wynkoop (Minister), Marsha Dietlein Bennett (Mother at Party), Timothy Adams (TV Cowboy), Jess Weixler (TV Cowgirl), Paul Borghese (Butcher), Sal Darigo (Barber), George Riddle (Frank), Calvin Brown (Old Man on the Street), Lynn Chen (Girl on the Street), Hasani Houston, Connor Hutcherson (Boys Who Throw Up), The Smokin' Section (Wedding Band), Chris Berger, Quincy Davis, Marcus Parsley (Loston Harris Band), Linda Thompson Williams (Wedding Singer)

Charlie Ray, Josh Hutcherson

Cast
Gabe **Josh Hutcherson**
Rosemary **Charlie Ray**
Adam **Bradley Whitford**
Leslie **Cynthia Nixon**
Ralph **Willie Garson**
Birdie **Tonye Patano**
Master Coles **J. Kyle Manzay**
Ronny **Josh Pais**
Mickey Telesco **Josh Dossett**
Jackie Telesco **Talia Balsam**
Sam **Jonah Meyerson**
Max **Michael Anthony Bush**

Willie Garson, Charlie Ray, Josh Hutcherson PHOTOS COURTESY OF 20TH CENTURY FOX

10-year-old Gabe, living on Manhattan's Upper West Side with his estranged parents, experiences his first feelings of true love when he falls for fellow karate student Rosemary.

Jeff Daniels, Laura Linney

Anna Paquin, Jeff Daniels

THE SQUID AND THE WHALE

(SAMUEL GOLDWYN) Producers, Wes Anderson, Peter Newman, Charlie Corwin, Clara Markowitz; Executive Producers, Reverge Anselmo, Miranda Bailey, Greg Johnson, Andew Lauren; Co-Executive Producer, Jennifer M. Roth; Director/Screenplay, Noah Baumbach; Photography, Robert D. Yeoman; Designer, Anne Ross; Costumes, Amy Westcott; Music, Dean Wareham, Britta Phillips; Editor, Tim Streeto; an Original Media, Ambush Entertainment presentation in association with Andrew Lauren Productions of an American Empirical Pictures, Peter Newman-Interal production; Dolby; DuArt color; Rated R; 80 minutes; Release date: October 5, 2005

Jesse Eisenberg, Owen Kline

Cast

Bernard Berkman **Jeff Daniels**
Joan Berkman **Laura Linney**
Walt Berkman **Jesse Eisenberg**
Frank Berkman **Owen Kline**
Sophie **Halley Feiffer**
Lili **Anna Paquin**
Ivan **William Baldwin**
Carl **David Benger**
Man with Joan **James Hamilton**
Otto **Adam Rose**
Lance **Henry Glovinsky**
Jeffrey **Eli Gelb**
Mrs. Greenberg **Peggy Gormley**
Mr. Greenberg **Peter Newman**
Greta Greenberg **Greta Kline**
Professor **Melissa Meyer**
Graduate Students **Molly Barton, Bo Berkman, Matthew Kaplan, Simon Kaplan, Matthew Kirsch, Daniella Markowicz, Elizabeth Meriwether, Ben Schrank, Amy Srebnick, Emma Straub, Alan Wilks**
Student with Puppets **Benjamin Smolen**

Owen Kline, William Baldwin

Laura Linney, Owen Kline, Jeff Daniels, William Baldwin

Laura Linney, Jeff Daniels

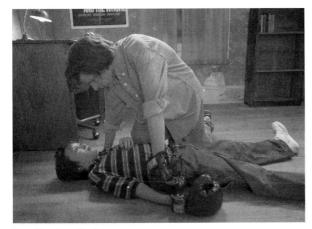

Owen Kline, Jesse Eisenberg

and Benjamin Smolen (Student with Puppets), Michael Countryman (Mr. Simic), Alexandra Daddario (Pretty Girl), Nico Baumbach (Jeb Gelber), Maryann Plunkett (Ms. Lemon), Hector Otero (Hector), Ken Leung (School Counselor), Jo Yang (Nurse)

Jeff Daniels

16-year-old Walt and 12-year-old Frank find themselves taking sides when their parents, he a once-successful author and she an up-and-coming novelist, decide to split up.

This film received an Oscar nomination for original screenplay.

Jesse Eisenberg PHOTOS COURTESY OF SAMUEL GOLDWYN

THE GOSPEL

(SCREEN GEMS) Producer, Will Packer; Executive Producers, Holly Davis-Carter, Fred Hammond; Director/Screenplay, Rob Hardy; Photography, Matthew MacCarthy; Designer, Frank Galline; Costumes, Paul Simmons; Music, Stanley A. Smith; Editor, Fernando Villena; Choreographer, Shayla "Shay Latte" Stevens; Casting, Robi Reed; a Rainforest Films production; Dolby; Deluxe color; Rated PG; 103 minutes; Release date: October 7, 2005

Cast
David Taylor **Boris Kodjoe**
Rev. Charles Frank **Idris Elba**
Charlene Taylor Frank **Nona Gaye**
Bishop Fred Taylor **Clifton Powell**
Ernestine **Aloma Wright**
Minister Hunter **Donnie McClurkin**
Wesley **Omar Gooding**
Rain Walker **Tamyra Gray**

Tamyra Gray, Omar Gooding, Boris Kodjoe

Idris Elba

Clifton Powell, Aloma Wright PHOTOS COURTESY OF SCREEN GEMS

Maya Walker **Keshia Knight Pulliam**
Young David **Michael J. Pagan**
Young Frank **Sean Nelson**
Brother Gordon **Hezekiah Walker**
Oscar **Dwayne Boyd**
Bishop Stackhouse **Tony Vaughn**

and Justin Hires (Youngster), China Anne McClain (Alexis), Leland L. Jones (Rev. Isaac Winston), Felicia Jeter (First Lady Winston), Delores Winans (Janet Perkins), Nard Holston (Sandstone), Donna Biscoe (Rev. Jones), Terrence Gibney (Physician), Aaliyah Franks (Lady), Will Packer (Attendant), Frank Ski (Marcus), John Nicholson (Bouncer), Rashan Ali (Reporter), Sasha the Diva (TV Reporter), Geoff McKnight (James Pelzer, Esq.), Rhoda Griffis (Lawyer #1), Rob Hardy (Church Announcer), Vince Canlas (Clark), Vickie Eng (Doctor), Birice Packer (Lady on Stairs), Tom Joyner, Myra J., Miss Dupree, Martha Munizzi, Yolanda Adams, Fred Hammond (Themselves)

Summoned back to Atlanta to see his ailing father, R&B star David Taylor seizes the chance to help a financially troubled church with a talented gospel choir.

Al Pacino, Matthew McConaughey

TWO FOR THE MONEY

(UNIVERSAL) Producers, James G. Robinson, Jay Cohen; Executive Producers, Dan Gilroy, Rene Russo, Guy McElwaine, David C. Robinson; Director, D. J. Caruso; Screenplay, Dan Gilroy; Co-Producer, Wayne Morris; Photography, Conrad W. Hall; Designer, Tom Southwell; Costumes, Marie-Sylvie Deveau; Music, Christophe Beck; Editor, Glen Scantlebury; Casting, Pam Dixon Mickelson, Amanda Mackey Johnson, Cathy Sandrich Gelfond; a James G. Robinson presentation of a Morgan Creek production; Dolby; Technicolor; Rated R; 122 minutes; Release date: October 7, 2005

Rene Russo, Al Pacino

Cast
Walter Abrams **Al Pacino**
Brandon Lang **Matthew McConaughey**
Toni **Rene Russo**
Novian **Armand Assante**
Jerry **Jeremy Piven**
Alexandria **Jaime King**
Southie **Kevin Chapman**
Reggie **Ralph Garman**
Milton **Gedde Watanabe**

Tammy **Carly Pope**
Chuck **Charles Carroll**
Herbie **Gerard Plunkett**
Amir **Craig Veroni**
Denny **James Kirk**
Julia **Chrislyn Austin**
Brandon's Mom **Denise Galik**
Brandon's Dad **Gary Hudson**
Mitch **Jeremy Guilbaut**

and Steve Makaj (Coach), Stephen Dimopoulos (Steve), Michael Rogers (Stu), William S. Taylor (Leon), Veena Sood (G.A. Hostess), Adrian Holmes, Trevor Roberts, Michael P. Northey (G.A. Members), Brad Kelly (Novian's Bodyguard), Jason Schombing (Mercedes Dealer), Louis Mustillo (Doorman), Luciana Carro (Gail), Kendall Cross (Makeup Artist), David Lovgren (TV Technician), Malcolm Scott (Man in Window), J. B. McEown (Teammate), Robin Mossley (Waiter at Restaurant), Raimund Stamm, Jonathan Bruce (Men at Restaurant), Barry LeBrock, Joel Myers, Ron Pitts (TV Announcers), Jim Rome (Himself)

Jeremy Piven

Matthew McConaughey, Al Pacino PHOTOS COURTESY OF UNIVERSAL

Former football player Brandon Lang, who has a knack for picking winners for the weekend's football matchup, is wooed by Walter Abrams into working for him in the sports gambling field.

David Strathairn

GOOD NIGHT, AND GOOD LUCK.

(WARNER INDEPENDENT PICTURES) Producer, Grant Heslov; Executive Producers, Todd Wagner, Mark Cuban, Marc Butan, Steven Soderbergh, Jennifer Fox, Ben Cosgrove, Jeff Skoll, Chris Salvaterra; Co-Producer, Barbara A. Hall; Director, George Clooney; Screenplay, George Clooney, Grant Heslov; Photography, Robert Elswit; Designer, Jim Bissell; Costumes, Louise Frogley; Music Supervisor, Allen Sviridoff; Editor, Stephen Mirrione; Casting, Ellen Chenoweth; a 2929 Entertainment, Participant Prods. presentation in association with Davis Films, Redbus Pictures, Tohokushinsha of a Section Eight production; Dolby; Black and white; Rated PG; 93 minutes; Release date: October 7, 2005

Cast

Edward R. Murrow **David Strathairn**
Joe Wershba **Robert Downey, Jr.**
Shirley Wershba **Patricia Clarkson**
Don Hollenbeck **Ray Wise**
William Paley **Frank Langella**
Sig Mickelson **Jeff Daniels**
Fred Friendly **George Clooney**
Jesse Zousmer **Tate Donovan**
Palmer Williams **Tom McCarthy**
Eddie Scott **Matt Ross**
John Aaron **Reed Diamond**
Charlie Mack **Robert John Burke**
Don Hewitt **Grant Heslov**
Natalie **Alex Borstein**
Millie Lerner **Rose Abdoo**
Colonel Anderson **Glenn Morshower**
Colonel Jenkins **Don Creech**
Mary **Helen Slayton-Hughes**
Don Surine **Robert Knepper**
Stage Manager **JD Cullum**
CBS Page **Simon Helberg**
Jimmy **Peter Jacobson**
Jazz Singer **Dianne Reeves**

George Clooney, David Strathairn

Patricia Clarkson, Robert Downey, Jr.

Ray Wise

Matt Ross, David Strathairn, Tate Donovan, Reed Diamond

The true story of how CBS news commentator Edward R. Murrow took an on-air stance against Senator Joseph R. McCarthy's unethical, witchhunt tactics in tracking down and exposing Americans the Senator believed were members of the Communist party.

This film received Oscar nominations for picture, actor (David Strathairn), director, original screenplay, cinematography, and art direction.

George Clooney, David Strathairn

Dianne Reeves

George Clooney, Glenn Morshower, Don Creech

Frank Langella

Tom McCarthy, David Strathairn PHOTOS COURTESY OF WARNER INDEPENDENT

IN HER SHOES

(20TH CENTURY FOX) Producers, Ridley Scott, Carol Fenelon, Lisa Ellzey, Curtis Hanson; Executive Producer, Tony Scott; Co-Producers, Mary Jo Winkler-Ioffreda, Erin Upson; Director, Curtis Hanson; Screenplay, Susannah Grant, based on her novel; Photography, Terry Stacey; Designer, Dan Davis; Costumes, Sophie de Rakoff; Music, Mark Isham; Editors, Craig Kitson, Lisa Zeno-Churgin; Casting, David Rubin; a Fox 2000 Pictures presentation of a Scott Free, Deuce Three production; Dolby; Panavision; Deluxe color; Rated PG-13; 129 minutes; Release date: October 7, 2005

Toni Collette

Toni Collette, Cameron Diaz

Cast

Maggie Feller **Cameron Diaz**
Rose Feller **Toni Collette**
Ella Hirsch **Shirley MacLaine**
Simon Stein **Mark Feuerstein**
Michael Feller **Ken Howard**
Sydelle Feller **Candice Azzara**
Mrs. Lefkowitz **Francine Beers**
The Professor **Norman Lloyd**
Lewis Feldman **Jerry Adler**
Amy **Brooke Smith**
Jim Danvers **Richard Burgi**

and Anson Mount (Todd), John Mastrangelo Sr., Emilio Mignucci (Di Bruno Bros. Cheese Guys), Terrance Christopher Jones (Lawyer), Nicole Randall Johnson (Rose's Assistant), Kateri DeMartino (Ferocious Shopper), Brandon Karrer (Canal House Guy), Jon Ingrassia (Bartender), Jason Peck (Cuervo Carl), Mary-Pat Green (Diner Waitress), Gene Bozzi (Doorman), Carlease Burke (Bea), Eric Balfour (Grant), Andy Powers (Tim), Karen Vicks (Amtrak Counter Woman), Carol Florence (Dog-Walking Woman), Maureen Torsney-Weir, William Spangler (Dog-Walking Couple), Chihiro Kawaymura (Sushi Waitress), Kevin Scott Anthony, Salih Abdul-Qawi, Earnie Philps, Bill Polk, Jacquin Rashad Walker (Sixers Fans at Pat's Cheesesteaks), Marcia Jean Kurtz (Mrs. Stein), Alan Blumenfeld (Mr. Stein), Jackie Geary (My Marcia), Jill Saunders (Lopey), Mel Alpern (Rabbi), Dorothy Kelly (Dora), Benton Jennings (Shoe Salesman), Marilyn

Cameron Diaz, Shirley MacLaine PHOTOS COURTESY OF 20TH CENTURY FOX

Raphael (Mimmy), Fran Gellatly (Mrs. Stempel), Joan Turner (Edie), Jeri Jordan (Jeri), Dan Fitzgerald (Altercocker in Golf Cart), Ruth Byler (Mrs. Haskell), David Shatraw (The Professor's Grandson), Richard Jah Ace & The Sons of Ace (Wedding Band), Cebert Hall, Ayana Mingo, Asabi Rich, Carole Robinson, Nicola Shirley, April Stewart (Jerk Hut Staff), John Draper, Len D'Errico, Ira Friedman, Bill Miller, George Randell, Mario Sandrelli, Ray Sullivan, Ray Wiersema (Shuffleboarders), Shirley Beehner, Sophie Klein, Marie Malocco, Betty Ricciardelli, Florence Ruprecht, Mike Schmidt (Pool Noodlers), Kenneth Beehner, Bob Koehler, Robert Miller, George Rosenberg, Fritz Rulli, Dale Schwant (The Bench), Jay Bressner, Jack Brown, Maxine Brown, Madeine S. Bruni, Rene Godin, Sandye Menduke, Tony Russo, Maureen Solomon (Tea Dancers)

Beautiful and selfish Maggie Feller crashes at the apartment of her more level-headed sister Rose, only to cause havoc on her sibling's personal life, leading her to jump at her last option, traveling south to search for the grandmother she had long thought dead.

Keira Knightley

DOMINO

(NEW LINE CINEMA) Producers, Samuel Hadida, Tony Scott; Executive Producers, Barry Waldman, Zach Schiff-Abrams, Lisa Ellzey, Toby Emmerich, Victor Hadida, Skip Chaisson; Co-Producers, Peter Toumasis, David Hadida; Director, Tony Scott; Screenplay, Richard Kelly; Story, Richard Kelly, Steve Barancik; Photography, Dan Mindel; Designer, Chris Seagers; Costumes, B.; Music, Harry Gregson-Williams; Editors, William Goldenberg, Christian Wagner; Special Effects Supervisor, John Frazier; Stunts, Chuck Picerni, Jr.; Casting, Denise Chamian; a Samuel Hadida presentation of a Scott Free, David Films production; Dolby; Panavision; Deluxe color; Rated R; 128 minutes; Release date: October 14, 2005

Cast

Domino Harvey **Keira Knightley**
Ed Moseby **Mickey Rourke**
Choco **Edgar Ramirez**
Claremont Williams **Delroy Lindo**
Lateesha Rodriguez **Mo'Nique**
Taryn Mills **Lucy Liu**
Mark Heiss **Christopher Walken**
Kimmie **Mena Suvari**
Lashandra Davis **Marcy Gray**
Sophie Wynn **Jacqueline Bisset**
Drake Bishop **Dabney Coleman**

and Brian Austin Green, Ian Ziering, Jerry Springer (Themselves), Stanley Kamel (Anthony Cigliutti), Peter Jacobson (Burke Beckett), T. K. Carter (Lester Kincaid), Kel O'Neill (Frances), Shondrella Avery (Lashindra Davis), Lew Temple (Locus Fender), Tom Waits (Wanderer), Rizwan Abbasi (Alf), Joseph Nunez (Raul), Dale Dickey (Edna Fender), Charles Paraventi (Howie Stein), Fred Koehler (Chuckie), Tabitha Brownstone (Young Domino, Age 8), Dusty Gilvaher (Fish Vendor), Chad Parker (Underwater Mobster), Cheryl Francis Harrington (Outraged Woman), Ashley Monique Clark (Kee Kee Rodriguez), Anthony Delan (Gas Attendant), Patrick Kerr (DMV Manager), Adam Clark (Agent Eric Cosgrove), Donna Scott (Agent Dina Wilson), Julie Valine (Sorority

Leader), Victor Manni (Bishop Goon #1), Mike Andolini (Mobster), Janet Gonzalez (Louise Maldonado), Michael Gonzalez (Hector Maldonado), Eddie Hernandez (Larenz "Creep" Dexter), Liza Lapira (Chinegro Woman), George Thabet (Alf, Age 14), Mark Newsom (Dr. Waldman), Jack McGee (Det. Christ Cudlitz), Rolando Molina (Security Manager), Morgan Nagler (Stacee Stevens), Ginger Kinison (Ariana Bower), Andy Milder, Neal Matarazzo (FBI Agents), Robbie Kaller (Zoo Brother), Melissa Lee (College Girl), Ash Christian (Zoo President), Michelle Fabiano (Mrs. Cigliutti), Philip Darlington (Zendejas), Leonidos Iraheta (Creep's Friend), Paul Nguyen (Asian Gang Banger), Julian Beriln, Lili Mirojnick (Sorority Girls), Richard Burch, Mike Rademaekers (BH Seminar Losers), Celeste Hodge (Runway Model), Abraham Ashley (Underwater Cop), Mark Kinsey Stephenson (Catholic Teacher), Leonardo Digirolamo (Priest), Richard Rand, Bruce Sparkes, Keith Dimmy, Frank Bilberg, Anne Chamberlain, Jeff Klein (FBI Agents), Jesse Rosales, David Riley, Adham Shalabi (Alf's Friends)

Edgar Ramirez, Mickey Rourke

Born into celebrity wealth, young Domino Harvey chucks her posh life style and instead becomes an L.A. bounty hunter.

Keira Knightley, Lucy Liu PHOTOS COURTESY OF NEW LINE CINEMA

Jason Isaacs, Robin Wright Penn

Lisa Gay Hamilton

Joe Mantegna, Kathy Baker

Dakota Fanning, Glenn Close PHOTOS COURTESY OF MAGNOLIA

NINE LIVES

(MAGNOLIA) Producer, Julie Lynn; Executive Producer, Alejandro Gonzalez Inarritu; Director/Screenplay, Rodrigo Garcia; Photography, Xavier Perez Grobet; Designer, Courtney Jackson; Music, Edward Shearmur; Editor, Andrea Folprecht; Associate Producers, Kelly Thomas, Amy Lippens; Casting, Amy Lippens; a Mockingbird Pictures production in association with Z Films; Dolby; Deluxe color; Super 16mm-to-35mm; Rated R; 115 minutes; Release date: October 14, 2005

Elpidia Carrillo

Cast
Camilla **Kathy Baker**
Lorna **Amy Brenneman**
Sandra **Elpidia Carrillo**
Maggie **Glenn Close**
Martin **Stephen Dillane**
Maria **Dakota Fanning**
Andrew **William Fitchner**
Holly **Lisa Gay Hamilton**
Sonia **Holly Hunter**
Damian **Jason Isaacs**
Richard **Joe Mantegna**
Larry **Ian McShane**
Lisa **Molly Parker**
Alma **Mary Kay Place**
Vanessa **Sydney Tamila Poitier**
Henry **Aidan Quinn**
Ron **Miguel Sandoval**
Samantha **Amanda Seyfried**
Ruth **Sissy Spacek**
Diana **Robin Wright Penn**

and Aomawa Baker, Andy Umberger (Guards), Andrew Borba (Paul), K Callan (Marisa), Mary Pat Dowhy (Nicole), Amy Lippens (Nurse), Daniel Edward Mora (Receptionist), Pat Musick (Mourner/Night Manager), Lawrence Pressman (Roman), Chelsea Rendon (Sandra's Daughter), Rebecca Tilney (Rebecca)

Nine brief glimpses into the lives of nine different women.

Orlando Bloom, Kirsten Dunst

ELIZABETHTOWN

(PARAMOUNT) Producers, Tom Cruise, Paula Wagner, Cameron Crowe; Executive Producer, Donald J. Lee, Jr.; Director/Screenplay, Cameron Crowe; Photography, John Toll; Designer, Clay A. Griffith; Costumes, Nancy Steiner; Music, Nancy Wilson; Editor, David Moritz; Casting, Gail Levin; a Cruise/Wagner Productions, Vinyl Films production; Dolby; Deluxe color; Rated PG-13; 123 minutes; Release date: October 14, 2005

Cast

Drew Baylor **Orlando Bloom**
Claire Colburn **Kirsten Dunst**
Hollie Baylor **Susan Sarandon**
Phil DeVoss **Alec Baldwin**
Bill Banyon **Bruce McGill**
Heather Baylor **Judy Greer**
Ellen Kishmore **Jessica Biel**
Jessie Baylor **Paul Schneider**
Uncle Dale **Loudon Wainright**
Charles Dean **Gailard Sartain**

and Jed Rees (Chuck Hasboro), Paula Deen (Aunt Dora), Dan Biggers (Uncle Roy), Alice Marie Crowe (Aunt Lena), Tim Devitt (Mitch Baylor), Ted Mason (Sad Joe), Maxwell Moss Steen, Reid Thopmson Steen (Samson), Shane E. Lyons (Starstruck Kid), Emily Rutherfurd (Cindy Hasboro), Michael Naughton (Another Cousin), Girffin Grabow (Griffin), Nina Jefferies (Staring Mona), Emily Goldwyn (Star Basketball Player), Kristin Lindquist (Connie), Allison Munn (Desk Clerk Charlotte), Tom Humbarger (Cremetory Concierge), Patty Griffin (Sharon), Gregory North (Helicopter Pilot), Steve Seagren (Dock Worker), Guy Stevenson, Jeff De Serrano (Security Guards), Jeannete O'Connor, Catherine McGoohan (Assistants), Sean Nepita (Mike Bohannon), Dena DeCola (Debbie), David Brandt (Hotel Manager), Jenny Stewart, Delaney Keefe (Loud Kids), Travis Howard (Electrician), Bobby Daniels (Des), Rod Burke (Raymond), Nate Mooney (Trent), Judy Trice (Woman in Finery), Jim Fitzpatrick (Rusty), Jim James, Two-Tone Tommy, Patrick Hallahan, Charlie "Bill" Crowe, Carl Broemel, Scott Sener (Jessie's Band), John M. Sullivan, Sonny King, Erwin Russell

Marlowe (Etown Veterans), Michael Hatch (Drew, Age 6), Masam Holden (Drew, Age 10), Kelly Pendygraft (Rebecca the Bridesmaid), Jennifer Woods (Bridesmaid), Alana Ball (Maid of Honor), Russell George (Russ from Ernestine and Hazel's), Ralph Conlee (Man on the Beach), Billy Tencza (Brett), Hailey Knight (Isis), Nicky Roos (Sharon's Son), Zane Rice (Little Chapel Boy), Kassie Bay Pinegar (Little Howling Girl), Daya Fernandez (Mercury Shoe Designer), Michael Karoscak (The Young Recruit), Nigel Patrick Miguel (Basketball Coach), Samantha Ray (Frightened Memorial-Goer), Nicole Spector (Other Girl in Red Hat)

Alec Baldwin, Orlando Bloom

After losing his company nearly a billion dollars, a suicidal Drew Baylor is asked by his mother to travel to Elizabethtown, Kentucky to claim his recently deceased father's body.

Susan Sarandon, Judy Greer, Orlando Bloom

Jessica Biel, Orlando Bloom   PHOTOS COURTESY OF PARAMOUNT

THE FOG

(COLUMBIA) Producers, Debra Hill, David Foster, John Carpenter; Executive Producers, Todd Garner, Dan Kolsrud, Derek Dauchy; Director, Rupert Wainright; Screenplay, Cooper Layne; Based on the film written by John Carpenter, Debra Hill; Photography, Nathan Hope; Designers, Michael Diner, Graeme Murray; Costumes, Monique Prudhomme; Music, Graeme Revell; Music Supervision, Budd Carr, Nora Felder; Editor, Dennis Virkler; Makeup/Character Effects Designer/Creator, Schminken Studio Inc.; Casting, Amanda Mackey, Cathy Sandrich Gelfond; a Revolution Studios presentation of a Debra Hill Production in association with David Foster Productions; Dolby; Deluxe color; Rated PG-13; 100 minutes; Release date: October 14, 2005

Selma Blair

Adrian Hough

Cast

Nick Castle **Tom Welling**
Elizabeth Williams **Maggie Grace**
Stevie Wayne **Selma Blair**
Spooner **DeRay Davis**
Tom Malone **Kenneth Welsh**
Father Malone **Adrian Hough**
Kath Williams **Sara Botsford**
Captain Blake **Rade Sherbedgia**

and Cole Heppell (Andy Wayne), Mary Black (Aunt Connie), Jonathon Young (Dan the Weatherman), R. Nelson Brown (Machen), Christian Bocher (Founding Father Malone), Douglas H. Arthurs (Founding Father Williams), Yves Cameron (Founding Father Wayne), Charles André (Founding Father Castle), Matthew Currie Holmes (Sean Castle), Sonja Bennett (Mandi), Meghan Heffern (Brandi/Jennifer), Alex Bruhanski (Uncle Hank), Dan Shea, Rick Pearce (Fishermen), Robert Harper (Mr. Latham), Eric Breker (Sheriff's Deputy), Caley Honeywell (EMT), Stefan Arngrim (Blake's Compadre), Steven Cree Molison (Local Fisherman), Bonnie Paynch (Fisherman's Wife), Sherri McLean (Grieving Woman), Xantha Radley (Mother in Hold), Abigail Winter-Culliford (Child in Hold), Tatiana Szalay (Woman in Hold), John Destry (Man in Hold)

Tom Welling

The small town of Antonio Bay is terrorized by a mysterious, malevolent force hidden with a thick and deadly fog. Remake of the 1980 Avco Embassy film that starred Adrienne Barbeau, Jamie Lee Curtis, Hal Holbrook, and Janet Leigh.

Maggie Grace PHOTOS COURTESY OF COLUMBIA

DREAMER:
INSPIRED BY A TRUE STORY

(DREAMWORKS) Producers, Mike Tollin, Brian Robbins; Executive Producers, Ashok Amritraj, Jon Jashni, Bill Johnson, Stacy Cohen, Caitlin Scanlon; Director/Screenplay, John Gatins; Photography, Fred Murphy; Designer, Brent Thomas; Costumes, Judy Ruskin Howell; Music, John Debney; Violin Solos, Joshua Bell; Editor, David Rosenbloom; Casting, Sarah Halley Finn, Randi Hiller; a Tollin/Robbins, Hunt Lowry production, presented in association with Hyde Park Entertainment; Dolby; Technicolor; Rated PG; 98 minutes; Release date: October 21, 2005

Cast

Ben Crane **Kurt Russell**
Cale Crane **Dakota Fanning**
Pop Crane **Kris Kristofferson**
Lilly **Elisabeth Shue**
Palmer **David Morse**
Manolin **Freddy Rodriguez**
Balon **Luis Guzman**
Prince Sadir **Oded Fehr**

Kris Kristofferson

Bill Ford **Ken Howard**
Doc Fleming **Holmes Osborne**
Prince Tariq **Antonio Albadran**

and John Moyer (Security Officer), Kayren Butler (Teacher), Tommy Barnes (Short Steward), Frank Hoyt Taylor (Chairman), David Shamieh (Man at Prince Sadir's Door), Varkas Everest (Prince Sadir's Horseman), Dick Allen (Veteran Gambler), Donna Barton Brothers, Adam Tomei (Reporters), Dan Beene (Emergency Vet), John Newberg (Beefeater), Rhoda Girffis (Classroom Mother), Hutchi Hancock (Betting Window Clerk), Rex Peterson (Emergency Medical Vet), Trevor Denman (Track Announcer/Breeders' Cup Announcer), Ed Burgart (Claiming Track Announcer), Mark Warrack (Texas Horseman)

A former horseman and his young daughter save the life of an injured racehorse and nurse her back to health with the intention of winning the Breeders' Cup Classic.

Elisabeth Shue, Luis Guzman, Dakota Fanning, Kris Kristofferson, Kurt Russell

Freddy Rodriguez, Luis Guzman

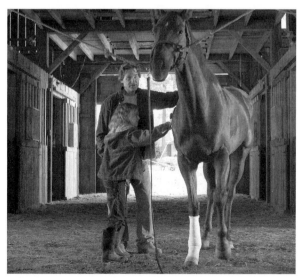

Dakota Fanning, Kurt Russell, Sacrifice PHOTOS COURTESY OF DREAMWORKS

Jason Schwartzman

SHOPGIRL

(TOUCHSTONE) Producers, Ashok Amritraj, Jon Jashni, Steve Martin; Executive Producer, Andrew Sugerman; Director, Anand Tucker; Screenplay, Steve Martin, based on his novella; Photography, Peter Suschitzky; Designer, William Arnold; Costumes, Nancy Steiner; Music, Barrington Pheloung; Editor, David Gamble; Co-Producer, Marcus Viscidi; Associate Producers, Nick Hamson, Simon Conder; Casting, Tricia Wood, Deborah Aquila, Jennifer Smith; a Hyde Park Entertainment presentation of an Ashok Amritraj production; Dolby; Panavision; CFI color; Rated R: 116 minutes; Release date: October 21, 2005

Steve Martin, Claire Danes

Cast

Ray Porter **Steve Martin**
Mirabelle Buttersfield **Claire Danes**
Jeremy **Jason Schwartzman**
Lisa Cramer **Bridgette Wilson-Sampras**
Dan Buttersfield **Sam Bottoms**
Catherine Buttersfield **Frances Conroy**
Christie Richards **Rebecca Pidgeon**
Loki **Samantha Shelton**
Del Rey **Gina Doctor**
Mr. Agasa **Clyde Kusatsu**
Loan Officer **Romy Rosemont**
Trey Bryan **Joshua Snyder**
Trey's Girlfriend **Rachel Nichols**
Chet **Shane Edelman**
Japanese Woman **Emily Kuroda**
Houseboy **Jayzel Samonte**
Luther **Mark Kozelek**
Hot Tears Band Members **Johnny Fedevich, Zak Sally**
Shrink **Ray Buktenica**
Karen **Alexandra Lee**
Saks Customer **Shannon Hile**
Businessman **Joe Bays**
Tom **Randy Oglesby**
Eli **Richard Fancy**

Claire Danes

Jason Schwartzman, Bridgette Wilson-Sampras

Claire Danes, Jason Schwartzman

Mirabelle, a lonely shopgirl, working in the glove department at Saks Fifth Avenue while hoping to make her mark as an artist, is wooed by the older, extremely wealthy Ray Porter. Meanwhile hapless Jeremy hopes to make up for his clumsy attempts at dating Mirabelle by turning himself from a slacker into a mature young man with a purpose.

Claire Danes, Steve Martin

Mandy **Anne Marie Howard**
Charley **Kevin Kilner**
The Volebeats **Matthew Smith, Troy Gregory, Scott Michalski, Russell Ledford, Jeff Oakes**
Armandi Seamstress **Kris Deskins**
Cosmetics Girl **Laura Grady**

Bridgette Wilson-Sampras

Claire Danes, Jason Schwartzman

Sam Bottoms, Frances Conroy, Claire Danes PHOTOS COURTESY OF TOUCHSTONE

NORTH COUNTRY

(WARNER BROS.) Producer, Nick Weschler; Executive Producers, Helen Bartlett, Nana Greenwald, Doug Claybourne, Jeff Skoll; Director, Niki Caro; Screenplay, Michael Seitzman; Inspired by the book *Class Action: The Landmark Case That Changed Sexual Harassment Law* by Clara Bingham, Laura Leedy Gansler; Photography, Chris Menges; Designer, Richard Hoover; Costumes, Cindy Evans; Music, Gustavo Santaolalla; Editor, David Coulson; Casting, Mali Finn; a Nick Weschler production, presented in association with Participant Productions; Dolby; Panavision; Technicolor; Rated R; 126 minutes; Release date: October 21, 2005

Richard Jenkins, Charlize Theron, Sissy Spacek

Frances McDormand, Sean Bean

Cast

Josey Aimes **Charlize Theron**
Glory **Frances McDormand**
Kyle **Sean Bean**
Hank Aimes **Richard Jenkins**
Bobby Sharp **Jeremy Renner**
Sherry **Michelle Monaghan**
Bill White **Woody Harrelson**
Alice Aimes **Sissy Spacek**
Big Betty **Rusty Schwimmer**
Peg **Jillian Armenante**
Sammy Aimes **Thomas Curtis**

Frances McDormand, Charlize Theron, Elle Peterson, Woody Harrelson

Karen Aimes **Elle Peterson**
Don Pearson **James Cada**
Lattavansky **Brad William Henke**
Young Josey **Amber Heard**
Judge Halsted **John Aylward**

and Xander Berkeley (Arlen Pavich), Corey Stoll (Ricky Sennett), Cole Williams (Young Bobby), Bryan Fagerstrom (Mac), Chris Mulkey (Earl Slangley), Aaron Shiver (Young Doctor), Clif Stokes (Good Guy), JD Garfield, Boots Southerland, John Hardman (Porta Guys), Forrest Norgaard (Mac's Buddy), Sage Coy (Stacey), Marcus Chait (Wayne), Dennis E. Garber (Real Estate Agent), Alex Layton (Number 3), Jacqueline Wright (Bobby's Wife), Catherine Campion (Stacey's Mom), Tom Bower (Gray Suchett), David Lislegard, Kurt Peterson, Pete Pellinen, Bruce Bohne (Union Members), Todd Anderson (Semen Man), Kit Gwin (Larynx Nurse), Monsignor Patrick McDowell (Priest), Raye Birk (Tom Motel Clerk), Sally Wingert (Kay Stollman), Katherine Ferrand (Sally Bullavina), Curtis Plagge (Burly Miner), Marc Miles (Digger Driver), J. C. Cutler (Union Rep #1), Gus Lynch (Pete Union Rep), Mark Sivertsen, Rand Kennedy (Bailiffs)

A single mother, struggling to put her life back together, takes a job at a Minnesota mine where she and the few other women on staff are subjected to sexual harassment by the male-dominated crew.

This film received Oscar nominations for actress (Charlize Theron) and supporting actress (Frances McDormand).

Rusty Schwimmer, Charlize Theron, Frances McDormand, Jillian Armenante, Michelle Monaghan PHOTOS COURTESY OF WARNER BROS.

KISS KISS BANG BANG

(WARNER BROS.) Producer, Joel Silver; Executive Producers, Susan Levin, Steve Richards; Co-Producer, Carrie Morrow; Director/Screenplay/Screenplay Story, Shane Black; Based in part on the novel *Bodies Are Where You Find Them* by Brett Halliday; Photography, Michael Barrett; Designer, Aaron Osborne; Costumes, Christopher J. Kristoff; Music, John Ottman; Music Supervisor, Randall Poster; Editor, Jim Page; Visual Effects Supervisors, Edson Williams, Greg Strause; Stunts, Kurt Bryant; Casting, Mary Gail Artz, Barbara Cohen; a Silver Pictures production; Dolby; Panavision; Technicolor; Rated R; 102 minutes; Release date: October 21, 2005

Cast

Harry Lockhart **Robert Downey, Jr.**
Gay Perry **Val Kilmer**
Harmony Faith Lane **Michelle Monaghan**
Harlan Dexter **Corbin Bernsen**
Mr. Frying Pan **Dash Mihok**
Dabney Shaw **Larry Miller**
Mr. Fire **Rockmond Dunbar**
Pink Hair Girl **Shannyn Sossamon**
Flicka **Angela Lindvall**
Harry, age 9 **Indio Falconer Downey**
Harmony, age 7 **Ariel Winter**
Chainsaw Kid **Duane Carnahan**
Rickie **Josh Richman**
Pistol Woman **Martha Hackett**

and Nancy Fish (NY Casting Woman), Bill McAdams, Jr. (NY Cop), Tanja Reichert (B-Movie Actress), Jake McKinnon (Creature), Stephanie Pearson (Teen Harmony), Chris Gilman (Protocop), Brendan Fehily (Local News Reporter), David Newsome (Agent Type), Judie Aronson (Gift Bag Girl), Ali Hillis (Marleah), Wiley Pickett (Homicide Cop), Joe Keyes (Lobby Cop), Bobby Tuttle (Hotel Concierge), Jake Eberle (Patrol Cop), Saida Rodriguez-Pagan (News Anchor), Lela Edgar (Party Girl), Daniel Browning Smith (Rubber Boy), Stevie (Pink Hair Girl's Dog), Teresa Herrera (Newswoman), Kathy Lamkin (Woman in Hospital Blues), Evan Parke (Dexter Clinic Guard), Vincent Laresca (Aurello), Brian Simpson, Cole McKay, Ben Bray (Dexter Goons), Harrison Young (Harmony's Dad)

Val Kilmer, Robert Downey, Jr.

A down-in-his-luck actor accidentally gets involved in a Hollywood murder mystery, helping to solve the case.

Michelle Monaghan PHOTOS COURTESY OF WARNER BROS.

Val Kilmer, Robert Downey, Jr.

BALLETS RUSSES

(ZEITGEIST) Producers, Dayna Goldfine, Dan Geller, Robert Hawk, Douglas Blair Turnbaugh; Directors, Dayna Goldfine, Dan Geller; Screenplay, Dan Geller, Dayna Goldfine, Gary Weimberg, Celeste Schaeffer Snyder; Photography, Dan Geller; Music, Todd Boekelheide, David Conte; Editors, Dan Geller, Dayna Goldfine, Gary Weimberg; Narrator, Marian Seldes; a Geller/Goldfine production; Color; Not rated; 121 minutes; Release date: October 26, 2005. Documentary on the six-decade history of the Ballets Russe company.

With

Ann Barzel, Irina Baronova, Yvonne Chouteau, Yvonne Craig, Frederic Franklin, Alan Howard, Nathalie Krassovska, Nina Novak, Marc Platt, Wakefield Poole, Tatiana Riabouchinska, Tatiana Stepanova, Maria Tallchief, Tamara Tchinarova Finch, Miguel Terekhov, Nini Theilade, Raven Wilkinson, Rochelle Zide, George Zoritch

Tatiana Riabouchinska, Tamara Toumanova, Irina Baronova in *Ballet Russes*
PHOTOS COURTESY OF ZEITGEIST

SAW II

(LIONS GATE) Producers, Mark Burg, Gregg Hoffman, Oren Koules; Executive Producers, Peter Block, Jason Constantine, Stacy Testro, James Wan, Leigh Whannell; Director, Darren Lynn Bousman; Screenplay, Darren Lynn Bousman, Leigh Whannell; Photography, David Armstrong; Designer, David Hackl; Costumes, Alex Kavanaugh; Music, Charlie Clouser; Editor, Kevin Greutert; Makeup, Patrick Baxter, Neil Morrill; Casting, Amy Lippens; a Twisted Pictures presentation of a Burg/Koules/Hoffman production; Dolby; Deluxe color; Rated R; 93 minutes; Release date: October 28, 2005

Cast

Eric Matthews	**Donnie Wahlberg**
Amanda	**Shawnee Smith**
Jigsaw	**Tobin Bell**
Xavier	**Franky G.**
Jonas	**Glenn Plummer**
Kerry	**Dina Meyer**

and Emmanuelle Vaugier (Addison), Beverley Mitchell (Laura), Erik Knudsen (Daniel), Timothy Burd (Obi), Lyriq Bent (Rigg), Noam Jenkins (Michael), Tony Nappo (Gus), Vincent Rother (SWAT Member Joe), Kelly Jones (SWAT Member Pete), John Fallon (Video Techie), Ho Chow (Security Officer), Linette Robinson (Mother in Cancer Ward), Gretchen Helbig (Nurse in Cancer Ward), Kofi Payton (Boy in Cancer Ward)

Police detectives Kerry and Eric find the hideout of sadistic killer Jigsaw where a video console reveals that nine people, including Eric's son, have been imprisoned together in an unidentified room.

Beverely Mitchell, Franky G. in *Saw II*

Dina Meyer, Donnie Wahlberg in *Saw II* PHOTOS COURTESY OF LIONS GATE

Nicholas Hoult, Nicolas Cage

THE WEATHER MAN

(PARAMOUNT) Producers, Todd Black, Steve Tisch, Jason Blumenthal; Executive Producers, William S. Beasley, David Alper, Norm Golightly; Director, Gore Verbinski; Screenplay/Co-Producer, Steve Conrad; Photography, Phedon Papamichael; Designer, Tom Duffield; Costumes, Penny Rose; Music, Hans Zimmer; Editor, Craig Wood; Casting, Denise Chamian; an Escape Artists presentation of an Escape Artists production; Dolby; Deluxe color; Rated R; 101 minutes; Release date: October 28, 2005

Cast
David Spritz **Nicolas Cage**
Robert Spritzel **Michael Caine**
Noreen **Hope Davis**
Shelly **Gemmenne De La Peña**
Mike **Nicholas Hoult**
Russ **Michael Rispoli**
Don **Gil Bellows**
Lauren **Judith McConnell**
DMV Guy **Chris Marris**
Andrea **Dina Facklis**
Clerk **DeAnna N.J. Brooks**
Nurse **Sia Moody**
Nipper Guy **Guy Van Swearingen**

and Alejandro Pina (Fast Food Employee), Jackson Bubala (Fast Food Child), Jennifer Bills (Fast Food Mom), Peter Grosz (Shelly's Archery Instructor), Joe Bianchi (Paul), Nick Kuehneman (Passenger with Frosty), Bruce Jarchow (Viewer), Joanne Sylvestrak (Viewer's Wife), Robyn Moler (Beer Girl), John D. Milinac (Beer Patron), Melanie Decelles Castro (Shelly's Companion), Jason Wells (Tim), Scott Benjaminson (Race Organizer), Ora Jones (Trust Counselor), Mike Bacarella (Takeout Clerk), Jennifer Joan Taylor (Reister Worker), Chuck Stubbings (Mark Dersen), Shané Williams, Dan Flannery (Hello America Producers), Sandy Whiteley (Hello America Director), Antoine McKay (Passing Pedestrian), Eddie Martinez (Pie Thrower), David Darlow (Robert's Friend), Will Zahrn (Priest), Poorna Jagannathan (NY Pedestrian), Bryant Gumbel, Ed

McMahon, Cristina Ferrare, Wolfgang Puck (Themselves), Anne Marie Howard, Juhong Xue (Co-Anchors), Stephen Hilger (Dave's Archery Instructor), Ron McClary (Guy in Park), Eric Amriz, Leah Rose Orleans (Elevator Kids), Tom Skilling (Station Assistant Director), Monica Weaver, John Francis Mountain (Living Funeral Guests)

Gemmenne De La Peña, Nicolas Cage

Michael Caine, Nicolas Cage

A successful but emotionally unfulfilled Chicago weatherman struggles to repair his strained relationships with his ailing father, his ex-wife, and his troubled children.

Hope Davis, Nicolas Cage PHOTOS COURTESY OF PARAMOUNT

PRIME

(UNIVERSAL) Producers, Suzanne Todd, Jennifer Todd; Executive Producers, Mark Gordon, Bob Yari; Co-Producers, Anthony Katagas, Brad Jenkel; Director/Screenplay, Ben Younger; Photography, William Rexer; Designer, Mark Ricker; Costumes, Melissa Toth; Music, Ryan Shore; Music Supervisor, Jim Black; Editor, Kristina Boden; Casting, Ellen Lewis; a Stratus Film Company presentation of a Team Todd, Younger Than You production; Dolby; Technicolor; Rated PG-13; 100 minutes; Release date: October 28, 2005

Meryl Streep

Recovering from a divorce, Rafi Gardet is thrilled to find herself falling in love with David Bloomberg, unaware that he is the son of her therapist.

Bryan Greenberg, Uma Thurman

Cast

Rafi Gardet **Uma Thurman**
Lisa Metzger **Meryl Streep**
David Bloomberg **Bryan Greenberg**
Morris **Jon Abrahams**
Bay Bridge Blonde **Adriana Biasi**
Brothers **David Younger, Palmer Brown**
Randall **Zak Orth**
Katherine **Annie Parisse**
Michelle **Aubrey Dollar**
Sam **Jerry Adler**
Blanch **Doris Belack**
Damien **Ato Essandoh**
Bodega Counterman **David Anzuelo**
Dinah Bloomberg **Noami Aborn**
Jack Bloomberg **John Rothman**

and Jonathan Roumie, Tadhg O'Mordha (Bakery Countermen), Madhur Jaffrey (Rita), Gil Deeble (Security Guard), Jason McDonald (Photographer/Basketball Player), Lotte Mandel (Bubi), Eboni Summer Cooper (Radjina), Mick de Lint (Fashion Shoot Client), Mini Anden (Sue), Tina Farris (Rafi's Assistant), Stretch Armstrong (House Party DJ), Susie Kantar (Carla), Sebastian Sozzi, Jade Yorker (Friends), David Costabile (Jason), Will McCormack (Palmer), Alex Webb (Art Collector), Seth Herzog (Rafi's Friend), Anne Joyce (Young Mother), Beth Skipp (Salesperson), Mitch Green (Bouncer), Christopher Innvar (Rafi's Date), Jennifer Marlowe (Il Buco Bartender)

Uma Thurman, Bryan Greenberg

John Rothman, Meryl Streep, Bryan Greenberg, Uma Thurman PHOTOS COURTESY OF UNIVERSAL

Nick Chinlund

THE LEGEND OF ZORRO

(COLUMBIA) Producers, Walter F. Parkes, Laurie MacDonald, Lloyd Phillips; Executive Producers, Steven Spielberg, Gary Barber, Roger Birnbaum; Director, Martin Campbell; Screenplay, Roberto Orci, Alex Kurtzman; Story, Roberto Orci, Alex Kurtzman, Ted Elliott, Terry Rossio; Photography, Phil Meheux; Designer, Cecilia Montiel; Costumes, Graciela Mazon; Music, James Horner; Editor, Stuart Baird; Visual Effects Supervisor, Kent Houston; Casting, Pam Dixon Mickelson; a Spyglass Entertainment presentation of an Amblin Entertainment production; Dolby; Deluxe color; Rated PG; 129 minutes; Release date: October 28, 2005

Cast

Zorro/Alejandro de la Vegas **Antonio Banderas**
Elena **Catherine Zeta-Jones**
Count Armand **Rufus Sewell**
Jacob McGivens **Nick Chinlund**
Frey Felipe **Julio Oscar Mechoso**
Pike **Shuler Hensley**
Harrigan **Michael Emerson**
Joaquin **Adrian Alonso**
Brother Ignacio **Alberto Reyes**
Cortez **Gustavo Sanchez Parra**

Blanca **Giovanna Zacarias**
Tabulador **Carlos Cobos**
Governor Riley **Pedro Armendariz**
Governor's Wife **Mary Crosby**
Don Verdugo **Mauricio Bonet**
Don Diaz **Fernando Becerril**
Don Robau **Xavier Marc**
Colonel Beauregarde **Leo Burmester**

and Pepe Olivares (Phineas), Alexa Benedetti (Lupe), Tony Amendola (Father Quintero), Brandon Wood (Ricardo), Alejandro Galan (Constable), Tina French (Peasant Woman), Rayo Rojas (Polo Attendant), Raúl Mendez (Ferroq), Mar Carrera (Marie), Pedro Altamirano (Saloon Owner), Silverio Palacios (Head Jailer), Alfredo Ramirez, Juan Manuel Vilchis (Guards), Antonio Gallegos (Jail Guard), Philip Meheux (Lord Dillingham), Matthew Stirling (Stoker), Pedro Mira (Abraham Lincoln)

Catherine Zeta-Jones, Antonio Banderas

Zorro springs back into action to thwart the efforts of Count Armand to prevent California from achieving statehood. Sequel to the 1998 Tri-Star release *The Mask of Zorro*, with Antonio Banderas and Catherine Zeta-Jones repeating their roles.

Antonio Banderas, Adrian Alonso PHOTOS COURTESY OF COLUMBIA

Chicken Little

CHICKEN LITTLE

(WALT DISNEY PICTURES) Producer, Randy Fullmer; Director, Mark Dindal; Screenplay, Steve Bencich, Ron J. Friedman, Ron Anderson; Story, Mark Dindal, Mark Kennedy; Designer, David Womersley; Music, John Debney; Associate Producer, Peter Del Vecho; Design, Mac George; Art Director, Ian Gooding; Editor, Dan Molina; Visual Effects Supervisor, Steve Goldberg; CG Supervisors, Kevin Geiger, Kyle Odermatt; Layout Supervisor, Terry Moews; Head of Story, Mark Kennedy; Animation Supervisor, Eamonn Butler; Casting, Jen Rudin Pearson; Dolby; Color; Rated G; 80 minutes; Release date: November 4, 2005

Fish Out of Water, Mr. Woolensworth

Goosey Loosey, Foxy Loxy

Voice Cast

Chicken Little **Zach Braff**
Buck Cluck **Garry Marshall**
Abby Mallard **Joan Cusack**
Runt of the Litter **Steve Zahn**
Foxy Loxy **Amy Sedaris**
Mayor Turkey Lurkey **Don Knotts**
Dog Announcer **Harry Shearer**
Mr. Woolensworth **Patrick Stewart**
Principal Fetchit **Wallace Shawn**
Mevlin—Alien Dad **Fred Willard**
Tina—Alien Mom **Catherine O'Hara**
Ace—Hollywood Chicken Little **Adam West**
Alien Cop **Patrick Warburton**

Runt of the Litter, Chicken Little, Abby Mallard

Chicken Little, Buck Cluck PHOTOS COURTESY OF WALT DISNEY PICTURES

and Mark Walton (Goosey Loosey), Mark Dindal (Morkubine Porcupine/Coach), Dan Molina (Fish Out of Water), Joe Whyte (Rodriguez/Acorn Mascot/Umpire), Sean Elmore, Evan Dunn, Matthew Josten (Kirby—Alien Kid), Kellie Hoover (Mama Runt), Will Finn (Hollywood Fish), Dara McGarry (Hollywood Abby), Mark Kennedy (Hollywood Runt)

Having destroyed his already tarnished reputation in town by telling the populace that the sky is falling, Chicken Little must save the day when he realizes that unexplainable forces are about to place the world in danger.

THE DYING GAUL

(STRAND) Producers, Campbell Scott, George Van Buskirk; Executive Producers, Joseph Caruso III, Shawn Fitzgerald, David Newman, Paul Cohen, Paul Manafort, Jerome Schwartz; Co-Producer, Kimberley Reiss; Director/Screenplay, Craig Lucas, based on his play; Photography, Bobby Bukowski; Designer, Vincent Jefferds; Costumes, Danny Clicker; Music, Steve Reich; Music Supervisor, Linda Cohen; Editor, Andy Keir; Casting, Douglas Aiken; a Holedigger Films Inc. presentation; Dolby; Fotokem color; Rated R; 101 minutes; Release date: November 4, 2005

Campbell Scott, Patricia Clarkson, Peter Sarsgaard

Campbell Scott, Peter Sarsgaard

Cast

Elaine Tishop **Patricia Clarkson**
Jeffrey Tishop **Campbell Scott**
Robert Sandrich **Peter Sarsgaard**
Max Tishop **Ryan Miller**
Debbon Tishop **Faith Jeffries**
Bella **Robin Bartlett**
Olaf **Ebon Moss-Bachrach**
Liz **Kelli O'Hara**
Emad **Dee Dee Flores**
Kelli **Elizabeth Marvel**
Male Guest **Don Johnson**
Malcolm Cartonis **Bill Camp**
Dr. Foss **Linda Emond**
Robert's Masseur **Jason-Shane Scott**

A gay writer, deeply in debt, accepts a $1 million offer for his script under the condition that he change the central gay couple to a heterosexual one.

Patricia Clarkson

Campbell Scott PHOTOS COURTESY OF STRAND RELEASING

JARHEAD

(UNIVERSAL) Producers, Douglas Wick, Lucy Fisher; Executive Producers, Sam Mercer, Bobby Cohen; Director, Sam Mendes; Screenplay, William Broyles, Jr.; Based on the book by Anthony Swofford; Photography, Roger Deakins; Designer, Dennis Gassner; Costumes, Albert Wolsky; Music, Thomas Newman; Music Supervisor, Randall Poster; Editor, Walter Murch; Co-Producer, Pippa Harris; Visual Effects Supervisor, Pablo Helman; Casting, Debra Zane; a MP Kappa Productions of a Lucy Fisher/Douglas Wick production in association with Neal Street Productions; Dolby; Deluxe color; Rated R; 127 minutes; Release date: November 4, 2005

Jamie Foxx, Jake Gyllenhaal

Cast

Anthony Swofford **Jake Gyllenhaal**
Allen Troy **Peter Sarsgaard**
Chris Kruger **Lucas Black**
Lt. Col. Kazinski **Chris Cooper**
Staff Sgt. Sykes **Jamie Foxx**
Fergus **Brian Geraghty**
Cortez **Jacob Vargas**
Escobar **Laz Alonso**
Fowler **Evan Jones**
Major Lincoln **Dennis Haysbert**
D. I. Fitch **Scott MacDonald**
Bored Gunny **Ming Lo**
Branded Marine **Kevin Foster**
Poitier **Damion Poitier**
Nurse **Riad Galayini**
Young Mr. Swofford **Craig Coyne**
Young Mrs. Swofford **Katherine Randolph**
Swoff's Sister **Rini Bell**

and Dendrie Taylor (Mrs. Swofford), James Morrison (Mr. Swofford), Arman Zajac (Boy Swofford), Brianne Davis (Kristina), Brian Casey (Paintball Marine), Ernest Ozuna (Sgt. Major), Tyler Sedustine (Harris),Jocko Sims (Julius), Jonathon R. Mize, Joel Prato (STA Graduates), Kristin Richardson (Stewardess), Ivan Fenyo (Pinko), Peter Gail (Doc John), Jamie Martz (Foster), Kareem Grimes (Welty), Donna Kimball (Reporter), Marty Papazian (Dettman), Becky Boxer (Dettman's Wife), Mark Davis (Dettman's Neighbor), John Krasinski (Corporal Harrigan), Christian Reeve, Mike Akrawi, Toufiq Tulsiram, Jubin K, Hari Bali (Bedouins), Kurt Larson (Arguing Corporal), Ammar Daraiseh, Al Faris (Iraqi Officers), V. J. Foster (Vietnam Vet)

Chris Cooper

Twenty-year-old Anthony Swofford enlists in the Marines in order to see combat and ends up being sent to Saudi Arabia to fight in the first Gulf War where he and his fellow soldiers wait anxiously and endlessly for their first mission.

Jake Gyllenhaal, Peter Sarsgaard

Jake Gyllenhaal, Laz Alonso, Peter Sarsgaard, Lucas Black PHOTOS COURTESY OF UNIVERSAL

Tory Kittles, Curtis "50 Cent" Jackson, Terrence Howard

GET RICH OR DIE TRYIN'

(PARAMOUNT) Producers, Jimmy Iovine, Paul Rosenberg, Chris Lighty, Jim Sheridan; Executive Producers, Gene Kirkwood, Stuart Parr, Van Toffler, David Gale, Arthur Lappin, Daniel Lupi; Co-Producer, Heather Parry; Director, Jim Sheridan; Screenplay, Terence Winter; Designer, Mark Geraghy; Costumes, Francine Jamison; Music, Quincy Jones, Gavin Friday, Maurice Seezer; Music Supervisors, John Houlihan, Sha Money XL; Editors, Conrad Buff, Roger Barton; Casting, Avy Kaufman; an Interscope/Shady/Aftermath Films, MTV production; Dolby; Super 35mm Widescreen; Color; Rated R; 118 minutes; Release date: November 9, 2005

Cast

Marcus	**Curtis "50 Cent" Jackson**
Charlene	**Adewale Akinnuoye-Agbaje**
Charlene	**Joy Bryant**
Keryl	**Omar Benson Miller**
Justice	**Tory Kittles**
Bama	**Terrence Howard**
Antwan	**Ashley Walters**
Young Marcus	**Marc John Jeffries**
Grandma	**Viola Davis**
Grandpa	**Sullivan Walker**
Katrina	**Serena Reeder**
Levar	**Bill Duke**
Junebug	**Mpho Koaho**
Odell	**Russell Hornsby**
Uncle Deuce	**Joseph Pierre**
Uncle Ray	**Ryan Allen**

and Vanessa Madden, Zainab Musa, Brendan Jeffers, Anastasia Hill, Shawn Singleton, Tchas "Toni" Goodridge (Marcus' Relatives), Leon (Slim), Rhyon Nicole Brown (Young Charlene), Lenno Britos (Carlos Delgato), Paulino Nunes, Arnold Pinnock (Detectives), Steve Cruz (Rodrigo), Frank Pellegrino (Det. Doyle), Bubba (Easy/Coke Dealer), Walter Alza (Raoul), Jer O'Leary (Valdez), Jorge Berrio (Cash Counting Machine Operator), Pedro Miguel Arce (Cash Counting Guard), Mercedez De Castro, Martha Chaves (Women), Pedro Salvín (Man), Beatriz Pizano (Rodrigo's Mom), Arelen Duncan (Judge Juvenile Court), Charles Anthony Burks (Car Salesman), Roland Rothchild (Marcus' Lawyer), Brian Paul (Doctor), Curtis "Ejyp" Johnson (Lizard Boot Man), George Randolph (School Security Guard), Conrad Bergschneider (Prison Guard), Tommy Chang (Store Owner), Vivian Lee (Store Owner's Wife), David Collins (Priest), Ethan James Duff (New Jerseyite), Malik Barnhardt (Gun Salesman), Michael Miller (Dangerous), Don Ritchie (Emergency Room Doctor), Jean Daigle (Prison Corrections Officer), Steve Prempeh (Young Antwan), Cinam Zee, Shane Smith, P. J. Fuller (Young Kids), Andrea Grant (Charlene's Mother), Victor Gomez (Tito), George Ghali (Landlord), Gouchy Boy (Club Bouncer), Rogue Johnston (Coin Fiend), Michael Colonesse (Raoul's Young Friend), Mike Santana (Fiend), Benz Antoine (Ray Wilmore), Mantee Murphy (Canary Cook), Quancetia Hamilton (Canary Waitress), Dan Duran (Journalist), Destan Owens (Charlene's Friend), Jerom White (Photographer), Bazil Williams, Juliette Nurse (Teachers), Dave Naughton (Prison Tattoo Artist), Lloyd Coke, Roger Moore (Majestic Thugs), Philip Akin (Reverend), Niguel Henry (Mourner), Dalecia Davis (Neighborhood Kid), Venice Grant (Hot Girl), Randy Brookes (ND Thug),

Adewale Akinnuoye-Agbaje, Joy Bryant, Curtis "50 Cent" Jackson PHOTOS COURTESY OF PARAMOUNT

Luis Fino (Studio Engineer), Sean Croft (Wilmore's Bodyguard), Paulina Berger (Receptionist), Boyd Banks (Prison Solitary Guard), Keisha Brown (Tammi), Keneisha Brown (Monique), Paul De La Rosa (Bailiff), Angelica Mengana (Reporter), Stefania Vommaro (Gangster's Girlfriend), DeAndra P. Mickel (Check Cashier), Anarosa Peguero (Drug Addict), Keith Schatt (NJ Guy), Victor Fischbarg (Mercedes Driver/Drug Buyer), Richardson Desil (Gun Store Bouncer), Rashaad Robert Devore (Subway Man), Josaline I. Espinal (Barbershop Customer), Melissa Russo (Store Owner), Daveed Ramsay, Matlok, James Ockimey (Teenage Thugs), Troy Oliver Patterson, Balford Gordon, Zachary Augustine, Scott Neil, Keifer John, Mark Alexander, Leaford Lewis, Anwan Ekpo, Jason Moore, Angus Bishop, Allan Alexander, Marlon Hull (Marcus Crew Guys)

Laying wounded after a botched robbery, Marcus looks back on how he got mixed up in the drug running trade and his efforts to break away from his dangerous life by becoming a rap musician.

Richard Gere, Juliette Binoche

Max Minghella, Richard Gere, Flora Cross

Max Minghella, Juliette Binoche, Flora Cross, Richard Gere

BEE SEASON

(FOX SEARCHLIGHT) Producers, Albert Berger, Ron Yerxa; Executive Producers, Arnon Milchan, Peggy Rajski, Mark Romanek; Directors, Scott McGehee, David Siegel; Screenplay, Naomi Foner Gyllenhaal; Based on the novel by Myla Goldberg; Photography, Giles Nuttgens; Designer, Kelly McGehee; Costumes, Mary Malin; Music, Peter Mashel; Editor, Martin Walsh; a Regency Entertainment presentation of a Bona Fide production; Dolby; Panavision; Deluxe color; Rated PG-13; 105 minutes; Release date: November 11, 2005

Cast

Saul Naumann **Richard Gere**
Miriam Naumann **Juliette Binoche**
Eliza Naumann **Flora Cross**
Aaron Naumann **Max Minghella**
Chali **Kate Bosworth**
National Spelling Bee Pronouncer **Corey Fischer**
National Spelling Bee Judge **Sam Zuckerman**
Ms. Bergermeyer **Joan Mankin**
Dr. Morris **Piers McKenzie**
Ms. Rai **Lorri Holt**
Mr. Julien **Brian Leonard**
Regional Bee Pronouncer **Kathy McGraw**
Regional Bee Judge **John Evans**
Young Miriam **Alisha Mullally**
State Bee Judge **Olivia Charles**

and Stephen Anthony Jones (Sergeant), Velina Brown (Hotel Housekeeper), Justin Alioto (Kevin), Ben Johnson (Orangutan Speller), Sophie Tamiko Oda ('Usurper' Speller), Shawn Smith ('Macrame' Speller), Mickey Boxwell, Alissa Anderegg, Jared Dorrance, Brandon Haas, Alexandra Rieger (Spelling Bee Student), Gaayatri Kaundinya ('Selenic' Speller), Charlotte Musengwa ('Duvetyn' Speller), Alison Doyle (National Spelling Bee Winner), Heather Barberie (Lab Assistant), Aida Bernardino (Student Mom), Mia Bernardino (Eliza's Classmate), Chandler Bolt (Student), Cathy Fithian (Elevator Mom), Deena Foley (Contestant Family Member), Aaron Guerra (Audience Member), David Hern (Bell Judge), Shaun Landry (Patient), Florentine Mocanu (Nurse), Scott Palmer (Congressman), Jennifer Robertson (Family Member), Angie Ruiz (Kabbalah Student)

Discovering that his young daughter has an aptitude for spelling, Berkeley professor Saul Naumann encourages her skills so that she can compete in the National Finals.

Max Minghella, Flora Cross PHOTOS COURTESY OF FOX SEARCHLIGHT

Reese Witherspoon, Joaquin Phoenix

WALK THE LINE

(20TH CENTURY FOX) Producers, Cathy Konrad, James Keach; Executive Producers, John Carter Cash, Alan C. Blomquist; Director, James Mangold; Screenplay, Gill Dennis, James Mangold; Based on *Man in Black* and *Cash: An Autobiography* by Johnny Cash; Photography, Phedon Papamichael; Designer, David J. Bomba; Costumes, Arianne Phillips; Music/Executive Music Producer, T Bone Burnett; Editor, Michael McCusker; Casting, Lisa Beach, Sarah Katzman; a Fox 2000 Pictures presentation of a Tree Line Films, Catfish Productions production; Dolby; Color; Rated PG-13; 136 minutes; Release date: November 11, 2005

Cast

John R. Cash **Joaquin Phoenix**
June Carter **Reese Witherspoon**
Vivian Cash **Ginnifer Goodwin**
Ray Cash **Robert Patrick**
Sam Phillips **Dallas Roberts**
Luther Perkins **Dan John Miller**
Marshall Grant **Larry Bagby**
Carrie Cash **Shelby Lynne**
Elvis Presley **Tyler Hilton**
Jerry Lee Lewis **Waylon Malloy Payne**
Waylon Jennings **Shooter Jennings**
Maybelle Carter **Sandra Ellis Lafferty**
Ezra Carter **Dan Beene**
W. S. "Fluke" Holland **Clay Steakley**
Roy Orbison **Johnathan Rice**
Carl Perkins **Johnny Holiday**
Young J. R. **Ridge Canipe**
Young Jack Cash **Lucas Till**
Young Reba Cash **Carly Nahon**
Tommy Cash, Age 5 **Wyatt Entrekin**
Roseanne Cash **Hailey Anne Nelson**
Kathy Cash **Kerris Dorsey**
Cindy Cash **Delaney Marie Keefe**
Carlene Carter **Victoria Hester**

and Deborah Rawlings (Diner Waitress), James DeForest Parker (Inmate), James Keach (Warden), Davielle Boyce (Maid at Door), Alan Gardner (Texarkana Stage Manager), Danny Vinson (Texarkana MC), Dave McPhail (Armory MC), Bob King (Armory Stage Manager), Natalie Canerday (Lady in the Aisle), Rhoda Griffis (Five and Dime Manager), Jeff Bailey (El Paso Taxi Driver), Ross Harkins (Record Executive), J. D. Evermore (FBI Man), Helen Ingebritsen (Bank Teller), J. W. Williams (Pill Man), Shane Bowen (JR's Agent), Tim Ware, Dolan Wilson (A&R Men), J. Allen Scott (Dyess Doctor), Clare Johnson (Lissome Girl), Michael Ingersoll (Donzil), Carter Thrower (Sheriff), Jean-Paul McNeely (Musician), Brian Deas (NCO), Glenda Pannell (Neighbor Woman), Amy Kudela (Wanda), Tracee Miller (Birdie Perkins)

Waylon Malloy Payne

The true story of country singer Johnny Cash's rise to fame and his pursuit of fellow performer June Carter to become his wife.

2005 Academy Award winner for Best Actress (Reese Witherspoon).
This film received additional nominations for actor (Joaquin Phoenix), costume design, editing, and sound.

Johnathan Rice PHOTOS COURTESY OF 20TH CENTURY FOX

Jonah Bobo, Kristen Stewart, Dax Shepard, Josh Hutcherson

ZATHURA: A SPACE ADVENTURE

(COLUMBIA) Producers, William Teitler, Scott Kroopf, Michael De Luca; Executive Producers, Ted Field, Louis D'Esposito; Co-Producer, Peter Billingsley; Director, Jon Favreau; Screenplay, David Koepp, John Kamps; Based on the book by Chris Van Allsburg; Photography, Guillermo Navarro; Designer, J. Michael Riva; Costumes, Laura Jean Shannon; Music, John Debney; Editor, Dan Lebental; Visual Effects Supervisor, Joe Bauer; Casting, Avy Kaufman; a Radar Films, Teitler Film, Michael De Luca production; Dolby; Deluxe color; Rated PG; 101 minutes; Release date: November 11, 2005

Cast
Danny **Jonah Bobo**
Walter **Josh Hutcherson**
Astronaut **Dax Shepard**
Lisa **Kristen Stewart**
Dad **Tim Robbins**
Voice of Robot **Frank Oz**

Josh Hutcherson, Kristen Stewart, Jonah Bobo

Josh Hutcherson, Jonah Bobo, Tim Robbins

Two squabbling brothers find themselves trapped in the midst of a space-age board game as they try to protect their home from alien obliteration.

Josh Hutcherson, Jonah Bobo

Jonah Bobo   PHOTOS COURTESY OF COLUMBIA

SARAH SILVERMAN: JESUS IS MAGIC

(ROADSIDE ATTRACTIONS) Producers, Heidi Herzon, Mark Williams, Randy Sosin; Director, Liam Lynch; Screenplay, Sarah Silverman; Photography, Rhet W. Bear; Designer, Henry Arce; Editor, Liam Lynch; Casting, Renita Whited; a Black Gold Films production; Dolby; Color; Not rated; 72 minutes; Release date: November 11, 2005. Comedian Sarah Silverman in performance.

With

Sarah Silverman (Herself), Brian Posehn (Friend), Bob Odenkirk (Manager), Laura Silverman (Friend), Steve Agee (Guy in Wings), Jon Cellini, Emily Petta (Funeral Attendees), Suzanne Fagan, Dee Kaye (Soccer Moms), Jonathan Kimmel (Harmonies), Kiyano La'vin, Eddie Bo Smith, Jr. (African American Guys), Ben Matthews (Grandma's Friend), Alexa Power, Harry Schatz, Robert Towers (Grandma's Friends), Joi Stanton (Old Folks), Brody Stevens (Jewish Agent), Phoebe Summersquash (Drummer)

Sarah Silverman in *Sarah Silverman: Jesus is Magic*   PHOTO COURTESY OF ROADSIDE ATTRACTIONS

DERAILED

(WEINSTEIN CO.) Producer, Lorenzo di Bonaventura; Executive Producers, Harvey Weinstein, Bob Weinstein, Jonathan Gordon; Co-Producer, Mark Cooper; Director, Mikael Håfström; Screenplay, Stuart Beattie; Based on the novel by James Siegel; Photography, Peter Biziou; Designer, Andrew Laws; Costumes, Natalie Ward; Music, Edward Shearmur; Editor, Peter Boyle; Casting, Avy Kaufman (US), Carrie Hitlon (UK); a Miramax Films presentation of a Di Bonaventura Pictures production in association with Patalex V Productions; Dolby; Super 35 Widescreen; Deluxe color; Rated R; 107 minutes; Release date: November 11, 2005

Cast

Charles Schine **Clive Owen**
Lucinda Harris **Jennifer Aniston**
Philippe LaRoche **Vincent Cassel**
Deanna Schine **Melissa George**
Det. Church **Giancarlo Esposito**
Sam Griffin **Sean Morrissey**

Jennifer Aniston in *Derailed*

Candy **Georgina Chapman**
Jerry the Lawyer **Denis O'Hare**
Elliot Firth **Tom Conti**
Amy Schine **Allison Timlin**
Dexter **Xzibit**
Winston Boyko **RZA**

and Sandra Bee (Train Conductor), William Armstrong (Accountant), Rachel Blake (Susan Davis), Richard Leaf (Hotel Clerk), Catherine McCord (Avery-Price Receptionist), David Oyelowo (Patrol Officer), Claire Lubert (Bank Teller), Jennifer Joan Taylor (Real Estate Agent), Sam Douglas (Homicide Detective), Ortis Deley (Lake Hotel Police Officer), Danny McCarthy (Correctional Officer Hank), Chiké Okonkwo (Paramedic), Joshua Brail (School Child), Christopher Fosh (Officer Townsend, Chicago Cop), Thaddeus Griebel (Arcade Gamer), Patricia E. Harrington, Big Kalvin, Alexandra Lo Russo, Angelina Riposta, Gary Sedlock, Joey Strobel, Richard Strobel, Ron Valdez, Anthony Velasco (Commuters), Georgiana Jianu (Business Woman), James Melody (Billy), Aimee Denaro (Waitress), Ike Ononye (Prison Inmate), Mel Raido (Business Executive), Georgie Smith (Business Woman)

As Charles Schine is about to consummate an illicit affair with a woman he has met on the train, the two are attacked, robbed, and assaulted at a motel, leaving Charles open for blackmail and his marriage in danger.

Clive Owen, Jennifer Aniston   PHOTOS COURTESY OF WEINSTEIN COMPANY

HARRY POTTER AND THE GOBLET OF FIRE

(WARNER BROS.) Producer, David Heyman; Executive Producers, David Barron, Tanya Seghatchian; Director, Mike Newell; Screenplay, Steve Kloves; Based on the novel by J. K. Rowling; Photography, Roger Pratt; Designer, Stuart Craig; Costumes, Jany Temime; Music, Patrick Doyle; Editor, Mick Audsley; Co-Producer, Peter MacDonald; Visual Effects Supervisor, Jim Mitchell; Casting, Mary Selway, Fiona Weir; a Heyday Films production; Dolby; JDC Widescreen; Technicolor; Rated PG-13; 157 minutes; Release date: November 18, 2005

Frances de la Tour, Beauxbaton Girls

Cast

Harry Potter **Daniel Radcliffe**
Ron Weasley **Rupert Grint**
Hermione Granger **Emma Watson**
Rubeus Hagrid **Robbie Coltrane**
Lord Voldemort **Ralph Fiennes**
Albus Dumbledore **Michael Gambon**
Alastor "Mad Eye" Moody **Brendan Gleeson**
Lucius Malfoy **Jason Isaacs**
Sirius Black **Gary Oldman**
Rita Skeeter **Miranda Richardson**
Severus Snape **Alan Rickman**
Minerva McGonagall **Maggie Smith**
Wormtail **Timothy Spall**
Barty Crouch **Roger Lloyd Pack**
Barty Crouch Junior **David Tennant**
Fred Weasley **James Phelps**
George Weasley **Oliver Phelps**
Amos Diggory **Jeff Rawle**
Cedric Diggory **Robert Pattinson**
Draco Malfoy **Tom Felton**
Viktor Krum **Stanislav Ianevski**
Cho Chang **Katie Leung**
Neville Longbottom **Matthew Lewis**
Argus Filch **David Bradley**
Filius Flitwick **Warwick Davis**

Daniel Radcliffe, Emma Watson, Miranda Richardson

Madame Olympe Maxime **Frances de la Tour**
Gabrielle Delacour **Clémence Poésy**
Moaning Myrtle **Shirley Henderson**
Frank Bryce **Eric Sykes**

and Mark Williams (Arthur Weasley), Bonnie Wright (Ginny Wealey), Robert Hardy (Cornelius Fudge), Philip Rham, Olivia Higginbottom, Ashley Artus, Alex Palmer, Paschal Friel, Richard "Rubber Ritchie" Rosson (Death Eaters), Sheila Allen, Su Elliot, Anne Lacy, Flip Webster (Ministry Witches), David Sterne, Christopher Whittingham, Liam McKenna, Campbell Graham (Ministry Wizards), Margery Mason (Food Trolley Lady), William Melling (Nigel), Devon Murray (Seamus Finnigan), Afshan Azad (Padma Patil), Shefali Chowdhury (Parvati Patil), Angelica Mandy (Gabrielle Delacour), Pedja Bjelac (Igor Karkaroff), Tolga Safer (Karkaroff's Aide), Alfie Enoch (Dean Thomas), Louis Doyle (Ernie MacMillan), Jamie Waylett (Vincent Crabbe), Josh Herdman (Gregory Goyle), Charlotte Skeoch (Hannah Abbott), Robert Wilfort (Photographer), Tiana Benjamin (Anglina Johnson), Henry Lloyd Hughes (Roger Davies), Jarvis Cocker (Band Lead Singer), Jonny Greenwood, Philip Selway, Steve Mackey, Jason Buckle, Steve Claydon (Band), Alan Watts (Assistant Judge), Adrian Rawlins (James Potter), Geraldine Somerville (Lily Potter)

Pedja Bjelac, Alan Rickman, Maggie Smith, Michael Gambon

Shefali Chowdhury, Daniel Radcliffe, Rupert Grint, Afshan Azad

Katie Leung

Brendan Gleeson

Robert Pattinson, Katie Leung

Rupert Grint

Rupert Grint, Emma Watson, Daniel Radcliffe

Against his wishes, Harry Potter is selected to participate in the dangerous Tri-Wizard tournament. The fourth film in the Warner Bros. series following *Harry Potter and the Sorcerer's Stone* (2001), *Harry Potter and the Chamber of Secrets* (2002), and *Harry Potter and the Prisoner of Azkaban* (2004), with most of the principals repeating their roles.

This film received an Oscar nomination for art direction.

Michael Gambon, Daniel Radcliffe

YOURS, MINE AND OURS

(PARAMOUNT/MGM/COLUMBIA) Producers, Robert Simonds, Michael Nathanson; Executive Producers, Ira Shuman, Richard Suckle; Director, Raja Gosnell; Screenplay, Ron Burch, David Kidd; Based on the 1968 motion picture screenplay by Melville Shavelson, Mort Lachman; Story, Madelyn Davis, Bob Carroll, Jr.; Photography, Theo Van De Sande; Designer, Linda DeScenna; Costumes, Marie-Sylvie Deveau; Music, Christophe Beck; Music Supervisor, Spring Aspers; Editors, Stephen A. Rotter, Bruce Green; Casting, Mary Vernieu, Shalimar Reodica; a Paramount Pictures, MGM, Nickelodeon Movies, Columbia Pictures presentation of a Robert Simonds production; Dolby; Color; Rated PG; 88 minutes; Release date: November 23, 2005

Rene Russo, Jessica Habib, Brecken Palmer, Ty Panitz, Nicholas Roget-King, Jennifer Habib, Bridger Palmer, Dennis Quaid

Rene Russo, Slade Pearce PHOTOS COURTESY OF PARAMOUNT

Rene Russo, Dennis Quaid

Cast

Frank Beardsley **Dennis Quaid**
Helen North **Rene Russo**
The Beardlsey Children:
William **Sean Faris**
Christina **Katija Pevec**
Harry **Dean Collins**
Michael **Tyler Patrick Jones**
Kelly **Haley Ramm**
Ely **Brecken Palmer**
Otter **Bridger Palmer**
Ethan **Ty Panitz**
The North Children:
Phoebe **Danielle Panabaker**
Dylan **Drake Bell**
Naoko **Miki Ishikawa**
Mick **Slade Pearce**
Jimi **Lil' JJ**
Joni **Miranda Cosgrove**
Lau **Andrew Vo**
Bina **Jennifer Habib**
Marisa **Jessica Habib**
Aldo **Nicholas Roget-King**

and Rip Torn (Commandant Sherman), Linda Hunt (Mrs. Munion), Jerry O'Connell (Max), David Koechner (Darrell), Jenica Bergere (Claudia), Josh Henderson (Nick De Pietro), Lisa Waltz (Reunion Classmate), Jimmy Bradley (Waiter), Mateo Arias, Jaelin Palmer, Connor Matheus, Jordan Wright (Bully Kids), Dan Mott (Pizza Delivery Guy), Rueben Grundy, Lisa Richman (Buyers), Beau Holden (Hardware Store Worker), Kirsten Gronfield (Bed Store Employee), Sydney Castillo (Helmsman), Ricky Fanté (Reunion Singer), Diane Woods Carter, Donna Taylor (Backup Singers), Jason Dunn, Aaron Tosti, Daniel Biro, Jonathan Steingard (Party Band, Hawk Nelson), Bradley Gosnell (School Jock)

Widowed Frank Beardsley and Helen North decide to marry, bringing their total number of kids to 18. Remake of the 1968 United Artists film which starred Lucille Ball and Henry Fonda.

Rene Russo, Jessica Habib, Miranda Cosgrove, Jennifer Habib, Lil' JJ, Slade Pearce, Andrew Vo, Drake Bell, Nicholas Roget-King, Miki Ishikawa, Danielle Panabaker

Chris Cooper, Jeffrey Wright

SYRIANA

(WARNER BROS.) Producers, Jennifer Fox, Michael Nozik, Georgia Kacandes; Executive Producers, George Clooney, Steven Soderbergh, Ben Cosgrove, Jeff Skoll; Director/Screenplay, Stephen Gaghan; Based on the book *See No Evil* by Robert Baer; Photography, Robert Elswit; Designer, Dan Weil; Costumes, Louise Frogley; Music, Alexandre Desplat; Editor, Tim Squyres; Casting, Lucinda Syson, Lora Kennedy, Avy Kaufman; a 4M Film, Section Eight production, presented in association with Participant Productions; Dolby; Color; Rated R; 128 minutes; Release date: November 23, 2005

Cast

Bob Barnes **George Clooney**
Bryan Woodman **Matt Damon**
Bennett Holiday **Jeffrey Wright**
Jimmy Pope **Chris Cooper**
Stan **William Hurt**
Wasim Khan **Mazhar Munir**
Danny Dalton **Tim Blake Nelson**
Julie Woodman **Amanda Peet**
Dean Whiting **Christopher Plummer**
Prince Nasir Al-Subaai **Alexander Siddig**
Prince Meshal Al-Subaai **Akbar Kurtha**

and Kayvan Kovak (Arash), Amr Waked (Mohammed Sheik Agiza), Robert Foxworth (Tommy Barton), Nicky Henson (Sydney Hewitt), Nicholas Art (Riley Woodman), Steven Hinkle (Max Woodman), Daisy Tormé (Rebecca), Peter Gerety (Leland Janus), Richard Lintern (Bryan's Boss), Jocelyn Quivrin (Vincent), Shahid Ahmed (Saleem Ahmed Khan), Bikram Singh Bhamra (Pakistani Translator), Roger Yuan (Chinese Engineer), Jayne Atkinson (Division Chief), Tom McCarthy (Fred Franks), Jamey Sheridan (Terry), Randall Boffman, Tony French (Distinguished Gentlemen), Max Minghella (Robby Barnes), Katie Foster (Nervous Daughter), Nadim Sawalha (Emir Hamed Al-Subaai), Ozzie Yue (Chinese Oil Executive), Sonell Dadral (Farooq), Jon Lee Anderson (Himself), Othman Bin Hendi (Arab Businessman), Bashar H. Atiyat (Nasir's Aide), Ali Al Amine (Older Kid at Pool), William C. Mitchell (Bennett Holiday, Sr.), Ahmed Aa Mohammed (Abu Khalifa), Ahmed Ayoub, Mohammed Asad Khan (Pakistani Teenagers), Atta Mohammed Saleh (Old Man), Aziz Zacca (Policeman), David Clennon (Donald), Omar Mostafa (The Cleric), Said Amadis (Reza Reyhani), David J. Manners (Egypt Bureau Chief), Jamil Jabbar (Supplicant), Badria Timimi (Nasir's Wife), Mohammed Majd (Said Hossein Hashimi), Mark Strong (Mussawi), Driss Roukhe (Guard), Katherine Hoskins Mackey, Linda E. Williams, Susan Allenbach, William L. Thomas (Paralegals), El Mahjoub Raji (Hashmi's Man), Michael Stone Forrest, Bob Baer (CIA Security Officers), Fritz Michel (Hotel Security Guard), Bob Fajkowski (Secretary of Defense), Jeff Baker (Tommy's Lawyer), Tarik Tamzali (Nasir's Secretary), Mitesh Soni (Martyr), Tootsie Duvall (Assistant at CIA), Nabeel Noman (Bedouin Leader), Ryan Murphy (Drone Tech), Will McCormack (Willy), Donna Mitchell (Pat Janus), James Plannette (Connex Functionary), Michael Allinson (Sir David)

An unexpected merger between two powerful oil companies hoping to gain a position in the Middle East leads to deception and tragedy.

2005 Academy Award winner for Best Supporting Actor (George Clooney). This film received an additional Oscar nomination for original screenplay.

Matt Damon, Amanda Peet

Tim Blake Nelson

Mark Strong, George Clooney PHOTOS COURTESY OF WARNER BROS.

Wilson Jermaine Heredia

Taye Diggs, Anthony Rapp, Adam Pascal

Tracie Thoms, Anthony Rapp

RENT

(COLUMBIA) Producers, Jane Rosenthal, Robert De Niro, Chris Columbus, Mark Radcliffe, Michael Barnathan; Executive Producers, Jeffrey Seller, Kevin McCollum, Allan S. Gordon, Lata Ryan; Co-Executive Producer, Tom Sherak; Co-Producer, Julie Larson; Director, Chris Columbus; Screenplay, Stephen Chbosky; Based on the musical with book, music and lyrics by Jonathan Larson; Song/Music Producer/Arranger, Rob Cavallo; Music Supervisor, Matt Sullivan; Vocal Conductor/Additional Arranger, Tim Weil; Choreographer, Keith Young; Editor, Richard Pearson; Photography, Stephen Goldblatt; Designer, Howard Cummings; Costumes, Aggie Guerard Rodgers; Casting, Bernard Telsey; a Revolution Studios presentation in association with 1492 Pictures of a Tribeca Production; Dolby; Panavision; Deluxe color; Rated PG-13; 136 minutes; Release date: November 23, 2005

Anthony Rapp, Idina Menzel

Rosario Dawson, Adam Pascal

Cast

Mark Cohen **Anthony Rapp**
Roger Davis **Adam Pascal**
Mimi Marquez **Rosario Dawson**
Tom Collins **Jesse L. Martin**
Angel Dumott Schunard **Wilson Jermaine Heredia**
Maureen Johnson **Idina Menzel**
Joanne Jefferson **Tracie Thoms**
Benjamin Coffin III **Taye Diggs**
Rent Tenants **Julia Roth, Porscha Radcliffe**
Homeless Squeegee Man **Stephen Payne**
Thugs **Darryl Chan, Ken Clark, R. C. Ormond**
Homeless Man on Range Rover **David Fine**
April **Mackenzie Firgens**
The Man **Jason Foster**
Paul **Daniel London**
Steve **Aaron Lohr**
Gordon **Wayne Wilcox**
Ali **Bianca Sams**
Pam **Heather Barberie**
Sue **Liisa Cohen**

Adam Pascal, Anthony Rapp PHOTOS COURTESY OF COLUMBIA

and Sharon Ferrol-Young, Liz Ramos, Kristin Medwick, Katie Weber, Angela McConnell, Feleciana Stevenson, Kim Williams (Cat Scratch Floor Dancers), Damia Foti, Laura Padierne (Cat Scratch Waitresses), Kevin Hagan, Brian Delate (Cops), Aisha de Haas (Blanket Woman), Marco De La Cruz, Erika Harden, Truc Long (Subway Passengers), Chris Chalk (Street Vendor Who Sells Coats), Cory Duval, Clarke Devereaux (Riot Cops), Corey Rosen (Life Cafe Manger), Shaun Earl (Life Cafe Waiter), Matthew Dickens, Tara Nicole Hughes, Troy Christian, Gigi Hunter, Kevin Stea, Robert Prescott Lee, Sebastien Poffet, Linda Cevallos, Roosevelt Flenoury (Bohemians)

Wilson Jermaine Heredia, Jesse L. Martin

Tracie Thoms, Idina Menzel

A group of bohemians living in New York's Alphabet City struggle against poverty, AIDS, and imperfect relationships as they try to express themselves through their art. Rapp, Pascal, Diggs, Menzel, Martin, and Heredia repeat their roles from the original 1996 Broadway production.

THE ICE HARVEST

(FOCUS) Producers, Albert Berger, Ron Yerxa; Executive Producers, Robert Benton, Richard Russo, Glenn Williamson; Director, Harold Ramis; Screenplay, Richard Russo, Robert Benton; Based on the novel by Scott Phillips; Photography, Alar Kivilo; Designer, Patrizia von Brandenstein; Costumes, Susan Kaufmann; Music, David Kitay; Editor, Lee Percy; Casting, Jeanne McCarthy; a Bona Fide production; Dolby; Rated R; 88 minutes; Release date: November 23, 2005

Cast

Charlie Arglist **John Cusack**
Vic Cavanaugh **Billy Bob Thornton**
Renata **Connie Nielsen**
Rusti **Lara Phillips**
Culligan **Bill Noble**
Bill Guerrard **Randy Quaid**
Pete Van Heuten **Oliver Platt**
Ronny **Brad Smith**
Sidney **Ned Bellamy**
Roy **Mike Starr**
Officer Tyler **T. J. Jagodowski**
Francie **Meghan Maureen McDonough**
Dennis **Tab Baker**
Restauranteur **Frank Gallo**
Manager **William Dick**
Councilman Williams **David Pasquesi**

Billy Bob Thornton, John Cusack

Oliver Platt, John Cusack

Mob lawyer Charlie Arglist and pornographer Vic Cavanaugh steal $2 million from a powerful mob boss only to have trouble leaving ice-covered Wichita on Christmas Eve.

Billy Bob Thornton, John Cusack

and Laura Whyte (Dottie), Steve King (Stan), Justine Bentley (Sarabeth), Max Kirsch (Spencer), Shana Goodsell (Christian Girl), Mick Napier (Stroke), Lindsay Porter (Gladys), Brendan Donaldson (Clerk), Shelby Hyman (Shelby), Meredith Maresh (Pearl), Matthew Campobasso, Lori Ann Gerdisch (Bar Patrons), Diana Frances Fisher (Lounge Patron), Michael Kilcullen (Restaurant Busboy), Michael Stailey (Restaurant Patron), Jenny Wade (Cupcake)

Connie Nielsen, Randy Quaid PHOTOS COURTESY OF FOCUS FEATURES

Anna Faris, Christopher Marquette

Amy Smart, Ty Olsson, Ryan Reynolds

Ryan Reynolds, Amy Smart, Julie Hagerty PHOTOS COURTESY OF NEW LINE CINEMA

JUST FRIENDS

(NEW LINE CINEMA) Producers, Chris Bender, JC Spink, Michael Ohoven, William Vince, Bill Johnson; Executive Producers, Toby Emmerich, Richard Brener, Cale Boyter, Marco Mehlitz; Director, Roger Kumble; Screenplay, Adam "Tex" Davis; Photography, Anthony B. Richmond; Designer, Robb Wilson King; Costumes, Alexandra Welker; Music, Jeff Cardoni; Music Supervisor, Patrick Houlihan; Editor, Jeff Freeman; Casting, Rick Montgomery; a Benderspink and Cinezeta production in association with Inferno Distribution, presented in association with Cinerenta; Rated PG-13; 94 minutes; Release date: November 23, 2005

Chris Klein, Amy Smart

Cast

Chris Brander **Ryan Reynolds**
Jamie Palamino **Amy Smart**
Samantha James **Anna Faris**
Carol Brander **Julie Hagerty**
Mike Brander **Christopher Marquette**
KC **Stephen Root**
Clark **Fred Ewanuick**
Dusty Dinkleman **Chris Klein**
Tim **Ty Olsson**
Darla **Amy Matysio**
Mr. Palamino **Barry Flatman**
Athena **Maria Arcé**

and James Bitoni (Bouncer), Annie Brebner (Sarah), Jason Bryant (Customer), Simon Chin (Sound Engineer), Cavan Cunningham (Ron, Record Producer), Owen Gieni (Bartender), Mircea Monroe (Betty), Jaden Ryan (Joey), Sky Brandon (Toady), Robin Dunne (Ray), Ashley Scott (Nurse Janice), Mike Simpson (Preacher)

A once-overweight high schooler, who has since slimmed down and made a killing in the music business, gets the chance to woo the once-popular girl whom he once desired.

AEON FLUX

(PARAMOUNT) Producers, Gale Anne Hurd, David Gale, Gary Lucchesi, Greg Goodman, Martha Griffin; Executive Producers, Tom Rosenberg, Van Toffler; Director, Karyn Kusama; Screenplay, Phil Hay, Matt Manfredi; Based on characters created by Peter Chung; Photography, Stuart Dryburgh; Designer, Andrew McAlpine; Costumes, Beatrix Aruna Pasztor; Music, Graeme Revell; Editors, Peter Honess, Plummy Tucker, Jeff Gullo; Visual Effects Supervisors, Jonathan Rothbart, Colin Strause, Greg Strause, Matthew Gratznere, David Sosalla, Scott Rader, Syd Dutton, Bill Taylor; Stunts, Charlie Croughwell; Casting, Laura Rosenthal, Karen Lindsay Stewart; a Lakeshore Entertainment presentation of a Valhalla Motion Pictures, MTV Films production; Dolby; Arri Widescreen; Deluxe color; Rated PG-13; 92 minutes; Release date: December 2, 2005

Charlize Theron

Sophie Okonedo

Marton Csokas, Jonny Lee Miller

Frances McDormand

Cast

Aeon Flux **Charlize Theron**
Trevo Goodchild **Marton Csokas**
Oren Goodchild **Jonny Lee Miller**
Sithandra **Sophie Okonedo**
Handler **Frances McDormand**
Keeper **Pete Postlethwaite**
Una Flux **Amelia Warner**
Freya **Caroline Chikezie**
Claudius **Nikolai Kinski**

and Paterson Joseph (Giroux), Yangzom Brauen (Inari), Aoibheann O'Hara, Thomas Huber, Weijian Liu (Scientists), Maverick Quek (Chemist), Ralph Herforth (Gardener), Megan Gay (Weaver), Rainer Will (Commander Puhl), Charlie Beall (Lt. Ord), Bruno Bruni (Armory Soldier), Ronald Marx (Bregnan Police Captain), Axel Schreiber (Policeman), Katie Mullins (Neighbor), Shaun Lawton (Man in Marketplace), Terry Bartlett, Betty Okino (Monican Spies), Anatole Taubman (Sasha Prillo's Father), Lavinia Wilson (Sasha Prillo's Mother), Khira Lilli Pobanz (Sasha Prillo), William Morts (Guard), Phil Hay (Soldier), Nils Dommning (Young Trevor), Bojan Heyn (Young Oren), Justin Schierlo (Boy at Wall), Marianne Sonneck (Boy's Mother), Joost Siedhoof, Tamara Röhl (Criers), Narges Rashidi (Pregnant Woman), Claas Würfel (Husband), Robin Gooch (Doctor), Anna De Carlo (Bregnan Victim), Martha Fessehatzion (Checkpoint Woman), Milton Welsh, Mehmet Yilmaz (Monican Men), Alex Benjamin, Natacza Boon, Clio Burggraeve, Alexander Flache, Lilja Löffler, Kim Pfeiffer, Michael Pink, Joachim Schönfeld (Monorail Passengers)

In the year 2415, when most of the Earth's population has been wiped out by a virus and the remaining citizens are ruled with military force, rebel assassin Aeon Flux seeks revenge for the government sanctioned murder of her sister.

Charlize Theron, Amelia Warner PHOTOS COURTESY OF PARAMOUNT

Kevin Zegers, Felicity Huffman

Felicity Huffman, Graham Greene

Felicity Huffman, Kevin Zegers PHOTOS COURTESY OF WEINSTEIN COMPANY

TRANSAMERICA

(WEINSTEIN CO.) Producers, Linda Moran, Rene Bastian, Sebastian Dungan; Executive Producer, William H. Macy; Director/Screenplay, Duncan Tucker; Photography, Stephen Kazmierski; Designer, Mark White; Costumes, Danny Glicker; Music, David Mansfield; Music Supervisor, Doug Bernheim; Song: "Travelin' Thru" by Dolly Parton; Editor, Pam Wise; Casting, Eva Battaglia; a Belladonna production; Dolby; Color; Super 16mm-to-35mm; Rated R; 103 minutes; Release date: December 2, 2005

Kevin Zegers, Felicity Huffman

Cast

Bree **Felicity Huffman**
Toby **Kevin Zegers**
Elizabeth **Fionnula Flanagan**
Margaret **Elizabeth Peña**
Calvin **Graham Greene**
Murray **Burt Young**
Sydney **Carrie Preston**
Arletty **Venida Evans**
Alex **Jon Budinoff**
Bobby Jensen **Raynor Scheine**
Hitchhiker **Grant Monohon**
Mary Ellen **Bianca Leigh**
Dr. Spikowsky **Danny Burstein**
Voice Coach **Andrea James**
Fernando **Maurice Orozco**

and Paul Borghese (NYC Cop), Kate Bayley (Tennessee Waitress), Stella Maeve (Taylor), Teala Dunn (Little Girl), Jim Frangione (Taylor's Father), Calpernia Addams (Calpernia), Forrie Smith (Sammy), Elayne Stein (Phoenix Lady), Amy Povich (Phoenix Cop), Matt Young (Wayne), Barbara Hubbard Barron (Ms. Swallow), Richard Poe (John)

Bree, a pre-operative transsexual, springs from jail the son she never knew she had, and journeys west with the lad who has no idea that "she" is a "he," let alone his father.

This film received Oscar nominations for actress (Felicity Huffman) and song ("Travelin' Thru").

Aslan, Skandar Keynes

Anna Popplewell

THE CHRONICLES OF NARNIA: THE LION, THE WITCH AND THE WARDROBE

(WALT DISNEY PICTURES) Producers, Mark Johnson, Philip Steuer; Executive Producers, Andrew Adamson, Perry Moore; Director, Andrew Adamson; Screenplay, Ann Peacock, Andrew Adamson, Christopher Markus, Stephen McFeely; Photography, Donald M. McAlpine; Designer, Roger Ford; Costumes, Isis Mussenden; Music, Harry Gregson-Williams; Editors, Sim Evan-Jones, Jim May; Co-Producer, Douglas Gresham; Visual Effects Supervisor, Dean Wright; Special Visual Effects/Animation, Sony Pictures Imageworks, Industrial Light & Magic; Casting, Pippa Hall, Gail Stevens; a Walden Media presentation of a Mark Johnson production; Dolby; Panavision; Technicolor; Rated PG; 136 minutes; Release date: December 9, 2005

Cast

Lucy Pevensie **Georgie Henley**
Edmund Pevensie **Skandar Keynes**
Peter Pevensie **William Moseley**
Susan Pevensie **Anna Popplewell**
White Witch **Tilda Swinton**
Mr. Tumnus **James McAvoy**
Professor Kirke **Jim Broadbent**

Georgie Henley, James McAvoy

Ginarrbrik **Kiran Shah**
Father Christmas **James Cosmo**
Mrs. Pevensie **Judy McIntosh**
Mrs. MacReady **Elizabeth Hawthorne**
Oreius **Patrick Kake**
General Otmin **Shane Rangi**
Voice of Aslan **Liam Neeson**
Voice of Mr. Beaver **Ray Winstone**
Voice of Mrs. Beaver **Dawn French**
Voice of Mr. Fox **Rupert Everett**
Voice of Gryphon **Cameron Rhodes**
Voice of Philip the Horse **Philip Steuer**
Voice of Vardan **Jim May**
Voice of Wolf **Sim Evan-Jones**

and Brandon Cook (Boy on Train), Cassie Cook (Girl on Train), Morris Lupton (Train Conductor), Shelley Edwards-Bishop, Susan Haldane, Margaret Bremner (Mothers), Jaxin Hall (Soldier), Terry Murdoch (German Pilot), Katrina Browne (Green Dryad), Lee Tuson (Rumblebuff the Giant), Elizabeth Kirk, Felicity Hamill, Kate O'Rourke, Sonya Hitchcock, Lucy Tanner, Tiggy Mathias (Hags), Greg Cooper, Richard King, Russell Pickering (Fauns), Ben Barrington, Charles Williams, Vanessa Cater, Allison Sarofim (Centaurs), Alina Phelan (Centaur Archer), Stephen Ure,

Jim Broadbent

Kiran Shah, Tilda Swinton

Sam Lahood (Satyrs), Ajay Ratilal Navi, Bhoja Kannada, Zakiuddin Mohd, Farooque, M. Ramaswami, Prapaphorn Chansantor, Nikhom Nusungnern, Doungdieo Savangvong (Red & Black Dwarfs), Rachael Henley (Lucy, Older), Mark Wells (Edmund, Older), Noah Huntley (Peter, Older), Sophie Winkleman (Susan, Older)

Skandar Keynes, William Moseley

Mr. and Mrs. Beaver

Sent away from London to live with Professor Kirke for the endurance of the war, the four Pevensie children stumble upon a wardrobe that magically opens into the wintry world of Narnia, ruled by the evil White Witch.

This film received Oscar nominations for visual effects, makeup, and sound.

Georgie Henley PHOTOS COURTESY OF WALT DISNEY PICTURES

Jake Gyllenhaal, Heath Ledger, Michelle Williams

Jake Gyllenhaal

Jake Gyllenhaal, Anne Hathaway

BROKEBACK MOUNTAIN

(FOCUS) Producers, Diana Ossana, James Schamus; Executive Producers, William Pohlad, Larry McMurtry, Michael Costigan, Michael Hausman, Alberta Film Entertinament; Co-Producer, Scott Ferguson; Director, Ang Lee; Screenplay, Larry McMutry, Diana Ossana; Based on the short story by Annie Proulx; Photography, Rodrigo Pietro; Designer, Judy Becker; Costumes, Marit Allen; Music, Gustavo Santaolalla; Music Supervisor, Kathy Nelson; Casting, Avy Kaufman; a River Road presentation; Dolby; Deluxe color; Rated R; 134 minutes; Release date: December 9, 2005

Cast

Ennis Del Mar **Heath Ledger**
Jack Twist **Jake Gyllenhaal**
Cassie **Linda Cardellini**
Lashawn Malone **Anna Faris**
Lureen Newsome **Anne Hathaway**
Alma **Michelle Williams**
Joe Aguirre **Randy Quaid**
L. D. Newsome **Graham Beckel**
Monroe **Scott Michael Campbell**
Randall Malone **David Harbour**

Heath Ledger, Michelle Williams

Jake Gyllenhaal, Heath Ledger

Alma Jr., Age 19 **Kate Mara**
Jack's Mother **Roberta Maxwell**
John Twist **Peter McRobbie**
Basque **David Trimble**
Jolly Minister **Larry Reese**
Timmy **Marty Antonini**
Bikers **Don Bland, Steven Cree Molison**
Announcer **Duval Lang**
Bartenders **Dan McDougall, Dean Barrett**
Alma Jr., Age 3 **Hannah Stewart**
Fayette Newsome **Mary Liboiron**
Jenny, Age 4 **Brooklynn Proulx**

and James Baker, Pete Seadon (Farmers), Sarah Hyslop (Alma Jr., Age 9–12), Jerry Callaghan (Judge), Cheyenne Hill (Alma Jr., Age 13), Ken Zilka, John Tench (Roughnecks), Will Martin (Carl), Gary Lauder (Killer Mechanic), Christian Fraser (Grease Monkey), Cam Sutherland (Assailant), Tom Carey (Rodeo Clown), Valerie Planche (Waitress), Victor Reyes, Lachlan Mackintosh (Chilean Sheepherders), Kade Philps (Ennis, Age 9), Steffen Cole Moser (K.E. Del Mar, Age 11), Keanna Dubé (Alma Jr., Age 5), Jacey Kenny (Jenny, Age 7–8), Cayla Wolever (Jenny, Age 11), Jake Church (Booby, Age 10).

Anne Hathaway

While herding sheep on Brokeback Mountain, Ennis Del Mar and Jack Twist find themselves releasing pent-up passions and become lovers, a secret they try to hide as they go about leading separate lives for the next two decades.

2005 Academy Award winner for Best Director, Adapted Screenplay, and Original Score. This film received additional Oscar nominations for picture, actor (Heather Ledger), supporting actor (Jake Gyllenhaal), supporting actress (Michelle Williams) and cinematography.

Heath Ledger, Jake Gyllenhaal

Michelle Williams

Heath Ledger PHOTOS COURTESY OF FOCUS FEATURES

MEMOIRS OF A GEISHA

(COLUMBIA/DREAMWORKS) Producers, Lucy Fisher, Douglas Wick, Steven Spielberg; Executive Producers, Roger Birnbaum, Gary Barber, Patricia Whitcher, Bobby Cohen; Director, Rob Marshall; Screenplay, Robin Swicord; Based on the book by Arthur Golden; Co-Producer, John DeLuca; Photography, Dione Beebe; Designer, John Myhre; Costumes, Colleen Atwood; Music, John Williams; Cello Solos, Yo-Yo Ma; Violin Solos, Itzak Perlman; Editor, Pietro Scalia; Casting, Francine Maisler; a Spyglass Entertainment presentation of an Amblin Entertainment/Red Wagon Entertainment production; Dolby; Panavision; Deluxe color; Rated PG-13; 140 minutes; Release date: December 9, 2005

Ken Watanabe, Suzuka Ohgo

Ziyi Zhang, Michelle Yeoh, Gong Li

Cast

Sayuri **Ziyi Zhang**
The Chairman **Ken Watanabe**
Mameha **Michelle Yeoh**
Nobu **Koji Yakusho**
Pumpkin **Youki Kudoh**
Mother **Kaori Momoi**
Auntie **Tsai Chin**
The Baron **Cary-Hiroyuki Tagawa**
Chiyo **Suzuka Ohgo**
Hatsumomo **Gong Li**
Young Pumpkin **Zoe Weizenbaum**
Mr. Bekku **Thomas Ikeda**
Tanaka **Togo Igawa**
Sakamoto **Mako**
Satsu **Samantha Futerman**
Sakamoto's Wife **Elizabeth Sung**

and David Okihiro (Shamisen Teacher), Miyako Tachibana (Dance Teacher), Kotoko Kawamura (Granny), Yune (Koichi Karl), Eugenia Yuan (Korin), Yoko Narahashi (Mameha's Maid), Kenneth Tsang (The General), Navia Nguyen (Geisha in Green), Natsuo Tomita (Geisha in Lavender), Fumi Akutagawa (Yukimoto Teahouse Matron), Koji Toyoda (Hairdresser), Steve Terada (Boy on Bike), Laura Miro, Diane Mizota (Yukimoto Teahouse Geisha), Yasusuke Uike (Sumo Referee), Shuhei Nagao (Small Sumo Wrestler), Kiyoshi Sugawa (Large Sumo Wrestler), Koji Yakusho (Nobu), Ren Urano (Sumo Ring Announcer), Ace Yonamine, Anthony

Begonia, Albert Lee, Dino Rivera (Sumo Wrestlers), Randall Duk Kim (Dr. Crab), Takayo Fischer (Tanizato Teahouse Owner), Asako Takasue (Tanizato Teahouse Matron), Clarissa Park (Dancer at Party), Nobuyuki Matsuhia (Kimono Artist), Jim Leung (Kimono Factory Worker), Chad Cleven, Richard J. Bell, Cameron Duncan (Drunken G.I.s), Faith Shin (Little Kiko), Brannon Bates (Military Police Officer), Ted Levine (Col. Derricks), Paul Adelstein (Lt. Hutchins), Shizuko Hoshi (Sayuri Narration), Michelle Camaya, Janelle Dote, Kim Hazel, Ashia Meyers, Laura Miro, Shiho Miyazawa, Diane Mizota, Minae Noji, Mami Saito, Kiyoka Miyazaki (Spring Festival Dancers), Shannon Abero, Kiyoko Ando, Miki Fujita, Chieko Hidaka, Wendy Lam, Kana Miyamoto, Brooke Miyasaki, Nao Nojima, Shelly Oto, Nikki Tuazon, Addie Yungmee (Willow Fan Dancers), Cassidy Adams, Celena Ahn, Allison Chan, Deziree Del Rosario, Emilie Endow, Rosie Endow, Emma Fusako Ishii, Hannah Hwang, Amy Saki Kawakami, Stefani Lee, Teanna Lee, Melissa Morinishi, Michelle Obi, Kasey Okazaki, Jacqueline Osaki, Ayaka Oyama, Jade Refuerzo, Meng Shi, Stacy Suzuki, Miwa Tachibana, Jordan Tamabra, Shaye Uyematsu (Student Dancers), Etsuo Hongo, Tateo Takahashi, Maza Yoshizawa (Shamisen Musicians)

Taken from her parents as a child, Sayuri grows up to become a legendary geisha, captivating countless men while always haunted by the one man out of her reach.

2005 Academy Award winner for Best Cinematography, Costume Design, and Art Direction. This film received additional nominations for original score, sound, and sound editing.

Koji Yakusho, Ken Watanabe PHOTOS COURTESY OF COLUMBIA

THE THREE BURIALS
OF MELQUIADES ESTRADA

(SONY CLASSICS) Producers, Michael Fitzgerald, Luc Besson, Pierre-Ange Le Pogam, Tommy Lee Jones; Director, Tommy Lee Jones; Screenplay, Guillermo Arriaga; Photography, Chris Menges; Designer, Merideth Boswell; Costumes, Kathleen Kiatta; Music, Marco Beltrami; Editor, Roberto Silvi; Casting, Jeanne McCarthy, Jo Edna Boldin (Texas), Manuel Teil (Mexico); a EuropaCorp, Javelina Film Company presentation; U.S.-French; Dolby; Panavision; Deluxe color; Rated R; 121 minutes; Release date: December 14, 2005

Barry Pepper, Tommy Lee Jones

Julio Cesar Cedillo, Tommy Lee Jones

Melissa Leo

Rosa **Cecilia Suarez**
Lucio **Ignacio Guadalupe**
Mariana **Vanessa Bauche**
Manuel **Irineo Alvarez**
Juan **Guillermo Arriaga**
Border Patrolman **Josh Berry**
Salesman **Rodger Boyce**
Don Casimiro **René Campero**

and Jorge Adrián Espíndola, Uriel Chávez (Cowboys), Sonny Carl Davis (Kruger), Maya Zapata, Montserrat de León (El Toston Women), Jesse De Luna (Miller), Jesse De Luna (Miller), Richard Dillard (Jim), Jourdan Henderson (Mary, Soap Opera Girl), Sean Hennigan (Chuck), Karen Jones (Dog Lady), Richard Jones (Bob), Victoria Jones (Immigrant Girl), Lonnie Nelson (Gravedigger), Juan Gabriel Pareja (Sands Guy #1), Terry Parks (Neil), Gustavo Sánchez Parra (Tomas), Hugo Pérez (Man), Charles Sanders (Doctor), Brent Smiga (Deputy Antonio), Spike Spencer (John, Soap Opera), Angelina Torres (Adriana), Barry Tubb (A. L.), Guillermo Von Son (Chino), Gabriel Olds (Ed)

Pete Perkins forces the Border Patrol guard who killed his best friend, Melquiades Estrada, to transport the body into Mexico in order to bury Estrada according to his wishes.

Tommy Lee Jones PHOTOS COURTESY OF SONY CLASSICS

Cast
Pete Perkins **Tommy Lee Jones**
Mike Norton **Barry Pepper**
Melquiades Estrada **Julio Cesar Cedillo**
Belmont **Dwight Yoakam**
Lou Ann Norton **January Jones**
Rachel **Melissa Leo**
Old Man with Radio **Levon Helm**
Captain Gomez **Mel Rodriguez**

Jack Black, John Sumner

KING KONG

(UNIVERSAL) Producers, Jan Blenkin, Carolynne Cunningham, Fran Walsh, Peter Jackson; Co-Producer, Philippa Boyens; Director, Peter Jackson; Screenplay, Fran Walsh, Philippa Boyens, Peter Jackson; Based on a story by Merian C. Cooper, Edgar Wallace; Photography, Andrew Lesnie; Designer, Grant Major; Costumes, Terry Ryan; Music, James Newton Howard; Editors, Jamie Selkirk, Jabez Olssen; Special Makeup/Creatures/Miniatures, Richard Taylor; Senior Visual Effects Supervisor, Joe Letteri; Casting, Liz Mullane, Victoria Burrows, John Hubbard, Dan Hubbard, Ann Robinson; Stunts, Shane Dawson, Chris Anderson, Kirk Maxwell; a Wingnut Films production; Dolby; Color; Rated PG-13; 187 minutes; Release date: December 14, 2005

Cast

Ann Darrow **Naomi Watts**
Carl Denham **Jack Black**
Jack Driscoll **Adrien Brody**
Captain Englehorn **Thomas Kretschmann**
Preston **Colin Hanks**
Kong/Lumpy **Andy Serkis**
Hayes **Evan Parke**
Jimmy **Jamie Bell**
Choy **Lobo Chan**
Herb **John Sumner**
Mike **Craig Hall**
Bruce **Kyle Chandler**
Manny **Willians Johnson**
Harry **Mark Hadlow**
Maude **Geraldine Brophy**
Taps **David Denis**
Weston **David Pittu**
Zelman **Pip Mushin**

and Jim Knobeloch (Thuggish Studio Guy), Ric Herbert (Sleazy Studio Guy), Lee Donahue (Studio Guy's Assistant), Tom Hobbs (Young Assistant), Tiriel Mora (Fruit Vendor), Lee Hartley (Venture Radio Operator), Ray Woolf (Venture Helmsman), Jed Brophy, Frank Edwards, Michael Lawrence, Crawford Thompson, Richard Kavanagh, Stephen Hall, William Wallace, Joe Folau, Tim Wong, Steve Reinsfield, John

Naomi Watts

Wraight, Matthew Chamberlain, Troy O'Kane, Louis Sutherland, Jason Whyte, Toa Waaka, John Clarke, David Dengelo, Greg Smith, Chris Bailey, Peter McKenzie, Peter Ford, Tamihana Nuku, Russell Dubois (Venture Crew), Phillip Grieve (Laughing Man), Vicky Haughton (Sharwoman), Jacinta Wawatai (Feral Child), Terence Griffiths (Skull Islander), Stephen Buckley (Cab Driver), Chic Littlewood (Old Security Guard), Rick Baker, Jim Dietz, Rodney Cook, Gene De Marco (Pilots), John Dybvig (Policeman), Tim Gordon (Hotel Clerk), Lee McDonald (Chorus Line Tap Dancer), Stig Eldred (Army Commander), Billy Jackson, Katie Jackson (NY Children), Tania Rodger, Samuel Taylor (Hooverville Mother & Child), Bob Burns, Kathy Burns, Jo Gertler, Jennifer Gertler (NY Standers), Geoff Timblick, Geoff Allen (Pressmen), Belindalee Hope, Crushanin Dixor-McIvor, Jodie Taylor (Burlesque Dancers), Hilton Denis, Geoff Dunstain,

Naomi Watts, Kong

Kong

Andy Serkis

Daniel Tusia, Paul & Shannon Wilson, Jesse Rasmussen, Sosina Wogayehu, Peter Corrigan, Collin Boggars, Susan Eastwood, Carol Dallas, Darryl John, Felicia O'Brien (Vaudeville Acts), Peter Jackson, Rick Porras, Frank Darabont, Hamish Bruce (Gunners), Latham Gaines (Photographer), Julia Walshaw (Broadway Ann), Luanne Gordon, Lorraine Ashbourne, Edwin Wright, Glen Drake (Theatre Actors), Lawrence Jarden (NY Police Chief), Ross Duncan (Audience Member), Jim McLarty, Matt Wilson (Photographers)

Adrien Brody, Jamie Bell, Evan Parke

Jack Black, Thomas Kretschmann

Obsessed filmmaker Carl Denham charts a ship to the mysterious Skull Island where he and his crew encounter a gigantic gorilla who takes a shine to Denham's leading lady. Remake of the 1933 RKO film which starred Fay Wray, Robert Armstrong, and Bruce Cabot, and of the 1976 Paramount film which starred Jeff Bridges, Jessica Lange, and Charles Grodin.

Naomi Watts, Adrien Brody

2005 Academy Award winner for Best Visual Effects, Sound, and Sound Editing. This film received an additional nomination for art direction.

Kyle Chandler PHOTOS COURTESY OF UNIVERSAL

Matthew Broderick, Will Ferrell, Nathan Lane

Nathan Lane, Uma Thurman

Matthew Broderick, Jon Lovitz

THE PRODUCERS

(UNIVERSAL/COLUMBIA) Producers, Mel Brooks, Jonathan Sanger; Director/Choreographer, Susan Stroman; Screenplay, Mel Brooks, Thomas Meehan; Based on their stage musical, from the screenplay of Brooks' film *The Producers*; Photography, John Bailey, Charles Minsky; Designer, Mark Friedberg; Costumes, William Ivey Long; Co-Producer, Amy Herman; Music/Lyrics, Mel Brooks; Associate Producer, Leah Zappy; Music Conductor/Supervisor, Patrick S. Brady; Orchestrations, Doug Besterman; Casting, Tara Rubin; a Brooksfilms production; Dolby; Panavision; Technicolor; Rated PG-13; 134 minutes; Release date: December 16, 2005

Nathan Lane, Matthew Broderick

Cast
Max Bialystock/Alvin's Mother **Nathan Lane**
Leo Bloom **Matthew Broderick**
Ulla **Uma Thurman**
Franz Liebkind **Will Ferrell**
Roger De Bris **Gary Beach**
Carmen Ghia **Roger Bart**
Hold Me-Touch Me **Eileen Essell**
Prison Trustee **Michael McKean**
Judge **David Huddleston**
Lick Me-Bite Me **Debra Monk**
Kiss Me-Feel Me **Andrea Martin**
Mr. Marks **Jon Lovitz**

and Bryn Dowling, Meg Gillentine (Usherettes), Kevin Ligon, Mike McGowan (Workmen), Ray Wills (Bum), Marilyn Sokol (Bag Lady), Brad Oscar (Cab Driver), Tory Ross (Misfit Showgirl), Brent Barrett (Brian the Set Designer), Peter Bartlett (Kevin the Costume Designer), Jim Borstelmann (Scott the Choreographer), Kathy Fitzgerald (Shirley Markowitz), Jai Rodriguez (Sabu the Houseboy), Mike Jackson (Injun Jack), Keith Kuhl (First Mate Kyle), Keith Lamelle Thomas (Patrolman Pete), Roland Rusinek (Jack Lapidus), Jim Borstelmann (Donald Dinsmore), Jason Antoon (Jason Green), Madeleine Doherty (Mildred the Audition Accompanyist), Jonathan Freeman (Ticket Taker), Timothy Gulan (Gunter), Patrick S. Brady (Conductor), John Barrowman (Lead Tenor),

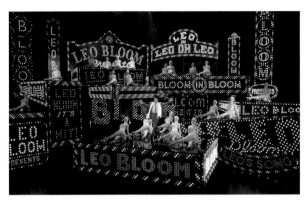

Matthew Broderick (center)

Gary Beach, Roger Bart

Nathan Lane, Matthew Broderick

Michael McCormick (Mr. Shocked), Susann Fletcher (Mrs. Bewildered), Michael Thomas Holmes (Stormtrooper Rolf), Ronn Carroll (Stormtrooper Mel), Ruth Williamson (Snooty Woman), John C. Vennema (Stuffy Man), Fred Applegate (Officer O'Toole), Jerry Richardson (Officer O'Reilly), Timothy Shew (Officer O'Rourke), Danny Mastrogiorgio (Jail Guard), Richard Kind (Jury Foreman), John Deyle (Juror), Naomi Kakuk (Stenographer), Thomas Meehan (Max's Attorney), Brian Rogalski, Jimmy Smagula (Convicts), James Biberi (Sing Sing Prison Guard), Mel Brooks (Hilda the Pigeon/Tom the Cat/Voice of Stormtrooper Mel/Himself), Rachel Montez Collins, John Treacy Egan, Robert Fowler, Jack Hayes, Angelique Ilo, Stephanie Michels, Dana Moore, Christopher Nilsson, Christina Norrup, Chris Peterson, Mia Price, Wayne Schroeder, John Sloman, Abe Sylvia, Craig Waletzo, Wendy Waring, Jeff Williams, Karen Ziemba (First Nighters), Matt Allen, Matt Baker, Ken Barnett, Alan Bennett, D. B. Bonds, Harry Bouvy, Patrick Boyd, Liam Burke, Eric Michael Gillett, Justin Greer, Peter Gregus, Timothy Gulan, Eric Gunhus, David Havasi, Jason Lacayo, Jamie LaVerdiere, Mark Ledbetter, David Lowenstein, Ira Mont, Joseph Mooradian, Patrick Mullaney, Marcus Nance, Chris Peterson, Nick Santa Maria, Denton Tarver, Craig Wetzel, Steve Wilson, Kent Zimmerman (Accountants), Leanne Bowman, Holly Cruikshank, Colleen Dunn, Jenny Gruby Field, Rhonda Kaufman, Charley Izabella King, Sarah Misiano, Kandice Pelletier, Katherine Marie Schwing, Michele Utzig, Wendy Waring (Girls with Pearls), Angie C. Creighton, Jennifer Lee Crowl, Bryn Dowling, Meg Gillentine, Kimberly

Jones, Naomi Kakuk, Renee Klapmeyer, Alison Levenberg, Mia Price (Girls with Pearls/Little Old Ladies), Melanie Allen, Jane Altman, Piper Lindsay Arpan, Mary Ellen Ashley, Margery Beddow, Mimi Bensinger, Jim Borstelmann, Pam Bradley, Maureen Brennan, Jane Brockman, Barbara Broughton, Kimberly Calore, Alice Cannon, Warren Carlyle, Eileen Casey, Erin Crouch, Madeline Doherty, Diane Findaly, Norma Fire, Kathy Fitzgerald, Robert Fowler, Sondra Gorney, James Gray, Justin Greer, Eric Gunhus, Ashley Amber Haase, James Hadley, Mary Ann Hannon, Marcia Haufrecht, Cynthia Leigh Heim, Kimberly Hester, Chris Holly, Stacey Todd Holt, Shauna Hoskin, Angelique Ilo, Joan Jaffe, Nancy Johnston, Shari Jordan, Kevin Ligon, Mary Looram, Dana Lorge, C. C. Loveheart, Melissa Rae Mahon, Patti Mariano, Peter Marinos, Mike McGowan, Lucy Martin, Liz McKendry, Jeannine Moore, Sarah Misiano, Jan Neuberger, Denise Nolin, Francine Myles, Christina Norrup, Nancy Ozelli, Sylvia Norman, Mia Price, Darcy Pulliam, Jessica Perrizo, Erika Rominger, Lisa Rothauser, Rita Rehn, Joy Seligsohn, Letty Serra, Jason Patrick Sands, Jessica Sheridan, Jennifer Smith, Karen Shallo, Cynthia Thole, Wendy Waring, Tracy Terstriep, Chryssie Whitehead, Jill Wolins, Patrick Wetzel, Courtney Young (Little Old Ladies)

A failing Broadway producer cons a meek accountant into helping him deceive his backers by producing a surefire flop musical, *Springtime for Hitler*. Lane, Broderick, Bart, and Beach repeat their roles from the original 2001 Broadway cast. Remake of the 1967 AVCO Embassy film *The Producers*, which starred Zero Mostel and Gene Wilder, and was directed and written by Mel Brooks.

Matthew Broderick PHOTOS COURTESY OF UNIVERSAL

HOODWINKED

(WEINSTEIN CO.) Producers, Maurice Kanbar, Sue Bea Montgomery, Preston Stutzman, David K. Lovegren; Director, Cory Edwards; Co-Directors, Tony Leech, Todd Edwards; Screenplay, Cory Edwards, Todd Edwards, Tony Leech; Music, John Mark Painter; Songs, Todd Edwards; Editor, Tony Leech; Overall 3-D/Digital Supervisor, Glenn Neufeld; Modeling/Animation Supervisor, Dennis Leech; a Kanbar Entertainment production in association with Kanbar Animation, Blue Yonder Films; Dolby; Color; Rated PG; 80 minutes; Release date: December 16, 2005

Red

Chief Grizzly, Nicky Flippers, Det. Bill Stork

Voice Cast

Red **Anne Hathaway**
Granny **Glenn Close**
The Woodsman **Jim Belushi**
The Wolf **Patrick Warburton**
Det. Bill Stork **Anthony Anderson**
Nicky Flippers **David Ogden Stiers**
Chief Grizzly **Xzibit**
Woolworth **Chazz Palminteri**
Boingo **Andy Dick**
Twitchy **Cory Edwards**
Japeth the Goat **Benjy Gaither**

The Wolf, The Woodsman, Granny, Red

The Woodsman PHOTOS COURTESY OF WEINSTEIN COMPANY

and Tye Edwards (Dolph), Todd Edwards (Sandwich Man), Joshua J. Greene (Jimmy Lizard), Preston Stutzman (Timmy), Ken Marino (Raccoon Jerry), Kevin Michael Richardson (P-Biggie), Tara Strong (Zorra), Vicki Edwards (Skunk Reporter), Dennis Leech (Walla Group), Troy Norton (Caterpillar 2), Kelly Stables (Schnitzel Kid 1)

Red, Granny, the Woodsman, and the Wolf all get a chance to tell their version of the Red Riding Hood fairy tale.

Twitchy

Sarah Jessica Parker, Dermot Mulroney

Dermot Mulroney, Luke Wilson, Rachel McAdams

Claire Danes, Dermot Mulroney, Diane Keaton, Craig T. Nelson

Rachel McAdams, Diane Keaton, Sarah Jessica Parker PHOTOS COURTESY OF 20TH CENTURY FOX

THE FAMILY STONE

(20TH CENTURY FOX) Producer, Michael London, Executive Producer, Jennifer Ogden; Director/Screenplay, Thomas Bezucha; Photography, Jonathan Brown; Designer, Jane Ann Stewart; Costumes, Shay Cunliffe; Music, Michael Giacchino; Editor, Jeffrey Ford; Casting, Mindy Marin; a Fox 2000 Pictures presentation of a Michael London production; Dolby; Deluxe color; Rated PG-13; 102 minutes; Release date: December 16, 2005

Craig T. Nelson, Sarah Jessica Parker, Ty Giordano, Savannah Stehlin, Elizabeth Reaser, Dermot Mulroney, Rachel McAdams, Diane Keaton, Brian White

Cast
Julie Morton **Claire Danes**
Sybil Stone **Diane Keaton**
Amy Stone **Rachel McAdams**
Everett Stone **Dermot Mulroney**
Kelly Stone **Craig T. Nelson**
Meredith Morton **Sarah Jessica Parker**
Ben Stone **Luke Wilson**
Thad Stone **Ty Giordano**
Patrick Thomas **Brian White**
Susannah Stonte Trousdale **Elizabeth Reaser**
Brad Stevenson **Paul Schneider**
Elizabeth Trousdale **Savannah Stehlin**
John Trousdale **Jamie Kaler**
David Silver **Robert Dioguardi**

and Carol Locatell (Jeweler), Ginna Carter (Jittery Cashier), Gus Buktenica (Bartender), Michale Pemberton, Ron Wall (Bus Drivers), Christopher Parker (Inn Receptionist)

Everett Stone brings his stuck-up fiancée, Meredith, home to meet his close-knit and highly judgmental family during the Christmas holidays.

Richard Jenkins, Téa Leoni, Jim Carrey

FUN WITH DICK AND JANE

(COLUMBIA) Producers, Brian Grazer, Jim Carrey; Executive Producers, Jane Bartelme, Peter Bart, Max Palevsky; Director, Dean Parisot; Screenplay, Judd Apatow, Nicholas Stoller; Based on the screenplay by Jerry Belson, David Giler, Mordecai Richler, from a story by Gerald Gaiser; Photography, Jerzy Zielinski; Designer, Barry Robison; Costumes, Julie Weiss; Music, Theodore Shapiro; Music Supervision, Randall Poster; Editor, Don Zimmerna; Associate Producer, Linda Fields Hill; Casting, Debra Zane; an Imagine Entertainment presentation of a Brian Grazer, JC 23 Entertainment, Bart/Palevsky production; Dolby; Deluxe color; Rated PG-13; 90 minutes; Release date: December 21, 2005

Cast

Dick Harper **Jim Carrey**
Jane Harper **Téa Leoni**
Jack McCallister **Alec Baldwin**
Frank Bascombe **Richard Jenkins**
Veronica Cleeman **Angie Harmon**
Garth **John Michael Higgins**
Joe Cleeman **Richard Burgi**
Oz Peterson **Carlos Jacott**
Billy Harper **Aaron Michael Drozin**
Blanca **Gloria Garayua**
Dick's Secretary **Michelle Arthur**
Jack's Receptionist **Stacey Travis**
Jack's Assistant **Timm Sharp**

and Dave Herman (Angry Caller), Dempsey Pappion (Production Assistant), Knox Grantham White (Sound Technician), Walter Addison (Sam Samuels), Ralph Nader (Himself), Deena Adar (Hysterical Globodyne Employee), Jorey Bernstein (Ficus Guy), Dilva Henry (Anchor), Luis Saguar (Hector), Rocael L. Rueda (Gardener), Peter Breitmayer, P. J. Byrne, Pete Gardner (Laughing Executives), Kym Whitley (Kostmart Training Leader), Gavin Grazer (Kostmart Job Applicant), Taso Papadakis (Gym Manager), James St. James (Scary Kostmart Shopper), Mary Gillis (Lactose Kostmart Shopper), Esther Scott (Disgruntled Kostmart Customer), Larry Dorf (Used Car Salesman), Dario Gonzalez, Emilio

Rivera, Jullian Dulce Vida (Day Laborers), Steve Seagren (Truck Guy), Ivan Brogger (Research Scientist), Clint Howard, Jack Conley, Huey Redwine (INS Agents), Wayne Flemming (Nosy Neighbor), Jason Marsden (Convenience Store Clerk), Scott L. Schwartz (Bigger Convenience Store Clerk), Bette Beatrice (Elderly Lady with Bags), Rick Overton (Head Shop Clerk), Kerry Hoyt (Coffee Shop Barrista), Kenji Nakamura, Rikio Nakashita, Brian Tee (Sushi Chefs), Phil Reeves (Car Dealer), Daniel Espeseth (Ameribanx Security Guard), Garrett M. Brown (Ameribanx Bank Manager), Stephnie Weir (Debbie), Peter Weireter (Police Leader at Ameribanx), Peter Conklin (Hunter), Steve Kehela (Bartender), Rob Nagle (Concerned Businessman), Oliver Muirhead (Senior Account Rep, Cayman Bank), Chris Ellis (Vice President, Cayman Bank), Bob Morrisey (Authorization Officer Spencer), Kevin Ruf (Karen Williams' Receptionist), Maggie Rowe (Karen Williams), Tony Lupo (Cop Outside Cayman Bank), Alejandro Furth (Cesar), Frank Levangie (Waiter), Staci Lawrence, Robert Alan Beuth (Globodyne Employees)

Jim Carrey, Téa Leoni

After being laid off and forced to give up his comfortable suburban life, Dick Harper and his wife Jane turn to a life of crime. Remake of the 1977 Columbia film which starred George Segal and Jane Fonda.

Alec Baldwin, Jim Carrey PHOTOS COURTESY OF COLUMBIA

CHEAPER BY THE DOZEN 2

(20TH CENTURY FOX) Producers, Shawn Levy, Ben Myron; Executive Producers, Jennifer Gibgot, Adam Shankman, Garrett Grant; Director, Adam Shankman; Screenplay, Sam Harper; Based on characters created by Craig Titley, based upon the novel *Cheaper by the Dozen* by Frank Bunker Gilbreth, Jr. and Ernestine Gilbreth Carey; Photography, Peter James; Designer, Cary White; Costumes, Joseph G. Aulisi; Music, John Debney; Music Supervisor, Buck Damon; Editors, Christopher Greenbury, Matthew Cassel; Casting, Monica Swann; a 21 Laps production; Dolby; Color; Rated PG; 93 minutes; Release date: December 21, 2005

Cast

Tom Baker **Steve Martin**
Kate Baker **Bonnie Hunt**
Sarah Baker **Alyson Stoner**
Mark Baker **Forrest Landis**
Kim Baker **Morgan York**
Jessica Baker **Liliana Mumy**
Jake Baker **Jacob Smith**
Charlie Baker **Tom Welling**
Nigel Baker **Brent Kinsman**
Kyle Baker **Shane Kinsman**
Lorraine Baker **Hilary Duff**
Mike Baker **Blake Woodruff**
Henry Baker **Kevin G. Schmidt**
Nora Baker-McNulty **Piper Perabo**

and Jonathan Bennett (Bud McNulty), Eugene Levy (Jimmy Murtaugh), Carmen Electra (Sarina Muraugh), Jamie King (Anne Murtaugh), Alexander Conti (Kenneth Murtaugh), Melanie Tonello (Becky Murtaugh), Robbie Amell (Daniel Murtaugh), Courtney Fitzpatrick (Lisa Murtaugh), Madison Fitzpatrick (Robin Murtaugh), Shawn Roberts (Calvin Murtaugh), William Copeland (The Commodore), Peter Keleghan (Mike Romanow), Sam Kalilieh (Doctor), Damon Runyan (Tennis Pro), Graham Losee (Theatre Usher), Seth Howard (Clam Bake Server), Matthew Knight (Theatre Kid), Lee MacDougall (Doobner Dad), Jenny Parsons (Doobner Mom), Dylan Rosenthal (Doobner Older Son), Haylee Wanstall (Doobner Daughter), Ely Henry (Doobner Younger Son), Tre Smith (Security Guard), Adam Shankman (Clam Bake Chef), Shawn Levy (Hospital Intern), Enid Rose (Announcer at Graduation), Kristen Dulmage (Clam Bake Piano Player)

Eugene Levy, Steve Martin PHOTO COURTESY OF 20TH CENTURY FOX

A family vacation pits Tom Baker and his vast brood against his arch rival Jimmy Murtaugh and his family. Sequel to the 2003 film *Cheaper by the Dozen* (20th Century Fox) with most of the principals repeating their roles.

Jed Rees, John Taylor, Johnny Knoxville, Bill Chott, Edward Barbanell, Geoffrey Arend
PHOTO COURTESY OF FOX SEARCHLIGHT

THE RINGER

(FOX SEARCHLIGHT) Producers, Peter Farrelly, Bradley Thomas, Bobby Farrelly; Executive Producer, Tom Shriver; Co-Producers, Marc S. Fischer, Clemens Emanuel Franek; Director, Barry W. Blaustein; Screenplay, Ricky Blitt; Photography, Mark Irwin; Designer, Arian Jay Vettier; Costumes, Lisa Jensen; Music, Mark Mothersbaugh; Music Supervisors, Tom Wolfe, Manish Raval; Editor, George Folsey Jr.; Casting, Nancy Foy; a Conundrum Entertainment; Dolby; Clairmont-Scope; Deluxe color; Rated PG-13; 94 minutes; Release date: December 23, 2005

Cast

Steve Barker **Johnny Knoxville**
Gary Barker **Brian Cox**
Lynn Sheridan **Katherine Heigl**
Winston **Geoffrey Arend**
Billy **Edward Barbanell**
Thomas **Bill Chott**
Jimmy Washington **Leonard Flowers**

and Leonard Earl Howze (Mark), Jed Rees (Glen), John Taylor (Rudy), Luis Avalos (Stavi), Zen Gesner (David Patrick), Steve Levy (Himself), Mohammada Ahmed (Dr. Ahmed), Nicole E. Bradley (Yolie), Mike Cerrone (Paulie), Camille Chen (Sarah), Michael Clossin (Closs), Kelly Cook, Eric Hernandez (Athlete), Alcides Dias (Michael), Lauren-Elaine Edleson (Brandi), Damian Fannin, Rajiv Patel (Special Olympics Volunteer), Terry Funk (Frankie), Charles E. Gray (Photographer), Diana Heart (Girl in Wheelchair), Kimberley R. Johnson (Sports Agent), Bo Kane (Matt), Brad Leland (Mr. Henderson), Brandie McMinn (Actress), Adam North (Popcorn Guy), Robert C. Pemleton (Office Worker), Steven Chester Prince (Peter Clemons), John Rothman (Priest), J. D. Stahr (Starting Gun Official), Jesse Ventura (Voice of Motivational Speaker), Santiago Villalobos (Soccer Referee/Field Judge), Katherine Willis (Ditzy Woman)

Finding himself deeply in debt, Steve Barker hits upon the outrageous idea of pretending to be mentally disabled in order to compete in the Special Olympics.

MUNICH

(UNIVERSAL/DREAMWORKS) Producers, Kathleen Kennedy, Steven Spielberg, Barry Mendel, Colin Wilson; Director, Steven Spielberg; Screenplay, Tony Kushner, Eric Roth; Based on the book *Vengeance* by George Jonas; Photography, Janusz Kaminski; Designer, Rick Carter; Costumes, Joanna Johnston; Music, John Williams; Editor, Michael Kahn; Special Effects Supervisor, Joss Williams; an Amblin Entertainment, Kennedy/Marshall, Barry Mendel production, in association with Alliance Atlantis Communications; Dolby; Arri Widescreen; Technicolor; Rated R; 164 minutes; Release date: December 23, 2005

Cast
Avner **Eric Bana**
Steve **Daniel Craig**
Carl **Ciaran Hinds**
Robert **Mathieu Kassovitz**
Hans **Hanns Zischler**
Daphna **Ayelet Zurer**
Ephraim **Geoffrey Rush**
Avener's Mother **Gila Almagor**
Papa **Michael Lonsdale**
Louis **Mathieu Amalric**
Andreas **Moritz Bleibtreu**

Eric Bana, Geoffrey Rush PHOTOS COURTESY OF FILMCOMPANY

Eric Bana, Ayelet Zurer

(Kamal Nasser), Rim Turki (Adwan's Wife), Jonathan Rozen (Ehud Barak), Charley H. Gilleran (Commando/Arab Guard), Jonathan Uziel, Guy Zu-Aretz, Yossi Sagie, Liron Levo, Ohad Knoller (Commandos), Lyes Salem, Carim Messalti, Hichem Yacoubi, Omar Mostafa (Arab Guards),

Eric Bana, Mathieu Kassovitz, Ciaran Hinds, Hanns Zischler, Daniel Craig

and Valeria Bruni-Tedeschi (Sylvie), Meret Becker (Yvonne), Marie-Josee Croze (Jeannette), Yvan Attal (Tony, Andreas' Friend), Ami Weinberg (Gen. Zamir), Lynn Cohen (Golda Meir), Amos Lavie (Gen. Yariv), Moshe Ivgy (Mike Harari), Michael Warshaviak (Attorney General Meir Shamgar), Ohad Shachar, Rafael Tabor (Ministers), Sharon Cohen Alexander (Gen. Nadev), Schmuel Calderon (Gen. Hofi), Oded Teomi (Mossad Accountant), Alon Abutul (Israeli Soldier with Zamir), Makram Khoury (Wael Zwaiter), Igal Naor (Mahmoud Hamshari), Hiam Abbass (Marie Claude Hamshari), Mouna Soualmen (Amina Hamshari), Mostefa Djadjam (Hussein Abad Al-Chir), Assi Cohen (Newly-Wed Man), Lisa Werlinder (Newly-Wed Bride), Djemal Barek (Zaid Muchassi), Derar Suleiman (Abu Youssef), Ziad Adwan (Kemal Adwan), Bijan Daneshmand

Mathieu Kassovitz, Hanns Zischler

Mahmoud Zemouri (Older Lebanese Man), Souad Amidou (Yussef's Wife), Amrou Alkadhi (Yussef's Son), Omar Metwally (Ali), Nasser Memarzia (Older Palestinian), Abdelhafid Metalsi (Palestinian in 30s), Karim Qayouhi (Young Palestinian), Mihalis Giannatos (Hotel Aristides Porter), Faruk Pruti, Rad Lazar (KGB Liaisons), Laurence Fevrier (Papa's Wife), Habir Yahya (Girl with Papa), Mehdi Nebbou (Ali Hassan Salameh), Hicham Nazzal, Lemir Guerfa, Hisham Silman (Salameh Guards), Brian Goodman, Richard Brake, Robert John Burke (Belligerent Americans),

Mathieu Kassovitz, Eric Bana

Yehuda Levi, Danny Zahavi (Tel Aviv Airport Soldiers), Itay Barnea (Israeli Deputy Consul NY), Elyse Klaits (Consulate Secretary), Nabil Yajjou (Young Tarifa Guard), Karim Saleh (Issa), Merik Tadros (Tony "The Cowboy"), Mousa Kraish (Badran, Moahmmed Safed), Karim Saidi (Kader, Adnan Al-Gashey), Mohammed Khouas (Samir, Jamal Al-Gashey), David Ali Hamade (Paulo), Ben Youcef (Saleh), Sami Samir (Abu Halla), Guri Weinberg (Moshe Weinberg), Sam Feuer (Yossef Romano), Sabi Dorr (Yossef Gutfruend), Wojchiech MacHnicki (Tuvia Sokolovsky), David Feldman (Kehat Shorr), Ori Pfeffer (Andre Spitzer), Shmuel Edleman (Jacov Spring), Joseph Sokolosky (Amirzur Shapira), Lior Perel (David Berger), Ossie Beck (Eliezer Halfin), Guy Amir (Mark Slavin), Haguy Wigdor (Zeev Friedman), Roei Avigdori (Gad Tsabari), Kevin Collin, Daniel Bess (American Athletes), Baya Belal, Ula Tabari (Palestinian Women Watching TV), Saida Bekkouche, Fettouma Bouamari (Aida Refugee Camp Women), Alexander Beyer (German Reporter in Munich Underground), Amos Shoub, Geoffrey Dowell, Rana Werbin (Israeli News Anchors), Jane Garda (Italian Girl in Car), Felicite Du Jeu (Young Swiss Bank Official), Gil Soriano (Man in Haifa Bar), Mordechai Ben Shachar (Older Man in Haifa Bar), Amina Al-Aidroos, Leda Mansour (Palestinian Teachers), Sasha Spielberg (Young Israeli Woman Watching TV), Renana Raz, Hagit Dasberg-Shamul (Israeli Women Watching TV), Patrick Kennedy (English Reporter in Munich Underground), Stephane Freiss (French Reporter in Munich Underground), Arturo Arribas (Spanish Reporter in Munich Underground), Yaron Josef Motolla (Israeli Reporter in Munich Underground), Jalil Naciri (Arab Reporter in Munich Underground), Martin Ontrop, Joram Voelklein (Camera Crew at Munich), Michael Schenk (Photographer at Munich), Andreas Lust, Tom Wlaschiha (News Crew at Furstenfeldbrook)

A covert Israeli hit squad is dispatched to eliminate the Palestinian group responsible for the murders of nine members of the Israeli team at the 1972 Olympics.

This film received Oscar nominations for picture, director, adapted screenplay, original score and editing.

Moshe Ivgy, Ami Weinberg, Lynn Cohen

Eric Bana, Ayelet Zurer PHOTOS COURTESY OF UNIVERSAL

Heath Ledger, Sienna Miller

CASANOVA

(TOUCHSTONE) Producers, Mark Gordon, Betsy Beers, Leslie Holleran; Executive Producers, Su Armstrong, Adam Merims, Gary Levinsohn; Director, Lasse Hallström; Screenplay, Jeffrey Hatcher, Kimberly Simi; Story, Kimberly Simi, Michael Cristofer; Photography, Oliver Stapleton; Designer, David Gropman; Costumes, Jenny Beavan; Co-Producer, Guido Cerasuolo; Music, Alexandre Desplat; Editor, Andrew Mondshein; Associate Producer, Mishka Cheyko; Italian Casting, Lilia Trapani; a Mark Gordon Company, Hallström/Holleran production; Dolby; Panavision; Technicolor; Rated R; 111 minutes; Release date: December 25, 2005

Cast

Giacomo Casanova	**Heath Ledger**
Francesca Bruni	**Sienna Miller**
Bishop Pucci	**Jeremy Irons**
Pietro Paprizzio	**Oliver Platt**
Andrea Bruni	**Lena Olin**
Lupo	**Omid Djalili**
Donato	**Stephen Greif**
Dalfonso	**Ken Stott**
Casanova's Mother	**Helen McCrory**
Mother's Lover (Tito)	**Leigh Lawson**
The Doge	**Tim McInnerny**
Giovanni Bruni	**Charlie Cox**
Victoria	**Natalie Dormer**
Guardi	**Phil Davis**

and Paddy Ward (Vittorio), Ben Moor (Andolini), Adelmo Togliani (Fulvio), Lidia Biondi (Casanova's Grandmother), Eugene Simon (Casanova, Age 11), Robert Levine (Cardinal Lopresta), Lauren Cohan (Sister Beatrice), Danielle Baker (Sister Magdalene), Clive Riche (Prof. Bennetto), Marta Bellocchio (Beautiful Masked Woman), Adriano Jurissevich (Masked Casanova Actor), Giorgio Bertan (Actor), Niall Buggy (Bookseller/Printer), Simonetta Bortolozzi (Beautiful Woman in Bookshop), Francis Pardeilhan (Custom Officer), Enzo Turrin (Maggiordomo), Carolina Levi (Bruni's Maid), Paola Pessot (Lolling Street Walker), Elisabeth Riva (Prostitute), Monica Vallerini (Whore #3), Nicholas Raymond Capriati (Boy), Naijke Rivelli (Dark Haired Beauty), Sara Guerra (Fair Haired Woman), Marta Paola Richeldi (Another Woman), Giorgia Riccardi (Another Beauty), Kristy

DiBiccari (Woman in Bookshop), Jessica Seaton (Plain Woman in Bookshop), Anna Gaia Marchioro (Plain Looking Woman), Lorenzo Felisatti (Laughing Man), Roy Doliner (Dalfonso's Secretary), Silvia Nanni (Whispering Woman), Paolo De Giorgio (Young Man), Alessandro Bressanello (Flunkey Captain), Katarina Volgyiova (Society Woman), Davide Bozzato (Drunken Reveller), Catherine Gault (Reveller), Renzo Martini (Beadle), Laura Pigozzo (Woman), Federico Scridel (Casanova Actor), Manuella Massimi (Lady Actress), Tommy Korberg (Gondola Singer), Bryan Korenberg (Man in Brothel), Bimba (Pig)

Natalie Dormer, Jeremy Irons

Lena Olin, Charlie Cox, Heath Ledger

Told he will be exiled from Venice unless he changes his randy ways, womanizing Giacomo Casanova sets out to find a wife and falls in love with the strong-willed Francesca Bruni only to discovered she has been promised in marriage to a wealthy lard merchant.

Lena Olin, Oliver Platt PHOTOS COURTESY OF TOUCHSTONE

RUMOR HAS IT...

(WARNER BROS.) Producers, Paula Weinstein, Ben Cosgrove; Executive Producers, George Clooney, Steven Soderbergh, Jennifer Fox, Michael Rachmil, Len Amato, Robert Kirby, Bruce Berman; Co-Producer, Frank Capra III; Director, Rob Reiner; Screenplay, T. M. Griffin; Photography, Peter Denning; Designer, Tom Sanders; Costumes, Kym Barrett; Music, Marc Shaiman; Music Supervisor, Chris Douridas; Editor, Robert Leighton; Casting, Jane Jenkins, Janet Hirshenson; a Section Eight, Spring Creek production, presented in association with Village Roadshow Pictures; Dolby; Technicolor; Rated PG-13; 97 minutes; Release date: December 25, 2005

Mark Ruffalo, Jennifer Aniston

Shirley MacLaine, Kevin Costner

Steve Sandvoss, Mena Suvari

Cast

Sarah Huttinger **Jennifer Aniston**
Beau Burroughs **Kevin Costner**
Katherine Richelieu **Shirley MacLaine**
Jeff Daly **Mark Ruffalo**
Earl Huttinger **Richard Jenkins**
Roger McManus **Christopher McDonald**
Scott **Steve Sandvoss**
Annie Huttinger **Mena Suvari**
Blake Burroughs **Mike Vogel**
New Year's Eve MC **Robert Lanza**
Young Katherine **Lisa Vachon**
Young Beau **Trevor Steck**
Jocelyn Richelieu **Jennifer Taylor**
Nikki **Jennifer Wade**
Donna **Erin Bartlett**

and Marcia Ann Burrs, Lynn Wanlass, Mary Anne McGarry (Pasadena Wives), Maree Cheatham, Gloria Grant, Gregory White, Jake Mailey, Frank Novak, William Kerr, Terrie Snell, Shannon Farnon (Party Guests), Allyson Bradford, Kate McClafferty (Bridesmaids), Googy Gress (Burly Man), Rolando Molina (Mover), Carmela Rappazzo (Party Planner), Erinn Hayes (Wedding Coordinator), Christopher Stapleton (Bartender), George F. Regas (Pastor), Jamie Ray Newman (Conference Greeter), Andy Milder, Gabriel Jarret, Clyde Kusatsu, John Sterling Carter (Conference Attendees), Mike Baldridge, Donna Cooper (Reporters), Erin McDonald (Waitress), Paul Ganus (Co-Pilot), Amos Levkovitch (Magician), Leigh French, Charlotte Ortiz Colavin, George Gerdes, Lyman Ward, Jordan Lund (Charity Dinner Guests), John E. Byrd (Doorman), Aida Bernardino (Restaurant Owner), Kathy Bates (Aunt Mitzi), George Hamilton (Himself)

Finding out that both her late mother and her grandmother slept with the same man, Sarah Huttinger starts to wonder if perhaps her family was the basis for *The Graduate* and that she is, in fact, the offspring of her mother's lover.

Jennifer Aniston, Kathy Bates PHOTOS COURTESY OF WARNER BROS.

THE NEW WORLD

(NEW LINE CINEMA) Producers, Bill Mechanic, Rolf Mittweg, Toby Emmerich, Mark Ordesky, Trish Hofmann; Director/Screenplay, Terrence Malick; Photography, Emmanuel Lubezki; Designer, Jack Fisk; Costumes, Jacqueline West; Music, James Horner; Editors, Richard Chew, Hank Corwin, Saar Klein, Mark Yoshikawa; Casting, Francine Meisler, Kathy Driscoll-Mohler; Native American Casting, Rene Haynes; Dolby; Panavision; Deluxe color; Rated PG-13; 149 minutes (cut to 135 minutes); Release date: December 25, 2005

Christian Bale, Christopher Plummer

Colin Farrell, Q'orianka Kilcher

Cast

Captain John Smith **Colin Farrell**
Pocahontas (Rebecca) **Q'orianka Kilcher**
Captain Christopher Newport **Christopher Plummer**
John Rolfe **Christian Bale**
Powhatan **August Schellenberg**
Opechancanough **Wes Studi**
Captain Edward Wingfield **David Thewlis**
Captain Argail **Yorick van Wageningen**
Ben **Ben Mendelsohn**
Tomocomo **Raoul Trujillo**
Lewes **Brian F. O'Byrne**
Pocahontas' Mother **Irene Bedard**
Savage **John Savage**
Emery **Jamin Harris**
Patawomeck **Thomas Clair**
Patawomeck's Wife **Alex Rice**
Rupewew **Michael Greyeyes**

and Ben Chaplin (Jehu Robinson), Jonathan Pryce (King James), Roger Rees (Virginia Company Representative), Noah Taylor (Selway), Kalani Queypo (Parahunt), Alexandra Malick (Queen Anne), Kirk Acevedo, Will Wallace (Sentry), Arturo Tointigh Adrian (Guide), Jason Aaron Baca (Parker), Blake Bess (Young Warrior), Yuriy Cherepnya, Anthony Parker, Cory Rodriguez, Gabriel Jones Roxas, Lawrence Santiago (Warriors), Greg Cooper (Boatman), Colin Cox, Chris Nelson (English Sailor), Martin Nigel Davey (London Gentleman), Janine Duvitski (Mary), John Esteban (Colonist), John Ghaly (English Soldier), Joe Inscoe (Ackley), Henry

August Schellenberg

Jaderlund (Lead Garlanded Man), Tayla Kean (Samual the Cabin Boy), Eddie Marsan (Edward), Josh Padgett (Joshua), Jeremy Radin (Jeremy), Myrton Running Wolf (Tockwhogh), Gary Sundown (Messenger), Rulan Tangen (Two Moons)

Arriving in what would become Virginia, the first group of British colonists make an effort to establish contact with the Native Americans. After his life is spared by Pocahontas, Captain John Smith manages to ingratiate himself with her tribe.

This film received an Oscar nomination for cinematography.

Thomas Clair, Alex Rice PHOTOS COURTESY OF NEW LINE CINEMA

Pierce Brosnan, Greg Kinnear

Greg Kinnear, Pierce Brosnan

THE MATADOR

(WEINSTEIN CO.) Producers, Pierce Brosnan, Beau St. Clair, Sean Furst, Bryan Furst; Executive Producers, Bob Yari, Mark Gordon, Adam Merims, Andreas Thiesmeyer, Josef Lautenschlager, Andy Reimer; Co-Producers, Brad Jenkel, Gerd Koechlin, Manfred Heid; Director/Screenplay, Richard Shepard; Photography, David Tattersall; Designer, Rob Pearson; Costumes, Catherine Thomas; Music, Rolfe Kent; Editor, Carole Kracetz-Akyanian; Associate Producers, Amanda J. Scarano, Susanne Bohnet; Casting, Carla Hool; a Stratus Film Co., DEJ Prods. presentation in association with Equity Pictures Medienfonds KG II of a Furst Films, Irish Dreamtime production; Dolby; FotoKem color; Rated R; 97 minutes; Release date: December 30, 2005

Pierce Brosnan

Cast

Julian Noble **Pierce Brosnan**
Danny Wright **Greg Kinnear**
Carolyn "Bean" Wright **Hope Davis**
Mr. Randy **Philip Baker Hall**
Lovell **Dylan Baker**
Phil Garrison **Adam Scott**
Genevieve **Portia Dawson**
Mr. Stick **William Raymond**
Ten Year Old Boy **Jonah Meyerson**
Skinny Mexican Man **Roberto Sosa**
Hotel Bartenders **Antonio Zavala, Jorge Robles**
Shooting Stand Owner **Ramon Alvarez**
Vienna Fling **Claudia Lobo**
Australian Bar Waitress **Maureen Muldoon**
Manila Target **Arturo Echeverria**

and Arlin Miller (Radio DJ), Carolyn Horwitz (Cantina Turista #1), Hanny Sáenz (Fat Man's Girlfriend), Gabriela Goldsmith (Flirting Woman at Outdoor Cafe), Bernice Alvarado, Adriana Dávila, Isabel Villa (Budapest Ballerinas), Guillermo Capetillo, Federico Pizarro (Matadors)

In Mexico City, Julian Noble, an aging hit man who's losing his grip, strikes up an unlikely friendship with down on his luck businessman Danny Wright, figuring they might be able to help one another out of their prospective ruts.

Greg Kinnear, Hope Davis   PHOTOS COURTESY OF WEINSTEIN COMPANY

Sven Garrett in *Murder-Set-Pieces* PHOTO COURTESY OF BLACKWATCH CINEMA

MURDER-SET-PIECES

(BLACKWATCH CINEMA) Producer/Director/Screenplay/Casting, Nick Palumbo; Executive Producers, Thomas Quinlin, Erlich Livingston; Photography, Brendan Flynt; Art Director, Nick Zito; Editor, Todd Ramsay; a Fright Flix production in association with Q-Vest Ventures; Dolby; Color; Not rated; 105 minutes; Release date: January 7, 2005. CAST: Sven Garrett (The Photographer), Jade Risser (Jade), Valerie Barber (Charlotte), Katie Richards (Megan), Tanja Grupp (German Mother), Gunnar Hansen (Nazi Mechanic), Tony Todd (Clerk), Ed Neal (Good Samaritan), Sherrie Winings (Psychic), Cerina Vincent (Beautiful Girl), Paul Bischot (Bus Driver), Jerami Cruise (Video Victim), Kylle Epperson (Green Ball Girl), Kendra Flynt (Baby Girl), Casie Gillespie (Candy), Liv Holley (Pole Girl), Cristie Whiles, Shelby Jackson (Dildo Girls), Stephanie Megrete (Dream Girl), Jena Peacock (Mirror Girl), Amber Richards (Toilet Girl), Destiny St. Claire (Weight Bench Girl), Ashley Twigg (Chainsaw Girl), Natalie Himmler, Ashley Richards, Hannah Keough, Brittni Truitt, Karri Jonas (Halloween Girls), Shandee Lang, Jamie Jent (High Chair Girls), Fred Vogel, Darren Williams (Masked Pyschos), Crissy Moran, Jenna Velanni (Tree Girls), Natalie Scytow, Sarah Murray (Strip Girls)

ELEKTRA

(20TH CENTURY FOX) Producers, Arnon Milchan, Gary Foster, Avi Arad; Executive Producers, Stan Lee, Mark Steven Johnson; Director, Rob Bowman; Screenplay, Zak Penn, Stuart Zicherman, Raven Metzner; Photography, Bill Roe; Designer, Graeme Murray; Costumes, Lisa Tomzzeskzyn; Music, Christophe Beck; Music Supervisor, Dave Jordan; Co-Producers, Kevin Feige, Josh McLaglen; Editor, Kevin Stitt; Stunts/Fight Choreographer, Mike Gunther; Casting, Dianne Crittenden, Coreen Mayrs, Heike Brandstatter; a New Regency, Horseshoe Bay production of a Regency Enterprises presentation in association with Marvel Enterprises, Inc.; Dolby; Panavision; Deluxe color; Rated PG-13; 96 minutes; Release date: January 14, 2005. CAST: Jennifer Garner (Elektra Natchios), Terence Stamp (Stick), Kirsten Prout (Abby), Goran Visnjic (Mark), Cary-Hiroyuki Tagawa (Roshi), Will Yun Lee (Kirigi), Chris Ackerman (Tattoo), Edson T. Ribeiro (Kinkou), Natassia Malthe (Typhoid), Bob Sapp (Stone), Colin Cunningham (McCabe), Hiro Kanagawa (Meizumi), Mark Houghton (Bauer), Laura Ward

(Young Elektra), Kurt Max Runte (Nikolas Natchios), Nathaniel Arcand, Aaron Au (Hand Ninjas), Kevan Ohtsji (Roshi Servant), Ian Tracey (Pool Shark), Jana Mitsoula (Young Elektra's Mother), Sean Akira, Taku Kawai (Glowering Ikurens), Kendall Cross, Ty Olsson, Nancy Wetzel (Paramedics), Paul Wu (Fight Instructor), Mark Driesschen (Weatherman)

SHORT CUT TO NIRVANA: KUMBH MELA

(MELA FILMS) Producers/Directors/Photography, Maurizio Benazzo, Nick Day; Music, Bob Muller; Editor, Nick Day; Dolby; Color; Not rated; 85 minutes; Release date: January 14, 2005. Documentary on India's Kumbh Mela, a sacred gathering held every twelve years; featuring Swami Krishnanand, Dyan Summers, Jasper Johal, Justin Davis, Vanessa Ramos, Pilot Baaba, Bharti Urdvahu, The Dalai Lama, Ramanand Puri, Kali Baaba, Devrahaha Hans Baba

ARAKIMENTARI

(TROOPERS FILMS) Producer, Jason Fried; Executive Producer, Regis Trigano; Director, Travis Klose; Photography, Brian Burgoyne; Music, DJ Krush; Editor, Masako Tsumura; Color; DV; Not rated; 74 minutes; Release date: January 21, 2005. Documentary on Japanese photographer/provocateur Nobuyoshi Araki, featuring Nobuyoshi Araki, Takeshi Kitano, Björk, Daido Moriyama, Richard Kern, Komari Shino, Yoshiko Kamikura.

WHEN ZACHARY BEAVER CAME TO TOWN

(ECHO BRIDGE) Producers, Amy Robinson, Michael Corrente, Jay Julien; Line Producer, Susan Kirr; Director/Screenplay, John Schultz; Photography, Shawn Maurer; Designer, Reiko Kobayashi; Costumes, Lee Hunsaker; Music, Richard Gibbs; Editor, John Pace; Casting, James Calleri; Color; Rated PG; 85 minutes; Release date: January 21, 2005. CAST: Jonathan Lipnicki (Toby Wilson), Sasha Neulinger (Zachary Beaver), Cody Linley (Cal McKnight), Eric Stoltz (Otto Wilson), Jane Krakowski (Mrs. Wilson), Kathleen Lancaster (Kate McKnight), Brady Coleman (Sheriff Fetterman), Amanda Alch (Scarlett Staling), Brett Brock (Mr. McKnight), Kevin Corrigan (Paulie), Ryan Harper Gray (Billy), Joanna McCray (Tara), Jesse Pennington (Wade), Kimberly Ann Shafter (Esther), Ken Thomas (Highway Patrolman), Lawrence Varnado (Officer McCollum)

Jennifer Garner in *Elektra* PHOTO COURTESY OF 20TH CENTURY FOX

Short Cut to Nirvana PHOTO COURTESY OF MELA FILMS

ALONE IN THE DARK

(LIONS GATE) Producer, Shawn Williamson; Executive Producers, Uwe Boll, Wolfgang Herold; Co-Executive Producers, Harry Rubin, Bruno Bonnell; Director, Uwe Boll; Screenplay, Elan Mastai, Michael Roesch, Peter Scheerer; Based on the Atari Video Game; Photography, Mathias Neumann; Designer, Tink; Costumes, Maria Livingstone; Music, Bernd Wendlandt; Editor, Richard Schwadel; Visual Effects, Doug Oddy, Geoff D. E. Scott; a Boll KG Prods. production in association with Herold Prods., Brightlight Pictures; Dolby; Panavision; Color; Rated R; 98 minutes; Release date: January 28, 2005. CAST: Christian Slater (Edward Carnby), Tara Reid (Aline Cedrac), Stephen Dorff (Cmdr. Burke), Frank C. Turner (Fischer), Matthew Walker (Prof. Hudgens), Will Sanderson (Agent Miles), Mark Acheson (Capt. Chernick), Darren Shahlavi (John Houghton), Karin Konoval (Sister Clara), Craig Bruhnanski ('80s Sheriff), Kwesi Ameyaw (Deputy Adams), Catherine Lough Haggquist (Krash), Ed Anders (James Pinkerton), Dustyn Arthurs (Young Edward), Brad Turner (Beat Cop), Michael P. Northey (Delivery Guy), Ryan Drescher (Young Boy), Sean Campbell (First Mate), Sarah Deakins (Linda), Daniel Cudmore (Agent Barr), Francoise Yip (Agent Cheung), Ho-Sung Pak (Agent Marko), Mike Dopud (Agent Turner), Brendan

Christian Slater, Tara Reid in *Alone in the Dark* PHOTO COURTESY OF LIONS GATE

Fletcher (Cabbie), Donna Lysell (Sarah Fischer), Ona Grauer (Agent Feenstra), John Fallon (Agent Yonek), Rebekah Postey (Sophie), Robert Bruce (Crewman Barnes), Dean Redman (Agent Richards), Antonio Mauriano (Agent Tony)

PEACE, PROPAGANDA & THE PROMISED LAND

(ARAB FILM DISTRIBUTION) Producer, Bathsheba Ratzkoff; Directors/Screenplay, Bathsheba Ratzkoff, Sut Jhally; Music, Thom Monahan; Editors, Bathsheba Ratzkoff, Sut Jhally, Kenyon King; a Media Education Foundation production; Color; Not rated; 80 minutes; Release date: January 28, 2005. Documentary on how U.S. reporting on the conflict in the Middle East has been distorted; featuring Seth Ackerman, Major Stav Adivi, Rabbi Arik Ascherman, Hanan Ashrawi, Noam Chomsky, Robert Fisk, Dr. Neve Gordon, Toufic Haddad, Sam Husseini, Hussein Ibish, Roebrt Jensen, Rabbi Michael Lerner, Karen Pfeifer, Alisa Solomon, Gila Svirsky.

FREAK WEATHER

(HKM FILMS) Producers, Andrea Sperling, Alexis Magagni-Seely; Director, Mary Kuryla; Photography, Arturo Smith; Designer, Macie Vener; Editor, Joe D'Augustine; Casting, Cassandra Kulukundis; Color; Not rated; 87 minutes; Release date: February 2, 2005. CAST: Jacqueline McKenzie (Penny), Jacob Chase (Albert), Aida Turturro (Glory), John Carroll Lynch (Ed), John Heard (David), Justin Pierce (Pizza Guy), James Ent (Jimmy)

Michael Bonsignore, Maggie Riley in *Assisted Living* PHOTO COURTESY OF COWBOY PICTURES

ASSISTED LIVING

(COWBOY PICTURES) Producers, Elliot Greenebaum, Archie Borders, Alex Laskey, Alan Oxman; Executive Producer, Andrew Herwitz; Director/Screenplay, Elliott Greenebaum; Photography, Marcel Cabrera; Music, Hub Moore; Editors, Alexandra Bodner, Adriana Pacheco, Paul Frank; an Economic Projections, MomoDog Productions presentation; Color; Rated R; 78 minutes; Release date: February 2, 2005. CAST: Michael Bonsignore (Todd), Maggie Riley (Mrs. Pearlman), Nancy Jo Boone (Nancy Jo), Malerie Boone (Malerie Skelley), Clint Vaught (Hance Purcell), Gail Benedict (Kathy Hogan), Jose Albovias (Jose)

WMD: WEAPONS OF MASS DECEPTION

(CINEMA LIBRE) Producer, Anna B. Pizarro; Executive Producers, Barbara Kopple, Danny Schechter, Anant Singh; Director, Danny Schechter; a Globalvision Inc. production; Color; Not rated; 98 minutes; Release date: February 4, 2005. Documentary on the media coverage of the war in Iraq.

Cole Williams, Bryce Johnson in *Harry + Max* PHOTO COURTESY OF TLA RELEASING

SONS OF PROVO

(HALESTONE) Producer/Casting, Peter Brown; Executive Producer, Will Swenson; Director, Will Swenson; Screenplay, Will Swenson, Peter Brown; Photography, John Lyde, Stephen Rose; Designer, John Shircliff; Costumes, Anne Rose; Editor, John Lyde; from Fresh-Mex productions; Color; Rated PG; 93 minutes; Release date: February 4, 2005. CAST: Will Swenson (Will Jensen), Kirby Heyborne (Kirby Laybourne), Danny Tarasevich (Danny Jensen), Jennifer Erekson (Jill Keith), Peter Brown (Grayson Jensen), Maureen Eastwood (Yvonne Bolschweiler), H. K. Baird (Uncle LaMarr), Karen C. Baird (Verda Jensen), Gavin Bentley (Taylor), Marion Bentley (Shirl Jensen), Michael Birkeland (Hotel Clerk), Danielle Rae Bryan (Sister Campbell), Alison Akin Clark (Shantel), Curt Dousett (Bishop Bestor), Joseph Draschil (Tyler) Jeremy Elliott (Jeremy Jackson), Rachel Emmers (Crying Girl), Sally Hale (Shirley Jensen), Jed Knudsen (Recording Engineer), Carrie Morgan (Shaela), Alan Osmond (Himself), Mark Pulham (Prof. Tufnel), Robert Swenson (Singing Zak)

THE LETTER: AN AMERICAN TOWN AND THE "SOMALI INVASION"

(ARAB FILM DISTRIBUTION) Producers, Ziad H. Hamzeh, Marc Sandler, Bert Brown; Director/Screenplay/Editor, Ziad H. Hamzeh; Music, Kareem Roustom; a Hamzeh Mystique Films production; Color; Not rated; 76 minutes; Release date: February 9, 2005. Documentary on the controversy over 1,100 Somali refugees being relocated to Lewiston, Maine, following the 9/11 terrorist attacks.

YOU THINK YOU REALLY KNOW ME: GARY WILSON

(GORGEOUS ENTERTAINMENT) Producers, Michael Wolk, Kumiko Yoshii; Director, Michael Wolk; Photography, Bob Green; Music, Gary Wilson; Editor, Mustafa

Bhagat; Color; Not rated; 74 minutes; Release date: February 16, 2005. Documentary on avant-garde musician Gary Wilson; featuring Gary Wilson, Rossie Harris, Adrian Milan, Frank Roma.

HARRY + MAX

(TLA RELEASING) Producers, Christopher Münch, Roni Deitz; Director/Screenplay/Editor, Christopher Münch; Photography, Rob Sweeney; Art Director, Doran Meyers; Costumes, Kristen Anacker; Music, Michael Tubbs; Casting, Joseph Middleton; an Antarctic Pictures production; Color; Not rated; 74 minutes; Release date: February 18, 2005. CAST: Bryce Johnson (Harry), Cole Williams (Max), Rain Phoenix (Nikki), Kate Ellis (Brandi), Roni Deitz (Roxanne), Tom Gilroy (Josiah), Michelle Phillips (Mother), Justin Zachary (Jordan), Max Picioneri (Max, Age 9), Mark L. Young (Harry, Age 15)

SON OF THE MASK

(NEW LINE CINEMA) Producers, Erica Huggins, Scott Kroopf; Executive Produces, Beau Marks, Mike Richardson, Toby Emmerich, Kent Alterman, Michele Weiss; Co-Producer, Stephen Jones; Director, Lawrence Gutterman; Screenplay, Lance Khazel; Photography, Greg Gardiner; Designer, Leslie Dilley; Costumes, Mary E. Vogt; Music, Randy Edelman; Editors, Malcolm Campbell, Debra Neil Fisher; Visual Effects Supervisor, James E. Price; Special Visual Effects Animation, Industrial Light & Magic; Special Makeup Effects Supervisor, Brian Sipe; Stunts, Glenn Boswell; Casting, Roger Mussenden, Christine King; a Radar Pictures production in association with Dark Horse Entertainment; Dolby; Deluxe color; Rated PG; 95 minutes; Release date: February 18, 2005. CAST: Jamie Kennedy (Tim Avery), Alan Cumming (Loki), Liam Falconer, Ryan Falconer (Alvey), Traylor Howard (Tonya Avery), Steven Wright (Daniel Moss), Kal Penn (Jorge), Ben Stein (Dr. Neuman), Bob Hoskins (Odin), Brett Pickup (Museum Boy), Peter Callan (Museum Redneck), Ashley Lyons (Museum Security Guard), Wayne McDaniel (Museum Person), Sandy Winton (Chris), Rebecca Massey (Clare), Isaac Longmuir, Tayzin Fahey-Leigh, Skyla Laginha, Lochie Nazer-Hennings, Andie Rogers (Chris & Clare's Child), Alyssa McClelland, Trilby Glover (Dream Nurses), Josephine Chu, Solomon Freer, Ethan Coker (Tour Kids), Ryan Johnson (Chad), Victoria Thaine (Sylvia), Duncan Young (Mansion Doorman), Amber Todd (Daniel's Assistant), Damon Herriman (Animagine Employee), Raj Ryan (Dr. Hamada), Emma Jackson (Delivery Nurse), Jerry Minor (Shopkeeper), Holly Austin (Hospital Nurse), Jeanette Cronin (Housewife), Magda Szubanski

Jamie Kennedy, Traylor Howard in *Son of the Mask* PHOTO COURTESY OF NEW LINE NEW LINE CINEMA

(Neighbor Betty), Peter Flett (Mr. Kemperbee), Amanda Smyth (Mrs. Babcock, Obese), Matt Passmore, Tina Bursill, Anthony Kierann (Network Execs), Colin Borgonon (NY Exec), Esosa Edmonds (Burly Female Traffic Cop Odin), Peter Plusch (Reporter), Michael Kelly (Doctor), Joyce Kurtz, Mona Marshall (Baby Alvey Voice), Mary Matilyn Mouser (Alvey Avery Voice), Neil Ross (Deep Alvey Voice), Richard Steven Horvitz (Otis Voice), Bill Farmer (Mask Otis Voice)

UNCLE NINO

(LANGE FILM RELEASING) Executive Producer, David James; Director/Screenplay, Robert Shallcross; Photography, Hugo Cortina; Designer, Martha Ring; Costumes, Ginger Cavalier; Music, Larry Pecorella; Editor, Dan Schalk; Casting, Mickie Paskal, Rachel Tenner; from Kick the Can Productions; Color; Rated PG; 104 minutes; Release date: February 11, 2005. CAST: Joe Mantegna (Robert Micelli), Anne Archer (Marie Micelli), Pierrino Mascarino (Uncle Nino), Trevor Morgan (Bobby Micelli), Gina Mantegna (Gina Micelli), Duke Doyle (Bones), Daniel Adebayo (Joey), Gary Houston (Jerry), Chelcie Ross (Stewert), Mindy Bell (Bonnie), Shanesia Davis-Williams (Lorita), Ned Schmidtke (The Executive),

Pierrino Mascarino, Joe Mantegna in *Uncle Nino* PHOTO COURTESY OF LANGE FILM RELEASING

Marcus Thomas, Amy Smart in *Bigger Than the Sky* PHOTO COURTESY OF NEVERLAND FILMS

Ian Belkanp (John Cummings), Freeman Coffey (Police Officer), Marilyn Dodds Frank (Store Customer), Maureen Gallagher (Ellen, Robert's Secretary), Ora Jones (Pinched Grocery Store Customer), John Judd (Grocery Store Worker), Keegan Michael Key (Airport Stranger), Margaret Kusterman (Sample Lady), Krista Lally (Airport Bathroom Lady), Carley Reiff (The Crush Girl), Dale Rivera (Limo Driver), Abby Sher (Pet Store Worker), Michael Stahl-David (Craig), Jessica Szohr (The MC)

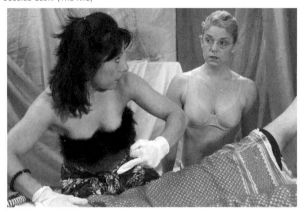

Leslie Shearing, Heather Smith in *Unscrewed* PHOTO COURTESY OF KANBAR ENTERTAINMENT

UNSCREWED

(KANBAR ENTERTAINMENT) formerly *Dogs in the Basement*; Producers, Leslie Shearing, Alan Oxman, Hans Hoffman; Director/Screenplay, Leslie Shearing; Photography, Peter Olsen; Music, Sabina Sciubba; Editor, Lilah Bankier; an Other Side Filmworks production; Color; Not rated; 75 minutes; Release date: February 11, 2005. CAST: Heather Smith (Mary St. John), Hans Hoffman (Joseph St. John), Donna Klimek (Gehan Brown-Cohen), Elizabeth Quinn (Tanya Nashold), Michael T. Rose (Todd Cohen), Douglas Manes (Dr. Emil Watson), Leslie Shearing (Dr. Nadia Pfelt), Jill Borher (Dr. Pfelt's Receptionist), Lulu (Herself), Amy Rush (Salon Receptionist), Libby Skala (Mary's Friend), Michael Scott Hill (The Frotteur), Jeff Matheny (Joe's Friend), Tiffany Lawrence (Woman in Park)

BIGGER THAN THE SKY

(NEVERLAND FILMS) Producers, Al Corley, Bart Rosenblatt, Eugene Musso, David Arquette, Steven Siebert, Mark Burton; Executive Producer, Jonathan Dana; Director, Al Corley; Screenplay, Rodney Vaccaro; Co-Producer, Craig M. Borden; Photography, Carl Nilsson; Designer, Stephen Lineweaver; Costumes, Julia Caston; Music, Rob Cairns; Music Supervisor, Barklie K. Griggs; Editor, Axel Hubert; Casting, Billy Hopkins, Suzanne Smith, Kerry Barden; Produced in association with Coquette Productions; Dolby; FotoKem color; Rated PG-13; 106 minutes; Release date: February 18, 2005. CAST: Marcus Thomas (Peter Rooker), John Corbett (Michael Degan), Amy Smart (Grace Hargrove), Sean Astin (Ken Zorbell), Clare Higgins (Edwina), Patty Duke (Mrs. Keene/Earline), Allan Corduner (Kippy), Greg Germann (Roger), Pam Mahon (Julie), James W. Crawford (Kirk), Victor Morris (Steve), Kenneth Jones (Scott), Brian Urspringer (Ted), Orianna Herrman (Susan), Ernie Garret (Paul), Matt Salinger (Mal), Nurmi Husa (David Nicolette), Michael Teufel (Sewer)

SUNSET STORY

(VITAGRAPH) Producers, Laura Gabbert, Eden Wurmfeld, Caroline Libresco; Consulting Producer, Emily Stevens; Director, Laura Gabbert; Photography, Shana Hagan; Music, Peter Golub; Editors, David Timoner, William Haugse; a Gabbert/Libresco Productions; Color; Not rated; 73 minutes; Release date: February 25, 2005. Documentary on residents of Sunset Hall, a Los Angeles home for senior citizens; featuring Lucille Albert, Irja Lloyd.

MAN OF THE HOUSE

(COLUMBIA) Producers, Steven Reuther, Todd Garner, Allyn Stewart; Executive Producers, Tommy Lee Jones, Derek Dauchy; Director, Stephen Herek; Screenplay, Robert Ramsey, Matthew Stone, John J. McLaughlin; Story, John J. McLaughlin, Scott Lobdell; Photography, Peter Menzies, Jr.; Designer, Nelson Coates; Music, David Newman; Editors, Chris Lebenzon, Joel Negron; Costumes, Betsy Heimann; Casting, Sharon Bialy, Sherry Thomas; a Revolution Studios presentation of a Steven Reuther production; Dolby; Panavision; Deluxe color; Rated PG-13; 97 minutes; Release date: February 25, 2005. CAST: Tommy Lee Jones (Roland Sharp), Cedric the Entertainer (Percy Stevens), Christina Milian (Anne), Paula Garces (Teresa), Monica Keena (Evie), Vanessa Ferlito (Heather), Kelli Garner (Barb), Anne Archer (Prof. Molly McCarthy), Brian Van Holt (Eddie Zane), Shea Whigham (Ranger Holt), Terry Parks (Ranger Riggs), R. Lee Ermey (Capt. Nichols), Paget Brewster (Binky), Shannon Marie Woodward (Emma), Liz Vassey (Maggie Swanson), Curtis Armstrong (Morgan Ball), Tom Reynolds (Carter), James Richard Perry (Himself), Turner Stephen Bruton (John Cortland), Nar Williams (Pizza Delivery Guy), Mark Hanson (Jimmy), Lucien Douglas (Cortland's Attorney), Bo Kane (Courthouse Reporter), Ash Christian (Razorback Mascot), Phil Aboussie (A/C Technician), Robert Southwell, Chase Jeffery, David Andrew Monahan (Campus Guys), Christopher Dahlberg (Local Stud), Brandon Johnson (Stud's Friend), Jesse De Luna, Mark Turner (Warehouse Officers), Luc Calhoun (Clay), Jimmy Ortega (Border Bus Driver), Timothy Crowley (Referee), Jim Baker (Football Coach), David Dunard (Announcer), William Bryant II (Organist), Carl F. Martin (Choir Director), Alan Atkins, Thomasina A. Atkins, Lorenzo Johnson, Denisha Missap, Elizabeth Millsap, Vania Reneau (Church Singers), James Burney II, Loren Davis, DeAnte Duckett, Whon Martin, Alethea Mills, Chavonne Morris, Sheven Morris, Aminah Ofumbi, Loren Turner, Clarissa Watkins (Choir Singers)

Kelli Garner, Christina Milian, Tommy Lee Jones, Paula Garces, Vanessa Ferlito, Monica Keena in *Man of the House* PHOTO COURTESY OF COLUMBIA

CRAZY LEGS CONTI: ZEN AND THE ART OF COMPETITIVE EATING

(OYSTER PRODS.) Producers/Directors/Photography, Danielle Franco, Christopher Kenneally; Music, Dinshaw Gobhai; Editor, Marc Senter; Color; DV; Not rated; 74 minutes; Release date: March 2, 2005. Documentary on Crazy Legs Conti's efforts to become the champ of competitive eating; featuring Crazy Legs Conti, Jeremy George, George Shea, Rick Shea, Rona Conti, Richard Conti, Little Jimmy, Takeru Kobayashi, Ed Cookie Jarvis, Eric Badlands Booker, Hungry Charles Hardy, Mo Ribs Molesky, Crawfish Nick Stipelcovich, Ray the Bison Meduna.

FACE

(INDICAN) Producers, Alexa L. Fogel, Joseph Infantolino, Bertha Bay-Sa Pan; Director, Bertha Bay-Sa Pan; Screenplay, Bertha Bay-Sa Pan, Oren Moveman; Photography, John Inwood; Designer, Teresa Mastropiero; Music, Leonard Nelson Hubbard; Editor, Gary Levy; Casting, Mercedes Danforth, Alexa L. Fogel; a Beech Hill Films, Centre Street production; Not rated; 89 minutes; Release date: March 4, 2005. CAST: Bai Ling (Kim), Kristy Wu (Genie), Kieu Chinh (Mrs. Liu), Treach (Michael), Will Yun Lee (Daniel), Tina Chen (Mrs. Chang), Ken Leung (Willie), Melissa Martinez (Sue), Deedee Magno (Kelly), Les J. N. Mau (Mr. Huang), Tina Factor (Asian Woman), Diane Cheng (Mrs. Mar), Christy Qin (Jenny), Ruth Zhang (Mrs. Huang), Jim Chu (Steve), Ben Wang (Mr. Leung), Susan Bigelow (Hospital Nurse), Paul J. C. Lee (Husband #2), Dena Atlantic (Clinic Nurse)

Michael Rodrick, Debbie Rochon in *Nowhere Man* PHOTO COURTESY OF FIRST INDEPENDENT

SHERIFF

(GO PICTURES) Producers, Daniel Kraus, Jason Davis; Executive Producer, John A. Davis III; Director/Photography/Editor, Daniel Kraus; Color; Mini-DV; Not rated; 76 minutes; Release date: March 11, 2005. Documentary on Ronald E. Hewett, the sheriff of Brunswick County, North Carolina.

MAIL ORDER WIFE

(FIRST INDEPENDENT PICTURES) Producers, Avram Ludwig, Kendall Morgan, Nina Yang, Andrew Weiner; Executive Producers, Gary Rubin, David Bartis, Doug Liman, Bo Hyde, Bobby Sheng; Directors/Screenplay, Huck Botko, Andrew Gurland; Photography, Luke Geissbuhler; Designer, Jon Nissenbaum; Costumes, Jennifer Galvelis; Editor, Kevin Napier; Casting, Lori Eastside; a Cherry Road Films, Double Edge Entertainment presentation of a Hypnotic production; Dolby;

Crazy Legs Conti in *Crazy Legs Conti* PHOTO COURTESY OF OYSTER PRODS.

Widescreen; Color; HD-to-35mm; Rated R; 92 minutes; Release date: March 11, 2005. CAST: Andrew Gurland (Andrew), Eugenia Yuan (Lichi), Adrian Martinez (Adrian), Deborah Teng (Deborah), Jose Canseco, Charles Debold, Luke Geissbuhler, Dan Johnson, David Mayer (Themselves), John Gramaglia (The Editor), Merritt Janson (Merritt), Sam Lisenco (Skaater), Paul Thornton (Curt Botko)

NOWHERE MAN

(FIRST RUN FEATURES) Producers, Tim McCann, Lawrence O'Neil, Mark Tchelistcheff; Director/Screenplay/Editor, Tim McCann; Photography, John Lazear; Designer, Laura Hyman; a King Cobra Films production; Color; Not rated; 78 minutes; Release date: March 11, 2005. CAST: Michael Rodrick (Conrad), Debbie Rochon (Jennifer), Frank Olivier (Daddy Mac), Lloyd Kaufman (Dr. Johnson), Bob Gosse (Hersh West), Michael Risley (Speed), Jim Burton (Larry), Mark Tchelistcheff (Shannon), Rod Razor (Little John), Steven Olivieri (Porn Producer), Aaron Parker (Gun Dealer), Eric Hill (Bartender), Paul Williams (Bar Patron), Kathy Good (Lisa), Elvira Sinani (Marie), Juliette Olivier (Samantha), Jim Harrison, Larry O'Neill, Joe Indusi (Pool Players)

NIGHT OF HENNA

(ILLUMINAIRE ENTERTAINMENT) Producer/Director/Screenplay, Hassan Zee; Co-Producers, Jeffrey Jones, Marc Meir; Photography, Hiro Narita; Designer, Phyllis Bowie; Music, George Gousis, Editors, Sharon Franklin, J. D. Sievertson; a Zee Films production; Dolby; Color; Not rated; 92 minutes; Release date: March 11, 2005. CAST: Joyce Carlin (Teacher), Nancy Carlin (Sue), Poni Chesser (Rafia), Reef Karim (Baboo), Pooja Kumar (Hava), Craig Marker (Justin), Jeanette Penley (Molly), Azhar Shah (Bashir), Girja Shankar (Abdul), Noor Shic (Zakia), Suhail Tayeb (Salman), Kevin Michael Walsh (Matt)

AFTER THE APOCALPYSE

(MEDAMA PRODS.) Producer/Director/Screenplay/Editor, Yasuaki Nakajima; Photography, Carolyn Macartney; Music, Hiro Ota; Black and white; Not rated;

72 minutes; Release date: March 16, 2005. CAST: Jacqueline Bowman, Vewlina Georgi, Zorikh Lequidre, Oscar Lowe, Moises Morales, Yasuaki Nakajima

THE VENETIAN DILEMMA

(PARNASSUSWORKS) Producers/Directors, Carole Rifkind, Richard Rifkind; Executive Producer, Rob Fruchtman; Photography, Giovanni Andreotta, Roberto Cimatti; Music, Joel Goodman; Editor, Joshua Waltezsky; Color; Not rated; 93 minutes; Release date: March 16, 2005. Documentary on the dual identity of Venice, as a city of history and as a tourist attraction; featuring Roberto D'Agostino, Paolo Pnapoppi, Danilo Palmiere, Michela Scibilia.

EATING OUT

(ARIZTICAL ENTERTAINMENT) Producer, Danielle Probst; Executive Producer, Michael Shoel; Director/Screenplay, Q. Allan Brocka; Photography, Keith J. Duggan; Designer, Melissa Fischer; Costumes, David Devincenzo; Music, Dominik Hauser; Editor, Phillip J. Bartell; Casting, Don Carroll, Cathy Reinking; Color; Not rated; 90 minutes; Release date: March 18, 2005. CAST: Rebekah Kochan (Tiffani), Scott Lunsford (Caleb Peterson), Jim Verraros (Kyle), Natalie Burge (Milkshake Marcy), Adrienne Pearson (Jenny the Beaver "Firecrotch"), Jillian Nusbaum (Jamie Peterson), Ryan Carnes (Marc Everhard), Christopher Michaels (Sebastian), Emily Stiles (Gwen Anderson), William Shepard (Joey), Maurice Grossman (Carnival Vendor), John Janezic (Richard), Ditte Lokon (Miko), Dani Millan (Ronnie), Stafford Williamson (Prof. Winston James), Donald Cline (Mr. Milford), Joy Ives (Mrs. Milford), Pete Kelly, Michael J. Shoel (Leather Guys), Murphy Michaels (Frank Peterson), Martie van der Voort (Susan Peterson)

After the Apocalypse PHOTO COURTESY OF MEDAMA PRODS.

A TALE OF TWO PIZZAS

(COCKEYED CARAVAN) Producer, Patricia Zagarella; Executive Producers, James L. Simon, Gary Kauffman, Mary Ellen Ashley, Neil McCurry, Frederic B. Vogel; Director/Screenplay, Vinnie Sassone; Photography, Peter Nelson; Designer, Ukachi Arinzeh; Costumes, Toni-Leslie James; Music, Peter Fish; Editor, Robert Pennington; Casting, Rob Decina; a Hot Pie production; Color; Rated PG; 82 minutes; Release date: March 18, 2005. CAST: Vincent Pastore (Vito Rossi), Frank Vincent (Frank Bianco), Robin Paul (Angela Rossi), Conor Dubin (Tony Bianco), Patti D'Arbanville (Margie Bianco), Louis Guss (Emilio), Angela Pietropinto (Beverly Rossi), Nick Giangiullo (Mooch), Kelly Karbacz (Lisa), Michael Carbonaro (Mikey), Melissa Marsala (Denise), Frankie Galasso (Tommy), Pooch Hall (Eugene), Mikey Romano (Sal), Mary Ellen Ashley (Eleanor), Jimmy Palumbo (Health Inspector), Brian Sullivan (Gas Burner Technician), Geoffrey Arend (Johnny), Pat Decina (Johnny's Dad), Richard V. Licata (Rocco), Eric Dorsey (Bouncer), Jack Martin (Anthony, Jr.), James L. Simon (Lone Customer), Simeon Guss, Luigi Petrozza (Gamblers), Amelia Borella (Club Waitress), Alisia Geanopulos (Mindy Abramsky), Jeremy Fonicello (Carmine)

Dudley Findlay, Jr., Clint Jordan in *Milk and Honey* PHOTO COURTESY OF WELLSPRING

MILK AND HONEY

(WELLSPRING) Producers, Matthew Myers, Thierry Cagianut; Executive Producers, Cedric Jeanson, John Quested; Director/Screenplay, Joe Maggio; Photography, Gordon Chou; Designer, Bryce Paul Mama; Music, Hal Hartley; Editor, Seth Anderson; Casting, Amy Gossels; a Concrete Films, Highbrow Entertainment, P-Kino production; Dolby; Color; Not rated; 90 minutes; Release date: March 18, 2005. CAST: Clint Jordan (Rick Johnson), Kirsten Russell (Joyce Johnson), Dudley Findlay, Jr. (Moses Jackson), Anthony Howard (Tony), Greg Amici (Dudley), Eric Wippo (Troy), Lizbeth Sant'Angelo (Maud)

MONDOVINO

(THINKFILM) Producer, Emmanuel Giraud, Jonathan Nossiter; Director/Editor, Jonathan Nossiter; Photography, Jonathan Nossiter, Stephanie Pommez; Line Producer, Catherine Hannoun; a Goatworks Films (NY),Les Films de la Croisade (Paris) production in association with Sophie Dulac Prods., Ricardo Preve Films, Michel Saint Jean, Diaphana Films with the participation of CNC; U.S.-French; Dolby; Color; DV-to-35mm; Not rated; 166 minutes; Release date: March 23, 2005. Documentary on the wine making industry; featuring Albiera Antinori, Allegra Antinori, Lodovico Antinori, Isanette Bianchetti, Jean-Charles Boisset, Marchioness Bona, Michael Broadbent, Antonio Cabezas, Battista Columbu, Lina Columbu, Xavier de Eizaguirre, Alix de Montille, Etienne de Montille, Hubert de Montille, Arnaldo Etchart, Marco Etchart, Salvatore Ferragamo, Marquis Dino Frescobaldi, Aime Guibert, Bill Harlan, Yvonne Hegoburu, Patrick Léon, Bernard Magrez, Margrit Mondavi, Michael Mondavi, Tim Mondavi, Jonathan Nossiter, Robert Parker, Michel Rolland, Neal Rosenthal, James Suckling, Inaldo Tedesco, Jean-Luc Thunevin, Massimo Vinci, Patrizia Vinci, Marquis Vittorio.

MISS CONGENIALITY 2: ARMED AND FABULOUS

(WARNER BROS.) Producers, Sandra Bullock, Marc Lawrence; Executive Producers, Mary McLaglen, John Kirby, Bruce Berman; Director, John Pasquin; Screenplay, Marc Lawrence; Based on characters created by Marc Lawrence, Katie Ford, Caryn Lucas; Photography, Peter Menzies; Designer, Maher Ahmad; Costumes, Deena Appel; Music, Christophe Beck; Editor, Garth Craven; Choreographer, Fatima; Casting, Nancy Foy; a Castle Rock presentation in association with Village Roadshow Pictures of a Fortis Films production; Dolby; Panavision; Technicolor; Rated PG-13; 115 minutes; Release date: March 24, 2005. CAST: Sandra Bullock (Gracie Hart), Regina King (Sam Fuller), Enrique Murciano (Jeff Foreman), William Shatner (Stan Fields), Ernie Hudson (McDonald), Heather Burns (Cheryl), Diedrich Bader (Joel), Treat Williams

Battista Columbu, Jonathan Nossiter, Lina Columbu in *Mondovino*

Hubert de Montille, Alix de Montille in *Mondovino* PHOTO COURTESY OF THINKFILM

Sandra Bullock, Regina King in *Miss Congeniality 2* PHOTO COURTESY OF WARNER BROS.

Heather Burns, Abraham Benrubi, William Shatner in *Miss Congeniality 2*

(Collins), Abraham Benrubi (Lou Steele), Nick Offerman (Karl Steele), Elisabeth Röhm (Janet), Leslie Grossman (Pam), Lusia Strus (Janine), Molly Gottlieb (Priscilla), Susan Chuang (Tobin), William O'Leary (Jenkins), John DiResta (Clonsky), Audrey Wasilewski (Mother in Bank), Marjorie Lovett (Bank Customer), Michelle Page (Punk Girl in Bank), Faith Minton, Eve Gordon, Kim Morgan Greene (Housewives), Rachel Iverson (Rachel), Regis Philbin, Joy Philbin, Dolly Parton, Ida Flammenbaum, Frank Marino (Themselves), Patricia Andrest Davis (Angela), Christopher Ford (Jason), Brian Shortall (Rob Okun), Vic Chao (Hills), Marcelo Tubert (Roberto Fenice), Adam LeFevre (Bartender), Stephen Tobolowsky (Tom Abernathy), Mary Ann Price (Dolly's Assistant), Megan Cavanagh (Shirley), Don Perry (Buster Harrison), Gregory Stenson (Sniper), Don Mirault (Griffin), L. Sidney (Agent Clark), Larry Edwards (Patti LaBelle Impersonator/Tina Impersonator #2), Brad Grunberg (Elizabeth Taylor Impersonator), Alan Luzietti (Liza Impersonator), Todd Sherry (Dolly Impersonator), Adam Austin (Agent Austin), Roxana Ortega (Mrs. Gordon), Thomas McGoldrick (Regis Show Propman), Esteban Cueto (Big Man in Bar), Octavia Spencer (Middle-Aged Woman), James DuMont (Man in Bookstore), Sue Tripathi (CNN Reporter), Brendan P. O'Connor (Affion Crockett (Attendants), Benny Nieves (Tracking Agent), Jayen Krashin, Cynthia Pepper, Lloyd Kino, Fusako Stevenson (Tourists), Rachel Smith (Vegas Anchorwoman), Mark S. Llewellyn (SWAT Leader)

THE HELIX…LOADED

(ROMAR ENTERTAINMENT) Producers, A. Raven Cruz, Ryan Francis, Sylwia Golonka, Samuel A. Levine, Antonio Aniano; Executive Producers, Jonathan Schneidman, Joel Jaffe, Robin Jaffe; Director/Screenplay, A. Raven Cruz; Photography, Tony Puyol; Designer, Julie Simpson; Costumes, Lisa Marie Harris; Music, Michael S. Patterson, Stephen Viens; Editors, Sylwia Golonka, Joel Rutkowski; Visual Effects Supervisor, Ryan Carter; Fight Choreographer, John Kreng; Casting, Dave Casper; Stained Iris Productions; Dolby; Color; Rated R; 97 minutes; Release date: March 25, 2005. CAST: Scott Levy (Nuyo), Vanilla Ice (Theo), Geremy Dingle (Agent Smak/Harold the Bum), Samantha Brooke (Infinitti), Dana Woods (Orpheum), Dane Moreton (Chad), Brigett Fink (Swatch), Eugene Kim (Ping), Moe Irvin (Tyrone), Christine Carlo (Dijonaise), Delia Copold (Agent Crack), Anthony Aniano (Agent Jonzen), Cylk Cozart (The Orafice), Jennifer Sky (Lola the Secretary), Joel South (Mr. Champion/Willy Twin), Tracy Workman (Danilly Twin), Joe Sperandeo (Prad Bitt), Edward Klau (Norton Edward), Ray Siegle (Captain Federale), Stephanie Swinney (Stacy), Amy Damkroger (Danice), Neal "Xingu" Rodil (The Hulky), Tony Tarasco (Pablo), Wendy E. Snyder (Angela the Post-Cog), Jody Jaress (Georgina), Steve Nave (5 Group Leader), Brian Ames (Neg 5 Clubgoer), Justin Baldoni (Jason), Joe Brent (Larry, Therapy Patient), Ken Gamble (Blade), Brenna Long (Bookworm Brenna), Brittany Long (Bowling Ball Brittany), Rane Miranda (Wallwalker Rane), Sofia Miranda (Fork Bending Sofia)

D.E.B.S.

(SAMUEL GOLDWYN FILMS) Producers, Angela Sperling, Jasmine Kosovic; Executive Producer, Larry Kennar; Director/Screenplay/Editor, Angela Robinson; Photography, M. David Mullen; Designer, Chris Anthony Miller; Costumes, Frank Helmer; Music, Steven Stern; Casting, Rick Montgomery; a Screen Gems, Destination presentation; Dolby; Panavision; 24p HD; Deluxe color; Rated PG-13; 91 minutes; Release date: March 25, 2005. CAST: Sara Foster (Amy Bradshaw), Jordana Brewster (Lucy Diamond), Meagan Good (Max Brewer), Devon Aoki (Dominique), Jill Ritchie (Janet), Geoff Stults (Bobby Matthews), Jimmi Simpson (Scud), Holland Taylor (Mrs. Petrie), Michael Clarke Duncan (Dr. Phipps), Jessica Cauffiel (Ninotchka Kaprova), Christina Kirk (Madeleine), J. B. Ghuman, Jr. (Dustin), Scoot McNairy (Stoner), Jean St. James (Waitress), Eric Dearborn (Eric), Jenny Mollen (German D.E.B.), Aimee Garcia (Maria), Roger Fan, Krista Conti (News Anchors), Gina Salemi, Kasey Stevens (Juniors), Jennifer Carpenter (Hysterical Student), Eric Bochniarz (David), Ryan Xavier (Hutch), Michael Mastro (Kirk), Tony Cecere (Proctor)

Meagan Good, Devon Aoki, Jill Ritchie in *D.E.B.S.* PHOTO COURTESY OF SAMUEL GOLDWYN FILMS

The Fabulous Moolah, Judy Grable in *Lipstick & Dynamite* PHOTO COURTESY OF KOCH LORBER

LIPSTICK & DYNAMITE, PISS & VINEGAR: THE FIRST LADIES OF WRESTLING

(KOCH LORBER FILMS) Producers, Ruth Leitman, James Jernigan, Debbie Nightingale, Anne Hubbell; Executive Producer, Lydia Dean Pilcher; Director, Ruth Leitman; Photography, Ruth Leitman, Nancy Segler; Editors, Ruth Leitman,

Colton Ford in *Naked Fame* PHOTO COURTESY OF REGENT/HERE!

M. Connie Diletti; a Ruthless Films, 100-to-One Films production in association with the Nightingale Co.; Black and white/color; Not rated; 77 minutes; Release date: March 25, 2005. Documentary on lady wrestlers; featuring Penny Banner, Lllian Ellison, Gladys Gillen, The Fabulous Moolah, Judy Grable, Cyndi Lauper, Ida May Martinez, Ella Waldek, Mae Young.

NAKED FAME

(REGENT/HERE! FILMS) Director, Christopher Long; Editor, J. D. Disalvatore; Color; Not rated; 84 minutes; Release date: March 25, 2005. Documentary on how porn star Colton Ford turned his back on his trade to return to a musical career; featuring Colton Ford, Blake Harper, Amber, Kevin Aviance, Marc Berkely, Chi Chi La Rue, Pepper Mashey, Tony Mills, Bruce Vilanch.

Robin Greenspan, Lacie Harmon in *Girl Play* PHOTO COURTESY OF WOLFE RELEASING

GIRL PLAY

(WOLFE RELEASING) Producers, Gina G. Goff, Laura Kellam; Executive Producer, Sean McVity; Director, Lee Friedlander; Screenplay, Lee Friedlander, Lacie Harmon, Robin Greenspan; Photography, Michael Negrin; Designer, Dahl Delu; Costumes, Shawnelle Cherry; Music, Laura Karpman; Editor, Christian White; a Goff-Kellam production; Color; Not rated; 73 minutes; Release date: April 1, 2005. CAST: Robin Greenspan (Robin), Lacie Harmon (Lacie), Mink Stole (Robin's Mother), Dom DeLuise (Gabriel), Katherine Randolph (Audrey), Lauren Maher (Cass), Gina DeVivo (Robin, Age 14), Shannon Perez (Young Robin, Age 6), Dominic Ottersbach (Gabriel's Assistant), Julie Briggs (Dr. Katherine), Peter Ente (Robin's Father), Graham T. McClusky (Parents' Friend), Skye Emerson (Bartender), Jessica Golden (Laura, Drunk Girl at Bar), Lynn A. Henderson (Attractive Girl at Bar), Sara Barielles (Singer in Bar), Lanre Idewu (Photographer), Sean Thomas Russell (Photographer's Assistant), Brian To (Photographer's Technician), Katlin Belcher (Girl in Robin's School), Kristen Evenson (Resort Waitress), G. Allan Brocka (Waiter)

DUST TO GLORY

(IFC FILMS) Producers, Scott Waugh, Mike McCoy; Executive Producer, C. Rich Wilson; Director/Screenplay, Dana Brown; Photography, Kevin Ward; Music, Nathan Furst; Editors, Dana Brown, Scott Waugh; Associate Producer, Marty

Fiolka; a BrownWa Pictures presentation in association with Score Intl.; Dolby; Color; HD/16mm-to-35mm; Rated PG; 97 minutes; Release date: April 1, 2005. Documentary on the Baja 1000 autorace; featuring Mario Andretti, Sal Fish, Robby Gordon, Ricky Johnson, Chad McQueen, Jimmy N. Roberts, Malcolm Smith.

Dust to Glory PHOTO COURTESY OF IFC FILMS

VOICES IN WARTIME

(CINEMA LIBRE) Producers, Jonathan King, Rick King; Executive Producer, Andrew Himes; Co-Executive Producers, Alix Wilbur; Director, Rick King; Photography, Eric Browne, Kevin Cloutier, Brian Dowley, Mike Fox, Chris Gallo, Joseph Hudson; Music, Anton Sanko; Editor, Daniel Lowenthal; a Two Careys Productions presentation; Color; DV; Not rated; 74 minutes; Release date: April 8, 2005. Documentary on war as reflected through poetry; featuring Chris Abani, Sinan Antoon, Rachel Bentham, David Connolly, Pamela Talene Hale, Sam Hamill, Chris Hedges, Lt. Gen. William Lennox Jr., Lt. Paul Mysliwiec, Marilyn Nelson, Sherman Pearl, Jonathan Schell, Alexandra Sanyal, Hashim Shafiq, Jonathan Shay, Jon Stallworthy, Emily Warn, Craig White, Saul Williams; VOICES: Chris Sarandon, Lisbeth Scott, Garrison Keillor, Gilbert Hines, Dorothy King, John Francis, Jason Williams, Graham Townsley, Kazuko Robertshaw, Humbert Hodgin, Jon Christensen.

STATE PROPERTY 2

(LIONS GATE) Producer/Director, Damon Dash; Executive Producers, Michael Paseornek, Beth Melillo; Screenplay, Adam Moreno; Story, Adam Moreno, Damon Dash; Photography, Tom Houghton; Designer, Anne Stuhler; Costumes, Crystal Streets; Music, Kerry Muzzey; Editor, Gary Levy; Casting, Kristen Paladino; a Dash Films, Lions Gate production; Super 16mm-to-HD-to-35mm, Color; Rated R; 94 minutes; Release date: April 13, 2005. CAST: Beanie Siegel (Beanie), Victor N.O.R.E. Santiago (El Loco), Damon Dash (Dame), Michael Bentt (Biggis, El Plaga), "Omillio Sparks" Kenneth Johnson (Baby Boy), Oschino (D-Nice), Freeway, Cam'ron, Julez Sanchez, Jimmy Jones, Kanye West, Denim, Nicole Wray, Winky Wright (Themselves), Neef, Young Chris (Young Gunz), Duan Grant (P-Nut), Sundy Carter (Aisha), Russell Jones (Dirt McGirt), "Fame" Jamal Grinnage, Billy Danz, Fox (MOP), Roselyn Sanchez (D.A.), Mariah Carey (Professionally Dressed Woman), Angie Martinez (Missy, Tuesday Night), Bernard Hopkins (O.G.), "Loon" Chauncey Haukins (Loco's Father), Omarah (Loco's Mother), "Smokey" Derron Edington, Rob Stapleton, Capone, Lil Cease,

Sal, Jeff Ward (Inmates), Big Face Gary, Shawn Arnold, Bobby Dash, Boola, Sha, Von (Dame Crew), Sade (Dancer), Bo Kaprall (Judge), Kevin Campbell (C-Zer), Tiana (Aja), Damon Dash II "Boogie" (Young Damon), Quasim Pressley (Young Baby Boy), Shakur Al Din Barry (Young Beans), Siddiq Cornish (Young D-Nice), Amir Grant (Young P-Nut), Steven Derry (Kid), Adam Moreno (Warden), Michelle Brown (Ceo), Virginia Torres (Fight Night), Joe Sherman (The Fist), Carlo D'Amore (Latino #1, Mario), René Ojeda, Cesar De Leon (Cuban Goons), Chance Kelly (Guard), Damien Achilles, Muse Abdullah (Loco's Crew), Tim House (Captain), Bobby Beckles (Insult Victim), Tim Gallin (Swat), James Lawrence (Shoe Thief), Derrick Simmons (Bound Man), Seymour Hewitt (Kitchen Inmate), Nik P. Jeternika (Philly Detective), Richardson Desil (Drug Dealer), Ted Landers (Detective), Lawrence Evans (Dame's Driver), Barry (Mariah's Bodyguard)

Voices in Wartime PHOTO COURTESY OF CINEMA LIBRE

WINNING GIRLS THROUGH PSYCHIC MIND CONTROL

(DIGITAL FILM GROUP) Producers, Dan Harnden, Joel Barkow, Terry Welch; Executive Producer, Sean O'Connor Dowd; Consulting Producer, Nathaniel Bonini; Director, Barry Alexander Brown; Screenplay, Dan Harnden; Photography, Ian Dudley, Scott Maher; Designers, Terry Welch, Joel Barkow; Costumes, Kate Quinlan; Music, Steve Ferrone, Adam Asarnow, Bill Simms Jr.; Editor, K. A. Chisholm; a Cannery Filmworks production; Dolby; Color; Not rated; 93 minutes; Release date: April 15, 2005. CAST: Bronson Pinchot (Devon Sharpe), Ruben Santiago-Hudson (Samuel Menendez), Amy Carlson (Kathy), Christopher Murney (Albert), Amy Wright (Psychiatrist), Larry Clarke (Bob), Lauren Braddock (Sarah), Lana Quintal (Camilla), Stuart Zamsky (Drunk on Steps), Kimberley Wurster (Store Owner), Karla Brown (Bob's Wife), Carey Hope (Lady with Tattoo), Sharon Raab, Jason Downs (Pregnant Couple), Bill Brecht (Man with Benign Biopsy), Tonya Lewis Lee (Woman with Cheating Boyfriend), Taij Ayodeji (Baseball Fan), Regina Spektor (Girl Who Lost Ring), June Leroy (Woman Asking Life's Purpose), Noora Telaranta (Kathy Lookalike), Roseanne Farano (Woman on Stairs), Brad Scribner (Man on Stairs), Jackie Enfield (Jesse), Tracy Lockhart (Tanya), William Laney (Kenny), Henry Yuk (Maintenance Guy), Hugh Karraker (Father of the Bride), Roger Schira (Club Stage Manager), Deyong Liu (Chinese Questioner), Lucia Grillo (Woman on Bench), Lisa Stagnitti (Woman in Park)

DOWN AND DERBY

(GS ENTERTAINMENT) Producers, Steele Hendershot, Dickilyn Johnson; Executive Producers, John Stone, Eric Hendershot; Director/Screenplay, Eric Hendershot; Photography, T. C. Christensen, Gordon Lonsdale; Designer, Arizona Taylor; Costumes, Hayley Hammond; Music, Chuck E. Myers; Editor, Tony Lombardo; Casting, Michael Fenton, Allison Cowitt; a Stonehaven Media production in association with First in Flight Media; Dolby; FotoKem color; Rated PG; 94 minutes; Release date: April 15, 2005. CAST: Greg Germann (Phil Davis), Lauren Holly (Kim Davis), Adam Hicks (Brady Davis), Perry Anzilotti (Big Jimmy), Deborah Ashton (Angel Scaldoni), Danny Shepherd (Danny Scaldoni), Ross Brockley (Blaine Moosman), Tammy Lier (Charlotte Moosman), Nicholas Nengas (Todd Moosman), Marc Raymond (Ace Montana), Hunter Tylo (Teri Montana), Eric Jacobs (A. J. Montana), Pat Morita (Uno Yakimoto), Joey Miyashima (Kyosho Yakimoto), Robert Costanzo (Claude), Don Murphy (Himself), Carmen Rasmusen (Marilyn), Sandy Hackett (Larry Savage), Scott Christopher (Delivery Guy), Craig Costello (Announcer), Megan Selensky (Jane)

Lauren Holly, Greg Germann in *Down and Derby* PHOTO COURTESY OF GS ENTERTAINMENT

Sandy Hackett, Pat Morita, Greg Germann, Joey Miyashima in *Down and Derby*

A WAKE IN PROVIDENCE

(MISTER P. PRODS.) Producers, Patrick Coppola, Vincent Pagano, William Redner; Director, Rosario Roveto, Jr.; Screenplay, Billy Van Zandt, Vincent Pagano, Jane Milmore, Mike Pagano; Photography, Mark Kohl; Music, Ed Alton; Editor, Gareth O'Neil; Color; Rated R; 94 minutes; Release date: April 15, 2005. CAST: Vincent Pagano (Anthony), Victoria Rowell (Alissa), Mike Pagano (Frankie), Adrienne Barbeau (Aunt Lidia), Billy Van Zandt (Louie), John Mariano (Brunie), Mark DeCarlo (Vinnie), Jane Milmore (Patty), Lisa Raggio (Claudia), Kaye Kingston (Gram Baldassarre), Louis Guss (Uncle Guy), Micole Mercurio (Aunt Elaine), Sam Coppola (Uncle Joe), Magda Harout (Aunt Alma), John Capodice (Uncle Sal), Esther Reaves Grande (Aunt Esther), Travis J. Feretic (Nicky), Sarah Thompson (Erica), Leigh Allyn Baker (Connie), Michele Maika (Gina), Thomas Grigsby (Ian), Dan Lauria (Rudy), Jerry Vale (Buddy Verona), Robert E. Weil (Mr. Scalsi), George Michael Jones (Lionel), John Randolph Jones (Priest), Melinda Sanford (Singer in Church), Mews Small (Voice of Casting Director), Michael Bearducci (Man in Funeral Home), Joe Mecca (Man in Bar), Rosario Roveto, Jr. (Man in Car)

THE YEAR OF THE YAO

(FINE LINE FEATURES) Producers, James D. Stern, Adam Del Deo; Executive Producers, Adam Silver, Gregg Winik, Bill Sanders; Co-Producers, Christopher Chen, Paul Hirschheimer; Co-Executive Producer, Laurence Weitzman; Directors, James D. Stern, Adam Del Deo; Photography, Michael Winik; Music,

Shaquille O'Neal, Yao Ming in *The Year of the Yao* PHOTO COURTESY OF FINE LINE FEATURES

Erik Palladino in *Dead & Breakfast* PHOTO COURTESY OF ANCHOR BAY

James L. Venable; Editors, Jeff Werner, Michael Tolajian; an Endgame Entertainment, NBA Entertainment production; Dolby; Color; Rated PG; 88 minutes; Release date: April 15, 2005. Documentary on Yao Ming, the first Chinese-born player to become a star player for the National Basketball Association; featuring Yao Ming, Charles Barkley, Steve Francis, Michael Irvin, Ernie Johnson, Cuttino Mobley, Shaquille O'Neal, Colin Pine, Glen Rice, Kenny Smith.

DEAD & BREAKFAST

(ANCHOR BAY) Producers, E. J. Heiser, Jun Tan; Executive Producers, Joe Madden, Ching I. Wang, Miranda Bailey; Director/Screenplay, Matthew Leutwyler; Story, Matthew Leutwyler, Jun Tan, Billy Burke; Photography, David Scardina; Designer, Don Day; Costumes, Molly Grundman; Music, Brian Vander Ark; Editor, Peter Devaney Flanagan; an Ambush Entertainment, Goal Line production; Color; Rated R; 87 minutes; Release date: April 20, 2005. CAST: Ever Carradine (Sara), Portia de Rossi (Kelly), David Carradine (Mr. Wise), Bianca Lawson (Kate), Jeffrey Dean Morgan (The Sheriff), Erik Palladino (David), Oz Perkins (Johnny), Gina Philips (Melody), Jeremy Sisto (Christian), Diedrich Bader (Chef Henri), Miranda Bailey (Lisa Belmont), Vincent Ventresca (Doc Riley), Mark Kelly (Enus), Brent David Fraser (The Drifter), Brooke Allison (Mrs. Kimble), Padraic Aubrey (Mullet Man), Ric Barbera (The Preacher), Theresa Burkharrt (Skanky Chick), Amy Claire (Waitress), Jeff Enden (Cletus), Brian Gattas (Farmer Bob), Devon Gummersall (Orange Cap), Evan Helmuth (Bass Player), Johnny Martin (Bartender), Barry J. Ratcliffe (Ear Guy), Zakareth Ruben (Bridesmaid), Zach Selwyn (Randall Keith Randall), Zed Starkovich (Harmonica Bob)

MADISON

(ADDISON STREET FILMS) Producers, Martin Wiley, Carl Amari; Executive Producers, Chris Dennis, Steve Salutric, Roy Millonzi; Director, William Bindley; Screenplay, William Bindley, Scott Bindley; Photography, James Glennon; Designers, Dorian Vernacchio, Deborah Raymond; Costumes, Jane Anderson; Music, Kevin Kiner; Editor, William Hoy; Casting, Amy Lippens; Presented in association with Genius Entertainment; Dolby; Panavision; Technicolor; Rated PG; 94 minutes; Release date: April 22, 2005. CAST: Jim Caviezel (Jim McCormick), Jake Lloyd (Mike McCormick), Mary McCormack (Bonnie McCormick), Bruce Dern (Harry Volpi), Paul Dooley (Mayor Vaughn), Brent Briscoe (Tony Steinhardt), Mark Fauser (Travis), Reed Diamond (Skip Naughton), Frank Knapp (Bobby Humphrey), Chelcie Ross (Roger Epperson), Byrne Piven (George Wallin), William Shockley (Rick Winston), Matt Letscher (Owen), Richard Lee Jackson (Buddy Johnson), Kristina Anapau (Tami Johnson), Vincent Ventresca (Walker Greif), Cody McMains (Bobby Epperson), John Watson, Sr. (Walter), Jim Andelin (Merle), Carl Amari (Jake Merrill), Len Foley (Bill Kittle), Jane Heitz (Audrey), Kathleen Ewing (Bank Secretary), Laura Whyte (Bonnie's Mom), Bernie Landis (Lyle Dayhoff), Jim Hendrick (Himself), Dean Biasucci (ABC Reporter), Bob North (Keith), Emily Salutric, Brie Larson, Will Bindley, Cully Smoller (Racers), Roger Wolski (Angry Citizen), W. E. Bindley (Sideburns), Don Youngblood (Another Man), Fran Williamson (Offended Woman), Chris Dennis (Man in Crowd), Don Keaton (Businessman), Sharon Bishop (Darlene), Greg Thomas (Construction Worker), Joy Ellison (Bonnie's Friend), Tony Steinhardt (Hydroplane Fan), Denise Dal Vera, Gabrielle Evans (Housewives), Kyle McClanahan (Kent), Randall Gienko (Peter), Mercedes Blanco (Autograph Seeker), Betsey Vonderheide (Gertie), Peter Marmentini, Zack Rosenfield (Crew Guys), Cynthia Elterman (Miami Race Registrar), Hank Johnston (Ricky), John Riley (Captain), Mel Vonderheide (Priest), Jan Lucas (Woman in Crowd), James Field (Davy Snyder), John Mellencamp (Narration)

Jim Caviezel in *Madison*

Jake Lloyd, Jim Caviezel in *Madison* PHOTO COURTESY OF ADDISON STREET FILMS

Wes Bentley in *The Game of Their Lives* PHOTO COURTESY OF IFC FILMS

THE GAME OF THEIR LIVES

(IFC FILMS) Producers, Ginger T. Perkins, Peter Newman, Howard Baldwin, Karen Baldwin; Executive Producers, William J. Immerman, Greg Johnson; Director, David Anspaugh; Screenplay, Angelo Pizzo; Based on the book by Geoffrey Douglas; Photography, Johnn E. Jensen; Designer, Linda Burton; Costumes, Jane Anderson; Music, William Ross; Editors, Bud Smith, Scott Smith, Ian Crafford, Lee Grubin; Stunts, Tim Davison; Casting, Amanda Mackey Johnson, Cathy Sandrich Gelfond; a Bristol Bay Productions presentation, in association with Peter Newman Prods./InterAL, Baldwin Entertainment Group; Dolby; Panavision; Technicolor; Rated PG; 96 minutes; Release date: April 22, 2005. CAST: Gerard Butler (Frank Borghi), Wes Bentley (Walter Bahr), Jay Rodan (Frank "Pee Wee" Wallace), Gavin Rossdale (Stanley Mortensen), Costas Mandylor (Charlie "Gloves" Columbo), Louis Mandylor (Gino Pariani), Zachery Bryan (Harry Keough), Jimmy Jean-Louis (Joe Gaetjens), Patrick Stewart (Older Dent McSkimming), Terry Kinney (Dent McSkimming), John Rhys Davies (Bill Jeffrey), Nelson Vargas (John "Clarkie" Souza), Maria Bertrand (Rosemary Borghi), Mike Bacarella (Silvio Capiello), Tom Brainard (Lt. Austin), Marilyn

Dodds Frank (Fara Borghi), Brooke Edwards (Fiora Abruzzo), Joe Erker (Chubby Lyons), Julie Granata (Janet Capiello), John Harkes (Ed McIlvenny), Craig Hawksley (Walter Giesler), Stephen Milton (Spike), Mike Nussbaum (Mr. Abruzzo), Bill Smitrovich (Gen. Higgins), Sally Stephens (Granddaughter of Dent), Stephen Alexander (Sideline Cameraman), James E. Ash (All-Star Game Head Referee), Patrick Belics (Grocery Delivery Boy), Vanna Bonta (Italian Bride), Ian Carrington (English Coach), Deborah Corday (Lady of the Evening), Pamela Fischer (Woman in Press Box), Steve Fucoloro (Man in Green-Blue Shirt), Rosemary Garris (Soccer Fan on Stairs), Cleve Gray (ENG Sound Man), Todd Gwin (Intense Fan), Paul Lancia, Rob Miley (Soccer Subs), Chris Lueken (Cigar Smoker at Banquet), Brenna McDonough (Woman in Press Box), Sarah Maria Newman (Wedding Singer)

KING'S RANSOM

(NEW LINE CINEMA) Producer, Darryl Taja; Executive Producers, Toby Emmerich, Matt Moore, J. David Brewington Jr., Mike Drake, Jeremy Barber; Director, Jeff Byrd; Screenplay, Wayne Conley; Photography, Robert McLachlan; Designer, Kalina Ivanov; Music, Marcus Miller; Music Supervisor, Melodee Sutton; Editor, Jeff Cooper; Associate Producer, Luke Ryan; Casting, Tracy "Twinkie" Byrd; a Catch 23's Alter Ego production; Dolby; Deluxe color; Rated PG-13; 97 minutes; Release date: April 22, 2005. CAST: Anthony Anderson (Malcolm King), Jay Mohr (Corey), Kellita Smith (Renee King), Nicole Parker (Angela Drake), Regina Hall (Peaches Clarke), Loretta Devine (Miss Gladys), Donald Faison (Andre), Leila Arcieri (Kim Baker), Charlie Murphy (Herb Clarke), Brooke D'Orsay (Brooke Mayo), Jackie Burroughs (Grandma), Lisa Marcos (Raven), Roger Cross (Byron), Millie Tresierra (Woman), Rob Smith (David), Brenda H. Crichlow (Anita), Carrie Colak (Lori), Lila Yee (Miss Ho), Nicolas Wright (Timmy), Kwasi Songui (Ronald), Mutsumi Takahashi (Chicago Newscaster), Lawrence Dane (Officer Conley), Christian Potenza (Officer Holland), Glenn Bang (Peking Palace Employee), Martin Thibaudeau (Handsome Cop), Jennifer Seguin (Happy Snack Customer), Randy Thomas, Larry Day (Cops), Luis Oliva (Pablo), Terry Simpson (Desk Sergeant), Robert Higden (Boyfriend), Deepak Massand (Karaoke Ninja Singer), Ralph Francois, Roberto Blizzard (Onlookers), Sean Spender, Freddy Bessa (Boneagra Cops), Nicole Jones, Karina Shalaby, Julie Applebee (Malcolm's Beauties), Jonathan Krespil (Valet with Andre)

Anthony Anderson, Regina Hall in *King's Ransom* PHOTO COURTESY OF NEW LINE CINEMA

Jay-Z, Devon Aoki, Damon Dash in *Death of a Dynasty* PHOTO COURTESY OF TLA RELEASING

DEATH OF A DYNASTY

(TLA RELEASING) Producers, Damon Dash, Steven C. Beer; Executive Producers, Ron Rothholz, Lisa Fragner; Director, Damon Dash; Screenplay, Mr. Blue; Photography, Dave Dahniel; Designer, Cecil Gentry; Costumes, Sarah Beers; Music, Big Chuck, Theron Feemster; Editor, Chris Fiore; Casting, Adrienne Stern; a Rock-A-Fella Films, R&B FM production in association with Intrinsic Value Films and Entertainment Funding Group; Dolby; Color; Rated R; 91 minutes; Release date: April 29, 2005. CAST: Ebon Moss-Bachrach (David), Devon Aoki (Picasso), Capone (Damon), Robert Stapleton (Jay-Z), Rashida Jones (Layna), Kevin Hart (P-Diddy/Lackey), Gerald Kelly (Biggs), Damon Dash (Harlem), Chloë Sevigny, Kari Wuhrer, Jamie-Lynn DiScala (Sexy Women), Mr. Blue (A&R Guy/Hipster/Lew Chaplin), Sale Johnson, Lorraine Bracco (Enchante R&B Singers), Duncan Sheik (Well-Dressed Man), James Toback (Lyor Cohen), Drina De Niro, Mo Rocca (Staff Writers), Mark Ronson (Engineer), Ashley Shelton (EZ), Richard Maldone (Mikey), Gerald Kelly (Funkmaster Flex/Biggs/Angry Blackman), Charles Q. Murphy (Dick James/Dukey Man/Sock Head), Boogie (C-10 Kid), Devron "Smokey" Edington (Street Team Kid/Chauffeur/Bootlegger No.2/Big Boi/Lil' Bow Wow), Tony Roberts (Town Car Driver/Host), Aliya Campbell (Vonda), Flavor Flav, Laverne Atkinson, Augustus Johnson (Reporters), John Michaelson (Porter), Ann Jones, Janelle (Bitchy Women), Caleb Oglosk (Video Girl), Peter Sarsgaard (Brendon III), Zofia Borucka (Damon Dash's Nanny), Andrew August King (Magician), Stewart Summers (Lawyer), Tobias Truvillion (Cool Guy), Ed Lover, Doctor Dre, Carson Daly, Walt Frazier, Michael Musto, Rell, Riddick Bowe, Zap Juddah, Jay-Z, Cam'ron, M.O.P., State Property, YoungSteffa, Mariah Carey, Shoshanna Losntein, Jimmy Rodriguez, Russell Simmons (Themselves)

STALIN'S WIFE

(CINETRON) Producers, Slava Tsukerman, Myra Todorovsky, Nina V. Korova; Director/Screenplay, Slava Tsukerman; Photography, Slava Tsukerman, Vlad Sladkoy, Victor Notov, Lina Tregubov, Ernst Kolobko; Music, Joel Diamond; Narrators, Tim Smallwood, Susan Doukas, Mik Cribben; a Myrabel Studios production; U.S.-Russian; Color; Not rated; 104 minutes; Release date: April 29, 2005. Documentary investigating the mysterious death of Nadezhda Alliluyeva, the second wife of dictator Joseph Stalin.

FUNNY HA HA

(GOODBYE CRUEL RELEASING) Producer, Ethan Vogt; Director/Screenplay/Editor, Andrew Bujalski; Photography, Matthias Grunsky; Associate Producers, Morgan Faust, Hagai Shaham; Color; Not rated; 89 minutes; Release date: April 29, 2005. CAST: Kate Dollenmayer (Marnie), Christian Rudder (Alex), Myles Paige (Dave), Jennifer L. Schaper (Rachel), Lissa Patton Rudder (Susan), Marshall Lewy (Wyatt), Andrew Bujalski (Mitchell), Mark Herlehy (Grady), Danny Miller (Gary), Mark Capraro (Travis), Sabrina Hawthorne (Laurie), William Westfall (Jeff), Jeb McCaleb (Lance), Sheila Dubman (Kimberly), Justin Rice (Jed), AnitRa Menning (Liz), Thomas Hansen (Prof. Garver), Justin Sheckler (Chris), Jonathan Clermont (Ben), Phillip Mighdoll (Rabbi), Morgan Faust (Gretchen), Victoria Haggblom (Jackie), Vanessa Bertozzi (Nina), Adam Mansbach (Wes), Randy Bell (Rodney), Sam Dollenmayer (Amos)

ANOTHER ROAD HOME

(GEOQUEST ENTERTAINMENT GROUP) Producer/Director, Danae Elon; Executive Producer, Liselle Mei; Photography, Andrew T. Dunn; Editor, Bryan Dunnar Cole; Color; Not rated; 77 minutes; Release date: April 29, 2005. Documentary in which an Israeli woman tries to find her Palestinian caregiver.

Danae Elon, Mahmoud "Musa" Obdeidallah in *Another Road Home*

Amos Elon in *Another Road Home* PHOTO COURTESY OF GEOQUEST ENTERTAINMENT

Ice Cube, Willem Dafoe in *XXX: State of the Union* PHOTO COURTESY OF COLUMBIA

XXX: STATE OF THE UNION

(COLUMBIA) Producers, Neal H. Moritz, Arne L. Schmidt; Executive Producers, Todd Garner, Rob Cohen, Derek Dauchy; Director, Lee Tamahori; Screenplay, Simon Kinberg; Photography, David Tattersall; Designer, Gavin Bocquet; Costumes, Sanja Milkovic Hays; Music, Marco Beltrami; Editors, Mark Goldblatt, Steven Rosenblum, Todd E. Miller; Visual Effects Supervisor, Scott Farrar; Casting, Margery Simkin; a Revolution Studios presentation of an Original Film production; Dolby; Super 35 Widescreen; Color; Rated PG-13; 100 minutes; Release date; April 29, 2005. CAST: Ice Cube (XXX, Darius Stone), Samuel L. Jackson (Agent Augustus Gibbons), Willem Dafoe (Gen. George Octavius Deckert), Scott Speedman (Agent Kyle Steele), Peter Strauss (Pres. James Sanford), Xzibit (Zeke), Michael Roof (Toby Lee Shavers), Sunny Mabrey (Charlie), Nona Gaye (Lola Jackson), John G. Connolly (Lt. Alabama "Bama" Cobb), Ramón De Ocampo (Agent Meadows), Barry Sigismondi (Bull), Michael Don Evans (Conductor), David Rountree (Agent), Ned Schmidtke (Col. Jack Pettibone), Scott Michael Morgan (Farmhand), Chris Johnson (Young Agent), Thom Gossom, Jr. (Baptist Preacher), Stan Sellers (Uptight Businessman), Paul Collins (NSA Director Bill Brody), Lisa Joyner (Field Reporter at Fire), Bruce Kirkpatrick (Police Capt. Davis), Lance Baldwin (Sharpshooter), Kent Shocknek, Glen Walker, Leyna Nguyen (Newscasters), Jeanne Sakata, Gina St. John, Paul Keeley (Field Reporters), Andrew Fiscella (Guard), J. Anthony Brown (Webster), Bruce Bruce (Maurice), Matt Gerald (Liebo), Dave Kennedy (Funeral Commander), Rene Ibarra (Casket Detail Commander), Sarah Mack (Presidential Aide), Jared Chandler (Firing Team Commander), Samantha Tyler (Corvette Girl), Gavin Lindsay Goode (SWAT Officer), Jeffrey Moon (Soldier), Toby Bronson (Tank Commander), Travis Hinson (Tank Gunner)

THE GIRL FROM MONDAY

(HART SHARP) Producers, Hal Hartley, Steven Hamilton; Director/Screenplay, Hal Hartley; Photography, Sarah Cawley; Designer, Inbal Weinberg; Costumes, Virginia Cook; Editor, Steve Hamilton; Casting, Ryan Bronz; a Possible Films, The Monday Company production; Color; Rated R; 84 minutes; Release date: May 4, 2005. CAST: Bill Sage (Jack), Sabrina Lloyd (Cecile), Tatiana Abracos (The Girl from Monday), Leo Fitzpatrick (William), D. J. Mendel (Abercrombie), James Urbaniak (Funk), Juliana Francis (Rita), Ryan Bronz (Benson), David Neumann (Soldier #1), Michael Cassidy (Ted), Normandy Sherwood (Emily), James

Stanley (Doc), Paul Urbanski (CEO), Edie Falco (Judge), Matt Kalman (Nick), Tanya Perez (Theresa), Jenny Seastone Stern (Martha), Gary Williams (Adjuster), Cordelia Reynolds (Gunn Saleswoman), Linda Horwatt (Rachel), Elizabeth Faulkner (Court Secretary), James Findlay (Taxi Driver), Adrienne Campbell-Holt, Adam D. Grant, Christel Halliburton, Jarah, Darius Safavi, Tana Sarntinoranont, Audrey Lynn Weston (Students)

FIGHTING TOMMY RILEY

(FREESTYLE RELEASING) Producers, Eddie O'Flaherty, J. P. Davis, Bettina Tendler O'Mara; Executive Producer, Diana Kessler; Director, Eddie O'Flaherty; Screenplay, J. P. Davis; Photography, Michael Fimognari; Designer, Marla Atlschuler; Costumes, Corena Gibson; Music, Tim Simonec; Editor, Aram Nigoghossian; Casting, Carlene Moore; a Visualeyes Productions, 1st Chance Productions presentation; Color; Rated R; 109 minutes; Release date: May 6, 2005. CAST: Eddie Jones (Marty Goldberg), J. P. Davis (Tommy Riley), Christina Chambers (Stephanie), Diane Tayler (Diane Stone), Scot Belsky (Mr. Riley), Paul Terrell Clayton (Oscar), Paul Raci (Bob Silver), Adam Harlan (Bob Silver's Assistant), Don Wallace (Leroy Kane)

Sabrina Lloyd, Bill Sage in *The Girl from Monday*

Bill Sage, Tatiana Abracos in *The Girl from Monday* PHOTO COURTESY OF HART SHARP

A HOLE IN ONE

(BEECH HILL FILMS) Producers, Joseph Infantolino, Alexa L. Fogel; Director/ Screenplay, Richard Ledes; Photography, Stephen Kazmierski; Designer, William Fleming; Costumes, Jeanie Kimber; Music, Stephen Trask; Editor, Susan Graef; Dolby; Color; Not rated; 97 minutes; Release date: May 6, 2005. CAST: Michelle Williams (Anna Watson), Meat Loaf Aday (Billy), Tim Guinee (Dr. Tom Franklin), Wendell Pierce (Dan), Bill Raymond (Dr. Harold Ashton), Jonathan Watton (Bobby), Merritt Wever (Betty), Louis Zorich (Sammy), Mark Day (Mark), Ileen Getz (Nurse Aphrodite), Gerry Mendocino (Johnny)

DOUBLE DARE

(BALCONY RELEASING) Producers, Danielle Renfrew, Karen Johnson; Director/Photography, Amanda Michelli; Music, Marco D'Ambrosio; Editor, Purcell Carson; a Map Point Pictures, Goodmovies Entertainment, Runaway Films production; Color; Not rated; 81 minutes; Release date: May 6, 2005. Documentary focusing on Hollywood's stunt women; featuring Jeannie Epper, Zoe Bell, Lynda Carter, Lucy Lawless, Eurlyne Epper, Ken Howard, Terry Leonard, Quentin Tarantino, Steven Spielberg, Conrad E. Palmisano.

Uma Thurman, Zoe Bell in *Double Dare* PHOTO COURTESY OF BALCONY

UP FOR GRABS

(CROOKED HEADS PRODS.) Producer/Director/Screenplay, Michael Wranovics; Photography, Josh Keppel, Zach Richard; Editor, Dave Claccio; Color; Video; Not rated; 90 minutes; Release date: May 6, 2005. Documentary on the legal battle that erupted over the ownership of the ball that Giants player Barry Bonds hit into the stands at Pacific Bell Park, thereby hitting his record-breaking 73rd home run.

LOST

(SILVERCREST) Producer, Kevin Matossian, Paul Emami; Executive Producers, Ralph Winter, John J. Kelly; Director/Screenplay, Darren Lemke; Photography, Paul Emami; Designer, Shane Richardson; Costumes, Robert Constant; Music, Russ Landau; Editor, Bob Joyce; Casting, Peter D'Alessio; Dolby; Color; Not rated; 90 minutes; Release date: May 13, 2005. CAST: Dean Cain (Jeremy Stanton), Ashley Scott (Judy, Operator), Danny Trejo (Edward James Archer), Irina Björklund (Cora Stanton), Justin Henry (Chester Gould), Griffin Armstorff

Michelle Williams, Meat Loaf Aday in *A Hole in One* PHOTO COURTESY OF BEECH HILL FILMS

(Tyler Stanton), Taylor Boggan (Young Jeremy), Steve Lee Allen (Young Jeremy's Father), Irini D'Alessio (Ginger), Robert Easton (Minister), Paul Green (Trooper), John Paul Lubran (Sylvester), Rob O'Malley (Maloney), Pasquale Solomon (Tim), David Weiss (Barry), David Willis (Riley), Joseph Berwick, Jonathan Bell (Thieves), Farrell Bender, Cindy Jo Hinkleman, Selma Pinkard (Bank Tellers), Lois Hall (Old Woman), Luis Chavez (Mexican Teen), Angela Finger-Erben (Bar Patron)

TELL THEM WHO YOU ARE

(THINKFILM) Producer/Director/Photography, Mark S. Wexler; Screenplay, Mark S. Wexler, Robert DeMaio; Music, Blake Leyh; Editor, Robert DeMaio; a Sundance Channel, Wexler's World production; Color; Rated R; 95 minutes; Release date: May 13, 2005. Mark Wexler's documentary on his famous cine-matographer father, Haskell Wexler; featuring Mark Wexler, Haskell Wexler, Peter Bart, Verna Bloom, Billy Crystal, Michael Douglas, Jane Fonda, Milos Forman, Troy Garity, Ronnie Gilbert, Conrad L. Hall, Conrad W. Hall, Tom Hayden, Dennis Hopper, Ron Howard, Norman Jewison, Irvin Kershner, George Lucas, Albert Maysles, Danny Moder, Paul Newman, Sidney Poitier, Julia Roberts, John Sayles, Martin Sheen, Lee Tamahori, Studs Terkel, Jonathan Winters

Haskell Wexler, Mark Wexler in *Tell Them Who You Are* PHOTO COURTESY OF THINKFILM

STOLEN CHILDHOODS

(BALCONY RELEASING) Producer/Director/Screenplay, Len Morris; Photography, Robin Romano; Music, Miriam Cutler; Narrator, Meryl Streep; Color; Not rated; 85 minutes; Release date: May 20, 2005. Documentary on the shocking number of children sold to do slave labor throughout the world; featuring Tom Harkin, Pharis Harvye, Kailash Satyrathi, Wangari Maathai, Bruce Harris, Inderjit Kurana.

Chris Barnes in *A League of Ordinary Gentlemen* PHOTO COURTESY OF MAGNOLIA

A LEAGUE OF ORDINARY GENTLEMEN

(MAGNOLIA) Director, Christopher Browne; Photography, Ken Seng; Music, Gary Meister; Editors, David S. Tung, Kurt Engfehr; Color; Not rated; 93 minutes; Release date: May 27, 2005. Documentary following a group of middle-aged bowlers who hope to revive interest in the sport; featuring Wayne Webb, Pete Weber, Walter Ray Williams.

Stolen Childhoods PHOTO COURTESY OF BALCONY

DOMINION: PREQUEL TO THE EXORCIST

(WARNER BROS.) Producer, James G. Robinson; Executive Producers, David Robinson, Guy McElwaine; Director, Paul Schrader; Screenplay, Caleb Carr, William Wisher; Photography, Vittorio Storaro; Designer, John Graysmark; Costumes, Luke Reichle; Music, Angelo Badalamenti; Editor, Tim Silano; Prosthetic Makeup Supervisor, Jake Garber; Special Effects Coordinator, Danilo Bollettini; a Morgan Creek International production; Dolby; Color; Rated R; 117 minutes; Release date: May 20, 2005. CAST: Stellan Skarsgård (Father Lankester Merrin), Gabriel Mann (Father Francis), Clara Bellar (Rachel Lesno), Billy Crawford (Cheche), Ralph Brown (Sgt. Major), Israel Aduramo (Jomo), Andrew French (Chuma), Antonie Kamerling (Kessel), Julian Wadham (Maj. Granville), Eddie Osei (Emekwi), Ilario Bisi-Pedro (Sebituana), Njall Refoy (Corporal—Thief), Lorenzo Camporese (Private—Thief), Burt Caesar (Dr. Lamu), Marcello Santoni (Dutch Farmer), Griet van Damme (Teenage Dutch Girl), Simon McLinden (Corporal), Pet Chege (Sebituana's Wife), Hamadi Mwapachu (Convulsive Worker), Evelyn Duah (Mara), Rick Warden (Cpl. Williams), Michele Mariotti (German Sgt.), Ben Meyjes, Oliver Maltman (Soldiers), Omari Carter (James), Adrian Black (Joseph), Nick Komornicki (Gun-Firing Soldier)

Gano Grills, Jade Yorker in *Bomb the System*

FEARLESS FREAKS

(SHOUT! FACTORY) Producer, Rick Fuller; Executive Producer, Dan Jacunich, Ryan Dolan; Director/Narrator, Bradley Beesley; Editor, JoLynn Garnes; Color; Not rated; 100 minutes; Release date: May 25, 2005. Documentary on the band The Flaming Lips; featuring Beck, Steve Burns, Wayne Coyne, Jonathan Donahue, Steven Drozd, Adam Goldberg, Michael Ivins, Juliette Lewis, Liz Phair, Cat Power, Christina Ricci, Jack White, Meg White.

Mark Webber, Jaclyn DeSantis in *Bomb the System* PHOTO COURTESY OF PALM PICTURES

BOMB THE SYSTEM

(PALM PICTURES) Producers, Sol Tyron, Ben Rekhi; Executive Producers, Mark Webber, Kanwal Rekhi; Director/Screenplay, Adam Bhala Lough; Photography, Ben Kutchins; Designer, Jon Nissenbaum; Costumes, Harwood Lee; Music, El-P; Editor, Jay Rabinowitz; a Drop Entertainment production; Color; Rated R; 91 minutes; Release date: May 27, 2005. CAST: Mark Webber (Anthony "Blest" Campo), Gano Grills (Justin "Bulk 50" Broady), Jade Yorker (Kevin "Lune" Broady), Jaclyn DeSantis (Alexandra), Joey Dedio (Jazer), Stephen Buchanan (Noble), Al Sapienza (Officer Bobby Cox), Bonz Malone (Officer Nole Shorts), Donna Mitchell (Diane Campo), Kumar Pallana (Kumar Baba), Blake Lethem (Lazaro), Dylan Mikson (Gabriel), Joshua Gustin (Young Blest), KaDee Strickland (Toni), Semz (Knife), Walter Masterson (Hyste), Nato Jude (Mayo), Lee Quinones (Himself), I'Kyori Swaby (Pharaoh), Aliya Campbell (Kim), Ned Stresen-Reuter (Brendan Pricely), David Ley (Randolph), Peter Linari (Custodial Boss), Manny Siverio (Sum5), Derrick Simmons (Tido), Elliott Santiago (Krazy), Mukc, Trina Grant (Hazar's Girlfriends), Nikklas Bates (Drug Dealer), Quinn (Man in Window), Daisy Rojas (Woman in Window), David Aldi, Rajan Rekhi (Yuppies), Tim Donlin (Drooling Junkie), Ajay Naidu (Moses Mundhra)

Invisible PHOTO COURTESY OF INDEPENDENT

Alison Folland, Troy Garity in *Milwaukee, Minnesota* PHOTO COURTESY OF TARTAN USA

Joe Pantoliano, Jennifer Tilly in *Second Best* PHOTO COURTESY OF VELOCITY FILMS

SECOND BEST

(VELOCITY FILMS) Producers, Joe Pantoliano, Callum Greene, Anthony Katagas; Executive Producer, Paul Mayersohn; Director/Screenplay, Eric Weber; Photography, Chris Norr; Designer, John Nyomarkay; Costumes, Kitty Boots; Editor, Craig Cobb; Casting, Lina Todd; a Keep Your Head, Tenfaly Film Company production; Color; Rated R; 86 minutes; Release date: May 27, 2005. CAST: Joe Pantoliano (Elliot), Boyd Gaines (Richard), Peter Gerety (Marshall), Bronson Pinchot (Doc Klingenstein), Matthew Arkin (Gerald), Jennifer Tilly (Carole), Stephen Bogardus (George), Barbara Barrie (Dorothea), Polly Draper (Paula), James Ryan (Danny), Stephen Sable (Lum Chin), Damian Young (Robert Stern), Melody Pantoliano (Waitress), Irma St. Paule (Beth), Frank McCombs (Frank), Jacob Weber (Checkout Person), Patricia Hearst (Alana), Fiona Gallagher (Tiffany), Marcella Lowery (Nurse), Milton James (Pakistani Man), Paulina Porizkova (Allison), Tara Gropt (Karolina), Jessica Weber (Saleswoman), Robert Montano (Mike)

INVISIBLE

(INDEPENDENT) Producer/Director, Konstantin Bojanov; Photography, Hristo Bozajiev; Music, Masami Tomihisa, J. J. McGeehan; Editors, Konstantin Bojanov, Stela Georgieva, Boryana Alexandrova; U.S.-Bulgarian; Dolby; Color; Not rated; 90 minutes; Release date: June 1, 2005. Documentary on the ordeal of heroin addiction.

MILWAUKEE, MINNESOTA

(TARTAN USA) Producers, Molly M. Mayeux, Michael J. Brody, Jeff Kirshbaum; Executive Producers, Frances Grill, Joseph Grill; Director, Allan Mindel; Screenplay, R. D. Murphy; Photography, Bernd Heinl; Designer, Dina Goldman; Costumes, Michael Wilkinson; Music, Michael Convertino, Robert Muzingo; Editor, David Rawlings; a Albert & Tuey Productions, Empire State Entertainment, Framework Entertainment Group production; Dolby; Color; Rated R; 95 minutes; Release date: June 3, 2005. CAST: Troy Garity (Albert Burroughs), Alison Folland (Tuey Stites), Randy Quaid (Jerry James), Bruce Dern (Sean McNally), Hank Harris (Stan Stites), Debra Monk (Edna Burroughs), Josh Brolin (Gary), Holly Woodlawn (Transvestite), John Judd (Bartender), Maren Lindow (Woman in Photo), Timothy Slaske (Man in Restaurant)

ROCK SCHOOL

(NEWMARKET) Producers, Don Argott, Sheena M. Joyce; Director/Photography, Don Argott; Editor, Demian Fenton; a 9.14 Pictures, A&E Indiefilms production; Dolby; Color; Rated R; 93 minutes; Release date: June 3, 2005. Documentary on a school where kids learn the fundamentals of rock music; featuring Paul Green, C. J. Tywmoniak, Asa, Napoleon Murphy Brock, Tucker Collins, Madi Diaz-Svalgard, Will O'Connor.

PATERNAL INSTINCT

(TWO SPIRIT PRODS.) Producers, Murray Nossel, Craig Harwood; Executive Producer, Sheila Nevins; Superivsing Producer, John Hoffman; Director, Murray Nossel; Photography, Edward Marritz; Music, Hahn Rowe; Editor, Susanne Rostock; Color; Not rated; 75 minutes; Release date: June 8, 2005. Documentary in which Mark and Erik search for a surrogate mother for their child.

Gabrielle Union, Cedric the Entertainer, Mike Epps, Regina Hall in *The Honeymooners*
PHOTO COURTESY OF PARAMOUNT

THE HONEYMOONERS

(PARAMOUNT) Producers, David T. Friendly, Marc Turtletaub, Eric C. Rhone, Julie Durk; Executive Producers, Hal Ross, Cedric the Entertainer, Mike Epps; Director, John Schultz; Screenplay, Danny Jacobson, David Sheffield, Barry W. Blaustein, Don Rhymer; Based on the characters from the CBS television series; Photography, Shawn Maurer; Designer, Charles Wood; Costumes, Joan Bergin; Music, Richard Gibbs; Music Supervisor, Jennifer Hawks; Co-Producer, Niles Kirchner; Editor, John Pace; Casting, Nancy Foy, Susie Farris; a Deep River production; Dolby; Deluxe color; Rated PG-13; 85 minutes; Release date: June 10, 2005. CAST: Cedric the Entertainer (Ralph Kramden), Mike Epps (Ed Norton), Gabrielle Union (Alice Kramden), Regina Hall (Trixie Norton), Eric Stoltz (William Davis), Jon Polito (Kirby), John Leguizamo (Dodge), Carol Woods (Alice's Mom), Ajay Naidu (Vivek), Arnell Powell (DJ Suckaslam), Leticia Castillo (Young Mother), Chuy Bravo (Grocer), Doreen Keogh (Miss Celestine), Camille Donegan (Lissa), Joanna Dickens (Bus Stop Woman), Kim Chan (Quinn), Alice Drummond (Miss Benvenuti), Jerry De Capua (Television Play-by-Play Announcer), Guss Gerard Williams, Andrew St. Clair James, James Akapotor, Kensika Monshengwo (Poolhall Heavies), Tim Dillard, Enrique Fonseca, Charlie Kranz (Sewer Workers), Dana Lee (Hitako Kawakami), John Tormey (Auctioneer),

Paul Green (right) in *Rock School* PHOTO COURTESY OF NEWMARKET

Lenny Venito (Lenny), Brad Adkins (Dog Handler), Bern Deegan (Chip), Fergal Brady (Valet), Tsisiana Lohmann, Marcus Valentine, Charlie Schultz, Jeffrey Rudom (Party Guest), Laura Wey (Kirby's Date), Maria Tecce (Race Track Party Coordinator), Liu Shi Lun, Xiao Bai Wong (Real Entertainers), Tom Lawrence (Lonnie), Arlin Miller (Race Track Announcer), Kevin Fitzgerald Corrigan (Larry the Bus Driver), Doug MacMillan (City Health Inspector), Iggy (Himself)

THE KEEPER: THE LEGEND OF OMAR KHAYYAM

(ARRIVAL PICTURES) Producers, Kayvan Mashayekh, Sep Riahl, Belle Avery: Executive Producers, Robert Guest, Ali King; Director, Kayvan Mashayekh; Screenplay, Kayvan Mashayekh, Belle Avery; Photography, Matthew Cantrell, Dusan Joksimovic; Designer, Michelle Milosh; Costumes, Jane Robinson; Music, Elton Ahi; Editor, Duncan Burns; Casting, Jeremy Zimmerman, Andrea Clark; a Guide Co. Films presentation of a Keeper production; Dolby; Color; Rated PG; 95 minutes; Release date: June 10, 2005. CAST: Adam Echahly (Kamran), Bruno Lastra (Omar Khayyam), Moritz Bleibtreu (Malikshah), Rade Sherbedgia (Imam Muaffak), Vanessa Redgrave (The Heiress), Christopher Simpson (Hassan Sabbah), Marie Espinosa (Darya), Diane Baker (Miss Taylor),

Bruno Lastra, Rade Serbedzija in *The Keeper* PHOTO COURTESY OF FILMCOMPANY

C. Thomas Howell (Coach Fielding), Kevin Anding (Timmy), Puya Behinaein (Nader), Daniel Black (Young Omar), Richard Dillard (Mr. Saxon), Sarah Hadaway (Omar's Mother), Darius Irannejat (Grandfather), Hanane Joumal-Echahly (Shahin), Andy Madadian (Ali Ben-Sabbah), Layla Lauren Mashayekh (Nessa), Yasmin Paige (Young Darya), Shani Rigsbee (Court Entertainer), Shahrad Vossoughhi (Mansour), Apik Youssfeian (Grandmother)

Casper Andreas, Jamie Hatchett in *Slutty Summer*

SLUTTY SUMMER

(EMBREM ENTERTAINMENT) Producers, Casper Andreas, Anton Shilov; Executive Producer, Runar Petursson; Director/Screenplay/Editor, Casper Andreas; Photography, Jon Fordham; Music, Scott Starrett; from Hot Summer Productions; Color; Not rated; 85 minutes; Release date: June 10, 2005. CAST: Casper Andreas (Markus), Jesse Archer (Luke), Jamie Hatchett (Tyler), Jeffrey Christopher Todd (Peter), Virginia Bryan (Marilyn), Cristos Klapsis (Julian), Lance Werth (Kevin), Colin Houston (Adam), J. R. Rolley (Derek), Lex Sosa (Steven), Nick Toren (Larry), Michael Rogers, Dan Elhedery (Luke's Tricks), Mat Ellenburg (Go-Go Boy), Christophe Fraire (Peter's Date), Huy Nguyen (Asian Kid), Ben Ryan (Julian's Trick/Markus' Trick), Dan Sanabria (Luke's Leatherman), Anton Shilov (Tyler's Trick), Carter Vonasik (Markus' Leatherman), Cynthia Powell, Jenny Cabrera (Upset Customers), Elizabeth Crowley (Distressed Customer), Rula Elyas (Hostess), John Samuel Jordan, Neal Utterback (Businessmen), Christopher Meister (Impatient Customer), Selcen Onsan (Thirsty Customer), Jarret Sumers (Doorman), Daniele Teodoro (Confused Customer), Fanney Voigt (Soup Customer)

Jesse Archer, Christopher Todd in *Slutty Summer* PHOTO COURTESY OF EMBREM

Chris Noth, Hilary Duff in *The Perfect Man*

Heather Locklear, Hilary Duff, Aria Wallace in *The Perfect Man* PHOTO COURTESY OF UNIVERSAL

THE PERFECT MAN

(UNIVERSAL) Producers, Marc Platt, Dawn Wolfrom, Susan Duff; Executive Producers, Billy Higgins, Adam Siegel; Director, Mark Rosman; Screenplay, Gina Wendkos; Story, Michael McQuown, Heather Robinson, Katherine Torpey; Photography, John R. Leonetti; Designer, Jasna Stefanovich; Costumes, Marie Sylvie Deveau; Music, Christophe Beck; Editor, Cara Silverman; Casting, Nancy Klopper; a Marc Platt production; Dolby; Fotokem color; Rated PG; 96 minutes; Release date: June 17, 2005. CAST: Hilary Duff (Holly Hamilton), Heather Locklear (Jean Hamilton), Chris Noth (Ben Cooper), Mike O'Malley (Lenny Horton), Ben Feldman (Adam Forrest), Vanessa Lengies (Amy Pearl), Caroline Rhea (Gloria), Kym Whitley (Dolores), Aria Wallace (Zoe), Carson Kressley (Lance), Michelle Nolden (Amber), Maggie Castle (Wichita Girl), Gerry Mendicino (Market Co-Worker), James McGowan (Jean's Suitor), Philip Akin (English Teacher), Jeff Lumby (Dr. Fitch), Monique Mojica (Principal Campbell), Marvin Kaye, Eldridge Hyndman, Sean Gallagher, Jung-Yul Kim (Construction Workers), Dennis DeYoung, John Blasucci, Matthew DeYoung, Thomas Dziallo, Allison "Hawk" Horton (Tribute Band), Ed Fielding (Orchid Thief), Eugene Oleksiuk (PTA Man), Richard Partington (Priest), Hazel Gorin (Landlady), Martin Doyle (Cake Contest MC), Laura Robinson (Saleslady), Sharise Mortfield (Student in Library), Evelyn Kaye (Spelling Bee Moderator), Len Wagner (Groom), Jerry Azzopardi (Highway Patrolman), Sue Parker (Dog Walker), Shelley Cook (Wedding Usher)

THE DEAL

(FRONT STREET FILMS) Producers, Harvey Kahn, Ruth Epstein, Chris Dorr; Executive Producers, Kevin Kennedy, David Leuschen, Christian Slater; Director, Harvey Kahn; Screenplay, Ruth Epstein; Photography, Adam Sliwinski; Designer, Andrew Deskin; Costumes, Matia Stand; Music, Christopher Lennertz; Editor, Richard Schwadel; a Myriad Pictures presentation of a Front Street Films, Clean Slate Prods. production; Dolby; Deluxe color; Rated R; 107 minutes; Release date: June 17, 2005. CAST: Christian Slater (Tom Hanson), Selma Blair (Abbey Gallagher), Robert Loggia (Jared Tolson), Colm Feore (Hank Weiss), Angie Harmon (Anna), John Heard (Prof. Roseman), Kevin Tighe (John Cortland), Philip Granger (Jerome Halliday), Francoise Yip (Janice Long), Jim Thorburn (Shane Waller), Paul McGillion (Richard Kester), Christine Lippa (Lucy Rahlston), Jennifer Clement (Sara Kester), Mike Dopud (Theo Gorbov), Vyacheslav Vinnik (Nicholai Chernoff), Peter Hall (Clark Jackwell), Jay Robert Inslee (Senator Lucas), Linda Darlow (Erma), Frida Betrani (Jared's Secretary), Tony Alcantar (Agent Grazer), Peter LaCroix (Rod), Aubrey Arnason (Deena Scott), Tom McBeath (Board Member #1), Marc Baur (Client #1), Nathaniel DeVeaux (Officer), Valentina Ballos (Cleaning Woman), Howard Storey (Armed Security Guard)

THE TALENT GIVEN US

(VITAGRAPH FILMS) Producers, Andrew Wagner, Chelsea Gilmore, Tom Hines; Executive Producers, Kevin Fortuna, Tim Farley; Director/Screenplay/ Photography, Andrew Wagner; Music, David Dyas; Editor, Terri Breed; a Daddy W. Prods. production; Color; DV; Not rated; 97 minutes; Release date: June 17, 2005. CAST: Allen Wagner (Allen), Judy Wagner (Judy), Emily Wagner (Emily), Maggie Wagner (Maggie), Judy Dixon (Bumby), Billy Wirth (Billy), Andrew Wagner (Andrew), Tom Hines (Disgruntled Actor)

Jerry in *Waging A Living* PHOTO COURTESY OF PUBLIC POLICY PRODS.

WAGING A LIVING

(PUBLIC POLICY PRODS.) Producer/Director, Roger Weisberg; Co-Producers, Pamela Harris, Frances Reid, Edward Rosenstein; Photography, Slawomir Grunberg; Music, Richard Fiocca; Editors, Christopher White, Lewis Erskine, Sandra Christie; Color; Not rated; 85 minutes; Release date: June 22, 2005. Documentary on the efforts of several working Americans to lift their families out of poverty.

THE LAST MOGUL:
THE LIFE AND TIMES OF LEW WASSERMAN

(THINKFILM) Producers, Tori Hockin, Nat Brescia; Executive Producers, Nat Brescia, Barry Avrich, Jeff Sackman; Director/Screenplay, Barry Avrich; Photography, Charles Haggart; Designer, Mark Vandervoet; Music, Jim McGarth, Frank Kitching; Editor, Alex Shuper; Associate Producer, Natalie Mitrovich; Narrator, Neil Shee; a Melbar Entertainment Group, mPIX production; Color; Not rated; 103 minutes; Release date: June 24, 2005. Documentary on agent-turned-Hollywood studio executive Lew Wasserman; featuring Peter Bart, David Brown, Helen Gurley Brown, David Carr, Jimmy Carter, Charles Champlin, George Christy, Kay Coleman, Janet De Codrova, Garth H. Drabinsky, Dominick Dunne, Robert Evans, Leonard Goldberg, Wendy Goldberg, Jay Kanter, Larry King, Alan Ladd Jr., Michael Ovitz, Suzanne Pleshette, Frank Price, Al Setnick, Kathleen Sharp, Jack Valenti, Richard Zanuck.

DALLAS 362

(THINKFILM) Producers, Kip Konwiser, Gregory Sabatino; Executive Producers, Beau Flynn, Brian Williamson; Director/Screenplay, Scott Caan; Photography, Phil Parmet; Designer, Chuck Voelter; Costumes, Sophie De Rakoff Carbonell; Music, Danny Saber, Blues Saraceno; Editor, Andrea Bottigliero; Casting, Mary Vernieu; a Sunlion Films, Konwiser Brothers production; Color; Rated R; 100 minutes; Release date: June 24, 2005. CAST: Scott Caan (Dallas), Jeff Goldblum (Bob), Shawn Hatosy (Rusty), Kelly Lynch (Mary), Heavy D (Bear), Bob Gunton (Joe), Marley Shelton (Amanda), Val Lauren (Christian), Selma Blair (Peg), Isla Fisher (Redhead), Freddy Rodriguez (Rubin), James Caan (Walter), Raymond T. Williams (Rasta), Tony Lee Boggs (Beard), Ann Scott (Lady), Sasha Perl-Raver (Girl #1), Kip Ren (Girl on the Couch), Rene Heger, Joey Simmrin (Kids), Joan May (Hot Asian Girl), Shannon Jones (Girl in Bar)

RIZE

(LIONS GATE) Producers, David LaChapelle, Marc Hawker, Ellen Jacobson-Clarke, Richmond Talauega, Tone Talauega; Executive Producers, Ishbel Whitaker, Barry Peele, Ellen Jacobson-Clarke, Stavros Merjos, Rebecca Skinner; Director, David LaChapelle; Photography, Morgan Susser; Music, Red Ronin Prods., Amy Marie

Miss Prissy in *Rize* PHOTO COURTESY OF LIONS GATE

Shawn Hatosy in *Dallas 362* PHOTO COURTESY OF THINKFILM

Beauchamp, Jose Cancella; Music Supervisor, Jonathan McHugh; Editor, Fernando Villena; an HSI, Darkfibre production; Dolby; Color; DV; Rated PG-13; 85 minutes; Release date: June 24, 2005. Documentary on how krumping, a combination of dancing and athletic movement, was developed on the streets of South Central L.A.; featuring Tommy the Clown, Lil Tommy, Larry Swoop, El Niño, Dragon, Lil C, Tight Eyez, Baby Tight Eyez, Daisy, Big X, Miss Prissy, La Niña, Quinesha.

THE WAR ON THE WAR ON DRUGS

(MAD DOG FILMS) Producer, Dan Kornfeld; Director/Screenplay, Cevin D. Soling; Music, Martin Trum; a Sponge Music Group production; Dolby; Color; Not rated; 87 minutes; Release date: June 24, 2005. CAST: Tara Platt (Leader Tara/Agnes/Anime Girl/Norma/Sara/Isabelle), Yuri Lowenthal (John/Biff/Glenn/Henry/Ted/Zombie/Judge Knott), Joseph Greene (Professor Science/Victim/V.O. Still/Man at Urinal/Drug Czar), Brett Colby (Mugger/Hitler/Brahma/Garuda/Ken Carumen/Narrator/Police Detective/Paco), Kenny Marshall (Kali/Officer Hummler/God/Sissy Boy/Cold Sufferer), Susie Schwartz (Shroomie/Tennis Player #1/Lackey/Repulsed Girl), Daniel J. Kornfeld (Cop/Nixon/Senor Syringe/Chemist/Mark McGuire/Bob Marley/Officer Mengela/

Jimmy Hendrix/Keith Moon/Orin/Narrator/Thug #1/Football Brawler/Parent/Welder/Man in Line/Man in Booth/Bad Puppeteer), Darren Fouse (Businessman/Dr. Burke), Carrie Keranen (Carrie/ Businesswoman), Kevin Mulhern (Narrator/Football Fan/Main in Line), Cevin D. Soling (Narrator/ Nimbus the Elder/Ticketing Officer/Frogman/Dr. Death/Director/Good Puppeteer), Craig Henneberry (High School Student), Stephen Kaplan (Businessman), Joe Rejeski (Nate/Laramie/Man in Line/ Janitor/Football Brawler), Phil Shafer (College Kid), Stephanie Silk (Mother)

THIS REVOLUTION

(INDEPENDENT) Producer, Lisa Kawamoto Hsu; Executive Producers, Bob Jason, Bob Kravitz; Co-Executive Producers, Jaid Barrymore, Michael Ellenbogenm, Adrienne Stern, Brenda Kravitz; Director/Screenplay, Stephen Marshall; Photography, Brian Jackson; Designer, Lisa Hsu; Music Supervisor, Raymond Leon Roker; Editors, Stephen Marshall, Nathan Crooker; a Co.OpC production of a Guerrilla News, Revolution Theory action; Color; DV; Not rated; 101 minutes; Release date: June 29, 2005. CAST: Rosario Dawson (Tina Santiago), Nathan Crooker (Jake Cassavetes), Amy Redford (Chloe Harden), Brett DelBuono (Richie Santiago), Brendan Sexton III (Daniel Sympton), Robert Bella (Bob Kramer), Cynthia Garrett (BCN News Anchor), Ned Silverman (Dexter), Brett Berg (Cody), Jermaine Chambers (Max), Gavin Bellour (Dante), Vija Brigita Grosgalvis (Mousy), James T. Williams II (Music Producer), Juan Hernandez (Cruz Santiago), Stephen Marshall (Silverback), Immortal Technique, Arthur Robins, Michael Kane, Ashleigh Banfield, Lloyd Grovbe, Cheri Honkala (Themselves), Akir, Toure Harris (Tech's Goons), Jeffrey Lloyd Lewis (Bluestockings Clerk), Danielle James (Woman at Party), Jack Hartnett (Republican at Party), Denis McKeown (NYPD Detective), Mike Casey (Undercover Detective)

TWIST OF FAITH

(ARTISTIC LICENSE) Producer, Eddie Schmidt; Executive Producer, Sheila Nevins; Supervising Producer, Nancy Abraham; Photography, Tom Hofbauer; Music, Blake Leyh; Editor, Matthew Clarke; an HBO Documentary Films, Chain Camera Pictures production; Color; Not rated; 87 minutes; Release date; July 1, 2005. Documentary in which a man confronts his sexual abuse as a boy by a Catholic priest; featuring Jeff Anderson, Tony Comes, Wendy Comes, Catherine Hoolahan, Dennis O'Loughlin, Matthew Simon, Father Stephen Stanberry.

Wendy Comes, Tony Comes in *Twist of Faith* PHOTO COURTESY OF ARTISTIC LICENSE

REBOUND

(20TH CENTURY FOX) Producer, Robert Simonds; Executive Producers, Martin Lawrence, Tracey Trench, Heidi Santelli, Paul Deason; Director, Steve Carr; Screenplay, Jon Lucas, Scott Moore; Story, William Wolf, Ed Decter, John J. Strauss; Photography, Glen MacPherson; Designer, Jaymes Hinkle; Music, Teddy Castellucci; Editor, Craig Herring; Casting, Jane Jenkins, Janet Hirshenson; a Robert Simonds, Runteldat production; Dolby; Deluxe color; Rated PG; 86 minutes; Release date: July 1, 2005. CAST: Martin Lawrence (Roy McCormick/Preacher Don), Wendy Raquel Robinson (Jeanie Ellis), Breckin Meyer (Tim Fink), Horatio Sanz (Mr. Newirth), Oren Williams (Keith Ellis), Patrick Warburton (Larry Burgess), Megan Mullaly (Principal Walsh), Eddy Martin (One Love), Steven C. Parker (Wes), Steven Anthony Lawrence (Ralph), Logan McElroy (Fuzzy), Gus Hoffman (Goggles), Tara Correa (Big Mac), Amy Bruckner (Annie), Alia Shawkat (Amy), Fred Stoller (Late Carl), Katt Micah Williams (Preacher Don's Sidekick), Dennis Cockrum (Refree Freddy), Beau Billingslea (NCBA Board Member), Michael Gallagher (OPU Assistant Coach), Gary Owen (Vulture Mascot), Robert Floyd (OPU Player Brill), Tara Mercurio (Bethanne), Hailey Noelle Johnson (Little Girl), Cody Linley (Larry Burgess, Jr.), Alex Vojdani (Guitar Student), Stacey Ford-Waters, Cole Evan Weiss (Opposing Players), Robert Rusler (Falcon Coach), Scott L. Treger (Falcon Asst. Coach), Ayla Kell (Cute Girl), Jason Matthew Smith (Referee Mike), Todd S. Glass (Referee Steve), Mark Griffin (Photographer), J. J. Chaback (Secretary Marge), Marlon Young (Visiting Coach), Vinnie Hughes (Walkman Kid), Jack K. Haley, Barry Hochberg (Announcers), Kimora Lee Simmons, Angela Oh (Reporters), Laura Kightlinger (Car Re-Po Lady), Brian Palermo, Matt McCoy (Alumni Associate Members), Kyle Chambers (American History Student), La Tya Benson, Daytona Borders, Jewell Burnett, Marquisha Henderson, Monica Irusta, Kelly Christine Jew, Stevie Larkin, Jasmine McGerr, Tevyn Page, Gabrielle Simmons, Clare Sofer, Aryelle Tomlinson (Cheerleaders)

Judy Marte, Danny Rivera in *On the Outs* PHOTO COURTESY OF KINDRED MEDIA

The Oil Factor PHOTO COURTESY OF FREE WILL PRODS.

Seth Macari (Michael), Alex Douglas (Paulie), Don Max (Dante), Dave Emerson (Guy), Paul Lekakis (Nick, Mr. Bang Bang), Lonnie Simpson (Rex), Hunter F. Roberts (Jeff), Gina Vetro (Veronica), Jonathan Zenz (Pascal), Devon Michael Jones (Blaire Edgewood), Lonnie Henderson (Billy), Ron Doyle (Mr. Miller), Barry Ashley (Old Sebastien), Ken Barrow (Old Billy), Tim Seltzer (Rod), Mick Page (Luis), Christine Reagan (Makeup Artist), Jimmy Steele (Cheater Boy), D. J. McGill (Bar Waiter), Robert John, Michael Reiner (Gossip Boys), Judith Dexter (Posh Waitress), Richard Taylor (Posh Waiter), Barry Parker (Old Queen), Mark Cirillo (Mickey Miata)

Martin Lawrence, Breckin Meyer in *Rebound* PHOTO COURTESY OF 20TH CENTURY FOX

SEX, POLITICS & COCKTAILS

(REGENT/HERE! FILMS) Producer/Director/Screenplay/Editor, Julien Hernandez; Photography, Hunter F. Roberts, Denise Brassard; Designer, Diane Hanamoto; Costumes, Vita Brown, Denise Hammond; Music, D.N.B. Pedergnana, Pedro Bromfman; a Kuba Pictures production; Color; Not rated; 90 minutes; Release date: July 1, 2005. CAST: Julien Hernandez (Sebastien), Marisa Petroro (Daria),

A SIDEWALK ASTRONOMER

(TELESCOPE PICTURES/JACOBS ENTERTAINMENT) Executive Producer/Director/ Photography, Jeffrey Jacobs; Music, John Angier; Editor, Jeanne Vitale; Color; Not rated; 78 minutes; Release date: July 8, 2005. Documentary on John Dobson, the inventor of the Dobsonian telescope mount.

ON THE OUTS

(KINDRED MEDIA GROUP) Producers/Directors, Lori Silverbush, Michael Skolnik; Screenplay, Lori Silverbush; Photography, Mariana Sánchez de Antuñano; Designer, Katya Blumenberg; Costumes, Liceika Rijfkogel; a Fader Films, Youth House Productions; Color; Rated R; 86 minutes; Release date: July 13, 2005. CAST: Anny Mariano (Suzette Williams), Judy Marte (Oz), Paola Mendoza (Marisol Pagan), Dominic Colon (Chewey), Flaco Navaja (Jimmy Ortiz), Danny Rivera (J Stutter), Don Parma (Tyrell), Earl Thomason (Pancake), Rokafella (Evelin), Kamilah Forbes (Frances), Raven Hamilton (Raven), Gloria Zelaya (Rosa), Autumn Collier (Autumn), Nikki Jean (Malia), Shanaine Osbourne (Jasmine), Hannah Schick (Delila), Gandhja Monteiro (Alexis), Maribel Lizardo (Ms. Herrera), Edward O'Blendis Jr. (Dr. Kendall), Levon Fickling (Quilmo), Bonz Malone (Jail Speaker)

THE RECEPTION

(STRAND) Producer, Paul Pagnucco; Executive Producers, Dexter Davis, Ramen Cromwell; Director/Screenplay, John G. Young; Photography, Derek Wiesehahn; Designer, Sally Bonython; Costumes, Amanda-Ray Clegg; Editor, J. Blake Fichera; a Black Water Films, D Street Pictures production; Color; Not rated; 80 minutes; Release date: July 15, 2005. CAST: Darien Sills-Evans (Andrew), Wayne Lamont Sims (Martin), Pamela Stewart (Jeannette)

THE OIL FACTOR:
BEHIND THE WAR ON TERROR

(FREE-WILL PRODUCTIONS) Directors/Screenplay, Audrey Brohy, Gerard Ungerman; Music, Fritz Heede; Editor, Jason Stelzel; Color; Not rated; 93 minutes; Release date: July 15, 2005. Documentary connecting the need for oil and the war in Iraq.

Grace in *Making Grace* PHOTO COURTESY OF FIRST RUN FEATURES

MAKING GRACE

(FIRST RUN FEATURES) Producer/Director, Catherine Gund; Music, Paul Armstrong; Editors, Catherine Gund, Aljernon Tunsil; an Aubin Pictures release; Color; Not rated; 86 minutes; Release date: July 22, 2005. Documentary on the efforts of Ann Krsul and Leslie Sullivan to become mothers and raise a child together.

Monumental PHOTO COURTESY OF FIRST RUN FEATURES

MONUMENTAL:
DAVID BROWER'S FIGHT FOR WILD AMERICA

(FIRST RUN FEATURES) Producer/Director, Kelly Duane; Executive Producer, Brian Maxwell; Co-Producers, Paul Barnett, Samantha Weaver; Photography, David Brower, Sophia E. Constantinou; Editors, Anne Flatte, Tony Saxe, Nathaniel Dorsky; a Loteria Films production; Color; Not rated; 88 minutes; Release date: July 22, 2005. Documentary on environmental activist David Brower; featuring David Brower, Martin Litton, Stewart Udall, Jerry Mander, Floyd Dominy, Kevin Starr, Rod Nash, Ken Brower, Barbara Brower, John Dyer, Michael McCloskey, Michael Cohen, Roderick Nash, Phillip Berry.

THE BALLAD OF GREENWICH VILLAGE

(INDEPENDENT) Producer/Director, Karen Kramer; Narrator, Lili Taylor; No other credits available; Color; Not rated; 70 minutes; Release date: July 22, 2005. Documentary in which filmmaker Karen Kramer interviews several famous New Yorkers about Greenwich Village; featuring Edward Albee, Woody Allen, Maya Angelou, Amiri Baraka, Judy Collins, Allen Ginsberg, Richie Havens, Roy Haynes, Norman Mailer, Tom Paxton; Peter, Paul & Mary; Tim Robbins, Artie Traum, Dave Van Ronk.

Norman Mailer, Karen Kramer in *The Ballad of Greenwich Village* PHOTO COURTESY OF INDEPENDENT

NOVEMBER

(SONY CLASSICS) Producers, Danielle Renfrew, Gary Winick, Jake Abraham; Executive Producers, Jonathan Sehring, Caroline Kaplan, John Sloss; Director/Editor, Greg Harrison; Screenplay, Benjamin Brand; Photography, Nancy Schreiber; Designer, Tracey Gallacher; Costumes, Danny Glicker; Music, Lew Baldwin; Casting, Sheila Jaffe, Georgianne Walken; an IFC Prods. presentation of an InDigEnt production in association with Map Point Pictures; Dolby; Color; DV; Rated R; 73 minutes; Release date: July 22, 2005. CAST: Courteney Cox (Sophie Jacobs), James LeGros (Hugh), Michael Ealy (Jesse), Nora Dunn (Dr. Fayn), Nick Offerman (Officer Roberts), Anne Archer (Carol Jacobs), Matthew Carey (The Shooter), Robert Wu (Juhn), Brittany Ishibashi (Lim), Amir Talai (George)

Courteney Cox, Michael Ealy in *November* PHOTO COURTESY OF SONY CLASSICS

THIS DIVIDED STATE

(MINORITY FILMS) Producer, Steven Greenstreet; Co-Producers, Philip Gordon, Kristi Haycock; Director/Editor, Steven Greenstreet; Photography, Matt Easlin, Wes Aldredge, Steven Greenstreet, Josh Ligiari; Color; DV; Not rated; 88 minutes; Release date: August 4, 2005. Documentary on an ultra-conservative Utah

Michael Moore in *This Divided State* PHOTO COURTESY OF MINORITY FILMS

RITTENHOUSE SQUARE

(MAX L. RAAB PRODUCTIONS) Producer, Max L. Raab; Director, Robert Downey, Sr.; No other credits available; Color; Not rated; 82 minutes; Release date: July 22, 2005. Documentary on the noted Philadelphia park, Rittenhouse Square; featuring Robert Downey Sr., Caeli Veronica Smith, Zach DePue, Ranaan Meyer, Sharon Pinkenson.

THE LAST DISPATCH

(FABRICATION FILMS) Producers, Shane Gilbert, Brady Nasfell, Kurt Schemper; Executive Producers, Keith Stoltz, Charles Heimbold; Director/Editor, Helmut Schleppi; a Sodium Entertainment production; Dolby; Color; Not rated; 81 minutes; Release date: July 29, 2005. The final concert of the rock group Dispatch, held in Boston in July of 2004; with Brad Corrigan, Pete Francis, Chad Urmston (Dispatch).

YOUNG REBELS

(GOWANUS PRODUCTIONS) Producers, Richard Sterling, Anna Boden; Co-Producer, Elise Wise; Directors, Anna Boden, Ryan Fleck; Photography, Ryan Fleck; Editor Anna Boden; U.S.-Cuban; Color; Not rated; 70 minutes; Release date: August 3, 2005. Documentary on five Cuban hip-hop groups; featuring Adrianci Gonzalez, Alexander Guerra Hoez, Alexis Rodriguez.

Jamie Bell in *The Chumscrubber* PHOTO COURTESY OF NEWMARKET

college's reaction to liberal filmmaker Michael Moore's appearance there for a lecture; featuring Michael Moore, Kay Anderson, Jim Bassi, Kenneth F. Brown, Alex Caldiero, Phil Clegg, Phil Gordon, Sean Hannity, Pierre LaMarche, Jason Nichols, Vegor Pederson, Dennis Potter, Bob Rasmussen, William Sederburg, Jessie Steele, Joe Vogel, Sean Vreeland

THE CHUMSCRUBBER

(NEWMARKET) Producers, Lawrence Bender, Bonnie Curtis; Executive Producers, Bob Yari, Josef Lautenschlager, Philip Levinson, Michael Beugg, Andreas Thiesmeyer; Director, Arie Posin; Screenplay, Zac Stanford; Story, Arie Posin, Zac Stanford; Photography, Lawrence Sher; Designer, Patti Podesta; Music, James Horner; Music Supervisor, Chris Douridas; Casting, Anya Colloff, Amy McIntyre; an El Camino Pictures, Equity Pictures Medienfonds GmbH & Co. KG II production; U.S.-German; Dolby; Widescreen; Color; Rated R; 107 minutes; Release date: August 5, 2005. CAST: Jamie Bell (Dean Stiffle), Camilla Belle (Crystal Falls), Justin Chatwin (Billy), Glenn Close (Carrie Johnson), Rory Culkin (Charlie Stiffle), Thomas Curtis (Charlie Bratley), Tim DeKay (Mr. Peck), William Fitchner (Bill Stiffle), Ralph Fiennes (Michael Ebbs), Kathy Copeland, Richard Gleason (Parents), Caroline Goodall (Mrs. Parker), John Heard (Officer Lou Bratley), Lauren Holly (Boutique Owner), Jason Isaacs (Mr. Parker), Allison Janney (Mrs. Stiffle), Joshua Janowicz (Troy), Carrie-Anne Moss (Jerri Falls), Lou Taylor Pucci (Lee), Rita Wilson (Terri Bratley), David Ellison, Eric Jungman, Max Van Ville (Students), Susan Hegarty, Jeff Parise (Aides to Mayor Ebbs), Laura Shanahan, Scott Spiro (Party Goers)

MY DATE WITH DREW

(SLOW HAND RELEASING) Producers, Kerry David, Jon Gunn, Brian Herzlinger, Brett Winn; Executive Producers, Clark Peterson, Andrew Reimer; Co-Producer, Steven Break; Directors, Jon Gunn, Brian Herzlinger, Brett Winn; Photography/Editors, Jon Gunn, Brian Herzlinger, Brett Winn; Music, Steven Stern, Stuart Hart; Music Supervisor, Joe Fischer; a Rusty Bear Entertainment, Lucky Crow Films production in association with DEJ Prods.; Color; DV; Rated PG; 90 minutes; Release date: August 5, 2005. Documentary in which filmmaker Brian Herzlinger attempts to get a date with his idol Drew Barrymore within 30 days; featuring Brian Herzlinger, John August, Drew Barrymore, Stephanie Bedell, Sara Berkowitz, Allison Burnett, Sonya Daka, Kerry David, George DelHoyo, Bill D'Elia, Corey Feldman, Mary Firestone, Ross Forooghi, Lisa Gunn, Jon Gunn, Lauren Hays, Eric Herzlinger, Stracey Herzlinger, Zita Herzlinger, Pam Levin, Jenna Lewis, John Mann, Kristin Mitzner, Kimberly Padula, Mikaela Austin Phillips, Mindi Phillips, Lily Rains, Eric Roberts, Dan Ryder, Susan Spano, Brett Winn

THE GREAT RAID

(MIRAMAX) Producers, Marty Katz, Lawrence Bender; Executive Producers, Bob Weinstein, Harvey Weinstein, Jonathan Gordon, Michelle Rimo Aboua; Director, John Dahl; Screenplay, Carlo Bernard, Doug Miro; Based on the books *The Great Raid on Cabanatuan* by William B. Breuer and *Ghost Soldiers* by Hampton Sides; Photography, Peter Menzies, Jr.; Designer, Bruno Rubeo; Costumes, Lizzy Gardiner; Music, Trevor Rabin; Editors, Pietro Scalia, Scott Chestnut; Casting, Bonnie Timmerman; a Marty Katz production in association with Lawrence Bender Prods.; Dolby; Panavision; Deluxe color; Rated R; 132 minutes; Release date: August 18, 2005. CAST: Benjamin Bratt (Lt. Col. Mucci),

James Franco (Capt. Prince), Connie Nielsen (Margaret Utinsky), Joseph Fiennes (Maj. Gibson), Marton Csokas (Capt. Redding), Motoki Kobayashi (Maj. Nagai), Robert Mammone (Capt. Fisher), Natalie Mendoza (Mina), Cesar Montano (Juan Pajota), Max Martini (1st Sgt. Side "Top" Wojo), James Carpinello (Cpl. Aliteri), Mark Consuelos (Cpl. Guttierez), Craig McLachlan (2nd Lt. Riley), Freddie Joe Farnsworth (2nd Lt. Foley), Laird Macintosh (2nd Lt. O'Grady), Jeremy Callaghan (Lt. Able), Scott McLean (Lt. LeClaire), Paolo Montalban (Sgt. Valera), Clayne Crawford (PFC Aldridge), Sam Worthington (PFC Lucas), Royston Innes (Sgt. Adams), Diarmid Heidenreich (PFC Daly), Luke Pegler (PFC Miller), Dale Dye (Gen. Kreuger), Jerome Ehlers (Col. H. White), Brett Tucker (Maj. Lapham), Peter Tkacz (PFC Cohen), Kristian Schmid (Cpl. Lee), Samuel Robinson (T/4 Gordon), Warwick Young (Sgt. Lyle), Steve Harman (PFC Chestnut), Tim Campbell (Cpl. Friedberg), Matt Doran (Ron Carlson), Logan Marshall-Green (Lt. Paul Colvin), Nicholas Bell (Duke), Kenny Doughty (Pitt), Iain Gardiner (McMahon), Christopher Baker (Monty), Christopher Morris (Sgt. Williams), Will Gluth (Wittinghill), Lucas Stribbard (Hewitt), Noel O'Neill (Katz), Elwyn Edwards (Campbell), Eugenia Yuan (Cora), Alvin Clifford Lorenz Anson (Rudi), Jose Rommel de Montano Manhilot (Miguel), Ramon Jose Leyran (Carlos), Marcelino Cavestany (Antonio Corcurea), Simon Maiden (Father McPherson), Neil Fitzpatrick (Father Connor), Laura Whitnall (Nurse, Manila Hospital), Romina Villanueva (Informer with Hood), Res S. Cortez, Rafael "Bembol" A. Roco, Jr. (Henchemen), Nikko Mackintosh (Nikko), Gotaro Tsunashima (Yamada), Masa Yamaguchi (Lt. Hikobe), Yutaka Izumihara (Sgt. Maj. Takeda), Paul Nakauchi (Sgt. Shigeno), Ken Senga (Col. Mori), Kuni

Brian Herzlinger in *My Date With Drew* PHOTO COURTESY OF SLOW HAND RELEASING

Hashimoto (Air Raid), Kentaro Hara (Lt. Okasaka), Koichi Kimura (Storage Room Soldier), Takayuki "Taka" Nagano (Japanese Cpt. Manila), David Chamberlain , Naoto Uchida (Tank Officers), Shingo Usami (Tower Guard SC201 208), Kazuhiro Muroyama, Akira Yoshikawa (Guardhouse Japanese Soldiers), Ebgon Joson (Capt. Joson), Leo Kooistra (Lt. Esteben), Chito Sayo (Manuel), Kenneth Moraleda (Monsod), Jourdan Lee Khoo (Filipino Commander), Leon Ford, Matthew Newton (American POW at Palawan), Ken Kikkawa (Commander Tanaka), Nor Domingo (Platero Doctor), Christine O'Neill (Pregnant Girl), Lena Cruz (Mother of Pregnant Girl), Den Patricio (Platero Girl #1), Alfred Nicdao (Platero Village Elder), Noel Trinidad Jr. (Young Filipino Collaborator), Valerie Berry (Refugee Woman), Ryan Eigennman (Refugee Profiteer), Jackson Raine (Truck Driver)

Evan Rachel Wood, Adi Schnall, Elisabeth Harnois in *Pretty Persuasion*
PHOTO COURTESY OF SAMUEL GOLDWYN

PRETTY PERSUASION

(SAMUEL GOLDWYN) Producers, Todd Dagres, Carl Levin, Marcos Siega, Matthew Weaver; Executive Producers, Joni Sighvatsson, Jason Barhydt, Eric Kopeloff, Robert Ortiz; Co-Producer, Skander Hallim; Director, Marcos Siega; Screenplay, Skander Halim; Photography, Ramsey Nickell; Designer, Paul Oberman; Costumes, Danny Glicker; Music, Gilad Benamram; Editor, Nicholas Erasmnus; Casting, Joseph Middleton, Barbara Fiorentino; a Prospect Pictures presentation; Dolby; Panavision; Color; Rated R; 110 minutes; Release date: August 12, 1005. CAST: Evan Rachel Wood (Kimberly Joyce), David T. Wagner (Morgan), Brent Goldberg (Rick), Adi Schnall (Randa), Elisabeth Harnois (Brittany), Stark Sands (Troy), Jane Krakowski (Emily Klein), Michael Hitchcock (Headmaster Charles Meyer), Danny Comden (Roger Nicholl), Jaime Kingh (Kathy Joyce), Josh Zuckerman (Josh Horowitz), James Snyder (Dave), Ron Livingston (Percy Anderson), Cody McMains (Kenny), Mike Erwin (Barry), James Woods (Hank Joyce), Ira Wood (Martin Stivers), Selma Blair (Grace Anderson), Johnny Lewis (Warren Prescott), David C. Taylor (Carlyle Cream), Lisa Arturo (Stephanie Swift), Alex Désert (Joe, Security Guard), Tina Holmes (Nadine), Christopher Thornton (Emmett Friedman), Clyde Kusatsu (Judge Carl Munro), Deprece Reddick (Sudan), Robert Joy (Larry Horowitz), Julie Wittner, Aydiee Vaughn (Bystanders), Navid Negahban (Mr. Azzouni), Veena Bidasha (Mrs. Azzouni), Octavia Spencer (Woman), Angelo Spizzirri (Cody)

Eddie Griffin, Rob Schneider in *Deuce Bigelow: European Gigolo* PHOTO COURTESY OF COLUMBIA

CHAOS

(DINSDALE) Producer, Steven Jay Bernheim; Executive Producer, Alan Kapilow; Director/Screenplay, David DeFalco; Based on an original idea by Steven Jay Bernheim, David DeFalco; Photography, Brandon Trost; Designer, Freddy Naff; Editors, Mark Leif, Peter Devaney Flanagan; Special Effects Supervisor, Ron Trost; a Dominion Entertainment presentation of a Steven Jay Bernheim production; Color; Rated R; 74 minutes; Release date: August 12, 2005. CAST: Kevin Gage (Chaos), Stephen Wozniak (Frankie), Kelly K. C. Quann (Daisy), Sage Stallone (Swan), Chantal Degroat (Emily), Maya Barovich (Angelica), Ken Medlock (Sheriff), Deborah Lacey (Emily's Mother), Scott Richards (Emily's Father)

11:14

(NEW LINE CINEMA) Producers, Raju Patel, Beau Flynn, John Morrissey; Executive Producers, Mark Damon, Hilary Swank, Stewart Hall, Jeff Kwatinetz, Sammy Lee, David Rubin, Tripp Vinson; Director/Screenplay, Greg Marcks; Photography, Shane Hurlbut; Designer, Devorah Herbert; Costumes, Christopher Lawrence; Music, Clint Mansell; Editors, Richard Nord, Dan Lebental; Casting, Mary Vernieu, Felicia Fasano; a Media 8 Entertainment, MDP Worldwide, Firm Films production; Dolby; Color; Rated R; 85 minutes; Release date: August 12, 2005. CAST: Henry Thomas (Jack), Blake Heron (Aaron), Barbara Hershey (Norma), Clark Gregg (Officer Hannagan), Hilary Swank (Buzzy), Shawn Hatosy (Duffy), Stark Sands (Tim), Colin Hanks (Mark), Ben Foster (Eddie), Patrick Swayze (Frank), Rachael Leigh Cook (Cheri), Jason Segel (Leon, Paramedic), Rick Gomez (Kevin, Paramedic)

DEUCE BIGELOW: EUROPEAN GIGOLO

(COLUMBIA) Producers, Jack Giarraputo, Adam Sandler, John Schneider; Director, Mike Bigelow; Screenplay, Rob Schneider, David Garrett, Jason Ward; Story, Rob Schneider; Based on character created by Harris Goldberg & Rob Schneider; Executive Producer, Glenn S. Gainor; Photography, Marc Felperlaan; Designer, Benedict Schillemans; Costumes, Linda Bogers; Music, James L. Venable; Music Supervisor, Michael Dilbeck; Editors, Peck Prior, Sandy Solowitz; Co-Producers, Nathan T. Reimann, Tom McNulty; Casting, Roger Mussenden; a Happy Madison production; Dolby; Deluxe color; Rated R; 83 minutes; Release date: August 12, 2005. CAST: Rob Schneider (Deuce Bigelow), Eddie Griffin (T. J. Hicks), Jeroen Krabbé (Gaspar Voorsboch), Til Schweiger (Heinz Hummer), Douglas Sills (Chadsworth Buckingham, III), Carlos Ponce (Rodrigo), Charles Keating (Gian-Carlo), Hanna Verboom (Eva), Kostas Sommer (Assapopolous Mariolis), Bastiaan Ragas (Anchorman), Zoe Telford (Lily), Miranda Raison (Svetlana), Federico Dordei (Mahmoud), Elisabetta Canalis (Lady in Castle), Johnny Vaughan (Himself), Skytriss (Marlene Alsmere), Alex Dimitriades (Enzo Giarraputo), Dana Goodman (Greta, The Hunchback Girl), Jimmy Gardner (Kaiser), Topper (Lil' Kim), Hilton Myburgh (Diego Verga), Alex Zane (Dan van der Hoek), Rachel Stevens (Louisa, The Dirty Girl), Joop Kasteel (Security Guard), Julia Wolov (The Big Eared Girl), Wimie Wilhelm (Heavy Set Maid), SuChin Pak (Newscaster), Wes Takahashi (News Reporter), Bobbi Sue Luther, Sylvana Simons, Heather Campbell (Newscasters), Willie Gault (Black Man in Airport), Kelly Brook (Beautiful Woman in Painting), Nicolette van Dam (Spa Attendant), Vincent Martella (Billy), Kris McKay (Jimmy), Micky Hoogendijk (Wealthy Woman in Car), Johnny De Mol, Matthew Segal (Canadian College Kids), Katie Downes (Sexy Window Washer), Joshua Rubin

(Production Assistant), Kenan Raen (Man in Robe), Chantal Janzen (Scandinavian Porn Star), Cees Geel (Manwhore Union Doorman), Rachel Bachofner, Monika Kuczowska, Astrid Knoop (Topless Weather Ladies), Daan Schuurmans (Belgian Gigolo), Edwin Adolfs (Porn Midget), Pilar M. Schneider (Woman in Airplane), Erik de Vogal (Cop), Narsingh Balwantsingh (Pakistani Man), Jean Challis (Older European Blind Woman), Bobbi Aron (Blind Woman in Net), Veronica Devenish (Older Blind Woman), Andreas Wolmuth (Dophin Handler), Rebecca Rule, Nikkala Scott, Melanie Walsh, Nicola Tappenden, Zoe McConnell, Krystle Gohel (Red Light District Girls), Adam Sandler (Javier Sandooski)

REEL PARADISE

(WELLSPRING) Producers, Steve James, Scott Mosier; Executive Producers, Kevin Smith, John Pierson, Janet Pierson; Photography/Co-Producer, P. H. O'Brien; Director/Editor, Steve James; Music, Norman Arnold; Line Producer, Gita Saedi; a View Askew production; Color; DV; Not rated; 113 minutes; Release date: August 17, 2005. Documentary on a remote cinema, the Meridian, located in Taveuni, Fiji; featuring John Pierson, Janet Pierson, Georgia Pierson, Wyatt Pierson.

THE UNTOLD STORY OF EMMETT LOUIS TILL

(THINKFILM) Producers, Keith Beauchamp, Yolande Geralds; Executive Producer, Ceola Beauchamp, Edgar Beauchamp, Ali Bey, Steve Laitmon, Jacki Ochs; Directors, Keith Beauchamp, Kevin A. Beauchamp; Music, Jim Papoulis; Color; Rated PG-13; 70 minutes; Release date: August 17, 2005. Documentary on the 1953 racially motivated murder of Emmett Louis Till who was accused of whistling at a white woman.

Emmett Till in *The Untold Story of Emmett Louis Till* PHOTO COURTESY OF THINKFILM

Wyatt Pierson, Janet Pierson, John Pierson, Georgia Pierson in *Reel Paradise*
PHOTO COURTESY OF WELLSPRING

Robert Patrick, Cameron Richardson, Mike Vogel in *Supercross* PHOTO COURTESY OF 20TH CENTURY FOX

SUPERCROSS

(20TH CENTURY FOX) Producers, Steve Austin, J. Todd Harris; Executive Producers, David Borg, Marc Toberoff, Jonathan Bogner, Richard Gabai; Director, Steve Boyum; Screenplay, Ken Solarz, Bart Baker; Based on a story by Bart Baker, Keith Alan Bernstein; Photography, William Wages; Designer, Max Biscoe; Costumes, Elaine Montalvo; Music, Jasper Randall; Editors, Alan Cody, Brett Hedlund; Casting, Janet Hirshenson, Jane Jenkins, Michelle Lewitt; Stunts, Jimmy N. Roberts; a TAG Entertainment production in association with Clear Channel Entertainment Motor Sports; Dolby; Color; Rated PG-13; 92 minutes; Release date: August 19, 2005. CAST: Steve Howey (K. C. Carlyle), Mike Vogel (Trip Carylyle), Cameron Richardson (Piper Cole), Sophia Bush (Zoe Lang), Aaron Carter (Owen Cole), Channing Tatum (Rowdy Sparks), J. D. Pardo (Chuy), Carolina Garcia (Starr), Ryan Locke (Jeff Johnson), Robert Patrick (Earl Cole), Robert Carradine (Clay Sparks), David Castillo (David Castillo), Erin Bates, Jamie Little, Terry Boyd, Tyler Evans, Ricky Johnson (Themselves), David Pingree (Billy), Alana Austin (Rider Girlfriend), Richard Danielsonn (Rowdy's Mechanic), Rick Johnson (Assistant), Erin Lear (Hairstylist), Joey Bucaro (Biker), Antonia Jones (Nurse), Dan Gunther (Dr. Simms), Adriana Bilan (Bike Girl), Kyle Dietz (Young K. C.), Ian Michael Kintzle (Taylor), Dylan McLaughlin (Young Trip), Jyoti Mittal (Girl #1), Kaya Redford (Pit Crew Team), Daniel Roebuck (Mr. Lang)

Ashlee Simpson, Pell James in *Undiscovered* PHOTO COURTESY OF LIONS GATE

KING OF THE CORNER

(ELEVATION FILMWORKS) Producer, Lemore Syvan; Executive Producer, Melissa Marr, Peter Sahagen, Anthony Mastromauro; Director, Peter Riegert; Screenplay, Peter Riegert, Gerald Shapiro; Photography, Mauricio Rubinstein; Designer, Ben Constable; Costumes, Lynn Falconer; Music, Al Kooper; Editor, Mario Ontal; Casting, Cindy Tolan; a Two Tequila Prods. production in association with Ardustry Entertainment, Pursuit Film; Dolby; Color; Super 16-to 35mm; Rated R; 93 minutes; Release date: August 21, 2005. CAST: Peter Riegert (Leo Spivak), Isabella Rossellini (Rachel Spivak), Jennifer Albano (Carolyn), Eric Bogosian (Rabbi Evelyn Fink), Dominic Chianese (Stan Marshack), Beverly D'Angelo (Betsy), Peter Friedman (Arthur Wexler), Jake Hoffman (Ed Shiffman), Alecia Hurst (Greta Braunsweig), Ashley Johnson (Elana Spivak), Rita Moreno (Inez), Eli Wallach (Sol Spivak), Frank Wood (Berenson), Harris Yulin (Hargrove)

THE BAXTER

(IFC FILMS) Producers, Daniela Taplin Lundberg, Galt Niederhoffer, Celine Rattray, Reagan Silber; Executive Producers, Jonathan Sehring, Caroline Kaplan, Holly Becker; Director/Screenplay, Michael Showalter; Photography, Tim Orr; Designer, Mark White; Costumes, Jill Kilber, Jill Newell; Music, Theodore Shapiro, Craig Wedren; Editors, Jacob Craycroft, Sarah Flack; Casting, Susie Farris; produced in association with Plum Pictures; Dolby; Color; Rated PG-13; 91 minutes; Release date: August 26, 2005. CAST: Michael Showalter (Elliot Sherman), Elizabeth Banks (Caroline Swann), Michelle Williams (Cecil Mills), Justin Theroux (Bradley Lake), Zak Orth (Wendall Wimms), Michael Ian Black (Ed), Catherine Lloyd Burns (Stella), Peter Dinklage (Benson Hedges), Paul Rudd (Dan Abbott), Katharine Powell (Sonya Simmons), John DeVries (Alan Swann), Donna Mitchell (Judy Swann), Haviland Morris (Kate), David Wain (Louis Lewis), Jim DeMarse (Leonard Sherman), Leslie Lyles (Sheila Sherman), A. D. Miles, Joe Lo Truglio, Seth Herzog, Jonathan Marc Sherman (Bar Baxters), Peter Stalden (Young Elliot Sherman), Abigail Wathen (Kimberly), Gabriel Millman (Max), Sarah Drew (Serena), Chris Spain (Tanner Bates), Marylouise Burke (Delores), Ken Marino (Jack Mechanic), Audrie Neenan (Pastor Pritchard), Bobby Tisdale (Emcee), Michael Portnoy (Interpretive Dancer), Maya Goldsmith (Muffy), Jenny Maguire (Peg), Melissa McGregor (Lilly)

UNDISCOVERED

(LIONS GATE) Producers, Michael Burns, Bic Tran, Marco Mehlitz, Michael Ohoven; Executive Producers, Joe Simpson, Michael Paseornek, Eberhard Kayser, Tom Rosenberg, Gary Lucchesi, Harley Tannenbaum, Jordan Schur; Director, Meiert Avis; Screenplay, John Galt; Photography, Danny Hiele; Designer, Philip Duffin; Costumes, Jen Rade; Editor, David Codron; Casting, Tricia Wood, Deborah Aquila, Jennifer Smith; a Lakeshore Entertainment, Cinerenta presentation of a Cinejota production; Dolby; Panavision; Technicolor; Rated PG-13; 98 minutes; Release date: August 26, 2005. CAST: Pell James (Brier Tucket), Steven Strait (Luke Falcon), Kip Pardue (Euan Falcon), Shannyn Sossamon (Josie), Carrie Fisher (Carrie), Peter Weller (Wick Treadway), Fisher Stevens (Garret Schweck), Stephen Moyer (Mick Benson), Ashlee Simpson (Clea), Perrey Reeves (Michelle), Melissa Lawner (Christy), Cameron Thor (Cameron), Brian Swibel (Jason from Acting Class), Ewan Chung (Brendon, Garrett's Asst.), Mann Alfonso (Bat Guy), Don Smith (Mint Bartender), Meghan Lynch (Mint Bargirl), Shaina Fewell, Rachel Sterling (Pretty Girls at Mint), Stephanie Mace (Waitress at Mint), Natasha Soudek (Stylist), Sasha Gelbart, Dan Callahan (Turks), Jesse Burch (Airline Rep), Megan Kuhlmann (Ticket Counter Agent), Earl Carroll (Airline Security Guard), Lori Heuring (Flight Attendant), Craig Watkinson (Onlooker), Tami Humphrey (Woman), Lauren

Lena Headey, Eddie Cibrian in *The Cave* PHOTO COURTESY OF SCREEN GEMS

Michelle Williams in *The Baxter* PHOTO COURTESY OF IFC FILMS

William J. Eggleston in *William Eggleston in the Real World* PHOTO COURTESY OF PALM PICTURES

Zelman (Bakery Waitress), Brittany Ishibashi (Trapeze Instructor), Carolina Cerisola, Hannah Feldner-Shaw, Vaitiare Au-Harehoe (Trippy Nightclub Dancers), Melissa Cross (Extra Reporter)

WE JAM ECONO: THE STORY OF THE MINUTEMEN

(ROCK FUEL FILMS) Producer, Keith Schieron; Director, Tim Irwin; Music, George Hurley, Mike Watt, D. Boon; a San Pedro Film Society production; Black and white/color; Not rated; 85 minutes; Release date: August 26, 2005. Documentary on early '80s punk band the Minutemen; featuring Richard Bonney, Flea, Greg Ginn, Richard Hell, George Hurley, Ian MacKaye, Thurston Moore, Henry Rollins, Mike Watt.

THE CAVE

(SCREEN GEMS) Producers, Richard Wright, Michael Ohoven, Tom Rosenberg, Gary Lucchesi, Andrew Mason; Executive Producers, Marco Mehlitz, Neil Bluhm, Judd Malkin; Director, Bruce Hunt; Screenplay, Michael Steinberg, Tegan West; Photography, Ross Emery; Designer, Pier Luigi Basile; Costumes, Wendy Partridge; Music, Johnny Klimek; Editor, Brian Berdan; Visual Effects Supervisors, James McQuaide, Gary Beach, Payam Shohadai; Creature Designer, Patrick Tatopoulos; Casting, Tricia Wood, Deborah Aquila; a Screen Gems, Lakeshore Entertainment, Cinerenta presentation of a Lakeshore Entertainment production in association with City Prods., Cineblue; Dolby; Arri Widescreen; Deluxe color; Rated PG-13; 97 minutes; Release date: August 26, 2005. CAST: Cole Hauser (Jack), Morris Chestnut (Top Buchanan), Eddie Cibrian (Tyler), Rick Ravanello (Briggs), Marcel Iures (Dr. Nicolai), Kieran Darcy-Smith (Strode), Daniel Dae Kim (Kim), Lena Headey (Kathryn), Piper Perabo (Charlie), Vlad Radescu (Dr. Bacovia), Simon Kunz (Mike, Caver #1), David Kennedy (Ian, Caver #2), Alin Panc (Razvan, Caver #3), Zoltan Butuc (Corvin, Caver #4), Brian Steele (Creature)

WILLIAM EGGLESTON IN THE REAL WORLD

(PALM PICTURES) Producers, Michael Almereyda, Jesse Dylan, Anthony Katagas; Executive Producers, Donald Rosenfeld, Alexis Zoullas; Director/Screenplay/Photography, Michael Almereyda; Music, Simon Fisher-Turner; Editors, Joshua Falcon, Karen Choy, Johannes Weuthen; a High Line Productions, Keep Your Head production; Color; Not rated; 86 minutes; Release date: August 31, 2005. Documentary examining the groundbreaking work of photographer William J. Eggelston.

9/11/03: A DAY IN THE LIFE OF NEW YORK

(KARZ ENTERTAINMENT) Producer/Director/Editor, Richard Karz; Associate Producer, Miami Meridy; Color; Not rated; 97 minutes; Release date: September 1, 2005. Documentary on a gathering at the Surrogate Courthouse in lower Manhattan on the second anniversary of the terrorist attacks on the World Trade Center; featuring Chang Tiu-Hua, Stanley Crouch, Paul McHale, Arthur Mitchell, Robert Morgenthau, Shirin Neshat, Drew Nieporent, Isaiah Owens, Peter G. Peterson, Charles Rangel, Lawrence Rinder, Christopher H. Rising, Rosanna Rosado, Salman Rushdie, John Sexton, Russell Simmons, Jessica Stern, Shashi Tharoor, Joe Torre, Alek Wek, Fareed Zakaria.

MARGARET CHO: ASSASSIN

(REGENT/HERE! RELEASING) Producer/Director (Opening & Closing Sequences), Konda Mason; Executive Producers, Margaret Cho, Rick Scott, Karen Taussig, Paul Colichman, Eric T. Feldman, Joel Lipman; Director, Kerry Asmussen; Screenplay, Margaret Cho; Photography, Sovonto Green; Music, Paula Gallitano; Editors, Adam Streit, Nancy Rosenblum; an Autonomy Inc., Cho Taussig Productions Inc. production; Color; Not rated; 90 minutes; Release date: September 2, 2005. Margaret Cho performs her stand-up comedy act.

Margaret Cho in *Margaret Cho: Assassin* PHOTO COURTESY OF REGENT/HERE!

Shawn Ashmore, Nick Cannon in *Underclassman* PHOTO COURTESY OF MIRAMAX

UNDERCLASSMAN

(MIRAMAX) Producers, Peter Abrams, Robert L. Levy, Andrew Panay; Executive Producers, Nick Cannon, Michael Goldman, Bob Weinstein, Harvey Weinstein, Bob Osher, James Dyer; Director, Marcos Siega; Screenplay, David T. Wagner, Brent Goldberg; Photography, David Hennings; Designer, Gary Frutkoff; Costumes, Tish Monaghan; Music, BT; Editor, Nicholas Smith; Casting, Christine Sheaks; a Tapestry Films production; Dolby; Panavision; Deluxe color; Rated PG-13; 94 minutes; Release date: September 2, 2005. CAST: Nick Cannon (Tracy Stokes), Shawn Ashmore (Rob Donovan), Roselyn Sanchez (Karen Lopez), Kelly Hu (Lisa Brooks), Ian Gomez (Det. Gallecki), Hugh Bonneville (Headmaster Powers), Cheech Marin (Capt. Delgado), Adrian Young (Jose), Art Bonilla (Cuervo), Bart McCarthy (Earl the Bum), Ryan Beil (Warren Williams), Peter Bryant (Michael Barry), Sam Easton (Oliver Horn), Mary Pat Gleason (Ms. Hagery), Kaylee DeFer (Des), Mycale (April), Nicole Garza (Candice), Pete Kasper (Botany Professor), NiCole Robinson (teacher), J. R. Dyer (Math Professor), Duke Shibley (Geek Math Guy), Johnny Lewis (Alexander Jeffries), Wayne King Jr. (Referee), Terry Chen (Sleepy Jones), Keith Dallas (Melvin the Security Guard), Jamie Kaler (Beach Police Officer), Dan Mellor (Holding Cell Officer), Don McManus (Julian Reynolds), Ben Cotton (Raver), Adrian Mcmorran (Buyer), Brandy Heidrick, Madeline Brown (High School Hotties), Zak Santiago (Anderson), Christopher Rosamond (Smith), Dan Shea (Weston), Biski Gugushe (Dispatcher), Angelo Fierro (Paramedic), Rob Bruner (Todd), Jeffrey Geniesse (Basketball Player), Amber Havens (Hot High School Girl), Rae'Ven Larrymore Kelly (Qweeshawn Johnson), David Michie (Voice of Police Officer on Bike), Sarah Morris (Jamie), Mark Pinkosh (Wesbury High Teacher)

A SOUND OF THUNDER

(WARNER BROS.) Producers, Moshe Diamant, Howard Baldwin, Karen Baldwin; Executive Producers, Elie Samaha, Romana Cisarova, John Hardy, Rick Nathanson, Jorg Westerkamp, William J. Immerman, Breck Eisner; Director/Photography, Peter Hyams; Screenplay, Thomas Dean Donnelly, Joshua Oppenheimer, Greg Poirier; Based on a story by Ray Bradbury; Designer, Richard Holland; Costumes, Esther Walz; Music, Nick Glennie-Smith; Editor, Sylvie Landra; Visual Effects Supervisor, Tim McGovern; Special Effects Supervisor, Joss Williams; Casting, Anja Dihrberg, Jessica Horathova; a Franchise Pictures presentation of an Apollomedia QI Quality Intl., MFF (Sound of Thunder) Limited, FilmGroup 111, Coco co-production in association with Crusader Films of a Scenario Lane, Jericho production; Dolby; Color; Rated PG-13; 101 minutes; Release date: September 2, 2005. CAST: Edward Burns (Travis Ryer), Catherine McCormack (Sonia Rand), Ben Kingsley (Charles Hatton), Jemima Rooper (Jenny Krase), David Oyelowo (Tech Officer Payne), Wilfried Hochholdinger (Dr. Andrew Lucas), August Zirner (Clay Derris), Corey Johnson (Christian Middleton), Armin Rhode (John Wallenbeck), Heike Makatsch (Alicia Wallenbeck), Alvin Van Der Kuech (Young Technician), Andrew Blanchard (George, the Doorman), William Armstrong (Ted Eckles), Nikita Le Spinasse (Newswoman on TV), Scott Bellefeville (Onlooker), Stuart Ong (Chinese Man), Antonin Hausknecht (Taxi Driver), Anezka Novakova (Elderly Woman), John Hyams (Delivery Man), Martin Svetlik (Grocery Boy), John Comer (Grocery Man), Kurt Van Der Basch (Armed Policeman), Vladimir Kulhavy (Man at Eckles'), Jiri Klenot (Man at Middleton's)

MUSIC FROM THE INSIDE OUT

(EMERGING PICTURES) Producer/Director, Daniel Anker; Associate Producer, Nate Smith; Photography, Tom Hurwitz; Editors, Jean Tsien, Bob Eisenhardt, Stanley Warnow; an Anker Productions, Inc., Independent Television Service (ITVS) production; Dolby; Color; Not rated; 89 minutes; Release date: September 9, 2005. Documentary in which members of the Philadelphia Orchestra talk about music.

CURANDERO

(MIRAMAX) Executive Producers, Robert Rodriguez, Elizabeth Avellan, Andre Rona, Harvey Weinstein, Bob Weinstein; Director, Eduardo Rodriguez; Screenplay, Robert Rodriguez; Photography, Jaime Reynoso; Art Director, Hannia Robledo; Costumes, Adriana Olivera; Music, Luis Ascanio; Editors, Eduardo Rodriguez, Mario Olivera; a Bad Egg production; Rated R; Release date: September 9, 2005. CAST: Carlos Gallardo (Curandero), Sergio Acosta (Oscar), Gizeht Galatea (Maggie), Gabriel Pingarrón (Castaneda), José Carlos Ruiz (Don Carlos), Ernesto Yáñez (Don Chi Chi), Jorge Zepeda (Comandante)

WALKING ON THE SKY

(NEWMARK/ECHELON) Producer, Josh Eggleston; Director/Screenplay, Carl T. Evans; Photography, Claudia Raschke; Music, Michael Tremante; from CTE Productions; Color; Not rated; 94 minutes; Release date: September 9, 2005.

Ben Kingsley, Edward Burns in *A Sound of Thunder* PHOTO COURTESY OF WARNER BROS.

CAST: Randall Batinkoff (Nick), Chris Henry Coffey (Jim), Carl T. Evans (Dylan), Nicole Fonarow (Liz), Kristen Marie Holly (Joann), Michael Knowles (Josh), Susan Misner (Sara), Jack Crocicchia (Young Dylan), Olivia Crocicchia (Lisa), Mike Marino (Karaoke Man)

Eugene Levy, Samuel L. Jackson in *The Man* PHOTO COURTESY OF NEW LINE CINEMA

THE MAN

(NEW LINE CINEMA) Producer, Rob Fried; Executive Producers, Toby Emmerich, Kent Alterman, Matthew Hart; Director, Les Mayfield; Screenplay, Jim Piddock, Margaret Oberman, Steve Carpenter; Story, Jim Piddock, Margaret Oberman; Photography, Adam Kane; Designer, Carol Spier; Costumes, Delphine White; Music, John Murphy; Editor, Jeffrey Wolf; Casting, Amanda Mackey Johnson, Cathy Sandrich Gelfond; a Fried Films production in association with Meradin Prods.; Dolby; Deluxe color; Rated PG-13; 83 minutes; Release date: September 9, 2005. CAST: Samuel L. Jackson (Derrick Vann), Eugene Levy (Andy Fiddler), Luke Goss (Joey/Kane), Miguel Ferrer (Agent Peters), Susie Essman (Lt. Rita Carbone), Anthony Mackie (Booty), Gigi Rice (Susan), Rachael Crawford (Dara Vann), Philip Akin (2nd L.A. Agent), Christopher Murray (Homeless Man), Joel Keller (Laptop Guy), John Hemphill (Ted), Kathryn Greenwood (Flight Attendant), Carrie Cain Sparks (Big Kim), George Ghali (Cab Driver), Leni Parker (Cashier), Matt Cooke (Uniform Cop on PA), Joe Sacco (Rookie), Neville Edwards (Tall Agent), Scott Wickware (Booking Officer), Tomorrow Baldwin Montgomery (Kate Vann), Geoff Bowes (Phone Agent), Randy Butcher (Guard), Jessica Kelly (Female Prisoner), Eldridge Hyndhman (Muscular Prisoner), Peter Oldring (Young Guard), Leonard Thomas (Mark), Max McCabe (Pinto Driver), Frank Spadone, Andrew Stelmack, Gordon Bolan (Conventioneers), J. J. Authors (Waiter), Toby Proctor (Cavity Search Guard), Peter Kosaka (Asian Man), Beatriz Yuste, Jackie Laidlaw, Dina Pino, Patricia Brown (Nuns), Lindsay Ames (Waitress), Michael Cameron (IA Driver), Jason Gautreau (Bicycle Cop), Kevin Rushton (Thug), Horatio Sanz (Diaz)

STEAL ME

(CINEVILLE INC.) Producer, Lisa Larrivee; Executive Producers, Carl Colpaert, Lee Caplin; Director/Screenplay, Melissa Painter; Designer, Andrea Soeiro; Costumes, Courtney Hess; Casting, Meg Morman, Betty Ann Conrad; a Picture Entertainment Corporation production; Color; Not rated; 95 minutes; Release date: September 9, 2005. CAST: Danny Alexander (Jake), Hunter Parrish (Tucker), Cara Seymour (Mother), John Terry (Father), Steven Brian Conrad (Officer Will), Chelsea Carlson (Cindy), Paz de la Huerta (Lily Rose), Miles Gravage (Kon), Vann Gravage (Alan), Keegan Nashan (Cindy's Friend), Justin O'Hair (Unshaved Man), Toby Poser (Grace), Zelda Poser (Baby Zelda), Clay Tuck (Billy)

MAKE IT FUNKY!

(TRIUMP) Producers, Cillisa Eberle, Michael Murphy; Executive Producer, Daniel Roth; Director/Screenplay, Michael Murphy; a Bottom of the Ninth Prods. II, Michael Murphy Prods. presentation; Color; Not rated; 110 minutes; Release date: September 9, 2005. Documentary on New Orleans' musical heritage; featuring Allen Toussaint, Bonnie Raitt, Big Sam's Funky Nation, Dirty Dozen Brass Band, Earl Palmer, Funky Meters, George Porter Jr., Irma Thomas, Irvin Mayfield, Ivan Neville, Jon Cleary, Keith Richards, Kermit Ruffins, Lloyd Price, Monk Boudreaux and the Golden Eagle Mardi Gras Indians, Neville Brothers, Poppa Funky's Boys, Snooks Eaglin, Troy Andrews, Walter "Wolfman" Washington.

CHAIN

(GRAVITY HILL FILMS) Producer, Mary Jane Skalski, Jem Cohen; Executive Producers, Guy Picciotto, Ian MacKaye, Jeffrey Levy-Hinte; Director/Screenplay/Photography, Jem Cohen; Music, God Speed You Black Emperor; Editors, Jem Cohen, David Frankel; an Antidote Films production; U.S.-German; Color; Not rated; 99 minutes; Release date: September 14, 2005. CAST: Miho Nikaido (Tamiko), Mira Billotte (Amanda Timms), Tarik O'Regan (Currency Trader), Rick Aquino, Douglas A. Scocco (Piano Store Salesmen), Bill Stuckey (TV Announcer), Minda Martin (Amanda's Half Sister), Robert C. Gibson (Motel Manager), Anne Truitt (Woman in Car and Parking Lot)

THE FUTURE OF FOOD

(CINEMA LIBRE STUDIO) Producer, Deborah Koons, Catherine Lynn Butler; Director/Screenplay, Deborah Koons; Photography, John Chater; Music, Todd Boekelheide; Editor, Vivien Hillgrove; a Lily Films production; Color; Not rated; 88 minutes; Release date: September 14, 2005. Documentary on the unlabeled, genetically engineered food that have crept onto America's grocery store shelves over the past decade.

Hunter Parrish, Paz de la Huerta, Danny Alexander in *Steal Me* PHOTO COURTESY OF CINEVILLE

ONE BRIGHT SHINING MOMENT

(FIRST RUN FEATURES) Producers, Stephen Vittoria, Frank Fischer; Executive Producer, Michael P. Donaldson; Director, Stephen Vittoria; Screenplay, Frank Cottrell Boyce; Photography, Patrick Kelly, Gilbert Yousefian; Music, Robert Guillroy; Editor, Jeffrey Sterling; a Street Legal Cinema production; Digital Betacam/Betacam/DV/16mm/35mm; Color; Not rated; 123 minutes; Release date: September 16, 2005. Documentary on former senator George McGovern's 1972 campaign for the presidency; featuring, George McGovern, James Abourezk, Warren Beatty, Chip Berlet, Malcolm Boyd, Jim Burton, Amy Goodman, Dick Gregory, Gary Hart, Thomas J. Knock, Harvey Kornberg, Ron Kovic, Frank Mankiewicz, Rick Stearns, Gloria Steinem, J. C. Svec, Gore Vidal, Howard Zinn.

HUMAN ERROR

(NEW DEAL PICTURES) a.k.a. *Below the Belt*; Producer, Joel Ehrlich; Executive Producers, Tom Bower, Hank Lightstone; Director, Robert M. Young; Screenplay, Richard Dresser, based on his play *Below the Belt*; Photography, Michael F. Barrow; Designer/Costumes, Hilary Rosenfeld; Music, A.I.; Editor, Roger Cohen; Dolby; Color; Not rated; 95 minutes; Release date: September 16, 2005. CAST: Xander Berkeley (Hanrahan), Tom Bower (Merkin), Caroline Ashley (Catherine), Robert Knott (Dobbitt), Sarah Clarke (Company Spokesperson), Michael D. Olmos (Factory Worker)

Julian Morris, Jared Padalecki, Lindy Booth, Kristy Wu in *Cry_Wolf*
PHOTO COURTESY OF ROGUE PICTURE

CRY_WOLF

(ROGUE) Producer, Beau Bauman; Executive Producers, David Bartis, Doug Liman; Director, Jeff Wadlow; Screenplay, Jeff Wadlow, Beau Bauman; Photography, Romeo Tirone; Designer, Martina Buckley; Costumes, Alysia Raycraft; Music, Michael Wandmacher; Editor, Seth Lewis Gordon; Visual Effects, CIS Hollywood; Casting, Fern Champion; a Hypnotic Prods. film; Dolby; Panavision; Technicolor; Rated PG-13; 89 minutes; Release date: September 16, 2005. CAST: Lindy Booth (Dodger), Julian Morris (Owen), Jared Padalecki (Tom), Kristy Wu (Regina), Sandra McCoy (Mercedes), Paul James (Lewis), Jon Bon Jovi (Rich Walker), Jesse Janzen (Randall), Gary Cole (Mr. Matthews), Anna Deavere Smith (Headmaster Tinsley), Jane Beard (Miss McNally), Ethan Cohn (Graham), Sabrina Gilbert, Ashleigh Pixley, Shauna Sauls, Ranel Johnson (Game Players), Michael Kennedy (Custodian), Ashley Davis (Laura), Jarvis George (Resident Advisor), Shannon Cusack (Field Hockey Player), Gregory Prunchak

George McGovern in *One Bright Shining Moment* PHOTO COURTESY OF FIRST RUN FEATURES

(Student Talking to Cop), Dan Geroe (Student in Dorm Hall), Sarah Satow (Student in Class), Marty Terry (Librarian), Stephanie Nicole Kelley (Girl in Manager's Office), Elaine Deichmeister (Angel Being Kissed), Steven Ritzi (Cop Outside Dance), Antonio D. Charity (Cop at Police Station)

VENOM

(DIMENSION) Producers, Kevin Williamson, Scott Faye, Karen Lauder; Executive Producers, Bob Weinstein, Harvey Weinstein, Andrew Rona; Director, Jim Gillespie; Screenplay, Flint Dille, John Zuur Platten, Brandon Boyce; Story, Flint Dille, John Zuur Platten; Photography, Steve Mason; Designer, Monroe Kelly; Costumes, Jennifer Parsons; Music, James L. Venable; Editor, Paul Martin Smith; Visual Effects Supervisors, Greg Strause, Colin Strause; Casting, Amanda Harding, Amanda Koblin; an Outerbanks Entertainment, Collision Entertainment production; Dolby; Panavision; Deluxe color; Rated R; 86 minutes; Release date: September 16, 2005. CAST: Agnes Bruckner (Eden), Jonathan Jackson (Eric), Laura Ramsey (Rachel), D. J. Cotrona (Sean), Rick Cramer (Ray), Meagan Good (Cece), Bijou Phillips (Tammy), Method Man (Deputy Turner), Pawel Szajda (Ricky), Davetta Sherwood (Patty), Stacey Travis (Laura), Marcus Brown (Terry), James Pickens, Jr. (Sheriff), Deborah Duke (Miss Emmie)

HELLBENT

(REGENT/HERE!) Producers, Steven J. Wolfe, Josh Silver; Executive Producers, Karen L. Wolf, Joseph Wolf, Michael Roth; Director/Screenplay, Paul Etheredge-Ouzts; Photography, Mark Mervis; Designer, Matthew "Flood" Ferguson; Music, Mike Shapiro; Editors, Claudia Finkle, Steven Dyson; a Sneak Preview Entertainment production; Color; Rated R; 85 minutes; Release date: September 16, 2005. CAST: Dylan Fergus (Eddie), Bryan Kirkwood (Jake), Hank Harris (Joey), Andrew Levitas (Chaz), Matt Phillips (Tobey), Samuel Phillips (Mikey), Kris Andersson (Drag Queen), Shaun Benjamin (Police Officer), Wren T. Brown (Police Captain), Miguel Caballero (Jorge), Danny Seckel, Nick Collins (Queens), Blake Davis (Frat Guy), Jerry Farmer (Tattoo Artist), Rafael Feldman, Yan Feldman, John P. Petrelli (Friends), Nick Name (Himself), Jazzmun (Pepper),

Jamila Jones (Waitress), Texas Terri (Tattoo Woman), Dionne Lea (Dog Owner), Paul Lekakis (Admirer), Nina Landey (Maria), Michael Louden (Costumed Man), Ryan McTavish (Fireman), Baron Rogers (Jared Reynolds), Joe Sabatino (Office Cop), Stanton Schnepp (EMT Guy), Rachel Sterling (Girl in Car), Eric Stiles (Boy in Car), Sam Levine (Mikey Fike)

Meagan Good, Laura Ramsey, Jonathan Jackson, Agnes Bruckner in *Venom* PHOTO COURTESY OF DIMENSION/MIRAMAX

Dylan Fergus in *Hellbent* PHOTO COURTESY OF REGENT/HERE!

G

(ALOHA RELEASING) Producers, Andrew Lauren, Judd Landon; Director, Christopher Scott Cherot; Screenplay, Christopher Scott Cherot, Charles E. Drew, Jr.; Story, Charles E. Drew, Jr., Andrew Lauren; Photography, Horacio Marquinez; Designer, Anne Stuhler; Costumes, Jennifer Bryan; Music, Bill Conti; Editors, Robert Reitano, Brad Lauren; Andrew Lauren Productions; Dolby; Deluxe color; Rated R; 96 minutes; Release date: September 16, 2005. CAST: Richard T. Jones (Summer G), Blair Underwood (Chip Hightower), Chenoa Maxwell (Sky Hightower), Andre Royo (Tre), Andrew Lauren (Adam Gordon), Laz Alonso (Craig Lewis), Lalanya Masters (Nicole Marshall), Nicoye Banks (B. Mo Smoov), Jillian Lindsey (Daizy Duke), Sonja Sohn (Shelly), Marcia Wright (Ladara), Damian Young (Gene Underhill), Alex Carr (Bill), Renet Kyles (Monica),

Johnny Russo (Ramon), Lisa Ferreira (Dierdre), Miko Tam (Peter), Brian d'Arcy James (Lloyd), Beth Dover (Nancy), Linda Marie Larson (Emily), Michael Quinlan (Charles), Sarah Schoenberg (Car Woman), Tara Ashley (Girl Fan #1), Christopher Michael Gerrard (Christopher)

LOUDMOUTH SOUP

(DENDROBIUM) Producers, Adam Watstein, Jennifer Lyne; Director/Photography/Editor, Adam Watstein; an Aloha Street Production; Color; Not rated; 95 minutes; Release date: September 22, 2005. CAST: Nancy Bell (Blake Barker), Kevin Chamberlin (Charlie Barker), Melanie Chapman (Catherine Grant), Joe Mellis (Jason Grant), Kit Pongetti (Kim White), Michael James Reed (Sam Ransom), James Tupper (Keith Miller)

DALTRY CALHOUN

(MIRAMAX) Producer, Danielle Renfrew; Executive Producers, Quentin Tarantino, Erica Steinberg; Director/Screenplay, Katrina Holden Bronson; Photography, Matthew Irving; Designer, Tracey Gallagher; Costumes, Mynka Draper; Music, John Swihart; Editor, Daniel R. Padgett; Casting, Sheila Jaffe; an L. Driver production in association with Map Point Pictures; Dolby; Panavision; Technicolor; Rated PG-13; 93 minutes; Release date: September 23, 2005. CAST: Johnny Knoxville (Daltry Calhoun), Juliette Lewis (Flora), Elizabeth Banks (May), Kick Gurry (Frankie), David Koechner (Doyle Earl), Sophie Traub (June), Andrew Prine (Sheriff Cabot), Beth Grant (Dee), James Parks (Arlo), Matthew Sharp (Eugene), Laura Cayouette (Wanda Banks), Thomas Jackson Burt (Farmer), Ken Jackson (Charlie), Linda Wylie (Beehive Woman), Carri O'Neill, Sammye Sowell (Housewives), Bob King (Ancient Farmer), Gatlin Green (Little Girl), Kelsey Stinson, Natalie Stinson (Baby June), Laura Gant, Rachel Gant (Young June), Craig Sawyer, James Holmes, Lawrence Bull Jr. (Repo Men), Preston Cook (Sandwich Shop Person), Kristin Shrader (Pretty Girl), Jonathan Stegman (Boy on Bus)

OCCUPATION: DREAMLAND

(RUMUR RELEASING) Producer, Garrett Scott; Directors/Editors, Garrett Scott, Ian Olds; Photography, Ian Olds; Color; Not rated; 78 minutes; Release date: September 23, 2005. Documentary on U.S. soldiers stationed in Falluja in Iraq; featuring Matthew Bacik, Christ Corzione, Eric Forbes, Patrick Napoli, Thomas Turner.

Johnny Knoxville, Sophie Traub in *Daltry Calhoun* PHOTO COURTESY OF MIRAMAX

CARLITO'S WAY: RISE TO POWER

(UNIVERSAL) Producer, Martin Bregman; Executive Producers, Bo Dietl, Nicholas Raynes; Director/Screenplay, Michael Bregman; Based on the novel *Carlito's Way* by Edwin Torres; Photography, Adam Holender; Designer, Dan Leigh; Costumes, Sandra Hernandez; Music, Joe Delia; Editor, David Ray; a Focus Pictures presentation of a Martin Bregman/Gravesend production; Dolby; Color; Rated R; 93 minutes; Release date: September 30, 2005. CAST: Jay Hernandez (Carlito Brigante), Mario Van Peebles (Earl), Luis Guzman (Nacho Reyes), Michael Kelly (Rocco), Sean Combs (Hollywood Nicky), Giancarlo Esposito (Little Jeff), Jaclyn DeSantis (Leticia), Burt Young (Artie Sr.), Mtumbe Grant (Reggie), Juan Carlos Hernandez (Sigredo), Dominick Lombardozzi (Artie Jr.), Tony Cucci (Big Jeff), Eric Nieves (Chucho), Jaime Tirelli (Leticia's Father), Nelson Vasquez (Manny Sanchez), Casper Martinez (Colorado), Stu "Large" Riley (Tiny), Edmonte Salvato III (Gino), Chuck Zito (Buck), Mary Hammett (Artie Jr.'s Wife), Chad Coleman (Clyde), Jaime Sanchez (Eddie the Bartender), Carmen Lopez (Leticia's Mother), Jaime Velez (Drunk Hood), Gene Canfield (Guard), Ramon Rodriguez (Angel Rodriguez), Annette Rosario (Rocco's Date), Chris Bergman (Valet Attendant), Nicholas Kepros (Tailor), Wass Stevens (Jerry), Misha Sedgwick (Ginger), Chandler Parker (Tenement Guy), Gary Swanson (Doctor), Chris Chalk (Shad), Mandel Butler (Lee), Janet Sarno (Artie Sr.'s Wife), Ron Cephas Jones (Activist), Greg Flippen (Co-Activist), Duke Valenti (Inmate), Duke Valenti (Inmate), Ruperto Vanderpool (Drug Dealer), Omar Evans (Young Runner), Amanda Loncar, Erin Williams (Woodstock Girls), Victor Pagan (Delivery Guy), Frank Pellegrino (Crooning Wiseguy), Pete Colapietro (Father Pete)

DIRTY LOVE

(FIRST LOOK) Producers, Trent Walford, Jenny McCarthy, John Asher; Executive Producer, Scott Saldana, Jim Cantelupe; Director, John Asher; Screenplay, Jenny McCarthy; Photography, Eric Wycoff; Designer, Frank Bollinger; Costumes, Paula Ellins; Editor, Warren Bowman; Music, D. A. Young; a Doubledown Entertainment presentation; Dolby; Deluxe color; Rated R; 91 minutes; Release date: September 23, 2005. CAST: Jenny McCarthy (Rebecca), Carmen Electra (Michelle), Eddie Kaye Thomas (John), Kam Heskin (Carrie), Victor Webster (Richard), Lochlyn Munro (Kevin), Kathy Griffin (Madame Belly), Jessica Collins (Mandy), David O'Donnell (Jake), Judith Benezra (Officer Davis), David Zappone (Officer Hooker), Elena Lyons (Cindy), Noah Harpster (Robert Rodale), Ingrid Rogers (Mindy), Teddy Lane, Jr. (Steroid Monster), Renee Albert (Sara), Frank Alvarez (Bouncer), Cris Borgnine (Officer Ellis), Guillermo Diaz (Magician), Colby Donaldson (Mike), Forbes March (Hot Bacon), Amy McCarthy (Lilly), Coyote Shivers, Sum 41, Steve Jocz (Themselves), Rob Steiner (Henry), Elvis Strange (Hollywood Rocker), Mary Dignan (Casting Director), Bob Glouberman (Producer), Jenna Hagel (Cashier), Tabitha Taylor (Sexy Woman), Jonathan Torrens (Mike), Shira Zimbeck (Runway Model), Joyce Bulifant (Rebecca's Mother)

INTO THE FIRE

(SLOWHAND CINEMA) Producers, Michael Phelan, David Crockett, Bryan Thomas; Director/Screenplay, Michael Phelan; Photography, Chris Norr; Designer, Steven J. Jordan; Costumes, Stephanie Maslansky; Music, Matt Athony, Stephen O'Reilly; Editor, Shawna Callahan; Casting, Kim Miscia, Beth Bowling; a Silent Thunder Entertainment production; Color; Not rated; 95 minutes;

Release date: September 23, 2005. CAST: Sean Patrick Flanery (Walter Hartwig, Jr.), Melina Kanakaredes (Catrina/Sabrina Hampton), JoBeth Williams (June Sickles), Pablo Schreiber (Sandy Manetti), Lydia Jordan (Quinn Sickles), Ron McLarty (Walter Hartwig, Jr.), Herb Lovelle (Arthur Jackson), Ed Lauter (Capt. Dave Cutler), Drew Cortese (Maraldi), Elizabeth Hobgood (Mandy Manetti), Michole White (Patty), Philip Levy (Det. Stack), Jeremy Johnson (NTSB Agent Parker), Chris Diamantopoulos (NTSB Agent #2), Alexander Mitchell (Ed Lynch), Leslie Elliard (Mr. Lynch), Marchell Williams (Waitress), Talia Balsam (Dr. Linda Boyle), Dawnnie Mercado (News Reporter), Charles Borland (Wilcox)

DORIAN BLUES

(TLA RELEASING) Producers, Tennyson Bardwell, Portia Kamons, Frank D'Andrea, Mary-Beth Taylor; Executive Producer, Steven C. Beer; Director/Screenplay, Tennyson Bardwell; Photography, Taylor Morrison; Designer, Len Clayton; Music, Will Severin; Editor, Ann Marie Lizzi; a Day Dreamer Films production; Color; Not rated; 88 minutes; Release date: September 23, 2005. CAST: Michael McMillian (Dorian Lagatos), Lea Coco (Nicky Lagatos), Steven C. Fletcher (Tom Lagatos), Mo Quigley (Maria Lagatos), Austin Basis (Spooky), Ryan Kelly Berkowitz (Tiffany), Chris Dallman (Andrew), Carl Dana (Priest), Leslie Elliard (Therapist), Sian Heder (Ellie), Cody Nickell (Ben), Jeff Paul (Social Worker), John Abele (Ben's Father), Richard Burke (Muscles), Ryan Garrett (Locker Bully), Portia Kamons (Mrs. Polk), Michelle Summerlin (Ben's Mother)

Carmen Electra, Jenny McCarthy, Kam Heskin in *Dirty Love* PHOTO COURTESY OF FIRST LOOK

Melina Kanakaredes, Sean Patrick Flanery in *Into the Fire* PHOTO COURTESY OF SLOWHAND CINEMA

FORTY SHADES OF BLUE

(FIRST LOOK) Producers, Margot Bridger, Ira Sachs, Mary Bing, Jawal Nga, Donald Rosenfeld; Executive Producers, Geoff Stier, Diane Von Furstenberg; Director, Ira Sachs; Screenplay, Michael Rohatyn, Ira Sachs; Photography, Julian Whatley; Designer, Teresa Mastropierro; Costumes, Eric Daman; Music, Dickon Hinchliffe; Editor, Affonso Goncalves; Casting, Avy Kaufman, Jordan Beswick; Dolby; DuArt color; Not rated; 108 minutes; Release date: September 28, 2005. CAST: Rip Torn (Alan James), Dina Korzun (Laura), Darren Burrows (Michael), Paprika Steen (Lonni), Red West (Duigan), Jenny O'Hara (Celia), Jerry Chipman (Shel), Stuart Greer (Tom Skolnick), Christy Hamilton (Tennis Player), Andrew Henderson (Sam James), Charles J. Ingram (Restaurant Owner), Charly Kayle (Karin), Howard Keltner (Sales Consultant), Todd Malta (Waiter), Mary Jean McAdams (Gina), Emily McKenna (April James), Joanne Pankow (Betty), Forrest Pruett (Gary)

Michael McMillian in *Dorian Blues* PHOTO COURTESY OF TLA RELEASING

THE RODNEES: WE MOD LIKE DAT!

(INDEPENDENT) Producer/Director/Screenplay/Music, Lindley Farley; Executive Producer, Stuart Rifkin; Photography, Michael J. Dennis; Editors, Kate Cunningham, Joshua Geisler; Casting, John Charles Thomas; Black and white; Not rated; 77 minutes; Release date: September 30, 2005. CAST: Charles Harding (Rodney Barnett), Alexandre Baptiste (Jhn Dodney), David McLeod (Rodney "Modney" Wolcott), Moogy Klingman (Wm. D. Kappelmeyer), Courtney Turner (Mrs. Davenport), Ashley Arnold (Young Fan)

3 DAYS OF RAIN

(ROGUE ARTS) Producer, Bill Stockton; Executive Producers, Christine U. King, Brad Hillstrom; Director/Screenplay, Michael Meredith; Photography, Cynthia Pusheck; Art Director, Scott Wittmer; Editor, Sabine Hoffman; a Maximone Pictures production; Dolby; Color; Not rated; 98 minutes; Release date: September 30, 2005. CAST: Don Meredith (John), Peter Falk (Waldo), Michael Santoro (Thunder), Joey Bilow (Denis), Merle Kennedy (Tess), Erick Avari (Alex), Lyle Lovett (Disc Jockey), Penelope Allen (Helen), Bruce Bohne (Jenkins), Blythe Danner (Beverly), Robert Carradine (Bus Driver), Robert Casserly (Ray), Chuck Cooper (Jim), Heather Kafka (Lisa), Christine Karl (Liza), George Kuchar (Vendor), Wayne Rogers (Business Man), Bill Stockton (Michael), Claire Kirk (Margaret), Maggie Walker (Jen), Laurie Coleman (Reporter), Jason Patric, Keir Dullea, Max Perlich, Mark Feuerstein, John Carroll Lynch

Rip Torn, Dina Korzun in *Forty Shades of Blue* PHOTO COURTESY OF FIRST LOOK

MY BIG FAT INDEPENDENT MOVIE

(ANCHOR BAY) Producer, Chris Gore; Executve Producers, Tim Miesnhimer, David Wiggins; Director/Editor, Philip Zlotorynski; Screenplay, Chris Gore, Adam Schwartz; Photography, Scott Peck; Designer, Kathleen Widomski; Costumes, Elizabeth Meredith; Music, Joe Kraemer; Casting, David Glanzer; an Aloha Pictures production; Color; Rated R; 80 minutes; Release date: September 30, 2005. CAST: Paget Brewster (Julianne), Neil Barton (Sam), Eric Hoffman (Harvey), Darren Reiher (Johnny Vince), Ashley Head (Anomalie), Brian Krow (Memento Guy), Neil Hopkins (Lanky Man), Rob Schrab (Bald Genius), Regnia Berger (Lola), Neil Dooley (Greek Father), David Douglas (Spike), Robert Eaton (Creepy Security Guard), John Fortson (Spader), Gregory Giles (Gay Husband), Paul Goebel (Crime Boss), Chris Gore (Gimp), Liam Hearne (Hitler), Clint Howard (The Mechanic), Pete Jones, Pauly Shore, Julie Strain (Themselves), Claudia Katz (Secretary), Amy Keranen (Confused Chick), Averill Kessee (Big Man), Abraham Kleiman (Head Rabbi), Hope Levy (Greek Wedding Girl), Henri Lubatti (Young Rabbi), Jasna Meshko (Blonde Lesbian), Dan Mirvish (Rabbi), Chi Chi Navarro (Old Greek Lady), Bob Odenkirk (Steve), Nicolas Read, Darren Richardson (Cockney Guys), Caroline Rivers (Girl in Tutu with Gun), Ward Roberts (Boy Scout), Eric Spitznagel (Animated Linklater), Manolo Travieso (El Mariachi Guy), Serena Viharo (Joey), Woodie Hade (Undercover Cop), Philip Zlotorynski (White Guy), Jim Agnew, Eric Campos, Jon Schnepp (Mexican Standoff Extras), Jason Mewes (Answering Machine)

Neil Barton, Paget Brewster, Eric Hoffman in *My Big Fat Independent Movie* PHOTO COURTESY OF ANCHOR BAY

GOING SHOPPING

(RAINBOW) Producer, Judith Wolinsky; Director, Henry Jaglom; Screenplay, Henry Jaglom, Victoria Foyt; Photography, Hanania Baer; Designer, John Mott; Costumes, Gail De Krassell; Music, Harriet Schock; a Revere Entertainment production; Color; Rated PG-13; 106 minutes; Release date: September 30, 2005. CAST: Victoria Foyt (Holly), Rob Morrow (Miles), Lee Grant (Winnie), Mae Whitman (Coco), Bruce Davison (Adam), Jennifer Grant (Quinn), Cynthia Sikes (Lisa), Martha Gehman (Melanie), Pamela Bellwood (Landlady), Juliet Landau (Isabella), Robert Romanus (Jimmy), Joseph Feury (Richie), Robyn Peterson (Nicole), Dilyn Cassel (Julie), Kim Kolarich (Miki, Waitress), Jenny Gabrielle (Waitress), Michael Panes (Waiting Man), Zoe Warner (Chloe), Jake Daniel Chapman (James), Angela Garcia Combs (Mother), Julia Garcia Combs (Teenage Daughter), Judi Davidson (Another Mother), Rachel Davidson (Pregnant Daughter), Claudio Knafo (Jeweler), Julie Inouye (Mom with 3 Young Girls), Sabrina Marie Jaglom (Young Girl Who Wants Purse), Chandler Rubottom, Madeleine Halyard (Young Girls), Charles Matthau (Sarcastic Boyfriend), Maja Alexander, Marcy Austin, Miriam Billington, Damessa Bell, Claudia Brown, Demetria Bragg, Rachel Case, Sarah Colonna, Deborah Corday, Pamela Demorest, Anna Gerfein, Donna Germaine, Gia Lauren Gittleson, Mignon Goetze, Martha Goldhirsh, Jeanie Hackett, Aloma Ichinose, Marcia

Jacobs, Dani Janssen, Tyger Kahn, Marya Kazakova, Silva Kelegian, Jennifer Kramer, Katharine Kramer, Aleksia Landau, Kimberly Lancaster, JoAnna Linn, Amy Lord, Roxie Moon, Aliza Murieta, Lorielle New, Shae Popovich, Viki Reed, Robin Reiser, Esther Rydell, Jeanne Sapienza, Helen Shin, Hilary Shepard Turner, Maggie Wagner, April Daisy White, Elisabeth Worzniak (Shoppers)

Mae Whitman, Martha Gehman, Victoria Foyt in *Going Shopping* PHOTO COURTESY OF FILMCOMPANY

SANTO DOMINGO BLUES

(MAMBO MEDIA) Director/Producer/Photography/Editor, Alex Wolfe; Screenplay, Alex Wolfe, Richard Fleming; Color/black and white; Not rated; 75 minutes; Release date: September 30, 2005. Documentary on the Dominican Republic's Bachata music; featuring Luis Vargas.

THE WAR WITHIN

(MAGNOLIA) Producers, Jason Kliot, Joana Vicente, Tom Glynn; Executive Producers, Todd Wagner, Mark Cuban; Director, Joseph Castelo; Screenplay, Joseph Castelo, Tom Glynn, Ayad Akhtar; Photography, Joseph White, Lisa Rinzler; Designer, Stephanie Carroll; Costumes, Sylvia Grieser; Music, David Holmes; Editor, Malcolm Jamieson; a co-production of HDNet Films, Coalition Films, 2929 Productions; Dolby; Color; Rated R; 90 minutes; Release date: September 30, 2005. CAST: Ayad Akhtar (Hassan), Firdous Bamji (Sayeed), Nandana Sen (Duri), Sarita Choudhury (Farida), Charles Daniel Sandoval (Khalid), Varun Sriram (Ali), Anjeli Chapman (Rasheeda), John Ventimiglia (Gabe), Mike McGlone (Mike O'Reilly), Aasid Mandvi (Abdul), Ajay Naidu (Naved), Kamal Marayati (Imam), Wayman Ezell (Izzy), James Rana (Saudi Man), Christopher Castelo (Steven), Christine Commesso (News Anchorwoman), John Zibell (Officer Carroll)

SCREEN DOOR JESUS

(INDICAN) Producers, David Stuart, Sam Adelman; Executive Producers, Elzbieta Szoka, Joe Bratcher III; Director/Screenplay, Kirk Davis; Stories, Christopher Cook; Photography, Dan Stoloff; Designer, Galen York; Costumes, Lee Hunsaker; Music, Max Lichtenstein; Editor, Sam Ademan; an FCM Productions Inc. production; Color; Rated R; 119 minutes; Release date: September 30, 2005. CAST: Terry Parks (Believer), Buck Taylor (Old Man Nickels), My Watford (Dawson), Cynthia Dorn (Mother Harper), Silivia Moore (Joycie Conroy), Julius Tennon

Luis Vargas in *Santo Domingo Blues* PHOTO COURTESY OF MAMBO MEDIA

Firdous Bamji (center) in *The War Within* PHOTO COURTESY OF MAGNOLIA

(Fallon), Scarlett McAlister (Ronette), Alaina Kalanj (Sharon Beaudry), Cliff Stevens (George Herbert), Josh Berry (Hank Jeters), Mark Dalton (Duane), Marc Menchaca (Little Red), Richard Dillard (Mayor)

Tracy Coogan, Graham Sibley in *Zombie Honeymoon* PHOTO COURTESY OF RAINBOW

Cynthia Dorn in *Screen Door Jesus* PHOTO COURTESY OF INDICAN

ZOMBIE HONEYMOON

(FABRICATION FILMS) Producers, David Gebroe, Christina Reilly; Executive Producers, Steven Beer, Sam Downey, Larry Fessenden; Director/Screenplay, David Gebroe; Photography, Ken Seng; Music, Michael Tremante; Editor, Gordon Grinberg; Casting, Liz Ortiz Mackes; Dolby; Color; Not rated; 83 minutes; Release date: October 5, 2005. CAST: Tracy Coogan (Denise), Graham Sibley (Danny), Tonya Cornelisse (Nikki), David M. Wallace (Buddy), Neal Jones (Officer Carp), Maria Bermudez (Nurse), Phil Catalano (Jack Birch), Gary Cerborino (Ice Cream Victim), Chris Chan (Bartender), Joe Cicalese (Old Man), Sue Cicalese (Old Woman), Barry Colicelli, Kevin Connell (Policemen), Louis Fattell (Nikki's Client), Mitch Goldberg (Zombie #1), Maria Iadonisi (Mrs. Catalano), John Kirby (The Priest), Nate Meyer (Irate Video Store Customer), Rachel Nord (Waitress), Dustin Smither (Video Store Owner), Soby (Doctor), Steve Szymanski (Fat Jogger)

Graham Sibley in *Zombie Honeymoon* PHOTO COURTESY OF FABRICATION FILMS

DANDELION

(INTERNATIONAL FILM CIRCUIT) Producer, Molly M. Mayeux; Executive Producer/Director, Mark Milgard; Screenplay, Mark Milgard, Robb Williamson, R. D. Murphy; Photography, Tim Orr; Designer, Judy Becker; Costumes, Jill Newell; Music, Robb Williamson; Editor, Amy E. Duddleston; Casting, Tracy Kaplan; a Ballistic Media Group production; Dolby; Color; Not rated; 93 minutes; Release date: October 7, 2005. CAST: Vincent Kartheiser (Mason Mullich), Taryn Manning (Danny Voss), Arliss Howard (Luke Mullich), Mare Winningham (Layla Mullich), Blake Heron (Eddie), Michelle Forbes (Mrs. Voss), Marshall Bell (Uncle Bobby), Shawn Reaves (Arlee), Robert Blanche (Sheriff Teft), Don Alder (Daryl), Wally Dalton (Train Guy), Edward Thomas, Jr. (Will Chavers), Donnie Stroud (Print Shop Clerk), Steven Weyte (Judge Cobb)

Vincent Kartheiser, Taryn Manning in *Dandelion* PHOTO COURTESY OF INTERNATIONAL FILM CIRCUIT

24 Hours on Craigslist PHOTO COURTESY OF ZEALOT PICTURES

24 HOURS ON CRAIGSLIST

(ZEALOT PICTURES) Executive Producer, Ian Reinhard; Director, Michael Ferris Gibson; Photography, Marty Shulman, Juri Kroll; Editor, Jennifer Leo Russ; from Yerba Buena Productions, Inc.; Color; Not rated; 82 minutes; Release date: October 7, 2005. Documentary on the Internet classified ad service, Craigslist, and some of the people who advertise on it; featuring Craig Newmark, Rachel Berney, Holly Dalton, Darleen Hollis, Tina McRee, Sadie, Mark Sargent, Michael Soldier, Daniel Trimble, Scott Trimble.

Shelly Frasier in *Never Been Thawed* PHOTO COURTESY OF SLIPPERY CHICKEN PICTURES

C.S.A.: THE CONFEDERATE STATES OF AMERICA

(IFC FILMS) Producer, Rick Cowan; Executive Producers, Andrew Herwitz, Marvin Voth; Director/Screenplay, Kevin Willmott; Photography, Matt Jacobson; Music, Erich L. Timkar; Editors, David Gramly, Sean Blake; a Hodcarrier Films production; Color/black and white; Not rated; 89 minutes; Release date: October 7, 2005. CAST: Fernando Arenas (Luis Arroyo), Sean Blake (Hitler), Richard A. Buswell (Truck Driver), Ryan L. Carroll (Bobby), Charles Frank (Narrator), Rodney Hill (White Trash Daddy), Evamarji Johnson (Patricia Johnson), Troy Moore ('Sambo X-15' Guy #2), Jon Niccum ("Pink List" Spokesman), Rupert Pate (Sherman Hoyle), Larry Peterson (John Ambrose Fauntroy V), Robert Sokol (Voice of Channel 6 Announcer), Wendy Thompson (Suffragette)

WAITING...

(LIONS GATE) Producers, Adam Rosenfelt, Stavros Merjos, Jay Rifkin, Jeff Balis, Rob Green; Executive Producers, Thomas Augsberger, Paul Fiore, Sam Nazarian, Malcolm Petal, Marc Schaberg, Chris Moore, Jon Shestack; Director/Screenplay, Rob McKittrick; Photography, Matthew Irving; Designer, Devorah Herbert; Costumes, Jillian Kreiner; Music, Adam Gorgoni; Editor, David Finfer, Andy Blumenthal; Casting, Anne McCarthy, Jay Scully; an Eden Rock Media, Element Films, Wisenheimer Films production; Dolby; Color; Rated R; 93 minutes; Release date: October 7, 2005. CAST: Ryan Reynolds (Monty), Anna Faris (Serena), Justin Long (Dean), David Koechner (Dan), Chi McBride (Bishop), Luis Guzman (Raddimus), John Francis Daley (Mitch), Emmanuelle Chriqui (Tyla), Kaitlin Doubleday (Amy), Andy Milonakis (Nick), Alanna Ubach (Naomi), Dane Cook (Floyd), Robert Patrick Benedict (Calvin), Vanessa Lengies (Natasha), Max Kasch (T-Dog), Jordan Ladd (Danielle), Wendie Malick (Monty's Mom), Monica Monica (Dean's Mom), Travis Resor (Chett), JD Evermoore (Redneck), Clay Chamberlain (Video Host), Skyler Stone (Cook #1), Melissa Morgan (Bitchy Lady), Don Brady (Old Man), Anne Ewen (Girl at Bar), Pat Hazell (Jack), Jordan Werner (Smooth Guy #1), Skylar Duhe (Girly #1), Ann Guidry (Dessert Woman), Lauren Swinney (Elderly Woman), Wayne Ferrara (Rocco), Richard Netzberger, Roland W. Hoffman (Germans)

THE AGGRESSIVES

(SEVENTH ART) Producer/Director, Daniel Peddle; Photography, Jeanny Tsai, Daniel Peddle; Music, LU...RRELAS, Ryan Donowho; a Secret Gallery production; Color; DV; Not rated; 73 minutes; Release date: October 7, 2005. Documentary on "aggressives," women who stress their masculine sides.

NEVER BEEN THAWED

(SLIPPERY CHICKEN PICTURES) Producer, Chuck LeVinus; Executive Producers, Gregg Ghelfi, Evan Astrowsky; Director, Sean Anders; Screenplay, Sean Anders, Chuck LeVinus, John Morris; Music, Thomas Luafenberg; Color; Not rated; 87 minutes; Release date: October 7, 2005. CAST: Sean Anders (Shawn Anderson), Shelly Frasier (Shelly Toue), Allen Zwolle (Al McTavish), Mike Gordon (Vince Coppecki), John Morris (Chris Anderson), Charles Arnold (Matt Dakin), S. Joseph Isham (Scott Baxter), John Angelo (Milo Binder), Greg Behrendt (Stan), C. J. Cotton (Alana Mavin), Chuck LeVinus (Chuck McTavish), Travis Randall (Trevor)

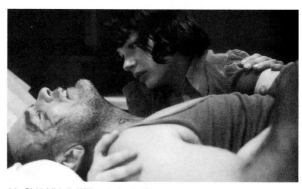

John Diehl, Michelle Williams in *Land of Plenty* PHOTO COURTESY OF IFC FILMS

Justin Long, Ryan Reynolds in *Waiting...* PHOTO COURTESY OF LIONS GATE

Marquise in *The Aggressives* PHOTO COURTESY OF SEVENTH ART

SACRED STAGE: THE MARLINSKY THEATER

(FIRST RUN FEATURES) Producer, Lisa Kirk Colburn; Director/Editor, Joshua Waletzky; Narrator, Richard Thomas; a Red Fire Films production; Color; Not rated; 90 minutes; Release date: October 7, 2005. Documentary on the Marlinsky Theatre in St. Petersburg; featuring Valery Gergiev, Yulia Makhalina, Yevgeny Nikitin, George Tyspin.

LAND OF PLENTY

(IFC FILMS) Producers, Samson Mucke, Jake Abraham, In-Ah Lee; Executive Producers, Jonathan Sehring, John Sloss, Peter Schwartzkopff, Caroline Kaplan; Director, Wim Wenders; Screenplay, Wim Wenders, Michael Meredith; Story, Wim Wenders, Scott Derrickson; Photography, Franz Lustig; Designer, Nathan Amondson; Costumes, Alexis Scott; Music, Thom; Editor, Moritz Laube; Casting, Victoria Thomas, Ellen Lewis; an Emotion Pictures, InDigEnt, Reverse Angle International production; U.S.-German; Dolby; Color; Not rated; 123 minutes; Release date: October 12, 2005. CAST: Michelle Williams (Lana), John Diehl (Paul), Shaun Toub (Hassan), Wendell Pierce (Henry), Richard Edson (Jimmy), Burt Young (Sherman), Yuri Elvin (Officer Elvin), Jeris Poindexter (Charles), Rhonda Stubbins White (Dee Dee), Bernard White (Youssef),

Matthew Kimbrough (News Announcer), Jeff Parise (Coroner's Assistant), Warren Stearns (Mortician), Gloria Stuart (Old Lady)

LOGGERHEADS

(STRAND) Producer, Gill Holland; Executive Producers, Stephen Hays, Lillian LaSalle; Director/Screenplay, Tim Kirkman; Photography, Oliver Bokelberg; Designer, "Jungle Jim" Shaughnessy; Costumes, Susan Oliver; Music, Mark Geary; Editor, Caitlin Dixon; Casting, Cindy Tolan; an Independent Dream Machine, LaSalleHolland production; Dolby; Color; Rated PG-13; 95 minutes; Release date: October 14, 2005. CAST: Tess Harper (Elizabeth Austin), Bonnie Hunt (Grace Bellamy), Michael Kelly (George), Michael Learned (Sheridan Bellamy), Kip Pardue (Mark Austin), Ann Owens Pierce (Ruth), Chris Sarandon (Rev. Robert), Valerie Watkins (Lola), Robin Weigert (Rachel), Adrian Lee (Linda), Tammy Arnold (Patti), Bill Ladd (Rick), Trevor Gagnon (Julian), R. Adam Williams (Hector), Joanne Pankow (Phyllis the Bartender), Michael Harding (Ray the Cop), Kelly Mizell (Gina the Receptionist), Ruth Reid (Ann the Agency Administrator), Craig Walker (Mike Sullivan the Bartender), Jeff Billak (Sam), Al Butler (Lou), Tyler Simmons (Aaron), J. R. Rodriguez (Gordy), Scott Brooks, Jim Nelson, Stephen Wolf, Greg Yoder (Movers), Michael Esper (Gill), David F. Maxwell (Farmer in Barbershop)

Rachel Weigert, Bonnie Hunt in *Loggerheads*

Michael Kelly, Kip Pardue in *Loggerheads* PHOTO COURTESY OF STRAND RELEASING

DON'T TELL

(QUANTUM ENTERTAINMENT) Producer, Peer J. Oppenheimer; Executive Producer, Amy Sommer; Director, Isaac H. Eaton; Screenplay, Julie Koehnen; Photography, Mike King; Designer, Erika Rice; Costumes, B. Kay Stein; Music, Larry Brown; Editor, Patrick Gallagher; Color; Not rated; 88 minutes; Release date: October 14, 2005. CAST: Robert Merrill (Ed), Matthew Christopher (Jessie), Alison Eastwood (Rachel), Colby French (Lee), Bonnie Root (Izzy), Gary Warden (Jack), James Wlcek (Yale), Nolan Flannery (Young Yale), Rachel Gibbs (Young Rachel), Vanessa Chace (Party Guest)

THREE OF HEARTS: A POSTMODERN FAMILY

(THINKFILM) Producers, Susan Kaplan, Sarie Horowitz; Executive Producer, David Friedson; Director, Susan Kaplan; Photography, Kramer Morgenthau, Don Lenzer, Sarah Cawley, Sam Henriques; Music, Catie Curtis, Ross Levinson; Editor, Toby Shimin; a Bravo Cable, Cactus Three, Hibiscus Films production; Color; Rated R; 95 minutes; Release date: October 19, 2005. Documentary on two gay men who share their apartment, and their bed, with a third roommate, a woman; featuring Sam Cagnina, Steven Margolin, Samantha Singh.

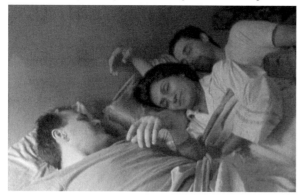

Sam Cagnina, Samantha Singh, Steven Margolin in *Three of Hearts* PHOTO COURTESY OF THINKFILM

PROTOCOLS OF ZION

(THINKFILM) Producers, Marc Levin, Steve Kalafer; Supervising Producers, Nancy Abraham, Daphne Pinkerson; Executive Producers, Sheila Nevins, Jeff Herr; Director, Marc Levin; Photography, Marc Benjamin; Music, John Zorn; Editor, Ken Eluto; an HBO, Cinemax Documentary production; Dolby; Color; Not rated; 93 minutes; Release date: October 21, 2005. Documentary about the rise of anti-Semitism in the United States following the terrorist attacks on the World Trade Center on September 11, 2001; featuring Marc Levin, Al Levin.

AFTER INNOCENCE

(NEW YORKER) Producers/Screenplay, Jessica Sanders, Marc H. Simon; Director, Jessica Sanders; Photography, Buddy Squires, Shana Hagan; Music, Charles Bernstein; Editor, Brian Johnson; an American Film Foundation, Showtime Independent Films production; Color; Not rated; 95 minutes; Release date: October 21, 2005. Documentary on wrongfully convicted men who have been freed after spending years in prison.

Emy Coligado, Stephanie Sherrin, Alex Anfanger, Caitlin Wachs, Crystal Celeste Grant, Chris Morris, Gregory Smith in *Kids in America* PHOTO COURTESY OF LAUNCHPAD/SLOWHAND

KIDS IN AMERICA

(LAUNCHPAD/SLOWHAND) Producer, Andrew Shaifer; Executive Producers, Scott Rosenfelt, B. Billie Greif; Director, Josh Stolberg; Screenplay, Josh Stolberg, Andrew Shaifer; Photography, Guy Livneh; Designer, Stephen Readmond; Costumes, Nikoya Gonzalez; Music, BC Smith; Editor, Tracy Curtis; Casting, Karen Meisels; a Kids in American production; Dolby; Deluxe color; CineAlta HD; Rated PG-13; 89 minutes; Release date: October 21, 2005. CAST: Gregory Smith (Holden Donovan), Stephanie Sherrin (Charlotte Pratt), Chris Morris (Chuck McGinn), Caitlin Wachs (Katie Carmichael), Emy Coligado (Emily Chua), Crystal Celeste Grant (Walanda Jenkins), Alex Anfanger (Lawrence Reitzer), Julie Bowen (Principal Weller), Malik Yoba (Will Drucker), Andrew Shaifer (Kip Stratton), Nicole Camille Richie (Kelly Stepford), Genevieve Cortese (Ashley Harris), George Wendt (Coach Thompson), Adam Arkin (Ed Mumsford), Jeff Chase (Asst. Coach Fasso), Leila Leigh (Jane Jordan), Damien Luvara (Rick Garcia), Rosanna Arquette (Abby Pratt), Steve Rosenbaum (Security Guard), Elizabeth Perkins (Sondra Carmichael), Matthew Brent (Nat French), Raymond Braun (Mo Williams/Teenage Stanley), Rakefet Abergel (Goth Kid), Tim Griffin (Tony), Antoinette Peragine (Tammy), W. Earl Brown (Boss McGinn), Rosalie Ward (Monica Rose), Charles Shaughnessy (Sgt. Carmichael), Kim Coles (Loretta Jenkins), Samantha Mathis (Jennifer Rose), Owen Williams (Cashier), Derek Webster (Police Officer #1), Mary Strong, Derrick Jones, Suzanne Krull (Reporters), Michelle Phillips, Rain Phoenix (Singers), Steve Kim, Michael Tubbs (Guitarists), Johnny Estes (Tim Spears), Justin Halliwell (Twan), Amy Hill (Mrs. Young)

Calvin Willis in *After Innocence* PHOTO COURTESY OF NEW YORKER FILMS

EMMANUEL'S GIFT

(FIRST LOOK) Producers/Directors, Nancy Stern, Lisa Lax; Screenplay, Nancy Stern, Lisa Lax, Liz Massie; Photography, Samson Chan; Music, Jeff Beal; Editors, April Wilson, Meredith Paige; Narrator, Oprah Winfrey; a Lookalike Production; Dolby; Color/black and white; Not rated; 80 minutes; Release date: October 21, 2005. Documentary on how Emmanuel Yeboah rode a bicycle across Ghana to prove that the disabled can contribute to society; featuring Emmanuel Yeboah, Rudy Garcia Tolson, Jim Maclaren.

Emmanuel Yeboah in *Emmanuel's Gift* PHOTO COURTESY OF FIRST LOOK

THE ROOST

(VITAGRAPH) Producer, Susan Leber; Executive Producer, Larry Fessenden; Director/Screenplay/Editor, Ti West; Photography, Eric Robbins; Designer, David Bell; Digital Effects, Quiet Man; Special Effects Coordinator, Glenn McQuaid; a Glass Eye Pix, ECR Prods.; Color/black and white; Super 16mm-to-DV; Not rated; 80 minutes; Release date: October 21, 2005. CAST: Tom Noonan (The Horro Host), Wil Horneff (Elliott), Karl Jacob (Trevor), Vanessa Horneff (Allison), Sean Reid (Brian), John Speredakos (Officer Mitchell), Richard Little (Elvin), Barbara Wilhide (May), Larry Fessenden (Tow Truck Driver), Tom Hamilton (Duncan), Graham Reznick (Local DJ), Heather Robb (Aubry Promise/Fake Shemp), Mary Schmidt (Sally), Ti West (Professor)

THE OPTIMISTS

(CASTLE HILL) Director, Jacky Comforty; Screenplay, Jacky Comforty, Lisa Comforty; Photography, Sid Lubitsch, Ivan Yarimezov, Yoay Ben-David; Music, Stuart Rosenberg; Editor, Jacky Comforty, Lissa Oliver; a Comforty Media Concepts production; Dolby; Color; Not rated; 83 minutes; Release date: October 21, 2005. Documentary on the rescue of 50,000 Bulgarian Jews from the Holocaust.

STAY

(20TH CENTURY FOX) Producers, Arnon Milchan, Tom Lassally, Eric Kopeloff; Executive Producers, Bill Garraro, Guymon Casady; Director, Marc Foster; Screenplay, David Benioff; Photography, Roberto Schaefer; Designer, Kevin Thompson; Costumes, Frank Fleming; Music, Asche & Spencer; Editor, Matt Chesse; Visual Effects Designer, Kevin Tod Haug; Casting, Francine Maisler, Alexa L. Fogel; a Regency Enterprises presentation of a New Regency produc-

Ika Comforty, Vicky Comforty in *The Optimists* PHOTO COURTESY OF CASTLE HILL

tion; Dolby; Super 35 Widescreen; Deluxe color; Rated R; 98 minutes; Release date: October 21, 2005. CAST: Ewan McGregor (Sam Foster), Naomi Watts (Lila Culpepper), Ryan Gosling (Henry Letham), Janeane Garofalo (Dr. Beth Levy), B. D. Wong (Dr. Ren), Bob Hoskins (Dr. Leon Patterson), Kate Burton (Mrs. Letham), Michael Gaston (Sheriff Kennedy/Security Officer), Mark Margolis (Business Man), Elizabeth Reaser (Athena), John Tormey (Custodian/Piano Mover #1), Jose Ramon Rosario (Cabbie/Piano Mover #2), Becky Ann Baker (Paramedic #1/Butch Cook), Lisa Kron (Paramedic #2), Gregory Mitchell (Dance Instructor), John Dominici (Boy/Young Henry), Jessica Hecht (Boy's Mother), Sterling K. Brown (Frederick/Devon), Amy Sedaris (Toni), Michael Devine (Security Guard), Jolly Abraham (Young Woman/Intern), Mark Margolis (Business Man), Mary Testa (Waitress #1), Angela Pietropinto (English Woman/Waitress #2), Oni Faida Lampley (Daisy/Waitress #3), Jarlath Conroy (English Man), Noah Bean (Clerk/Student Guide), Isaach De Bankolé (Professor), G. A. Aguilar (Bicyclist), Riley G. Matthews Jr., Vitto Violante (Officers), Douglas Crosby, Blaise Corrigan (Psych Ward Paramedics), Hank Eulau (Noodle Man)

Ewan McGregor, Naomi Watts in *Stay* PHOTO COURTESY OF 20TH CENTURY FOX

THE TIME WE KILLED

(SPANKY PICTURES) Producers, Jennifer Todd Reeves, Randy Sterns; Director/Screenplay/Photography/Editor, Jennifer Todd Reeves; a Peeping Jane Production; Black and white; Not rated; 94 minutes; Release date: October 21, 2005. CAST: Lisa Jarnot (Robyn Taylor), Chris Tann (Voice of Newsreader), Susan Arthur, Rainer Dragon, Valeska Peschke, Jennifer Todd Reeves

EL VACILÓN: THE MOVIE

(TELEVISA CINE) Producers, Agustin, Darryl Neverson; Executive Producers, Alma, Luis Jimenez; Director, Agustin; Screenplay, Luis Jimenez; Photography, Tony Morales; Costumes, Liza Montoya; Music, DJ Chucky; Editor, Omar Tinoco; Casting, Trina Bardusco; a Babylegs Entertainment Inc. production; Dolby; Color; Rated R; 80 minutes; Release date: October 21, 2005. CAST: Luis Jimenez, Moonshadow, Paul Rodriguez, Findingo (Themselves), Ruperto Vanderpool (Platanoman), John Sialiano (Cop), Caridad de la Luz (Bruja), Agustin, Speedy (Hospital Orderlies), Maria E. Alma (Dominatrix), Dita de Leon (Sexy Girl at Bar), A. Michael Elian (Arabe), Juan Manuel Lebron (Oyente), Casper Martinez (Puneta's Boyfriend), Alessandra Ramos (Elba Nano), Marilyn Torres (Coochie)

NAKED IN ASHES

(PARADISE FILMWORKS) Producer, Tina Kettle; Executive Producer/Director, Paula Fource; Screenplay, Paula Fource, William Haugse, Lisa Leeman; Photography, Christopher Tufty; Music, Tony Humecke, Stephen Day; Dolby; Color; Not rated; 108 minutes; Release date: October 21, 2005. Documentary on some of the 13 million yogis in India.

NEW YORK DOLL

(FIRST INDEPENDENT PICTURES) Producers, Ed Cunningham, Seth Gordon; Director, Greg Whiteley; Photography, Roderick A. Santiano; Music, Brett Boyett; Editors, Greg Whiteley, Seth Gordon; a One Potato Production; Color; Rated PG-13; 75 minutes; Release date: October 28, 2005. Documentary on Arthur Kane, former member of the band the New York Dolls who has since become a Mormon; featuring Arthur Kane, Nina Antonia, Bishop Bragg, Clem Burke, Lee Black Childers, Steve Conte, Bob Geldof, Chrissie Hynde, Frank Infante, David Johansen, Mick Jones, Barbara Kane, Brian Koonin, Dawn Laureen, Don Letts, Bishop MacGregor, Morrissey, Iggy Pop, Sylvain Sylvain, Sirius Trixon, Sammy Yaffa.

Arthur Kane, David Johansen in *New York Doll* PHOTO COURTESY OF FIRST INDEPENDENT

DERAILROADED

(UBIN TWINZ PRODS.) Producer, Jeremy Lubin; Executive Producer, Faithe Raphael; Director, Josh Rubin; Photography, Bryan Newman; Music, Larry "Wild Man" Fischer; Editors, Josh Rubin, Jeremy Lubin; DV; Color; Not rated; 86 minutes; Release date: November 3, 2005. Documentary on cult musician Larry "Wild Man" Fischer; featuring, Larry "Wild Man" Fischer, Harold Bronson, Solomon Burke, Josephine Chuey, Irwin Chusid, Dr. Demento, Dennis P. Eichhorn, Miguel Ferrer, David Fischer, Richard Foos, Freak, Robert Haimer, Fugly the Klown, Mark Mothersbaugh, Bill Mumy, Dr. Louis Sass, Gigi Shepard, "Weird Al" Yankovic.

Naked in Ashes PHOTO COURTESY OF PARADISE FILMWORKS

WAL-MART: THE HIGH COST OF LOW PRICE

(BRAVE NEW FILMS) Producers, Robert Greenwald, Jim Gilliam, Devin Smith; Director, Robert Greenwald; Photography, Kristy Tully; Music, John Frizzell; Editors, Douglas Cheek, Jonathan Brock, Robert Florio, Chris M. Gordon; Color; Not rated; 95 minutes; Release date: November 4, 2005. Documentary on the retail chain Wal-Mart; featuring James Cromwell (Bob Whitebread), Frances Fisher (Wendy Whitebread), Julie R. Lee, Dane Ritter (Employees).

THE COMEDIANS OF COMEDY

(VITAGRAPH) Producer, D. J. Paul, Ted Sarandos; Executive Producers, Patton Oswalt, Michael Blieden; Co-Producers, David Rath, Cindy Holland; Director/Editor, Michael Blieden; Photography, Brandon Hickman; Music, Michael Penn; a NetFlix production in association with Lord Loudon, the Comedians of Comedy LLC, Flaming Liberal Prods. LLC; DV, Color; Not rated; 103 minutes; Release date: November 4, 2005. Documentary on four "alternative" comedians, Maria Bamford, Zach Galifiankiis, Patton Oswalt, Brian Posehn.

BROOKLYN LOBSTER

(MEADOWBROOK) Producers, Kevin Jordan, Darren Jordan, Chris Valentino; Director/Screenplay, Kevin Jordan; Photography, David Tumblety; Designer, Jesse Nemeth; Costumes, Laquita Matthews; Music, Craig Maher; Editor, Mako Kamitsuna; Casting, Phyllis Huffman; a Red Claw Inc. production; Color; Not rated; 90 minutes; Release date: November 4, 2005. CAST: Danny Aiello (Frank Giorgio), Jane Curtin (Maureen Giorgio), Daniel Sauli (Michael Giorgio), Marisa Ryan (Lauren Giorgio-Wallace), Ian Kahn (Justin Wallace), Heather Burns (Kerry Miller), Sam Freed (James Miller), Tom Mason (Chuck Miller), Barbara Garrick (Lynn Miller), Henry Yuk (Bill Lau), Jo Yang (Jen Lau), John Rothman (Sal Guardino), Olivia Archer (Aimee Giorgio-Wallace), Rick Aiello

(Tommy C.), Moises Belizario (Court Clerk), Frank Bongiorno (Tony Annelli), Mike Colter (Jamal), Matt Huffman (Joey), Austin Lysy (David Miller), John O'Brien (Doug), Upendran Pan'cker (Salim), Frank Pellegrino (Judge Astarita), Stephen Schnetzer (Mr. Hammon), Cheryl Stern (Shelly Stutz), Angel Sing (Ron Lau), Connie Teng (Mindy Lau), Myra Lucretia Taylor (Beth Myra), Tony Anelli (Waiter), Aimee Golden Jordan, Allison Moran (Waitresses), Thomas Mulachy, Thomas Golden, Lynne Kelly, William Sweeney, Thomas Kelly (Bidders), Darren Jordan (FDIC Assistant), William Jordan (John Evans), Eileen Jordan (Lady Singing at Piano), Brian Jordan (Sammy Taylor), Max Von Essen (Piano Player), Jeanine Bartel (Dawn), Phyllis Huffman (Judge Williams), Tony Sherry (Diner Cook), Cousin Brucie (Radio DJ), Marni Lustig (Karen), Travis Guba (Deckhand), Moet Meira (Jodi), Maryann Plunkett (Kathy Mulachey), Arlen Dean Snyder (Herman)

GAY SEX IN THE 70S

(FRAMELINE) Producers/Photography, Joseph Lovett, Michael Sean Kaminsky; Director, Joseph Lovett; Music, Art Labriola; Editor, Jason Szabo; a Lovett, Heartlove Production; Color; Not rated; 67 minutes; Release date: November 4, 2005. Documentary on gay New York in the post-Stonewall, pre-AIDS era; featuring Bob Alvarez, Alvin Baltrop, Barton Benes, Tom Bianchi, Scott Bromley, Mel Cheren, Arnie Kantrowitz, Larry Kramer, Larry Mass, Rodger McFarlane, Susan Tomken, Ken Unger, Joe Lovett.

Gay Sex in the 70s PHOTO COURTESY OF FRAMELINE

I LOVE YOUR WORK

(THINKFILM) Producers, David Hillary, Chris Hanley, Tim Peternel, Joshua Newman, Adam Goldberg; Executive Producers, Jay Firestone, Daniel Diamond, Damon Martin, Chad Troutwine, Boro Vukadinovic; Director, Adam Goldberg; Screenplay, Adam Goldberg, Adrian Butchart; Photography, Mark Putnam; Designer, Erin Smith; Costumes, Dawn Weisberg; Music, Steven Drozd, Adam Goldberg; Editors, Zack Bell, Adam Goldberg, John M. Valerio; Casting, Shannon Makhanian; a Fireworks presentation of a Muse production in association with Cyan Pictures, Departure Entertainment, Miracle Mile Films, Rice/Walter Prods.; Dolby; Widescreen; FotoKem color; Rated R; 110 minutes; Release date: November 4, 2005. CAST: Giovanni Ribisi (Gray Evans), Franka Potente (Mia), Joshua Jackson (John), Marisa Coughlan (Jane), Christina Ricci (Shana), Jared Harris (Yehud), Elvis Costello (Himself), David Alan Graf (Zoo Policeman), Rick Hoffman (Louis), Kathleen Robertson (Interviewer), Eric Siegel (Phil), Jason Lee (Disheveled Man), Nicky Katt (Handsome Man), Lake Bell (Felicia), Dan Bucatinsky (Director), Judy Greer (Samantha), Shalom Harlow (Charlotte), Clark McCutcheon (Photographer), Beth Riesgraf (Elizabeth), Bob Sattler (Detective), Vince Vaughn (Stiev), Randall Batinkoff, Glenn Campbell, Haylie Duff, Pat Healy, Holly King

Wal-Mart: The High Cost of Low Price PHOTO COURTESY OF BRAVE NEW FILMS

Patton Oswalt in *The Comedians of Comedy* PHOTO COURTESY OF VITAGRAPH

Giovanni Ribisi, Franka Potente in *I Love Your Work* PHOTO COURTESY OF THINKFILM

Naomi Watts, Scott Coffey in *Ellie Parker* PHOTO COURTESY OF STRAND RELEASING

Nicole Conn, Nicholas, Gwen Baba in *Little Man* PHOTO COURTESY OF JOUR DE FÊTE

LITTLE MAN

(JOUR DE FÊTE) Producers, Danny Jacobsen, Nicole Conn; Executive Producer, David Bohnett; Director, Nicole Conn; Photography, Brian Hoven, K. C. Kaufman, Joe Van Witsen, Therese Sherman; Music, Mark Chait; Editor, Sean Presant; from Little Man Productions; Color; Not rated; 112 minutes; Release date: November 4, 2005. Documentary on a mico-preemie baby.

CHRISTMAS IN THE CLOUDS

(MAJESTIC FILMS) Producers, Kate Montgomery, Mitchell Stein, Sarah Wasserman; Executive Producers, Alfred Lin, Anthony Hsieh, The Stockbridge-Munsee Community Band of Mohican Indians; Director/Screenplay, Kate Montgomery; Photography, Steven Bernstein; Designer, Mark Worthington; Costumes, Glenn Ralston; Music, Stephen McKeon; Editors, Alan Baumgarten, Maysie Hoy; Casting, Katy Wallin, Cate Praggastis; a Random Ventures production; Color; Rated PG; 96 minutes; Release date: November 4, 2005. CAST: M. Emmet Walsh (Stu O'Malley), Timothy Vahle (Ray Clouds on Fire), Mariana Tosca (Tina Little Hawk), Sam Vlahos (Joe Clouds on Fire), Sheila Tousey (Mary), Rosalind Ayres (Mabel), Graham Greene (Earl), Jonathan Joss (Phil), Rita Coolidge (Ramona), Lois Red Elk (Grammy), Wes Studi (Bingo Caller), Shirley Cheechoo (Betty), Georgina Lightning (Louise), Karina Moeller (Annie), Kaesi Belen Soto (Katie), Brian Wescott (Barney), Gerald T. Olson (TV Announcer),

Larry Cesspooh (Floyd), Patrick Shining Elk (Bingo MC), Heather Rae (Buffy), Carla Plante (Muffy), Phillip Blanchett (Singing Cook), Jeff Pehrson (Snake), Steve Sandalis (Buffalo Thunder), Mindy Lawson (Eileen), Joetta Bitsuie (Miss Sky Mountain), Randall Carlisle (Newscaster), Millie Chou (Millie), Anthony Hsieh (Tony), Mace Melonas (Danny)

ELLIE PARKER

(STRAND) Producer, Naomi Watts; Director/Screenplay, Scott Coffey; Music, BC Smith; a Dream Entertainment Inc. production; Color; Rated R; 95 minutes; Release date: November 11, 2005. CAST: Naomi Watts (Ellie Parker), Rebecca Riggs (Sam), Scott Coffey (Chris), Mark Pellegrino (Justin), Chevy Chase (Dennis), Blair Mastbaum (Smash), Jennifer Syme (Casting Chick), Johanna Ray (Casting Director), David Baer (Acting Teacher), Keanu Reeves (Himself), Robbi Chong (Acting Student), Fanshen Cox (Hostile Receptionist), Cyrus Pahlavi (Producer)

DUANE HOPWOOD

(IFC FILMS) Producers, Melissa Marr, Marc Turtletaub, Lemore Syvan; Director/Screenplay, Matt Mulhern; Photography, Mauricio Rubinstein; Designer, Ben Conable; Costumes, Lynn Falconer; Music, Michael Rohatyn; Editor, Tom McArdle; an Elevation Filmworks, Deep River Production; Color; Rated R; 84 minutes; Release date: November 11, 2005. CAST: David Schwimmer (Duane Hopwood), Janeane Garofalo (Linda), Judah Friedlander (Anthony), Susan Lynch (Gina), Dick Cavett (Fred), Steve Schirripa (Steve), Jerry Grayson (Carl), Bill Buell (Wally), John Krasinski (Bob Flynn), Ramya Pratt (Mary), Rachel Covey (Kate), Brian Tarantina (Mr. Alonso), Irma St. Paule (Mrs. Fillipi), Isiah Whitlock, Jr. (William), Lenny Venito (Cop), Bernie McInerney, Mia Dillon (Judges), Jim Fyfe (Linda's Lawyer), Chance Kelly (Tommy the Security Guard), Jeffrey V. Thompson (Rahmn), Josh Flitter (Jake), Sayra Player (Kate's Teacher), Vincent Riviezzo (Aldo), Marty Dunn (Beefy Bartender), Jama Williamson, Pauline Tully (Joggers), Daisy Ang (Frank)

ARISTIDE AND THE ENDLESS REVOLUTION

(FIRST RUN FEATURES) Producers, Nicolas Rossier, Roopa De Choudhury; Director, Nicolas Rossier; Music, Lubo Astinov; Editor, Cameron Clendaniel; Narrator, Ross Douglas; a Baraka Production; U.S.-Swiss; Color; Not rated; 84 minutes;

David Schwimmer, Janeane Garofalo in *Duane Hopwood* PHOTO COURTESY OF IFC FILMS

Release date: November 17, 2005. Documentary on how the U.S. removed Haiti's president Jean-Bertrand Aristede; featuring Jean-Bertrand Aristede.

39 POUNDS OF LOVE

(BALCONY FILMS) Producers, Dani Menkin, Daniel J. Chalfen; Executive Producers, Lynn Roth, Davil Gil, John Matlick, Ed Priddy, John Priddy; Director, Dani Menkin; Screenplay, Dani Menkin, Ilan Heitner; Photography, Yoav Kleinman; Music, Chris Gubisch; an HBO/Cinemax Documentary, Priddy Brothers, Hey Jude production; Color; Not rated; Not rated; 74 minutes; Release date: November 23, 2005. Documentary on Ami Ankilewitz, a 34-year old man unable to move any part of his body.

Vera Farmiga, Hugh Dillon in *Down to the Bone* PHOTO COURTESY OF LAEMMLE/ZELLER

IN THE MIX

(LIONS GATE/20TH CENTURY FOX) Producer, John Dellaverson; Executive Producers, Usher, Holly Davis-Carter, Bill Borden, Michael Paseornek; Co-Producer, Chanel Capra; Director, Ron Underwood; Screenplay, Jacqueline Zambrano; Story, Chanel Capra, Cara Dellaverson, Brian Rubenstein; Photography, Clark Mathis; Designer, Cynthia Charette; Costumes, Ha Nguyen; Music, Aaron Zigman; Editor, Don Brochu; Casting, Barbara Fiorentino, Rebecca Mangieri; a J&C Entertainment, Ush Entertainment production; Dolby; Deluxe color; Rated PG-13; 96 minutes; Release date: November 23, 2005. CAST: Usher (Darrell), Chazz Palminteri (Frank), Emmanuelle Chriqui (Dolly), Robert Davi (Fish), Matt Gerald (Jackie), Robert Costanzo (Fat Tony), Anthony Fazio (Frankie Junior), Geoff Stults (Chad), K. D. Aubert (Cherise), Kevin Hart (Busta), Isis Faust (Lexi), Nick Mancuso (Salvatore), Chris Tardio (Angelo), Deezer D (Jojo), Page Kennedy (Twizzie), Jennfer Echols (Big Momma), Robert Gallo (Dr. Rizzoli), Dwight Hicks (Bouncer), Mieko (Hottie), Erin Cardillo (Rachelle), Lana Underwood (Carly), Misti Traya (Maya), Kristen Renton (Skye), Dominic Testa (Frank's Guest), Lucille Oliver (LaShonda), Kellie Williams (Cami), Mat Gifford (Aqua Receptionist), Alfred "A. J." Jackson, Labyron "Chaos" Walton, Gary "G 1000" Randolph (Street Performers), John David Conti (Gino), Griffin Dellaverson (Griffin), Holly Bonelli, Tamara Garfield (Club Dancers), Elise Cameron (Dolly's Friend), Nito Larioza (Breakdancer), Jennifer Lauren (Yoga Student), Joe Rosario (Frank's Henchman)

SEAMLESS

(SUBMARINE ENTERTAINMENT) Producers, Douglas Keeve, Sabrina Tubio-Cid; Executive Producers, Tom Florio, Josh Braun; Director, Douglas Keeve; Photography, Rob Featherstone, Marcus Burnett, Joseph Van Harken; Music, James Sizemore; Editors, David S. Tung, Kurt Engfehr; a Douglas Keeve Studios production; Color/black and white; Not rated; 75 minutes; Release date: November 25, 2005. Documentary on up and coming fashion designers; featuring Isaac Mizrahi, Vera Wang, Anna Wintour.

DOWN TO THE BONE

(LAEMMLE/ZELLER) Producers, Susan Leber, Anne Rosellini; Director, Debra Granik; Screenplay, Debra Granik, Richard Lieske; Photography, Michael McDonough; Designer, Mark White; Costumes, Nancy Brous; Editor, Malcolm Jamieson; a Down to the Bone, Susie Q production; Color; Not rated; 104 minutes; Release date: November 25, 2005. CAST: Vera Farmiga (Irene), Hugh Dillon (Bob), Clint Jordan (Steve), Caridad "La Bruja" De La Luz (Lucy), Jasper Daniels (Ben), Taylor Foxhall (Jason), Tom Brangle (Policeman), Edward Crawford (Kevin), Chris Heitzman (James), Terry McKenna (Gene), Gia Mitchell (April), Crystal Verdachizzi (Tina)

Usher, Chazz Palminteri in *In the Mix*

Robert Costanzo, Usher in *In the Mix* PHOTOS COURTESY OF LIONS GATE

THE BOYS OF BARAKA

(THINKFILM) Producers/Directors, Rachel Grady, Heidi Wing; Photography, Tony Hardmon, Marco Franzoni; Editor, Enat Sidi; a Loki Films production; Color; Not rated; 84 minutes; Release date: November 25, 2005. Documentary about twenty boys from Baltimore's inner city who were sent to an experimental boarding school in Kenya; featuring Devon Brown, Darius Chambers, Richard Keyseer, Justin Mackall, Montrey Moore, Romesh Vance.

The Boys of Baraka PHOTO COURTESY OF THINKFILM

EXIST: NOT A PROTEST FILM

(ESTHER BELL PRODS.) Producers, Isen Robbins, Aimee Schoof, Esther Bell; Executive Producers, Edward Gregory, Morgan Pehme; Director, Esther Bell; Screenplay, Esther Bell, Nic Mevoli, Ben Bartlett; Photography, Tracy Gudwin; Art Director, Brad Raider; Music, Jeremy Faquhar, Clayton Rychik; Editor, Yasunari Rowan; Color; Not rated; 80 minutes; Release date: December 1, 2005. CAST: Nic Mevoli, Ben Bartlett, Tunde Adebimpe, Mary Christmas, Maya Alexander, Shira Zimbeck, George Crowley

FIRST DESCENT: THE STORY OF THE SNOWBOARDING REVOLUTION

(UNIVERSAL) Producers, Kevin Harrison, Kemp Curley; Executive Producers, Dave Burwick, John Galloway, Jaime Weinstein, Tera Hanks, Chris Moore, Larry Tanz; Directors, Kevin Harrison, Kemp Curley; Screenplay, Kevin Harrison; Photography, Scott Duncan; Music, Mark Mothersbaugh; Music Supervisor, Christopher Covert; Editor, Kemp Curley; Narrator, Henry Rollins; a Transition production in association with Embassy Row, Live Planet, Davie-Brown Entertainment, presented in association with MD Films; Dolby; Arri Widescreen; Color; DV-to-35mm; Rated PG-13; 110 minutes; Release date: December 2, 2005. Documentary on snowboarding; featuring Shaun White, Hannah Teter, Shawn Farmer, Nick Perata, Treje Haakonsen, Travis Rice, Chuck Barfoot, Jake Barton, Tom Sims.

THE KID AND I

(SLOWHAND CINEMA) Producers, Tom Arnold, Penelope Spheeris, Brad Wyman; Executive Producers, Marie L. Fyhrie, Jordan Katz; Director, Penelope Spheeris;

Arielle Kebbel, Eric Gores in *The Kid and I* PHOTO COURTESY OF SLOWHAND

Screenplay, Tom Arnold; Photography, Robert E. Seaman; Designer, Linda Spheeris; Music Supervisor, Damon Fox; Editors, Jay Northrop, John Wesley Whitton; a Wheels Up Films presentation of a The Kid and I Prods. film; Color; Not rated; 93 minutes; Release date: December 2, 2005. CAST: Tom Arnold (Bill

Nic Mevoli in *Exist: Not a Protest Film* PHOTO COURTESY OF ESTHER BELL PRODS.

First Descent PHOTO COURTESY OF UNIVERSAL

Williams), Eric Gores (Aaron "A-Dog" Roman), Linda Hamilton (Susan Mandeville), Joe Mantegna (Davis Roman), Henry Winkler (Johnny Bernstein), Richard Edson (Guy Prince), Shannon Elizabeth (Shelby Roman), Brenda Strong (Bonnie Roman), Arielle Kebbel (Arielle), Yvette Nicole Brown (Bunny), Gabby Sanalitro (Val), Laura Michel Kahwaji (Laura), Shaquille O'Neal, Bill Goldberg, Pat O'Brien, Jamie Lee Curtis, Arnold Schwarzenegger, Penelope Spheeris (Themselves), Alejandro Patino (Apartment Manager), Felicia Lee (Bad Girl), Eric Dickerson (Coach), Branden Morgan, Lisa Wilhoit (Fake Reporters), Melissa Price (Melissa), Brianne Davis (Marla), Melissa Steach (Receptionist), Michael Gores, Ricky Lee Lawson (Paparazzi Kids), Mark Chadwick (Blind Guy), Pablo Eskabar (Chloe)

BE HERE TO LOVE ME: A FILM ABOUT TOWNES VAN ZANDT

(PALM PICTURES) Producers, Margaret Brown, Sam Brumbaugh; Executive Producers, Chris Mattsson, Louis Black, Paul Stekler; Director, Margaret Brown; Photography, Lee Daniel; a Rike Films production; Color; Not rated; 99 minutes; Release date: December 2, 2005. Documentary on songwriter-musician Townes Van Zandt; featuring Townes Van Zandt, Steve Earle, Emmylou Harris, Kris Kristofferson, Willie Nelson.

Townes Van Zandt in *Be Here to Love Me* PHOTO COURTESY OF PALM PICTURES

Arlo Guthrie (left), Pete Seeger (right) in *Isn't This A Time!* PHOTO COURTESY OF SEVENTH ART

ISN'T THIS A TIME! A TRIBUTE TO HAROLD LEVENTHAL

(SEVENTH ART) Producers, Jim Brown, William Eigen, Michael Cohl; Executive Producers, Arlo Guthrie, Harold Leventhal; Director, Jim Brown; Editors, Adam Browne, Samuel D. Pollard, Paul Petreissans; a Ginger Group, L. K. Cohl production; Color; Not rated; 90 minutes; Release date: December 9, 2005. Concert documentary featuring Leon Bibb, Theodore Bikel, Erik Darling, Ronnie Gilbert, Arlo Guthrie, Fred Hellerman, Harold Leventhal; Peter Seeger, Peter, Paul & Mary.

HAPPY HERE AND NOW

(IFC FILMS) Producers, Anthony Katagas, Callum Greene; Director/Screenplay, Michael Almereyda; Photography, Jonathan Herron; Designer, Leonard R. Spears; Costumes, Marco Cattoretti; Music, David Julyan; Editor, Kristina Boden; Casting, Lina Todd; a Keep Your Head production; Dolby; Color; Rated R; 89 minutes; Release date: December 14, 2005. CAST: Karl Geary (Eddie Mars/Tom), Shalom Harlow (Muriel), Clarence Williams III (Bill), Ally Sheedy (Lois), Josephine Martin (Josephine), Gloria Reuben (Hannah), Liane Balaban (Amelia), David Arquette (Eddie), Isabel Gillies (Isabel), Quintron (Quintron), Nic Ratner (Peter), John Sinclair, Ernie K-Doe, Anoinette K-Doe (Themselves), Larry Fessenden (Clifton), Kyle Jason Louque (Police Officer), Billy Slaughter (Napoleon Bonaparte)

Liane Balaban in *Happy Here and Now* PHOTO COURTESY OF IFC FILMS

THE GRACE LEE PROJECT

(LEE LEE FILMS) Producer/Director, Grace Lee; Executive Producers, In-Ah Lee; Co-Producer/Editor, Amy Ferraris; Screenplay, Grace Lee, Amy Ferraris; Photography, Jerry A. Henry; Music, Woody Pak; Color; Not rated; 68 minutes; Release date: December 14, 2005. Documentary in which filmmaker Grace Lee tries to find out why there are so many Asian-American women who share her name.

Grace Lee, Grace Lee in *The Grace Lee Project* PHOTO COURTESY OF LEE LEE FILMS

Frank Stallone in *Angels with Angels* PHOTO COURTESY OF SION ENTERTAINMENT

ANGELS WITH ANGLES

ISION ENTERTAINMENT) Producers, Melissa Wegman, Paul Greenberg, Scott Edmond Lane; Executive Producers, Howard Silver, Gary Arnold, Steven M. Berez; Co-Producers, Mitchell L. Cohen, Larry D. Hansen, Steve Vosburgh; Director, Scott Edmund Lane; Screenplay, Scott Edmund Lane, Mark Pietri; Photography, Holly Fink; Designer, Peter Kanter; Costumes, Shon LeBlanc; Music, Tim Kobza, Scott Edmund Lane; Editor, Steven Vosburgh; Sierra Mar Pictures; Color/Black and white; Rated PG; 87 minutes; Release date: December 16, 2005. CAST: Julie Carmen (Graciella), Frank Gorshin (George Burns/Shelleen), Scott Edmund Lane (Shoomie), Henry Darrow (Raul), David Proval (Howie Gold), Rodney Dangerfield (God), Dawn Maxey (Mary), Branscombe Richmond (El Capitan), Soupy Sales (Cigar Salesman), Frank Stallone (Elvis Presley), Adam West (Alfred the Butler), Carmen Argenziano

(Rico), Christopher Durmick (Chico), Holly Farris (Mae West), Arturo Gil (Announcer Angel), Karin Hallen (Ella the Elevator Lady), Dwayne Hickman (Maynard G. Gillis), Victor Marcel (Soldier #2), Don Marino (Harpo Marx/Fanasito), Jerry Mathers (Mr. Cohiba), Richard Moll (Robert), Gino Montesinos (Shipping Manager), Miguel Perez (Delgado), Zelda Rubinstein (Zelad the Angel), Whitney Rydbeck (Jack Benny), Jeffrey Sherrard (Angel), David Springhorn (W. C. Fields), Lisa Thayer (Hollywood Icon), Jeffrey Weissman (Groucho), Amy Wieczorek (Graice Allen), Jay Wright (Fidel Castro)

TRAPPED BY THE MORMONS

(JEFF GOODE ENTERTAINMENT) Producers, Tony Greenberg, Declan Murphy, Mark Osele, Elizabeth Engel, Eric Simpson; Director/Screenplay, Ian Allen; Adapted from the novel by Winifred Graham and the 1922 screenplay by Frank Miller; Photography, Christopher McKenzie; Costumes, Rhonda Key; Music, Richard Renfield; Casting, Rabbi Weiss; a Cherry Red production; Black and white; Not rated; 69 minutes; Release date: December 16, 2005. CAST: Johnny Kat (Isoldi Keane), Emily Riehl-Bedford (Nora Prescott), Monique LaForce (Sadie Keane), Richard Renfield (Elder Kayler), Mark Osele (Elder Marz), Tony Greenberg (Mr. Prescott), Catherine Aselford (Mrs. Prescott), Judith Baicich (Tilly), Brent Lowder (Jim), Marcus Lawrence (Fairfax), Jennifer Ambrosino (Mormon Follower), Jay Barber, Gabriel Fry, Dave Guess, John Horn (Policemen), Fiona Blackshaw (Girl #1/Mormon Follower/Nightclub Patron), Melissa Leigh Douglas (Slutty Dancer), Danielle Drakes (Singer), Dana Edwards, Marissa Molnar, Sica Neilson, Adrienne Nelson, Lynette Morris (Girls), Rhonda Key (Tarty Girl/Mormon Follower), Andy Kuester (Police Sarge), Brian Laycock, Erik Morrison (Mormon Followers), Dee Ann Lehr (Nightclub Patron), Dallas Miller (Uke Player), Paul Morton (Piano Player), Glee Murray, Karen Joan Topping (Mormon Followers/Nightclub Patrons), Antonio Ordonez (Waiter), David Patrician, Allyn Weber (Nightclub Patron), Emily Rems (Boss Lady), Paul Vodra (Mormon Follower/Policeman)

Johnny Kat in *Trapped by the Mormons* PHOTO COURTESY OF JEFF GOODE ENTERTAINMENT

FOREIGN FILMS

RELEASED IN THE U.S. IN 2005

WHITE NOISE

(UNIVERSAL) Producers, Paul Brooks, Shawn Williamson; Executive Producers, Scott Niemeyer, Norm Waitt, Simon Brooks, Stephen Hegyes; Director, Geoffrey Sax; Screenplay, Niall Johnson; Photography, Chris Seager; Designer, Michael S. Bolton; Costumes, Karen Matthews; Music, Claude Foisy; Editor, Nick Arthurs; Casting, Maureen Webb; a Gold Circle Films presentation; Canadian-British; Dolby; Super 35 Widescreen; Technicolor; Rated PG-13; 95 minutes; American release date: January 7, 2005

Nicholas Elia

Michael Keaton, Deborah Kara Unger, Ian McNeice

Cast

Jonathan Rivers **Michael Keaton**
Anna Rivers **Chandra West**
Sarah Tate **Deborah Kara Unger**
Raymond Price **Ian McNeice**
Jane **Sarah Strange**
Mike Rivers **Nicholas Elia**
Detective Smits **Mike Dopud**
Police Woman **Marsha Regis**
Minister **Brad Sihvon**
Work Man **Mitchell Kosterman**
Business Man **L. Harvey Gold**
Susie Tomlinson **Amber Rothwell**
Mary Freeman **Suzanne Ristic**
Mirabelle Keegan **Connor Tracy**

and Miranda Frigon (Car Crash Woman), Aaron Douglas (Young Father), Anthony Harrison (Doctor), Bruce Dawson (Mark), Benita Ha (TV Reporter), Anastasia Corbett (Young Girl, EVP), Miki Maunsell (Edith Tomlinson), Ross Birchall (Young Boy, EVP), Peter Bryant (Man, EVP), Bill Tarling, Chuck Walkinshaw, Colin Chapin (Presences), April Telek (John's Secretary), Michale Ascher (Woman)

Deborah Kara Unger

A man whose wife has recently died becomes obsessed with trying to contact her by using electric audio and video static.

Michael Keaton PHOTOS COURTESY OF UNIVERSAL

Asanee Suwan PHOTO COURTESY OF REGENT/HERE

BEAUTIFUL BOXER

(REGENT) Producer, Ekachai Uekrongtham; Executive Producers, Phaiboon Damrongchaiyatham, Boosaba Daoreong, Choophong Rattanbanthoon, Ekachai Uekrongtham; Director, Ekachai Uekrongtham; Screenplay, Ekachai Uekrongtham, Desmond Sim, Kim Jim; Photography, Choochart Nantitanyatada; Designer, Nopphadol Arkart; Costumes, Tasakorn Tragulpadetkrai; Music, Amornbhong Methakunbudh; Editor, Dusanne Puinongpho; Fight Choreographer, Sanae Tuptimtong; a GMM Pictures presentation of a Spicy Apple production; Thai, 2004; Dolby; Color; Not rated; 108 minutes; American release date: January 21, 2005

Cast

Nong Toom/Parinaya Charoemphol **Asanee Suwan**
Pi Chart **Sorapong Chatree**
Nong Toom's Mother **Orn-Anong Panyawong**
Nong Toom's Father **Nukkid Boonthong**
Nat **Sitiporn Niyom**
Herself **Kyoko Inoue**
Jack the Reporter **Keagan Kang**

and Yuka Hyodo (Japanese Fan), Somsak Tuangmkuda (Pi Moo), Tanyabuth Songsakul (Tam), Sarawuth Tangchit (Nong Toom as a Boy), Natee Pongsopol (Nong Toom, as a Novice Monk), Samnuan Sangpali (Anaconda), Natawuth Singlek (Ramba), Pat Sasipragym (Hercules), Denkamol Kiatbussaba (Power King), Ittipol Varuthirakorn (Samson), Lampangchai Kiatsunanta (Mountain Top), Payakpanlan Kiatmongeorn (Night Tiger), Pi Day (Cabaret Show Girl), Narisara Soneaim (Prostitute), Watchkarn Krinmueng (Reporter), Kazuhiko Nobukane (Japanese Ringmaster), Erik Markus Schuetz (Hooligan)

While hoping to realize his ultimate desire of becoming a woman, Nong Toon finds fame and success as a Thai kickboxer.

MONSIEUR N.

(EMPIRE) Producers, Marie-Castille Mention-Schaar, Pierre Kubel; Executive Producer for South Africa, Teri-Lin Robertson; Director, Antoine de Caunes; Screenplay, Rene Manzor; Based on an original idea by Pierre Kubel; Photography, Pierre Aim; Designer, Patrick Durand; Costumes, Carine Sarfati; Music, Stephan Eicher; Editor, Joëlle Van Effenterre; Casting, Frederique Modin (France), Sarah Beardsall (U.K.); a Loma Nasha Prods. presentation of a Loma Nasha, Studio Canal, France 3 Cinema (France), Scion Films, IMGS Prods. (U.K.) co-production with the participation of Canal Plus, Studio Images 9, France Television Images 2; French-British, 2003; Dolby; Super 35 Widescreen; Color; Not rated; 128 minutes; American release date: January 21, 2005

Cast

Napoleon Bonaparte **Philippe Torreton**
Hudson Lowe **Richard E. Grant**
Basil Heathcote **Jay Rodan**
Albine de Montholon **Elsa Zylberstein**
Marshal Bertrand **Roschdy Zem**
Cipriani **Bruno Putzulu**
Gen. Montholon **Stephane Freiss**
Gen. Gourgaud **Frederic Pierrot**

Philippe Torreton, Richard E. Grant PHOTOS COURTESY OF EMPIRE FILMS

and Siobhan Hewlett (Betsy Balcombe), Peter Sullivan (Thomas Reade), Stanley Townsend (Dr. O'Meara), Igor Skreblin (Ali), Blanche de Saint-Phalle (Fanny Bertrand), Jake Nightingale (Carpenter), Bernard Bloch (Von Holdendorp), Christopher Bowen (Col. Bingham), Michael Culkin (Adm. Cockburn)

Lieutenant Basil Heathcoate looks back upon when he and his fellow British soldiers were assigned to St. Helena where they were responsible for keeping an eye upon the exiled Napoleon Bonaparte.

Birol Ünel, Sibel Kekilli

HEAD-ON

(STRAND) a.k.a. *Gegen die Wand*; Producers, Ralph Schwingel, Stefan Schubert; Co-Producers, Faith Akin, Andreas Thiel, Mehmet Kurtulus; Director/Screenplay, Faith Akin; Photography, Rainer Klausmann; Designer, Tamo Kunz; Music Consultant, Alexander Hacke; Editor, Andrew Bird; Casting, Mai Seck; a Wueste production, in co-production with Corazon Intl., NDR/Arte; German, 2004; Dolby; Color; Not rated; 122 minutes; American release date: January 28, 2005

Cast

Cahit Tomruk **Birol Ünel**
Sibel Güner **Sibel Kekilli**
Maren **Catrin Striebeck**
Seref **Güven Kiraç**
Selma **Meltem Cumbul**
Nico **Stefan Gebelhoff**

and Cem Akin (Yilmaz Güner), Aysel Iscan (Birsen Güner), Demir Gokgol (Yunus Güner), Hermann Lause (Dr. Schiller), Adam Bousdoukos (Lukas), Ralph Misske (Ammer), Mehmet Kurtulus (Huseyin)

Birol Ünel

Birol Ünel, Sibel Kekilli

Sibel Kekilli

Birol Ünel, Sibel Kekilli PHOTOS COURTESY OF STRAND RELEASING

Self-destructive Cahit agrees to marry spirited Sibel to help her escape from the dominance of her parents, the two Turks agreeing to live separately in Germany.

LOST EMBRACE

(NEW YORKER) a.k.a. *El Abrazo partido*; Producer, Jose Maria Morales; Supervising Producer, Sebastian Ponce; Executive Producer, Diego Dubcovsky; Director, Daniel Burman; Screenplay, Daniel Burman, Marcelo Birmajer; Photography, Ramiro Civita; Art Director, Maria Eugenia Sueiro; Costumes, Roberta Pesci; Music, Cesar Lerner; Editor, Alejandro Brodersohn; a BD Cinea production with the participation of Paradis Films, Classic Film, Wanda Vision; Argentine-French-Italian-Spanish, 2003; Dolby; Color; Not rated; 100 minutes; American release date: January 28, 2005

Daniel Hendler, Adriana Aizenberg, Jorge D'Elia in *Lost Embrace*

Silvina Bosco, Daniel Hendler in *Lost Embrace*

Cast
Ariel **Daniel Hendler**
Sonia **Adriana Aizenberg**
Elias **Jorge D'Elia**
Joseph **Sergio Boris**
Mitelman **Diego Korol**
Senior Saligani **Atilio Pozzobón**
Rita **Silvina Bosco**
and Isaac Fajn (Osvaldo), Salo Pasik (Marcos "El Colorado"), Melina Petriella (Estela), Norman Erlich (Rabbi Benderson), Rosita Londner (Grandmother), Juan José Quispe (Ramón), Francisco Pinto (Geraldo), Eduardo Wigutow (Moshe Levin), Catalina Cho (Ho Kim), Pablo Kim (Kim)

Ariel longs to leave his dead-end job in Buenos Aires and move to Poland, hoping somehow to discover why his family was abandoned by his father, who chose to fight in the Yom Kippur War.

Daniel Hendler, Jorge D'Elia in *Lost Embrace* PHOTOS COURTESY OF NEW YORKER FILMS

NOBODY KNOWS

(IFC FILMS) a.k.a. *Dare mo shirani*; Producer, Hirokazu Kore-eda; Executive Producer, Yutaka Shigenobu; Director/Screenplay/Editor, Hirokazu Kore-eda; Photography, Yutaka Yamazaki; Art Directors, Toshihiro Isomi, Keiko Mitsumatsu; Music, Gontiti; a TV Man Union production, in association with Bandai Visual Co., Engine Film, c-style, Cine Qua Non production; Japanese, 2004; Dolby; Color; Rated PG-13; 141 minutes; American release date: February 4, 2005

Cast
Akira **Yuya Yagira**
Kyoko **Ayu Kitaura**
Shigeru **Hiei Kimura**
Yuki **Momoko Shimizu**
Saki **Hanae Kan**
Keiko Fukushima **You**
Baseball Coach **Susumu Terajima**
Mini-Market Teller **Takoko Take**

Left abandoned in a small apartment by their irresponsible mother, four children have no choice but to fend for themselves.

Ayu Kitaura, Momoko Shimizu in *Nobody Knows* PHOTOS COURTESY OF IFC FILMS

SWIMMING UPSTREAM

(MGM) Producers, Howard Baldwin, Karen Baldwin, Paul Pompian; Executive Producers, Andrew Mason, William J. Immerman, Anthony Fingleton; Director, Russell Mulcahy; Screenplay, Anthony Fingleton; Based on the book by Anthony Fingleton and Diane Fingleton; Line Producer, Carol Hughes; Co-Producer, Nick Morton; Photography, Martin McGrath; Designer, Roger Ford; Costumes, Angus Strathie; Music, Johnny Klimek, Reinhold Heil; Editor, Marcus D'Arcy; Casting, Ann Robinson; a Crusader Entertainment presentation; Australian, 2003; Dolby; Color; Rated PG-13; 97 minutes; American release date: February 4, 2005

Jesse Spencer, Tim Draxl

Tim Draxl, Geoffrey Rush

Cast

Harold Fingleton **Geoffrey Rush**
Dora Fingleton **Judy Davis**
Tony Fingleton **Jesse Spencer**
John Fingleton **Tim Draxl**
Billie **Deborah Kennedy**
Harold Fingleton, Jr. **David Hoflin**
Ronald Fingleton **Craig Horner**
Diane Fingleton **Brittany Byrnes**
Young Tony **Mitchell Dellevergin**
Young John **Thomas Davidson**
Young Harold Jr. **Kain O'Keeffe**
Young Ronald **Robert Quinn**
Young Diane **Keeara Byrnes**
Tommy **Mark Hembrow**

and Simon Burvill-Holmes (Brother Campbell), Bob Newman (Panno), Andrew Nason (Burly Labourer), Barrie Young, Michael Earnshaw (Pub Patrons), Remi Broadway (Murray Rose), Melissa Thomas (Dawn Fraser), Andrew Booth (Bruce Humphrey), Brett Bullock (Gary Humphrey), Todd Leigh, Steven O'Donnell (Lifeguards), Christopher Morris (Medic), Anneliese Fegan (Nurse), Gyton Grantley, Tudor Valise (Swimmers), Dayle Marriott (Melbourne Swimmer), Nick Crilly (Jason Saunders), Laura Donaldson (Young Girl Fan with Dog), Courtney Ayre, Joanne Dobbin (Young Girl Fans), Todd Levi (Well-Dressed Man), Russell Krause, Ron Kelly, Murray Rose, Paul Raynor (Reporters), Dawn Fraser (Dawn Fraser's Coach), Justine Anderson (Tearoom Waitress), Chris Herden (North Sydney Race Starter), Cameron Watt, Christopher Betts, Terry Bone (Valley Pool Starters), Peter Marshall (Empire Games Race Starter), Bruce Wainright (Empire Games Official), Peter Jeremijenko (Pool Marshall), Bruce Shapiro (Pool Man), Chas Green, Aaron Aash (Strikes), Ray McCabbin (Catholic Priest), Katherine Lyall-Watson (Grocery Woman), Raj Ryan (Raido Commentator)

The true story of how Tony Fingleton overcame a troubled homelife, often made unbearable by his abusive, alcoholic father, to become a champion Australian swimmer.

Judy Davis   PHOTOS COURTESY OF MGM

RORY O'SHEA WAS HERE

(FOCUS) a.k.a. *Inside I'm Dancing*; Producers, James Flynn, Juanita Wilson; Executive Producers, Tim Bevan, Eric Fellner, Natascha Wharton, Morgan O'Sullivan; Director, Damien O'Donnell; Screenplay, Jeffrey Caine; Story, Christian O'Reilly; Photography, Peter J. Robertson; Designer, Tom Conroy; Costumes, Lorna Marie Mugan; Music, David Julyan; Music Supervisor, Nick Angel; Editor, Frances Parker; a Universal Pictures, Studio Canal, Working Title Films presentation in association with the Irish Film Board of a WT2/Octagon production; British-Irish-U.S.; Dolby; Super 35 Widescreen; Color; Rated R; 103 minutes; American release date: February 4, 2005

Romola Garai

Suffering from cerebral palsy, Michael Connolly finds his life changed for the better when rebellious, exuberant Rory O'Shea, paralyzed from muscular dystrophy, arrives at the Carrigmore nursing home and encourages the shy lad to share a house with him so they can have something akin to a normal life.

Steven Robertson

Cast

Rory O'Shea **James McAvoy**
Michael Connolly **Steven Robertson**
Siobhan **Romola Garai**
Fergus Connolly **Gerald McSorley**
Con O'Shea **Tom Hickey**
Eileen **Brenda Fricker**
Tommy **Alan King**
Annie **Ruth McCabe**
Alice **Anna Healy**
Girls in Pub **Sarah Jane Drummey, Rachel Hanna**

and Emmet Kirwan (Angry Man), Pat Shortt (Nightclub Doorman), Stanley Townsend, Derbhle Crotty, Donal Toolan (Interview Panelists), Tony Kenny (Cabaret Singer), Keith Dunphy (Estate Agent), Michele Forbes (Fergus' Secretary), Emaonn Hunt (Foreman), Michael Higgins, Frank McCusker, Deirdre O'Kane, Owen Monaghan, Lucas Verbist, Conor McPherson (Job Applicant), Lauren Carr, Paul Lee, Jonathan Mitchell, Keith O'Brien (racing Kids), Michael Hayes (Garda Sergeant), John Finegan (Garda at Station), Adam Fergus (Declan), Mary Kate O'Flanagan (Geisha), Ofo Uhiara (Peter), Justine Mitchell (Doctor), Frank Corry S.M. (Priest)

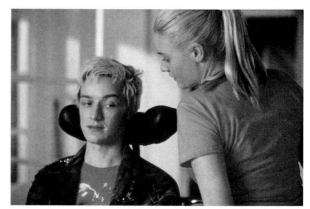

James McAvoy, Romola Garai

Romola Garai, Steven Robertson PHOTOS COURTESY OF FOCUS FEATURES

BRIDE & PREJUDICE

(MIRAMAX) Producer, Deepak Nayar, Gurinder Chadha; Executive Producers, Francois Ivernel, Cameron McCracken, Duncan Reid; Director, Gurinder Chadha; Screenplay, Paul Mayeda Berges, Gurinder Chadha; Inspred by the novel *Pride and Prejudice* by Jane Austen; Photography, Santosh Sivan; Designer, Nick Ellis; Costumes, Ralph Holes, Eduardo Castro; Editor, Justin Krish; Background Music, Craig Pruess; Song Music, Anu Malik; Lyrics, Zoya Akhtar, Farhan Akhtar, Chaman Lal Chaman, Paul Mayeda Berges, Dev Kholi; Choreographer, Saroj Khan; Casting, Susie Figgis; a Pathe Pictures presentation, in association with U.K. Film Council, Kintop Picture and Bend It Films, of a Nayar Chadha production, in association with Inside Track; British, 2004; Dolby; Super 35 Widescreen; Color; Rated PG-13; 111 minutes; American release date: February 11, 2005

Aishwarya Rai

Cast

Lalita Bakshi **Aishwarya Rai**
William Darcy **Martin Henderson**
Mrs. Bakshi **Nadira Babbar**
Mr. Bakshi **Anupam Kher**
Balraj Bingley **Naveen Andrews**
Jaya Bakshi **Namrata Shirodkar**
Johnny Wickham **Daniel Gillies**
Kiran Bingley **Indira Varma**
Chandra Lamba **Sonali Kulkarni**
Mr. Kohli **Nitin Chandra Ganatra**
Meghnaa **Meghna Kothari**
Lakhi Bakshi **Peeya Rai Choudhuri**
Georgina "Georgie" Darcy **Alexis Bledel**
Catherine Darcy **Marsha Mason**
Herself **Ashanti**
Mrs. Lamba **Harvey Virdi**
Bride **Shivani Ghai**
Anne **Georgina Chapman**
Bijili **Mellan Mitchell**
Neighbor **Rick Warden**

Martin Henderson, Aishwarya Rai

In this modern day version of *Pride and Prejudice* Lalita Bakshi finds herself inexplicably drawn to the well-to-do and very disagreeable Will Darcy.

Aishwarya Rai, Martin Henderson PHOTOS COURTESY OF MIRAMAX

Tony Jaa

ONG-BAK

(MAGNOLIA) Producers, Prachya Pinkaew, Sukanya Vongsthapat; Executive Producer, Somsak Techaratanaprasert; Director, Prachya Pinkaew; Screenplay, Suphachai Sithiamphian; Story, Prachya Pinkaew, Phanna Rithikrai; Photography, Nattawut Kittikhun; Designer, Akhadaet Kaewchote; Music, Atomix Clubbing; Editor, Thanat Sunshin; Martial Arts/Stunt Choreographer, Phanna Rithikrai; a Sahamongkol Film Intl. presentation of a Baa-Ram-Ewe production; Thailand, 2003; Dolby; Color; Rated R; 105 minutes; American release date: February 11, 2005

Tony Jaa   PHOTOS COURTESY OF MAGNOLIA

Cast
Ting **Tony Jaa**
Humlae/Dirty Balls/George **Perttary Wongkamlao**
Muay Lek **Pumwaree Yodkamol**
Komtuan **Suchao Pongwilai**
Don **Wannakit Sirioput**
Uncle Mao **Chumphorn Thepphithak**
Saming **Chattapong Pantanaunkul**
Peng **Chatewut Watcharakhun**

and Rungrawee Barijindakul (Ngek), Nudhapol Asavabhakin (Yoshiro), Pornpimol Chookanthong (Mae Waan), Udom Chouncheun (Ta Meun), Boonsri Yindee (Yai Hom), Arirat Ratanakaitkosol (Tang On), Worayit

Tanochitsirkul (Sia Pao), Chalongsak Sirimahasan (Hia Lao), Swanag Rodnuch (Noi), Sutin Rodnuch (Jamnean), Woranard Tantipidok (Pra Cru), Paul Gaius (Lee), David Ismalone (Mad Dog), Sukanya Kongkwaong (Waitress), Hans Eric (Pearl Harbour), Nick Kara (Big Bear)

Ting, an expert in Thai kick boxing, journeys to Bangkok to retrieve a stolen Buddhist statue which is now in the possession of a ruthless crime boss.

Karl Fred Müller, Horst Krause, Harald Warmbrunn in *Schultze Gets the Blues*
PHOTOS COURTESY OF PARAMOUNT CLASSICS

SCHULTZE GETS THE BLUES

(PARAMOUNT CLASSICS) Producer, Jens Körner; Director/Screenplay, Michael Schorr; Photography, Axel Schneppat; Designer, Natascha Tagwerk; Music, Dirk Niemeier, Thomas Wittenbecher; Editor, Tina Hillman; Casting, Michael Schorr, Karen Wendland; a co-production of Filmkombinat GmbH & Co., Zweites Deutsches Fernsehen (ZDF); German, 2003; Dolby; Color; Rated PG; 114 minutes; American release date: February 18, 2005

Cast
Schultze **Horst Krause**
Jürgen **Harald Warmbrunn**
Manfred **Karl Fred Müller**
Jürgen's Wife **Ursula Schubert**
Gatekeeper **Wolfgang Boos**
Head of Music Club **Leo Fischer**
Schultze's Mother **Loni Frank**
Nurse **Elke Rümmler**
Frau Lorant **Rosemarie Deibel**
Physician **Hans-Peter Robiger**

and Marylu Poolman, Ilse Holtmann, Eva Bodnar (Seniors), Gunnar Schlafmann (Cooking Show Host), Wilhelmine Horschig (Lisa), Volkr Robiger (Priest), Alozia St. Julien (Josephine), Kerry Christensen (Yodeler), Raimond Darilek, Freddie Hirsch, Chris Pilat, Richard Gaerkner (Domino Players), Frances Pilat (Barmaid), Charles Pilat (Barkeeper), Marie Bourque (Dancing Partner), Kirk Guidry (Captain Kirk), Anne V. Angelle (Aretha), Danielle Krause (Shareen)

A retired East German miner and polka enthusiast gets hooked on zydeco music and plans to travel to a zydeco festival in America.

DOWNFALL

(NEWMARKET) *a.k.a. Der Untergang*; Producer/Screenplay, Bernd Eichinger; Based on the book *Inside Hitler's Bunker: The Last Days of the Third Reich* by Joachim Fest and the memoir *Until the Final Hour: Hitler's Last Secretary* by Traudl Junge and Melissa Muller; Director, Oliver Hirschbiegel; Photography, Rainer Klausmann; Designer, Bernd Lepel; Costumes, Claudia Bobsin; Music, Stephan Zacharias; Editor, Hans Funck; Makeup, Waldemar Pokromski; Associate Producer, Christine Rothe; Casting, An Dorthe Braker; a Constantin Film, Bernd Eichinger presentation, in association with EOS Prod., RAI Cinema, with the participation of ARD Degeto Film, ORF; German, 2004; Dolby; Color; Rated R; 154 minutes; American release date: February 18, 2005

Cast

Adolf Hitler **Bruno Ganz**
Traudl Junge **Alexandra Maria Lara**
Magda Goebbels **Corinna Harfouch**
Joseph Goebbels **Ulrich Matthes**
Eva Braun **Juliane Koehler**
Albert Speer **Heino Ferch**
Dr. Ernst-Gunter Schenck **Christian Berkel**
Dr. Werner Haase **Matthias Habich**
Herman Fegelein **Thomas Kretschmann**
Heinrich Himmler **Ulrich Noethen**
Otto Guensche **Goetz Otto**
Peter Kranz, The Hilter Youth **Donevan Gunia**

and Michael Mendl (Gen. Helmuth Weidling), Andre Hennicke (Wilhelm Mohnke), Birgit Minichmayr (Gerda Christian), Rolf Kanies (Gen. Hans Krebs), Justus von Dohnanyi (Gen. Wilehlm Burgdorf), Dieter Mann (Field Marshal Wilehlm Keitel), Christian Redl (Gen. Alfred Jodl), Thomas Limpinsel (Heinz Linge), Thomas Thieme (Martin Bormann), Alexander Held (Walter Hewel), Bettina Redlich (Constanze Manziarly), Heinrich Schmieder (Rochus Misch), Anna Thalbach (Hanna Reitsch), Dietrich Hollinderbaumer (Field Marshal Robert Ritter von Greim), Ulrike Krumbiegel (Dorothee Kranz), Karl Kranzkowski (Wilhelm Kranz), Thorsten Krohn (Dr. Ludwig Stumpfegger), Jurgen Tonkel (Erich Kempka), Devid Striesow (Feldwebel Tornow), Fabian Busch (Stehr), Christian Hoenig (Dr. Ernst-Robert Grawitz), Alexander Slastin (Gen. Tschuikow), Aline Sokar (Helga Goebbels), Amelie Menges (Heide Goebbels), Charlotte Stoiber (Hilde Goebbels), Gregory Borlein (Helmut Goebbels), Julia Bauer (Heda Goebbels), Laura Borlein (Holde Goebbels), Andrey Blagoslovenski (Solder in Ruinenkeller), Dikr Borchard (Tank Commander), Lisa Boyarskaya (Schwester Erna), Michael Bradner (Hans Fritzsche), Igor Bubenchikov (Schadle), Leopold von Buttlar (Sohn Grawitz), Martin Butzke, Dimitry Bykovsky (SS Soldiers), Sergej Evseyev (Adjutant to General Mohnke), Mathias Gnadinger (Hermann Goring), Boghdan Graczyk (Clausen), Sergei Halturin (SS Adjutant), Norbert Heckner (Registrar Wagner), Enno Hesse (Lt. Col.), Yevgeni Ilovaiskij, Valeri Solomakhin (Older Civilians), Julia Jentsch (Hanna Potrowski), Oleg Khoroshilov (Henker), Michael Kind (SA-Mann in Ruinenkeller), Elisabeth von Koch (Margarete Lorenz), Marie Sarah Linke (Hedwig Brandt), Michael Lippold (Junger Officer #1), Konstantin Lukashev (Older Soldier), Stefan Mehren (Casualty Soldier), Ilya Mozgovoi (Soldier #1), Silke

Bruno Ganz

Nikowski (Frau Grawitz), Alexei Oleinikov (SS Officer Brauerei), Alexander Orlov (HJ Fuhrer), Oleg Piminov (Adjutant of General Weidling), Silke Popp (Ursula Puttkamer), Vasily Reutov (Adjutant of General Krebs), Igor Romanov (SS Officer Hogel), Tanya Schleiff (Russian Artist), Christian Schmidt (SS-Mann Commando), August Schmolzer (Hans Baur), Jurij Schrader (Dolmetscher), Boris Schwarzmann (Matwej Blanter), Maria Semenova (Rothaarige Frau), Igor Sergeyev (Russian Soldier), Valeri Slavinski (Man), Hans H. Steinberg (Karl Koller), Klaus Jurgen Steinmann (Officer #1), Oliver Stritzel (Machinist Hentschel), Veit Stubner (Tellermann), Mikhail Tryasorukov (Adjutant Muller), Vsevolod Tsurilo (Russian Adjutant), Klaus B. Wolf (Young Marine), Yelena Zelenskaya (Inge Dombrowski), Tatjana Zhuravleva (Old Woman)

Thomas Kretschmann, Juliane Koehler, Bruno Ganz PHOTOS COURTESY OF NEWMARKET

An account of the last ten days of Adolf Hitler while he hid out in a bunker, as the certainty of Germany losing the war brought him to the brink of madness. This film received an Oscar nomination for Foreign Language Feature. Previous film on the same period was the 1973 Paramount drama *Hitler: The Last Ten Days*, starring Alec Guinness.

Alessio Boni, Luigi Lo Cascio

THE BEST OF YOUTH

(MIRAMAX) a.k.a. *La Meglio Gioventu*; Producer, Angelo Barbagallo; Executive Producer, Alessandro Calosci; Director, Marco Tullio Giordana; Screenplay, Sandro Petraglia, Stefano Rulli; Photography, Roberto Forza; Designer, Franco Ceraolo; Costumes, Esliabetta Montaldo; Editor, Roberto Missiroli; Casting, Barbara Melega; a Rai presentation of a Rai Fiction production; Italian, 2003; Color; Super 16mm-to-35mm; Rated R; 366 minutes; American release date: March 2, 2005

Cast

Nicola Carati **Luigi Lo Cascio**
Matteo Carati **Alessio Boni**
Adriana Carati **Adriana Asti**
Giulia Monfalco **Sonia Bergamasco**
Carolo Tommasi **Fabrizio Gifuni**
Mirella Utano **Maya Sansa**
Francesca Carati **Valentina Carnelutti**
Giorgia **Jasmine Trinca**
Angelo Carati **Andrea Tidona**
Giovanna Carati **Lidia Vitale**
Sara Carati **Camilla Fillippi**
Sara Carati, Age 8 **Greta Cavuoti**
Sara Carati, Age 5 **Sara Pavoncello**
Vitale Micavi **Claudio Gioe**
Luigino **Paolo Bonanni**
Medicine Professor **Mario Schiano**
Berto **Giovanni Scifoni**
Literature Professor **Michele Melega**

and Paolo De Vita (Don Vito), Mimmo Mignemi (Saro), Marcello Prayer (Sottotenente), Nila Carnelutti (Francesca Carati, Age 8), Therese Vaddem (Therese), Riccardo Scamarcio (Andrea Utano, adult), Stefano Abbati (Spacciatore), Giovanni Martorana (Maghrebino), Domenico Centamore (Enzo), Pippo Montalbano (Sicilian Commissario), Gaspare Cucinella (Viddanu), Dario Veca (Macellaio), Nicola Vigiliante (Infermiere), Walter Da Pozzo (Mario), Krum De Nicola (Brigo), Maurizio Di Carmine (Terrorist), Roberto Accornero (President of Turin Tribunal), Fabio Camilli (Detenuto Tangentopoli), Antonello Puglisi (Sacerdote Palermo), Patrizia Punzo (Gallerista), Emilia Marra (Dootressa), Nina Carnelutti (Francesca Carati, Age 8), Francesco La Macchina (Andrea Utano, Age 6), Valeria Colangelo (Elena), Laura Di Mariano (Paola), Massimiliano Petrucci (Fabio), Claudia Fiorentini (Cati), Giorgio Crisafi (Chief Doctor at Villa Quieta), Paolo Emilio Alvarez de Castro (Man in Jaguar), Rosa Canova (Moglie di Saro), Aldo Mansi (Ravenna Barman), Ferdinando Martin (Station Barman), Angelo Giuliano, Angelino Costabile (Train Station Police), Enzo Marcelli (Celio Sentry), Aldo Innocenti (Experienced Soldier), Stefano Biscotti (Inexperienced Soldier), Siur Midttun, Rasmus Bu, Mohammed Essaje, Cinzia Cartei (Young Travellers), Assia Pallavicino, Lavinia Matteucci (Riccobaldi Sisters), Danilo Maria Valli (Marino), Fabio Roscillo (Felice), Alberto Pozzo (Rosario), Maddalena Recino (Anita), Massimo Del Sette (Manilo), Letterio Micalizzi (Giovanbattista), Roberto Faglia (Fulgenzio), Giovanni Tormen (Patient), Zefferino Stefanic (The Accused), Giusto Lo Piparo (Lawyer for the Defense), Marcella Mariotti (Assistant Judge), Manuela Massarenti (Director of Psychiatric Hospital), Matteo Ceccarelli (Cabinieri Marshal), Alessandro Trotta (Palermo Policeman), Giuseppe Gandini (Local Administrator), Angelica Zanardi (Neighbor), Joana Jimenez (Lolita), Maria Grazia Bon (Portiera), Mattia Osti (Office Policeman), Giuseppe Mascia (Secondary School Student), Leonardo Antiri (Orlando as a Child), Fabio Rossi (Orlando), Alessio Brilli (Ludovico), Giovanni Giordana (Michele Tomassi), Fausto Maria Sciarappa (A Doctor), Kristine M. Opheim (Ermione)

The very different lives of two brothers, the free-spirited Nicola and the introverted Matteo, are contrasted over a forty-year period.

Alessio Boni, Luigi Lo Cascio

Jasmine Trinca, Alessio Boni PHOTOS COURTESY OF MIRAMAX

Gerard Butler, Jack McElhone

Gerard Butler, Jack McElhone

Emily Mortimer, Gerard Butler PHOTOS COURTESY OF MIRAMAX

DEAR FRANKIE

(MIRAMAX) Producer, Caroline Wood; Executive Producers, Stephen Evans, Angus Finney, Francois Ivernel, Cameron McCracken, Duncan Reid; Co-Producers, Gillian Berrie, Matthew T. Gannon; Director/Photography, Shona Auerbach; Screenplay, Andrea Gibb; Designer, Jennifer Kernike; Costumes, Carole K. Millar; Music, Alex Heffes; Editor, Oral Norrie Ottey; Casting, Des Hamilton; British-Scottish, 2004; Dolby; Deluxe color; Rated PG-13; 105 minutes; American release date: March 4, 2005

Emily Mortimer, Jack McElhone, Gerard Butler

Cast
Lizzie **Emily Mortimer**
Frankie **Jack McElhone**
The Stranger **Gerard Butler**
Nell **Mary Riggans**
Marie **Sharon Small**
Serious Girl **Sophie Main**
Miss MacKenzie **Katy Murphy**
Ricky Monroe **Sean Brown**
Catriona **Jayd Johnson**
Headmistress **Anna Hepburn**
Post Officer Clerk **Rony Bridges**
Stamp Shop Keeper **Douglas Stewart-Wallace**
Librarian **Elaine Mackenzie Ellis**
Barmaid **Carolyn Calder**

and John Kazek (Ally), Garry Collins (Waiter), Anne Marie Timoney (Janet), Maureen Johnson (Singer), Andrea Gibb (Waitress), Cal Macaninch (Davey), Sharon MacKenzie (Staff Nurse), Jonathan Pender (Frankie's Voice-Over)

Hoping to appease her deaf son, who believes his father has been away at sea for years, Lizzie offers money to a stranger to pass himself off as the boy's dad.

WALK ON WATER

(ROADSIDE/SAMUEL GOLDWYN) Producer, Amir Harel; Executive Producers, Micki Rabinovich, Leon Edery, Moshe Edery, Eytan Fox, Gal Uchovsky, Dudi Zilber; Director, Eytan Fox; Screenplay, Gal Uchovsky; Photography, Tobias Hochstein; Designer, Christoph Merg, Avi Fahima; Costumes, Peter Pohl, Ron Doron; Music, Ivri Lider; Editor, Yosef Grumfeld; Casting, Yael Aviv, Chunlei Tan; a Hot, Israeli Film Fund, Fond Européen Media co-production; Israeli-Swedish, 2004; Color; Rated R; 103 minutes; American release date: March 4, 2005

Cast

Eyal **Lior Ashkenazi**
Axel Himmelman **Knut Berger**
Pia Himmelman **Caroline Peters**
Menachem **Gideon Shemer**
Axel's Mother **Carola Reginer**
Axel's Father **Hanna Zischler**
Alfred Himmelman **Ernest Lenart**
Jello **Eval Rozales**
Rafik **Yousef "Joe" Sweid**

Knut Berger, Caroline Peters, Lior Ashkenazi PHOTOS COURTESY OF ROADSIDE

and Imad Jabarin (Rafik's Uncle), Sivan Sasson (Weapons Instructor), Natali Shilman (Iris), Hugo Yarden (Kibbuz Manager), Joshua Simon, Tom Rahay (Kibbuz Singers), Imke Barnstedt (Helga), Yuval Semo (Guy with a Cell Phone), Nesrin Cevadzade (Arab Mother), Adi Eisenman (Mossad Agent), Ahmed Saydam (Arab Child), Mahir Tuocu (Arab Father), Shay Rokach (Tel Aviv Bartender), Hubertus Regou; Biggi van Blond, Paisley Dalton (Drag Queens), Sascha Remkuf (Berlin Bartender), Itimar Ziv (Eyal and Pia's Baby)

An Israeli officer assigned to assassinate a Nazi war criminal has second thoughts about the mission when he befriends the man's grandson.

Knut Berger, Caroline Peters

Specialist Tom Susdorf in *Gunner Palace* PHOTO COURTESY OF PALM PICTURES

GUNNER PALACE

(PALM PICTURES) Producers/Directors/Editors, Michael Tucker, Petra Epperlein; Photography, Michael Tucker; Music, Robert Cimino; a Nomados Films production; Dolby; Color; Rated PG-13; 85 minutes; German-U.S.; American release date: March 4, 2005. Documentary in which American soldiers of the 2/3 Field Artillery talk about their experiences in Baghdad during the Iraq War.

With

Bryant Davis, Devon Dixon, Javorn Drummond, Elliott Lovett, Nick Moncrief, Richmond Shaw, Terry Taylor, Stuart Wilf, Tom Susdorf

Lior Ashkenazi

Bernard Hill, Colm Meaney in *The Boys & Girl from County Clare* PHOTO COURTESY OF FIRST LOOK

THE BOYS & GIRL FROM COUNTY CLARE

(FIRST LOOK/PALISADES) Producers, Ellen Dinerman Litle, Wolfgang Esenwein, Evzen Kolar; Executive Producers, David Korda, Martyn Auty, Jim Reeve, Antony Rufus-Isaacs, Dieter Stempnierwsky; Line Producer, Matthew Kuipers; Director, John Irvin; Screenplay, Nicholas Adams; Photography, Thomas Burstyn; Designer, Tom McCullagh; Music, Fiachra Trench; Editor, Ian Crafford; Casting, John Hubbard, Mary Maguire; a Studio Hamburg-WorldWide Pictures production; Irish-British-German, 2003; Dolby; Color; Rated R; 90 minutes; American release date: March 11, 2005

Cast
Jimmy **Colm Meaney**
John Joe **Bernard Hill**
Anne **Andrea Corr**
Alex **Phil Barantini**
Maisie **Charlotte Bradley**
Teddy **Shaun Evans**
Padjo **Patrick Bergin**
Pat **Eamonn Owens**
Ben **Malachy Bourke**

and Brendan O'Hare (Brendan), Leslie Bingham (Leslie), Frank Twomey (Roger), Emmet Kirwan (Clive), Noel Bridgeman (Johnny), Russell Smith (Terry), Aidan Mulholland (Aidan), Margi Clarke (Dove), Pat Laffan (Gerry, the Custom Officer), Jo Taylor (Sean, the Postie), Bridie Canning (The Woman of the House), Cha Cha Seigne (Hippie Girl), Rob Kolar (American Hippie), Philip Richey (English Hippie), Marc O'Shea (Barry), James Doran (Dave), Nuala O'Neill (Hotel Receptionist), Brian Devlin(Registration Official), Catherine Byrne (Bernie), Sean Brown (Tall Black Man), Aiden McKenna (Rory), Mary Jordan (Rory's Mother), Bill Boylan (The Adjudicator), Pascal Scott (The Official), Alan Crozier (The Soundman), T. P. McKenna (The Announcer), Frank Kelly (The Chairman), Horace Oliver (Paul Francis), Zela Gayle (Aisling McCaffrey), Zelia Attzs (Elliot Ngubane)

Two long estranged brothers reignite their rivalry when their bands compete in a Ceili music festival.

DOT THE I

(SUMMIT ENTERTAINMENT) Producers, Meg Thomson, George Duffield; Executive Producers, David Garrett, Bob Hayward, Patrick Wachsberger, Erik Feig, Francisco Ramos; Director/Screenplay, Matthew Parkhill; Photography, Affonso Beato; Designer, Tom Burton; Costumes, Louise Stjernsward; Music, Javier Navarrete; Editor, Jon Harris; Casting, Kate Rhodes James; an Arcane Pictures, Summit Entertainment production presented in association with Alquinia Cinema; British-Spanish, 2003; Dolby; Technicolor; Rated R; 92 minutes; American release date: March 11, 2005

Cast
Kit Winter **Gael Garcia Bernal**
Carmen Colazzo **Natalie Verbeke**
Barnaby R. Caspian **James D'Arcy**
Tom **Tom Hardy**
Theo **Charlie Cox**
Matire D' **Yves Aubert**
Carmen's Friend **Myfanwy Waring**
Landlord **Michael Webber**

and Jonathan Kydd (Burger Bar Manager), Michael Elwyn (Hotel Manager), Len Collin (Hotel Security), John Pearson (Kit's Father), Tasha de Vasconcelos (Kit's Mother), Tito Heredia (Flamenco Guitarist), Olayo Gimenez (Flamenco Singer), Richard Clifford (Registrar), Mark Spalding (Policeman), Paul Shelley (Presenter), Graham McTavish, Michael Nardone (Detectives), Jonathan Emmanuel (Doorman), David Decio (Waiter)

Natalie Verbeke, Gael Garcia Bernal in *Dot the I* PHOTO COURTESY OF SUMMIT ENTERTAINMENT

Flamenco dancer Carmen Colazzo regrets marrying her well-to-do but dull husband and begins an affair with out-of-work actor Kit Winter, which becomes increasingly deceitful and dangerous.

MILLIONS

(FOX SEARCHLIGHT) Producers, Andrew Hauptman, Graham Broadbent, Damian Jones; Executive Producers, Francois Ivernel, Cameron McCracken, Duncna Reid, David M. Thompson; Director, Danny Boyle; Screenplay, Frank Cottrell Boyce; Photography, Anthony Dod Mantle; Designer, Mark Tildesley; Costumes, Susannah Buxton; Music, John Murphy; Editor, Chris Gill; Visual Effects Supervisor, Peter Bach; Casting, Gail Stevens, Beverley Keogh; a Pathe Pictures presentation, in association with U.K. Film Council, BBC Films, of a Mission Pictures Ltd. production, in association with Inside Track; British; Dolby; Color; Rated PG-13; 97 minutes; American release date: March 11, 2005

Lewis McGibbon, Alex Etel

Alex Etel, Jane Hogarth

Cast

Damian Cunningham	**Alex Etel**
Anthony Cunningham	**Lewis McGibbon**
Ronnie Cunningham	**James Nesbitt**
Dorothy	**Daisy Donovan**
The Poor Man	**Christopher Fulford**
Community Policeman	**Pearce Quigley**
Mum	**Jane Hogarth**
St. Peter	**Alun Armstrong**
St. Francis	**Enzo Cilenti**
St. Joseph	**Nasser Memarzia**
St. Clare	**Kathryn Pogson**
St. Nicholas	**Harry Kirkham**
Gonzaga	**Cornelius Macarthy**
Ambrosio	**Kolade Agboke**
Himself	**Leslie Phillips**

and James Quinn (Estate Agent), Mark Chatterton (Head Teacher), Toby Walton (Damian's Teacher), Frank Cottrell Boyce (Nativity Teacher), Christy Cullen (Surveyor), Gunnar Winbergh (Eli), Christian Pedersen (Jerome), Guy Flanagan (All Saint 3), Philippa Howarth (Tricia), Billy Hyland (Keegan), John Nugent (Graham), Steve Garti (Terry), Alice Grice (Maria), Dale Stringer (Fairclough), Warren Donnelly (Sweet Shop Owner), Emily Aston, Denny James Smith (Big Issue Sellers), Nicky Evans (Scruffy Young Man), Bina Patel, Lisa Millett (Cashiers), Neville Skelly (Pizza Hut Waiter), Daniel Weyman (Bright Eyed Young Man), Tara Moran

Alex Etel

(Applicant #2), Michelle Whitehad (Skinny Woman), Maggie Norris (Professional Woman), Ian Cunningham (Zealous Applicant), Richard Styles (Hedgehog Applicant), Jo Hicks (Young Santa Woman)

Two brothers come across a bagful of money, which they have only two weeks to spend before the British pound switches over to the Eurodollar.

Alex Etel, Lewis McGibbon PHOTOS COURTESY OF MIRAMAX

IN MY COUNTRY

(SONY CLASSICS) a.k.a. *Country of My Skull*; Producers, Robert Chartoff, Mike Medavoy, John Boorman, Kieran Corrigan, Lynn Hendee; South African Producer, David Wicht; Executive Producers, Chris Auty, Neil Peplow, Mfundi Vundla, Duncan Reid, Sam Bhembe, Jamie Brown; Director, John Boorman; Screenplay, Ann Peacock; Based on the book *Country of My Skull* by Antjie Krog; Photography, Seamus Deasy; Designer, Derek Wallace; Costumes, Jo Katsaras; Music Supervisor, Philip King; Editor, Ron Davis; Associate Producers, Peter Fudakowski, Niles Helmboldt; Casting, Moonyeenn Lee, Janet Meintjies; a Phoenix Pictures, Film Consortium, Merlin Pictures presentation, in association with the U.K. Film Council, Industrial Development Corp. of South Africa, of a Studio Eight Prods. (U.K.), Country Merlin (Ireland) production in association with Inside Track Prods., Skoop, Skiet, Drama; British-Irish-U.S.-South African; Dolby; Deluxe color; Rated R; 102 minutes; American release date: March 11, 2005

Juliette Binoche, Samuel L. Jackson

Owen Sejake, Genesis Canda

Brendan Gleeson

Cast

Langston Whitfield	**Samuel L. Jackson**
Anna Malan	**Juliette Binoche**
De Jager	**Brendan Gleeson**
Dumi Mkhalipi	**Menzi "Ngubs" Ngubane**
Anderson	**Sam Ngakane**
Elsa	**Aletta Bezuidenhout**
Edward Morgan	**Lionel Newton**
Boetie	**Langley Kirkwood**
Reverend Mzondo	**Owen Sejake**
Albertina Sobandia	**Harriet Manamela**
Willem Malan	**Louis Van Niekerk**
Old Man in Wheelbarrow	**Jeremiah Ndlovu**
Felicia Rheinhardt	**Fiona Famsay**
De Smidt	**Daniel Robbertse**

and Robert Hobbs (Van Deventer), Lwando Nondzaba (Peter Makeba), Trix Pienaar (B&B Lady), Greg Latter (Sgt. Dreyer), Albert Maritz (Farmer), Sizwe Msutu (Gilbert), Dumisani Mbebe (Kenneth), Sunu Gonera (Lionel), Nick Boraine (Jack Marlon), Charley Boorman (Adam Hartley), Connie Chiume (Mrs. Tabata), Seumus Keir (Simon), Nicholas Andrews, Julian Creasy (Chris), Grant Swanby (Johan), Paul Eilers (Police General), Bheki Vilakazi (Perpetrator #1), Louw Venter (Alec), Wayne Harrison (Brian), Terry Norton (Lilly), Andre Jacobs (Judge), Alyce Chavunduka (Newsreader), Lillian Dube, Namhla Ndlovu, Lee Duru, Nambitha Mpumlwana (Women), Garrick Hagon (Pilot), Andrew Johnson (Taxi Driver)

Washington D.C. reporter Langston Whitfield arrives in South Africa to cover the 1995 Truth and Reconciliation Committee hearings in which opposing views on apartheid are raised.

Samuel L. Jackson PHOTOS COURTESY OF SONY CLASSICS

DON'T MOVE

(NORTHERN ARTS) a.k.a. *Non ti muovere*; Producers, Riccardo Tozzi, Marco Chimenez, Giovanni Stabilini; Line Producer, Matteo De Laurentiis; Director, Sergio Castellitto; Screenplay, Sergio Castellitto, Margaret Mazzantini; Based on the novel by Margaret Mazzantini; Photography, Gianfilippo Corticelli; Designer, Francesco Frigeri; Costumes, Isabella Rizza; Music, Lucio Godoy; Editor, Patrizio Marone; a Cattleya, Medusa production, in association with Alquimia Cinema, the Producers Films; Italian-Spanish-British, 2004; Dolby; Color; Not rated; 125 minutes; American release date: March 11, 2005

Cast

Italia **Penelope Cruz**
Timoteo **Sergio Castellitto**
Elsa **Claudi Gerini**
Nora **Lina Bernardi**
Alfredo **Pietro De Silva**
Ada **Angela Finocchiaro**
Manlio **Marco Giallini**
Pino **Renato Marchetti**

and Paola Cerimele (Nurse), Gianni Musi (Padre di Elsa), Marit Nissen (Martine), Elena Perino (Angela), Vittoria Piancastelli (Raffaella)

A doctor whose daughter has been badly injured in a motorcycle accident thinks back upon the affair he had with a prostitute shortly before the girl was born.

Penelope Cruz, Sergio Castellitto in *Don't Move* PHOTO COURTESY OF NORTHERN ARTS

STEAMBOY

(TRIUMPH) a.k.a. *Suchîmubôi*; Producers, Hideyuki Tomioka, Shinji Komori; Executive Producer, Shigeru Watanabe; Director, Katsuhiro Otomo; Screenplay, Katsuhiro Otomo, Sadayuki Murai; Art Director, Shinji Kimura; Music, Steve Jablonsky; Editor, Takeshi Seyama; a Steamboy Committee, Studio 4°C, Sunrise production; Japanese, 2004; Dolby; Color; Rated PG-13; 126 minutes; American release date: March 18, 2005.

VOICE Cast

Ray Steam **Anna Paquin**
Dr. Eddie Steam **Alfred Molina**
Dr. Lloyd Steam **Patrick Stewart**
Scarlett O'Hara **Kari Wahlgren**
David **Robin Atkin Downes**
Jason **David S. Lee**
Paula J. Newman **Emma**

and Moira Quirk (Cliff/Tommy/Additional Voices), Juilan Stone (Additional Voices)

Young Ray Steam comes into possession of a powerful steam ball which plays a key part in the battle between his father and grandfather.

Ray Steam in *Steamboy*

Ray Steam in *Steamboy* PHOTOS COURTESY OF TRIUMPH

LOOK AT ME

(SONY CLASSICS) a.k.a. *Comme une image*; Producers, Jean-Philippe Andraca, Christian Berard; Director, Agnès Jaoui; Screenplay, Agnès Jaoui, Jean-Pierre Bacri; Photography, Stephane Fontaine; Designer, Olivier Jacquet; Costumes, Jackie Budin; Music, Philippe Rombi; Editor, Francois Gedigier; Casting, Brigitte Moidon; a Les Films A4, Studio Canal, France 2 Cinema, Lumiere, Eyescreen production with the participation of Canal Plus; French, 2004; Dolby; Super 35 Widescreen; Color; Rated PG-13; 111 minutes; American release date: April 1, 2005

Keine Bouhiza, Marilou Berry

Lolita, a talented young singer with a weight problem, finds herself craving the approval of her egotistical father, a famed writer and publisher who is more interested in the new novel by Pierre, the husband of Lolita's music teacher.

Marilou Berry, Virginie Desarnauts

Cast

Lolita Cassard **Marilou Berry**
Sylvia Millet **Agnès Jaoui**
Étienne Cassard **Jean-Pierre Bacri**
Pierre Millet **Laurent Grévill**
Karine Cassard **Virginie Desarnauts**
Sébastien **Keine Bouhiza**
Vincent **Grégoire Oestermann**
Félix **Serge Riaboukine**
Édith **Michèle Moretti**
Taxi Driver **Jean-Pierre Lazzerini**
Bouncer **Jacques Boko**

and Yves Verhoeven, Samir Guesmi (Onlookers), Bob Zaremba (Guy Seen Everywhere), Roberte Kiehl (Conservatoire Pianist), Jean-Baptiste Blanc (Conservatoire Singer), Emma Beziaud (Louna), Julien Baumgartner (Mathieu), Zelie Berger (Mathieu's Girlfriend), Dimitri Rataud (Doctor), Camille Dereux (Pretty Singer), Henri Boyer (Pierre and Sylvia's Pianist), Guillaume Huet (Nicolas), Olivia Lancelot (Painter), Elodie Clairin (Étienne's Waitress), Olivier Claverie (Mr. Tessier), Bernard Blancan (Village Cafe Waiter), Sébastien Andrieu (Young Man Who Looks at Sylvia), Marie Sarrasin (Young Girl Mathieu Kisses), Antonia Cornin-Navarro (Guardian), Philippe Tran (Edith and Sylvia's Waiter), Erick Desmaretz (New Teacher), Didier Brice (New Teacher's Assistant), Olivier Doran (François Galland), Catherine Morin (Tastycat Actress), Alain Debruyne (Usher)

Agnès Jaoui, Marilou Berry

Jean-Pierre Bacri, Virginie Desarnauts PHOTOS COURTESY OF SONY CLASSICS

Stephen Chow (center)

KUNG FU HUSTLE

(SONY CLASSICS) a.k.a. *Kung Fu*; Producers, Stephen Chow, Chui Po-chu, Jeff Lau; Executive Producers, Yang Buting, Wang Zhongjun; Co-Producers, Bill Borden, David Hung; Director, Stephen Chow; Screenplay, Stephen Chow, Tsang Kan-cheong, Lola Huo, Chan Man-keung; Associate Director, Wellson Chin; Photography, Poon Hang-seng; Designer, Oliver Wong; Costumes, Shirley Chan; Music, Raymond Wong; Editor, Angie Lam; Makeup, Maggie Choy; Action Choreographer, Yuen Wo-ping; Visual Effects, Centro Digital Pictures; a Columbia Pictures Film Production Asia (Hong Kong)/Huyai Brothers & Taihe Film Investment Co., Beijing Film Studio of China Gilm Group Corp. (China) presentation of a Star Overseas (Hong Kong) production, in association with China Film Co-Production Co.; Hong Kong-Chinese; Dolby; Super 35 Widescreen; Color; Rated R; 99 minutes; American release date: April 8, 2005

Cast

Sing	**Stephen Chow**
Landlord	**Yuen Wah**
Landlady	**Yuen Qiu**
The Beast	**Leung Siu-lung**
Donut	**Doug Zhihua**
Tailor	**Chiu Chi-ling**
Coolie	**Xing Yu**
Brother Sum	**Chan Kwok-kwan**
Fong	**Huang Shengyi**
Bone, Sing's Sidekick	**Lam Tze-chung**
Crocodile Gang Boss	**Feng Xiaogang**
Axe Gang Vice-General	**Lam Suet**
Axe Gang Advisor	**Tin Kai Man**
Beggar	**Yuen Cheung-yan**
Inspector Chan	**Bai Zhang Yi**
Suzie	**Ren Si Lu**
Mr. Gold	**Ding Xiao Lung**
Mr. Silver	**Zhang Ming Ming**
Inspector	**Oliver Wong**
Rabbit-Tooth Jane	**Chen Kai Shi**

Chan Kwok-kwan

Lam Tze-chung, Stephen Chow

and Chin Wellson, Yeung Lun, Liu Chao Xia (Neighbors), He Wen Hui (Jiang Bao), David Hung (Mr. Big), Billy Ma (Axe Gang Member), Yuan Hao Tian (Little Sing), Fung Min Hun (Four Eye Clerk)

In a slum area known as Pig Sty Alley, drifter and gangster-wannabe Sing clashes with the powerful Axe Gang that rules the community through terror and violence.

Yuen Qiu PHOTOS COURTESY OF SONY CLASSICS

EROS

(WARNER INDEPENDENT) Producers, Raphael Berdugo, Stephane Tchal Gadjieff, Jacques Bar, Domenico Procacci; Linking Sequences, Lorenzo Mattotti, in collaboration with Studio Eye; a Roissy Films, Solaris, Cite Films Prods., Fandango, Delux production with Block2 Pictures, Ipso Facto; French-Italian-Luxembourg; Dolby; Color; Rated R; 109 minutes; American release date: April 8, 2005.

THE HAND: Producers, Wong Kar-wai, Jacky Pang Yee Wah; Executive Producer, Chan Ye Chang; Director/Screenplay, Wong Kar-wai; Photography, Christopher Doyle; Production & Costume Designer, William Chang Suk Ping.

> **Cast:** Gong Li (Miss Hua), Chang Chen (Zhang), Tin Fung (Master Jin), Auntie Luk (Ying), Zhou Jianjun (Zhao, Hua's Lover), Sheung Wing Ton, Wong Kim Tak, Ting Siu Man, Yim Lai Fu, Shin Cheng You, Siu Wing Kong, Lee Kar Fai (Tailors), Un Chi Keong (Hotel Concierge)

A tailor's apprentice falls in love with a prostitute when he comes to her home for a dress fitting.

EQUILIBRIUM: Producer, Gregory Jacobs; Director/Screenplay, Steven Soderbergh; Photography, Peter Andrews; Designer, Philip Messina; Costumes, Milena Canonero; Music, Chico O'Farrill, Tito Puente; Editor, Mary Ann Bernard; Casting, Debra Zane.

> **Cast:** Robert Downey, Jr. (Nick Penrose), Alan Arkin (Dr. Pearl/Hal), Ele Keats (The Woman/Cecelia)

A distressed New York ad exec tells his problems and erotic dreams to his psychiatrist.

THE DANGEROUS THREAD OF THINGS: Producers, Raphael Berdugo, Tchal Gadjieff, Jacques Bar, Domenico Procacci; Executive Producer, Danielle Rosencranz; Director, Michelangelo Antonioni; Screenplay, Michelangelo Antonioni, Tonino Guerra; Based on the book *Quel Bowling sul Tevere* by Michelangeo Antonioni; Photography, Marco Pontecorvo; Designer, Stefano Lucci; Costumes, Carin Berger; Music, Enrica Antonioni, Vinicio Milani; Editor, Claudio Di Mauro.

Sanna Brading in *A Hole in My Heart* PHOTO COURTESY OF NEWMARKET

Cast: Christopher Buchholz (Christopher), Regina Nemni (Cloe), Luisa Ranieri (The Girl/Linda), Cecilia Luci, Karima Machehour (Girls by the Cascade), Riccardo Manfredi (Barman), Valerio Burroni (Waiter), Pelino Tarantelli (Gardener), Maria Bosio, Carla Milani, Vinicio Milani, Jason Cardone, Carin Berger, Enrica Antonioni (Guests at the Restaurant)

Christopher and Cloe's unraveling marriage causes him to sleep with a beautiful horseback rider.

Regina Nemni, Christopher Buchholz in *Eros* PHOTOS COURTESY OF WARNER INDEPENDENT

A HOLE IN MY HEART

(NEWMARKET) a.k.a. *Ett hål i mitt hjärta*; Producer, Lars Jonsson; Co-Producers, Gunnar Carlsson, Tomas Eskilsson, Peter Aalbaek Jensen; Director, Lukas Moodysson; Screenplay, Lukas Moodysson, Bjorn Almroth, Sanna Brading, Thorsten Flinck, Malin Fornander, Jesper Kurlandsky, Goran Marjanovic, Karl Strandlind; Photography, Malin Fornander, Jesper Kurlandsky, Lukas Moodysson, Karl Strandlind; Art Director/Costumes/Casting, Malin Fornander, Jesper Kurlandsky, Lukas Moodysson, Karl Strandlind; a Memfis Film Rights 3 AB-production in association with Film I Vast, Swedish Television Gothenburg, Zentropa Entertainments5 ApS, Nordic Film- & TV-fond, with support from the Swedish Film Institute and the Danish Film Institute, in cooperation with Canal Plus Television AB; Swedish; Dolby; Color; DV-to-35mm; Not rated; 98 minutes; American release date: April 8, 2005

> **Cast**
> Rickard **Thorsten Flinck**
> Eric   **Bjorn Almroth**
> Tess   **Sanna Brading**
> Geko   **Goran Marjanovic**

While shooting an amateur porno film in his apartment, Rickard and his actors cross into disturbing territory with their uninhibited behavior.

Matthew McConaughey

SAHARA

(PARAMOUNT) Producers, Howard Baldwin, Karen Baldwin, Mace Neufeld, Stephanie Austin; Executive Producers, Matthew McConaughey, Gus Gustawes, William J. Immerman, Vicki Dee Rock; Director, Breck Eisner; Screenplay, Thomas Dean Donnelly, Joshua Oppenheimer, John C. Richards, James V. Hart; Based on the novel by Clive Cussler; Photography, Seamus McGarvey; Designer, Allan Cameron; Costumes, Anna Sheppard; Music, Clint Mansell; Music Supervisor, Lindsay Fellows; Editor, Andrew MacRitchie; Co-Producers, Denise O'Dell, Mark Albela, David Barron, Nick Morton; Visual Effects Supervisor, Mara Bryan; Casting, Anne McCarthy; Stunts, Lee Sheward; a Bristol Bay Productions presentation in association with Baldwin Entertainment Group of a j.k. livin production, a Kanzman production; British-Spanish-German-U.S.; Dolby; Super 35 Widescreen; Deluxe color; Rated PG-13; 127 minutes; Release date: April 8, 2005

Cast

Dirk Pitt **Matthew McConaughey**
Al Giordano **Steve Zahn**
Dr. Eva Rojas **Penelope Cruz**
Yves Massarde **Lambert Wilson**
Dr. Frank Hopper **Glynn Turman**
Carl **Delroy Lindo**
Admiral Sandecker **William H. Macy**
Rudi **Rainn Wilson**
Imam **Jude Akuwudike**
Lawyer **Mark Aspinall**
Mrs. Nwokolo **Rakie Ayiola**
Train Driver **Christopher Bello**
Captain Tombs **Robert Cavanah**
Oshodi **Clint Dyer**

and Nicholas Beveney (Gunboat 1 Officer), Empotoe Bosage (Pick Up Truck Guard), Matthew Flynn (1st Lieutenant, Ironclad), Paulin F. Fodouop (Modibo), Ouahbou Houcine, Lahcen Ouezgane (Tuareg Village Boys), Emmanuel Ighobdaro (Kazim's Officer Asselar), Lennie James (Zakara), Daniel Lobe (Tuareg Sangare), Francis Magee (Fuse Cutter), Partick

William H. Macy, Matthew McConaughey

William H. Macy, Matthew McConaughey

Malahide (Ambassador Polidori), Thierno Amath Mbaye (Pick Up Truck Driver), Femi Ogunbanjo (Modibo's Tuareg #2), Eddie Osei (Train Guard), Nathan Osgood (Gun Captain), Robert Paterson (NUMA Crew Member), Abdul Salis (Oumar), Tosin Sanyalo (Azikiwe Nwokolo), Christopher Saul (Pilot, Ironclad), Billy Seymour (Powder Monkey), Mark Springer (Solar Plant Guard), Celestine Vita (Old Woman in Labbezanga), Mark Wells (Sailor Who Drops Gold)

After coming across a fabled coin linked to a historical legend, adventurer Dirk Pitt travels to West Africa to find a long-lost Civil War battleship that contains a secret cargo.

Matthew McConaughey, Penelope Cruz, Steve Zahn PHOTOS COURTESY OF PARAMOUNT

LADIES IN LAVENDER

(ROADSIDE ATTRACTIONS) Producers, Nik Powell, Nicolas Brown, Elizabeth Karlsen; Executive Producers, Robert Jones, Bill Allan, Emma Hayter, Charles Dance; Director/Screenplay, Charles Dance; Based on a short story by William J. Locke; Photography, Peter Biziou; Designer, Caroline Amies; Costumes, Barbara Kidd; Music, Nigel Hess; Solo Violin, Joshua Bell; Editor, Michael Parker; Associate Producer, Ian Prior; Casting, Sarah Bird; a Tale Partnerships presentation of a Scala Prod., Lakeshore Entertainment production; British, 2004; Dolby; Technicolor; Rated PG-13; 103 minutes; American release date: April 29, 2005

Maggie Smith, Judi Dench

Maggie Smith, Judi Dench

Cast

Ursula Widdington **Judi Dench**
Janet Widdington **Maggie Smith**
Andrea Marowski **Daniel Bruhl**
Dorcas **Miriam Margolyes**
Olga Danilof **Natascha McElhone**
Jan Pendered **Freddie Jones**
Dr. Francis Mead **David Warner**
Adam Penruddocke **Clive Russell**
Barry **Richard Pears**
Hedley **Toby Jones**
Mrs. Pendered **Joanna Dickens**
Mr. Penhaligan **Geoffrey Bayldon**
Mr. Hallett **Timothy Bateson**

and Rebecca Hulbert (Fiancée), Roger Booth (Arthur), Finty Williams (Pretty Local Girl), Jimmy Yuill (Constable Timmins), Alan Cox (Obsequious Man), Peter Cellier (BBC Announcer), Trevor Ray, John Boswell (Very Old Men), Gregor Henderson-Begg (Luke Pendered), Ian Marshall (Fisherman)

In Cornwall, England, on the brink World War II, a pair of elderly sisters find a young Polish man washed up on the beach and nurse him back to health.

Daniel Bruhl

Natascha McElhone PHOTOS COURTESY OF ROADSIDE ATTRACTIONS

THE HOLY GIRL

(FINE LINE FEATURES) a.k.a. *La Niña Santa*; Producer, Lita Stantic; Executive Producers, Pedro Almodovar, Agustin Almodovar, Esther Garcia; Director/ Screenplay, Lucrecia Martel; Photography, Felix Monti; Designer, Graciela Oderigo; Costumes, Julio Suarez; Music, Andres Gerszenzon; Editor, Santiago Ricci; Casting, Nicolas Levin, Natalia Smirnoff; a Lita Stantic, El Deseo, Senso producciones, La Passionaria, Teodora, R&C Produzioni production; Argentine-Spanish-Italian, 2004; Dolby; Color; Rated R; 106 minutes; American release date: April 29, 2005

Carlos Belloso, Mercedes Moran

Mercedes Moran, Carlos Belloso

Cast
Helena **Mercedes Moran**
Dr. Jano **Carlos Belloso**
Freddy **Alejandro Urdapilleta**
Amalia **Maria Alche**
Josefina **Julieta Zylberberg**
Inés **Mía Maestro**
Mirta **Marta Lubos**
Dr. Vesalio **Arturo Goetz**
Dr. Cuesta **Alejo Mango**

and Mónica Villa (Josefina's Mother), Leandro Stivelman (Julian), Manuel Schaller (Thermin Player), Miriam Diaz (Miriam), Rodolfo Cejas (Josefina's Father), Maria Victoria Mosca Coll, Ornella Velazco, Guadalupe Pardo Hernandez, Ana Carolina Beltran (Local Girls), Rodolfo Cabrera (Manuel the Plumber), Maria Susana Falcon (Josefina's Aunt), Guillermo Enrique Castro (Lad in Accident), Victor Anuch (Juan Pablo), Sebastian Diaz Sabala (Juan Pablo's Friend), Maria Micol Ellero, Maria Emilia Martinez (Josefina's Sisters), Sebastián Montagna (Josefina's Brother), Guido Nunez (Medical Consultant), Nilda Silvia Suarez (Photocopier Woman), Ana Maria Fernandez (Jano's Wife), Carlos Silvio Poma (Dr. Lara), Eduardo Jesus Chaig, Juan Solis, Roberto Bernacki, Oscar Victoriano Sarmiento, David Daniel Torino (Doctors), Eliana Santillan (Servant), Alejandro Leonidas Diaz (Pool Worker), Florinda Rosa Guamante (Caretaker), David Mansilla, Pablo Arias (Hotel Porters), Marcos Reynoso (Phone Assistant)

Maria Alche, Carlos Belloso

When a young girl mistakes a physical gesture from a visiting doctor as something sexual, she makes it her mission to save his soul, not realizing that it is her mother who has, in fact, caught the man's attention.

Maria Alche, Julieta Zylberberg PHOTOS COURTESY OF FINE LINE FEATURES

3-IRON

(SONY CLASSICS) a.k.a. *Bin-Jip*; Producer/Director/Screenplay/Editor, Kim Ki-duk; Executive Producers, Michio Suzuki, Choi Yong-bae; Co-Producers, Kang Yeong-gu, Suh Young-joo; Photography, Jang Seung-baek; Art Director, Jun Jin-mo; Costumes, Gu Jae-hyeon; Music, Slvian; a Happinet Pictures (Japan), Kim Ki-duk Film (South Korea) presentation, in association with Chungeorahm Film, of a Kim Ki-duk Film production, in association with Cineclick Asia; Japanese-South Korean, 2004; Dolby; Color; Rated R; 87 minutes; American release date: April 29, 2005

Cast
Sun-hwa **Lee Seung-yeon**
Tae-suk **Lee Hyun-kyoon**
Min-gyu **Kwon Hyuk-ho**
Inspector Cho **Ju Jin-mo**
Jailor **Choi Jeong-ho**
Son of Old Man **Lee Ju-seok**
Daughter-in-Law of Old Man **Lee Mi-suk**
Sung-hyuk **Moon Sung-hyuk**
Jee-ah **Park Jee-ah**
Hyun-soo **Jang Jae-yong**
Ji-eun **Lee Dah-hae**

and Kim Han (Man in Studio), Park Se-jin (Woman in Studio), Park Dong-jin (Detective Lee), Lee Jong-su (Man Who Came Back from Family Trip), Lee Ui-soo (Woman Who Came Back from Family Trip), Ryoo Jong-hwa (Boy Who Came Back from Family Trip), Kang Sung-hoon (Boyfriend of Girl Who Got Hit by Golf Ball), Jung Suyng-hoon, Jang Ji-yong, Kim

Maeng-sung (Prisoners), Jang Hoon (Guy Who Stares), Jang Seok-bin, Kim Hyung-suk (CIS Team), Shin Tae-suk, Lee Hong-suk, Lee Byung-hun, Park Nam-min (Policemen)

A young drifter settles into the home of a model with whom he falls in love after rescuing her from her abusive spouse.

Lee Seung-yeon, Lee Hyun-kyoon in *3-Iron* PHOTO COURTESY OF SONY CLASSICS

HOUSE OF WAX

(WARNER BROS.) Producers, Joel Silver, Robert Zemeckis, Susan Levin; Executive Producers, Herbert W. Gains, Steve Richards, Bruce Berman; Director, Jaume Collet-Serra; Screenplay, Chad Hayes, Carey W. Hayes; Story, Charles Belden; Photography, Stephen Windon; Designer, Graham "Grace" Walker; Costumes, Alex Alvarez; Music, John Ottman; Editor, Joel Negron; Visual Effects Supervisor, John Breslin; Visual Effects, Photon VFX; Special Makeup Effects, KNB EFX Group; Casting, Mary Gail Artz, Barbara Cohen, Tom McSweeney; a Dark Castle Entertainment production, presented in association with Village Roadshow; Australian-U.S.; Dolby; Technicolor; Rated R; 107 minutes; American release date: May 6, 2005

Cast
Carly Jones **Elisha Cuthbert**
Nick Jones **Chad Michael Murray**
Bo/Vincent **Brian Van Holt**
Paige Edwards **Paris Hilton**
Wade **Jared Padalecki**
Dalton Chapman **Jon Abrahams**
Blake **Robert Ri'chard**
Trudy Sinclair **Dragicia Debert**
Young Bo **Thomas Adamson**
Dr. Sinclair **Murray Smith**
Young Vincent **Sam Harkess**
Roadkill Driver **Damon Herriman**
Sheriff **Andy Anderson**

A group of teens, lost en route to a football game, make the mistake of entering a shuttered house made of wax.

Chad Michael Murray, Elisha Cuthbert in *House of Wax* PHOTO COURTESY OF WARNER BROS.

KINGDOM OF HEAVEN

(20TH CENTURY FOX) Producer/Director, Ridley Scott; Executive Producers, Branko Lustig, Lisa Elizey, Terry Needham; Co-Producers, Mark Albela, Denise O'Dell, Henning Molfenter, Thierry Potok; Screenplay, William Monahan; Photography, John Mathieson; Designer, Arthur Max; Costumes, Janty Yates; Music, Harry Gregson-Williams; Editor, Dody Dorn; Special Effects and Prosthetics Supervisor, Neil Corbould; Visual Effects Supervisor, Wesley Sewell; Makeup Designer, Paul Engelen; Stunts, Phil Neilson; Casting, Debra Zane, Jina Jay; a Scott Free production, BK-Reino del Cielo-KOH-Babelsberg Film co-production in association with Inside Track 3 LLP; British-Spanish-U.S.-German; Dolby; Super 35 Widescreen; Technicolor; Rated R; 145 minutes; American release date: May 6, 2005

Cast

Balian **Orlando Bloom**
Sibylla **Eva Green**
Tiberias **Jeremy Irons**
Hospitaler **David Thewlis**
Reynald **Brendan Gleeson**
Guy de Lusignan **Marton Cskoas**
Priest **Michael Sheen**
Godfrey **Liam Neeson**
King Baldwin **Edward Norton**
Saladin **Ghassan Massoud**
Nasir **Alexander Siddig**

Jeremy Irons

Edward Norton

Orlando Bloom, Liam Neeson

and Khaled Nabawy (Mullah), Kevin McKidd (English Sergeant), Velibor Topi (Almaric), Jon Finch (Patriarch), Ulrich Thomsen (Templar Master), Nikolaj Coster-Waldau (Village Sheriff), Iain Glenn (Richard Coeur de Lion), Martin Hancock (Gravedigger), Nathalie Cox (Balian's Wife), Eriq Ebouaney (Firuz), Jouko Ahola (Odo), Philip Glenister (Squire), Bronson Webb (Apprentice), Steven Robertson (Angelic Priest), Michael Shaeffer (Young Sergeant), Nasser Memarzia (Muslim Grandee), Lofti Yahya Jedidi (Old Ibelin Housekeeper), Samira Draa (Sibylla's Maid), Matthew Rutherford (Rider), Michael Fitzgerald (Humphrey), Karim Saeh (Saracen Messenger), Shane Attwooll (Reynald's Templar Knight), Giannina Facio

Orlando Bloom, David Thewlis PHOTOS COURTESY OF 20TH CENTURY FOX

(Saldin's Sister), Emilio Doorgasingh (Saracen Engineer), Peter Cant (Peasant Boy), Angus Wright (Richard's Knight)

A young blacksmith is recruited by his long absent father to join the Crusades, where he hopes to make peace between the warring Muslims and Christians.

Nikolaj Lie Kaas, Ulrich Thomsen PHOTO COURTESY OF IFC FILMS

BROTHERS

(IFC FILMS) a.k.a. *Brødre*; Producers, Sisse Graum Jorgensen, Peter Aalbaek Jensen; Executive Producer, Peter Garde; Director, Susanne Bier; Screenplay, Anders Thomas Jensen; Story, Susanne Bier, Anders Thomas Jensen; Photography, Morten Soborg; Art Director, Viggo Bentzon; Costumes, Signe Sejlund; Music, Johan Soderqvist; Editor, Pernille Bech Christensen; a Zentropa Entertainments14 Aps production, in association with Two Brothers Ltd., Sigma Films Ltd., Memfis Film Intl. ABC, Fjellape Film AS, in cooperation with DR, Invicta Capital, with support from the Danish Film Institute, the Swedish Film Institute, Nordic Film & TV Fund; Danish, 2004; Dolby; Color; DV-to-35mm; Rated R; 110 minutes; American release date: May 6, 2005

Cast
Sarah **Connie Nielsen**
Michael **Ulrich Thomsen**
Jannik **Nikolaj Lie Kaas**
Natalia **Sarah Juel Werner**
Camilla **Rebecca Løgstrup**
Henning **Bent Mejding**
Else **Solbjørg Højfeldt**
Allentoft **Niels Olsen**
Soldier **Paw Henriksen**
Prebens **Lars Hjortshøj, Lars Ranthe**

and André Babikian (Nadeem), Lene Maria Christensen (Jeanette), Tom Mannion (Miles), Karzan Sherabyani (Makmuhd), William El Gardi (Samial-Tariq), Alex Caan (Farid), Sam Vincenti (Wisam), Hossein Karimbeik (Hossein), Hassni Shapi (Hassan), Bjarne Antnoisen (Fåborg), Morten Kirkskov, Clause Flygare (Officers)

After being captured while fighting in Afghanistan, Michael is forced to commit a barbaric act of violence that leaves him a shattered and changed man when he finally returns home to his family, who had believed him to be dead.

JIMINY GLICK IN LALAWOOD

(GOLD CIRCLE/MGM) Producers, Paul Brooks, Martin Short, Bernie Brillstein, Peter Safran; Executive Producers, Norm Waitt, Scott Niemeyer; Director, Vadim Jean; Screenplay, Martin Short, Paul Flaherty, Michael Short; Based on the character created by Martin Short; Photography, Mike J. Fox; Designer, Tony Devenyi; Costumes, Loraine Carson; Music, David Lawrence; Editor, Matt Davis; Makeup, Kristina Vogel; a Gold Circle Films, Brillstein-Grey production, in association with Dolshor Prods.; Canadian-U.S.; Dolby; Color; Rated R; 90 minutes; American release date: May 6, 2005

Cast
Jiminy Glick/David Lynch **Martin Short**
Dixie Glick **Jan Hooks**
Natalie Coolidge **Linda Cardellini**
Dee Dee **Janeane Garofalo**
Andre Devine **John Michael Higgins**
Miranda Coolidge **Elizabeth Perkins**
Haygood Lewkin **Larry Joe Campbell**
Sharon **Mo Collins**
Mario "Fa Real" Greene **DeRay Davis**
Barry King **Carlos Jacott**
Ben DiCarlo **Corey Pearson**
Gunnar "MC Gun" Jorge **Aries Spears**
Jay Schiffer **Robert Trebor**
Randall Bookerton **Gary Anthony Williams**
Matthew Glick **Landon Hansen**
Modine Glick **Jake Hoffman**

and Alex Diakun (Bellhop/Barber), Peter Breck (Tibor), Ellie Harvie (June), Darren Shahlavi (Johnny Stompanato), Courtney Andersen (Lana Turner), Randi Lynne (Rowena), Olivia Yung (Chinese Maid), Ari Solomon (Rabbi Schleckman), Christine Willes (Arlene Sheehy), Susan Gillan, Peter Kelamis (Hotel Clerks), Zahf Paroo (Gandhi's Manager), Allison Warnyca (Gandhi's Girlfriend), Natasha Wilson (Sexy Girl), Jano Frandsen, Anira Brown (Award Presenters), Christopher Lazar (Rap Fan), Sara Willey (Lana Turner's Daughter), Kiefer Sutherland, Whoopi Goldberg, Kevin Kline, Pat O'Brien, Jake Gyllenhaal, Forest Whitaker, Susan Sarandon, Kurt Russell, Rob Lowe, Steve Martin, Emmanuelle Béart, Willem Dafoe, Roger Ebert (Themselves)

Inept, obnoxious, rotund celebrity interviewer Jiminy Glick attends the Toronto Film Festival where he becomes involved in a murder.

DeRay Davis, Martin Short, Aries Spears PHOTO COURTESY OF GOLD CIRCLE

KINGS AND QUEEN

(WELLSPRING) a.k.a *Rois et reine*; Producer, Pascal Cauchteux; Director, Arnaud Desplechin; Screenplay, Arnaud Desplechin, Roger Bohbot; Photography, Eric Gautier; Designer, Dan Bevan; Costumes, Nathalie Raoul; a Why Not Prods., France 2 Cinema, Rhone-Alpes Cinema production; French, 2004; Dolby; Color; Not rated; 150 minutes; American release date: May 13, 2005

Cast

Nora Cotterelle **Emmanuelle Devos**
Ismael Vuillard **Mathieu Amalric**
Mme. Vasset, Psychiatrist **Catherine Deneuve**
Louis Jenssens **Maurice Garrel**
Chloe Jenssens **Nathalie Boutefeu**
Abel Vuillard **Jean-Paul Roussillon**
Arielle **Magalie Woch**
Marc Mamanne **Hippolyte Girardot**
Elizabeth **Noémie Lvovsky**
Dr. Devereaux **Elsa Wolliaston**
Claude **Geoffrey Carey**

Mathieu Amalric

and Valentin Lelong (Elias Cotterelle), Thierry Bosc (M. Mader), Olivier Rabourdin (Jean-Jacques), Olivier Borle (Instructor), Didier Sauvegrain (Surgeon), Francois Toumarkine (Prospero), Miglen Mirtchev (Caliban), Marc Bodnar (Psychiatrist), Chatherine Rouvel (Monioque Vuillard), Jan Hammenecker (Nicolas), Marie-Francoise Gonzales (Nurse), Joachim Salinger (Pierre Cotterelle), Daniel Cohen (Gynecologist), Frederic Epauyd (Town Hall Employee), Claude Phor (Loony), Karim Belkhadra (Intern), Gaëlle Dill (Victorine), Shulamit Adar (Mme Seyvos), Marc Betton (Leopold Virag), Gilles Cohen (Simon), Francis Leplay (Christian), Bernard Garnier (Physician), Joël Dahan (Author), Rachid Hami (Marcello), Marion Touitou (Delphine), Yann Coridian (Fidele), Andrée Tainsy (Grandmother), Sarah Lefevre (Nora's Friend), Denis Falgoux (Cop)

Mathieu Amalric, Catherine Deneuve

Valentin Lelong, Mathieu Amalric

In a pair of crisscrossing tales, art gallery director Nora is on the verge of marrying her third husband, while Ismael, a neurotic violinist, ends up in a mental institution because of his eccentric behavior.

Emmanuelle Devos PHOTOS COURTESY OF WELLSPRING

Jet Li, Morgan Freeman

Jet Li (left)

Bob Hoskins (center)

Kerry Condon, Jet Li PHOTOS COURTESY OF ROGUE PICTURES

UNLEASHED

(ROGUE) a.k.a. *Danny the Dog*; Producers, Pierre Ange Le Pogam, Luc Besson; Executive Producers, Steven Chasman, Bernard Grenet; Co-Producer, Pierre Spengler; Director, Louis Leterrier; Screenplay, Luc Besson; Photography, Pierre Morel; Designer, Jacques Bufnoir; Costumes, Olivier Beriot; Music, Massive Attack; Editor, Nicolas Trembasiewicz; Choreographer, Yuen Wo-ping; Stunts, Philippe Guegan; a EuropaCorp presentation of a EuropaCorp, TF1 Films Prods. (France), Danny the Dog (U.K.) production, in association with Qian Yang Intl., Current Entertainment, with the participation of Canal Plus; French-British; Dolby; Widescreen; Color; Rated R; 102 minutes; American release date: May 13, 2005

Cast

Danny **Jet Li**
Sam **Morgan Freeman**
Bart **Bob Hoskins**
Victoria **Kerry Condon**
Raffles **Vincent Regan**
Lefty **Dylan Brown**
Georgie **Tamer Hassan**
Wyeth **Michael Jenn**
Distinguished Lady **Phyllida Law**

and Carole Ann Wilson (Maddy), Michael Ian Lambert (The Stranger), Jaclyn Tze Wey (Danny's Mother), Puthirith Chou (Teen Danny), Tony Theng (Little Danny), Owen Lay, Frack Xie Cheng (Baby Danny), Georgina Chapman, Danielle Louise Harley (Floozies), Andy Beckwith (Righty), Michael Webber (Boxing Boss), Jeff Rudom (Boxing Giant), Laurence Ashley Taboulet (Shower Woman), Alex Lawson, Stuart Lawson, Audifax Kinga, Eric Mondoloni (Maddy's Market Fighters), Vanessa Mateo (Maddy's Market Cashier), Alain Figlarz (Boss First Fight), Maurice Chan, Grégory Feurté, Amadeo Cazzella, Emmanuel Lanzi, Afif Ben Badra, Cyrille Hertel (Tough Men), Santi Sudaros, Scott Adkins, Valérie Hénin, Seydina Baldé (Swimming Pool Fighters), Christian Bergner, Patrick Medioni, Jean-Francois Lenogue, Malik Attar, Serge Beuchat, Christophe Weyer, Vincent Haquin, Tarik Zitouni (Raffles' Thugs), Joseph Beddelem, Frédéric Dessains, Carlos Bonelli, Michel Bouis, William Cagnard, Thierry Saelens (Jewelry Security Men), Ksénia Zarouba (Sales Person), Grégory Loffredo, Mouloud Ikhaddalene, Marc Chung, Oumar Diaouré, Eric Etje, Sylvain Gabet, Pierre Rousselle, Marc Hoang, Karim Hocini, Loïc Molla, Louis-Marie Nyee, Patrick Oliver, Sébastien Soudais, Patrick Tang, Mickaël Troudé, Patrick Vo, Frédéric Alhinho, Gabriel Chatelain, Tarick Hadouch (Bart's Thugs), Pascal Lopez (Bart's Young Thug), Pascal Lavanchy (Bart's Driver), Eudes Clara Creantor, Christelle Senechal, Isabelle Didier, Gwenael Mairey, Ariadna Cascaval (Bart's Girls)

Danny, trained to attack violently whenever his metal collar is removed from his neck, escapes from his deadly trainer and is befriended by a blind piano tuner.

Daniel Craig, Sienna Miller

George Harris, Daniel Craig

Kenneth Cranham, Michael Gambon PHOTOS COURTESY OF SONY CLASSICS

LAYER CAKE

(SONY CLASSICS) Producers, Adam Bohling, David Reid, Matthew Vaughn; Executive Producer, Stephen Marks; Director, Matthew Vaughn; Screenplay, J. J. Connolly, based on his novel; Photography, Ben Davis; Designer, Kave Quinn; Costumes, Stephanie Collie; Music, Lisa Gerrard; Music Supervisor, Liz Gallacher; Editor, Jon Harris; Casting, Leo Davis, Jina Jay; a Matthew Vaughn production, presented in association with Marv Films; British; Dolby; Super 35 Widescreen; Color; Rated R; 105 minutes; American release date: May 13, 2005

Colm Meaney, George Harris, Daniel Craig

Cast
XXXX **Daniel Craig**
Gene **Colm Meaney**
Jimmy Price **Kenneth Cranham**
Morty **George Harris**
Duke **Jamie Foreman**
Tammy **Sienna Miller**
Eddie Temple **Michael Gambon**
Slavo **Marcel Iures**
Clarkie **Tom Hardy**
Crazy Larry **Jason Flemyng**
Slasher **Sally Hawkins**
Gazza **Burn Gorman**
Terry **Tamer Hassan**
Cody **Dexter Fletcher**

and Francis Magee (Paul the Boatman), Dimitri Andreas (Angelo), Garry Tubbs (Brian), Nathalie Lunghi (Charlie), Marvyn Benoit (Kinky), Rab Affleck (Mickey), Steve John Shepherd (Tiptoes), Ben Whishaw (Sidney), Paul Orchard (Lucky), Stephen Walters (Shanks), Louis Emerick (Trevor), Darren Healy, Matt Ryan (Junkies), Ivan Kaye (Freddie Hurst), Ben Brasier (Jerry Kilburn), Neil Finnighan (Troop), Budge Prewitt (Golf Host), Don McCorkindale (Albert Carter), Dragan Micanovic (Dragan)

Hoping to retire from the criminal trade, a drug dealer is asked by his boss to track down the missing daughter of another powerful gangster.

Emma de Caunes, Louis Garrel

MA MÈRE

(TLA RELEASING) Producers, Paulo Branco, Bernard-Henri Lévy; Co-Producers, Gabriele Kranzelbinder, Alexander Dumreicher-Ivanceanu; Associate Producer, Stéphane Sorlat, Dimitri de Clercq; Director/Screenplay, Christophe Honoré; Based on the novel by Georges Bataille; Photography, Hélène Louvart; Designer, Laurent Allaire; Costumes, Pierre Canitrot; Editor, Chantal Hymans; Casting, Richard Rousseau; a Gemini Films presentation of a Paulo Branco, Bernard Henri Levy presentation; French, 2004; Dolby; Color; Rated NC-17; 110 minutes; American release date: May 13, 2005

Isabelle Huppert, Louis Garrel

Cast

Hélène **Isabelle Huppert**
Pierre **Louis Garrel**
Hansi **Emma de Caunes**
Réa **Joana Preiss**
Loulou **Jean-Baptiste Montagut**
Marthe **Dominique Reymond**
Robert **Olivier Rabourdin**

Isabelle Huppert

The Father **Philippe Duclos**
Klaus **Pascal Tokatlian**
Ian **Théo Hakola**

and Nuno Lopes (The Doctor), Patrick Fanik (Eric), Susi Egetnheimer (Woman in Dunes), Sylvia Johnson (Woman of Couple)

Following the unexpected death of his father, restless 17-year-old Pierre finds his relationship with his free spirited mother becoming too intense for comfort.

Louis Garrel, Emma de Caunes

Joana Preiss, Isabelle Huppert PHOTOS COURTESY OF TLA RELEASING

August Diehl, Bibiana Beglau, Ulrich Matthes in *The Ninth Day*

THE NINTH DAY

(KINO) a.k.a. *Der Neunte Tag*; Producer, Jurgen Haase; Executive Producer, Wolfgang Plehn; Director, Volker Schlondorff; Screenplay, Eberhard Goerner, Andreas Pflueger; Based on the memoir *Pfarrerblock Z4587* by Father Jean Bernard; Photography, Tomas Erhart; Designer, Ari Hantke; Costumes, Jarmila Konecna; Music, Alfred Schnittke; Editor, Peter R. Adam; a Provobis Film production, in association with Bayerische Rundfunk, Video Press (Luxembourg), Arte; German, 2004; Dolby; Fujicolor; Not rated; 97 minutes; American release date: May 27, 2005

Cast

Abbe Henri Kremer **Ulrich Matthes**
Unterstrumfuehrer Gebhardt **August Diehl**
Roger Kremer **Germain Wagner**
Marie Kremer **Bibiana Beglau**
Raymond Schmitt **Jean-Paul Raths**
Armando Bausch **Ivan Jirik**
Father Laurant Koltz **Karel Hromadka**
Father Marcel Bour **Miroslav Sichmann**

and Adolf Filip (Klimek), Vladimir Fiser (Bishop Kozal), Petr Varga (Jozef), Petr Janis (Father Nansen), Zdenek Pechacek (Camp Commander), Karel Dobry (Bertram), Gotz Burger (Secretary Gerard Mersch), Hilmar Thate

Ulrich Matthes, August Diehl in *The Ninth Day* PHOTO COURTESY OF PARAMOUNT CLASSICS

(Bishop Philipp), Vaclav Kratky (SS), Marcel Svidrman (Gestapo), Michael Konig (Gauletier Simon), Vladimir Gut (Kapo in Kleiderablage)

A priest is released from Dachau and given nine days to persuade the Luxembourg church to cooperate with the Nazis.

Daniel Auteuil in *Après Vous...*

APRÈS VOUS...

(PARAMOUNT CLASSICS) Producer, Philippe Martin; Associate Producer, David Thion; Director, Pierre Salvadori; Screenplay, Pierre Salvadori, Benoît Graffin, David Léotard; Based on an idea by Danièle Dubroux; Photography, Gilles Henry; Designer, Yves Fournier; Costumes, Virginie Montel; Music, Camille Bazbaz; Editor, Isabelle Devinck; Casting, Alain Charbit; a Les Films Pelleas, France 2 Cinema, Gimages Films, Gimages Developpement, Glem Film, Tovo Films co-production with the participation of Centre national de la Cinematographie (CNC), Canal Plus; French, 2004; Dolby; Color; Rated R; 110 minutes; American release date: June 3, 2005

Cast

Antoine Letoux **Daniel Auteuil**
Louis **José Garcia**
Blanche Grimaldi **Sandrine Kiberlain**
Christine **Marilyne Canto**
Martine **Michèle Moretti**
Karine **Garance Clavel**
André **Fabio Zenoni**

and Ange Ruzé (Young Waiter), Andrée Tainsy (Louis' Grandmother), Jean-Luc Abel (The Inspector), Caroline Brunner (Andre's Girlfriend), Jocelyne Desverchère (Sandrine the Florist), Didier Menin (Man at Thai Restaurant), Jean-Charles Dumay (Serge the Sommelier), Jean-Claude Lecas (Cook), Elise Otzenberger (Hairdresser), Bladine Pélissier (Nurse), Santha Leng (Thai Waiter), Eric Chevalier, Claude-Bernard Perot (Businessmen), Suzanne Sinnet (Corked Wine Customer)

After saving Louis's life, restaurant manager Antoine Letoux makes it his mission to get the self-pitying man's life in order.

Frederica Sbrenna, Alice Teghil in *Caterina in the Big City* PHOTO COURTESY OF EMPIRE FILMS

CATERINA IN THE BIG CITY

(EMPIRE) a.k.a. *Caterina va in città*; Producers, Riccardo Tozzi, Giovanni Stabilini, Marco Chimenz; Executive Producer, Guido De Laurentiis; Director, Paolo Virzì; Screenplay, Francesco Bruni, Paolo Virzì; Photography, Arnaldo Catinari; Designer, Tonino Zera; Costumes, Bettina Potiggia; Music, Carlo Virzì; Editor, Cecilia Zanuso; a RAI Cinema, Cattleya production in association with Sky; Italian, 2003; Dolby; Color; Not rated; 90 minutes; American release date: June 3, 2005

Cast

Caterina Iacovoni **Alice Teghil**
Giancarlo Iacovoni **Sergio Catellitto**
Agata Iacovoni **Margherita Buy**
Cesarino **Antonio Carnevale**
Fabietto Cruciani **Silvio Vannucci**
Daniela Germano **Federica Sbrenna**
Margherita Rossi Chaillet **Carolina Iaquaniello**
Edward **Zach Wallen**
Gianfilippo **Martino Reviglio**
Manlio Germano **Claudio Amendola**
Lorenzo Rossi Chaillet **Flavio Bucci**
Aunt Marisa **Paola Tiziana Cruciani**
Uncle Alfredo **Luigi Grilli**
Teresa **Tereza Paula Da Rosa**
Aunt Adelina **Renata Orso**

and Margerita Mazzola (Martina), Martina Tasquetta (Alessia), Giulia Gorietti (Glada), Emanuele Aiello (Mirko), Ottavia Virzi (Zecca Roscia), Giacomo Rivera (Zecca Rasta), Riccardo Morra (Zecca Gaber), Leo Cappelletto (Piccoletto Vispo), Carola Di Mambro (Pariola), Giuditta Avossa (Altra Pariola), Marina Benetti (Precisa), Lorenza Tedesco (Precisona), Beatrice Nalin (Precisina), Chadlee Dasalla (Orientale), Filippo Festuccia (Pariolo), Antongiulio Borrelli (Pariolone), Valentina Molé (Prima Normale), Francesca Zarfati (Seconda Normale), Omar Abusuis (Seconda Gemello), Jari Abusuis (Secondo Gemello), Gemma Andreini, Bob Messini (Professors), Raffaelle Vannoli (Marcello the

Chauffeur), Paola Rota (Lucilla), Galatea Ranzi (Livia, Margherita's Mother), Gennaro Migliaccio (Vittorio Germano), Alessandra Celi (Signora Germano), Pasquale Anselmo (Riccardo), Milly Corinaldi (Nonna Cesira), Bruno Pavoncello (Armando), Luisella Boni (Andreina, Gianfilippo's Mother), Giovanna Melandri, Maurizio Costanzo, Simonetta Martone, Andrea Pancani, Michele Placido, Roberto Bengini (Themselves)

Fifteen-year-old Caterina becomes socially and politically enlightened when her family moves from a seaside town to Rome where she falls in with all sorts of odd characters.

Dana Ivgy, Ronit Elkabetz in *Or, My Treasure* PHOTO COURTESY OF KINO

OR, MY TREASURE

(KINO) a.k.a. *Mon trésor*; Producers, Itai Tamir, Emmanuel Agneray, Marek Rosenbaum, Jérôme Bleitrach; Director, Keren Yedaya; Screenplay, Keren Yedaya, Sari Ezouz; Photography, Laurent Brunet; Designer, Avi Fahima; Editor, Sari Ezouz; a Transfax Film Productions, Bizibi production with the participation of Canal Plus; French-Israeli, 2004; Dolby; Color; Not rated; 100 minutes; American release date: June 1, 2005

Cast

Ruthie **Ronit Elkabetz**
Or **Dana Ivgy**
Ido **Meshar Cohen**
Katia Zinbris **Katia Zimbris**
Shmuel **Shmuel Edelman**
School Career Adviser **Siyalit Tamir**
Iris **Sarit Vino-Elad**

Or finds a housekeeping job for her mother Ruthie to keep her from returning to her previous profession of turning tricks for money.

Maïwenn in *High Tension*

HIGH TENSION

(LIONS GATE) a.k.a. *Haute tension*; Producers, Alexandre Arcady, Robert Benmussa; Executive Producer, Andrei Boncea; Director, Alexandre Aja; Screenplay, Alexandre Aja, Grégory Levasseur; Photography, Maxime Alexandre; Designer, Tony Egry; Music, Francois Eudes; Editor, Baxter; Special Effects Supervisor, Adrian Popescu; Casting, Florin Chevorchian; an Alexandre Films, Europa Corp. production; French, 2003; Dolby; Color; Rated NC-17; 89 minutes; American release date: June 10, 2005

Cast
Marie **Cécile De France**
Alexia **Maïwenn**
The Killer **Philippe Nahon**
Jimmy **Franck Khalfoun**
Alex's Father **Andrei Finti**
Alex's Mother **Oana Pellea**
and Marco Claudiu Pascu (Tom), Jean-Claude de Goros (Police Captain), Bogdan Uritescu (Gendarme), Gabriel Spahiu (Car Man)

A mysterious killer terrifies two college friends on holiday in the country.

Cecile De France in *High Tension* PHOTOS COURTESY OF LIONS GATE

THE BRIDGE OF SAN LUIS REY

(FINE LINE) Producers, Samuel Hadida, Michael Lionello Cowan, Garrett McGuckian, Mary McGuckian, Denise O'Dell; Executive Producers, Jeff Abberley, Craig Darian, Victor Hadida, Peter James, Howard Kazanjian, James Simpson; Co-Producers, Elvira Bolz, Jason Piette; Director/Screenplay, Mark McGuckian; Based on the novel by Thornton Wilder; Photography, Javier Aguirresarobe; Art Director, Gil Parrondo; Costumes, Yvonne Blake; Music, Lalo Schifrin; Editor, Sylvie Landra, Kant Pan; a Tribeca Prods., Metropolitan Filmexport presentation of a Pembridge Pictures, Bridge SLP, Spice Factory (U.K.), Kanzman (Spain), Davis Films (France) production in association with Movision Entertainment, Scion Films; British-Spanish-French, 2004; Dolby; Color; Rated PG; 124 minutes; American release date: June 10, 2005

Émilie Dequenne in *The Bridege of San Luis Rey* PHOTO COURTESY OF FINE LINE FEATURES

Cast
Viceroy of Peru **F. Murray Abraham**
The Marquesa **Kathy Bates**
Brother Juniper **Garbiel Byrne**
The Abbess **Geraldine Chaplin**
Archbishop of Peru **Robert De Niro**
Doña Clara **Émilie Dequenne**
Pepita **Adriana Domínguez**
Uncle Pio **Harvey Keitel**
Captain Alvarado **John Lynch**
Manuel **Mark Polish**
Esteban **Michael Polish**
and Samuel Le Bihan (Doña Clara's Husband), Pilar López de Ayala (Camila Villegas), Dominique Pinon (His Excellency's Fop), Jim Sheridan (The King of Spain), Javier Conde (Camila's Matador)

A Franciscan monk investigates the cause behind the collapse of a Peruvian bridge as well as the stories of the people tragically killed in the accident. Earlier films of the novel were released in 1944 and 1929.

Sophie, Howl

HOWL'S MOVING CASTLE

(WALT DISNEY PICTURES) Producer, Toshio Suzuki; Director/Screenplay, Hayao Miyazaki; Based on the novel by Diana Wynne Jones; Supervising Animators, Akihiko Yamashita, Takeshi Inamura, Kitaro Kosaka; Music, Joe Hisaishi; U.S. Production: Executive Producer, John Lasseter; Producers, Rick Dempsey, Ned Lott; Directors, Pete Docter, Rick Dempsey; English Language Adaptation, Cindy Davis Hewitt, Donald H. Hewitt; Casting, Ned Lott; a Tokuma Shoten, Studio GHIBLI, Nippin Television Network, Dentsu, Buena Vista Home Entertainment, Mitsubishi and Toho presentation; Japanese; Dolby; Technicolor; Rated PG; 118 minutes; American release date: June 10, 2005

Voice Cast
Grandma Sophie **Jean Simmons**
Howl **Christian Bale**
Witch of the Waste **Lauren Bacall**
Madame Suliman **Blythe Danner**
Young Sophie **Emily Mortimer**
Markl **Josh Hutcherson**
Calcifer **Billy Crystal**
Lettie **Jena Malone**
Heen **Daijiro Harada**
Turnip **Crispin Freeman**
King **Mark Silverman**
Honey **Mari Devon**
Madge **Liliana Mumy**
and Carlos Alazraqui, Newell Alexander, Rosemary Alexander, Julia Barnett, Susanne Blakeslee, Leslie Carrara, Mitch Carter, David Cowgill, Holly Dorff, Moosie Drier, lake Eissinmann, Will Friedle, Bridget Hoffman, Richard Horvitz, Sherry Hursey, Hope Levy, Christian MacGregor, Joel McCrary, Edie Mirman, Peter Renaday, Kristen Rutherford, Warren Sroka (Additional Voices)

After being turned into a 90-year-old woman by the conniving Witch of the Waste, Sophie journeys to Howl's magical moving castle in hopes of breaking the spell.

This film received an Oscar nomination for animated feature.

The Moving Castle

Howl, Sophie

Heen, Markl, Turnip

Calcifer, Sophie PHOTOS COURTESY OF WALT DISNEY PICTURES

Valeria Bruni Tedeschi, Stéphane Freiss

5X2

(THINKFILM) Producers, Olivier Delbose, Marc Missonier; Director, Francois Ozon; Screenplay, Francois Ozon, Emmanuele Bernheim; Photography, Yorick Le Saux; Designer, Katia Wyszkop; Costumes, Pascaline Cavanne; Music, Philippe Rombi; Editor, Monica Coleman; Casting, Antoinette Boulat; a Fidelite presentation of a Fidelite, France 2 Cinema, FOZ production, with participation of Canal Plus; French, 2004; Dolby; Color; Rated R; 90 minutes; American release date: June 10, 2005

Valeria Burni Tedeschi, Stéphane Freiss PHOTOS COURTESY OF THINKFILM

Cast
Marion **Valeria Burni Tedeschi**
Gilles **Stéphane Freiss**
Valérie **Géraldine Pailhas**
Monique **Françoise Fabian**
Bernard **Michael Lonsdale**
Christophe **Antoine Chappey**
Mathieu **Marc Ruchmann**
American **Jason Tavassoli**
Judge **Jean-Pol Brissart**

After Marion and Gilles have decided to divorce they look back in reverse order on how they got to this point in their relationship.

Nathalie Press, Emily Blunt in *My Summer of Love* PHOTO COURTESY OF FOCUS FEATURES

MY SUMMER OF LOVE

(FOCUS) Producers, Tanya Seghatchian, Chris Collins; Executive Producers, David M. Thompson, Chris Auty, Emma Hayter; Director, Pawel Pawlikowski; Screenplay, Pawel Pawlikowski, Michael Wynne; Based on the novel by Helen Cross; Photography, Ryszard Lenczewski; Designer, John Stevenson; Costumes, Julian Day; Music, Alison Goldfrapp, Will Gregory; Editor, David Charap; Casting, Buffy Hall; a BBC Films, the Film Consortium presentation, in association with Baker Street, of a Take Partnerships production of an Apocalypso picture; British; Dolby; Color; Rated R; 83 minutes; American release date: June 17, 2005

Cast
Mona **Nathalie Press**
Tamsin **Emily Blunt**
Phil **Paddy Considine**
Ricky **Dean Andrews**
Ricky's Wife **Michelle Byrne**
Tamsin's Father **Paul Antony-Barber**
Tamsin's Mother **Lynette Edwards**
Sadie **Kathryn Sumner**

A lonely, restless sixteen-year-old girl, stuck living with her born-again Christian brother, finds solace and romance with a confident, well-to-do neighboring girl.

Stephanie Leonidas, Joan Allen

YES

(SONY CLASSICS) Producers, Christopher Sheppard, Andrew Fierberg; Executive Producers, John Penotti, Paul Trijbits, Fisher Stevens, Cedric Jeanson; Director/Screenplay, Sally Potter; Photography, Alexei Rodionov; Designer, Carlos Conti; Costumes, Jacqueline Durran; Editor, Daniel Goddard; Line Producer, Nick Laws; Casting, Irene Lamb; a Greenstreet Films, UK Film Council presentation of an Adventure Pictures production in association with Studio Fierberg; British; Dolby; Eclair Color; Super 16mm; Rated R; 99 minutes; American release date: June 24, 2005

Cast
She **Joan Allen**
He **Simon Abkarian**
Anthony **Sam Neill**
Cleaner **Shirley Henderson**
Aunt **Sheila Hancock**
Kate **Samantha Bond**
Grace **Stephanie Leonidas**
Billy **Gary Lewis**
Virgil **Wil Johnson**
Whizzer **Raymond Waring**

Simon Abkarian, Joan Allen PHOTOS COURTESY OF SONY CLASSICS

and Barbara Oxley (Cleaner in Swimming Pool), Kev Orkian (Waiter), George Viasoumi (Kitchen Boss), Beryl Scott (Cleaner in Laboratory), Lol Coxhill (Father Christmas), Father Charles Owen (Priest), Mandy Coombes, Beti Owen (Nuns), Dot Bond (Cleaner in Nursing Home), Dorca Reyes Sánchez (Woman in Cuban Apartment), Antoine Agoudjian, Christina Galstian (Friends in Beirut)

With her marriage falling apart, a biologist embarks upon an affair with a cook.

Jing Jue, Zhao Tao in *The World* PHOTO COURTESY OF ZEITGEIST

THE WORLD

(ZEITGEIST) a.k.a. *Shi Jie*; Producers, Chow Keung, Shozo Ichiyama, Hengameh Panahi; Director/Screenplay, Jia Zhang-ke; Photography, Yu Lik-wai; Art Director, Wu Li-zhong; Music, Lim Glong; Editor, Kong Jin-glei; an Office Kitano, Xtreem Pictures, Lumen Films production in association with Bandai Visual, Tokyo FM, Dentsu, TV Asahi, Bitters End, Shanghai Film Studios; Chinese-Japanese-French, 2004; Dolby; Color; Not rated; 140 minutes; American release date: July 1, 2005

Cast
Tao **Zhao Tao**
Taisheng **Chen Taisheng**
Xiaowei **Jing Jue**
Niu **Jiang Zhongwei**
Qun **Wang Yiqun**
Sanlai **Wang Hongwei**
Tao's Ex-Boyfriend **Liang Jingdong**
Youyou **Xiang Wan**
Yanqing **Liu Juan**

A look at some of the inhabitants and workers at World Park, a theme park outside of Beijing featuring reproductions of famous world landmarks.

THE BEAT THAT MY HEART SKIPPED

(WELLSPRING) a.k.a *De battre mon coeur s'est arrêté*; Producer, Pascal Caucheteux; Director, Jacques Audiard; Screenplay, Jacques Audiard, Tonino Benacquista; Based on the film *Fingers* written and directed by James Toback; Photography, Stéphane Fontaine; Designer, François Emmanuelli; Costumes, Virginie Montel; Music, Alexandre Desplat; Editor, Juliette Welfling; a Why Not Prods., Sedif, France 3 Cinema production; French; Dolby; Color; Not rated; 107 minutes; American release date: July 1, 2005

Romain Duris

Aure Atika, Romain Duris

Cast

Thomas Seyr **Romain Duris**
Robert Seyr **Niels Arestrup**
Miao-Lin **Linh-Dan Pham**
Aline **Aure Atika**
Chris **Emmanuelle Devos**
Fabrice **Jonathan Zaccaï**
Sami **Gilles Cohen**
Minskov **Anton Yakovlev**
Minskov's Girlfriend **Mélanie Laurent**
Woman **Agnès Aubé**
Old Man **Etienne Dirand**
Metreur **Denis Falgoux**
Man **Serge Onteniente**
Mr. Fox **Sandy Whitelaw**

and Emmanuel Finkiel (Conservatory Professor), Jian-Zhang (Jean-Pierre), Omar Habib (Assad), Jamal Djabou (Mounir), Vladislav Galard (Clerk), Walter Shnorkell (Verodin), Narianne Puech (Notaire), Alphonse Cemin (Pianist), David Birgé-Cotte (Young Thomas)

Niels Arestrup, Romain Duris

A young man finds himself torn between a life of crime and the possibility of honoring his mother's memory by becoming a concert pianist. Remake of the 1978 film *Fingers* which starred Harvey Keitel.

Romain Duris PHOTOS COURTESY OF WELLSPRING

SARABAND

(SONY CLASSICS) Producer, Pia Ehrnvall; Director/Screenplay, Ingmar Bergman; Photography, Raymond Wemmenlov, Sofi Stridh, P. O. Lantto; Art Director, Goran Wassberg; Costumes, Inger Elvira Pehrson; Music, J. S. Bach, Anton Bruckner; Editor, Sylvia Ingemarsson; a Swedish Television production, in association with DR (Denmark), NRK (Norway), YLE1 (Finland), RAI (Italy), ZDF/Arte (Germany), ORF (Austria); Swedish-Danish-Finnish-Italian-German-Austrian, 2003; Stereo; Color; DV; Rated R; 107 minutes; American release date: July 8, 2005

Julia Dufvenius, Börje Ahlstedt

Cast

Marianne **Liv Ullmann**
Johan **Erland Josephson**
Henrik **Börje Ahlstedt**
Karin **Julia Dufvenius**
Martha **Gunnel Ford**

Marianne decides to visit the ex-husband she has not seen in years, opening old wounds about their failed relationship. A sequel to Bergman's *Scenes from a Marriage* (1973).

Erland Josephson, Liv Ullmann PHOTOS COURTESY OF SONY CLASSICS

Damian Alcázár, John Leguizamo in *Crónicas* PHOTO COURTESY OF PALM PICTURES

CRÓNICAS

(PALM PICTURES) Producers, Bertha Navarro, Isabel Davalos, Guillermo Del Toro, Jorge Vergara, Alfonso Cuaron; Executive Producer, Frida Torresblanco; Co-Producer, Thierry Forte; Director/Screenplay, Sebastian Cordero; Photography, Enrique Chediak; Designer, Eugenio Caballero; Costumes, Monica Rui Ziegler; Music, Antonio Pinto; Editors, Luis Carballar, Ivan Mora; Casting, Mauricio Samaiego; a Producciones Anhelo presentation of an Anhelo, Cabezahueca, Tequila Gang production; Mexican; Dolby; Color; Rated R; 98 minutes; American release date: July 8, 2005

Cast

Manolo Bonilla **John Leguizamo**
Marisa Burralde **Leonor Watling**
Vinicio Cepeda **Damián Alcázar**
Ivan Suarez **José María Yazpik**
Capt. Bolivar Rojas **Camilo Luzuriaga**
Esperanza **Gloria Leiton**
Robert **Luiggi Pulla**
Don Lucho **Henry Layana**

and Hugo Idrovo (Orestes Zambrano), Tamara Navas (Dona Etelvina), Alfred Molina (Victor Hugo Puente), Peky Andino (Sargento Saltos), Manolo Sarmiento (Maestro), Jaime Estrada (Senor Limpieza)

Citizens of a small Ecuadorian village suffering from the murder of three local children react with intense hostility towards a traveling salesman who has accidentally hit and killed a boy with his car.

THE BEAUTIFUL COUNTRY

(SONY CLASSICS) Producers, Petter J. Borgli, Tomas Backstrom, Terrence Malick, Edward R. Pressman; Director, Hans Petter Moland; Screenplay, Sabina Murray, Larry Gross; Story, Lingard Jervey; Based on an idea by Terrence Malick; Photography, Stuart Dryburgh; Designer, Karl Juliusson; Costumes, Anne Pedersen; Music, Zbigniew Preisner; Editor, Wibecke Ronseth; Casting, Avy Kaufman, Tran Anh Hoa, Alice Chan; a Dinamo Story (Norway), Sunflower Prods. (U.S.) production, in association with Samy Boy Entertainment, SF Norge, Filmpartners; Norwegian-U.S.; Dolby; Super 35 Widescreen; Cinecolor; Rated R; 125 minutes; American release date: July 8, 2005

Cast

Binh **Damien Nguyen**
Steve **Nick Nolte**
Capt. Oh **Tim Roth**
Ling **Bai Ling**
Snakeshead **Temuera Derek Morrison**
Tam **Tran Dang Quoc Thinh**
Hairdresser **Nguyen Thi Huong Dung**
Mai **Chau Thi Kim Xuan**
Mrs. Hoa **Anh Thu**
Mrs. Hoa's Son **Khuong Duc Thuan**
Head Servant **Vu Tang**
Riley **Nguyen Than Kien**
Crippled Woman **Bui Ti Hong**
Jerry **John Hussey**

and Chapman To (Chingmy), Glen Bradford (Wayne), Devin Carbaugh (Yuppie), Cleve Chamberlain (Vietnam Veteran), Chu Dora (Bartender), Phyllis Cicero (Receptionist), Dins Xuan Phuc (Pham), Kirk Griffith (Ranch Owner), He Be (Grandfather), Hoang Phat Trieu (Captain on Junk), Damien Hung (Eng), Richard Black (Postal Clerk), Loke Wee Suu (Official), Victor Macias (Mexican Man), Mai Thi Hoa (Wa), Don McCoy (Police Officer), Ganrasha Moorthy (Officer), Arthur J. Nascarella (Gruff), Nguyen Thi Linh Phoung (Exquisite), Nguyen Thu An (Old Woman), Nguyen Van Hai (Git Wo), Pham Minh Quoc (Guard #1), Carl Savering (Truck Driver), Libby Villari (Steve's Servant)

Damien Nguyen, Bai Ling, Chau Thi Kim Xuan in *Beautiful Country* PHOTO COURTESY OF SONY CLASSICS

Binh, a young man of mixed race living in Vietnam, treks to Ho Chi Minh City to find the mother he never knew.

Stipe Erceg, Daniel Bruhl, Julia Jentsch in *The Edukators* PHOTO COURTESY OF IFC FILMS

THE EDUKATORS

(IFC FILMS) a.k.a. *Die Fetten Jahre sind Vorbei*; Producers, Hans Weingartner, Antonin Svoboda; Director, Hans Weingartner; Screenplay, Katharina Held, Hans Weingartner; Photography, Mtthias Schellenberg; Designer, Christian M. Goldbeck; Costumes, Silvia Pernegger; Music, Andreas Wodraschke; Editors, Dirk Octelshoven, Andreas Wodraschke; Casting, Silke Koch, Suse Marquardt; a Y3 Film (Germany), Coop99 (Austria) production in association with Sudwestrundfunk, Arte; German-Austria, 2004; Dolby; Color; DV-to-35mm; Rated R; 124 minutes; American release date: July 22, 2005

Cast

Jan **Daniel Brühl**
Jule **Julia Jentsch**
Peter **Stipe Erceg**
Hardenberg **Burghart Klaussner**
Villenbesitzer **Pee Martiny**
Villenesitzerin **Petra Zieser**
Tochter **Laura Schmidt**
Sohn **Sebastian Butz**

and Olivier Bröcker (Aggressive Global), Knut Berger (Glob), Hanns Zischler (Vermieter), Caludio Caiolo (Paolo), Bernhard Bettermann (Jules Chef), Sylvia Haider, Claudia Jakobshagen (Neureiche Women), Reiner Heise (Fahrscheink), Heinz Kreitzen (Obdachloser), Lara Schutzsack (Peters Bekannte), Heinz Fitz (Wanderer), Albert Gurtler (Betrunkener)

Political activist Jan hooks up with Peter and his girlfriend Jule to rile against the injustices of capitalistic society and end up kidnapping a wealthy businessman whose home they have broken into.

9 SONGS

(TARTAN) Producer, Andrew Eaton: Screenplay, Michael Winterbottom; Executive Producer, Melissa Parmenter; Photography, Marcel Zyskind; Editors, Matt Whitecross, Michael Winterbottom; a Revolution Films production; British; Dolby; Color; Not rated; 69 minutes; American release date: July 22, 2005

Cast
Matt **Kieran O'Brien**
Lisa **Margo Stilley**

and Huw Bunford, Cian Ciaran, The Dandy Warhols, Elbow, Franz Ferdinand, Bobby Gillespie, Bob Hardy, Dafydd Ieuan, Alex Kapranos, Mani, Nick McCarthy, Michael Nyman, Guto Pryce, Gruff Rhys, Courtney Taylor-Taylor, Robert Young (Themselves)

Matt looks back on his first encounter with Lisa at a rock concert and the subsequent physical expression of their passion.

Kieran O'Brien, Margo Stilley in *9 Songs*

Kieran O'Brien, Margo Stilley in *9 Songs* PHOTOS COURTESY OF TARTAN USA

BALZAC AND THE LITTLE CHINESE SEAMSTRESS

(EMPIRE) a.k.a. *Xiao cal feng*; Producer, Lise Fayolle; Executive Producer, Pujian Wang, Bernard Lorain; Director, Dai Sijie; Screenplay Dai Sijie, Nadine Perront; Based on the novel by Dai Sijie; Photography, Jean-Marie Dreujou; Designer, Cao Juiping; Costumes, Tong Huamiao; Music, Wang Pujian; Editor, Luc Barnier, Julia Gregory; a Les Films de la Suane, TF1 Films Productions; French-Chinese, 2002; Dolby; Color; Not rated; 110 minutes; American release: July 29, 2005

Cast
Little Chinese Seamstress **Zhou Xun**
Luo **Chen Kun**
Ma **Liu Ye**
Head of the Village **Wang Shuangbao**
Old Tailor **Cong Zhijun**
Four Eyes **Wang Hong Wei**
Mother of Four Eyes **Xiao Xiong**

and Tang Zuohui (Old Mill Worker), Chen Wei (Wife of the Head of the Village), Chen Tianlu (Director of the Village), Fan Qing-yun (Doctor)

During the Great Proletarian Cultural Revolution, Ma and Luo, sons of urban professionals, are sent to a re-education program where they form a bond with a Chinese seamstress.

Zhou Xun in *Balzac and the Little Chinese Seamstress* PHOTO COURTESY OF EMPIRE PICTURES

TONY TAKITANI

(STRAND) Producer, Motoki Ishida; Director/Screenplay, Jun Ichikawa; Based on the novel by Haruki Murakami; Photography, Taishi Hirokawa; Art Director, Yoshikazu Ichida; Music, Ryuichi Sakamoto; Editor, Tomoh Sanjo; a Wilco Co. Ltd. production; Japanese, 2004; Color; Not rated; 75 minutes; American release date: July 29, 2005

Cast

Tony Takitani/Schozaburo Takitani **Issei Ogata**
Konuma Eiko/Hisako **Rie Miyazawa**
Young Tony Takitani **Shinohara Takahumi**
Narrator **Hidetoshi Nishijima**

A man who has known only isolation and loneliness finds himself awakening to the outside world at the age of 37, when he falls in love.

Rie Miyazawa, Issei Ogata in *Tony Takitani* PHOTO COURTESY OF STRAND RELEASING

and Chris Poszczansky (Hulk), Paulette Sinclair (Secretary Roddy), Lubica Kucerova (Woman in Shower), Ben Gans, Jock McLeod (Senior Citizens), Jeff Baxter (Cattana), Daniel Karasik (Bolan), Jonathan Walker (Mr. Collins), Keir Gilchrist (Kid Collins), Jonathan Wilson (Father Gregg), Rob Smith (Santa Claus), Joan Massiah (Mrs. Scarlet), Gerard Parkes (Longboat), Boyd Banks, Henry Alessandroni (Workers), Fiona Highet (Nurse), Brandon Barre (Road Runner), John Blakey, Naomi Emmerson (Spectators), Sean Cullen (Children's Aid Officer), Barry Stillwell (Mr. Jones), Jonathan Higgins (Boston Announcer), Michael David Brown (John Bannon), Miranda Black (Nurse Riggin), Brian Bannan (Priest), Peter Feniak, Tufford Kennedy (Reporters)

At an Ontario Catholic High School, 14-year-old troublemaker Ralph Walker is ordered to join the cross-country track team as a means of discipline.

Campbell Scott, Adam Butcher in *Saint Ralph*

SAINT RALPH

(SAMUEL GOLDWYN) Producer, Michael Souther, Teza Lawrence, Seaton McLean, Andrea Mann; Executive Producers, Peter Sussman, Marguerite Pigott; Director/Screenplay, Michael McGowan; Photography, René Ohashi; Designer, Matthew Davies; Costumes, Anne Dixon; Music, Andrew Lockington; Editor, Susan Maggi; Casting, Jenny Lewis, Deirdre Bowen; an Alliance Atlantis Communications, Amaze Film + Television; Canadian, 2004; Dolby; Color; Rated PG-13; 98 minutes; American release date: August 5, 2005

Cast

Ralph Walker **Adam Butcher**
Father George Hibbert **Campbell Scott**
Father Fitzpatrick **Gordon Pinsett**
Nurse Alice **Jennifer Tilly**
Emma Walker **Shauna MacDonald**
Claire Collins **Tamara Hope**
Mr. Karl **Frank Crudele**
Chester Jones **Michael Kaney**

Adam Butcher (center) in *Saint Ralph* PHOTOS COURTESY OF SAMUEL GOLDWYN

2046

(SONY CLASSICS) Producer/Director/Screenplay, Wong Kar Wai; Co-Producers, Eric Heumann, Amedeo Pagani, Marc Sillam; Line Producer, Chan Wai-Chung; Photography, Christopher Doyle; Designer/Costumes, William Chang Suk Ping;Music, Peer Raben, Shigeru Umebayashi; a Block 2 Pictures presentation in association with Paradis Films, Orly Films (France), Classic (Italy), Shanghai Film Corp. (China), of a Jet Tone Films production, with the participation of Arte France, France 3 Cinema, ZDF-Arte; Hong Kong-French-Italian-Chinese; Dolby; Black and white/color; Rated R; 127 minutes; American release date: August 5, 2005

Zhang Ziyi, Tony Leung Chiu-wai

Tony Leung Chiu-wai

Cast

Chow Mo-wan **Tony Leung Chiu-wai**
Su Li Zhen **Gong Li**
Tak/Wang Jin Wen's Boyfriend **Takuya Kimura**
Wang Jin Wen **Faye Wong**
Bai Ling **Zhang Ziyi**
Lulu/Mimi/Android on 2046 Train **Carina Lau**
Mimi's Boyfriend **Chang Chen**
Mr. Wang/Train Captain **Sum Wang**
Ah Ping **Siu Ping Lam**
Su Li Zhen (1960) **Maggie Cheung**
Bird **Thongchai McIntyre**
Wang Jie Wen **Dong Jie**

Over the course of three Christmas Eves, Chow, a struggling sci-fi writer living in a hotel, experiences relationships with three different women, all of whom reside in Room 2046.

Takuya Kimura, Faye Wong

Zhang Ziyi   PHOTOS COURTESY OF SONY CLASSICS

Natasha Richardson, Hugh Bonneville in *Asylum* PHOTO COURTESY OF PARAMOUNT CLASSICS

ASYLUM

(PARAMOUNT CLASSICS) Producers, Laurence Borg, David E. Allen, Mace Neufeld; Executive Producers, Michael Barlow, Natasha Richardson, Robert Rehme, Baron Davis, Steven Markoff, Bruce McNall, Chris Curling, Harmon Kaslow, John Buchanan; Co-Producer, David Collins; Director, David Mackenzie; Screenplay, Patrick Marber, Chrys Balis; Based on the novel by Patrick McGrath; Photography, Giles Nuttgens; Designer, Laurence Dorman; Costumes, Consolata Boyle; Music, Mark Mancina; Editors, Colin Monie, Steven Weisberg; a Seven Arts Pictures (U.K.), Samson Films (Ireland), Mace Neufeld Prods. (U.S. production); British-Irish-U.S.; Dolby; Widescreen; Color; Rated R; 99 minutes; American release date: August 12, 2005

Cast

Stella Raphael **Natasha Richardson**
Max Raphael **Hugh Bonneville**
Charlie Raphael **Gus Lewis**
Dr. Peter Cleave **Ian McKellen**
Jack Straffen **Joss Ackland**
Edgar Stark **Martin Csokas**
Bridie Straffen **Wanda Ventham**
Mrs. Rose **Sarah Thurstan**
Monica **Alwyne Taylor**
Claudia Greene **Maria Aitken**
Lilly **Hazel Douglas**

and Anna Keaveney (Mrs. Bain), Robert Willox (John Archer), Judy Parfitt (Brenda Raphael), Sean Harris (Nick), Andy de la Tour (Inspector Easton), Roy Boyd (Trevor Williams), Rhydian Jones (Mr. Griffin), Nick Chadwin (Chaplain), Susie Gossling Valerio (Patient), Julia Hickman (Patient at Ball), Jason Thornton (George)

The wife of a new asylum administrator falls in love with patient Edgar Stark, an artist with a personality disorder who has been committed for having killed his wife.

VALIANT

(WALT DISNEY PICTURES) Producer, John H. Williams; Executive Producers, Barnaby Thompson, Ralph Kamp, Neil Braun, Robert Jones, Keith Evans; Director, Gary Chapman; Screenplay, Jordan Katz, George Webster, George Melrod; Original Story, George Webster; Co-Producers, Eric M. Bennett, Curtis Augspurger, Buckley Cullum; Music, George Fenton; Editor, Jim Stewart; Associate Producer, Marci Levine; Animation Director, Richard Purdum; Photography, John Fenner; CG Supervisors, Gray Horsfield, Ron Brinkmann; Casting, Celestia Fox; a Vanguard Animation Production in association with Ealing Studios, Odyssey Entertainment, the UK Film Council, Take Film Partnerships; British; Dolby; Technicolor; Rated G; 75 minutes; Release date: August 19, 2005

Voice Cast

Valiant **Ewan McGregor**
Bugsy **Ricky Gervais**
Von Talon **Tim Curry**
Sergeant **Jim Broadbent**
Gutsy **Hugh Laurie**
Mercury **John Cleese**
Felix **John Hurt**
Lofty **Pip Torrens**
Cufflink **Rik Mayall**
Victoria **Olivia Williams**

and Jonathan Ross (Big Thug), Brian Lonsdale (Toughwood), Dan Roberts (Tailfeather), Michael Schlingmann (Underlingk), Sharon Horgan (Charles De Girl), Sean Samuels (Jacques), Buckley Collum (Rollo), Annette Badland (Elsa), Harriet Jones (Barmaid), Harry Peacock (Recruiting Officer), Corin Mellinger (Wing Pigeon), Gary Chapman (Pigeon Officer), Curtis Augspurger (Pigeon Guard), Mike Harbour (Little Thug), Mike Jenn (Messenger Pigeon), Heidi Fecht (Sacy Pigeon), Robert Lence ("Tweet" Pigeon), Ali Dowling, Chris Fairbanks, Rupert Farley, Dan Flynn, Kris Milne, Stephen Pacey, James Dale Robinson, Emma Tate (Additional Voices)

An undersized pigeon gets his chance to be a hero when he is chosen to lead a dangerous mission during World War II.

Lofty, Tailfeather, Toughwood, Valiant in *Valiant* PHOTO COURTESY OF WALT DISNEY PICTURES

THE BROTHERS GRIMM

(DIMENSION) Producers, Charles Roven, Daniel Bobker; Executive Producers, John D. Schofield, Chris McGurk, Bob Weinstein, Harvey Weinstein, Jonathan Gordon, Andrew Rona; Co-Producers, Jake Myers, Michael Solinger; Director, Terry Gilliam; Screenplay, Ehren Kruger; Photography, Newton Thomas Sigel; Designer, Guy Hendrix Dyas; Costumes, Gabriella Pescucci, Carlo Poggioli; Music, Dario Marianelli; Editor, Leslie Walker; Makeup, Chrissie Beveridge; Visual Effects Supervisor, Kent Houston; Special Effects Supervisors, Simon Taylor, Mike Kelt; Casting, Irene Lamb; a Dimension Films, Metro-Goldwyn-Mayer Pictures presentation of a Mosaic Media Group, Daniel Bobker production; British-Czech Republic; Dolby; Deluxe color; Rated PG-13; 118 minutes; American release date: August 26, 2005

Heath Ledger, Matt Damon

Lena Headey, Matt Damon

Cast

Wilhelm Grimm **Matt Damon**
Jacob Grimm **Heath Ledger**
Cavaldi **Peter Stormare**
Angelika **Lena Headey**
Delatombe **Jonathan Pryce**
Mirror Queen **Monica Bellucci**
Hidlick **Mackenzie Crook**
Bunst **Richard Ridings**
Letorc **Julian Bleach**
Dax **Bruce McEwan**

and Petr Ratimec (Young Will), Barbara Lukêsova (Mother Grimm), Anna Rust (Sister Grimm), Jeremy Robson (Young Jacob), Radim Kaldova, Martin Hofmann (Gendarmes), Josef Pepa Nos (German War Veteran), Harry Gilliam (Stable Boy), Miroslav Táborsky (Old Miller), Roger Ashton-Griffiths (Mayor), Marika Sarah Procházková (Miller's Daughter), Alena Jakobova (Red Hooded Girl), Rudolf Pellar (Watchman), Dana Dohnalova, Petra Dohnvalova (Twin Sisters), Hanus Bor (Twins' Father), Ota Filip (Tavern Owner), Audrey Hamm, Annike Murjahn (Travelers), Lukás Bech (Barman), Karel Kohlicek (Bald French Soldier), Martin Kavan (Delatombe's Valet), Eva Reitererova (Serving Wench), Denisa Vokurkova (Greta), Martin Svetlik (Hans), Jan Unger (Gregor), Laura Greenwood (Sasha), Frantisek Velecky (Old Crone), Jakub Zindulka (Minister), Milan Gargula (Contemptuous Villager), Drahomira Fialkova (Grandmother),

Ludek Elias (Grizzled Elder), Jana Radojcicová (Angry Woman), Tomás Hanák (Woodsman), Denisa Malinovska (Young Angelika), Josef Vajnar (Bishop), Petr Vrsek (The King), Bara Rudlova, Andrea Milackova, Andrea Sochurkova, Daniela Kubickova (Angelika's Sisters), Veronika Loulova (Elsie), Vera Uzelacova (Elsie's Mother), Julie Venhaureova (Goose Girl), Deborah Hyde (Corpse Queen), Václav Chapula (Aide de Camp), Jiri Krejcir (Fat Soldier), Kamila Bruderova (Dumpy Farm Girl)

The Brothers Grimm, a pair of con men who pretend to exterminate supernatural spirits, find themselves combating real evil when young girls from the village of Marbaden start disappearing mysteriously.

Monica Bellucci

FORMULA 17

(STRAND) a.k.a. *Shi qi sui de tian kong*; Producers, Aileen Li, Michelle Yen; Line Producer, Roger Huang; Director, D. J. Chen; Screenplay, Rady Fu; Photography, Chen Hsi-Sheng; Art Director, Gu Zac; Music, George Chen, Hung Tze-li; Editor, Chen Hsiao-tong; a Three Dots Entertainment Co. production; Taiwanese, 2004; Dolby; Color; Not rated; 93 minutes; American release date: August 26, 2005

Cast

Tien **Tony Yang**
Bai Tieh-nan **Duncan**
Yu **Chin King**
C. C. **Ji Dada**
Alan **Jimmy Yang**
Jun **Jason Chang**
Kevin **Yu Ladder**
Jay **Huang Guan-Jie**
Tapiei Plumber **Yang Tze-Long**
Ray **Jeff Locker**

A gay teen moves to Taipei to find love but instead falls for a smooth lothario who is more interested in sex than a long-term relationship.

Tony Yang, Duncan in *Formula 17* PHOTO COURTESY OF STRAND RELEASING

Jan Decleir, Deborah Ostrega in *The Memory of a Killer* PHOTOS COURTESY OF SONY CLASSICS

Hilde De Baerdemaeker in The Memory of a Killer PHOTOS COURTESY OF SONY CLASSICS

THE MEMORY OF A KILLER

(SONY CLASSICS) a.k.a. *De Zaak Alzheimer*; Producers, Hilde De Laere, Erwin Provoost; Executive Producer, Mark De Geest; Director, Erik Van Looy; Screenplay, Erik Van Looy, Carl Joos; Based on the novel by Jef Geeraerts; Photography, Danny Elsen; Art Director, Johan Van Essche; Costumes, Kristin Van Passel; Music, Stephen Warbeck; Editor, Phillippe Ravoet, Yoohan Leyssens; Casting, Gunter Schmid; a co-production of TV1, PVPictures, TROS Bridge Rights; Belgian-Netherlands; Dolby; Color; Rated R; 120 minutes; American release date: August 26, 2005

Cast

Eric Vincke **Koen De Bouw**
Freddy Verstuyft **Werner De Smedt**
Angelo Ledda **Jan Decleir**
Linda de Leenheer **Hilde De Baerdemaeker**
Tom Coemans **Geert Van Rampelberg**
Baron Gustave de Haeck **Jo De Meyere**
Jean de Haeck **Tom Van Dyck**
Joseph Vlerick **Vic de Wachter**
Henriette Seynaeve **Lone van Roosendaal**
Seynaeve **Gene Bervoets**
Bob Van Camp **Lucas van den Eijnde**
Evan Van Camp **Els Dootermans**
Ine Van Camp **Anaïs Terryn**

and Patrick Descamps (Gilles Resnais), Johan van Assche (Van Parys), Jappe Claes (Prosecutor Bracke), Filip Peeters (Major De Keyzer), Bart Slegers (Lemmens), Marc Peeters (Opdebeeck), Tom Waes (Verheyen), Eddy Vereycken (Dr. Abbeloos), Dirk Roofthooft (Vader Cuypers), Laurien Van den Broeck (Bieke Cuypers), Deborah Ostrega (Anja), Ludo Hoogmartens (Businessman), Roland De Jonghe (Paolo Ledda), Peter Borghs (Guard), Jan Van Loovren (Police Motorcyclist), Kristine Arras (Housekeeper), Marc Janssen (Chaplain), Katrien Vandendries (Nurse), Mick van Bocxstaele (Receptionist), Jan Dyck (Taxi Driver), Babett Manalo (Masseuse), Anne-Caroline Suberville (Dienster)

Angelo Ledda, an aging professional assassin in the early stages of Alzheimer's, refuses the assignment of killing an underage call girl and finds himself targeted for death.

THE CONSTANT GARDENER

(FOCUS) Producer, Simon Channing Williams; Executive Producers, Gail Egan, Robert Jones, Donald Ranvaud, Jeff Abberley, Julia Blackman; Co-Producers, Henning Molfenter, Thierry Potok; Director, Fernando Meirelles; Screenplay, Jeffrey Caine; Based on the novel by John le Carre; Photography, Cesar Charlone; Designer, Mark Tildesley; Costumes, Odile Dics-Mireaux; Music, Alberto Iglesias; Editor, Claire Simpson; Casting, Leo Davis; a Potboiler production in association with Scion Films, presented in association with the U.K. Film Council; British-German; Dolby; Color; Rated R; 128 minutes; American release date: August 31, 2005

Cast

Justin Quayle **Ralph Fiennes**
Tessa Quayle **Rachel Weisz**
Sandy Woodrow **Danny Huston**
Arnold Bluhm **Hubert Koundé**
Sir Bernard Pellegrin **Bill Nighy**
Lorbeer **Pete Postlethwaite**
Arthur Hammond **Richard McCabe**
Tim Donohue **Donald Sumpter**
Gloria Woodrow **Juliet Aubrey**
Ghita Pearson **Archie Panjabi**
Sir Kenneth Curtiss **Gerald McSorley**
Mustafa **Samuel Otage**
Birgit **Anneke Kim Sarnau**
Miriam **Daniele Harford**

and Packson Ngugi (Office in Morgue), Damaris Itenyo Agweyu (Journo's Wife), Bernard Otieno Oduor (Journo), Keith Pearson (Porter Coleridge), John Sibi-Okumu (Dr. Joshua Ngaba), Nick Reding (Crick), Jacqueline Maribe (Wanza Kiluhu), Donald Apiyo (Kioko), Mumbi Kaigwa (Grace Makanga), John Moller (Athletic Unshaven Man), Andree Leenheer (Shaven-Headed Man), Lydia M. Manyasi (Kenyan Newsreader), Stennie Njoroge, Stuart Wheeler (Journalists), Chris Payne (Mike Mildren), Nyajima Jial (Esmeralda), Brigid M. Kakenyi (Hospital Administrator), Katherine Damaris (Nurse), Christopher Okinda (Doctor), Ainea Ojiambo (Police Driver), Peter King Nzioko, Ng'ang'a Kirumburu (Policemen), Ben

Ralph Fiennes, Danny Huston

Parker (Det. Inspector Deasey), John Keogh (Immigration Official), Jeffrey Caine (Club Servant), Rupert Simonian (Guido Hammond), Teresa Harder (Birgit's Secretary), Thomas Chemnitz (Uniformed Policeman), Joe Christopher Rhode, Edgar Nicholas Rhode (Karl), Eva Plackner (Crossing Guard), Claire Simpson (Maude Donohue), Sidede Onyulo (Jonah Andika), Chris Lightburn-Jones (Aid Worker), Ann Achan (Ana), Dan Wuor Dew (Sudanese Man), Ben Gardiner (Harry Woodrow)

An English diplomat investigates the situation behind his wife's death, realizing that she had caused an uproar after discovering how new drugs were being tested on unsuspecting Kenyans.

Ralph Fiennes, Pete Postlethwaite PHOTOS COURTESY OF FOCUS FEATURES

2005 Academy Award-winner for Best Supporting Actress (Rachel Weisz). This film received additional nominations for adapted screenplay, film editing, and original score.

Rachel Weisz, Ralph Fiennes

TRANSPORTER 2

(20TH CENTURY FOX) Producer/Screenplay, Luc Besson; Executive Producers, Terry Miller, Steve Chasman; Director, Louis Leterrier; Photography, Mitchell Amundsen; Designer, John Mark Harrington; Costumes, Bobbie Read; Music, Alexandre Azaria; Editors, Vincent Taballion, Christine Lucas Navarro; Fight Choreographer, Cory Yuen; a EuropaCorp, TF1 Films Production in association with Current Entertainment with participation of Canal Plus, TPS Star; French; Dolby; Widescreen; Color; Rated PG-13; 88 minutes; American release date: September 2, 2005

Cast

Frank Martin **Jason Statham**
Gianni **Alessandro Gassman**
Audrey Billings **Amber Valletta**
Lola **Kate Nauta**
Mr. Billings **Matthew Modine**
Dimitri **Jason Flemyng**
Stappleton **Keith David**
Jack Billings **Hunter Clary**

Kate Nauta, Jason Statham in *Transporter 2* PHOTO COURTESY OF 20TH CENTURY FOX

and Shannon Briggs (Max), François Berléand (Tarconi), Raymond Tong (Rastaman), George Kapetun (Dr. Sonovitch), Jeff Chase (Vasily), Gregg Weiner (Tipov), Gregg Davis (Techie at Billings), Marty Wright (Commander), Anna Lynne (Car Jacking Girl), Reggie Pierre, Elie Thompson, Adam Faldetta, Michael House (Car Jackers), Tim Ware (Hoffman), Liv Davalos Maier (TV News Announcer), Damaris Justamante (Receptionist), Andy Horne (Dr. Koblin), Doug MacKinnon (Marshal Smith), Marc Macaulay (Marshal Brown), Bill Wilson (Agent at Billings House), Robert Small (Government Doctor), Jim Campbell (Robot Tech), Heath Kelts, Chris Campbell (Security Agents), Paul Tei (Tech in Van), Ernest Harden, Jr. (Billings Aide), Tim Powell (Marshal at Robot Site), Shelah Rhoulhac (Nurse), Tom Derek (Homeless Man), Serafin Falcon (Sniper), Max Osterweis (The Phone's Man), Laurence Gormezano (TV News Announcer, Helicopter)

Special forces operative-turned-chauffeur Frank Martin must save the son of an anti-drug crusader after the boy is injected with a deadly virus, with those responsible expecting a huge ransom in exchange for the antidote.

Jean-Marc Barr, Gilbert Melki, Valeria Bruni-Tedeschi, Jacques Bonnaffé in *Cote D'Azur*
PHOTO COURTESY OF STRAND RELEASING

COTE D'AZUR

(STRAND) a.k.a. *Crustacés et coquillages*; Producer, Nicolas Blanc; Associate Producer, Robert Guédiguian; Directors/Screenplay, Olivier Ducastel, Jacques Martineau; Photography, Matthieu Poirot-Delpech; Designer, Lise Petermann; Costumes, Ann-Marie Giacalone; Music, Philippe Miller; Editor, Dominique Galliéni; a co-production of Bac Films, Agat Films & Cie, in association with Cofimage 16; French; Dolby; Color; Not rated; 93 minutes; American release date: September 9, 2005

Cast

Béatrix **Valeria Bruni Tedeschi**
Marc **Gilbert Melki**
Didier **Jean-Marc Barr**
Mathieu **Jacques Bonnaffé**
Martin **Edouard Collin**
Charly **Romain Torres**
Laura **Sabrina Seyvecou**
Michaël **Yannick Baudin**
Sylvain **Julien Weber**
Laura's New Friend **Sébastien Cormier**
Billiard Player **Marion Roux**

A family encounters a myriad of romantic complications during a vacation by the sea.

GARÇON STUPIDE

(PICTURE THIS!) Producer, Robert Boner; Director, Lionel Baier; Screenplay, Lionel Baier, Laurent Guido; Photography, Lionel Baier; Séverine Barde; Music, Sergei Rachmaninov; Editor, Christine Hoffet; a Saga Productions film; French-Swiss; Dolby; Color; Not rated; 94 minutes; American release date: September 16, 2005

Cast
Loïc **Pierre Chatagny**
Marie **Natacha Koutchoumov**
Rui **Rui Pedro Alves**
Lionel **Lionel Baier**
Videostore Trader **Jean-Stéphane Bron**
Guy in Museum **Laurent Guido**

and Marlyse Bonvin, Marianne Bruchez, Noah Canete Alves, Hervë D., Mikele D., Robin Harsch, Khaled Khoury, Ursula Meier, Rachel Noël, Michel Rochat, Joëlle Rübli, Vincent Verselle

A young man who indulges in random sexual encounters, wonders if love is a possibility and if there might be more to life than meaningless sex.

Pierre Chatagny in *Garçon Stupide* PHOTO COURTESY OF PICTURE THIS!

Emily Watson, Rupert Everett in *Separate Lies*

Tom Wilkinson, Rupert Everett in *Separate Lies* PHOTOS COURTESY OF FOX SEARCHLIGHT

SEPARATE LIES

(FOX SEARCHLIGHT) Producers, Christian Colson, Steven Clark-Hall; Executive Producer, Paul Smith; Director/Screenplay, Julian Fellowes; Based on the novel *A Way Through the Wood* by Nigel Balchin; Photography, Tony Pierce-Roberts; Designer, Alison Riva; Costumes, Michelle Clapton; Music, Stanislas Syrewicz; Editor, Alex Mackie, Martin Walsh; Casting, Janey Fothergill; a Celador Films, DNA Films presentation of a Celador Films production, in association with the U.K. Film Council, Film Four; British; Dolby; Deluxe color; Rated R; 87 minutes; American release date: September 16, 2005

Cast
James Manning **Tom Wilkinson**
Anne Manning **Emily Watson**
William Bule **Rupert Everett**
Priscilla **Hermione Norris**
Simon **John Warnaby**
Sarah Tufnell **Richenda Carey**
Maggie **Linda Bassett**
Nurse **Christine Lohr**
Maggie's Daughter **Alice O'Connell**
Lord Rawston **John Neville**

and Peregrine Kitchener-Fellowes (Bill's Son, Charles), Henry Drake (Bill's Son, Freddy), David Harewood (Inspector Marshall), Sabine Tourtellier (Receptionist), Philip Rham (French Lawyer), Jeremy Child (Angus Burrell)

Growing bored with her marriage to a powerful lawyer, Anne Manning indulges in an affair with heir William Bule, who may have the answer to who was responsible for a hit-and-run accident that killed the husband of one of the Manning servants.

Jamie Foreman

OLIVER TWIST

(SONY PICTURES) Producers, Robert Benmussa, Alain Sarde, Roman Polanski; Executive Producers, Timothy Burrill, Petr Moravec; Director, Roman Polanski; Screenplay, Ronald Harwood; Based on the novel by Charles Dickens; Photography, Pawel Edelman; Designer, Allan Starski; Costumes, Anna Sheppard; Music, Rachel Portman; Edtior; Herve de Luze; Casting, Celestia Fox; a TriStar Pictures, R.P. Prods. presentation of an R.O. Films, Runteam II Ltd., Etic Films S.R.O. co-production; French-British-Czech; Dolby; Panavision; Color; Rated PG-13; 130 minutes; American release date: September 23, 2005

Cast

Fagin **Ben Kingsley**
Oliver Twist **Barney Clark**
Bill Sykes **Jamie Foreman**
Artful Dodger **Harry Eden**
Nancy **Leanne Rowe**
Mr. Brownlow **Edward Hardwicke**
Mr. Limbkins **Ian McNeice**
Toby Crackit **Mark Strong**

Mr. Bumble **Jeremy Swift**
Mrs. Bedwin **Frances Cuka**
Mr. Sowerberry **Michael Heath**
Mrs. Sowerberry **Gillian Hanna**
Magistrate Fang **Alun Armstrong**
Workhouse Master **Andy De La Tour**
Dining Hall Master **Peter Copley**

and Joseph Tremain (Hungry Boy), Andreas Papadopoulos, Laurie Athey, Filip Hess (Workhouse Boys), Lewis Chase (Charley Bates), Jake Curran (Barney), Chris Overton (Noah Claypole), Richard Durden (Unkind Board Member), Timothy Bateson (Parson/Old Man with a Punch), Andy Linden (Mr. Garmfield, The Chimney Sweep), John Nettleton (First Magistrate), Teresa Churcher (Charlotte), Gerard Horan (Farmer), Morgane Polanski (Farmer's Daughter), Liz Smith (Old Woman), Levi Hayes (Nicky), Ophelia Lovibond (Bet), Elvis Polanski (Boy with Hoop), Patrick Godfrey (Bookseller), Anezka Novak, Andrea Miltner, Kaeren Revell (Women in Street), Andy Camm (Policeman), Frank Mills (Elderly Officer), Turbo (Bullseye), David Meeking (Policeman in Court), Paul Brooke (Mr. Grimwig), Kay Raven (Woman at Window), Lizzy Le Quesne (Barmaid), Robert Orr (Man in Pub), Paul Eden (Barman), Nick Stringer (Inspector Blather), James Babson (Policeman), Richard Ridings (Warder)

Lewis Chase, Barney Clark, Harry Eden

An orphan boy runs away to London where he falls in with Fagin and his gang of young pickpockets. Earlier versions of *Oliver Twist* include those starring Lon Chaney and Jackie Coogan (Paramount, 1922), Alec Guinness and John Howard Davies (1948, U.S.: Universal, 1951), Ron Moody and Mark Lester (*Oliver!*, Columbia, 1968), animated (*Oliver & Company*, Disney, 1988), and *Twist* (Strand Releasing, 2003).

Ben Kingsley, Barney Clark PHOTOS COURTESY OF SONY PICTURES

Gina McKee

Gina McKee (right)

Stephanie Leonidas PHOTOS COURTESY OF SAMUEL GOLDWYN

MIRRORMASK

(SAMUEL GOLDWYN) Producer, Simon Moorhead; Executive Producers, Lisa Henson, Michael Polis, Martin G. Baker; Director/Designer, David McKean; Screenplay, Neil Gaiman; Story, Neil Gaiman, David McKean; Photography, Antony Shearn; Costumes, Robert Lever; Digital Animation/Effects, Hourglass Studios; Music, Ian Ballamy; Editor, Nicolas Gaster; Casting, Louis Hammond; a Destination Films presentation of a Jim Henson production; British-U.S.; Dolby; Soho Images Color; Rated PG; 96 minutes; American release date: September 30, 2005

Cast
Helena **Stephanie Leonidas**
Joanne/Queen of Darkness/Queen of Light **Gina McKee**
Helena's Father/Prime Minister **Rob Brydon**
Valentine **Jason Barry**
Nan **Dora Bryan**
Gryphon **Robert Llewellyn**
Small Hairy **Andy Hamilton**
Librarian **Stephen Fry**
Receptionist **Fiona Reynard**
Pingo **Nik Robson**

Believing she is responsible for her mother's death, young Helena runs off from her circus life and journeys into the Dark Lands.

BEFORE THE FALL

(PICTURE THIS!) a.k.a. *Napola*; Producers, Viola Jäger, Haral Kügler, Molly von Fürstenberg; Director, Dennis Gansel; Screenplay, Dennis Gansel, Maggie Peren; Photography, Torsten Breuer; Costumes, Natascha Curtius-Noss; Music, Angelo Badalamenti; Editor, Jochen Ritter; Casting, Nessie Nesslauer; a Seven Pictures, Olga Film GmbH production; German, 2004; Dolby; Color; Not rated; 110 minutes; American release date: October 7, 2005

Max Riemelt in *Before the Fall*

Cast

Friedrich Weimer **Max Riemelt**
Albrecht Stein **Tom Schilling**
Heinrich Vogler **Devid Striesow**
Dr. Karl Klein **Joachim Bissmeier**
Gauletier Heinrich Stein **Justus von Dohanyi**
Josef Peiner **Michael Schenk**
Justus von Jaucher **Florian Stetter**
Herr Weimer **Alexander Held**
Frau Weimer **Sissy Höfferer**

and Jonas Jägermyr (Christoph Schneider), Leon A. Kersten (Tjaden), Thomas Drechsel (Hefe), Martin Goeres (Siegfried "Siggi" Gladen), Claudia Michelsen (Frau Stein), Julie Engelbrecht (Katharina), Max Dombrovka (Hans), Michael Lerchenberg (Latein-Lehrer), Johannes Zirner (Torben Send)

Tom Schilling, Max Riemelt in *Before the Fall* PHOTOS COURTESY OF PICTURE THIS!

Because of his boxing skills young Friedrich Weimer is recruited to join one of Germany's Nazi training schools, where he befriends the sensitive Albrecht Stein.

Carlos Padilla, Leonor Varela, Ana Paulina Caceres in *Innocent Voices* PHOTO COURTESY OF SLOWHAND

INNOCENT VOICES

(SLOWHAND) a.k.a. *Voces inocentes*; Producers, Lawrence Bender, Louis Mandoki; Executive Producers, Monica Lozano Serrano, Miguel Necoechea, Anna Roth, Federico Gonazlez Compeán, Francisco Gonzalez Compeán; Director, Luis Mandoki; Screenplay, Luis Mandoki, Oscar Orlando Torres; Story, Oscar Orlando Torres; Photography, Juan Ruiz Anchia; Designer, Antonio Muño-Hierro; Music, Andre Abujamra; Editor, Aleshka Ferrero; Casting, Carla Hool; a MUVI Films, Lawrence Bender Productions, Organizacion Santo Domingo, A Band Apart, Altavista Films production; Mexican-U.S.-Puerto Rican; Dolby; Color; Rated R; 120 minutes; American release date: October 14, 2005

Cast

Chava **Carlos Padilla**
Kella **Leonor Varela**
Cristina Maria **Xuna Primus**
Ancha **Gustavo Muñoz**
Uncle Beto **José María Yazpik**
Mama Toya **Ofelia Medina**
Priest **Daniel Giménez Cacho**
Chele **Adrian Alonso**

and Alejandro Felipe (Ricardito), Andrés Márquez (Marcos), Edgar Mencos (Soldier Shooting Speakers at Church), Ignacio Retes (Don Chico), Jorge Angel Toriello (Fito)

Abandoned by his father during the civil war in El Salvador, eleven-year-old Chava has no choice but to take charge of his family to help them survive.

WHERE THE TRUTH LIES

(THINKFILM) Producer, Robert Lantos; Executive Producers, Atom Egoyan, Colin Leventhal, Daniel J. B. Taylor, Donald A. Star; Co-Producers, Chris Chrisafis, Sandra Cunningham; Director/Screenplay, Atom Egoyan; Based on the novel by Rupert Holmes; Photography, Paul Sarossy; Designer, Philip Barker; Costumes, Beth Pasternak; Music, Mychael Danna; Editor, Susan Shipton; Casting, Mali Finn, John Buchan, Leo Davis; a Serendipity Point Films presentation in association with First Choice Films, the Movie Network, in association with Telefilm Canada, Movie Central, Ego Film Arts of a Robert Lantos production; Canadian-British; Dolby; Super 35 Widescreen; Deluxe color; Rated NC-17; 108 minutes; American release date: October 14, 2005

Alison Lohman

Colin Firth, Kevin Bacon

Cast

Lanny Morris **Kevin Bacon**
Vince Collins **Colin Firth**
Karen O'Connor **Alison Lohman**
Maureen O'Flaherty **Rachel Blanchard**
Reuben **David Hayman**
Sally Sanmarco **Maury Chaykin**
Alice **Kristin Adams**
Bonnie Trout **Sonja Bennett**
Mrs. O'Flaherty **Deborah Grover**
Jack Scaglia **Beau Starr**
Denise **Rebecca Davis**
Greg **Don McKellar**
Irv **John Moraitis**
John Hillman **Michael J. Reynolds**
Gina **Anna Silk**
Stanley **Simon Sinn**

and Deborah Grover (Mrs. O'Flaherty), Kathryn Winslow (PR Publicist), Sean Cullen (Telethon Announcer), Gigi Dalka (Showgirl), Adurey Dwyer (Receptionist), Sarah Wateridge, Kate Harrell (Stewardesses), David Hemblen (NY Hotel Concierge), Stuart Hughes, Shannon Lawson (Journalists), Arsinée Khanjian, Gabrielle Rose (Publishing Executives), Aliska Malish (Grotto Club Woman), Rosalba Martinni (NY Hotel Maid), Erika Rosenbaum (Legal Assistant), Vee Vimolaml (Room Service Girl)

Kevin Bacon, Rachel Blanchard, Colin Firth

A reporter hopes to uncover the truth behind the scandal that caused the comedy team of Lanny Morris and Vince Collins to break up at the height of their popularity in the 1950s.

Alison Lohman, David Hayman PHOTOS COURTESY OF THINKFILM

USHPIZIN

(PICTUREHOUSE) Producers, Rafi Bukaee, Gidi Dar; Director, Gidi Dar; Screenplay, Shuli Rand; Photography, Amit Yasur; Designer, Ido Doliev; Music, Nethaniel Mechaly; Editors, Isaac Sehayek, Nadav Harel; a Gilgamesh Prods. presentation of an Eddie King Ltd., Gilgamesh Prods. production; Israeli; Dolby; Color; Rated PG; 90 minutes; American release date: October 19, 2005

Michal Bat-Sheva Rand, Shuli Rand

Shuli Rand

Cast

Moshe **Shuli Rand**
Mali **Michal Bat-Sheva Rand**
Eliahu **Shaul Mizrahi**
Yosef **Ilan Ganani**
Ben Baruch **Avraham Abutboul**
Gabai **Yonathan Danino**
The Rabbi **Daniel Dayan**

and Michael Vaigel (Ethrog Assessor), Daniel Rand (Elazar), Yizhak Levkovits (Charity), Shmuel Ovadia (Wolf)

On the eve of Sukkot, impoverished ultra-Orthodox Moshe and his wife Mali pray for a miracle and are overjoyed when they receive $1,000 left over from the Yeshiva fund.

Shaul Mizrahi, Ilan Ganani

Shuli Rand, Michal Bat-Sheva Rand PHOTOS COURTESY OF PICTUREHOUSE

DOOM

(UNIVERSAL) Producers, Lorenzo di Bonaventura, John Wells; Executive Producer, John D. Schofield; Director, Andrzej Bartkowiak; Screenplay, David Callaham, Wesley Strick; Story, David Callaham; Based on the videogame by id Software; Photography, Tony Pierce-Roberts; Designer, Stephen Scott; Costumes, Carlo Poggioli; Music, Clint Mansell; Editor, Derek G. Brechin; Visual Effects Supervisor, Jon Farhat; Animattronics and Makeup Effects Designers & Creators, Stan Winston Studio; Stunts, Joe Dunne, Pavel Cajzl; a John Wells Productions, Di Bonaventure Pictures production; British-Czech-German-U.S.; Dolby; Technicolor; Rated R; 100 minutes; American release: October 21, 2005

The Rock, Karl Urban, Rosamund Pike PHOTO COURTESY OF UNIVERSAL

Cast

John Grimm **Karl Urban**
Samantha Grimm **Rosamund Pike**
Destroyer **DeObia Opearei**
Goat **Ben Daniels**
Duke **Raz Adoti**
Portman **Richard Brake**
The Kid **Al Weaver**
Pinky **Dexter Fletcher**
Hell Knight **Brian Steele**
Sarge **The Rock**
Mac **Yao Chin**
Dr. Carmack **Robert Russell**
Lt. Huengs **Daniel York**
Sanford Crosby **Ian Hughes**

and Blanka Jarosova (Dr. Hillary Tallman/Imp), Vladislav Dyntera (Dr. Steve Willits), Petr Hnetkovksy (Dr. Olsen), Jaroslav Psenicka (Dr. Turman), Marek Motlicek (Dr. Clay), Doug Jones (Dr. Carmack Imp/Sewer Imp)

A mercenary team arrives at a remote scientific facility on Mars to ensure that a nightmarish menagerie of creatures that have taken over the planet do not escape.

Miriam Yeung in *Three... Extremes* PHOTO COURTESY OF LIONS GATE

THREE…EXTREMES

(LIONS GATE) an Applause Pictures, CJ Entertainment, Kadokawa Pictures presentation of an Applause Pictures, B.O.M. Film Prod., Kadokawa Pictures production; Hong Kong-Korean-Japanese, 2004; Dolby; Color; Rated R; 125 minutes; American release date: October 28, 2005

DUMPLINGS: Producer, Peter Ho-Sun Chan; Executive Producer, Eric Than; Director, Fruit Chan; Screenplay, Lilian Lee, based on her novella; Photography, Christopher Doyle; Designer, Yee Chung-Man; Costumes, Dora Ng; Music, Chan Kwong-Wing; Editors, Tin Sam-Fat, Chan Ki-Hop; Special Visual Effects, Su Chun-Hung.

    Cast: Miriam Yeung (Qing Li), Bai Ling (Mei), Tony Ka-Fai Leung (Sije Li), Pauline Lau, Meme, Miki Yeung, Wong Su-Fun

CUT: Producer, Ahn Soo-Hyun; Executive Producers, Oh Jung-Wan, Lee Eu-Gene; Director/Screenplay, Park Chan-Wook; Photography, Chung Chung-Hoon; Designer, Yoo Seong-hee; Costumes, Cho Sang-Kyung; Music, Peach; Editors, Kim Sang-Beom, Kim Jae-Bum.

    Cast: Lee Byung-Hun, Kim Won-Hee, Gang Hye-Jung, Lee Jun Goo, Lee Mi Mi

BOX: Producers, Naoki Sato, Shun Shimizu, Fumio Inoue; Executive Producer, Kazuo Kuroi; Director, Takashi Miike; Screenplay, Haruko Fukushima; Story, Bun Saiko; Photography, Koichi Kawakami; Designer, Takashi Sasaki; Music, Koji Endo; Editor, Yasushi Shimamura.

    Cast: Kyoko Hasegawa, Atsuro Watabe, Mai Suzuki, Yuu Suzuki, Mitsuru Akaboshi

Three tales of horror: an aging actress hopes to rejuvenate herself through a magic dumpling; a film director and his wife are taken hostage by a disgruntled extra; and novelist is haunted by a tragedy from her past.

Ali Suliman, Kais Nashef

Kais Nashef, Ali Suliman

PARADISE NOW

(WARNER INDEPEDENT PICTURES) a.k.a. *Al-Jenna-an*; Producers, Hengameh Panahi, Amir Harel, Gerhard Meixner, Roman Paul, Bero Beyer; Director, Hany Abu-Assad; Screenplay, Hany Abu-Assad, Bero Beyer; Photography, Antoine Heberlé; Designer, Olivier Meidinger; Costumes, Walid Maw'ed; Editor, Sander Vos; Casting, Lara Zoabi; an Augustus Film presentation, with Lama Films, Razor Film, Lumen Films, Arte France Cinema, Hazazah Films; Dutch-Israeli-German-French; Dolby; Widescreen; Color; Rated PG-13; 90 minutes; American release date: October 28, 2005

Cast
Saïd **Kais Nashef**
Khaled **Ali Suliman**
Suha **Lubna Azabal**
Jamal **Amer Hlehel**
Saïd's Mother **Hiam Abbass**
Abu-Karem **Ashraf Barhoum**
Abu-Salim **Mohammed Bustami**

Kais Nashef (center), Ali Suliman (right)

Kais Nashef PHOTOS COURTESY OF WARNER INDEPENDENT

Kais Nashef, Hiam Abbass

A look at the lives of two Palestinian suicide bombers leading up to their terrorist mission in Tel Aviv.

This film received an Oscar nomination for foreign language film.

PRIDE & PREJUDICE

(FOCUS) Producers, Tim Bevan, Eric Fellner, Paul Webster; Executive Producers, Debra Hayward, Liza Chasin; Co-Producer, Jane Frazer; Director, Joe Wright; Screenplay, Deborah Moggach; Based on the novel by Jane Austen; Photography, Roman Osin; Designer, Sarah Greenwood; Costumes, Jacqueline Durran; Music, Dario Marianelli; Editor, Paul Tothill; Casting, Jina Jay; a Universal Pictures presentation, in association with StudioCanal, of a Working Title production; British-U.S.; Dolby; Super 35 Widescreen; Deluxe color; Rated PG; 126 minutes; American release date: November 11, 2005

Rosamund Pike, Keira Knightley, Simon Woods

Judi Dench

Cast

Elizabeth Bennet **Keira Knightley**
Mr. Darcy **Matthew Macfadyen**
Mrs. Bennet **Brenda Blethyn**
Mr. Bennet **Donald Sutherland**
William Collins **Tom Hollander**
Lady Catherine de Bourg **Judi Dench**
Jane Bennet **Rosamund Pike**
Lydia Bennet **Jena Malone**
Caroline Bingley **Kelly Reilly**
Charlotte Lucas **Claudie Blakley**
Mr. Gardiner **Peter Wright**

Matthew Macfadyen, Keira Knightley

Mrs. Gardiner **Penelope Wilton**
Charles Bingley **Simon Woods**
Lt. Wickham **Rupert Friend**
Gorgiana Darcy **Tamzin Merchant**

and Talulah Riley (Mary Bennet), Carey Mulligan (Kitty Bennet), Sylvester Morand (Sir William Lucas), Pip Torrens (Netherfield Butler), Janet Whiteside (Mrs. Hill), Sinead Matthews (Betsy), Roy Holder (Mr. Hill), Jay Simpson (Meryton Milliner), Rosamund Stephen (Miss de Bourg), Samantha Bloom (Rosings Governess), Cornelius Booth (Col. Fitzwilliam), Meg Wynn Owen (Mrs. Reynolds), Moya Brady (Lambton Maid)

Strong-willed Elizabeth Bennet finds herself inexplicably drawn to the stand-offish, well-to-do Mr. Darcy. Earlier version was distributed by MGM in 1940 and starred Greer Garson and Laurence Olivier. Modern version *Bride and Prejudice* was released earlier in 2005.

This film received Oscar nominations for actress (Keira Knightley), costume design, art direction, and original score.

Jena Malone, Rupert Friend

Brenda Blethyn, Donald Sutherland

GOOD MORNING, NIGHT

(WELLSPRING) a.k.a. *Buongiorno, notte* ; Producers, Marco Bellocchio, Sergio Pelone; Director, Marco Bellocchio; Screenplay, Marco Bellocchio, Daniela Ceselli; Based on the novel by Anna Laura Braghetti, Paola Tavella; Photography, Pasquale Mari; Designer, Marco Dentici; Costumes, Sergio Ballo; Muisc, Riccardo Giagni; Editor, Francesca Calvelli; Casting, Béatrice Kruger; a Rai Cinemafiction, Filmalbatros S.r.1. production; Italian, 2003; Dolby; Color/black and white; Not rated; 106 minutes; American release date: November 11, 2005

Maya Sansa

Pier Giorgio Bellocchio, Giovanni Calcagno, Maya Sansa, Luigi Lo Cascio

Cast
Mariano **Luigi Lo Cascio**
Chiara **Maya Sansa**
Aldo Moro **Roberto Herlitzka**
Ernesto **Pier Giorgio Bellocchio**
Primo **Giovanni Calcagno**
Enzo **Paolo Briguglia**
Zia di Chiara **Letizia Bellocchio, Maria Luisa Bellocchio**
Paolo VI **Giulio Bosetti**
Sandra **Roberta Spagnuolo**

In 1978, Aldo Moro president of Italy's Democrazia Cristiana, is kidnapped and murdered by the Red Brigade.

Maya Sansa

Maya Sansa, Pier Giorgio Bellocchi, Giovanni Calcagno PHOTOS COURTESY OF WELLSPRING

Cillian Murphy

Cillian Murphy, Laurence Kinlan

BREAKFAST ON PLUTO

(SONY CLASSICS) Producers, Alan Moloney, Neil Jordan, Stephen Wooley; Director, Neil Jordan; Screenplay, Neil Jordan, Patrick McCabe; based on the novel by Patrick McCabe; Photography, Declan Quinn; Designer, Tom Conroy; Costumes, Elmer Ni Mhaoldomhnaigh; Editor, Tony Lawson; Casting, Susie Figgis; a Pathe Pictures presentation, in association with Bord Scannan na hEireann of a Parallel Films, Number 9 Films production; Irish-British; Dolby; Technicolor; Rated R; 130 minutes; American release date: November 16, 2005

Cast

Patrick "Kitten" Braden **Cillian Murphy**
Father Bernard **Liam Neeson**
Bertie **Stephen Rea**
John-Joe **Brendan Gleeson**
Elly Bergin **Eva Birthistle**
Mosher **Liam Cunningham**
Mr. Silky String **Bryan Ferry**
Billy Hatchet **Gavin Friday**
PC Wallis **Ian Hart**
Irwin **Laurence Kinlan**
Ma Braden **Ruth McCabe**
Charlie **Ruth Negga**
Inspector Routledge **Steven Waddington**
and Conor McEvoy (Patrick, 10), Seamus Reilly (Laurence), Sid Young (Elly's Boy), Mark Doherty (Running Bear), Ciaran Nolan (Horse Killane), Eamonn Owens (Jackie Timlin), Tony Devlin (White Dove), Bianca O'Connor (Charlie, 10), Charlene McKenna (Caroline Braden), Jo Jo Finn (Squaddie), Neil Jackson (Soldier), Paraic Breathnach (Benny Feely), James McHale (Biker No. 1), Owen Roe (Dean), Mary Coughlan (Housekeeper), Mary Regan (Mrs. Feely), Patrick McCabe (Peepers Egan), Gerry O'Brien, Chris McHallem (Punters), Peter Gowan (Brother Barnabas), Antonia Campbell-Hughes (Stripper), Jonathan Ryan (Garda), Chris Robinson (Orderly), Rynagh O'Grady (Mrs. Coyle), Derek Elroy (Rasta Son), Britta Smith (Mrs. Clarke), Doreen Keogh (Assistant in Haberdashery), Tom Hickey (Bishop), Malcolm Douglas (Bishop's

Ruth Negga, Cillian Murphy

Secretary), Emmet Lawlor McHugh (Irwin, 10), Steve Blount (Bouncer #1), Morne Botes (Jason), Rachel Donovan (Nurse), Kathryn Pogson (Mrs. Henderson)

The many adventures of the androgynous Kitten Braden as he searches the British Isles for the mother he has never known.

Brendan Gleeson PHOTO COURTESY OF SONY CLASSICS

THE LIBERTINE

(WEINSTEIN CO.) Producers, Lianne Halfon, John Malkovich, Russell Smith; Executive Producers, Chase Bailey, Steve Christian, Marc Samuelson, Peter Samuelson, Ralph Kamp, Louise Goodsill; Director, Laurence Dunsmore; Screenplay, Stephen Jeffreys, based on his play; Photography, Alexander Melman; Designer, Ben Van Os; Costumes, Dien van Straalen; Music, Michael Nyman; Editor, Jill Bilcock; Hair/Makeup Designer, Peter Owen; Casting, Mary Selway, Lucy Bevan; an Odyssey Entertainment presentation, in association with the Isle of Man, of a Mr. Mudd production; British-U.S.; Dolby; Super 35 Widescreen; Color; Rated R; 114 minutes; American release date: November 25, 2005

Johnny Depp

Cast

Earl of Rochester **Johnny Depp**
Elizabeth Barry **Samantha Morton**
King Charles II **John Malkovich**
Elizabeth Malet **Rosamund Pike**
Sir George Etherege **Tom Hollander**
Charles Sackville **Johnny Vegas**
Jane **Kelly Reilly**
Harris **Jack Davenport**
Alcock **Richard Coyle**
Countess **Francesca Annis**
Billy Downs **Rupert Friend**
Molly Luscombe **Claire Higgins**
Chiffinch **Paul Ritter**
Keowen **Stanley Townsend**
Ratcliffe **Hugh Sachs**
Vaughan **Tom Burke**
Rose **Trudi Jackson**
Betterton **Freddie Jones**
Huysmans **Robert Wilfort**
Sackville's Servant **Jake Curran**
Barrillon **Paul Chahidi**
Constable **Kevin Doyle**
Trooper **Morgan Walters**
Chaplain **Niall Buddy**

Rosamund Pike, Johnny Depp

and Peter Howell (Bishop), T. P. McKenna (Black Rod), Louis Bawden (Orange Seller), Susie Gossling Valerio, Julia Hickman (Dancers), Cara Horgan, Maimie McCoy, Liam McKenna, Habib Nasib Nader, Laurence Spellman (Acting Troop), Shane MacGowan (17th Century Bard), Davo Brandon McKenzie (Pie Seller)

The true story of the Earl of Rochester, a 17th century poet who debauched himself to an early grave.

Samantha Morton, Johnny Depp PHOTOS COURTESY OF WEINSTEIN COMPANY

MRS. PALFREY AT THE CLAREMONT

(CINEVILLE) Producers, Lee Caplin, Zachary Matz, Carl Colpaert; Executive Producer, Gustavas Prinz; Co-Executive Producers, Martin Donovan, Harry Gregson Williams; Screenplay, Dan Ireland; Screenplay, Ruth Sacks; Based on the novel by Elizabeth Taylor; Photography, Claudio Rocha; Designer, Julian Nagel; Costumes, Maja Meschede; Music, Stephen Barton; Editor, Nigel Galt, Virginia Katz; a Picture Entertainment production; British; Dolby; Color; Not rated; 108 minutes; American release date: November 25, 2005

Cast

Mrs. Palfrey **Joan Plowright**
Ludovic "Ludo" Meyer **Rupert Friend**
Gwendolyn **Zoe Tapper**
Mrs. Arbuthnot **Anna Massey**
Mr. Osborne **Robert Lang**
Mrs. Post **Marcia Warren**
Mrs. Burton **Georgina Hale**
Mrs. De Salis **Millicent Martin**
Willie De Salis **Michael Culkin**
Elizabeth **Anna Carteret**
Desmond **Lorcan O'Toole**

Rupert Friend, Joan Plowright

Rupert Friend

Joan Plowright PHOTOS COURTESY OF CINEVILLE

Rupert Friend, Joan Plowright

and Clare Higgins (Mrs. Meyer), Emma Pike (Violet), Carl Proctor (The Manager), Sophie Linfield (Rosie), Olivia Caffrey (Nurse Clara)

A widow's lonely days in residence at the senior-oriented Claremont Hotel are brightened by a young aspiring writer whom she passes off as her grandson.

Patrick Flueger, Anthony Hopkins

THE WORLD'S FASTEST INDIAN

(MAGNOLIA) Producers, Roger Donaldson, Gary Hannam; Executive Producers, Masaharu Inaba, Charles Hannah, Megumi Fukasawa, Satoru Iseki, Barrie M. Osborne; Co-Producer, John J. Kelly; Director/Screenplay, Roger Donaldson; Photography, David Gribble; Designers, J. Dennis Washington (U.S.), Rob Gillies (N.Z.); Costumes, Nancy Cavallaro (U.S.), Jane Holland (N.Z.); Music, J. Peter Robinson; Editor, John Gilbert; Casting, Dianne Crittenden (U.S.), Diana Rowan (N.Z.); an OLC/Rights Entertainment, Tanlay, the New Zealand Film Production Fund, the New Zealand Film Commission presentation in association with 3 Dogs & a Pony of a Roger Donaldson, Gary Hannam production; New Zealand; Dolby; Panavision; FotoKem/Atlab color; Rated PG-13 ; 127 minutes; American release date: December 7, 2005

Cast
Burt Munro **Anthony Hopkins**
Ada **Diane Ladd**
Tom **Aaron Murphy**
Fernando **Paul Rodriguez**
Fran **Annie Whittle**
Tina Washington **Chris Williams**
Jim Moffet **Chris Lawford**
Wendy **Jessica Cauffiel**
Jake **Saginaw Grant**
Bob Higby **Chris Bruno**

and Carlos Lacamara (Cabbie), Patrick Flueger (Rusty), Walton Goggins (Marty Dickerson), Bruce Greenwood (Jerry), Joe Howard (Otto Donner), Gavin Grazer (Mike), William Lucking (Rolly Free), Eric Pierpoint (Earl), Laruel Moglen (Ali), Iain Rea (George), Tessa Mitchell (Sarah), Tim Shadbolt (Frank), Greg Johnson (Duncan), Antony Starr (Jeff), Kate Sullivan (Doris), Craig Hall (Antarctic Angel), Jim Bowman (Cook), Alison Bruce (Doctor), Phoebe Falconer (Janice), Charles Pierard (Bank Manager), Bill Richardson (Burt's Neighbor), Mick Rose (Brian), Tony Wilson (Captain), Wesley Dowdell (Troy), Todd Emerson (Purser), Daniel Sing (Ken), Mark Ruka (Crewman), Campbell Cooley (Engineer), James Gaylyn (Customs Official), Latham Gaines (Passport Officer), Steve

O'Neill (Interrogating Officer), Dan Moody (Second Officer), Martha Carter (Girl), Noelle Lee Kaine (Hooker), Kristen Marie Hullinger (Waitress), Tom Jacobsen, David Stevens (Clerks), Charles Halford (Gas Station Attendant #2), Mark Holodziej, Jr. (Kid), James Stevens (Attendant), Juliana Bellinger (Jackie), Annette Wright (Rhonda), Morgan Lund (Leroy the Cowboy), Bill Osborne (Cop), Tim Farmer (Warren), Michael Mantell (Glenn), Nicholas Lanier (Bystander), Brian Clark, Christ Kendrick (Nevada Cops), Lana Antonova (Sexy Woman in Pink), Joseph Hamilton (Passenger), Jim Jepson, Aaro Njustesen (Jim's Crew), Grant Lee Peterson (Binocular Guy), Aaron Radl (Official), Tim Sabuco (Mechanic), Bijan Zaimi (Black Widow Driver)

The true story of how 72-year-old Burt Murno rode his Indian Scout motorcycle across Utah's Bonneville Flats to set a world record. This film's director, Roger Donaldson, also directed the 1971 documentary *Offerings to the God of Speed* about the same subject.

Anthony Hopkins, Chris Lawford

Aaron Murphy, Anthony Hopkins PHOTOS COURTESY OF MAGNOLIA

MRS. HENDERSON PRESENTS

(WEINSTEIN CO.) Producer, Norma Heyman; Executive Producers, Bob Hoskins, David Aukin; Executive Producers for BBC Films, David M. Thompson, Tracey Scoffield; Executive Producers for Pathé, Francois Ivernel, Cameron McCracken; Director, Stephen Frears; Screenplay, Martin Sherman; Photography, Andrew Dunn; Designer, Hugo Luczc-Wyhowski; Costumes, Sandy Powell; Music, George Fenton; Editor, Lucia Zucchetti; Choreographers, Eleanor Fazan, Debbie Astell; Special Effects Supervisor, Graham Longhurst; Casting, Leo Davis; a Pathé Pictures, BBC Films presentation in association with Future Films, Micro-Fusion, the Weinstein Co., U.K. Film Council of a Heyman Hoskins production; British; Dolby; Technicolor; Rated R; 103 minutes; American release date: December 9, 2005

Kelly Reilly

Cast

Laura Henderson **Judi Dench**
Vivian Van Damm **Bob Hoskins**
Bertie **Will Young**
Lord Cromer **Christopher Guest**
Maureen **Kelly Reilly**
Lady Conway **Thelma Barlow**

and Anna Brewster (Doris), Rosalind Halstead (Frances), Sarah Solemani (Vera), Natalia Tena (Peggy), Sir Thomas Allen (Eric Woodburn), Richard Syms (Ambrose), Ralph Nossek (Leslie Pearkes), Camille O'Sullivan (Jane), Doraly Rosen (Maggie), Matthew Hart (Frank Lawson), Tony De La Fou (Victor Thornton), Dorian Ford (Christian), Lloyd Hutchinson (Harry), Toby Jones (Gordon), Christopher Logan (Ken), Michael Culkin (Lord Cromer's Secretary), Samuel Barnett (Paul), Dinah O'Brien, Maria Rohsean O'Brien, Rebecca O'Brien (The Deering Sisters), Richard Dormer (Comic), Shona McWilliams (Gracie Kramer), Waris Hussein (Maharajah), Antony Carrick, Ann Queensberry (Mourners), Anne Lambton (Chairwoman), Sandy McDade (Civil Servant), Andrzej Borkowski (Count Banderdene), Joseph Long (Harry), Billy Seymour (Serviceman), Matt Blair (G.I.), Patrick Kennedy (Pilot), Patti Love (Natalie Van Damm), Elise Audeyev, Vanessa Barmby, Sophie Brown, Vicki Davids, Charlene Ford, Frances Garvey, Victoria Hay, Rachel Lawrence, Kate Power, Melody Squire (Millerettes), Ciaran Connolly, Joseph McMurray (Chorus Boys)

Kelly Reilly, Judi Dench

Widowed Laura Henderson buys London's shuttered Windmill Theatre and turns it into a popular destination for soldiers during World War II because of her idea to include nudity in her revues.

This film received Oscar nominations for actress (Dench) and costume design.

Bob Hoskins, Judi Dench PHOTOS COURTESY OF WEINSTEIN COMPANY

THE WHITE COUNTESS

(SONY CLASSICS) Producer, Ismail Merchant; Executive Producers, Andre Morgan, Patrick Ko; Co-Producers, Paul Bradley, Richard Hawley; Director, James Ivory; Screenplay, Kazuo Ishiguro; Photography, Christopher Doyle; Designer, Andrew Sanders; Costumes, John Bright; Music, Richard Robbins; Editor, John David Allen; Casting, Celestia Fox; a Merchant Ivory Prods., Shanghai Film Group Corp. presentation of a VIP Medienfonds 3 production; British-U.S.-German-Canadian; Dolby; Color; Rated PG-13; 135 minutes; American release date: December 21, 2005

Ralph Fiennes, Natasha Richardson

Hiroyuki Sanada, Ralph Fiennes

Allan Corduner, Natasha Richardson

Cast
Todd Jackson **Ralph Fiennes**
Sofia Belinsky **Natasha Richardson**
Aunt Sara **Vanessa Redgrave**
Olga **Lynn Redgrave**
Greshenka **Madeleine Potter**
Matsuda **Hiroyuki Sanada**
Uncle Peter **John Wood**
Samuel Feinstein **Allan Corduner**
Kao **Ying Da**
Katya **Madeleine Daly**
Frenchman **Dan Herzberg**
Crane **Lee Pace**
Russian Singer **Pierre Seznec**
Liu **Luoyong Wang**
Maria **Aislin McGucklin**
Dancing Harlequin **Kyle Rothstein**

In 1936 Shanghai a blind American buys a nightclub and invites an impoverished Russian countess-turned-prostitute to serve as the club's hostess.

Ralph Fiennes, Natasha Richardson, Madeleine Daly PHOTOS COURTESY OF SONY CLASSICS

CACHE (HIDDEN)

(SONY CLASSICS) Producers, Margaret Menegoz, Veit Heiduschka; Co-Producers, Michael Weber, Valerio De Paolis; Director/Screenplay, Michael Haneke; Photography, Christian Berger; Designers, Emmanuel De Chauvigny, Christoph Kanter; Editors, Michael Hudecek, Madine Muse; a Les Films du Losange (France), Wega Film (Austria), Bavaria Film (Germany), Bim Distribuzione (Italy) co-production; French-Austrian-German-Italian; Dolby; Color; Rated R; 111 minutes; American release date: December 23, 2005

Nathalie Richard, Daniel Duval

Daniel Auteuil, Juliette Binoche

Lester Makedonsky

Cast
Georges Laurent **Daniel Auteuil**
Anne Laurent **Juliette Binoche**
Georges' Mom **Annie Girardot**
Majid **Maurice Bénichou**
Georges' Editor-in-Chief **Bernard Le Coq**
Majid's Son **Walid Afkir**
Pierrot Laurent **Lester Makedonsky**
Pierre **Daniel Duval**
Mathilde **Nathalie Richard**
Yvon **Denis Podalydès**
Chantal **Aïssa Maïga**
Nurse **Caroline Baehr**

and Christian Benedetti (Georges' Father, Young), Philippe Besson, Jean-Jacques Brochier, Mazarine Pingeot, Jean Teulé (TV Guests), Laurent Suire, Loïc Brabant (Police Officers), Paule Daré (The Orphanage Attendant), Louis-Do de Lencquesaing (Bookstore Owner), Annette Faure (Georges' Mother, Young), Hugo Flamigni (Georges as a Child), Peter Stephan Jungk (Writer), Diouc Koma (Cyclist), Marie Kremer (Jeannette), Nicky Marbot (The Orphanage Driver), Malik Nait Djoudi (Majid as a Child), Marie-Christine Orry (Housekeeper), Julie Recoing (Georges' Assistant), Karla Suarez (Novelist)

Bernard Le Coq, Daniel Auteuil PHOTOS COURTESY OF SONY CLASSICS

TV host Georges Laurent and his wife Anne are disturbed to receive a videotape of the outside of their house being watched over a period of time, suggesting someone is checking up on their lives for a reason.

Katia Golubeva in *The Intruder*

THE INTRUDER

(WELLSPRING) a.k.a. *L'Intrus*; Producer, Humbert Balsan; Executive Producer, Jean-Marie Gindraux; Director, Claire Denis; Screenplay, Clare Denis, Jean-Pol Fargeau, Jean-Luc Nanvy; Photography, Agnès Godard; Designer, Arnaud de Moleron; Costumes, Judy Shrewsbury; Music, S. A. Staples; Editor, Nelly Quettier; an Ognon Pictures, Arte France Cinema production; French; Dolby; Color; Not rated; 130 minutes; American release date: December 23, 2005

Cast

Louis Trebor **Michel Subor**
Sidney **Grégoire Colin**
Young Russian Woman **Katia Golubeva**
Pharmacist **Bambou**
Antoinette **Florence Loiret-Caille**
The Wild Woman **Lolita Chammah**
The Priest **Alex Descas**

and Kim Dong-Ho (Ship Owner), Chang Se-tak (Ship Owner's Associate), Park Hong-suk (Man at Fish Market), Edwin Alin (Hardware Store Patron), Henri Tetainanuaril (Henri), Jean-Marc Teriipaia (Tony), Anna Tetuaveroa (The Mother), Béatrice Dalle (Queen of the Northern Hemisphere)

A heart transplant patient searches the world for his long lost son.

Michel Subor in *The Intruder* PHOTO COURTESY IF OGNON PICTURES

WOLF CREEK

(WEINSTEIN CO.) Producers, Greg Mclean, David Lightfoot; Executive Producers, Matt Hearn, Gary Hamilton, Simon Hewitt, Martin Fabinyi, George Adams, Michael Gudinski; Director/Screenplay, Greg Mclean; Photography, Will Gibson; Designer, Robert Webb; Costumes, Nicola Dunn; Music, Francois Tetaz; Editor, Jason Ballentine; Special Makeup Effects, Connelly Make-Up FX Team; Casting, Angela Heesom; a Dimension Pictures release of a True Crime Channel production in association with Darclight Films, Mushroom Pictures, Arclight Films, Film Finance Corp. Australia, 403 Films, South Australian Film Commission; Australian; Dolby; Color; HD-to-35mm; Rated R; 95 minutes; American release date: December 25, 2005

Kestie Morassi in *Wolf Creek* PHOTO COURTESY OF WEINSTEIN COMPANY

Cast

Mick Taylor **John Jarratt**
Ben Mitchell **Nathan Phillips**
Liz Hunter **Cassandra Magrath**
Kristy Earl **Kestie Morassi**
Police Officer **Peter Alchin**
Bazza **Andy McPhee**

and Guy Petersen, Jenny Starwall (Swedish Backpackers), Gordon Poole (Attendant), Aaron Sterns (Bazza's Mate)

Three friends on a trip through Australia find their lives in peril when their car breaks down near Wolf Creek National Park and they are captured by a menacing bushman.

MATCH POINT

(DREAMWORKS) Producers, Letty Aronson, Gareth Wiley, Lucy Darwin; Executive Producer, Stephen Tenenbaum; Director/Screenplay, Woody Allen; Co-Producers, Helen Robin, Nicky Kentish Barnes; Co-Executive Producers, Jack Rollins, Charles H. Joffe; Photography, Remi Adefarasin; Designer, Jim Clay; Costumes, Jill Taylor; Editor, Alisa Lepelter; Casting, Juliet Taylor, Gail Stevens, Patricia Kerrigan DiCerto; a Jada production, presented in association with BBC Films, Thema Production SA; British; Dolby; Technicolor; Rated R; 124 minutes; American release date: December 28, 2005

Jonathan Rhys Meyers, Matthew Goode, Scarlett Johansson

Jonathan Rhys Meyers, Rupert Penry-Jones

Penelope Wilton

Cast
Chris Wilton **Jonathan Rhys Meyers**
Nola Rice **Scarlett Johansson**
Chloe Hewett Wilton **Emily Mortimer**
Tom Hewett **Matthew Goode**
Alec Hewett **Brian Cox**
Eleanor Hewett **Penelope Wilton**
Mrs. Eastby **Margaret Tyzack**
Detective Parry **Steve Pemberton**
Inspector Dowd **Ewen Bremner**
Detective Banner **James Nesbitt**
Mr. Townsend **Alexander Armstrong**
Estate Agent **Paul Kaye**
La Traviata Performers **Janis Kelly, Alan Oke**
Ping-Pong Player **Mark Gatiss**
Waiter **Philip Mansfield**
Rod Carver **Simon Kunz**
Alan Sinclair **Geoffrey Streatfield**
Rigoletto Performer **Mary Hegarty**
John the Chauffeur **John Fortune**
Henry **Rupert Penry-Jones**

Brian Cox, Jonathan Rhys Meyers

Tennis instructor Chris Wilton finds himself in a dicey position when he marries well-to-do Chloe Hewett while carrying on an affair with her brother's girl-friend, Nola.

This film received an Oscar nomination for original screenplay.

Jonathan Rhys Meyers, Emily Mortimer PHOTOS COURTESY OF DREAMWORKS

HITLER'S HIT PARADE

(DEUTSCHE MODERNE FILMKINST) Producer, C. Cay Wesnigk; Directors, Oliver Axer, Susanne Benze; Digital Post-Production Director, Klaus Schafer; a C. Cay Wesnigk Filmproduckion production in association with ZDF/Arte; German, 2004; Black and white/color; Not rated; 76 minutes; American release date: January 5, 2005. Documentary in which the Third Reich is seen through the eyes of German citizens of the time.

TRAVELERS AND MAGICIANS

(ZEITGEIST) Producers, Malcolm Watson, Raymond Steiner; Executive Producer, Jeremy Thomas; Director/Screenplay, Khyentse Norbu; Photography, Alan Kozlowski; Designer, Raymond Steiner; Costumes, Claudia Bahls; Editor, Andrew McCormick; a Prayer Flag Pictures production; Australian-Bhutan, 2003; Dolby; Color; Not rated; 108 minutes; American release date: January 7, 2005. CAST: Tsewang Dandup (Dondup), Sonam Lhamo (Sonam), Lhakpa Dorji (Tashi), Deki Yangzom (Deki), Sonam Kinga (The Monk), Sumcho Budha (Kingzang Wangchuk), Lama Yeshi Dendup, Pelden Dorji (Magic Students), Ap Dochu (Appleman), Namgay Dorjee (Karma), Jigme Drukpa (Phunsok), Venerable Lungataen Gyatso (Magic Teacher)

Hitler's Hit Parade PHOTO COURTESY OF DEUTSCHE MODERNE

ABOUT BAGHDAD

(ARAB FILM DISTRIBUTION) Producer, Adam Shapiro; Directors, Sinan Antoon, Adam Shapiro; Photography, Suzy Salamy, Bassam Haddad, Maya Mikdashi, Adam Shapiro; Music, Amer Tawfiq; Editor, Carol Mansour; from InCounter Productions; Iraqi-U.S.; Color; Not rated; 90 minutes; American release date: January 12, 2005. Documentary in which an exiled Iraqi writer interviews citizens of Baghdad, with Sinan Antoon.

APPLESEED

(GENEON) Producers, Fumihiko Sori, Hidenori Ueki, Naoko Watanabe; Executive Producer, Sumiji Miyake; Director, Shinji Aramaki; Screenplay, Haruka Handa, Tsutomu Kamishiro; Based on the manga by Masamune Shirow; Character Designer, Masaki Yamada; Background Designer, Nobuhito Sue; CG Producer, Yusaku Toyoshima; Music, Paul Oakenfeold, Ryuichi Sakamoto, T. Raumschmiere; a Micott & Basara, TBS, Geneone Entertainment, Yamato, Toho, TYO, Digital Frontier, MBS production; Japanese, 2003; Dolby; Color; Not rated; 105 minutes; American release date: January 14, 2005. VOICE CAST: Mia Bradly (Hitomi), James Lyon (Briareos), Jennifer Proud (Deunan Knute), Jack Aubree, Frederick Bloggs, Russell Thor, William Frederick, Steve Kramer, Michael McConnohie, Melissa Williamson, William Markham, John Smallberries, Ray Michaels, Deborah Sale Butler, David Lelyveld

MACHUCA

(MENEMSHA) Producers, Gerardo Herrero, Mamoun Hassan, Andres Wood; Director, Andres Wood; Screenplay, Roberto Brodsky, Mamoun Hassan, Andres Wood; Photography, Miguel J. Littin; Designer, Rodrigo Bazaes; Costumes, Maya Mora; Music, Miguel Angel Miranda, Jose Miguel Tobar; Editor, Fernando Pardo; Casting, Carlos Johnson; an Andres Wood Producciones

Deki Yangzom in *Travelers and Magicians* PHOTO COURTESY OF ZEITGEIST FILMS

(Chile), Tornasol Films (Spain), Mamoun Hassan (U.K.), Paraiso (France) production in association with Chilefilms, with the participation of Canal Plus Spain, Television Espanola; Chilean-Spanish-British-French, 2004; Dolby; Color; Not rated; 121 minutes; American release date: January 19, 2005. CAST: Matías Quer (Gonzalo Infante), Ariel Mateluna (Pedro Machuca), Manuela Martelli (Silvana), Ernesto Malbran (Father McEnroe), Aline Küppenheim (María Luisa Infante), Federico Luppi (Roberto Ochagavía (Federico Luppi), Francisco Reyes (Patricio Infante), Luis Dubó (Ismael Machuca), Tamara Acosta (Juana), Maria Olga Matte (Miss Gilda), Gabriela Medina (Lucy), Tiago Correa (Pablo), Alejandro Trejo (Willi), Andrea García-Huidobro (Isabel), Pablo Krögh (Colonel Sotomayor), Sebastian Trautmann (Gaston)

WATERMARKS

(KINO) Producers, Yaron Zilberman, Yonatan Israel; Co-Producer, Philippa Kowarsky; Director/Screenplay, Yaron Zilberman; Photography, Tom Hurwitz; Editors, Ruben Korenfeld, Yuval Shar; a Yofi Films, Cinephil (Israel), Jetlag Films (U.S.), Zadig Prods. (France) production, in association with Arte, ORF, HBO/Cinemax, Keshet Broadcast; Israeli-U.S.-French, 2004; Dolby; Color/black and white; DigiBeta/Super 16-to-35mm; Not rated; 80 minutes; American release date: January 21, 2005. Documentary on Vienna's Haokah sports club who made it their goal to train Jewish athletes to beat gentiles at swimming, in order to prove Hitler wrong about their inferiority at the sport; featuring Judith Haspel, Trude Hirschler, Anni Lampl, Hanni Lux, Ann Marie Pisker, Nanne Selinger, Greta Stanton, Elisheva Susz.

SHE'S ONE OF US

(LEISURE TIME FEATURES) a.k.a. *Elle est des nôtres* and *For She's a Jolly Good Fellow*; Producer, Béatrice Caufman; Director, Siegrid Alnoy; Screenplay, Siegrid Alnoy, Jérôme Beaujour, François Favrat; Photography, Christophe Pollock; Designer, Michel Vandestien; Costumes, Mic Cheminal; Music, Gabriel Scotti; Editor, Benoît Quinon; a BC Films, Rhone-Alpes Cinéma production, in association with Gimages 5, with the participation of Canal Plus, Centre National de la Cinématographie; French, 2004; Color; Not rated; 100 minutes; American release date: January 21, 2005. CAST: Sasha Andres (Christine Blanc), Catherine Mouchet (Patricia), Carlo Brandt (Degas), Eric Caravaca (Eric), Pierre-Félix Gravière (Sébastien), Daniel Ceccaldi (Christine's Father), Jacques

Watermarks PHOTO COURTESY OF KINO INTERNATIONAL

Sasha Andres, Pierre-Félix Gravière in *She's One of Us* PHOTO COURTESY OF LEISURE TIME FEATURES

Spiesser (Danjard), Mireille Roussel (Pascale), Pascal Cervo (Police Receptionist), Alexis Perret (Employment Agent), Dominique Valdadié (Marie-Noelle), Clotilde Mollet (Carole), Stanislas Stanic (Inspector Brebion), Rodolphe Congé (Inspector Cazalis), Marcial Di Fonzo Bo (Customer), Laurent Pointrenaux (Jean-Michel), Nathalie Pescançon (Waitress), Thomas Chabrol (Manager), Hélène Alexandridis (Saleswoman), Delphine Elliet (Accountant), Laurent Bateau (Promocash Employee), Florence Viala (Continent Cashier), Violaine Schwartz (Continent Client), Agathe Dronne (Promocash Secretary), Lise Lamétrie (Pool Cashier), Geneviève Mnich (Christine's Mother), Valérie de Dietrich (Sonia), Monique Couturier (Mme. Imbert)

ARMY OF ONE

(RED STORM PRODS.) Producers, Sarah Goodman, Erik Paulsson, Arlene Ami; Consulting Producer, Brad Lichtenstein; Director/Screenplay, Sarah Goodman; Photography, Andrew Bowley, Alexandra Kondracke; Music, Paul Watson, Mark Stewart; Editor, Caroline Christie; from Fovea Productions; Canadian-U.S.; Color; Not rated; 69 minutes; American release date: January 26, 2005. Documentary on joining the army; featuring Sara Miller, Thaddeus Ressler, Nelson Reyes.

Matías Quer, Manuela Martelli, Ariel Mateluna in *Machuca* PHOTO COURTESY OF MENEMSHA FILMS

Jacqueline Bisset, Adam Garcia in *Fascination* PHOTO COURTESY OF MGM

FASCINATION

(MGM) Producer/Director/Screenplay, Klaus Menzel; Based on a screenplay by Daryl Haney, John Jacobs; Executive Producers, Ingo Deinert, Armin Stieler; Co-Producer, Peter McRae; Line Producer, Edward Cathell III; Photography, Reinhart Peschke; Designer, Marc Greville-Masson; Costumes, Susanna Puisto; Music, John Du Prez; Editor, Toby Yates; Casting, Lucy Jenkins, Gary Davies, Leonard Finger; a Quality Films, Classicmap production; German-British, 2004; Dolby; Color; Rated R: 95 minutes; American release date: January 28, 2005. CAST: Jacqueline Bisset (Maureen), Adam Garcia (Scott Doherty), Alice Evans (Kelly Vance), James Naughton (Patrick Doherty), Stuart Wilson (Oliver Vance), Craig Cady (Philip Shields), Vincent Castellanos (District Attorney), Jaime Bello (Martin Earnhardt), Ann Michele Fitzgerald (Sammi Russell), Ted Richard, Gary-Michael Davies (Detectives), Cucho Viera (Pharmacist), William Sloan (E.R. Doctor), Elia Enid Cadilla (Justice of the Peace), Idee B. Charriez Millet (Nurse), J. C. Love (Doctor)

FEAR X

(SILVER NITRATE) Producer, Henrik Danstrup; Executive Producers, Kenneth D. Plummer, Joseph Cohen, Gary Phillips, Mark Vennis, Donald C. Archbold, Nadia Redier; Director, Nicolas Winding Refn; Screenplay, Nicolas Winding Refn, Hubert Selby Jr.; Photography, Larry J. Smith; Designer, Peter De Neergaard; Costumes, Darena Snowe; Music, Brian Eno, J. Peter Schwaim; Editor, Anne Osterud; Casting, Penny Perry; a Moviehouse Entertainment presentation of a NWR/ApS, FearX Ltd. production; Danish-British-Canadian, 2003; Dolby; Widescreen; Color; Rated PG-13; 91 minutes; American release date: January 28, 2005. CAST: John Turturro (Harry), Deborah Kara Unger (Kate), Stephen McIntyre (Phil), William Allen Young (Agent Lawrence), Eugene M. Davis (Ed), Mark Houghton (Diner Cop), Jacqueline Ramel (Claire), James Remar (Peter), Frank Adamson (Adamson), Sharon Bajer (Sally), Megan Basaraba (Amy), John Bluethner (Steadman), Gerry Caplap (Steve), Kekoa Charlot (Directory Voice), Thane Chartrand (Agent Wolfson), Liv Corfixen (Hotel Waitress), Victor Cowie (Bill Craven), Spencer Duncanson (Man), Fradley Garner (Radio Voice), Robert Huculak (Roger), Jennifer Lynn Keef (Dept. of Tourism Voice), Susan Kelso (Mrs. Craven), Jeffrey R. Lawrence (Sgt. Frank), Nadia Litz (Ellen), Brock MacGregor (Quinn), Amanda Ooms (Prostitute), Dan K. Toth (Hotel Clerk), Garfield Williams (Guard)

DAYBREAK

(NEWMARKET) a.k.a. *Om jag vänder mig om*; Producer, Clas Gunnarsson; Executive Producer, Mattias Nohrborg; Director/Screenplay, Björn Runge; Photography, Ulf Brantås; Art Director, Catarina Schiffer; Costumes, Anna Ågren; Music, Ulf Dageby; Editor, Lena Dahlberg; Casting, Sophia Olsson; an Auto Images, Film i Väst production; Swedish, 2003; Dolby; Color; Rated R; 108 minutes; American release date: February 2, 2005. CAST: Pernilla August (Agnes), Jakob Eklund (Rickard), Marie Richardson (Sofie), Leif Andrée (Mats), Peter Andersson (Olof), Ann Petrén (Anita), Sanna Krepper (Petra), Ingvar Hirdvall (Knut), Marika Lindström (Mona), Magnus Krepper (Anders), Camilla Larsson (Helen), Johan Kvanrnström (Jonas), Angelica Olsson (Hanna), Hampus Penttinen (Peter), Peter Lorentzon (Torsten)

Marika Lindström, Ingvar Hirdvall in *Daybreak* PHOTO COURTESY OF NEWMARKET

OH! UOMO

(INDEPENDENT) Producers/Directors/Screenplay/Editors, Yervant Gianikian, Angela Ricci Lucchi; Solo Voice, Giovanna Marini; a Trento Historical Museum, Rovereto War Museum, Province of Trento, City of Rovereto, Fallen of Rovereto Foundation production; Italian, 2004; Black and white; Not rated; 71 minutes; American release date: February 3, 2005. Documentary/montage of archival images from World War I showing the devastating effects of the conflict.

BLACK

(YASH RAJ FILMS) Producers, Anshumaan Shwami, Sanjay Leela Bhansali; Director, Sanjay Leela Bhansali; Screenplay, Bhavani Iyer, Prakash Kapadia, Sanjay Leela Bhansali; Photography, Ravi K. Chandran; Art Director, Omung Kumar; Costumes, Sabyasachi; Background Music, Monty; Lyrics, Prasoon Joshi; an Applause Entertainment, SLB Films production; Indian; Dolby; Widescreen; Color; Not rated; 124 minutes; American release date: February 4, 2005. CAST: Amitabh Bachchan (Debraj Sahai), Rani Mukherjee (Michelle McNally), Shernaz Patel (Catherine McNally), Ayesha Kapoor (Young Michelle McNally), Dhritiman Chatterjee (Paul McNally), Sillo Majava (Mrs. Gomes), Mahabanoo Mody-Kotwal (Mrs. Nair), Chippy Gangjee (Principal Fernades), Salomi Roy Kapur (Martha), Kenny Desai (Dr. Mehta), Arif Shah (Marc Brugger), Bomie E. Dotiwala (Mr. Brugger), Jeroo Shroff (Mrs. Brugger), Shehnaz Anand (Teacher), Polly Shroff (Nun), Richard Lane Smith (Priest), Marriane Deruz

(Singer at Party), Bomi Kapadia, Kamal Adib, Zul Vellani (Trustees), Tiara Gandhi (Baby Sara), Trish Xavier (Baby Michelle), Nandana Sen (Sarah McNally)

THE NOMI SONG

(PALM PICTURES) Producers, Thomas Mertens, Annette Piscane, Andrew Horn; Director/Screenplay, Andrew Horn; Photography, Mark Daniels; Designer, Ruth Peyser; Editors, Angela Christlieb, Guido Krajewski; a CV Films, Cameo Filmproduktion, ZDF/Arte productions with the support of Film Stifung NRW; German, 2004; Dolby; Color/black and white; DigiBeta-to-35mm; Not rated; 99 minutes; American release date: February 4, 2005. Documentary on German stage artiste Klaus Nomi; featuring Ann Magnuson, Gabriele Lafari, David McDermott, Page Wood, Tony Frere, Man Parrish, Kristian Hoffman, Ron Johnsen, Kenny Scharf, Anthony Scibelli, Alan Platt, Adrian, Joseph Arias, Calvin Churchman, Jay Jay French, Michael Halsband, Janus, Pamela Rosenthal, Ira Siff

BAD GUY

(LIFESIZE ENTERTAINMENT) a.k.a. *Nabbeun namja*; Producer, Lee Seung-jae; Executive Producer, Kim Seung-beom; Director/Screenplay, Kim Ki-duk; Photography, Hwang Cheol-hyeon; Music, Park Ho-jun; Editor, Hang Seong-won; a LJ Film production; South Korean, 2001; Color; Not rated; 100 minutes; American release date: February 11, 2005. CAST: Jo Jae-hyeon (Han-ki), Seo Won (Sun-hwa), Kim Yun-tae (Yun-tae), Choi Duek-mun (Myoung-soo), Choi Yoon-young (Hyun-ja), Shin Yoo-jin (Min-jung), Kim Jung-yeong (Eun-hye), Nam Gung-Min (Hyun-su)

Jo Jae-hyeon, Seo Won in *Bad Guy* PHOTO COURTESY OF LIFESIZE ENTERTAINMENT

MY MOTHER'S SMILE

(NEW YORKER) a.k.a. *L'ora di religione*; Producers, Marco Bellocchio, Sergio Pelone; Director/Screenplay, Marco Bellocchio; Photography, Pasquale Mari; Designer, Marco Dentiel; Costumes, Sergio Ballo; Music, Riccardo Giagni; Editor, Francesca Calvelli; Casting, Beatrice Kruger; a co-production of Rai Cinemafiction, Filmalbatros, and Tele+; Italian, 2003; Dolby; Color; Not rated; 103 minutes; American release date: February 11, 2005. CAST: Sergio Castellitto (Ernesto Picciafuocco), Jacqueline Lustig (Irene Picciafuocco), Chiara Conti (Diana Sereni), Gigio Alberti (Ettore Picciafuocco), Alberto Mondini

Klaus Nomi in *The Nomi Song* PHOTO COURTESY OF PALM PICTURES

(Leonardo Picciafuocco), Gianfelice Imparato (Erminio Picciafuocco), Gianni Schicchi Gabrieli (Filippo Argenti), Maurizio Donadoni (Cardinal Piumini), Donato Placido (Egidio Picciafuocco), Renzo Rossi (Baldracchi), Pietro De Silva (Curzio Sandali), Bruno Cariello (Don Pugni), Piera Degli Esposti (Aunt Maria), Toni Bertorelli (Count Ludovico Bulla), Maria Luisa Bellocchio, Letizia Bellocchio (Zia Ernesto), Giovanni Cappelli (Autista), Ada Ferrata (Madre Ernesto), Lino Bonanni (Eugenio), Hubert Grieco (Gaspare)

Sergio Castellitto in *My Mother's Smile* PHOTO COURTESY OF NEW YORKER FILMS

TURTLES CAN FLY

(IFC FILMS) a.k.a. *Lakposhtha ham parvaz mikonand*; Producers, Bahman Ghobadi, Babak Amini, Hamid Ghavami, Hamid Karim Batin Ghobadi; Executive Producer, Abbas Ghazali; Director/Screenplay/Designer, Bahman Ghodabi; Photography, Shahram Assadi; Music, Hossein Alizadeh; Editors, Mustafa Kherquepush, Haydeh Safi-Yari; a Bac Films, Mij Film Co. production; Iranian-French; Dolby; Color; Rated PG-13; 95 minutes; American release date: February 18, 2005. CAST: Soran Ebrahim (Satellite), Avaz Latif (Agrin), Saddam Hossein Feysal (Pashow), Hiresh Feysal Rahman (Hengov), Abdol Rahman Karim (Riga), Ajil Zibari (Shirkooh)

Jiri Machacek, Natasa Burger in *Up and Down* PHOTO COURTESY OF SONY CLASSICS

SEXUAL DEPENDENCY

(CINEMA TROPICAL) Producers, Rodrigo Bellott, Ara Katz; Executive Producer, Gregory Leonarczyk; Director, Rodrigo Bellott; Screenplay, Rodrigo Bellott, Lenelle N. Moise; Photography, Rodrigo Bellott, Daryn De Luco; Designer, Carlos Pardo; Music, John Dobry, Jeremiah Vancans; Editor, Adriana Pacheco; Bolivian-U.S.; Color; Not rated; 104 minutes; American release date: February 23, 2005. CAST: Alexandra Aponte (Jessica), Roberto Urbina (Sebastian), Jorge Antonio Saavedra (Choco), Ronica V. Reddick (Adinah), Matthew Guida (Tyler), Matt Cavenaugh (Sean), Rodrigo Mendez-Roca (Fabian, Sebastian's Cousin), Liv Fruyano (Love, Choco's Girlfriend), David Budd (Nick), Damien Carter (Jeremiah), Pablo Fernandez (Joaquin), Elba Flores (Mrs. Lopez), Ronald Flores (Josue), Ignacio Ichazo (Chichito), Melina Logan (Obnoxious R.A.), Arturo Lora (Jessica's Dad), Franco Nogales (Mr. Lopez), Sandra Paz (Clemencia), Chichita Pena (Choco's Mom), Ryan Prozer (Gay Activist), Rodolfo Quizbert (Professor), Carlos Rocabado (Dante), Charitio Rojas (Jessica's Mom), Maria Elva Saucedo (Isabel), Eliana Sosa (Camila), Carolian Suarez (Guadalupe), Javier Yabeta (Jessica's Brother), Jared Zeus (Tyler's Boyfriend), Fred Nunez, Yuri Lora (Drag Queens)

THE OTHER SIDE OF THE STREET

(STRAND) a.k.a. *O Outro Lado da Rua*; Producers, Marcos Bernstein, Katia Machado; Executive Producer, Mariza Figueiredo; Director/Story, Marcos Bernstein; Screenplay, Melanie Dimantas; Photography, Toca Seabra; Art Director, Bia Junqueira; Costumes, Cristina Kangussu; Music, Guilherme Bernstein Seixas; Editor, Marcelo Moraes; a Neanderthal, Cinema Passaro

Soran Ebrahim in *Turtles Can Fly* PHOTO COURTESY OF IFC FILMS

Films production; Brazilian-French, 2004; Color; Not rated; 97 minutes; American release date: February 25, 2005. CAST: Fernanda Montenegro (Regina), Raul Cortez (Camargo), Laura Cardoso (Patolina), Luiz Carlos Persy (Alcides), Miguel Lunardi (Regina's Son), Caio Ramos (Regina's Grandson), Eliana César (Camargo's Daughter), Milene Pizarro (Celia), Marcio Vito (Walmir)

UP AND DOWN

(SONY CLASSICS) a.k.a. *Horem pádem*; Producer, Ondrej Trojan; Executive Producer, Milan Kuchynka; Director, Jan Hrebejk; Screenplay, Jan Hrebejk, Petr Jarchovsky; Photography, Jan Malír; Designer, Milan Bycek; Costumes, Katarina Bielikova; Music, Ales Brezina; Editor, Vladimír Barák; a co-production of Ceská Televize, Total Help Art T.H.A.; Czech, 2004; Dolby; Color; Rated R; 108 minutes; American release date: February 25, 2005. CAST: Petr Forman (Martin Horecky), Emília Vásáryová (Vera Horecká), Jirí Machácek (Fantisek Fikes), Natasa Burger (Miluska), Jan Tríska (Prof. Otakar Horecky), Ingrid Timková (Hana Svobodová), Kristyna Liska-Boková (Lenika Horecká), Pavel Liska (Eman), Marek Daniel (Lubos), Jan Budar (Milan), Zdenek Suchy (Goran), Jaroslav Dusek (Colonel), Martin Huba (Doctor), Jirina Trebická (Jeno Matka), Miroslav Kaman (Z. Policista), Josef Kolinsky (Fetak), Roman Holub (Amir), Maria Tusa (Peggy), Ester Geislerova, Jakub Sommer (Students), Václav Havel (The President)

Fernanda Montenegro, Raul Cortez in *The Other Side of the Street*
PHOTO COURTESY OF STRAND RELEASING

THE RED ORCHESTRA

(HYBRID FILMS) Producers, Stefan Roloff, Daniel Elias, David Houts; Director, Stefan Roloff; Screenplay, Stefan Roloff, Rebecca Runze; Music, Martin Rey; Editor, Rebecca Runze; Photography, Rainer Fetting, Eberhard Kredel, Sebastian Quakc, Johannes Roloff, Ralf Schulze, Txuspo, Gerald Wesolowski; a When 6 is 9 Productions, Zweites Deutsches Fernsehen (ZDF) presentation; Black and white/color; Not rated; 85 minutes; American release date: March 2, 2005.

María del Carmen Jiménez in *Intimate Stories* PHOTO COURTESY OF NEW YORKER FILMS

Chris William Martin, Ian McKellen in *Emile* PHOTO COURTESY OF CASTLE HILL FILMS

EMILE

(CASTLE HILL) Producers, Jacquelyn Renner, Carl Bessai; Executive Producers, Jonthan English, Bjorg Veland, Carl Bessai; Director/Screenplay/Photography, Carl Bessai; Designer, Dina Zecchel; Costumes, Lara Lupish; Music, Vince Mal; Editor, Julian Clarke; Casting, David Hall, Susan Taylor; a Raven West Films Ltd. presentation in association with Meltemi Entertainment, BV Intl. Pictures, Redbus Film Distribution Ltd. and Seville Pictures; Canadian, 2003; Dolby; Alpha Cine color; Rated R; 91 minutes; American release date: March 4, 2005. CAST: Ian McKellen (Emile), Deborah Kara Unger (Nadia/Nadia's Mother), Theo Crane (Maria/Nadia, Age 10), Chris William Martin (Carl), Tygh Runyan (Freddy), Ian Tracey (Tom), Janet Wright (Alice), Nancy Sivak (Superintendent), Frank Borg (Taxi Driver)

INTIMATE STORIES

(NEW YORKER) Executive Producer, Martin Bardi; Director, Carlos Sorin; Screenplay, Pablo Solarz; Photography, Hugo Colace; Art Director, Margarita Jusid; Costumes, Ruth Fischerman; Music, Nicolas Sorin; Editor, Mohamed Rajid; Casting, Argentina Northern; a Guacamole Films, Nirvana Films, Wanda Vision production; Argentine-Spanish, 2002; Dolby; Cinecolor; Not rated; 92 minutes; American release date: March 4, 2005. CAST: Javier Lombardo (Roberto), Antonio Benedicti (Don Justo Benedictis), Javiera Bravo (Maria Flores), Julia Solomonoff (Julia), Laura Vagnoni (Estela), Enrique Otranto (Carlos), Mariela Diaz (Maria's Friend), Maria Rosa Cianferoni (Ana), Cesar Garcia (Himself), Mariá del Carmen Jiménez, Mario Splanguño, Rosa Valsecchi (Bakers)

SCHIZO

(PICTURE THIS!) Producers, Sergei Bodrov, Sergei Seiyanov, Sergei Azimov; Director, Gulshad Omarova; Screenplay, Gulshad Omarova, Sergei Bodrov; Photography, Hasanbek Kidiraliev; Designer, Talgan Asirankulov; Music, Sig; Editor, Ivan Lebedev; a CTB Films Co. (Russia), Kazakh Film Studio (Kazakhstan) production, in association with Le Petite Lumieres (France), Kinofabrika GmbH (Germany) with the support of the Ministry of Culture (Russia), Fonda Sud, CNC, Ministry of Foreign Affairs (France); Russian-Kazakhstan-French-German, 2004; Dolby; Color; Not rated; 86 minutes; American release date: March 18, 2005. CAST: Oldzhas Nusuphayev (Shiza), Olga Landina (Zinka), Eduard Tabishev (Sakura), Viktor Sukhorukov (Doctor), Guinara Yeraliyeva (Kulyash), Hurtaj Kanagat (Sandzhik), Khorabek Musabayev (Almaz), Bakhytbek Bajmukhanbetov (Dzhaken), Mukhit Izimov (Nurlan), Gajratdzhan Tokhgibakiyev (Uzbek), Emine Ismailova (Ballet Dancer), Dzhasulan Makhanov (Almaz's Bodyguard)

Olga Landina, Hurtaj Kanagat in *Schizo*

Oldzhas Nusuphayev in *Schizo* PHOTO COURTESY OF PICTURE THIS!

Susan Lynch, Kevin McKidd in *Sixteen Years of Alcohol* PHOTO COURTESY OF TARTAN FILMS

SIXTEEN YEARS OF ALCOHOL

(TARTAN) Producers, Hamish McAlpine, Richard Jobson, Mark Burton; Executive Producers, Steve McIntyre, Wouter Barendrecht, Michael J. Werner; Director/Screenplay, Richard Jobson, based on his book; Photography, John Rhodes; Designer, Adam Squires; Costumes, Carole Millar; Music, Keith Atack, Malcolm Lindsay; Editor, Ioannis Chalkiadakis; Casting, Sarah Crowe; a Scottish Screen presentation, in association with Metro Tartan and Fortissimo Film Sales, of a Tartan Works production; British, 2003; Dolby; Digitalscope Widescreen; Sony HD CAM-to-35mm; Color; Rated R; 102 minutes; American release date: March 18, 2005. CAST: Kevin McKidd (Frankie Mac), Laura Fraser (Helen), Susan Lynch (Mary), Stuart Sinclair Blyth (Miller), Jim Carter (Director), Ewen Bremner (Jake), Elaine C. Smith (AA Meeting Woman), Kate Robbins, Jim Cunningham (Fighting Couple), Marcia Rose, Gerald Lepkowski (Actors), Lewis Macleod (Frankie's Father), Lisa May Cooper (Frankie's Mother), Iain De Caestecker (Frankie as a Boy), Russell Anderson (Kill), Michael Moreland (Budgie), Allison McKenzie (Dad's Lover), Naoufal Ousellam, Nabi Stuart (Rival Gang Boys), John Comerford (Barman), Colvin Cruickshank (Record Shop Assistant), Louise Irwin, Pauline Goldsmith (Brewery Women), Carole O'Brien (Clothes Shop Assistant), David Gallagher (Art Critic), Anne Downie (Art Critic's Friend), John Yule (Referee), Anthony Strachan (Parent's Friend), Jenny Hogarth (Helen's Friend)

Choi Min-sik (right) in *Old Boy* PHOTO COURTESY OF TARTAN FILMS

THE RIDER NAMED DEATH

(KINO) a.k.a. *Vsadnik po imeni smert*; Producer/Director, Karen Shakhnazarov; Executive Producer, Galina Shadur; Screenplay, Alexander Borodyansky, Karen Shakhnazarov: Based on the novel *Pale Horse* by Boris Savinko; Photography, Vladimir Kilmov; Designer, Ludmila Kusakova; Music, Anatoly Kroll; Editor, Lidia Milloti; a Mosfilm Cinema Concern presentation of a Mosfilm production; Russian, 2004; Widescreen; Color; Not rated; 106 minutes; American release date: March 18, 2005. CAST: Andrei Panin (Georges), Kseniya Rappoport (Erna), Artyom Semakin (Vanya), R. Bershauer (Fyodor), Anastasya Makeyeva (Elan), Aleksei Kazakov (Heinrich), Dimitri Dyuzhev (Azef), Valeri Storozhik (Elena's Husband), Vasiliy Zotov (The Grand Prince Sergei Aleksandrovich)

Andrei Panin in *Rider Named Death* PHOTO COURTESY OF KINO INTERNATIONAL

Anat Waxman, Alon Abutbul in *Nina's Tragedies* PHOTO COURTESY OF WELLSPRING

OLD BOY

(TARTAN FILMS) Producer, Kim Dong-ju; Executive Producer, Kim Jang-wook; Director, Park Chan-wook; Screenplay, Hwang Jo-yun, Lim Jun-hyeong, Park Chan-wook; Story, Garon Tsuchiya, Nobuaki Minegishi; Photography, Jeong Jeong-hun; Designer, Ryu Seong-Hie; Costumes, Jo Sang-gyeong; Music, Shim Heyon-jeong; Editor, Kim Sang-beom; a Show East production, in association with Egg Films; South Korean, 2003; Dolby; Super 35 Widescreen; Color; Not rated; 118 minutes; American release date: March 25, 2005. CAST: Choi Min-sik (Oh Dae-su), Yu Ji-tae (Lee Woo-jin), Kang Hye-jeong (Mi-do), Ji Dae-han (No Joo-hwan), Oh Dal-su (Park Cheol-woong), Kim Byeong (Mr. Han), Lee Seung-Shin (Yoo HyungOja), Yun Jin-seo (Lee Soo-ah), Lee Dae-yeon (Beggar),

Oh Kwang-rok (Suicidal Man), Oh Tae-kyung (Young Dae-su), Ahn Yeon-suk (Young Woo-jin), Oo Il-han (Young Joo-hwan), Yong Yi (Deliver Boy)

BEYOND THE SEA

(CINEMA TROPICAL) a.k.a. *Más allá del mar*; Director/Screenplay/Photography/ Editor, Lisandro Perez-Rey; Music, Carl Ferrari; Cuban-U.S.; Color; Not rated; 80 minutes; American release date: March 25, 2005. Documentary on the Mariel Boatlift.

Vitaliano Trevisan, Michela Cescon in *Primo Amore* PHOTO COURTESY OF STRAND RELEASING

NINA'S TRAGEDIES

(WELLSPRING) Producers, Anat Assoulin, Savi Gabizon; Director/Screenplay, Savi Gabizon; Photography, David Garfunkel; Designer, Shahar Bar-Adon; Costumes, Tsipi Englisher; Music, Assaf Amdurky; Editor, Tali Halter Shanker; an Anat Assoulin presentation of an A.A. production; Israeli, 2004; Color; Not rated; 106 minutes; American release date: March 25, 2005. CAST: Ayelet July Zurer (Nina), Yoram Hattab (Haimon/Alex), Alon Abutbul (Avinoam), Aviv Elkabeth (Nadav), Shmil Ben Ari (Amnon), Dov Navon (Menahem), Anat Waxman (Alona), Jonathan Bar-Giora (Braslav Singer/Guitarist), Jenya Dodina (Galina), Shmuel Edelman (Shlomi), Osnat Fishman (Lihi), Gili Shushan (Rafi)

ODESSA…ODESSA!

(MOBY DICK FILMS) Director, Michale Boganim; Photography, Jackob Ihre; Editor, Valerio Bonelli; French-Israeli; Color; Not rated; 96 minutes; American release date: March 30, 2005. A look at the vanishing Odessa Jewish community in the Ukraine, New York, and Israel.

KONTROLL

(THINKFILM) Producer, Tamás Hutlassa; Director, Nimród Antal; Screenplay, Nimród Antal, Jim Adler; Photography, Gyula Pados; Designer, Balázs Hujber; Costumes, János Breckl; Music, Neo; Editor, István Király; Casting, Syzilivia Nemesdedi, Veronika Varjasi; a Bonfire, Café Film production; Hungarian, 2003; Dolby; Color; Rated R; 105 minutes; American release date: April 1, 2005. CAST: Sándor Csányi (Bulcsú), Zoltán Mucsi (Professor), Csaba Pindroch (Muki), Sándor Badár (Lecsó), Zsolt Nagy (Tibi), Bence Mátyási (Gyalogkukk), Gyözö

Szabó (Shadow), Eszter Balla (Szofi), László Nádasi (Laci), Péter Scherer (Chief), Lajos Kovács (Béla), Károly Horváth (Tamás), György Cserhalmi (Big Boss), János Kulka (Feri), László Bicksei Kris (Doki), Zsolt László (Nub)

IN SATMAR CUSTODY

(YONA PRODUCTIONS) Producer/Director/Screenplay, Nitzan Giladi; Photography, Yaron Orbach; Music, Ophir Leibovitch; Editor, Ron Goldman; Israeli, 2003; Color; Not rated; 70 minutes; American release date: April 6, 2005.

PRIMO AMORE

(STRAND) Producer, Domenico Procacci; Director, Matteo Garrone; Screenplay, Matteo Garrone, Vitaliano Trevisan, Massimo Gaudioso; Based on the novel by Carlo Mariolini; Photography, Marco Onorato; Designer, Paolo Bonfini; Costumes, Francesca Leondeff; Music, Banda Osiris; Editor, Marco Spoletini; Casting, Salvatore Sansone, Gianni Di Gregorio; Italian, 2004; Dolby; Color; Not rated; 94 minutes; American release date: April 6, 2005. CAST: Vitaliano Trevisan (Vittorio), Michela Cescon (Sonia), Elvezia Allari (Anna), Paolo Capoduro (Paolo), Roberto Comacchio (Sonia's Brother), Paolo Cumerlato (Waiter), Claudio Manuzzato (Cook), Marco Manzardo (Marco), Antonella Mazzuccato (Antonella), Gianluca Moretto (Mopi), Alberto Re (Doctor), Pierpaolo Speggiorin (Real Estate Agent), Antonio Viero (Mario), Deni Viero (Mario's Son)

Sándor Csányi, Eszter Balla in *Kontroll* PHOTO COURTESY OF THINKFILM

Sándor Csányi, Sándor Badár in *Kontroll* PHOTO COURTESY OF THINKFILM

HAPPILY EVER AFTER

(KINO) a.k.a. *Ils se marièrent et eurent beaucoup d'enfants*; Producer, Claude Berri; Executive Producer, Pierre Grunstein; Director/Screenplay, Yvan Attal; Photography, Rémy Chevrin; Designer, Katia Wyszkop; Costumes, Jacqueline Bouchard; Music, Brad Mehldau, Christian Chevalier; Editor, Jennifer Augé; Casting, Laurent Soulet, Antoinette Boulat; a Pathe Renn Productions, Hirsch, TF1 Films Production; French; Color; Not rated; 100 minutes; American release date: April 8, 2005. CAST: Charlotte Gainsbourg (Gabrielle), Yvan Attal (Vincent), Alain Chabat (Georges), Alain Cohen (Fred), Emmanuelle Seigner (Nathalie), Angie David (The Mistress), Anouke Aimee (Vincent's Mother), Claude Berri (Vincent's Father), Aurore Clément (Vincent's Mistress's Mother), Marie-Sophie Wilson-Carr (Florence), Stéphanie Murat (Géraldine), Ruben Marx (Little Antoine), Kitu Gidwani (Mme Gibson), Sujay Sood (M. Gibson), Keith Allen (Man at Pool), Carolina Gynning (Zoé), Chloé Combret (Chloé), Johnny Depp (Man at Record Store), Ben Attal (Joseph), Jérôme Bertin (Client from Garage), Sarah Delorme (Ludivine), Nicolas Vaude (Spectator), Sébastien Vidal (Thibault)

Luca Zingaretti (right) in *Perlasca* PHOTO COURTESY OF CASTLE HILL FILMS

THE FRIEND

(FILM PHILOS) a.k.a. *Fremder Freund*; Producers, Sabine Lamby, Michael Amtmann, Giulio Ricciarelli; Director, Elmar Fischer; Screenplay, Elmar Fischer, Tobias Kniebe; Photography, Florian Emmerich; Designer, Dörte Schreiterer; Costumes, Anina Diener; Music, Matthias Beine; Editor, Antje Zynga; a co-production of Naked Eye Filmproduktion, Shot by Shot Filmproduktion, Zweites Deutches Fernsehen (ZDF); German, 2003; Dolby; Color; Not rated; 105 minutes; American release date: April 8, 2005. CAST: Navid Akhavan (Yunes), Fatih Alas

Frankie Wild in *It's All Gone Pete Tong* PHOTOS COURTESY OF FILMCOMPANY

Charlotte Gainsbourg, Yvan Attal in *Happily Ever After* PHOTO COURTESY OF KINO INTERNATIONAL

(Raid), Ercan Durmaz (Imam's Assistant), Elmar Fischer (Roommate), Mavie Hörbiger (Nora), Wolfgang Liese (Old Man on Road), Judith Rauschenberger (University Employee), Mina Tander (Julia), Anna Vielhaben (Movie Cashier), Patrick von Blume (Young Man on Road), Antonio Wannek (Chris)

PERLASCA

(CASTLE HILL) Producers, Carlo Degli Esposito, Anna Giolitti; Director, Alberto Negrin; Screenplay, Stefano Rulli, Sandro Patraglia; Based on the book *The Banality of Goodness* by Enrico Deaglio; Photography, Stefano Ricciotti; Designer, Lazlo Gardonyi; Costumes, Agnes Gyarmathy; Music, Ennio Morricone; Editor, Antonio Siciliano; Casting, Rita Forzano, Istvan Kolos; a Castle Hill Prods., RAI Television presentation of an RAI Fiction, Palomar-Endemol, Focus Film (Budapest), France 2 (Paris), Hamster Prods. (Paris), SVT Fiktion (Stockholm); Italian; Dolby; Color; Not rated; 125 minutes; American release date: April 15, 2005. CAST: Luca Zingaretti (Giorgio Perlasca), Jerome Anger (Farkas), Amanda Sandrelli (Magda), Gyorgy Cserhalmi (Bleiber), Elena Arvigo (Anna), Lorenzo Lavia (Daniel), Franco Castellano (Adam), Marco Bonini (Sandor), Jean Francois Garreaud (Balasz Professor), Dezso Garas (Rabbi), Palle Granditzky (Jacob), Giuliana Lojodice (Mme. Tourne), Mathilda May (Contessa Eleonora), Alvaro Gradella (Szarka)

IT'S ALL GONE PETE TONG

(MATSON FILMS) Producers, Allan Niblo, James Richardson, Elizabeth Yake; Executive Producers, Rob Morgan, Rupert Preston, Kim Roberts; Director/Screenplay, Michael Dowse; Photography, Balasz Bolygo; Designer, Paul Burns; Music, Graham Massey; Editor, Stuart Gazzard; an Alliance Atlantis, Odeon Films presentation of a Vertigo Films in association with True West Films production; Canadian-British; Dolby; Widescreen; Color; Not rated; 89 minutes; American release date: April 15, 2005. CAST: Paul Kaye (Frankie Wilde), Beatriz Batarda (Penelope), Mike Wilmot (Max Hagger), Dave Lawrence (Horst), Paul J. Spence (Alfonse), Kate Magowan (Sonia)

TORREMOLINOS 73

(FIRST RUN FEATURES) Producers, Tomás Cimadevilla, Mohamed Khashoggi; Co-Producers, Bo Ehrhardt, Lars Bredo Rahbek; Director/Screenplay, Pablo Berger; Photography, Kiko de la Rica; Costumes, Estibaliz Markiegi; Casting, Luis San

Narciso; a co-production of Mama Films, Estudios Picasso; Spanish-Danish, 2003; Color/black and white; Not rated; 91 minutes; American release: April 15, 2005. CAST: Javier Cámara (Alfredo), Candela Peña (Carmen), Juan Diego (Carlos), Malena Alterio (Vanessa), Fernando Tejero (Juan Luis), Mads Mikkelsen (Magnus), Ramón Barea (José Carlos Romerales), Thomas Bo Larsen (Dennis), Nuria González (Señora de Romerales), Mariví Bilbao (Señora de Anasagasti), Ana Wagener (Dependienta), Jaime Blanch (Gynecologist), Máximo Valverde (Himself), Carmen Machi (Client), Tina Sáinz (Doña Isabel), Bjarne Henriksen (Lauritz), Miguel Alcíbar (Taxista), Carmen Belloch (Sra. Bronte), Tom Jacobsen (Erik), Mari-Anne Jespersen (Frida), Ruth Lewin (Novia)

Candela Peña, Mads Mikkelsen in *Torremolinos 73* PHOTO COURTESY OF FIRST RUN FEATURES

SAVE THE GREEN PLANET!

(KOCH LORBER) a.k.a. *Jigureul Jikyeora!*; Producers, Cha Seung-jau, Noh Jong-yun; Executive Producer, Lee Kang-bok; Director/Screenplay, Jang Jun-hwan; Photography, Hong Gyeong-pyu; Art Directors, Jang Geun-yeong, Kim Gyeong-heul; Music, Michael Staudahcer; Editor, Park Gok-ji; Martial Arts Supervisors, Kim Min-su, Yu Sang-seob; a CJ Entertainment presentation, in association with Sidus, Discovery Venture Capital, of a Sidus production; South Korean, 2003; Dolby; Color; Not rated; 116 minutes; American release date: April 20, 2005. CAST: Shin Ha-kyun (Lee Byeong-gu), Baek Yun-shik (Kang Man-shik),

Lazaro Ramos in *The Man Who Copied* PHOTO COURTESY OF TLA RELEASING

Shin Ha-kyun, Baek Yun-shik in *Save the Green Planet!* PHOTO COURTESY OF KOCH LORBER FILMS

Hwang Jeong-min (Su-ni), Lee Jae-yong (Inspector Choo), Lee Ju-hyeon (Inspector Kim), Gi Ju-bong (Suqad Leader Lee)

ONE MISSED CALL

(MEDIA BLASTERS) a.k.a. *Chakushin Ari*; Producers, Naoki Sato, Yoichi Arishige, Fumio Inoue; Director, Takashi Miike; Screenplay, Minako Daira, Yasushi Akimoto; Photography, Hideo Yamamoto; Art Director, Hisao Inagaki; Music, Koji Endo; Editor, Yasushi Shimamura; a Kadokawa-Daiei Pictures production; Japanese, 2004; Dolby; Color; Rated R; 111 minutes; American release date: April 22, 2005. CAST: Kou Shibasaki (Yumi Nakamura), Shin'ichi Tsutsumi (Hiroshi Yamashita), Kazue Fukiishi (Natsumi Konishi), Renji Ishibashi (Motomiya, Detective), Goro Kishitani (Oka, Undertaker), Anna Nagarata (Yoko Okazaki), Atsushi Ida (Kenji Kawai), Yutaka Matsushige (Ichiro Fujieda), Mariko Tsutsui (Marie Mizunuma)

THE MAN WHO COPIED

(TLA RELEASING) a.k.a. *O Homem Que Copiava*; Producers, Luciana Tomasi, Nora Goulart; Director/Screenplay, Jorge Furtado; Photography, Alex Sernambi; Designer, Fiapo Barth; Music, Leo Henkin; Editor, Giba Assis Brasil; a Casa de Cinema de Porto Alegre production in association with Sony Corp. of America, Columbia Pictures, Columbia TriStar; Brasilian, 2003; Dolby; Color; Rated R; 123 minutes; American release date: April 22, 2005. CAST: Lazaro Ramos (Andre), Leandra Leal (Silvia), Luana Piovani (Marines), Pedro Cardoso (Cardoso), Julio Andrade (Feitosa), Kike Barbosa (Bebado), Carlos Chunha (Antunes), Paulo Jose (Paulo), Janaina Kremer (Dona Maria), Ivo Schergl (Office Boy), Heitor Schmidt (Gomide)

CASUISTRY: THE ART OF KILLING A CAT

(ROUGH AGE PROJECTILES) Producer, Linda Feesey; Director/Screenplay/Editor, Zev Asher; Photography, Zev Asher, Linda Feesey; Music, Jen Morris; Canadian; Color; Not rated; 91 minutes; American release date: April 27, 2005. Documentary in which a man tortures and kills his cat while declaring it art; featuring Christie Blatchford, Daniel Borins, Jubal Brown, Matthew Kaczorowski, Istvan Kantor, John Margetson, Jesse Power, Anthony Wennekers.

THE TUNNEL

(AVATAR FILMS) Producers, Ariane Krampe, Nico Hofmann; Executive Producer, Alicia Remirez; Director, Roland Suso Richter; Screenplay, Johannes W. Betz; Photography, Martin Langer; Editor, Peter R. Adam; German, 2001; Dolby; Color/Black and white; Not rated; 167 minutes; American release date: April 29, 2005. CAST: Harry Melchior (Heino Ferch), Nicolette Krebitz (Friederike "Fritiz" Scholz), Sebastian Koch (Matthis Hiller), Alexandra Maria Lara (Lotte Lohmann), Claudia Michelsen (Carola Hiller), Felix Eitner (Fred von Klausnitz), Mehmet Kurtulus (Vic), Heinrich Schmieder (Theo Lohmann), Uwe Kockisch (Oberst Kruger), Karin Baal (Marianne von Krausnitz), Rainer Sellien (Georg Himmrich), Wolf-Dietrich Sprenger (Gruner), Sarah Kubel (Ina Lohmann), Florian Panzner (Heiner), Dorothea Moritz (Hermine), Wilfried Hochholdinger (Bellofs), Gode Benedix (Herbert Konig), Simon von Parys (William Ogilvie), Luis Lamprecht (Ewald Mezger), Shaun Lawton (Gerald McLoud), Uwe Zerbe (Friedrich Meyer)

Isild Le Besco, Ouassini Embarek in *À Tout de Suite* PHOTO COURTESY OF CINEMA GUILD

À TOUT DE SUITE

(CINEMA GUILD) Producers, Georges Benayoun, Raoul Saada; Executive Producer, Francoise Guglielmi; Director/Screenplay, Benoît Jacquot; Story, Elisabeth Fanger; Photography, Caroline Champetier; Designer/Costumes, Antoine Platteau; Editor, Luc Barnier; a Natan Productions, Arte France Cinema co-production; French, 2004; Dolby; Black and white; Not rated; 95 minutes; American release date: April 29, 2005. CAST: Isild Le Besco (Lili), Ouassini Embarek (Bada), Nicolas Duvauchelle (Alain), Laurence Cordier (Joelle)

WRITER OF O

(ZEITGEIST) Producer, Sylvie Cazin; Executive Producer, Anne Schuchman; Director, Pola Rapaport; Photography, Wolfgang Held; Music, Hélène Blazy; Editor, Variety Moszynski; an INA Films, Blinding Light production; French-U.S.; Black and white/color; Not rated; 80 minutes; American release date: May 4, 2005. Documentary on the scandalous best-seller *The Story of O*; featuring Dominique Aury, Cyril Corral, Thierry de Carbonnieres, John de St. Jorre, Catherine Mouchet, Penelope Puymirat, Alain Rimoux, Barney Rosset.

LE GRAND RÔLE

(FIRST RUN FEATURES) Director, Steve Suissa; Screenplay, Steve Suissa, Daniel Cohen, Sophie Tepper; Based on the book by Daniel Goldenberg; Photography, Guillaume Schiffman; Designer, Éric Barboza; Costumes, Aline Dupays; Music,

Stéphane Freiss, Bérénice Bejo in *Le Grand Rôle* PHOTO COURTESY OF FIRST RUN FEATURES

David Marouani; Editor, Monica Coleman; an Egerie Productions, Les Films de l'Espoir production; French; Color; Not rated; 89 minutes; American release date: May 6, 2005. CAST: Stéphane Freiss (Maurice Kurtz), Bérénice Bejo (Perla Kurtz), Peter Coyote (Rudolph Grichenberg), Lionel Abelanski (Simon Laufer), François Berléand (Benny Schwarz), Olivier Sitruk (Samy Rebbot), Laurent Bateau (Elie Weill), Mickaël Sabah (Ben), Rufus (M. Silberman), Stéphan Guérin-Tillié (Edouard), Valérie Benguigui (Viviane), Danièle Denie (Mme. Silberman), Smadi Wolfman (Sarah), Steve Suissa (Doron), Clément Sibony (Benoît)

A MAN'S GOTTA DO

(HOPSCOTCH PRODS.) Producer, John Winter; Director/Screenplay, Chris Kennedy; Photography, Kim Batterham; Art Director, Nell Hanson; Music, Peter Best; Editor, Emma Hay; Casting, Christine King; Australian, 2004; Dolby; Color; Not rated; 93 minutes; American release date: May 6, 2005. CAST: John Howard (Eddy), Rebecca Frith (Yvonne), Alyssa McClelland (Chantelle), Gyton Grantley (Dominic), Amie Mckenna (Delores), Rohan Nicol (Paul), Tony Barry (Dr. Savage), Helen Thompson (Tina), Jo-Anne Cahill (Sylvia), Lynne McGimpsy (Josephina), Manuel Terron (Rudi), Nicholas Brown (Young Doctor), Grant Bennett (Police Officer), Rowan Jackson (Nigel), Robyn Ormiston (Photographer), Vasa Gavrilovska (Svetlana)

Penelope Puymirat, Cyril Corra in *Writer of O* PHOTO COURTESY OF ZEITGEIST FILMS

MINDHUNTERS

(DIMENSION) Producers, Jeffrey Silver, Bobby Newmyer, Cary Brokaw, Rebecca Spikings; Executive Producers, Moritz Borman, Guy East, Nigel Sinclair, Renny Harlin; Co-Executive Producers, Bob Weinstein, Harvey Weinstein; Co-Producers, Scott Strauss, Erwin Godschalk, Hans De Weers; Director, Renny Harlin; Screenplay, Wayne Kramer, Kevin Brodbin; Story, Wayne Kramer; Photography, Robert Gantz; Designer, Charles Wood; Costumes, Louise Frogley; Music, Tuomas Kantelinen; Editors, Paul Martin Smith, Neil Farrell; Visual Effects, Brian M. Jennings, Harry Wiessenhaan; Casting, Monika Mikkelsen; an Intermedia Films presentation of an Outlaw, Avenue Pictures production, in association with Weed Road Pictures; British-Netherlands-Finnish-U.S.; Dolby; Widescreen; Color; Rated R; 106 minutes; American release date: May 13, 2005. CAST: LL Cool J (Gabe Jensen), Jonny Lee Miller (Lucas Harper), Kathryn Morris (Sara Moore), Patricia Velasquez (Nicole Willis), Clifton Collins, Jr. (Vince Sherman), Eion Bailey (Bobby Whitman), Will Kemp (Rafe Perry), Val Kilmer (Jake Harris), Christian Slater (J. D. Reston), Cassandra Bell (Jen), Anthonie Kamerling, Daniel Boissevain (Men in Bar), Jasmine Sendar (Friend of Jen), Trevor White (Attacker)

Patricia Velasquez, Christian Slater in *Mindhunters* PHOTO COURTESY OF DIMENSION/MIRAMAX

RED PASSPORT

(CANDELA FILM) a.k.a. *Pasaporte rojo*; Producers, Albert Xavier, Michael Masucci; Director/Screenplay, Albert Xavier; Story, Albert Xavier, Freddy Vargas; Photography, Brendan Flynt; Music, Luis Columna, Fulanito; Editor, Mako Kamitsuna; Dominican Republic, 2003; Dolby; Color; Not rated; 93 minutes; American release date: May 13, 2005. CAST: Sharon Angela (Theresa), Maite Bonilla (Sonia), Amanda Carneiro (Gavi), Stan Carp (Sal), Danilda Cruz (Lola), Bobby DeJesus (Gari), J. Teddy Garces (Juan), Jules Graciolett (Chory), Michael Masucci (Vinny), Frank Medrano (El Cojo), Frank Molina (Fabio), Ruperto Vanderpool (Josie)

MODIGLIANI

(INNOVATION FILM GROUP) Producers, Stephane Martinez-Campeau, Philippe Martinez, Andre Djaoui, Alan Latham; Executive Producers, Andy Garcia, Antony Blakey, Stephen Marsden, Paul Feetum, D. Miller, Karinne Behr, Marcos Zurinaga, Gary Ungar, Donald A. Barton; Director/Screenplay, Mick Davis; Photography, Emmanuel Kadosh; Designer, Giantito Burchiellaro; Costumes,

Pam Downe; Music, Guy Farley; Editor, Emma E. Hickox; a Bauer Martinez presentation of a UKFS production in co-production with Framewerk Produktion, Mediapro Pictures, Aliceleo, Buskin Film in collaboration with Cineson Prods. with Lucky 7 Prods., the Tower, Instituto Luce, Dealfilm, France 3 Cinema; British-German-Romanian-French-Italian; Dolby; Color; Rated R; 126 minutes; American release date: May 13, 2005. CAST: Andy Garcia (Amedeo Modigliani), Elsa Zylberstein (Jeanne Hebuterne), Hippolyte Girardot (Utrillo), Omid Djalili (Pablo Picasso), Eva Herzigova (Olga), Udo Kier (Max Jacob), Susie Amy (Beatrice Hastings), Peter Capaldi (Jean Cocteau), Louis Hilyer (Zborowski), Stevan Rimkus (Soutine), Dan Astilean (Diego Rivera), George Ivascu (Moise Kisling), Michelle Newell (Eudoxie Hebuterne), Frederico Ambrosino (Little Dedo), Miriam Margolyes (Gertrude Stein), Irina Dinescu (Paulette), Theodor Danetti (Renoir), Ion Siminie (Claude Monet), Andrei Boncea (City Official), George Stanciu (Starving Artist), Ciprian Dumitrascu (Swarthy Man #1), Dominique Schowebel (Salon Manager), Bianca Brad (Francesca), Jim Carter (Achilles Hebuterne), Dan Bordeianu (Androgynous Man), Cristina Piaget (Marie), Doru Stan (Young Walter), Mihai Niculescu (Priest), Joe Drago (Flaminio Modigliani), Adrian Dumitru (Cocteau's Boy), George Robu (Tram Driver), Alina Talmofte (Hashish Girl), Colin McCabe (Bartender), Marina Rotaru (Berthe Weill), Tomi Cristin, Emilia Danetti (Concierges), Ruza Madarevic (Doctor), Oana Zavoranu (Eugenia Modigliani), Ernest Maftei (Grandfather Modigliani), Philippe Vidal (Maitre d'), Sandu Mihai Gruia (Phillipe), Lance Henriksen (Foster Kane), Gratiana Cristache (Natascha), Lia Bugnar (Natascha's Mother), Constantin Florescu (Police Sergeant), Dorina Lazar (Stout Woman), Bryan Jardine (American), Loredana Groza (Singer), Beatrice Chiriac (Frida Kahlo), Cristina Liciman (Waitress)

Roméo Dallaire in *Shake Hands with the Devil* PHOTO COURTESY OF CALIFORNIA NEWSREEL

SHAKE HANDS WITH THE DEVIL: THE JOURNEY OF ROMÉO DALLAIRE

(CALIFORNIA NEWSREEL) Producer/Director, Peter Raymont; Photography, John Westheuser; Music, Mark Korven; Editor, Michèle Hozer; a co-production of White Pine Pictures, Societe Radio-Canada, the Canadian Broadcasting Company; Canadian, 2004; Color; Not rated; 90 minutes; American release date: May 13, 2005. Documentary on Lt. Gen. Roméo Dallaire's command of the UN mission to Rwanda at the time of the 1994 genocide.

Panyopas Lalita (left) in *6ixtyNin9* PHOTO COURTESY OF PALM PICTURES

6IXTYNIN9

(PALM PICTURES) a.k.a. *Ruang talok 69*; Producer/Director/Screenplay, Ratanaruang Pen-Ek; Photography, Chamnivikaipong Chankit; Editor, Yukol Patamanadda; a Five Stars Production Company, The Film Factory production; Thai, 1999; Dolby; Color; Rated R; 115 minutes; American release date: May 20, 2005. CAST: Panyopas Lalita (Tum), Ongartittichai Tasanawalai (Jim), Phomtong Black (Kanchit), Wannarbodeewong Arun (Mr. Tong), Lee Prompop (Shop Owner)

Nakamura Toru, Jang Dong-Kun in *2009: Lost Memories* PHOTO COURTESY OF ADV FILMS

2009: LOST MEMORIES

(ADV FILMS) Executive Producer, Kim Stanley; Director, Lee Si-myung; Photography, Pak Hyun-chul; Designer, Kim Ki-chul; Music, Lee Dong-jun; a CJ Entertainment, Indecom Cinema, Tube Entertainment production; South Korean, 2002; Dolby; Color; Rated R; 136 minutes; American release date: May 20, 2005. CAST: Ahn Kil-Kang (Lee Myung-Hak), Jang Dong-Kun (Sakamoto Masayuki), Kim Min-sun (Kindergarten Teacher), Ken Mitsuishi (Hideyo), Nakamura Toru (Saiko Shojiro), Seo Jin-ho (Oh Hye-Rin), Shin Goo (Takahashi), Yoshimura Miki (Saiko's Wife)

SEQUINS

(NEW YORKER) a.k.a. *Brodeuses*; Producers, Alain Benguigui, Bertrand Van Effenterre; Executive Producer, Thomas Verhaeghe; Director/Screenplay, Éléonore Faucher; Adaptation/Dialogue, Gaëlle Macé; Photography, Pierre Cottereau; Designer, Philippe van Herwijnen; Costumes, Pacaline Suty; Music, Michael Galasso; Editor, Joële Van Effenterre; a co-production of Sombrero Productions, Mallia Films, Rhone-Alpes cinema, Department de la Charente, Fondation GAN pour le Cinema; French; Dolby; Color; Not rated; 89 minutes; American release date: May 27, 2005. CAST: Lola Naymark (Claire Moutiers), Ariane Ascaride (Mme. Mélikian), Marie Félix (Lucile), Thomas Laroppe (Guillaume), Arthur Quehen (Thomas), Jacky Berroyer (M. Lescuyer), Anne Canovas (Mme. Lescuyer), Marina Tomé (Gynecologist), Elisabeth Commelin (Mme. Moutiers), Christophe Hatey (Butcher), François Noël (Bike Guy), Yasmine Modestine (Nurse), Annie-Claude Sauton (Baker), Nathalie Kirzin (Round Woman), Ludivine Morissonaud (Clotilde)

Lola Naymark, Ariane Ascaride in *Sequins* PHOTO COURTESY OF NEW YORKER FILMS

THE WHITE DIAMOND

(WERNER HERZOG FILMPRODUKTION) Executive Producer, Annettte Scheurich; Director/Narrator, Werner Herzog; Photography, Klaus Scheurich, Henning Brümmer; Music, Eric Spitzer, Ernst Reijsiger; Editor, Joe Bini; a Marco Polo Film, NDR Naturfilm (Germany), NHK (Japan), BBC (U.K.) production; German-Japanese-British; Color; Not rated; 88 minutes; American release date: June 1, 2005. Documentary on exploring the rainforest by using a Jungle Airship; featuring Dr. Graham Dorrington, Mark Anthony Yhap.

Deep Blue PHOTO COURTESY OF MIRAMAX

MCLIBEL

(CINEMA LIBRE) Producer/Director, Franny Armstrong; Executive Producer, Peter Armstrong; Photography, Franny Armstrong, Peter Armstrong, Neve Cunningham, Mick Duffield; Dramatic Segments Director, Ken Loach; Editors, David G. Hill, Gregers Sall; British; Color; Video; Not rated; 84 minutes; American release date: June 10, 2005. Documentary covering the U.K.'s longest trial in history, between McDonald's and two activists whom the corporation sued for libel; featuring Helen Steel, Dave Morris, Eric Schlosser, Morgan Spurlock, Colin Campbell, Sue Dibb, Dan Gallin, Stephen Gardner, Geoff Giuliano, Charlie Kervons, Howard Lyman, Charles O'Leary, Paul Preston, Charles Secrett, Keir Starmer, Fran Tiller; Bruce Alexander, Pip Donaghy, Ian Flintoff, Oliver Ford Davies, Richard Hope, William Hope, Linda McQuire, Nick Miles, Fred Pearson, Malcolm Tierney.

Helen Steel, Dave Morris in *McLibel* PHOTO COURTESY OF CINEMA LIBRE

WILD SIDE

(WELLSPRING) Producer, Gilles Sandoz; Executive Producer, Christian Tison; Director, Sebastien Lifshitz; Screenplay, Sebastien Lifshitz, Stephane Bouquet; Photography, Agnes Godard; Designer, Veronique Melery, Roseanna Sacco; Costumes, Elisabeth Mehu; Music, Jocelyn Pook; Editor, Stephanie Mahet; a co-production of Maïa Films, YV Alligator Films, Zephyr Films, Arte France Cinema; French-Belgian-British; Color; Not rated; 93 minutes; American release date: June 10, 2005. CAST: Stéphanie Michelini (Stéphanie), Yasmine Belmadi (Djamel), Edouard Nikitine (Mikhail), Josiane Stoléru (Mother), Antony Hegarty (Singer)

Edouard Nikitine, Yasmine Belmadi in *Wild Side* PHOTO COURTESY OF WELLSPRING

Dr. Graham Dorrington in *The White Diamond* PHOTO COURTESY OF WERNER HERZOG FILMPRODUKTION

DEEP BLUE

(MIRAMAX) Producers, Alix Tidmarsh, Sophokles Tasioulis; Executive Producers, Stefan Beiten, Nikolaus Weil, Andre Sikojev; Directors, Andy Byatt, Alastair Fothergill; Photography, Rick Rosenthal, Michael deGruy; Music, George Fenton; Editor, Martin Elsbury; Narrator, Pierce Brosnan; a co-production of BBC Natural History, BBC Worldwide, Greenlight Media; British-German, 2003; Dolby; Color; Not rated; 91 minutes; American release date: June 3, 2005. Documentary on the history of the world's oceans.

BUSTIN' BONAPARTE

(FREESTYLE RELEASING) a.k.a. *The Story of an African Farm*; Executive Producer, Bonnie Rodini; Line Producer, Cindy Rodkin; Director, David Lister; Screenplay, Bonnie Rodini, Thandi Brewer; Photography, Peter Tischhauser; a Rodini Films production; South African; Color; Rated PG; 97 minutes; American release date: June 3, 2005. CAST: Luke Gallant (Waldo), Richard E. Grant (Bonaparte Blenkins), Kasha Kropinski (Lyndall), Armin Mueller-Stahl (Otto), Karin van der Laag (Tant Sannie), Anneke Weidemann (Em)

Wheel of Time PHOTO COURTESY OF HEMISPHERIC PICTURES

Jerry Hernandez, Jun Hee Lee in *Ethan Mao* PHOTO COURTESY OF MARGIN FILMS

CAFE LUMIERE

(DIAPHANA FILMS) a.k.a. *Kohi Jikou*; Producers, Hideshi Miyajima, Liao Ching-sung, Ichiro Yamamoto, Fumiko Osaka; Director, Hou Hsiao-Hsien; Screenplay, Hou Hiso-Hsien, Chu Tien-Wen; Photography, Lee Ping-Bing; Designer, Tashiharu Aida; Costumes, Kazumi Hoshino, Yoji Yamada; a Shochiku, Asahi Shimbun, Sumimoto, Eisei Gekijo, IMAGICA co-production; Japanese, 2004; Dolby; Color; Not rated; 102 minutes; American release date: June 10, 2005. CAST: Yo Hioto (Yoko), Tadanobu Asano (Hajime Takeuchi), Masato Hagiwara (Seiji), Kimiko Yo (Yoko's Stepmother), Nenji Kobayashi (Yoko's Father)

JOINT SECURITY AREA

(PALM PICTURES) Producer, Lee Eun Soo; Director, Park Chan-wook; Screenplay, Park Chan-wook, Kim Heyon-seok, Jeong Seong-san, Lee Mu-yeong; Based on the novel *DMZ* by Park Sang-yeon; Photography, Kim Sung-Bok; Costumes, Park Sang-hoon; Music, Bang Jun-Seok, Jo Yeong-wook; Editor, Kim Sang-Beom; a CJ Entertainment, Intz.com, KTB Network production; South Korean; Dolby; Color; Not rated; 110 minutes; American release date: June 15, 2005. CAST: Lee Yeong-ae (Maj. Sophie E. Jean), Lee Byung-hun (Sgt. Lee Soo-hyeok), Song Kang-ho (Sgt. Oh Kyeong-pil), Kim Tae-woo (Nam Sung-shik), Shin Ha-kyun (Jeong Woo-jin), Christoph Hofrichter (Maj. Gen. Bruno Botta)

WHEEL OF TIME

(HEMISPHERIC PICTURES/518 MEDIA) Producer/Director/Screenplay, Werner Herzog; Executive Producer, Andre Singer; Photography, Peter Zeitlinger; Editor, Joe Bini; a Werner Herzog Filmproduktion; German, 2003; Dolby; Color; Not rated; 80 minutes; American release date: June 15, 2005. Documentary on twin Buddhist ceremonies.

THE GREAT WATER

(PICTURE THIS!) Producers, Robert Pazadziski, Suki Medencevic, Ivo Trajkov; Supervising Producer, Anita Elsani; Director, Ivo Trajkov; Screenplay, Ivo Trajkov, Vladimir Blazevski; Based on the novel by Zhivko Chingo; Photography, Suki Medencevic; Music, Kiril Dzajokovski; Editor, Atanas Georgiev; Casting, Mykola Hejko, Ivo Trajkov; a Kaval Film, Castor Productions, World Circle Foundation, Artis 3 production; Macedeonian-Czech-U.S.-German; Dolby; Color; Not rated;

93 minutes; American release date: June 17, 2005. CAST: Saso Kekenovski (Lem), Maja Stankovska (Isak Keyten), Mitko Apostolovski (Warden), Verica Nedeska (Komrade Olivera), Risto Gogovski (Bellman), Nikolina Kujaca (Verna), Meto Jovanovski (Old Lem), Aleksandar Ribak (Metodija Griskoski), Vladimir Svetiev (Sekule, Geography Teacher), Petar Mircevski (Dervutoski, Gym Teacher), Goce Deskoski (Klimoski), Marina Cakalova (Lence), Zoran Popovski (Niholce), Oliver Trinfunov (Spasko)

Vahina Giocante, Mohammed Khouas in *Lila Says* PHOTO COURTESY OF SAMUEL GOLDWYN FILMS

Mitko Apostolovski in *The Great Water* PHOTO COURTESY OF PICTURE THIS!

ETHAN MAO

(MARGIN FILMS) Producers, Quentin Lee, Stanley Yung; Associate Producers, Joan Huang, Julie Asato, Ernesto Foronda; Director/Screenplay, Quentin Lee; Photography, James C. Yuan; Designer, Rodney Hom; Costumes, Steve Norman Lee; Music, Steven Pranoto; Editor, Christine Kim; Casting, Joan Huang; a Trailing Johnson production; Color; Canadian-U.S.; Color; Not rated; 87 minutes; American release date: June 17, 2005. CAST: Jun Hee Lee (Ethan Mao), Raymond Ma (Abraham Mao), Julia Nickson (Sarah Mao), Kevin Kleinberg (Josh), Jerry Hernandez (Remigio), David Tran (Noel Mao), Mary Gilbert (Mrs. Harvisham), René St. Leon (Teenage Boy), Jyane Taini (Waitress), Erik Robinson (Rich Man), Gregory Paul Daniels (Unseen Man), Dana Pan (Ethan's Mom), Michael Mesirow (Voice of Sheriff Black)

LILA SAYS

(SAMUEL GOLDWYN) a.k.a. *Lila dit ça*; Producer, Marina Gefter; Executive Producer, Andrew Rouhemann, Paul Trijbits; Director, Ziad Doueiri; Screenplay, Ziad Doueiri, Mark Lawrence, Joelle Touma; Photography, John Daly; Designer, Yves Bernard; Costumes, Pierre Matard; Music, Nitin Sawhney; Editor, Tina Baz; Casting, Maya Sevleyan, Juliette Ménager; a Pyramide Productions, France 2 Cinema, Passion Picture, Huit et Demi Productions production; French-British, 2004; Dolby; Color; Rated R; 89 minutes; American release date: June 24, 2005. CAST: Vahina Giocante (Lila), Mohammed Khouas (Chimo), Karim Ben Haddou (Mouloud), Carmen Lebbos (Chimo's Mother), Hamid Dkhissi (Big Jo), Lotfi Chakri (Bakary), Edmonde Franchi (Lila's Aunt), Stéphanie Fatout (Claire Soulier), Barbara Chossis (Chinese Prostitute), Dominique Bluzet (Priest), Bruno Esposito (Police Inspector), Ghandi Assad (Sammy)

MEMORIES OF MURDER

(PALM PICTURES) a.k.a. *Salinui chueok*; Producers, Cha Seoung-Jae, Kim Moo Ryung, No Jong-yun; Executive Producer, Lee Kang-bok; Director, Bong Joon-ho; Screenplay, Bong Joon-ho, Shim Sung Bo, Kim Kwang-rim; Photography, Kim Hyeong-guy; Designer, Yu Seong-hie; Music, Taro Iwashiro; Editor, Kim Seon Min; Martial Arts Choreographer, Lee Eung Jun; a Sidus Pictures, CJ Entertainment production; South Korean, 2003; Dolby; Color; Not rated; 132 minutes; American release date: June 24, 2005. CAST: Song Kang-ho (Det. Park

Kim Sang-kyung, Song Kang-ho in *Memories of Murder* PHOTO COURTESY OF PALM PICTURES

Doo-Man), Kim Sang-kyung (Det. Seo Tae-Yoon), Kim Roe-ha (Det. Cho Yong-koo), Song Jae-ho (Sgt. Shin Dong-chul), Byeon Hie-bong (Sgt. Koo Hee-bong), Ko Seo-hie (Officer Kwon Kwi-ok), Park No-shik (Baek), Park Hae-il (Park), Choi Jong-ryol (Du-man's Father), Jeon Mi-seon (Kwok Seol-yung)

A Decent Factory PHOTO COURTESY OF FIRST RUN ICARUS

A DECENT FACTORY

(FIRST RUN/ICARUS) Producers, Thomas Balmes, Kaarle Aho; Director/Screenplay/Photography, Thomas Balmes; Editor, Catherine Gouze; a Margot Films, BBC, Making Movies production; Finnish-British-French; Color; DV; Not rated; 79 minutes; American release date: June 29, 2005. Documentary on outsourced factories in China owned by Germans and run by English managers; featuring Hanna Kaskinen, Louise Jamison.

Sakda Kaewbuadee, Banlop Lomnoi in *Tropical Malady* PHOTO COURTESY OF STRAND RELEASING

TROPICAL MALADY

(STRAND) a.k.a. *Sud Pralad*; Producer, Charles de Meaux; Co-Producers, Paiboon Damrongehaitham, Marco Muller, Christoph Thoke, Axel Moebius, Pantham Thongsangl; Director/Screenplay, Apichatpong Weerasethakul; Photography, Vichit Tanapanitch, Jarin Pengpanitch, Jean-Louis Vialard; Editors, Lee Chatametikool, Jacopo Quadri; an Anna Sanders Films, Tifa, Downtown, Thoke + Moebius, Kick the Machin co-production in association with Backup Films, RAI Cinema, Fabrica Cinema; French-Thai-Italian-German, 2004; Dolby; Color; Not rated; 118 minutes; American release date: June 29, 2005. CAST: Bankop Lomnoi (Keng), Sakda Kaewbuadee (Tong), Huai Dessom, Sirivech Jareonchon, Udom Promma

Felicity Mason in *Undead* PHOTO COURTESY OF LIONS GATE

UNDEAD

(LIONS GATE) Producers/Directors/Screenplay/Editors, The Spierig Brothers; Photography, Andrew Strahorn; Designer, Matthew Putland; Costumes, Chintamani Aked; Music, Cliff Bradley; Casting, Ben Parkinson; a Spierigfilm; Australian, 2003; Dolby; Color; Rated R; 100 minutes; American release date: July 1, 2005. CAST: Felicity Mason (Rene), Mungo McKay (Marion), Rob Jenkins (Wayne), Lisa Cunningham (Sallyanne), Dirk Hunter (Harrison), Emma Randall (Molly), Steve Grieg (Agent), Noel Sheridan (Chip), Gaynor Wensley (Aggie), Eleanor Stillman (Ruth), Robyn Moore (Officer in Locker Room), Robert Jozinovic (Man in Office), Peter Mensforth (Cricket Batsman), Jacob Andriolo (Young Cricketer), Michele Steel (Screamer), William John King (Angry Father), Tim Dickenson, Brad Sheriff (Fishermen), Georgia Potter-Cowie (Young Zombie Girl), Francesca Arakelian (General Store Owner), Kyan Marie Salter (Baby in Crib), David Whitcomb (Newsreader), Paul Guthrie (Disco Zombie), Rob Doran (Bullet Wound Victim), Kristijana Maric (Marion's Ex-Wife), Kathleen McGowan, Chintamani Aked, Steven O'Donnell (Zombies)

STEVE + SKY

(LIFESIZE ENTERTAINMENT) Producer, Dirk Impens; Supervising Producer, Jozefien Tsebie; Director/Screenplay, Felix Van Groeningen; Photography, Ruben Impens; Costumes, Hilde Destoop; Music, Soulwax; a Favourite Films production; Belgian, 2004; Dolby; Color; Not rated; 95 minutes; American release date: July 8, 2005. CAST: Titus De Voogdt (Steve), Delfine Bafort (Sky), Johan Heldenbergh (Jean-Claude), Romy Bollion (Charlotte), Wine Dierickx (Nikita), Vanessa Van Durme (Moeder Marc), Sylvie Buytaert (Kelly), Didier De Neck (Taxichauffeur), Bart Dauwe (Cipier), Sam Bogaerts (Vader), Wouter Bruneel (Zoon), Herwig Deweerdt (Klant Sky), Jonas Boel (Marc), Francoise Vanhecke (Verpleegster)

RETURN TO THE LAND OF WONDER

(ARAB FILM DISTRIBUTION) Producer/Director/Editor, Maysoon Pachachi; No other credits available; Color; Not rated; 88 minutes; American release date: July 13, 2005. Documentary on the efforts to draft Iraq's temporary constitution and bill of rights.

SEARCHING FOR THE WRONG-EYED JESUS

(SHADOW DISTRIBUTION) Producers, Andrew Douglas, Martin Rosenbaum, Jonathan Shoemaker; Executive Producers, Steve Golin, Anthony Qall; Director, Andrew Douglas; Screenplay, Steve Haisman; Photography, Flor Collins; Art Director, Clive Howard; Music, Jim White; Editor, Michael Elliot; an Andrew Douglas Co., Lone Star Prods. (U.K.), Anonymous Content (U.S.) production for BBC Arena; Color, 16mm-to-DigiBeta; Not rated; 84 minutes; American release date: July 13, 2005. Documentary in which British filmmaker Andrew Douglas looks at America's Deep South; featuring Jim White, The Handsome Family, Johnny Dowd, David Johansen, Lee Sexton, Harry Crews, Rev. Gary Howington, David Eugene Edwards, Trailer Bride Melissa Swingle.

GOD'S SANDBOX

(INDICAN) Producer, Yoav Halevy; Director, Doron Eran; Screenplay, Yoav Halevy, Hanita Halevy; Photography, Klaudio Shtainberg; an Open Doors Films production; Israeli, 2002; Color; Not rated; 86 minutes; American release date: July 15, 2005. CAST: Meital Dohan (Layla), Razia Israeli (Liz), Amos Lavi (Bedouin Sorcerer), Juliano Mer (Nagim), Orli Perl (Rachel), Sami Samir (Mustafa)

THE WARRIOR

(MIRAMAX) Producer, Bertrand Faivre; Executive Producers, Hanno Huth, Paul Webster; Line Producer, Mark Hubbard; Director/Screenplay, Asif Kapadia; Photography, Roman Osin; Designer, Adrian Smith; Costumes, Louise Stjernsward; Music, Dario Marianelli; Editor, Ewa Lind; Casting, Tigmanshu; a co-production of Film Four, The Bureau, with the participation of British Screen; British-French-German, 2001; Dolby; Deluxe color; Rated R; 86 minutes; American release date: July 15, 2005. CAST: Irfan Kahn (Lafcadia), Puru Chibber (Katiba), Aino Annuddin (Biswas), Manoj Mishra, Nanhe Khan, Chander Singh, Hemant Maahaor (Warriors), Mandakini Goswami (Rabia), Sunita Sharma (The Girl), Shauket (Clerk), Gori Shanker (Tarang Village Headman), Prabhuram (Blacksmith), Wagaram (Blacksmith's Son), Ajai Rohilla (Qaurrey Foreman), Noor Mani (Riaz), Anupam Shyam (Lord), Amit Kumar (Market Trader), Damayanti Marfatia (Blind Woman), Trilok Singh (Cart Driver), Anuradha Advanti (Lord's Wife), Sitaram Panchal (Dhaba Stall Owner), Chander Prakash Vyas, Sanjal (Dhaba Stall Men), Pushpa Negi (Restaurant Owner), Karuna Sarah Davis (Restaurant Girl), Rakesh Mehra (Rude Customer), Madhu (Singer)

Delfine Bafort, Titus De Voogdt in *Steve + Sky* PHOTO COURTESY OF LIFESIZE ENTERTAINMENT

Jim White in *Searching for the Wrong-Eyed Jesus* PHOTO COURTESY OF SHADOW DISTRIBUTION

Meital Dohan in *God's Sandbox* PHOTO COURTESY OF INDICAN

THROW DOWN

(TAI SENG ENTERTAINMENT) a.k.a. *Yau doh lung fu bong*; Producer/Director, Johnny To; Executive Producer, Charles Heung; Screenplay, Kin Yee Au, Nai-Ho Yau, Tin-Shing Yip; Photography, Siu-keung Cheng; Editor, David Richardson; a Sil-Metropole presentation of a China Star Entertainment, Milky Way Images production; Hong Kong-Chinese, 2004; Dolby; Color; Not rated; 95 minutes; American release date: July 22, 2005. CAST: Aaron Kwok (Tony), Louis Koo (Szeto Bo), Tony Leung Ka Fai (Kong), Cherrie Ying (Mona), Jordan Chan (Mona's Agent), Siu-Fai Cheung (Brother Savage), Yat-Chi Choi (Jing), Jack Kao (Mona's Dad), Hoi-Pang Lo (Master Cheng)

THE 3 ROOMS OF MELANCHOLIA

(INDEPENDENT) a.k.a. *Melancholian kolme huonetta*; Producer, Kristina Pervila; Director/Screenplay/Photography, Pirjo Honkasalo; Music, Sanna Salmenkallio; Editors, Niels Pagh Andersen, Pirjo Honkasalo; a Millennium Film (Finland), Lisbet Gabrielsson Film (Sweden), Magic Hour Films (Denmark), Ma Ja.De Prods. (Germany) production in association with ZDF/ARTE Germany, YLA, SVT, the Finnish Film Foundation, AVEK, the Danish Film Institute, the Swedish Film Institute, the Nordic Film & TV Fund, MEDIA Program; Finnish-Swedish-Danish-

German, 2004; Dolby; Color; Not rated; 104 minutes; American release date: July 27, 2005. Documentary on the Chechen war's effect on children, as told in three sections: "Nostalgia" set in the Kronstadt Cadet Academy, "Breathing" set in bombed Grozny, and "Remembering" set in Ingushetia.

OYSTER FARMER

(THE CINEMA GUILD) Producers, Anthony Buckley, Piers Tempest; Executive Producers, Robert Bevan, Mikael Borglund, Hilary Davis, Keith Hayley, Andrew Mackie, Stephen Margolis, Cyril Megret, Richard Peyton, Charlie Savill, Emile Sherman, Jonathan Shteinman; Director/Screenplay, Anna Reeves; Photography, Alun Bollinger; Designer, Steven Jones-Evans; Music, Stephen Warbeck; Editors, Jamie Trevill, Peter Beston; a Tempo Productions Limited production; Australia-British, 2004; Dolby; Color; Not rated; 91 minutes; American release date: July 29, 2005. CAST: Alex O'Loughlin (Jack), Jim Norton (Mumbles), Diana Glenn (Pearl), David Field (Brownie), Kerry Armstrong (Trish), Claudia Harrison (Nikki), Alan Cinis (Slug), Jack Thompson (Skippy), Bob Yearley (Bruce), Brady Kitchingham (Heath), Gary Henderson (Oyster Farmer Barry), Ian Johnson, Peter Johnson (Oyster Farmers), Natalie McCurry (Pearl's Mom)

Diana Glenn, Alex O'Loughlin in *Oyster Farmer* PHOTO COURTESY OF CINEMA GUILD

The 3 Rooms of Melancholia PHOTOS COURTESY OF INDEPENDENT

EDGAR G. ULMER—THE MAN OFF-SCREEN

(KINO) Producers, Georg Misch, Ralph Wieser, Arianne Ulmer Cipes; Director, Michael Palm; Photography, Joerg Burger; Editors, Michael Palm, Marek Kralovsky; a Mischief Films (Austria), Edgar G. Ulmer Preservation Corp. (US) production in association with Westdeutscher Rundfunk; Austrian-U.S.; Color/black and white; Not rated; 77 minutes; American release date: July 29, 2005. Documentary on filmmaker Edgar G. Ulmer; featuring Peter Bogdanovich, Christian Cargnelli, Arianne Ulmer Cipes, Roger Corman, Joe Dante, Stefan Grissemann, Alexander Horwath, Noah Isenberg, John Landis, Jimmy Lydon, Gregory W. Mank, Peter Marshall, Michael Omasta, Michael Palm, Ann Savage, John Saxon, William Schallert, Tom Weaver, Wim Wenders.

Pedro Perez, Mia Maestro in *Secuestro Express* PHOTO COURTESY OF MIRAMAX

SECUESTRO EXPRESS

(MIRAMAX) Producers, Jonathan Jakubowicz, Salomon Jakubowicz, Sandra Condito; Executive Producers, Elizabeth Avellan, Eduardo Jakubowicz; Director/Screenplay, Jonathan Jakubowicz; Photography, David Chalker; Art Director, Andrés Zawisza; Costumes, Belica; Music, Angelo Milli; Editor, Ethan Maniquis; Venezuelan, 2005; Dolby; Color; Rated R; 86 minutes; American release date: August 5, 2005. CAST: Mía Maestro (Carla), Rubén Baldes (Carla's Father), Carlos Julio Molina (Trece), Pedro Perez (Budu), Carlos Madera (Niga

Joseph Goebbels in *The Goebbels Experiment* PHOTO COURTESY OF FIRST RUN FEATURES

Sibilino), Jean Paul Leroux (Martin), Dimas Gonzalez (Guardia), Blamore Moreno (Official Briceno), Ermahn Osphina (Marcelo), Rider (Cangrejo)

DARWIN'S NIGHTMARE

(INTERNATIONAL FILM CIRCUIT) Producers, Hubert Sauper, Barbara Albert, Martin Gschlacht, Edouard Mauriat, Antonin Svoboda, Hubert Toint; Director/Screenplay/Photography, Hubert Sauper; Editor, Denise Vindevogel; a Coop 99, Saga Film, Mille en Une Productions production; Austrian-Belgian-French-Canadian-Finnish-Swedish, 2004; Dolby; Color; Not rated; 107 minutes; American release date: August 5, 2005. Documentary on how the Nile perch fish caught in Tanzania's Lake Victoria are sold in European markets while the Tanzanian families starve.

A STATE OF MIND

(KINO) Executive Producer, John Battsek; Director, Daniel Gordon; Editor, Peter Haddon; North Korean-British; Color; Not rated; 93 minutes; American release date: August 10, 2005. Documentary on two North Korean girls as they prepare for the Mass Games gymnastics competition; featuring Kim Jong-il, Kim Song Yun, Pak Hyon Sun.

A State of Mind PHOTO COURTESY OF KINO INTERNATIONAL

THE GOEBBELS EXPERIMENT

(FIRST RUN FEATURES) Producer, Guenter van Endert; Director, Lutz Hachmeister; Screenplay, Michael Kloft, Lutz Hachmeister; Additional Material, Christian Wagner, Mathias von der Heide; Photography, Hajo Schomerus; Music, Hubert Bittman; Editor, Guido Krajewski; Narrator, Kenneth Branagh; a Spiegel TV, ZDT (Germany), BBC Storyville (U.K.) presentation of an HMR Prod. production; German-British; Color/black and white; Not rated; 107 minutes; American release date: August 12, 2005. Documentary on Nazi leader Joseph Goebbels, based mostly on excerpts from his diaries.

SYMPATHY FOR MR. VENGEANCE

(TARTAN) a.k.a. *Boksuneun naui geot*; Producers, Lee Jae-sun, Lim Jing-guy; Executive Producers, Lee Kang-bok, Seok Dong-jun; Director, Park Chan-wook; Screenplay, Park Chan-wook, Lee Jae-sun, Lee Mu-yeong, Lee Yong-jong; Photography, Kim Sang-Beom; Designer, Choe Jung-hwa; Editor, Kim Sang-Beom; Costumes, Shin Seung-heui; a CJ Entertainment, Studio Box production; South Korean, 2002; Dolby; Color; Rated R; 117 minutes; American release date: August 19, 2005. CAST: Song Kang-ho (Park Dong-jin), Shin Ha-kyn (Ryu), Bae Du-na (Cha Yeong-mi), Lim Ji-Eun (Ryu's Sister), Han Bo-bae (Yu-sun), Kim Se-dong (Chief of Staff), Lee Dae-yeon (Choe), Jeong Jae-yeong (Husband of Dong-jin's Ex-Wife), Lee Han-hie (Park Dong-jin's Ex-Wife), Oh Kwang-rok (Anarchist)

Penelope Velasco, Guillermo Toledo in *El Crimen Perfecto* PHOTO COURTESY OF VITAGRAPH

EL CRIMEN PERFECTO

(VITAGRAPH) Producers, Alex de la Iglesia, Roberto Di Girolamo, Gustavo Ferrada; Line Producer, Juanma Pagazaurtandua; Director, Alex de la Iglesia; Screenplay, Alex de la Iglesia, Jorge Guerricaechevarria; Photography, Jose L. Moreno; Designer, Arturo Garcia Otaduy; Costumes, Paco Delgado; Music, Roque Baños; Editor, Alejandro Lázaro; Casting, Mamen Moya, Amaya Diez; a co-production of Panico Films, Planet Pictures, Digital +, Sogecine S.A.; Spanish-Italian; Dolby; Color; Not rated; 105 minutes; American release date: Augsut 19, 2005. CAST: Guillermo Toledo (Rafael González), Mónica Cervera (Lourdes), Luis Varela (Don Antonio Fraugas), Enrique Villén (Comisario Campoy), Fernando Tejero (Alonso), Javier Gutiérrez (Jaime), Kira Miró (Roxanne), Rosario Pardo (Senor Despistada), Gracia Olayo (Concha), Penélope Velasco (Susana), Montserrat Mostaza (Helena), Eduardo Gómez (Taxista), Alicia Andújar (Desiree), Juan Viadas (Julian), Hector Gomez (Vendedor), Isabel Osca (Doña Asución), Alicia Alvarez (Sonia), Ines Maria Guzman (Señora Enfadada)

NOW & FOREVER

(ARDUSTRY) Producers, Leanne Arnott, David Doerksen; Executive Producers, Cameron White, Tim Gamble, Kent Wingerak; Director, Bob Clark; Screenplay, Bill Boyle; Photography, Jan Kiesser; Designer, Wendy Morrow; Costumes, Koreen Heaver; Music, Paul Zaza; Editor, Lenka Syab; an Edge Entertainment Inc., Shoreline Entertainment production; Canadian, 2002; Dolby; Color; Not rated; 101 minutes; American release date: August 19, 2005. CAST: Mia Kirshner (Angela Wilson), Adam Beach (John Myron), Gordon Tootoosis (Ghost Fox), Theresa Russell (Dori Wilson), Gabriel Olds (T. J. Bolt), Callum Keith Rennie (Carl Mackie), Simon Baker (Young John Myron), Alexandra Purvis (Young Angela), Nicholas Treeshin (Jake Dube), Benson McCulloch (Brian Pressman), Rob Roy (Alex Wilson), Lyndon Linklater (Older Boy), Bernelda Wheeler (Old Woman), Dan MacDonald (Director), Kent Allen (Max), Calvert Chiefcalf (Reservation Officer), Louisa Ferguson (Movie Director), Collin Smenoff (Actor T. J.), David Millbern (Guardian)

Wall PHOTO COURTESY OF LIFESIZE ENTERTAINMENT

WALL

(LIFESIZE ENTERTAINMENT) a.k.a. *Mur*; Producer, Thierry Lenouvel; Director/Screenplay, Simone Bitton; Photography, Jacques Bouquin; Editors, Jean-Michel Perez, Catherine Poitevin-Meyer; a Ciné-Sud Promotion, Arna Productions presentation; French-Israeli, 2004; Dolby; Color; Not rated; 96 minutes; American release date: August 26, 2005. Documentary on the separation fence in Israel-Palestine.

Wall PHOTO COURTESY OF LIFESIZE ENTERTAINMENT

Thomas Dumerchez, Salim Kechiouche in *Three Dancing Slaves* PHOTO COURTESY OF TLA RELEASING

ETERNAL

(REGENT/HERE! FILMS) a.k.a. *Éternelle*; Producers, Wilhelm Liebenberg, Federico Sanchez, Tommaso Calevi; Executive Producer, Bruce Robertson; Directors/Screenplay, Wilhelm Leibenberg, Federico Sanchez; Photography, Jamie Thompson; Designer, Perri Gorrara; Costumes, Claire Nadon, Stefania Svizzeretto; Music, Mysterious Art; Editor, Isabelle Levesque; Casting, Aldo Tirelli, Elisabetta Giacomelli; a TVA Films, Wildkoast Entertainment production; Canadian, 2004; Dolby; Color; Rated R; 107 minutes; American release date: August 26, 2005. CAST: Sarah Manninen (Wildcat), Caroline Néron (Elizabeth Kane), Victoria Sanchez (Irina), Conrad Pla (Raymond Pope), Ilona Elkin (Nancy Cusack), Nick Baillie (Dean Cusack), Luke Bélanger (French Cop), Liane Balaban (Lisa), Joey Pla (Nathan), James A. Woods (Tom), Suzanna Lenir (Brenda), Arthur Holden (Mr. Renault), Justin Bradley (Teenage Basketball Player), Kathleen Munroe (Connie), Yves Corbeil (Captain Gérard), Romano Orzari (Det. Angie Manning), Jennifer Moorehouse (French Singer, Helene), Ella (Pianist), Suzanne Jacquart (Vanessa), John Dunn-Hill (Inspector Thurzo), Genevieve Sabourin (Mr. Renaud's Secretary), Concita Puglisi (Waitress Piazza San Marco), Cristina Bertini (Gypsy Girl), Ted Rusoff (Garibaldi), Francesco Loi (Water Taxi Driver), Luca Sinigallia (Masked Guard), Natacha Noël (Chained Woman), Stephanie Dixon, Anna Rubin (Feline Women), Valérie Wiseman (Tall Woman), Valentina Bordin (Predator), Maura Leone (First Victim), Sylvia Cohen (Elegant Woman), Manon Madia Umbertelli (Second Victim), Juliana Kögler (Third Victim).

GAMES OF LOVE AND CHANCE

(NEW YORKER) a.k.a. *L'Esquive*; Producer, Jacques Ouaniche; Director, Abdellatif Kechiche; Screenplay, Abdellatif Kechiche, Ghalia Lacroix; Photography, Lubomir Bakchev; Designer, Michel Gionti; Costumes, Mario Beloso Hall; Editor, Ghalia Lacroix, Antonella Bevenja; from Lola Films, Ciné Cinémas, Noé Productions; French, 2003; Dolby; Color; Not rated; 123 minutes; American release date: August 31, 2005. CAST: Osman Elkharraz (Krimo), Sara Forestier (Lydia), Sabrina Ouazani (Frida), Nanou Benhamou (Nanou), Hafet Ben-Ahmed (Fathi), Aurelie Ganito (Magalie), Carole Franck (French Professor), Hajar Hamlili (Zina), Rachid Hami (Rachid), Meryem Serbah (Krimo's Mother), Hanane Mazouz (Hanane), Sylvain Phan (Slam)

THREE DANCING SLAVES

(TLA RELEASING) a.k.a. *Le Clan*; Producer, Philippe Jacquier; Executive Producer, Bertrand Guerry; Director, Gaël Morel; Screenplay, Gaël Morel, Christophe Honoré; Photography, Jean-Max Bernard; Art Director, Zé Branco; a Sépia Productions, Rhône-Alpes Cinéma co-production, with the participation of Centre Européen Cinématographique Rhône-Alples, Centre National de la Cinématographie (CNC), Procirep, Angoa-Agioca; French, 2004; Dolby; Color; Not rated; 90 minutes; American release date: September 2, 2005. CAST: Nicolas Cazalé (Marc), Stéphane Rideau (Christophe), Thomas Dumerchez (Olivier), Salim Kechiouche (Hicham), Bruno Lochet (Father), Vincent Martinez ("Professor"), Jackie Berroyer (Robert), Aure Atika (Emilie), Nicolas Paz (Montana), Mathias Olivier (Ryan), Gary Mary (Luc), Geordie Piseri-Diaz (Jérémy), Clément Dettli (Henry), Pierre Vallin (Sly), Janine Ribollet (Sly's Mother), Gilles Taurand (Man at Farm), Fabien Reboux, Geoffroy Rippoz (Boys at Farm), Claude Carilglionne (Horse Trainer), Olivier Perez (Zora the Transexual), Kérédine Defdaf (Montana's Henchman), Jean-Jerôme Landue (Bruno), Joyce Edorh (Blanche-Neige), Paul Morel (François), Pierre Blériot (Boy at School), Nathanël Maïni (Hang-gliding Monitor), Yves Jacquemard (Physical Therapist)

TOUCH THE SOUND

(SHADOW RELEASING) Producers, Stefan Tolz, Leslie Hills, Trevor Davies; Director/Photograph/Editor, Thomas Riedelsheimer; Music, Evelyn Glennie, Fred Frith; a Filmquadrat GbR, Skyline production; German-British; Dolby; Color; Not rated; 99 minutes; American release date: September 7, 2005. Documentary on deaf Scottish percussionist Evelyn Glennie; featuring Evelyn Glennie, Fred Frith.

EDGE CODES.COM: THE ART OF MOTION PICTURE EDITING

(TRAVESTY RELEASING) Producers, Wyeth Clarkson, Phillip Daniels; Director, Alex Shuper; Screenplay, Alex Shuper, Phillip Daniels; an Astral Media, Inc., Bravo Network Canada, Mpix production; Canadian, 2004; Color; Not rated; 75 minutes; American release date: September 8, 2005. Documentary on film editing; featuring Mathilde Bonnefoy, Dody Dorn, Sarah Flack, Norman Jewison,

Sara Forestier (right) in *Games of Love and Chance* PHOTO COURTESY OF NEW YORKER FILMS

George Lucas, Andrew Mondshein, Michael Ondaatje, Ronald Sanders, Thelma Schoonmaker, Susan Shipton, Zach Staenberg, Mary Stephen, Christopher Tellefsen, David Wu.

KAMIKAZE GIRLS

(VIZ MEDIA) a.k.a. *Shimotsuma monogatari*; Producers, Satoru Ogura, Takashi Hirano, Yuuji Ishida; Executive Producers, Yokichi Osato, Kunikatsu Kondo; Director/Screenplay, Tetsuya Nakashima; Based on the comics by Nobara Takemoto; Photography, Masakazu Ato; Designer, Towako Kuwashima; Editor, Chiaki Toyama; a co-production of Amuse Pictures Inc., Tokyo Broadcasting System, Hori Production, Hakuhodo DY Media Partners; Japanese, 2004; Dolby; Color; Not rated; 102 minutes; American release date: September 9, 2005. CAST: Kyoko Fukada (Momoko Ryugasaki), Ana Tsuchiya (Ichigo Shirayuri), Hiroyuki Miyasako (Momoko's Father), Sadao Abe (Designer and Owner), Eiko Koike (Akimi), Shin Yazawa (Miko), Hirotaro Honda (Yakuza Boss), Kirin Kiki (Momoko's Grandmother), YosiYosi Arakawa (Grocery Store Manager), Katsuhisa Namase (Pachinko Parlor Manager), Ryoko Shinohara (Momoko's Mother), Yoshinori Okada (Baby, "The Stars Shine Bright" Owner)

Kyoko Fukada, Ana Tsuchiya in *Kamikaze Girls* PHOTO COURTESY OF VIZ MEDIA

Moshe Ivgy, Hani Furstenberg, Maya Maron in *Campfire* PHOTO COURTESY OF FILM MOVEMENT

CAMPFIRE

(FILM MOVEMENT) Executive Producers, David Mandil, Eyal Shiray; Director/Screenplay, Joseph Cedar; Photography, Ofer Inov; Designer, Miguel Markin; Costumes, Laura Sheim; Editor, Einat Glaser-Zarhin; a Cinema Post Production in association with Israeli Film Fund production; Israeli; Color; Not rated; 96 minutes; Release date: September 9, 2005. CAST: Michaela Eshet (Rachel Gerlik), Hani Furstenberg (Tami Gerlik), Moshe Ivgy (Yossi), Maya Maron (Esti), Assi Dayan (Motken), Oshri Cohen (Rafi), Yehoram Gaon (Moshe Weinstock), Yehuda Levi (Yoel), Avi Grainik (Oded), Edith Teperson (Shula), Itay Turgeman (Gozlan), Barak Lizork (Yaniv), Danny Zahavi (Ilan), Dina Senderson (Inbal), Ofer Seker (Yair)

THE WEEPING MEADOW

(NEW YORKER FILMS) Producers, Theo Angelopoulos, Amedeo Pagani, Phoebe Economopoulos, Amedeo Pagani; Executive Producer, Nikos Sekeris; Director, Theo Angelopoulos; Screenplay, Theo Angelopoulos, Petros Markaris, Tonino Guerra, Giorgio Silvagni; Photography, Andreas Sinanos; Designers, Giorgos Patsas, Costas Dimitriadis; Music, Eleni Karaindrou; Editor, Giorgos Triantanfillou; Casting, Haria Papadopoulos; Greek-French-German-Italian; Color; Not rated; 170 minutes; American release date: September 14, 2005. CAST: Alexandria Aidini (Eleni), Nikos Poursadinis (Young Man), Giorgos Armenis (Nikos, the Fiddler), Vassilis Kolovos (Spyros), Eva Kotamandiou (Cassandra), Toula Stathopoulou (Woman in Coffee House), Michalis Yannatos (Zissis, the Clarinet Player), Thali Argiriou (Danae), Grigoris Evangelatos (Teacher)

HARD GOODBYES: MY FATHER

(INDEPENDENT) Producers, Thanos Karanthanos, George Louzios, Kostas Lambropoulos; Director/Screenplay, Penny Panayotopoulou; Editor, Petar Markovic; a co-production of CL Productions, Greek Film Center, Alpha TV, Anima-Film, Max Productions, K.L. Production, Hellenic Radio & Television, Twenty Twenty Vision Filmproduktion GmbH; Greek-German; Dolby; Fujicolor; Not rated; 113 minutes; American release date: September 16, 2005. CAST: Yorgos Karayannis (Elias), Stelios Mainas (Elias' Father), Ioanna Tsirigouli (Elias' Mother), Hristos Boyotas (Aris), Despo Diamantidou (Grandmother), Christos Stergioglu (Theodosius)

Hristos Boyotas, Ioanna Tsirigouli in *Hard Goodbyes: My Father* PHOTOS COURTESY OF INDEPENDENT

I AM CUBA: THE SIBERIAN MAMMOTH

(TRES MUNDOS PRODUCCIONES) Producer, Isabel Martinez; Director/Screenplay, Vicente Ferraz; Editors, Dull Janiel, Mair Tavares; Music, Jenny Padron; Brazilian; Color/black and white; Not rated; 90 minutes; American release date: September 16, 2005. Documentary on the making and rediscovery of the 1963 documentary *I Am Cuba*, which celebrated the Castro revolution in Cuba.

NOVO

(IFC FILMS) Producer, Hengameh Panahi; Director, Jean-Pierre Limosin; Screenplay, Jean-Pierre Limosin, Christophe Honoré; Photography, Julien Hirsch; Designer, Christian Vansteenkiste; Costumes, Maripol; Music, Zenda Avesta, Mathieu Dury, Loïc Dury; Editor, Cristina Otero Roth; Casting, Stéphane Batut; a Lumen Films, Alta Films S.A., Amka Films Productions S.A.; Swiss-French-Spanish, 2002; Dolby; Color; Rated R; 98 minutes; American release date: September 21, 2005. CAST: Eduardo Noriega (Graham), Anna Mouglalis (Irene), Nathalie Richard (Sabine), Eric Caravaca (Fred), Paz Vega (Isabelle), Lény Bueno (Antoine), Julie Gayet (Julie), Agathe Dronne (Céline), Bernard Bloch (Dr. Sagem), Vincent Dissez (Simon), Catherine Bidaut (Nadine), Pascal Tokatlian (Gérard), Dominic Gould (Gilles), Stéphanie Picard (Waitress), André S. Labarthe (Man at Museum)

DEAR WENDY

(WELLSPRING) Producer, Sisse Graum Jorgensen; Executive Producers, Peter Aalbaek Jensen, Bo Ehrhardt, Birgitte Hald; Director, Thomas Vinterberg; Screenplay, Lars von Trier; Photography, Anthony Dod Mantle; Designer, Karl Juliusson; Costumes, Annie Perier; Music, Benjamin Wallfisch; Editor, Mikkel E. G. Nielsen; Casting, Avy Kaufman; a Lucky Punch I/S presentation of a Nimbus, Zentropa production in co-production with Pain Unlimited Filmproduktion GmbH, Slot Machine Sarl, Liberator2 Sari, Dear Wendy Ltd., Sigma III Films Ltd.; Danish-German-British-French; Dolby; Color; Not rated; 104 minutes; American release date: September 23, 2005. CAST: Jamie Bell (Dick Dandelion), Bill Pullman (Krugsby), Michael Angarano (Freddie), Danso Gordon (Sebastian), Novella Nelson (Clarabelle), Chris Owen (Huey), Alison Pill (Susan), Mark Webber (Stevie), Trevor Cooper (Dick's Dad), Matthew Géczy (Young Officer), William Hootkins (Marshall Walker), Teddy Kempner (Mr. Salomon), Thomas Bo Larsen (Customer)

Jamie Bell, Danso Gordon in *Dear Wendy* PHOTO COURTESY OF WELLSPRING

I Am Cuba: The Siberian Mammoth PHOTO COURTESY OF TRES MUNDOS

SHOUJYO: AN ADOLESCENT

(INDICAN) Producers, Eiji Okuda, Ben Yamamoto; Executive Producer, Henri Ishii; Director, Eiji Okuda; Screenplay, Katsuhiko Manabe, Izuru Narushima; Based on the short story *Shōjo* by Mikihiko Renjo; Photography, Hirokazu Ishii; Art Director, Katsuhiko Hibino; Music, Shigeru Umebayashi; a Zero Pictures Co. production; Japanese; Color; Not rated; 132 minutes; American release date: September 30, 2005. CAST: Eiji Okuda (Tomokawa), Mayu Ozawa (Yoko), Akira Shoji (Sukemasa), Marii Natsuki (Yukie), Hideo Murota (Shozo)

THE OVERTURE

(KINO) a.k.a. *Hom rong*; Producers, Ittisoontorn Vichailak, Pisamai Laodara, Chatrichalerm Yukol; Executive Producers, Duangkamol Limcharoen, Nonzee Nimibutr; Director/Editor, Ittisoontorn Vichailak; Screenplay, Ittisoontorn Vichailak, Peerasak Saksiri, Dolkamol Sattatip; Photography, Nattawut Kittikhun; Music, Nick Chaiyapak; a Sahamongkolfilm Co. Ltd. production; Thai, 2004; Color; Not rated; 103 minutes; American release date: October 7, 2005. CAST: Adul Dulyarat (Elderly Sorn), Sumeth Ong-ard (Prasit), Phoovarit Phumpuang (Terd), Anuchit Sapanpong (Sorn), Arratee Tanmahapran (Chote, 1880s), Chumphorn Thepphithak (Tew), Narongrit Tosa-nga (Kun In), Pongpat Wachirabunjong (Lt. Col. Veera)

HENRI LANGLOIS: PHANTOM OF THE CINEMATHEQUE

(LEISURE TIME FEATURES) Producer/Director/Screenplay, Jacques Richard; Photography, Jacques Richard, Jérôme Blumberg; Music, Liam Farrell, Nicolas Baby; Editor, Fabrice Radenac; a La Cinémathèque Française Présentation, Les Films Elementaries production; French; Black and white; Not rated; 210 minutes; American release date: October 12, 2005. Documentary on Henri Langlois, the founder of the Cinematheque Française; featuring Henri Alekan, Catherine Allegret, Jean-Michael Arnold, Christian Auboire, Francois Barat, Raphael Bassan, Claude Berri, Marie-Charlotte Bridant, Freddy Buache, Raymonde Carasco, Pierre Cardin, Francoise Carviliani, Jean Casol, Claude Chabrol,

Jacques Champreux, Odile Chapel, Michel Ciment, Daniel Cohn-Bendit, Claudia Collao, Henri Colpi, Frederic Compain, Herve de Luze, Sybile de Luze, Philippe de Pardaillan, Ghislaine Dewind, Jean Diard, Jean Douchet, Max Douy, Brigitte Duvivier, Bernard Eisenschitz, Lotte Eisner, Gerard Fallin, Zahra Farzanef, Feri Farzaneh, Francoise Foucault, Alain Gabet, Philippe Garrel, Farokh Ghafari, Noelle Giret, Jean-Luc Godard, George Goldfayn, Romain Goupil, Hiroko Govars, Laurent Heynemann, Robert Hossein, Henri Hudrister, Francois Husard, Leone Jaffin, Miklos Jancso, Marie-Josee Jeannet, Valerie Jeannet, Andre S. Labarthe, Marguerite Laloi-Diard, Valerie Lalonde, Xavier Lambours, Henri Langlois, Hugues Langlois, Jean-Louis Langlois, Paul Lanteri, Richard Leacock, Jean-Pierre Leaud, Maurice Lemaitre, Luce Leray-Mauriac, Eric le Roy, Roland Lesaffre, Lucie Lichtig, Renee Lichtig, Serge Losique, Marc Maintigneaux, Bernard Martinand, Mary Meerson, Marie-Helene Melies-Leherissey, Frederic Mitterrand, Pierre Moinot, Maud Molyneaux, Laurent Muratet, Glenn Myrent, Jean Narboni, Luc Passerau-Supervielle, Veronique Perles, Olivier Petitjean, Pierre Philippe, Jack Ralite, Jean Reznikov, Patrick Rinoux, Jacques Robiolles, Pascal Rogard, Eric Rohmer, Muriel Rosé, Jean Rouch, Ambroise Roux, Eva Rudling, Jacques Salom, Peter Scarlet, Daniel Schmidt, Werner Schroeter, Jean Charles Tacchella, Lionel Tardif, Max Tessier, Serge Toubiana, Francois Truffaut, Jean Tualrd, Jack Valenti, Agathe Vannier, Agnes Varda, Benedicte Veilloux, Luce Vigo, Michael Warren.

Anuchit Sapanpong in *The Overture* PHOTO COURTESY OF KINO INTERNATIONAL

THE DARK HOURS

(FABRICATION FILMS) Producer, Brent Barclay; Director, Paul Fox; Screenplay, Wil Zmak; Photography, Steve Cosens; Designer, Aidan Leroux; Costumes, Joanna Syrokomla; Music, E. C. Woodley; Editor, Marlo Miazga; Casting, Robin D. Cook, Sara Kay; a Calder Road Films, Feature Film Project production; Canadian; Dolby; Color; Rated R; 80 minutes; American release date: October 13, 2005. CAST: Kate Greenhouse (Samantha Goodman), Aidan Devine (Harlan Pyne), Gordon Currie (David Goodman), Iris Graham (Melody), Dov Tiefenbach (Adrian), David Calderisi (Dr. Lew Lanigan), Jeff Seymour (Radiologist), Trevor Hayes (Doctor), Bruce McFee (Donald Wegman), Kathryn Haggis (Waitress)

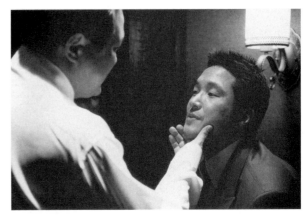

Jeong Wong-jung, Han Suk-kyu in *The President's Last Bang* PHOTO COURTESY OF KINO INTERNATIONAL

THE PRESIDENT'S LAST BANG

(KINO) Producer, Shin Chul; Executive Producers, Sim Jae Myeong, Choi Jin-hwa, Lee Eun Soo; Director/Screenplay, Im Sang-soo; Photography, Kim Woo-hyeong; Designer, Lee Min-bok; Music, Kim Hong-jib; Editor, Lee Eun Soo; an MK Pictures production; South Korean; Dolby; Color; Not rated; 102 minutes; American release date: October 14, 2005. CAST: Song Jae-ho (President Park Chun-hee), Han Suk-kyu (KCIA Chief Agent Ju), Baek Yun-shik (KCIA Director Kim), Jeong Wong-jung (President's Chief Bodyguard Cha), Kim Sang-ho (KCIA Agent Jang), Kwun Byung-gil (President's Chief Secretary Yang), Lee Jae-gu (KCIA Agent Kwon), Cho Sang-gun (KCIA Safehouse Caretaker Shim), Kim Eung-soo (KCIA Agent Colonel Min), Kim Seung-wook (KCIA Agent Won), Kim Tae-han (KCIA Agent Song), Kim Yoon-ah (Singer)

ROOMS FOR TOURISTS

(CONDOR MEDIA) Producer, Sebastian Fretes; Executive Producers, Rodrigo Ordenes Miro, Hernán Moyano; Director, Adrián García Bogliano; Screenplay, Adrián García Bogliano, Ramiro García Bogliano; Photography, Dario Bermeo, Veronica Padron; Designers, Pheonia Veloz, Catalina Oliva; Music, Rodrigo Franco; Editors, Adrián García Bogliano, Hernán Moyano; Casting, Maria Angelica Castro; a Mondo Trasho Productions, Roman Porno Eiga production; Argentine, 2004; Black and white; Not rated; 90 minutes; American release date: October 20, 2005. CAST: Jimena Krouco (Elena), Elena Siritto (Theda), Mariela Mujica (Silvia), Brenda Vera (Ruth), Victoria Witemburg (Lydia), Eliana Polonara (Young Tamara), Alejandro Lise (Maxi), Trajano Leydet (Ismael), Rolf García (Néstor), Oscar Ponce (Horacio)

WHITE KING, BLACK RUBBER, BLACK DEATH

(ARTMATTAN) Producer, Paul Pauweis; Director/Screenplay, Peter Bate; Photography, Renaat Lambeets; Music, Howard Davidson; Editor, Hugh Williamson; Narrator, Nick Fraser; Periscope Productions; Belgian-Australian-Canadian-Danish-Finnish-French-German-Netherlands-British; Color/black and white; Not rated; 84 minutes; American release date: October 21, 2005. Documentary on King Leopold II's reign of terror over the Congo; featuring Elie Lison, Roger May, Steve Driesen, Imotep Tshilombo, Annette Kelly.

The Swenkas PHOTO COURTESY OF SEVENTH ART

THE SWENKAS

(SEVENTH ART) Producers, Rasmus Thorsen, Anne Diemer; Director, Jeppe Ronde; Screenplay, Jeppe Ronde, Kim Leona; Photography, Lars Skree, Sebastian Wintero, Nic Hofmeyr; Music, Povi Kristian; Editor, Olivier Bugge Coutte; a Cosmo Film production in association with DR2 Denarmk, YLE Finland; Swedish, 2004; DV/16mm-to-35mm; Color/black and white; Not rated; 72 minutes; American release date: November 9, 2005. Documentary on Zulu men of Johannesburg who compete in amateur fashion contests; featuring Sabelo Hlatswayo, Dingani Zulu, Yule Mahsiteng.

PULSE

(MAGNOLIA) Director/Screenplay, Kiyoshi Kurosawa; Photography, Junichirô Hayashi; Designer, Tomoyuki Maruo; a Toho Company Ltd. production; Japanese, 2001; Dolby; Color; Not rated; 118 minutes; American release date: November 9, 2005. CAST: Haruhiko Katô (Ryosuke Kawashima), Kumiko Aso (Michi Kudo), Koyuki (Harue Karasawa), Kurume Arisaka (Junko Sasano), Masatoshi Matsuro (Toshio Yabe), Shinji Takeda (Yoshizaki), Jun Fubuki (Michi's Mother), Shun Sugata (Boss), Sho Aikawa (Employee), Kôji Yakusho (Ship Captain), Kenji Mizuhashi (Taguchi), Takumi Tanji (Man with Bag), Hassie Takano, Atsushi Yuki, Go Takashima (Students), Kaori Ichijô (Girl with Long Hair), Teruo Ono (Doroningen), Ken Furusawa (Convenience Store Employee)

Haruhiko Katô, Koyuki in *Pulse* PHOTO COURTESY OF MAGNOLIA

CAPE OF GOOD HOPE

(ARTISTIC LICENSE) Producers, Genevieve Hofmeyr, Suzanne Kay Bamford; Director, Mark Bamford; Screenplay, Mark Bamford, Suzanne Kay Bamford; Photography, Larry Fong; Music, J. B. Eckl; Editors, Frank Reynolds, Tanja Hagen; Casting, Eyde Belasco; a Wonder View Films, Moonlight Films production; South African-U.S.; Dolby; Deluxe color; Rated PG-13; 107 minutes; American release date: November 11, 2005. CAST: Debbie Brown (Kate), Eriq Ebouaney (Jean Claude), Nthati Moshesh (Lindiwe), Morne Visser (Morne), Quanita Adams (Sharifa), David Isaacs (Habib), Kamo Masilo (Tahbo), Nick Boraine (Stephen van Heern), Clare Marshall (Penny), Yule Masiteng (Rev. Poswa), Lillian Dube (Mama), Gregg Viljoen (Bruce), Fahrug Valley-Omar (Indian Hotel Husband), Bo Peterson (Shella), Wayne Harrison (Mr. Nell), Rick Bacon (Consulate Official), Tayo Oyekoya (Algerian Neighbor), Gideon Emery (Dance Instructor Miles), Hugh Masebenza (Township Mugger), Pharyn Leonard (Little Girl Who Wants Mutt), Sean Michael (Father Who Doesn't), Mary-Ann Barlow (Lisa Van Heern), Tom Fairfoot (Dr. Radford), Heather Middleton (Tipsy Woman at Party)

Debbie Brown, Gideon Emery in *Cape of Good Hope* PHOTO COURTESY OF ARTISTIC LICENSE

UNDERTAKING BETTY

(MIRAMAX) a.k.a. *Plots with a View*; Produced by Jason Piette, Michael Cowan, Suzanne Lyons, Kate Robbins. Executive Producers, Marie Vine, David Rogers, Alex Marshall, Terry Chase Chenowith. Director, Nick Hurran; Screenplay, Frederick Ponzlov; Photography, James Welland; Designer, Keith Maxwell; Costumes, Ffion Elinor; Music, Rupert Gregson-Williams; Editor, John Richards; a Vine Intl. Pictures/Great British Films presentation of a Spice Factory/Snowfall Films production; British-U.S.-German, 2002; Dolby; Widescreen; Color; Rated PG-13; 94 minutes; American release date: November 11, 2005. CAST: Brenda Blethyn (Betty Rhys-Jones), Alfred Molina (Boris Plots), Christopher Walken (Frank Featherbed), Naomi Watts (Meredith), Lee Evans (Delbert Butterfield), Robert Pugh (Councilor Hugh Rhys-Jones), Miriam Margolyes (Thelma/Selma), Jerry Springer (Himself), Ena Cohen (Candace), Malcolm Cousins (Rev. Price), Howell Evans (Dr. Owen), Maggs Harries (Pianist), Beverly Hotsprings (Andrea Cass), Dafydd Hywel (Gravedigger), Padrig Owen Jones (Willie), Pat Kane (Kindly Old Lady), Peggy Mason, Stevie Parry (Mourners), Robert Page (Bob Murdock), Dawn Pritchard (Vegas Showgirl), Dafydd Wyn Roberts (Pharmacist), Stan Stennet (Albert Edwards), Menna Trussler (Dilys Rhys-Jones), Noel Williams (Rev. Price)

Emmanuelle Devos in *Gilles' Wife* PHOTO COURTESY OF IFC FILMS

GILLES' WIFE

(IFC FILMS) a.k.a. *La Femme de Gilles*; Producers, Patrick Quinet, Claude Waringo; Executive Producers, Olivier Rausin, Stephan Quinet; Director, Frédéric Fonteyne; Screenplay, Frédéric Fonteyne, Marion Hänsel, Philippe Blasband; Based on the novel by Madeleine Bourdouxhe; Photography, Virginie Saint-Martin; Designer, Véronique Sacrez; Music, Vincent D'Hondt; Editor, Ewin Ryckaert; Casting, Richard Rousseau; a co-production of Artemis Productions, Liaison Cinematographique, Samsa Films; Belgian-French-Luxembourg-Italian-Swiss, 2004; Dolby; Color; Not rated; 103 minutes; American release date: November 16, 2005. CAST: Emmanuelle Devos (Elisa), Clovis Cornillac (Gilles), Laura Smet (Victorine), Alice Verlinden, Chloé Verlinden (Binoculars), Colette Emmanuelle (Elisa's Mother), Gil Lagay (Elisa's Father), Frédéric Fonteyne (Worker Friend of Gilles), Patrick Quinet (Maréchal)

Clara Khoury (center) in *The Syrian Bride* PHOTO COURTESY OF KOCH LORBER FILMS

THE SYRIAN BRIDE

(KOCH LORBER) Producers, Eran Riklis, Antoine de Clermont-Tonnerre, Michael Eckelt, Bettina Brokemper; Director, Eran Riklis; Screenplay, Eran Riklis, Suha Arraf; Photography, Michael Wiesweg; Designer, Avi Fahima; Costumes, Inabl Shuki; Music, Cyril Moran; Editor, Tova Asher; Casting, Yael Aviv; a France

Cinema Productions, Eran Riklis Productions, Neue Impuls Film GbR, MACT Productions; French-German-Israeli; Dolby; Color; Not rated; 96 minutes; American release date: November 16, 2005. CAST: Hiyam Abbass (Amal), Makram J. Khoury (Hammed), Clara Khoury (Mona), Ashraf Barhoum (Marwan), Eyad Sheety (Hattem), Evelyne Kaplun (Evelyna), Julie-Anne Roth (Jeanne), Adnan Trabshi (Amin), Marlene Bajjali (The Mother), Uri Gabriel (Simon), Alon Dahan (Arik), Robert Hoenig (Joseph), Derar Sliman (Tallel), Ranin Boulos (Mai), Hanan Abou-Manneh (Rama), Norman Issa (The Syrian Officer), Loutof Mousser (The Senior Elder), Maisra Masri (Fahdi), Imad Jabrin (Imad Jabarin)

Yannis Tsimitselis (left) in *Blackmail Boy* PHOTO COURTESY OF PICTURE THIS!

BLACKMAIL BOY

(PICTURE THIS!) a.k.a *Oxygono*; Producer, Elena Hatzialexandrou; Directors/Screenplay, Thanasis Papathanasiou, Michalis Reppas; Set Decoration, Antonis Daglidis; Costumes, Evelyn Sioupi; Music, Nikos Kypourgos, Dimitris Papadimitriou; Editor, Ioanna Spillopoulou; a Mega Channel, FilmNet, Greek Film Center, Odeon, Safe Company production; Greek, 2003; Dolby; Color; Not rated; 100 minutes; American release date: November 18, 2005. CAST: Nena Menti (Magda), Yannis Tsimitselis (Christos), Akilas Karazisis (Yiorgos), Jeannie Papadopoulou (Yiota), Alexis Georgoulis (Stelios), Joys Evidi (Tzia), Maria Kavoyianni (Vicky), Alexandros Antonpoulos (Manolis), Anna Kyriakou (Anneta)

PRIVATE

(TYEPCAST) Producer, Mario Gianani; Director, Saverio Costanzo; Screenplay, Saverio Costanzo, Camilla Costanzo, Alessio Cremonini, Sayed Oashua; Photography, Luigi Martinucci; Music, Alter Ego; Editor, Francesca Calvelli; an Offiside, Istituo Luce production; Italian; Color; Not rated; 90 minutes; American release date: November 18, 2005. CAST: Mohammed Bakri (Mohammad B.), Lior Miller (Commander Ofer), Hend Ayoub (Mariam B.), Tomer Russo (Private Eial), Arin Omary (Samiah B.)

ZIZEK!

(ZEITGEIST) Producer, Lawrence Konner; Director, Astra Taylor; Photography, Jesse Epstein, Martina Radwan; Music, Jeremy Barnes; Editor, Laura Hanna; a Hidden Driver Productions, The Documentary Campaign production; Canadian-U.S.; Color; Not rated; 71 minutes; American release date: November 18, 2005. Documentary on Slavoj Zizek.

Slavoj Zizek in *Zizek!* PHOTO COURTESY OF ZEITGEIST FILMS

Jasmin Tabatabai, Anneke Kim Sarnau in *Unveiled* PHOTO COURTESY OF WOLFE RELEASIN

UNVEILED

(WOLFE RELEASING) Producer, Ulrike Zimmermann; Director, Angelina Maccarone; Screenplay, Angelina Maccarone, Judith Kaufmann; Photography, Judith Kaufmann; Designer, Thomas Stromberger; Costumes, Regina Tiedeken, Friederike von Wedel-Parlow; Music, Hartmut Ewert, Jacob Hansonis; Editor, Bettina Bohler; Casting, Tina Bockenhauer; a Fischer Film production; German-Austrian; Dolby; Color; Not rated; 97 minutes; American release date: November 18, 2005. CAST: Jasmin Tabatabai (Fariba Tabrizi), Navid Akhavan (Siamak), Bern Tauber (Beamter BAFL), Majid Faraht (Dolmetscher), Georg Friedrich (Burkhardt), Atischeh Hannh Braun (Alev), Mikhail Dersim Sefer (Cem), Haranet Minlik (Velma), Frank Frede, Barbara Falter (Beamtins BGS), Ruth Wohlschlegel (Frau Gabriel), Jevgenij Sitochin (Maxim), Dmitri Dykhovichnij (Dmitri), Dominik Glaubitz (Pfarrer), Blerim Bala (Arton), Jens Munchow (Andi), Anneke Kim Sarnau (Anne), Monika Hansen (Waltraut), Jurgen Mielke

(Hermann), Nina Vorbrodt (Sabine), Hinnerk Schonemann (Uwe), Simon Schwarz (Lachle), Leon Philipp Hofmann (Melvin)

FAR SIDE OF THE MOON

(TLA RELEASING) a.k.a. *La Face cachée de la lune*; Producers, Bob Krupinski, Mario St-Laurent; Executive Producers, Robert Lepage, Daniel Langlois; Director/Screenplay, Robert Lepage; Photography, Ronald Plante; Designer, Jean Le Bourdais; Music, Benoit Jutras; Editor, Philippe Gagnon; an FCL Films, Media Principia Inc. production; Canadian, 2003; Dolby; Color; Not rated; 105 minutes; American release date: December 2, 2005. CAST: Robert Lepage (Phillippe/André), Anne-Marie Cadieux (Phillippe and André's Mother), Marco Poulin (Carl), Céline Bonnier (Nathalie), Lorraine Côté (Marie-Madeleine Bonsecours), Richard Fréchette (The Doctor), Gregory Hlady (Interpreter), Érika Gagnon (Philippe's Supervisor), Sophie Faucher (Presenter)

Pietro Sibille (right) in *Días de Santiago* PHOTO COURTESY OF CINEMA TROPICAL

DÍAS DE SANTIAGO

(CINEMA TROPICAL) Producers, Tito Bonicelli, Enid Campos; Executive Producers, Josue Mendez, Asa Greenberg, Stephen Dembitzer; Director, Josue Mendez; Screenplay, Josue Mendez, Analía Laos; Photography, Juan Duran; Designer, Eduardo Camino; Costumes, Leslie Hinojosa Cortijo; Music, Manuel Larroche; Editor, Roberto Benavides Espino; a Chullachaki Production; Peruvian, 2004; Dolby; Black and white/color; Not rated; 83 minutes; American release date:

Shinya Tsukamoto in *Marebito* PHOTO COURTESY OF TARTAN FILMS

December 8, 2005. CAST: Pietro Sibille (Santiago Roman), Milagros Vidal (Andrea), Marisela Pucicon (Elisa), Alheli Castillo (Mari), Lili Urbina (Mama), Ricardo Mejía (Papa), Erick Garcia (Coco), Ivy La Noire (Ines), Giselle Bedon (Rita), Sandro Calderón (Sandro Castro)

Robert Lepage in *Far Side of the Moon* PHOTO COURTESY OF TLA RELEASING

MAREBITO

(TARTAN) Producer, Tatsuhiko Hirata; Director, Takashi Shimizu; Screenplay, Chiaki Konaka, based on his novel; Photography, Tsukasa Tanabe; Designer, Atsuo Hirai; Costumes, Kuniko Hôjô; Music, Toshiyuki Takine; Editor, Masahiro Ugajin; a Euro Space, Adness, At Entertainment, Culture Publishers, Japan CableCast, Panorama Communications production; Japanese; Color; Not rated; 92 minutes; American release date: December 9, 2005. CAST: Shinya Tsukamoto (Masuoka), Tomomi Miyashita (F), Kazuhiro Nakahara (Arei Furoki), Miho Ninagawa (Aya Fukumoto), Shun Sugata (MIB)

THE POWER OF NIGHTMARES: THE RISE OF THE POLITICS OF FEAR

(BRITISH BROADCASTING CORP.) Producer/Director/Screenplay/Narrator, Adam Curtis; Executive Producer, Peter Horrocks; Not other credits available; British; Color; Not rated; 157 minutes; American release date: December 9, 2005. Documentary on how fear is used to gain political power; featuring Milton Bearden, Robert Bork, David Brock, Jason Burke, Vincent Cannistraro, David Cole, Joe Conason, Mikhail Gorbachev, Ron Hansen, Stephen Holmes, Gilles Kepel, Irving Kristol, William Kristol, Michael Ledeen, Richard Perle, Richard Pipes, Paul Weyrich.

NEAL 'N' NIKKI

(YASH RAJ FILMS) Producer, Yash Chopra; Director/Screenplay, Arjun Sablok; Photography, P. S. Vinod; Designers, Guruji Brothers; Music, Salim Merchant, Suleman Merchant; Editor, Ritesh Soni; Indian; Color; Not rated; 122 minutes; American release date: December 9, 2005. CAST: Tanisha (Nikita "Nikki" Bakshi), Uday Chopra (Gurneal "Neal" Ahluwalia), Abihishek Bachchan (Guy at Bar), Pawan Chopra, Gaurav Gera, Kamini Khanna, Samantha McLeod, Zain Meghji, Richa Pallod, Susheel Parashara

KRISANA

(KINO KOMBAT/SCREEN VISION) Producer/Director/Screenplay/Photography/Designer, Fred Kelemen; Music, Ramachandra Bocar; Editors, Fred Kelemen, Franka Pohl, Klaus Charbonier; Latvian-German; Color; Not rated; 90 minutes; American release date: December 9, 2005. CAST: Egons Dombrovskis (Matiss Zelcs), Nikolaj Mesetzkis (Alexej Mesetzkis), Vigo Roga (Inspector), Aija Dzerve (Alina), Gundars Silakaktins (Bartender), Andris Keiss (Alina's Husband), Rihards Gailiss (Alina's Son)

ELECTRIC SHADOWS

(FIRST RUN FEATURES) a.k.a. *Meng ying tong nian*; Producer, Derek Yee; Executive Producer, John Sham; Director, Xiao Jiang; Screenplay, Xiao Jiang, Qinsong Cheng; Photography, Chen Hong, Yang Lien; Designer, Fu Delin; Music, Zhao Lin; Editor, Lei Qin; a Happy Pictures Culture Communications Co. Ltd. production; Chinese, 2004; Color; Not rated; 93 minutes; American release date: December 16, 2005. CAST: Xia Yu (Mao Dabing), Li Haibin (Pan Daren), Zhang Yijing (Ling Ling as a Teenager), Jiang Shan (Policewoman), Liu Yang (Middle-Aged Woman), Jiang Yihong (Jiang Xuehua), Qi Zhongyang (Ling Ling, Young Woman), Guan Xiaotong (Ling Ling, Small Girl), Zhang Yijing (Ling Ling, Teenager), Wang Zhengija (Mao Xiaobing)

Li Haibin in *Electric Shadows*

Li Haibin, Qi Zhongyang in *Electric Shadows* PHOTO COURTESY OF FIRST RUN FEATURES

Henry Hübchen, Hannelore Elsner, Anja Franke in *Go For Zucker!*
PHOTO COURTESY OF FIRST RUN FEATURES

GO FOR ZUCKER!

(FIRST RUN FEATURES) a.k.a. *Alles auf Zucker!*; Producer, Manuela Stehr; Executive Producers, Barbara Buhl, Bettina Ricklefs, Andreas Schreitmüller; Director, Dani Levy; Screenplay, Dani Levy, Holger Franke; Photography, Carl F. Koschnick; Designer, Christian M. Goldbeck; Costumes, Lucie Bates; Music, Niki Reiser; Editor, Elena Bromund; an X-Filme Creative Pool, Bayerischer Rundfunk (BR), Westdeutcher Rundfunk (WDR) production; German, 2004; Dolby; Color; Not rated; 90 minutes; American release date: December 16, 2005. CAST: Henry Hübchen (Zucker), Hannelore Elsner (Marlene), Udo Samel (Samuel), Gold Tencer (Golda), Steffen Groth (Thomas), Anja Franke (Jana), Sebastian Blomberg (Joshua), Elena Uhlig (Lilly), Rolf Hoppe (Rabbi Ginsberg), Inga Busch (Irene), Antonia Adamik (Sarah), Renate Krößner (Linda), Axel Werner (Eddy Dürr), Gada Hammoudah (Janice), Tatjana Blacher (Tatjana), Juri Rossteaninji (Ukrainer), Bernd Stegemann (Bailiff), Tino Lau (Giant), Ulrich Voß (Druken Guest), Andreas Herder, Marc Bischoff (Male Nurses), Holger Franke (Billiard Pub Host), Manfred Möck (Hearse Driver), Victoria Deutschmann (Bar Woman), Peter König (Policeman), Adriana Altaras (Shop Assistant), Sven Markholz (Telegram Messenger), Klaus Müller (Cemetery Keeper), Rolf Hahn (Clinic Policeman), Suzanne Vogt (Doctor, Clinic), Kirsten Sprick (Taxi Driver)

THE BIG WHITE

(ECHO BRIDGE ENTERTAINMENT) Producers, Christopher Eberts, David Faigenblum, Chris Roberts; Executive Producers, Jane Barclay, Hannah Leader, Michael Birnbaum, Andreas Schmid, Andy Grosch, John Schimmel, Kia Jam; Director, Mark Mylod; Screenplay, Colin Frieson; Photography, James Glennon; Designer, John Billington; Costumes, Darena Snowe; Music, Mark Mothersbaugh; Editor, Julie Monroe; Casting, Tricia Wood, Deborah Aquila; a Capitol Films, VIP Medienfonds 2, Ascendant Filmproduktion production in association with Rising Star; Canadian-New Zealand; Dolby; Deluxe color; Rated R; 105 minutes; American release date: December 16, 2005. CAST: Robin Williams (Paul Barnell), Holly Hunter (Margaret Barnell), Giovanni Ribisi (Ted), Tim Blake Nelson (Gary), W. Earl Brown (Jimbo), Woody Harrelson (Raymond Barnell), Alison Lohman (Tiffany), Marina Stephenseon Kerr (Avis), Ralph J. Alderman (Mr. Branch), Frank Adamson (Det. Boyle), Ryan Miranda (Korean Teenager), Craig March (Howard), Ty Wood (Paperboy), Frank C. Turner (Dave), Brenda McDonald (Mrs. Wherry), Deena Fontaine (Cop), Joanne Rodriguez (TV Reporter), Eric Epstein (Minister), Harry Nelken (Warehouse Owner), Jeff Skinner (Arnith)

MY NAME WAS SABINA SPIELREIN

(FACETS MULTIMEDIA) Producer, Helgi Felixson; Director, Elizabeth Márton; Screenplay, Elizabeth Márton, Yolande Knobel, Signe Mähler, Kristina Hjertén von Gedda; Photography, Robert Nordström; Designer, Öqvist; Music, Vladimir Dikanski; Editors, Björn Engström, Yolande Knobel; Narrators, Lasse Almebäck, Eva Österberg; a co-production of SVT Sergies Television, Les Films du Centaure, Ide Film Felixsoon, Haslund Film Aps, Maximage GmbH, Hysteria Film ABC, Millennium Film OY; French-German-Swedish-Danish-Finish-Swiss, 2002; Black and white/color; Not rated; 90 minutes; American release date: December 28, 2005.

THE PROMISE

(MOONSTONE) Producers, Han Sanping, Chen Hong, Kim Dong-ju, Ernst Etchie Stroh; Executive Producer, Yang Bu Ting; Director/Screenplay, Chen Kaige; Photography, Peter Pau; Music, Klaus Badelt; a Moonstone Entertainment/Show East production; Chinese-Hong Kong-Japanese-South Korean; Dolby; Color; Not rated; 128 minutes; American release date: December 30, 2005. CAST: Jang Dong-Kun (Kunlun), Hiroyuki Sanada (General Guangming), Cecilia Cheung (Princess Qingcheng), Nicholas Tse (Wuhuan), Liu Ye (Snow Wolf), Chen Hong (Goddess Manshen), Qian Cheng (The Emperor)

Nicholas Tse, Cecilia Cheung in *The Promise* PHOTO COURTESY OF MOONSTONE

INITIAL D

(TAI SENG ENTERTAINMENT) Producer, Wai Keung Lau; Executive Producer, Yang Ying, John Chong; Directors, Wai Keung Lau, Siu Fai Mak; Screenplay, Felix Chong; Based on the comic by Shuichi Shigeno; Photography, Lai Yiu-Fai, Wai Keung Lau, Ng Man-Ching; Designer, Silver Cheung; Music, Kwong Wing Chan; Eidtor, Wong Hoi; an Avex Inc., Basic Pictures, Media Asia Group Ltd. production; Chinese-Hong Kong; Dolby; Color; Not rated; 95 minutes; American release date: December 30, 2005. CAST: Jay Chou (Takumi Fujiwara), Anne Suzuki (Natsuki Mogi), Edison Chen (Ryousuke Takahashi), Anthony Wong Chau-Sang (Bunta Fujiwara), Shawn Yue (Takeshi Nakazato), Chapman Yo (Itsuki Tachibana), Jordan Chan (Kyouichi Sudou), Kenny Bee (Yunichi Tachibana)

PROMISING NEW ACTORS OF 2005

Chris "Ludacris" Bridges (*Crash, Hustle & Flow*)

Taraji P. Henson (*Four Brothers, Hustle & Flow*)

Brady Corbet (*Mysterious Skin*)

Idina Menzel (*Rent*)

Matthew Goode (*Match Point*)

Michelle Monaghan (*Kiss Kiss Bang Bang, Mr. & Mrs. Smith, North Country, Winter Solstice*)

Josh Hutcherson (*Kicking & Screaming, Little Manhattan, Zathura: A Space Adventure*)

Charlie Ray (*Little Manhattan*)

Lou Taylor Pucci (*The Chumscrubber, Thumbsucker*)

Kelly Reilly (*Mrs. Henderson Presents, The Libertine, Pride & Prejudice*)

Victor Rasuk (*Lords of Dogtown*)

Tracie Thoms (*Rent*)

ACADEMY AWARD WINNERS & NOMINEES

Nona Gaye, Brendan Fraser

Ryan Phillippe

Jennifer Esposito, Don Cheadle, Kathleen York

BEST PICTURE
CRASH

(LIONS GATE) Producers, Cathy Schulman, Don Cheadle, Bob Yari, Mark R. Harris, Bobby Moresco, Paul Haggis; Executive Producers, Andrew Reimer, Tom Nunan, Jan Körbelin, Marina Grasic; Co-Producer, Betsy Danbury; Director/Story, Paul Haggis; Screenplay, Paul Haggis, Bobby Moresco; Photography, J. Michael Muro; Designer, Laurence Bennett; Costumes, Linda Bass; Music, Mark Isham; Song: "In the Deep" by Kathleen York and Michael Becker/performed by Bird York; Editor, Hughes Winborne; Casting, Sarah Halley Finn, Randi Hiller; a Bob Yari Prods. and DEJ Prods. presentation of a Black Friar's Bridge and Harris Co./Apollo-Proscreen/Bull's Eye Entertainment production; Dolby; Panavision; CFI Color; Rated R; 112 minutes; Release date: May 6, 2005

Jack McGee, Jayden Lund, Shaun Toub, Bahar Soomekh

Cast

Jean Cabot	**Sandra Bullock**
Graham Waters	**Don Cheadle**
Officer John Ryan	**Matt Dillon**
Ria	**Jennifer Esposito**
Flanagan	**William Fitchner**
Rick Cabot	**Brendan Fraser**
Cameron Thayer	**Terrence Howard**

Thandie Newton, Matt Dillon

Tony Danza, Terrence Howard

Larenz Tate, Chris "Ludacris" Bridges

Anthony **Chris "Ludacris" Bridges**
Christine Thayer **Thandie Newton**
Officer Tom Hansen **Ryan Phillippe**
Peter **Larenz Tate**
Karen **Nona Gaye**
Daniel **Michael Peña**
Farhad **Shaun Toub**
Fred **Tony Danza**
Lt. Dixon **Keith David**
Shaniqua **Loretta Devine**
Elizabeth **Karina Arroyave**
Lucien **Dato Bakhtadze**
Ken Ho **Art Chudabala**
Motorcycle Cop **Sean Cory**
Georgie **Ime N. Etuk**
Officer Gomez **Eddie Fernandez**
Store Owner **Howard Fong**
Officer Hill **Billy Gallo**
Bruce **Ken Garito**

and Octavio Gómez (Hispanic Passenger), James Haggis (Lara's Friend), Sylva Kelegian (Nurse Hodges), Daniel Dae Kim (Park), Bruce Kirby (Pop Ryan), Jayden Lund (Security Guard), Jack McGee (Gun Store Owner), Amanda Moresco (First Assistant Director), Martin Norseman (Conklin), Joe Ordaz (Hispanic Driver), Greg Joung Paik (Choi), Yomi Perry (Maria), Alexis Rhee (Kim Lee), Ashlyn Sanchez (Lara), Molly Schaffer (Woman at

Locksmith's), Paul E. Short (Officer Stone), Marina Sirtis (Shereen), Bahar Soomekh (Dorri), Allan Steele (Paramedic), Kate Super (Receptionist), Glenn Taranto (Country DJ), Beverly Todd (Graham's Mother), Kathleen York (Officer Johnson)

Various lives intersect throughout Los Angeles as racial tensions simmer and some explosive situations bring out the best and worst in human behavior.

2006 Academy Award Winner for Best Picture, Original Screenplay, and Editing. This film received additional nominations for supporting actor (Matt Dillon), Director, and Song ("In the Deep").

Michael Peña

Sandra Bullock PHOTOS COURTESY OF LIONS GATE

BEST FEATURE DOCUMENTARY
MARCH OF THE PENGUINS

(WARNER INDEPENDENT PICTURES) a.k.a. *La marche de l'empereur*; Producers, Yves Darondeau, Christophe Lioud, Emmanuel Priou; Executive Producer, Ilann Girard; Director, Luc Jacquet; Screenplay, Jordan Roberts; Based on the story by Luc Jacquet and the screenplay by Luc Jacquet, Michel Fessler; Photography, Laurent Chalet, Jerôme Maison; Music, Alex Wurman; Editor, Sabine Emiliani; Narrator, Morgan Freeman; a National Geographic Feature Films presentation of a Bonne Pioche production in association with Wild Bunch, with the participation of Buena Vista International Film Production (France), Canal Plus, a co-production with APC in association with the French Polar Institute (IPEV); French; Dolby; Color; Rated G; 80 minutes; American release date: June 24, 2005. Documentary on penguin mating rituals.

March of the Penguins

BEST FOREIGN LANGUAGE FEATURE
TSOTSI

(MIRAMAX) Producer, Peter Fudakowski; Executive Producers, Sam Bhembe, Robbie Little, Doug Mankoff, Basil Ford, Joseph D'Morais, Alan Howden, Rupert Lywood; Co-producer, Paul Raleigh; Director/Screenplay, Gavin Hood, based on a novel by Athol Fugard; Photography, Lance Gewer; Designer, Emelia Weavind; Costumes, Nadia Kruger, Pierre Vienings; Music, Mark Kilian, Paul Hepker; Editor, Megan Gill; Casting, Moonyeenn Lee; a U.K. Film + TV Production Co., Industrial Development Corp. of South Africa, National Film and Video Foundation of South Africa production, in association with Moviworld; British-South African, 2005; Dolby; Color; Rated R; 94 minutes; American release date: February 24, 2006.

Terry Pheto, Presley Chweneyagae

Zola, Zenzo Ngqobe, Kenneth Nkosi

Aap **Kenneth Nkosi**
Soekie **Thembi Nyandeni**
Captain Smit **Ian Roberts**
John Dube **Rapulana Seiphemo**
Gumboot Dlamini **Owen Sejake**
Fela **Zola**

A ruthless young thug dwelling in the slums of Soweto displays an unexpected streak of humanity when he finds a baby in the car he has stolen.

Presley Chweneyagae

Cast
Tsotsi **Presley Chweneyagae**
Boston **Mothusi Magano**
Miriam **Terry Pheto**
Tsotsi's Father **Israel Makoe**
Sgt. Zuma **Percy Matsemela**
Morris **Jerry Mofokeng**
Young Tsotsi **Benny Moshe**
Pumla Dube **Nambitha Mpumlwana**
Old Man at Tap **Jeremiah Ndlovu**
Butcher **Zenzo Ngqobe**

Mothusi Magano, Zenzo Ngqobe, Kenneth Nikosi, Presley Chweneyagae

BEST ANIMATED FEATURE

WALLACE & GROMIT:
THE CURSE OF THE WERE-RABBIT

(DREAMWORKS) Producers, Claire Jennings, Carla Shelley, Peter Lord, David Sproxton, Nick Park; Executive Producers, Michael Rose, Cecil Kramer; Directors, Nick Park, Steve Box; Screenplay, Steve Box, Nick Park, Mark Burton, Bob Baker; Photography, Dave Alex Riddett, Tristan Oliver; Music, Julian Nott; Editors, David McCormick, Gregory Perler; Supervising Animator, Lloyd Price; Voice Casting, Jenny Duffy; an Aardman Features presentation; British; Dolby; Color; Rated G; 82 minutes; American release date: October 5, 2005

Bunnies, Gromit

Wallace, Lady Campanula Tottington

Wallace, Gromit

Gromit

Voice Cast

Wallace **Peter Sallis**
Victor Quartermaine **Ralph Fiennes**
Lady Campanula Tottington **Helena Bonham Carter**
PC Mackintosh **Peter Kay**
Reverend Clement Hedges **Nicholas Smith**
Mrs. Mulch **Liz Smith**
Mr. Windfall **John Thomson**
Miss Blight **Mark Gatiss**
Mr. Caliche **Vincent Ebrahim**
Miss Thripp **Geraldine McEwan**

Gromit

Victor Quartermaine

Gromit, Were-Rabbit PHOTOS COURTESY OF DREAMWORKS

Lady Campunula Tottington

Mr. Growbag **Edward Kelsey**
Mr. Mulch **Dicken Ashworth**
Mr. Dibber **Robert Horvath**
Mr. Crock **Peter Atkin**
Mrs. Girdling **Noni Lewis**
Mr. Leaching **Ben Whitehead**

and Christopher Fairbank, James Mather, William Vanderpuye (Additional Voices)

Lady Campunula Tottington, Victor Quartermaine

Wallace's efforts to keep the town's bunny population from eating everyone's vegetable gardens backfires, producing a monstrous "were-rabbit."

ACADEMY AWARD FOR BEST ACTOR

PHILIP SEYMOUR HOFFMAN in *Capote*

ACADEMY AWARD FOR BEST ACTRESS
REESE WITHERSPOON in *Walk the Line*

ACADEMY AWARD FOR BEST SUPPORTING ACTOR
GEORGE CLOONEY in *Syriana*

ACADEMY AWARD FOR BEST SUPPORTING ACTRESS
RACHEL WEISZ in *The Constant Gardener*

ACADEMY AWARD NOMINEES FOR BEST ACTOR

Terrence Howard in *Hustle & Flow*

Joaquin Phoenix in *Walk the Line*

Heath Ledger in *Brokeback Mountain*

David Strathairn in *Good Night, and Good Luck.*

ACADEMY AWARD NOMINEES FOR BEST ACTRESS

Judi Dench in *Mrs. Henderson Presents*

Keira Knightley in *Pride & Prejudice*

Felicity Huffman in *Transamerica*

Charlize Theron in *North Country*

ACADEMY AWARD NOMINEES FOR BEST SUPPORTING ACTOR

Matt Dillon in *Crash*

Jake Gyllenhaal in *Brokeback Mountain*

Paul Giamatti in *Cinderella Man*

William Hurt in *A History of Violence*

ACADEMY AWARD NOMINEES FOR BEST SUPPORTING ACTRESS

Amy Adams in *Junebug*

Frances McDormand in *North Country*

Catherine Keener in *Capote*

Michelle Williams in *Brokeback Mountain*

TOP BOX OFFICE STARS & FILMS OF 2005

TOP BOX OFFICE STARS OF 2005

(Clockwise from top left corner)

1. Tom Cruise
2. Johnny Depp
3. Brad Pitt
4. Angelina Jolie
5. Vince Vaughn
6. George Clooney
7. Will Smith
8. Reese Witherspoon
9. Adam Sandler
10. Tom Hanks

TOP 100 BOX OFFICE FILMS OF 2005

1. **Star Wars Episode III: Revenge of the Sith** (20th) $380,270,000
2. **The Chronicles of Narnia:**
   The Lion, the Witch and the Wardrobe (Dis) $291,480,000
3. **Harry Potter and the Goblet of Fire** (WB) $290,000,000
4. **War of the Worlds** (Par/DW) $234,280,000
5. **King Kong** (Univ) $218,100,000
6. **Wedding Crashers** (NL) $209,220,000
7. **Charlie and the Chocolate Factory** (WB) $206,460,000
8. **Batman Begins** (WB) $205,350,000
9. **Madagascar** (DW) $193,210,000
10. **Mr. & Mrs. Smith** (20th) $186,340,000
11. **Hitch** (Col) $177,580,000
12. **The Longest Yard** (Par/Col) $158,120,000
13. **Fantastic Four** (20th) $154,690,000
14. **Chicken Little** (BV) $135,390,000
15. **Robots** (20th) $128,210,000
16. **Walk the Line** (20th) $119,460,000
17. **The Pacifier** (Dis) $113,100,000
18. **Fun with Dick and Jane** (Col) $110,340,000
19. **The 40 Year Old Virgin** (Univ) $109,290,000
20. **Flightplan** (BV) $89,710,000
21. **Saw II** (Lions Gate) $86,100,000
22. **Brokeback Mountain** (Focus) $82,980,000
23. **Monster-in-Law** (NL) $82,940,000

Brittany Murphy in *Sin City* PHOTO COURTESY OF DIMENSION/MIRAMAX

Russell Crowe, Renée Zellweger in *Cinderella Man* PHOTO COURTESY OF DREAMWORKS

Star Wars Episode III: Revenge of the Sith PHOTO COURTESY OF DREAMWORKS

Georgie Henley, Anna Popplewell, William Moseley, Skandar Keynes in *The Chronicles of Narnia: The Lion, The Witch and the Wardrobe* PHOTO COURTESY OF WALT DISNEY PICTURES

24. **Are We There Yet?** (Col) $82,610,000
25. **Cheaper by the Dozen 2** (20th) $81,470,000
26. **The Dukes of Hazzard** (WB) $80,280,000
27. **March of the Penguins** (WIP) $77,440,000
28. **Constantine** (WB) $75,970,000
29. **The Exorcism of Emily Rose** (Screen Gems) $75,100,000
30. **The Ring Two** (DW) $74,950,000
31. **Four Brothers** (Par) $74,490,000
32. **Sin City** (Mira) $74,110,000
33. **The Interpreter** (Univ) $72,560,000
34. **Guess Who** (Col) $68,890,000
35. **Sahara** (Par) $68,670,000
36. **Coach Carter** (Par) $67,270,000
37. **Herbie Fully Loaded** (BV) $66,100,000
38. **The Amityville Horror** (MGM) $64,540,000
39. **Sky High** (Dis) $63,940,000
40. **Bewitched** (Col) $63,270,000
41. **Jarhead** (Univ) $62,580,000
42. **Cinderella Man** (Univ/Mir) $61,650,000
43. **The Family Stone** (20th) $60,100,000
44. **Red Eye** (DW) $57,900,000
45. **Memoirs of a Geisha** (Col) $57,100,000
46. **Wallace & Gromit: The Curse of the Were-Rabbit** (DW) $56,100,000
47. **White Noise** (Univ) $55,900,000
48. **Be Cool** (MGM) $55,850,000
49. **Crash** (Lions Gate) $54,560,000

50. **Tim Burton's Corpse Bride** (WB) $53,360,000
51. **Yours, Mine & Ours** (Par/MGM/Col) $53,100,000
52. **Kicking and Screaming** (Univ) $52,670,000
53. **Hide and Seek** (20th) $51,120,000
54. **The Hitchhiker's Guide to the Galaxy** (Touchstone) $51,110,000
55. **Hoodwinked** (Weinstein) $51,100,000
56. **Syriana** (WB) $50,770,000
57. **Diary of a Mad Black Woman** (Lions Gate) $50,410,000
58. **Racing Stripes** (WB) $49,780,000
59. **Just Like Heaven** (DW) $48,320,000
60. **The Skeleton Key** (Univ) $47,830,000
61. **Miss Congeniality 2: Armed & Fabulous** (WB) $47,480,000
62. **Kingdom of Heaven** (20th) $47,400,000
63. **Munich** (Univ) $47,380,000
64. **Boogeyman** (Screen Gems) $46,730,000
65. **The Legend of Zorro** (Col) $45,360,000
66. **Must Love Dogs** (WB) $43,900,000
67. **Rumor Has It...** (WB) $43,000,000
68. **Transporter 2** (20th) $42,110,000
69. **Fever Pitch** (20th) $42,100,000
70. **The Adventures of Shark Boy and Lava Girl 3-D** (Mir) $39,180,000
71. **The Sisterhood of the Traveling Pants** (WB) $39,100,000
72. **Pride & Prejudice** (Focus) $38,220,000
73. **The Brothers Grimm** (Dimension) $37,920,000
74. **Beauty Shop** (MGM) $36,360,000
75. **Derailed** (Weinstein) $36,000,000

Djimon Hounsou, Queen Latifah in *Beauty Shop* PHOTO COURTESY OF MGM

Ewan McGregor, Scarlett Johansson in *The Island* PHOTO COURTESY OF DREAMWORKS

76. **The Island** (DW) $35,820,000
77. **The Ringer** (Fox Search) $35,430,000
78. **Hostage** (Mir) $34,640,000
79. **The Constant Gardener** (Focus) $33,580,000
80. **In Her Shoes** (20th) $32,890,000
81. **Bad News Bears** (Par) $32,790,000
82. **Dreamer: Inspired by a True Story** (DW) $32,710,000
83. **Just Friends** (New Line) $32,600,000
84. **Because of Winn-Dixie** (20th) $32,240,000
85. **House of Wax** (WB) $32,100,000
86. **The Wedding Date** (Universal) $31,630,000
87. **Good Night, and Good Luck.** (WIP) $31,510,000
88. **A History of Violence** (New Line) $31,500,000
89. **Stealth** (Col) $31,210,000
90. **Get Rich or Die Tryin'** (Para) $30,990,000
91. **The Fog** (Col) $29,520,000
92. **Rent** (Col) $29,100,000
93. **Capote** (Sony/UA) $28,400,000
94. **Zathura: A Space Adventure** (Col) $28,110,000
95. **Doom** (Univ) $28,100,000
96. **Elizabethtown** (Para) $26,780,000
97. **Aeon Flux** (Para) $25,780,000
98. **Dark Water** (BV) $25,480,000
99. **Serenity** (Univ) $25,380,000
100. **Unleashed** (Rogue) $24,540,000

Curtis "50 Cent" Jackson, Joy Bryant in *Get Rich or Die Tryin'* PHOTO COURTESY OF PARAMOUNT

Cameron Diaz in *In Her Shoes* PHOTO COURTESY OF 20TH CENTURY FOX

BIOGRAPHICAL DATA

Jessica Alba

Christian Bale

Drew Barrymore

Orlando Bloom

Aames, Willie (William Upton) Los Angeles, CA, July 15, 1960.
Aaron, Caroline Richmond, VA, Aug. 7, 1954. Catholic U.
Abbott, Diahnne NYC, 1945.
Abraham, F. Murray Pittsburgh, PA, Oct. 24, 1939. U Texas.
Ackland, Joss London, England, Feb. 29, 1928.
Adams, Amy Italy, Aug. 20, 1975.
Adams, Brooke NYC, Feb. 8, 1949. Dalton.
Adams, Catlin Los Angeles, CA, Oct. 11, 1950.
Adams, Edie (Elizabeth Edith Enke) Kingston, PA, Apr. 16, 1927. Juilliard, Columbia.
Adams, Jane Washington, DC, Apr. 1, 1965.
Adams, Joey Lauren Little Rock, AR, Jan. 6, 1971.
Adams, Julie (Betty May) Waterloo, IA, Oct. 17, 1926. Little Rock, Jr. College.
Adams, Maud (Maud Wikstrom) Lulea, Sweden, Feb. 12, 1945.
Adjani, Isabelle Paris, June 27, 1955.
Affleck, Ben Berkeley, CA, Aug. 15, 1972.
Affleck, Casey Falmouth, MA, Aug. 12, 1975.
Aghdashloo, Shohreh Tehran, Iran, May 11, 1952.
Agutter, Jenny Taunton, England, Dec. 20, 1952.
Aiello, Danny NYC, June 20, 1933.
Aiken, Liam NYC, Jan. 7, 1990.
Aimee, Anouk (Dreyfus) Paris, France, Apr. 27, 1934. Bauer Therond.
Akers, Karen NYC, Oct. 13, 1945, Hunter College.
Alba, Jessica Pomona, CA, Apr. 28, 1981.
Alberghetti, Anna Maria Pesaro, Italy, May 15, 1936.
Albert, Edward Los Angeles, CA, Feb. 20. 1951. UCLA.
Albright, Lola Akron, OH, July 20, 1925.
Alda, Alan NYC, Jan. 28, 1936. Fordham.
Aleandro, Norma Buenos Aires, Argentina, Dec. 6, 1936.
Alejandro, Miguel NYC, Feb. 21, 1958.
Alexander, Jane (Quigley) Boston, MA, Oct. 28, 1939. Sarah Lawrence.
Alexander, Jason (Jay Greenspan) Newark, NJ, Sept. 23, 1959. Boston U.
Alice, Mary Indianola, MS, Dec. 3, 1941.
Allen, Debbie (Deborah) Houston, TX, Jan. 16, 1950. Howard U.
Allen, Joan Rochelle, IL, Aug. 20, 1956. East Illinois U.
Allen, Karen Carrollton, IL, Oct. 5, 1951. U Maryland.

Allen, Nancy NYC, June 24, 1950.
Allen, Tim Denver, CO, June 13, 1953. Western Michigan U.
Allen, Woody (Allan Stewart Konigsberg) Brooklyn, NY Dec. 1, 1935.
Alley, Kirstie Wichita, KS, Jan. 12, 1955.
Allyson, June (Ella Geisman) Westchester, NY, Oct. 7, 1917.
Alonso, Maria Conchita Cuba, June 29, 1957.
Alt, Carol Queens, NY, Dec. 1, 1960. Hofstra U.
Alvarado, Trini NYC, Jan. 10, 1967.
Ambrose, Lauren New Haven, CT, Feb. 20, 1978.
Amis, Suzy Oklahoma City, OK, Jan. 5, 1958. Actors Studio.
Amos, John Newark, NJ, Dec. 27, 1940. Colorado U.
Anderson, Anthony Los Angeles, CA, Aug. 15, 1970.
Anderson, Gillian Chicago, IL, Aug. 9, 1968. DePaul U.
Anderson, Kevin Waukeegan, IL, Jan. 13, 1960.
Anderson, Loni St. Paul, MN, Aug. 5, 1946.
Anderson, Melissa Sue Berkeley, CA, Sept. 26, 1962.
Anderson, Melody Edmonton, Canada, Dec. 3, 1955. Carlton U.
Anderson, Michael, Jr. London, England, Aug. 6, 1943.
Anderson, Richard Dean Minneapolis, MN, Jan. 23, 1950.
Andersson, Bibi Stockholm, Sweden, Nov. 11, 1935. Royal Dramatic School.
Andress, Ursula Bern, Switzerland, Mar. 19, 1936.
Andrews, Anthony London, England, Dec. 1, 1948.
Andrews, Julie (Julia Elizabeth Wells) Surrey, England, Oct. 1, 1935.
Angarano, Michael Brooklyn, Dec. 3, 1987.
Anglim, Philip San Francisco, CA, Feb. 11, 1953.
Aniston, Jennifer Sherman Oaks, CA, Feb. 11, 1969.
Ann-Margret (Olsson) Valsjobyn, Sweden, Apr. 28, 1941. Northwestern.
Ansara, Michael Lowell, MA, Apr. 15, 1922. Pasadena Playhouse.
Anspach, Susan NYC, Nov. 23, 1945.
Anthony, Lysette London, England, Sept. 26, 1963.
Anthony, Tony Clarksburg, WV, Oct. 16, 1937. Carnegie Tech.
Anton, Susan Yucaipa, CA, Oct. 12, 1950. Bemardino College.
Antonelli, Laura Pola, Italy, Nov. 28, 1941.
Anwar, Gabrielle Lalehaam, England, Feb. 4, 1970.
Applegate, Christina Hollywood, CA, Nov. 25, 1972.
Archer, Anne Los Angeles, CA, Aug. 25, 1947.
Ardant, Fanny Monte Carlo, Monaco, Mar 22, 1949.

Arkin, Adam Brooklyn, NY, Aug. 19, 1956.
Arkin, Alan NYC, Mar. 26, 1934. LACC.
Armstrong, Bess Baltimore, MD, Dec. 11, 1953.
Arnaz, Desi, Jr. Los Angeles, CA, Jan. 19, 1953.
Arnaz, Lucie Hollywood, CA, July 17, 1951.
Arness, James (Aurness) Minneapolis, MN, May 26, 1923. Beloit College.
Arquette, David Winchester, VA, Sept. 8, 1971.
Arquette, Patricia NYC, Apr. 8, 1968.
Arquette, Rosanna NYC, Aug. 10, 1959.
Arthur, Beatrice (Frankel) NYC, May 13, 1924. New School.
Asher, Jane London, England, Apr. 5, 1946.
Ashley, Elizabeth (Elizabeth Ann Cole) Ocala, FL, Aug. 30, 1939.
Ashton, John Springfield, MA, Feb. 22, 1948. USC.
Asner, Edward Kansas City, KS, Nov. 15, 1929.
Assante, Armand NYC, Oct. 4, 1949. AADA.
Astin, John Baltimore, MD, Mar. 30, 1930. U Minnesota.
Astin, MacKenzie Los Angeles, CA, May 12, 1973.
Astin, Sean Santa Monica, CA, Feb. 25, 1971.
Atherton, William Orange, CT, July 30, 1947. Carnegie Tech.
Atkins, Christopher Rye, NY, Feb. 21, 1961.
Atkins, Eileen London, England, June 16, 1934.
Atkinson, Rowan England, Jan. 6, 1955. Oxford.
Attenborough, Richard Cambridge, England, Aug. 29, 1923. RADA.
Auberjonois, Rene NYC, June 1, 1940. Carnegie Tech.
Audran, Stephane Versailles, France, Nov. 8, 1932.
Auger, Claudine Paris, France, Apr. 26, 1942. Dramatic Cons.
Aulin, Ewa Stockholm, Sweden, Feb. 14, 1950.
Auteuil, Daniel Alger, Algeria, Jan. 24, 1950.
Avalon, Frankie (Francis Thomas Avallone) Philadelphia, PA, Sept. 18, 1939.
Aykroyd, Dan Ottawa, Canada, July 1, 1952.
Azaria, Hank Forest Hills, NY, Apr. 25, 1964. AADA, Tufts U.
Aznavour, Charles (Varenagh Aznourian) Paris, France, May 22, 1924.
Azzara, Candice Brooklyn, NY, May 18, 1947.

Bacall, Lauren (Betty Perske) NYC, Sept. 16, 1924. AADA.
Bach, Barbara Queens, NY, Aug. 27, 1946.
Bach, Catherine Warren, OH, Mar. 1, 1954.
Backer, Brian NYC, Dec. 5, 1956. Neighborhood Playhouse.
Bacon, Kevin Philadelphia, PA, July 8, 1958.
Bain, Barbara Chicago, IL, Sept. 13, 1934. U Illinois.
Baio, Scott Brooklyn, NY, Sept. 22, 1961.
Baker, Blanche NYC, Dec. 20, 1956.
Baker, Carroll Johnstown, PA, May 28, 1931. St. Petersburg, Jr. College.
Baker, Diane Hollywood, CA, Feb. 25, 1938. USC.
Baker, Dylan Syracuse, NY, Oct. 7, 1959.
Baker, Joe Don Groesbeck, TX, Feb. 12, 1936.
Baker, Kathy Midland, TX, June 8, 1950. UC Berkley.
Bakula, Scott St. Louis, MO, Oct. 9, 1955. Kansas U.
Balaban, Bob Chicago, IL, Aug. 16, 1945. Colgate.
Baldwin, Adam Chicago, IL, Feb. 27, 1962.
Baldwin, Alec Massapequa, NY, Apr. 3, 1958. NYU.
Baldwin, Daniel Massapequa, NY, Oct. 5, 1960.
Baldwin, Stephen Massapequa, NY, May 12, 1966.
Baldwin, William Massapequa, NY, Feb. 21, 1963.

Bale, Christian Pembrokeshire, West Wales, Jan. 30, 1974.
Balk, Fairuza Point Reyes, CA, May 21, 1974.
Ballard, Kaye Cleveland, OH, Nov. 20, 1926.
Bana, Eric Melbourne, Australia, Aug. 9, 1968.
Banderas, Antonio Malaga, Spain, Aug. 10, 1960.
Banerjee, Victor Calcutta, India, Oct. 15, 1946.
Banes, Lisa Chagrin Falls, OH, July 9, 1955. Juilliard.
Banks, Elizabeth Pittsfield, MA, Feb. 19, 1974. U of PA.
Baranski, Christine Buffalo, NY, May 2, 1952. Juilliard.
Barbeau, Adrienne Sacramento, CA, June 11, 1945. Foothill College.
Bardem, Javier Gran Canaria, Spain, May 1, 1969.
Bardot, Brigitte Paris, France, Sept. 28, 1934.
Barkin, Ellen Bronx, NY, Apr. 16, 1954. Hunter College.
Barnes, Christopher Daniel Portland, ME, Nov. 7, 1972.
Barr, Jean-Marc Bitburg, Germany, Sept. 27, 1960.
Barrault, Marie-Christine Paris, France, Mar. 21, 1944.
Barrett, Majel (Hudec) Columbus, OH, Feb. 23, 1939. Western Reserve U.
Barrie, Barbara Chicago, IL, May 23, 1931.
Barry, Gene (Eugene Klass) NYC, June 14, 1919.
Barry, Neill NYC, Nov. 29, 1965.
Barrymore, Drew Los Angeles, Feb. 22, 1975.
Baryshnikov, Mikhail Riga, Latvia, Jan. 27, 1948.
Basinger, Kim Athens, GA, Dec. 8, 1953. Neighborhood Playhouse.
Bassett, Angela NYC, Aug. 16, 1958.
Bateman, Jason Rye, NY, Jan. 14, 1969.
Bateman, Justine Rye, NY, Feb. 19, 1966.
Bates, Jeanne San Francisco, CA, May 21, 1918. RADA.
Bates, Kathy Memphis, TN, June 28, 1948. S. Methodist U.
Bauer, Steven (Steven Rocky Echevarria) Havana, Cuba, Dec. 2, 1956. U Miami.
Baxter, Keith South Wales, England, Apr. 29, 1933. RADA.
Baxter, Meredith Los Angeles, CA, June 21, 1947. Interlochen Academy.
Baye, Nathalie Maineville, France, July 6, 1948.
Beach, Adam Winnipeg, Canada, Nov. 11, 1972.
Beacham, Stephanie Casablanca, Morocco, Feb. 28, 1947.
Beals, Jennifer Chicago, IL, Dec. 19, 1963.
Bean, Orson (Dallas Burrows) Burlington, VT, July 22, 1928.
Bean, Sean Sheffield, Yorkshire, England, Apr. 17, 1958.
Béart, Emmanuelle Gassin, France, Aug. 14, 1965.
Beatty, Ned Louisville, KY, July 6, 1937.
Beatty, Warren Richmond, VA, Mar. 30, 1937.
Beck, John Chicago, IL, Jan. 28, 1943.
Beck, Michael Memphis, TN, Feb. 4, 1949. Millsap College.
Beckinsale, Kate England, July 26, 1974.
Bedelia, Bonnie NYC, Mar. 25, 1946. Hunter College.
Begley, Ed, Jr. NYC, Sept. 16, 1949.
Belafonte, Harry NYC, Mar. 1, 1927.
Bell, Jamie Billingham, England, Mar. 14, 1988.
Bell, Tom Liverpool, England, Aug. 2, 1933.
Beller, Kathleen NYC, Feb. 10, 1957.
Bellucci, Monica Citta di Castello, Italy, Sept. 30, 1964.
Bellwood, Pamela (King) Scarsdale, NY, June 26, 1951.
Belmondo, Jean Paul Paris, France, Apr. 9, 1933.
Belushi, James Chicago, IL, June 15, 1954.

Belzer, Richard Bridgeport, CT, Aug. 4, 1944.

Benedict, Dirk (Niewoehner) White Sulphur Springs, MT, March 1, 1945. Whitman College.

Benedict, Paul Silver City, NM, Sept. 17, 1938.

Benigni, Roberto Tuscany, Italy, Oct. 27, 1952.

Bening, Annette Topeka, KS, May 29, 1958. San Francisco State U.

Benjamin, Richard NYC, May 22, 1938. Northwestern.

Bennent, David Lausanne, Switzerland, Sept. 9, 1966.

Bennett, Alan Leeds, England, May 9, 1934. Oxford.

Bennett, Bruce (Herman Brix) Tacoma, WA, May 19, 1909. U Washington.

Bennett, Hywel Garnant, South Wales, Apr. 8, 1944.

Benson, Robby Dallas, TX, Jan. 21, 1957.

Bentley, Wes Jonesboro, AR, Sept. 4, 1978.

Berenger, Tom Chicago, IL, May 31, 1950, U Missouri.

Berenson, Marisa NYC, Feb. 15, 1947.

Berg, Peter NYC, March 11, 1964. Malcalester College.

Bergen, Candice Los Angeles, CA, May 9, 1946. U Pennsylvania.

Bergen, Polly Knoxville, TN, July 14, 1930. Compton, Jr. College.

Berger, Helmut Salzburg, Austria, May 29, 1942.

Berger, Senta Vienna, Austria, May 13, 1941. Vienna School of Acting.

Berger, William Austria, Jan. 20, 1928. Columbia.

Bergerac, Jacques Biarritz, France, May 26, 1927. Paris U.

Bergin, Patrick Dublin, Feb. 4, 1951.

Berkley, Elizabeth Detroit, MI, July 28, 1972.

Berkoff, Steven London, England, Aug. 3, 1937.

Berlin, Jeannie Los Angeles, CA, Nov. 1, 1949.

Berlinger, Warren Brooklyn, NY, Aug. 31, 1937. Columbia U.

Bernal, Gael García Guadalajara, Mexico, Oct. 30, 1978.

Bernhard, Sandra Flint, MI, June 6, 1955.

Bernsen, Corbin Los Angeles, CA, Sept. 7, 1954. UCLA.

Berri, Claude (Langmann) Paris, France, July 1, 1934.

Berridge, Elizabeth Westchester, NY, May 2, 1962. Strasberg Institute.

Berry, Halle Cleveland, OH, Aug. 14, 1968.

Berry, Ken Moline, IL, Nov. 3, 1933.

Bertinelli, Valerie Wilmington, DE, Apr. 23, 1960.

Best, James Corydon, IN, July 26, 1926.

Bettany, Paul London, England, May 27, 1971.

Bey, Turhan Vienna, Austria, Mar. 30, 1921.

Beymer, Richard Avoca, IA, Feb. 21, 1939.

Bialik, Mayim San Diego, CA, Dec. 12, 1975.

Biehn, Michael Anniston, AL, July 31, 1956.

Biggerstaff, Sean Glasgow, Scotland, Mar. 15, 1983.

Biggs, Jason Pompton Plains, NJ, May 12, 1978.

Bikel, Theodore Vienna, Austria, May 2, 1924. RADA.

Billingsley, Peter NYC, Apr. 16, 1972.

Binoche, Juliette Paris, France, Mar. 9, 1964.

Birch, Thora Los Angeles, CA, Mar. 11, 1982.

Birkin, Jane London, England, Dec. 14, 1947.

Birney, David Washington, DC, Apr. 23, 1939. Dartmouth, UCLA.

Birney, Reed Alexandria, VA, Sept. 11, 1954. Boston U.

Bishop, Joey (Joseph Abraham Gotllieb) Bronx, NY, Feb. 3, 1918.

Bishop, Kevin Kent, England, June 18, 1980.

Bisset, Jacqueline Waybridge, England, Sept. 13, 1944.

Black, Jack Edmonton, Alberta, Canada, Apr. 7, 1969.

Black, Karen (Ziegler) Park Ridge, IL, July 1, 1942. Northwestern.

Black, Lucas Speake, AL, Nov. 29, 1982.

Blackman, Honor London, England, Aug. 22, 1926.

Blades, Ruben Panama City, Florida, July 16, 1948. Harvard.

Blair, Betsy (Betsy Boger) NYC, Dec. 11, 1923.

Blair, Janet (Martha Jane Lafferty) Blair, PA, Apr. 23, 1921.

Blair, Linda Westport, CT, Jan. 22, 1959.

Blair, Selma Southfield, MI, June 23, 1972.

Blake, Robert (Michael Gubitosi) Nutley, NJ, Sept. 18, 1933.

Blakely, Susan Frankfurt, Germany, Sept. 7, 1950. U Texas.

Blakley, Ronee Stanley, ID, 1946. Stanford U.

Blanchett, Cate Melbourne, Australia, May 14, 1969.

Bledel, Alexis Houston, TX, Sept. 16, 1981.

Blethyn, Brenda Ramsgate, Kent, England, Feb. 20, 1946.

Bloom, Claire London, England, Feb. 15, 1931. Badminton School.

Bloom, Orlando Canterbury, England, Jan. 13, 1977.

Bloom, Verna Lynn, MA, Aug. 7, 1939. Boston U.

Blount, Lisa Fayettville, AK, July 1, 1957. U Arkansas.

Blum, Mark Newark, NJ, May 14, 1950. U Minnesota.

Blyth, Ann Mt. Kisco, NY, Aug. 16, 1928. New Waybum Dramatic School.

Bochner, Hart Toronto, Canada, Oct. 3, 1956. U San Diego.

Bogosian, Eric Woburn, MA, Apr. 24, 1953. Oberlin College.

Bohringer, Richard Paris, France, Jan. 16, 1941.

Bolkan, Florinda (Florinda Soares Bulcao) Ceara, Brazil, Feb. 15, 1941.

Bologna, Joseph Brooklyn, NY, Dec. 30, 1938. Brown U.

Bond, Derek Glasgow, Scotland, Jan. 26, 1920. Askes School.

Bonet, Lisa San Francisco, CA, Nov. 16, 1967.

Bonham-Carter, Helena London, England, May 26, 1966.

Boone, Pat Jacksonville, FL, June 1, 1934. Columbia U.

Boothe, Powers Snyder, TX, June 1, 1949. Southern Methodist U.

Borgnine, Ernest (Borgnino) Hamden, CT, Jan. 24, 1917. Randall School.

Bosco, Philip Jersey City, NJ, Sept. 26, 1930. Catholic U.

Bosley, Tom Chicago, IL, Oct. 1, 1927. DePaul U.

Bostwick, Barry San Mateo, CA, Feb. 24, 1945. NYU.

Bottoms, Joseph Santa Barbara, CA, Aug. 30, 1954.

Bottoms, Sam Santa Barbara, CA, Oct. 17, 1955.

Bottoms, Timothy Santa Barbara, CA, Aug. 30, 1951.

Boulting, Ingrid Transvaal, South Africa, 1947.

Boutsikaris, Dennis Newark, NJ, Dec. 21, 1952. Catholic U.

Bowie, David (David Robert Jones) Brixton, South London, England, Jan. 8, 1947.

Bowker, Judi Shawford, England, Apr. 6, 1954.

Boxleitner, Bruce Elgin, IL, May 12, 1950.

Boyd, Billy Glasgow, Scotland, Aug. 28, 1968.

Boyle, Lara Flynn Davenport, IA, Mar. 24, 1970.

Boyle, Peter Philadelphia, PA, Oct. 18, 1933. LaSalle College.

Bracco, Lorraine Brooklyn, NY, Oct. 2, 1949.

Bradford, Jesse Norwalk, CT, May 27, 1979.

Braeden, Eric (Hans Gudegast) Kiel, Germany, Apr. 3, 1942.

Braff, Zach South Orange, NJ, Apr. 6, 1975.

Braga, Sonia Maringa, Brazil, June 8, 1950.

Branagh, Kenneth Belfast, Northern Ireland, Dec. 10, 1960.

Brandauer, Klaus Maria Altaussee, Austria, June 22, 1944.

Brandon, Clark NYC, Dec. 13, 1958.

Chris "Ludacris" Bridges

Adrien Brody

Nicolas Cage

Kim Cattrall

Brandon, Michael (Feldman) Brooklyn, NY, Apr. 20, 1945.
Brantley, Betsy Rutherfordton, NC, Sept. 20, 1955. London Central School of Drama.
Bratt, Benjamin San Francisco, CA, Dec. 16, 1963.
Brennan, Eileen Los Angeles, CA, Sept. 3, 1935. AADA.
Brenneman, Amy Glastonbury, CT, June 22, 1964.
Brialy, Jean-Claude Aumale, Algeria, 1933. Strasbourg Cons.
Bridges, Beau Los Angeles, CA, Dec. 9, 1941. UCLA.
Bridges, Chris "Ludacris" Champagne, IL, Sept. 11, 1977.
Bridges, Jeff Los Angeles, CA, Dec. 4, 1949.
Brimley, Wilford Salt Lake City, UT, Sept. 27, 1934.
Brinkley, Christie Malibu, CA, Feb. 2, 1954.
Britt, May (Maybritt Wilkins) Stockholm, Sweden, Mar. 22, 1936.
Brittany, Morgan (Suzanne Cupito) Los Angeles, CA, Dec. 5, 1950.
Britton, Tony Birmingham, England, June 9, 1924.
Broadbent, Jim Lincoln, England, May 24, 1959.
Broderick, Matthew NYC, Mar. 21, 1962.
Brody, Adrien NYC, Dec. 23, 1976.
Brolin, James Los Angeles, CA, July 18, 1940. UCLA.
Brolin, Josh Los Angeles, CA, Feb. 12, 1968.
Bron, Eleanor Stanmore, England, Mar. 14, 1934.
Brookes, Jacqueline Montclair, NJ, July 24, 1930. RADA.
Brooks, Albert (Einstein) Los Angeles, CA, July 22, 1947.
Brooks, Mel (Melvyn Kaminski) Brooklyn, NY, June 28, 1926.
Brosnan, Pierce County Meath, Ireland. May 16, 1952.
Brown, Blair Washington, DC, Apr. 23, 1947. Pine Manor.
Brown, Bryan Panania, Australia, June 23, 1947.
Brown, Georg Stanford Havana, Cuba, June 24, 1943. AMDA.
Brown, James Desdemona, TX, Mar. 22, 1920. Baylor U.
Brown, Jim St. Simons Island, NY, Feb. 17, 1935. Syracuse U.
Browne, Leslie NYC, 1958.
Browne, Roscoe Lee Woodbury, NJ, May 2, 1925.
Bruckner, Agnes Hollywood, CA, Aug. 16, 1985.
Brühl, Daniel (Daniel Domingo) Barcelona, June 16, 1978.
Buckley, Betty Big Spring, TX, July 3, 1947. Texas Christian U.
Bujold, Genevieve Montreal, Canada, July 1, 1942.
Bullock, Sandra Arlington, VA, July 26, 1964.

Burghoff, Gary Bristol, CT, May 24, 1943.
Burgi, Richard Montclair, NJ, July 30, 1958.
Burke, Paul New Orleans, July 21, 1926. Pasadena Playhouse.
Burnett, Carol San Antonio, TX, Apr. 26, 1933. UCLA.
Burns, Catherine NYC, Sept. 25, 1945. AADA.
Burns, Edward Valley Stream, NY, Jan. 28, 1969.
Burrows, Darren E. Winfield, KS, Sept. 12, 1966.
Burrows, Saffron London, England, Jan. 1, 1973.
Burstyn, Ellen (Edna Rae Gillhooly) Detroit, MI, Dec. 7, 1932.
Burton, LeVar Los Angeles, CA, Feb. 16, 1958. UCLA.
Buscemi, Steve Brooklyn, NY, Dec. 13, 1957.
Busey, Gary Goose Creek, TX, June 29, 1944.
Busfield, Timothy Lansing, MI, June 12, 1957. East Tennessee State U.
Butler, Gerard Glasgow, Scotland, Nov. 13, 1969.
Buttons, Red (Aaron Chwatt) NYC, Feb. 5, 1919.
Buzzi, Ruth Westerly, RI, July 24, 1936. Pasadena Playhouse.
Bygraves, Max London, England, Oct. 16, 1922. St. Joseph's School.
Bynes, Amanda Thousand Oaks, CA, Apr. 3, 1986.
Byrne, David Dumbarton, Scotland, May 14, 1952.
Byrne, Gabriel Dublin, Ireland, May 12, 1950.
Byrnes, Edd NYC, July 30, 1933.

Caan, James Bronx, NY, Mar. 26,1939.
Caesar, Sid Yonkers, NY, Sept. 8, 1922.
Cage, Nicolas (Coppola) Long Beach, CA, Jan. 7, 1964.
Cain, Dean (Dean Tanaka) Mt. Clemens, MI, July 31, 1966.
Caine, Michael (Maurice Micklewhite) London, England, Mar. 14, 1933.
Caine, Shakira (Baksh) Guyana, Feb. 23, 1947. Indian Trust College.
Callan, Michael (Martin Calinieff) Philadelphia, Nov. 22, 1935.
Callow, Simon London, England, June 15, 1949. Queens U.
Cameron, Kirk Panorama City, CA, Oct. 12, 1970.
Camp, Colleen San Francisco, CA, June 7, 1953.
Campbell, Bill Chicago, IL, July 7, 1959.
Campbell, Glen Delight, AR, Apr. 22, 1935.
Campbell, Neve Guelph, Ontario, Canada, Oct. 3, 1973.
Campbell, Tisha Oklahoma City, OK, Oct. 13, 1968.
Canale, Gianna Maria Reggio Calabria, Italy, Sept. 12, 1927.

Cannon, Dyan (Samille Diane Friesen) Tacoma, WA, Jan. 4, 1937.

Capshaw, Kate Ft. Worth, TX, Nov. 3, 1953. U Misourri.

Cara, Irene NYC, Mar. 18, 1958.

Cardinale, Claudia Tunis, North Africa. Apr. 15, 1939. College Paul Cambon.

Carey, Harry, Jr. Saugus, CA, May 16, 1921. Black Fox Military Academy.

Carey, Philip Hackensack, NJ, July 15, 1925. U Miami.

Cariou, Len Winnipeg, Canada, Sept. 30, 1939.

Carlin, George NYC, May 12, 1938.

Carlyle, Robert Glasgow, Scotland, Apr. 14, 1961.

Carmen, Julie Mt. Vernon, NY, Apr. 4, 1954.

Carmichael, Ian Hull, England, June 18, 1920. Scarborough College.

Carne, Judy (Joyce Botterill) Northampton, England, 1939. Bush-Davis Theatre School.

Caron, Leslie Paris, France, July 1, 1931. Nationall Conservatory, Paris.

Carpenter, Carleton Bennington, VT, July 10, 1926. Northwestern.

Carradine, David Hollywood, CA, Dec. 8, 1936. San Francisco State.

Carradine, Keith San Mateo, CA, Aug. 8, 1950. Colo. State U.

Carradine, Robert San Mateo, CA, Mar. 24, 1954.

Carrel, Dany Tourane, Indochina, Sept. 20, 1932. Marseilles Cons.

Carrera, Barbara Managua, Nicaragua, Dec. 31, 1945.

Carrere, Tia (Althea Janairo) Honolulu, HI, Jan. 2, 1965.

Carrey, Jim Jacksons Point, Ontario, Canada, Jan. 17, 1962.

Carriere, Mathieu Hannover, West Germany, Aug. 2, 1950.

Carroll, Diahann (Johnson) NYC, July 17, 1935. NYU.

Carroll, Pat Shreveport, LA, May 5, 1927. Catholic U.

Carson, John David California, Mar. 6, 1952. Valley College.

Carsten, Peter (Ransenthaler) Weissenberg, Bavaria, Apr. 30, 1929. Munich Akademie.

Cartwright, Veronica Bristol, England, Apr 20, 1949.

Caruso, David Forest Hills, NY, Jan. 7, 1956.

Carvey, Dana Missoula, MT, Apr. 2, 1955. San Francisco State U.

Casella, Max Washington D.C. June 6, 1967.

Casey, Bernie Wyco, WV, June 8, 1939.

Cassavetes, Nick NYC, 1959, Syracuse U, AADA.

Cassel, Jean-Pierre Paris, France, Oct. 27, 1932.

Cassel, Seymour Detroit, MI, Jan. 22, 1935.

Cassel, Vincent Paris, France, Nov. 23, 1966.

Cassidy, David NYC, Apr. 12, 1950.

Cassidy, Joanna Camden, NJ, Aug. 2, 1944. Syracuse U.

Cassidy, Patrick Los Angeles, CA, Jan. 4, 1961.

Cates, Phoebe NYC, July 16, 1962.

Cattrall, Kim Liverpool, England, Aug. 21, 1956. AADA.

Caulfield, Maxwell Glasgow, Scotland, Nov. 23, 1959.

Cavani, Liliana Bologna, Italy, Jan. 12, 1933. U Bologna.

Cavett, Dick Gibbon, NE, Nov. 19, 1936.

Caviezel, Jim Mt. Vernon, WA, Sept. 26, 1968.

Cedric the Entertainer (Cedric Kyles) Jefferson City, MO, Apr. 24, 1964.

Chakiris, George Norwood, OH, Sept. 16, 1933.

Chamberlain, Richard Beverly Hills, CA, March 31, 1935. Pomona.

Champion, Marge (Marjorie Belcher) Los Angeles, CA, Sept. 2, 1923.

Chan, Jackie Hong Kong, Apr. 7, 1954.

Channing, Carol Seattle, WA, Jan. 31, 1921. Bennington.

Channing, Stockard (Susan Stockard) NYC, Feb. 13, 1944. Radcliffe.

Chapin, Miles NYC, Dec. 6, 1954. HB Studio.

Chaplin, Ben London, England, July 31, 1970.

Chaplin, Geraldine Santa Monica, CA, July 31, 1944. Royal Ballet.

Chaplin, Sydney Los Angeles, CA, Mar. 31, 1926. Lawrenceville.

Charisse, Cyd (Tula Ellice Finklea) Amarillo, TX, Mar. 3, 1922. Hollywood Professional School.

Charles, Josh Baltimore, MD, Sept. 15, 1971.

Charles, Walter East Strousburg, PA, Apr. 4, 1945. Boston U.

Chase, Chevy (Cornelius Crane Chase) NYC, Oct. 8, 1943.

Chaves, Richard Jacksonville, FL, Oct. 9, 1951. Occidental College.

Chaykin, Maury Canada, July 27, 1954.

Cheadle, Don Kansas City, MO, Nov. 29, 1964.

Chen, Joan (Chen Chung) Shanghai, China, Apr. 26, 1961. Cal State.

Cher (Cherilyn Sarkisian) El Centro, CA, May 20, 1946.

Chiles, Lois Alice, TX, Apr. 15, 1947.

Cho, John Seoul, Korea, June 16, 1972.

Cho, Margaret San Francisco, CA, Dec. 5, 1968.

Chong, Rae Dawn Vancouver, Canada, Feb. 28, 1962.

Chong, Thomas Edmonton, Alberta, Canada, May 24, 1938.

Christensen, Erika Seattle, WA, Aug. 19, 1982.

Christensen, Hayden Vancouver, British Columbia, Apr. 19, 1981.

Christian, Linda (Blanca Rosa Welter) Tampico, Mexico, Nov. 13, 1923.

Christie, Julie Chukua, Assam, India, Apr. 14, 1941.

Christopher, Dennis (Carrelli) Philadelphia, PA, Dec. 2, 1955. Temple U.

Christopher, Jordan Youngstown, OH, Oct. 23, 1940. Kent State.

Church, Thomas Hayden El Paso, TX, June 17, 1961.

Cilento, Diane Queensland, Australia, Oct. 5, 1933. AADA.

Clark, Candy Norman, OK, June 20, 1947.

Clark, Dick Mt. Vernon, NY, Nov. 30, 1929. Syracuse U.

Clark, Matt Washington, DC, Nov. 25, 1936.

Clark, Petula Epsom, England, Nov. 15, 1932.

Clark, Susan Sarnid, Ont., Canada, Mar. 8, 1943. RADA.

Clarkson, Patricia New Orleans, Dec. 29, 1959.

Clay, Andrew Dice (Andrew Silverstein) Brooklyn, NY, Sept. 29, 1957, Kingsborough College.

Clayburgh, Jill NYC, Apr. 30, 1944. Sarah Lawrence.

Cleese, John Weston-Super-Mare, England, Oct. 27, 1939, Cambridge.

Clooney, George Lexington, KY, May 6, 1961.

Close, Glenn Greenwich, CT, Mar. 19, 1947. William & Mary College.

Cody, Kathleen Bronx, NY, Oct. 30, 1953.

Coffey, Scott HI, May 1, 1967.

Cole, George London, England, Apr. 22, 1925.

Coleman, Dabney Austin, TX, Jan. 3, 1932.

Coleman, Gary Zion, IL, Feb. 8, 1968.

Coleman, Jack Easton, PA, Feb. 21, 1958. Duke U.

Colin, Margaret NYC, May 26, 1957.

Collet, Christopher NYC, Mar. 13, 1968. Strasberg Institute.

Collette, Toni Sydney, Australia, Nov. 1, 1972.

Collins, Clifton, Jr. Los Angeles, June 16, 1970.

Collins, Joan London, England, May 21, 1933. Francis Holland School.

Collins, Pauline Devon, England, Sept. 3, 1940.

Collins, Stephen Des Moines, IA, Oct. 1, 1947. Amherst.

Colon, Miriam Ponce, PR., Aug. 20, 1936. UPR.

Coltrane, Robbie Ruthergien, Scotland, Mar. 30, 1950.

Combs, Sean "Puffy" NYC, Nov. 4, 1969.

Comer, Anjanette Dawson, TX, Aug. 7, 1942. Baylor, Texas U.
Conant, Oliver NYC, Nov. 15, 1955. Dalton.
Conaway, Jeff NYC, Oct. 5, 1950. NYU.
Connelly, Jennifer NYC, Dec. 12, 1970.
Connery, Jason London, England, Jan. 11, 1963.
Connery, Sean Edinburgh, Scotland, Aug. 25, 1930.
Connick, Harry, Jr. New Orleans, LA, Sept. 11, 1967.
Connolly, Billy Glasgow, Scotland, Nov. 24, 1942.
Connors, Mike (Krekor Ohanian) Fresno, CA, Aug. 15, 1925. UCLA.
Conrad, Robert (Conrad Robert Falk) Chicago, IL, Mar. 1, 1935. Northwestern.
Constantine, Michael Reading, PA, May 22, 1927.
Conti, Tom Paisley, Scotland, Nov. 22, 1941.
Converse, Frank St. Louis, MO, May 22, 1938. Carnegie Tech.
Conway, Gary Boston, MA, Feb. 4, 1936.
Conway, Kevin NYC, May 29, 1942.
Conway, Tim (Thomas Daniel) Willoughby, OH, Dec. 15, 1933. Bowling Green State.
Coogan, Keith (Keith Mitchell Franklin) Palm Springs, CA, Jan. 13, 1970.
Coogan, Steve Manchester, England, Oct. 14, 1965.
Cook, Rachael Leigh Minneapolis, MN, Oct. 4, 1979.
Coolidge, Jennifer Boston, Aug. 28, 1963.
Cooper, Ben Hartford, CT, Sept. 30, 1930. Columbia U.
Cooper, Chris Kansas City, MO, July 9, 1951. U Misourri.
Cooper, Jackie Los Angeles, CA, Sept. 15, 1921.
Copeland, Joan NYC, June 1, 1922. Brooklyn College, RADA.
Corbett, Gretchen Portland, OR, Aug. 13, 1947. Carnegie Tech.
Corbett, John Wheeling, WV, May 9, 1961.
Corbin, Barry Dawson County, TX, Oct. 16, 1940. Texas Tech. U.
Corcoran, Donna Quincy, MA, Sept. 29, 1942.
Cord, Alex (Viespi) Floral Park, NY, Aug. 3, 1931. NYU, Actors Studio.
Corday, Mara (Marilyn Watts) Santa Monica, CA, Jan. 3, 1932.
Cornthwaite, Robert St. Helens, OR, Apr. 28, 1917. USC.
Corri, Adrienne Glasgow, Scotland, Nov. 13, 1933. RADA.
Cort, Bud (Walter Edward Cox) New Rochelle, NY, Mar. 29, 1950. NYU.
Cortesa, Valentina Milan, Italy, Jan. 1, 1924.
Cosby, Bill Philadelphia, PA, July 12, 1937. Temple U.
Coster, Nicolas London, England, Dec. 3, 1934. Neighborhood Playhouse.
Costner, Kevin Lynwood, CA, Jan. 18, 1955. California State U.
Courtenay, Tom Hull, England, Feb. 25, 1937. RADA.
Courtland, Jerome Knoxville, TN, Dec. 27, 1926.
Cox, Brian Dundee, Scotland, June 1, 1946. LAMDA.
Cox, Courteney Birmingham, AL, June 15, 1964.
Cox, Ronny Cloudcroft, NM, Aug. 23, 1938.
Coyote, Peter (Cohon) NYC, Oct. 10, 1941.
Craig, Daniel Chester, England, Mar. 2, 1968. Guildhall.
Craig, Michael Poona, India, Jan. 27, 1929.
Craven, Gemma Dublin, Ireland, June 1, 1950.
Crawford, Michael (Dumbel-Smith) Salisbury, England, Jan. 19, 1942.
Cremer, Bruno Saint-Mande, Val-de-Varne, France, Oct. 6, 1929.
Cristal, Linda (Victoria Moya) Buenos Aires, Argentina, Feb. 25, 1934.
Cromwell, James Los Angeles, CA, Jan. 27, 1940.
Crosby, Denise Hollywood, CA, Nov. 24, 1957.
Crosby, Harry Los Angeles, CA, Aug. 8, 1958.

Crosby, Mary Frances Los Angeles, CA, Sept. 14, 1959.
Cross, Ben London, England, Dec. 16, 1947. RADA.
Crouse, Lindsay NYC, May 12, 1948. Radcliffe.
Crowe, Russell New Zealand, Apr. 7, 1964.
Crowley, Pat Olyphant, PA, Sept. 17, 1932.
Crudup, Billy Manhasset, NY, July 8, 1968. UNC, Chapel Hill.
Cruise, Tom (T. C. Mapother, IV) July 3, 1962, Syracuse, NY.
Cruz, Penélope (P.C. Sanchez) Madrid, Spain, Apr. 28, 1974.
Cruz, Wilson Brooklyn, Dec. 27, 1973.
Cryer, Jon NYC, Apr. 16, 1965, RADA.
Crystal, Billy Long Beach, NY, Mar. 14, 1947. Marshall U.
Culkin, Kieran NYC, Sept. 30, 1982.
Culkin, Macaulay NYC, Aug. 26, 1980.
Culkin, Rory NYC, July 21, 1989.
Cullum, John Knoxville, TN, Mar. 2, 1930. U Tennessee.
Cullum, John David NYC, Mar. 1, 1966.
Culp, Robert Oakland, CA, Aug. 16, 1930. U Washington.
Cumming, Alan Perthshire, Scotland, Jan. 27, 1965.
Cummings, Quinn Hollywood, Aug. 13, 1967.
Cummins, Peggy Prestatyn, North Wales, Dec. 18, 1926. Alexandra School.
Curry, Tim Cheshire, England, Apr. 19, 1946. Birmingham U.
Curtin, Jane Cambridge, MA, Sept. 6, 1947.
Curtis, Jamie Lee Los Angeles, CA, Nov. 22, 1958.
Curtis, Tony (Bernard Schwartz) NYC, June 3, 1924.
Cusack, Joan Evanston, IL, Oct. 11, 1962.
Cusack, John Chicago, IL, June 28, 1966.
Cusack, Sinead Dalkey, Ireland, Feb. 18, 1948.

Dafoe, Willem Appleton, WI, July 22, 1955.
Dahl, Arlene Minneapolis, Aug. 11, 1928. U Minnesota.
Dale, Jim Rothwell, England, Aug. 15, 1935.
Dallesandro, Joe Pensacola, FL, Dec. 31, 1948.
Dalton, Timothy Colwyn Bay, Wales, Mar. 21, 1946. RADA.
Daltrey, Roger London, England, Mar. 1, 1944.
Daly, Tim NYC, Mar. 1, 1956. Bennington College.
Daly, Tyne Madison, WI, Feb. 21, 1947. AMDA.
Damon, Matt Cambridge, MA, Oct. 8, 1970.
Damone, Vic (Vito Farinola) Brooklyn, NY, June 12, 1928.
Dance, Charles Plymouth, England, Oct. 10, 1946.
Danes, Claire New York, NY, Apr. 12, 1979.
D'Angelo, Beverly Columbus, OH, Nov. 15, 1953.
Daniels, Jeff Athens, GA, Feb. 19, 1955. Central Michigan U.
Daniels, William Brooklyn, NY, Mar. 31, 1927. Northwestern.
Danner, Blythe Philadelphia, PA, Feb. 3, 1944. Bard College.
Danning, Sybil (Sybille Johanna Danninger) Vienna, Austria, May 4, 1949.
Danson, Ted San Diego, CA, Dec. 29, 1947. Stanford, Carnegie Tech.
Dante, Michael (Ralph Vitti) Stamford, CT, 1935. U Miami.
Danza, Tony Brooklyn, NY, Apr. 21, 1951. U Dubuque.
D'arbanville-Quinn, Patti NYC, May 25, 1951.
Darby, Kim (Deborah Zerby) North Hollywood, CA, July 8, 1948.
Darcel, Denise (Denise Billecard) Paris, France, Sept. 8, 1925. U Dijon.
Darren, James Philadelphia, PA, June 8, 1936. Stella Adler School.
Darrieux, Danielle Bordeaux, France, May 1, 1917. Lycee LaTour.
Davenport, Nigel Cambridge, England, May 23, 1928. Trinity College.

Erika Christensen   Kevin Costner   Alan Cumming   Claire Danes

David, Keith NYC, June 4, 1954. Juilliard.
Davidovich, Lolita Toronto, Ontario, Canada, July 15, 1961.
Davidson, Jaye Riverside, CA, Mar. 21, 1968.
Davidson, John Pittsburgh, Dec. 13, 1941. Denison U.
Davidtz, Embeth Lafayette, IN, Jan. 1, 1966.
Davies, Jeremy (Boring) Rockford, IA, Oct. 28, 1969.
Davis, Clifton Chicago, IL, Oct. 4, 1945. Oakwood College.
Davis, Geena Wareham, MA, Jan. 21, 1957.
Davis, Hope Tenafly, NJ, Mar. 23, 1964.
Davis, Judy Perth, Australia, Apr. 23, 1955.
Davis, Mac Lubbock, TX, Jan. 21,1942.
Davis, Nancy (Anne Frances Robbins) NYC, July 6, 1921. Smith College.
Davis, Sammi Kidderminster, Worcestershire, England, June 21, 1964.
Davison, Bruce Philadelphia, PA, June 28, 1946.
Dawber, Pam Detroit, MI, Oct. 18, 1954.
Dawson, Rosario NYC, May 9, 1979.
Day, Doris (Doris Kappelhoff) Cincinnati, Apr. 3, 1924.
Day, Laraine (Johnson) Roosevelt, UT, Oct. 13, 1917.
Day-Lewis, Daniel London, England, Apr. 29, 1957. Bristol Old Vic.
Dayan, Assi Israel, Nov. 23, 1945. U Jerusalem.
Deakins, Lucy NYC, 1971.
Dean, Jimmy Plainview, TX, Aug. 10, 1928.
Dean, Loren Las Vegas, NV, July 31, 1969.
DeCarlo, Yvonne (Peggy Yvonne Middleton) Vancouver, BC, Canada, Sept. 1, 1922. Vancouver School of Drama.
Dee, Joey (Joseph Di Nicola) Passaic, NJ, June 11, 1940. Patterson State College.
Dee, Ruby Cleveland, OH, Oct. 27, 1924. Hunter College.
DeGeneres, Ellen New Orleans, LA, Jan. 26, 1958.
DeHaven, Gloria Los Angeles, CA, July 23, 1923.
DeHavilland, Olivia Tokyo, Japan, July 1, 1916. Notre Dame Convent School.
Delair, Suzy (Suzanne Delaire) Paris, France, Dec. 31, 1916.
Delany, Dana NYC, March 13, 1956. Wesleyan U.
Delon, Alain Sceaux, France, Nov. 8, 1935.
Delorme, Daniele Paris, France, Oct. 9, 1926. Sorbonne.
Delpy, Julie Paris. Dec, 21, 1969.

Del Toro, Benicio Santurce, Puerto Rico, Feb. 19, 1967.
DeLuise, Dom Brooklyn, NY, Aug. 1, 1933. Tufts College.
DeLuise, Peter NYC, Nov. 6, 1966.
Demongeot, Mylene Nice, France, Sept. 29, 1938.
DeMornay, Rebecca Los Angeles, CA, Aug. 29, 1962. Strasberg Institute.
Dempsey, Patrick Lewiston, ME, Jan. 13, 1966.
DeMunn, Jeffrey Buffalo, NY, Apr. 25, 1947. Union College.
Dench, Judi York, England, Dec. 9, 1934.
Deneuve, Catherine Paris, France, Oct. 22, 1943.
De Niro, Robert NYC, Aug. 17, 1943. Stella Adler.
Dennehy, Brian Bridgeport, CT, Jul. 9, 1938. Columbia U.
Depardieu, Gérard Chateauroux, France, Dec. 27, 1948.
Depp, Johnny Owensboro, KY, June 9, 1963.
Derek, Bo (Mary Cathleen Collins) Long Beach, CA, Nov. 20, 1956.
Dern, Bruce Chicago, IL, June 4, 1936. UPA.
Dern, Laura Los Angeles, CA, Feb. 10, 1967.
DeSalvo, Anne Philadelphia, PA, Apr. 3, 1949.
Deschanel, Zooey Los Angeles, CA, Jan. 17, 1980.
Devane, William Albany, NY, Sept. 5, 1939.
DeVito, Danny Asbury Park, NJ, Nov. 17, 1944.
Dey, Susan Pekin, IL, Dec. 10, 1953.
DeYoung, Cliff Los Angeles, CA, Feb. 12, 1945. California State U.
Diamond, Neil NYC, Jan. 24, 1941. NYU.
Diaz, Cameron Long Beach, CA, Aug. 30, 1972.
DiCaprio, Leonardo Hollywood, CA, Nov. 11, 1974.
Dickinson, Angie (Angeline Brown) Kulm, ND, Sept. 30, 1932. Glendale College.
Diesel, Vin (Mark Vincent) NYC, July 18, 1967.
Diggs, Taye (Scott Diggs) Rochester, NY, Jan. 2, 1972.
Diller, Phyllis (Driver) Lima, OH, July 17, 1917. Bluffton College.
Dillman, Bradford San Francisco, CA, Apr. 14, 1930. Yale.
Dillon, Kevin Mamaroneck, NY, Aug. 19, 1965.
Dillon, Matt Larchmont, NY, Feb. 18, 1964. AADA.
Dillon, Melinda Hope, AR, Oct. 13, 1939. Goodman Theatre School.
Dixon, Donna Alexandria, VA, July 20, 1957.
Dobson, Kevin NYC, Mar. 18, 1944.
Dobson, Tamara Baltimore, MD, May 14, 1947. Maryland Institute of Art.

Doherty, Shannen Memphis, TN, Apr. 12, 1971.
Dolan, Michael Oklahoma City, OK, June 21, 1965.
Donat, Peter Nova Scotia, Canada, Jan. 20, 1928. Yale.
Donnelly, Donal Bradford, England, July 6, 1931.
D'Onofrio, Vincent Brooklyn, NY, June 30, 1959.
Donohoe, Amanda London, England, June 29 1962.
Donovan, Martin Reseda, CA, Aug. 19, 1957.
Donovan, Tate NYC, Sept. 25, 1963.
Dooley, Paul Parkersburg WV, Feb. 22, 1928. U West Virginia.
Dorff, Stephen Atlanta, GA, July 29, 1973.
Doug, Doug E. (Douglas Bourne) Brooklyn, NY, Jan. 7, 1970.
Douglas, Donna (Dorothy Bourgeois) Baywood, LA, Sept. 26, 1935.
Douglas, Illeana Quincy, MA, July 25, 1965.
Douglas, Kirk (Issur Danielovitch) Amsterdam, NY, Dec. 9, 1916. St. Lawrence U.
Douglas, Michael New Brunswick, NJ, Sept. 25, 1944. U California.
Douglass, Robyn Sendai, Japan, June 21, 1953. UC Davis.
Dourif, Brad Huntington, WV, Mar. 18, 1950. Marshall U.
Down, Lesley-Anne London, England, Mar. 17, 1954.
Downey, Robert, Jr. NYC, Apr. 4, 1965.
Drake, Betsy Paris, France, Sept. 11, 1923.
Drescher, Fran Queens, NY, Sept. 30, 1957.
Dreyfuss, Richard Brooklyn, NY, Oct. 19, 1947.
Drillinger, Brian Brooklyn, NY, June 27, 1960. SUNY/Purchase.
Driver, Minnie (Amelia Driver) London, England, Jan. 31, 1971.
Duchovny, David NYC, Aug. 7, 1960. Yale.
Dudikoff, Michael Torrance, CA, Oct. 8, 1954.
Duff, Hilary Houston, TX, Sept. 28, 1987.
Dugan, Dennis Wheaton, IL, Sept. 5, 1946.
Dukakis, Olympia Lowell, MA, June 20, 1931.
Duke, Bill Poughkeepsie, NY, Feb. 26, 1943. NYU.
Duke, Patty (Anna Marie) NYC, Dec. 14, 1946.
Dullea, Keir Cleveland, NJ, May 30, 1936. San Francisco State College.
Dunaway, Faye Bascom, FL, Jan. 14, 1941, Florida U.
Duncan, Sandy Henderson, TX, Feb. 20, 1946. Len Morris College.
Dunne, Griffin NYC, June 8, 1955. Neighborhood Playhouse.
Dunst, Kirsten Point Pleasant, NJ, Apr. 30, 1982.
Duperey, Anny Paris, France, June 28, 1947.
Durbin, Deanna (Edna) Winnipeg, Canada, Dec. 4, 1921.
Durning, Charles Highland Falls, NY, Feb. 28, 1923. NYU.
Dushku, Eliza Boston, Dec. 30, 1980.
Dussollier, André Annecy, France, Feb. 17, 1946.
Dutton, Charles Baltimore, MD, Jan. 30, 1951. Yale.
DuVall, Clea Los Angeles, CA, Sept. 25, 1977.
Duvall, Robert San Diego, CA, Jan. 5, 1931. Principia College.
Duvall, Shelley Houston, TX, July 7, 1949.
Dysart, Richard Brighton, ME, Mar. 30, 1929.
Dzundza, George Rosenheim, Germany, July 19, 1945.

Easton, Robert Milwaukee, WI, Nov. 23, 1930. U Texas.
Eastwood, Clint San Francisco, CA, May 31, 1931. LACC.
Eaton, Shirley London, England, Jan. 12, 1937. Aida Foster School.
Eckemyr, Agneta Karlsborg, Sweden, July 2, 1950 Actors Studio.
Eckhart, Aaron Santa Clara, CA, Mar. 12, 1968.

Edelman, Gregg Chicago, IL, Sept. 12, 1958. Northwestern.
Eden, Barbara (Huffman) Tucson, AZ, Aug. 23, 1934.
Edwards, Anthony Santa Barbara, CA, July 19, 1962. RADA.
Edwards, Luke Nevada City, CA, Mar. 24, 1980.
Eggar, Samantha London, England, Mar. 5, 1939.
Eichhorn, Lisa Reading, PA, Feb. 4, 1952. Queens Ont. U RADA.
Eikenberry, Jill New Haven, CT, Jan. 21, 1947.
Eilber, Janet Detroit, MI, July 27, 1951. Juilliard.
Eisenberg, Jesse NYC, Oct. 5, 1983.
Ekberg, Anita Malmo, Sweden, Sept. 29, 1931.
Ekland, Britt Stockholm, Sweden, Oct. 6, 1942.
Eldard, Ron Long Island, NY, Feb. 20, 1965.
Elfman, Jenna (Jennifer Mary Batula) Los Angeles, CA, Sept. 30, 1971.
Elizondo, Hector NYC, Dec. 22, 1936.
Elliott, Alison San Francisco, CA, May 19, 1970.
Elliott, Chris NYC, May 31, 1960.
Elliott, Patricia Gunnison, CO, July 21, 1942. U Colorado.
Elliott, Sam Sacramento, CA, Aug. 9, 1944. U Oregon.
Elwes, Cary London, England, Oct. 26, 1962.
Ely, Ron (Ronald Pierce) Hereford, TX, June 21, 1938.
Embry, Ethan (Ethan Randall) Huntington Beach, CA, June 13, 1978.
Englund, Robert Glendale, CA, June 6, 1949.
Epps, Omar Brooklyn, NY, July 23, 1973.
Erbe, Kathryn Newton, MA, July 2, 1966.
Erdman, Richard Enid, OK, June 1, 1925.
Ericson, John Dusseldorf, Germany, Sept. 25, 1926. AADA.
Ermey, R. Lee (Ronald) Emporia, KS, Mar. 24, 1944.
Esposito, Giancarlo Copenhagen, Denmark, Apr. 26, 1958.
Estevez, Emilio NYC, May 12, 1962.
Estrada, Erik NYC, Mar. 16, 1949.
Evans, Chris Sudbury, MA, June 13, 1981.
Evans, Josh NYC, Jan. 16, 1971.
Evans, Linda (Evanstad) Hartford, CT, Nov. 18, 1942.
Everett, Chad (Ray Cramton) South Bend, IN, June 11, 1936.
Everett, Rupert Norfolk, England, May 29, 1959.
Evigan, Greg South Amboy, NJ, Oct. 14, 1953.

Fabares, Shelley Los Angeles, CA, Jan. 19, 1944.
Fabian (Fabian Forte) Philadelphia, Feb. 6, 1943.
Fabray, Nanette (Ruby Nanette Fabares) San Diego, Oct. 27, 1920.
Fahey, Jeff Olean, NY, Nov. 29, 1956.
Fairchild, Morgan (Patsy McClenny) Dallas, TX, Feb. 3, 1950. UCLA.
Falco, Edie Brooklyn, NY, July 5, 1963.
Falk, Peter NYC, Sept. 16, 1927. New School.
Fallon, Jimmy Brooklyn, NY, Sept. 19, 1974.
Fanning, Dakota Conyers, GA, Feb. 23, 1994.
Farentino, James Brooklyn, NY, Feb. 24, 1938. AADA.
Fargas, Antonio Bronx, NY, Aug. 14, 1946.
Farina, Dennis Chicago, IL, Feb. 29, 1944.
Faris, Anna Baltimore, MD, Nov. 29, 1976. Univ of Washington.
Farr, Felicia Westchester, NY, Oct. 4. 1932. Penn State College.
Farrell, Colin Castleknock, Ireland, Mar. 31, 1976.
Farrow, Mia (Maria) Los Angeles, CA, Feb. 9, 1945.
Faulkner, Graham London, England, Sept. 26, 1947. Webber-Douglas.

Julie Delpy

Will Ferrell

Jane Fonda

Ioan Gruffud

Favreau, Jon Queens, NY, Oct. 16, 1966.
Fawcett, Farrah Corpus Christie, TX, Feb. 2, 1947. Texas U.
Feinstein, Alan NYC, Sept. 8, 1941.
Feldman, Corey Encino, CA, July 16, 1971.
Feldon, Barbara (Hall) Pittsburgh, Mar. 12, 1941. Carnegie Tech.
Feldshuh, Tovah NYC, Dec. 27, 1953, Sarah Lawrence College.
Fellows, Edith Boston, MA, May 20, 1923.
Fenn, Sherilyn Detroit, MI, Feb. 1, 1965.
Ferrell, Conchata Charleston, WV, Mar. 28, 1943. Marshall U.
Ferrell, Will Irvine, CA, July 16, 1968.
Ferrer, Mel Elbeton, NJ, Aug. 25, 1912. Princeton.
Ferrer, Miguel Santa Monica, CA, Feb. 7, 1954.
Ferrera, America Los Angeles, CA, Apr. 18, 1984.
Ferris, Barbara London, England, July 27, 1942.
Field, Sally Pasadena, CA, Nov. 6, 1946.
Field, Shirley-Anne London, England, June 27, 1938.
Field, Todd (William Todd Field) Pomona, CA, Feb. 24, 1964.
Fiennes, Joseph Salisbury, Wiltshire, England, May 27, 1970.
Fiennes, Ralph Suffolk, England, Dec. 22, 1962. RADA.
Fierstein, Harvey Brooklyn, NY, June 6, 1954. Pratt Institute.
Finch, Jon Caterham, England, Mar. 2, 1941.
Finlay, Frank Farnworth, England, Aug. 6, 1926.
Finney, Albert Salford, Lancashire, England, May 9, 1936. RADA.
Fiorentino, Linda Philadelphia, PA, Mar. 9, 1960.
Firth, Colin Grayshott, Hampshire, England, Sept. 10, 1960.
Firth, Peter Bradford, England, Oct. 27, 1953.
Fishburne, Laurence Augusta, GA, July 30, 1961.
Fisher, Carrie Los Angeles, CA, Oct. 21, 1956. London Central School of Drama.
Fisher, Eddie Philadelphia, PA, Aug. 10, 1928.
Fisher, Frances Milford-on-the-Sea, England, May 11, 1952.
Fitzgerald, Tara London, England, Sept. 17, 1968.
Flagg, Fannie Birmingham, AL, Sept. 21, 1944. U Alabama.
Flanagan, Fionnula Dublin, Dec. 10, 1941.
Flannery, Susan Jersey City, NJ, July 31, 1943.
Fleming, Rhonda (Marilyn Louis) Los Angeles, CA, Aug. 10, 1922.
Fletcher, Louise Birmingham, AL, July 22 1934.

Flockhart, Calista Stockton, IL, Nov. 11, Rutgers U.
Foch, Nina Leyden, Holland, Apr. 20, 1924.
Foley, Dave Toronto, Canada, Jan. 4, 1963.
Follows, Megan Toronto, Canada, Mar. 14, 1968.
Fonda, Bridget Los Angeles, CA, Jan. 27, 1964.
Fonda, Jane NYC, Dec. 21, 1937. Vassar.
Fonda, Peter NYC, Feb. 23, 1939. U Omaha.
Fontaine, Joan Tokyo, Japan, Oct. 22, 1917.
Foote, Hallie NYC, 1953. U New Hampshire.
Ford, Glenn (Gwyllyn Samuel Newton Ford) Quebec, Canada, May 1, 1916.
Ford, Harrison Chicago, IL, July 13, 1942. Ripon College.
Forlani, Claire London, England, July 1, 1972.
Forrest, Frederic Waxahachie, TX, Dec. 23, 1936.
Forrest, Steve Huntsville, TX, Sept. 29, 1924. UCLA.
Forslund, Connie San Diego, CA, June 19, 1950. NYU.
Forster, Robert (Foster, Jr.) Rochester, NY, July 13, 1941. Rochester U.
Forsythe, John (Freund) Penn's Grove, NJ, Jan. 29, 1918.
Forsythe, William Brooklyn, NY, June 7, 1955.
Fossey, Brigitte Tourcoing, France, Mar. 11, 1947.
Foster, Ben Boston, MA, Oct. 29, 1980.
Foster, Jodie (Ariane Munker) Bronx, NY, Nov. 19, 1962. Yale.
Foster, Meg Reading, PA, May 14, 1948.
Fox, Edward London, England, Apr. 13, 1937. RADA.
Fox, James London, England, May 19, 1939.
Fox, Michael J. Vancouver, British Columbia, June 9, 1961.
Fox, Vivica A. Indianapolis, July 30, 1964.
Foxworth, Robert Houston, TX, Nov. 1, 1941. Carnegie Tech.
Foxx, Jamie Terrell, TX, Dec. 13, 1967.
Frain, James Leeds, England, Mar. 14, 1969.
Frakes, Jonathan Bethlehem, PA, Aug. 19, 1952. Harvard.
Franciosa, Anthony (Papaleo) NYC, Oct. 25, 1928.
Francis, Anne Ossining, NY, Sept. 16, 1932.
Francis, Connie (Constance Franconero) Newark, NJ, Dec. 12, 1938.
Francks, Don Vancouver, Canada, Feb. 28, 1932.
Franklin, Pamela Tokyo, Feb. 4, 1950.
Franz, Arthur Perth Amboy, NJ, Feb. 29, 1920. Blue Ridge College.
Franz, Dennis Chicago, IL, Oct. 28, 1944.

Fraser, Brendan Indianapolis, IN, Dec. 3, 1968.
Frazier, Sheila NYC, Nov. 13, 1948.
Frechette, Peter Warwick, RI, Oct. 1956. U Rhoad Island.
Freeman, Al, Jr. San Antonio, TX, Mar. 21, 1934. CCLA.
Freeman, Mona Baltimore, MD, June 9, 1926.
Freeman, Morgan Memphis, TN, June 1, 1937. LACC.
Frewer, Matt Washington, DC, Jan. 4, 1958, Old Vic.
Fricker, Brenda Dublin, Ireland, Feb. 17, 1945.
Friels, Colin Glasgow, Scotland, Sept. 25, 1952.
Fry, Stephen Hampstead, London, England, Aug. 24, 1957.
Fuller, Penny Durham, NC, July 21, 1940. Northwestern.
Funicello, Annette Utica, NY, Oct. 22, 1942.
Furlong, Edward Glendale, CA, Aug. 2, 1977.
Furneaux, Yvonne Lille, France, May 11, 1928. Oxford U.

Gable, John Clark Los Angeles, CA, Mar. 20, 1961. Santa Monica College.
Gabor, Zsa Zsa (Sari Gabor) Budapest, Hungary, Feb. 6, 1918.
Gail, Max Derfoil, MI, Apr. 5, 1943.
Gaines, Boyd Atlanta, GA, May 11, 1953. Juilliard.
Galecki, Johnny Bree, Belgium, Apr. 30, 1975.
Gallagher, Peter NYC, Aug. 19, 1955. Tufts U.
Galligan, Zach NYC, Feb. 14, 1963. Columbia U.
Gallo, Vincent Buffalo, NY, Apr. 11, 1961.
Gam, Rita Pittsburgh, PA, Apr. 2, 1928.
Gamble, Mason Chicago, IL, Jan. 16, 1986.
Gambon, Michael Dublin, Ireland, Oct. 19, 1940.
Gandolfini, James Westwood, NJ, Sept. 18, 1961.
Ganz, Bruno Zurich, Switzerland, Mar. 22, 1941.
Garber, Victor Montreal, Canada, Mar. 16, 1949.
Garcia, Adam Wahroonga, New So. Wales, Australia, June 1, 1973.
Garcia, Andy Havana, Cuba, Apr. 12, 1956. FlaInt.
Garfield, Allen (Allen Goorwitz) Newark, NJ, Nov. 22, 1939. Actors Studio.
Garfunkel, Art NYC, Nov. 5, 1941.
Garland, Beverly Santa Cruz, CA, Oct. 17, 1926. Glendale College.
Garner, James (James Baumgarner) Norman, OK, Apr. 7, 1928. Oklahoma U.
Garner, Jennifer Houston, TX, Apr. 17, 1972.
Garofalo, Janeane Newton, NJ, Sept. 28, 1964.
Garr, Teri Lakewood, OH, Dec. 11, 1949.
Garrett, Betty St. Joseph, MO, May 23, 1919. Annie Wright Seminary.
Garrison, Sean NYC, Oct. 19, 1937.
Gary, Lorraine NYC, Aug. 16, 1937.
Gavin, John Los Angeles, CA, Apr. 8, 1935. Stanford U.
Gaylord, Mitch Van Nuys, CA, Mar. 10, 1961. UCLA.
Gaynor, Mitzi (Francesca Marlene Von Gerber) Chicago, IL, Sept. 4, 1930.
Gazzara, Ben NYC, Aug. 28, 1930. Actors Studio.
Geary, Anthony Coalsville, UT, May 29, 1947. U Utah.
Gedrick, Jason Chicago, IL, Feb. 7, 1965. Drake U.
Geeson, Judy Arundel, England, Sept. 10, 1948. Corona.
Gellar, Sarah Michelle NYC, Apr. 14, 1977.
Geoffreys, Stephen (Miller) Cincinnati, OH, Nov. 22, 1959. NYU.
George, Susan West London, England, England, July 26, 1950.
Gerard, Gil Little Rock, AR, Jan. 23, 1940.
Gere, Richard Philadelphia, PA, Aug. 29, 1949. U Mass.
Gerroll, Daniel London, England, Oct. 16, 1951. Central.

Gershon, Gina Los Angeles, CA, June 10, 1962.
Gertz, Jami Chicago, IL, Oct. 28, 1965.
Getty, Balthazar Los Angeles, CA, Jan. 22, 1975.
Getty, Estelle NYC, July 25, 1923. New School.
Gholson, Julie Birmingham, AL, June 4, 1958.
Ghostley, Alice Eve, MO, Aug. 14, 1926. Oklahoma U.
Giamatti, Paul NYC, June 6, 1967. Yale.
Giannini, Giancarlo Spezia, Italy, Aug. 1, 1942. Rome Academy of Drama.
Gibb, Cynthia Bennington, VT, Dec. 14, 1963.
Gibson, Henry Germantown, PA, Sept. 21, 1935.
Gibson, Mel Peekskill, NY, Jan. 3, 1956. NIDA.
Gibson, Thomas Charleston, SC, July 3, 1962.
Gift, Roland Birmingham, England, May 28 1962.
Gilbert, Melissa Los Angeles, CA, May 8, 1964.
Giles, Nancy NYC, July 17, 1960, Oberlin College.
Gillette, Anita Baltimore, MD, Aug. 16, 1938.
Gilliam, Terry Minneapolis, MN, Nov. 22, 1940.
Gillis, Ann (Alma O'Connor) Little Rock, AR, Feb. 12, 1927.
Ginty, Robert NYC, Nov. 14, 1948. Yale.
Girardot, Annie Paris, France, Oct. 25, 1931.
Gish, Annabeth Albuquerque, NM, Mar. 13, 1971. Duke U.
Givens, Robin NYC, Nov. 27, 1964.
Glaser, Paul Michael Boston, MA, Mar. 25, 1943. Boston U.
Glass, Ron Evansville, IN, July 10, 1945.
Gleason, Joanna Winnipeg, Canada, June 2, 1950. UCLA.
Gleason, Paul Jersey City, NJ, May 4, 1944.
Gleeson, Brendan Belfast, Nov. 9, 1955.
Glenn, Scott Pittsburgh, PA, Jan. 26, 1942. William and Mary College.
Glover, Crispin NYC, Sept 20, 1964.
Glover, Danny San Francisco, CA, July 22, 1947. San Francisco State U.
Glover, John Kingston, NY, Aug. 7, 1944.
Glynn, Carlin Cleveland, Oh, Feb. 19, 1940. Actors Studio.
Goldberg, Whoopi (Caryn Johnson) NYC, Nov. 13, 1949.
Goldblum, Jeff Pittsburgh, PA, Oct. 22, 1952. Neighborhood Playhouse.
Golden, Annie Brooklyn, NY, Oct. 19, 1951.
Goldstein, Jenette Beverly Hills, CA, Feb. 4, 1960.
Goldthwait, Bob Syracuse, NY, May 1, 1962.
Goldwyn, Tony Los Angeles, CA, May 20, 1960. LAMDA.
Golino, Valeria Naples, Italy, Oct. 22, 1966.
Gonzales-Gonzalez, Pedro Aguilares, TX, Dec. 21, 1926.
Gonzalez, Cordelia Aug. 11, 1958, San Juan, PR. UPR.
Goodall, Caroline London, England, Nov. 13, 1959. Bristol U.
Gooding, Cuba, Jr. Bronx, N.Y., Jan. 2, 1968.
Goodman, Dody Columbus, OH, Oct. 28, 1915.
Goodman, John St. Louis, MO, June 20, 1952.
Gordon, Keith NYC, Feb. 3, 1961.
Gordon-Levitt, Joseph Los Angeles, CA, Feb. 17, 1981.
Gortner, Marjoe Long Beach, CA, Jan. 14, 1944.
Gosling, Ryan London, Ontario, Nov. 12, 1980.
Goss, Luke London, England, Sept. 28, 1968.
Gossett, Louis, Jr. Brooklyn, NY, May 27, 1936. NYU.
Gould, Elliott (Goldstein) Brooklyn, NY, Aug. 29, 1938. Columbia U.
Gould, Harold Schenectady, NY, Dec. 10, 1923. Cornell.
Gould, Jason NYC, Dec. 29, 1966.

Goulet, Robert Lawrence, MA, Nov. 26, 1933. Edmonton.
Grace, Topher NYC, July 12, 1978.
Graf, David Lancaster, OH, Apr. 16, 1950. Ohio State U.
Graff, Todd NYC, Oct. 22, 1959. SUNY/Purchase.
Graham, Heather Milwauke, WI, Jan. 29, 1970.
Granger, Farley San Jose, CA, July 1, 1925.
Grant, David Marshall Westport, CT, June 21, 1955. Yale.
Grant, Hugh London, England, Sept. 9, 1960. Oxford.
Grant, Kathryn (Olive Grandstaff) Houston, TX, Nov. 25, 1933. UCLA.
Grant, Lee NYC, Oct. 31, 1927. Juilliard.
Grant, Richard E Mbabane, Swaziland, May 5, 1957. Cape Town U.
Graves, Peter (Aurness) Minneapolis, Mar. 18, 1926. U Minnesota.
Graves, Rupert Weston-Super-Mare, England, June 30, 1963.
Gray, Coleen (Doris Jensen) Staplehurst, NB, Oct. 23, 1922. Hamline.
Gray, Linda Santa Monica, CA, Sept. 12, 1940.
Grayson, Kathryn (Zelma Hedrick) Winston-Salem, NC, Feb. 9, 1922.
Green, Kerri Fort Lee, NJ, Jan. 14, 1967. Vassar.
Green, Seth Philadelphia, PA, Feb. 8, 1974.
Greene, Ellen NYC, Feb. 22, 1950. Ryder College.
Greene, Graham Six Nations Reserve, Ontario, June 22, 1952.
Greenwood, Bruce Quebec, Canada, Aug. 12, 1956.
Greer, Michael Galesburg, IL, Apr. 20, 1943.
Greist, Kim Stamford, CT, May 12, 1958.
Grey, Jennifer NYC, Mar. 26, 1960.
Grey, Joel (Katz) Cleveland, OH, Apr. 11, 1932.
Grieco, Richard Watertown, NY, Mar. 23, 1965.
Grier, David Alan Detroit, MI, June 30, 1955. Yale.
Grier, Pam Winston-Salem, NC, May 26, 1949.
Griffin, Eddie Kansas City, MO, July 15, 1968.
Griffith, Andy Mt. Airy, NC, June 1, 1926. U North Carolina.
Griffith, Melanie NYC, Aug. 9, 1957. Pierce Collge.
Griffith, Thomas Ian Hartford, CT, Mar. 18, 1962.
Griffiths, Rachel Melbourne, Australia, June 4, 1968.
Griffiths, Richard Tornaby-on-Tees, England, July 31, 1947.
Grimes, Gary San Francisco, June 2, 1955.
Grimes, Scott Lowell, MA, July 9, 1971.
Grimes, Tammy Lynn, MA, Jan. 30, 1934. Stephens College.
Grizzard, George Roanoke Rapids, NC, Apr. 1, 1928. U North Carolina.
Grodin, Charles Pittsburgh, PA, Apr. 21, 1935.
Groh, David NYC, May 21, 1939. Brown U, LAMDA.
Gross, Mary Chicago, IL, Mar. 25, 1953.
Gross, Michael Chicago, IL, June 21, 1947.
Gruffud, Ioan Cardiff, Wales, Oct. 6, 1973.
Guest, Christopher NYC, Feb. 5, 1948.
Guest, Lance Saratoga, CA, July 21, 1960. UCLA.
Guillaume, Robert (Williams) St. Louis, MO, Nov. 30, 1937.
Guiry, Thomas Trenton, NJ, Oct. 12, 1981.
Gulager, Clu Holdenville, OK, Nov. 16 1928.
Guttenberg, Steve Massapequa, NY, Aug. 24, 1958. UCLA.
Guy, Jasmine Boston, Mar. 10, 1964.
Guzman, Luis Cayey, Puerto Rico, Jan. 1, 1957.
Gyllenhaal, Jake Los Angeles, CA, Dec. 19, 1980.
Gyllenhaal, Maggie Los Angeles, CA, Nov. 16, 1977.

Haas, Lukas West Hollywood, CA, Apr. 16, 1976.
Hack, Shelley Greenwich, CT, July 6, 1952.
Hackman, Gene San Bernardino, CA, Jan. 30, 1930.
Hagerty, Julie Cincinnati, OH, June 15, 1955. Juilliard.
Hagman, Larry (Hageman) Weatherford, TX, Sept. 21, 1931. Bard.
Haid, Charles San Francisco, June 2, 1943. Carnegie Tech.
Haim, Corey Toronto, Canada, Dec. 23, 1972.
Hale, Barbara DeKalb, IL, Apr. 18, 1922. Chicago Academy of Fine Arts.
Haley, Jackie Earle Northridge, CA, July 14, 1961.
Hall, Albert Boothton, AL, Nov. 10, 1937. Columbia U.
Hall, Anthony Michael Boston, MA, Apr. 14, 1968.
Hall, Arsenio Cleveland, OH, Feb. 12, 1959.
Hamel, Veronica Philadelphia, PA, Nov. 20, 1943.
Hamill, Mark Oakland, CA, Sept. 25, 1952. LACC.
Hamilton, George Memphis, TN, Aug. 12, 1939. Hackley.
Hamilton, Linda Salisbury, MD, Sept. 26, 1956.
Hamlin, Harry Pasadena, CA, Oct. 30, 1951.
Hampshire, Susan London, England, May 12, 1941.
Hampton, James Oklahoma City, OK, July 9, 1936. Northern Texas State U.
Han, Maggie Providence, RI, 1959.
Handler, Evan NYC, Jan. 10, 1961. Juillard.
Hanks, Colin Sacramento, CA, Nov. 24, 1977.
Hanks, Tom Concord, CA, Jul. 9, 1956. California State U.
Hannah, Daryl Chicago, IL, Dec. 3, 1960. UCLA.
Hannah, Page Chicago, IL, Apr. 13, 1964.
Harden, Marcia Gay LaJolla, CA, Aug. 14, 1959.
Hardin, Ty (Orison Whipple Hungerford, II) NYC, June 1, 1930.
Harewood, Dorian Dayton, OH, Aug. 6, 1950. U Cinncinatti.
Harmon, Mark Los Angeles, CA, Sept. 2, 1951. UCLA.
Harper, Jessica Chicago, IL, Oct. 10, 1949.
Harper, Tess Mammoth Spring, AK, 1952. South Western Misourri State.
Harper, Valerie Suffern, NY, Aug. 22, 1940.
Harrelson, Woody Midland, TX, July 23, 1961. Hanover College.
Harrington, Pat NYC, Aug. 13, 1929. Fordham U.
Harris, Barbara (Sandra Markowitz) Evanston, IL, July 25, 1935.
Harris, Ed Tenafly, NJ, Nov. 28, 1950. Columbia U.
Harris, Jared UK, Aug. 24, 1961.
Harris, Julie Grosse Point, MI, Dec. 2, 1925. Yale Drama School.
Harris, Mel (Mary Ellen) Bethlehem, PA, 1957. Columbia U.
Harris, Neil Patrick Albuquerque, NM, June 15, 1973.
Harris, Rosemary Ashby, England, Sept. 19, 1930. RADA.
Harrison, Gregory Catalina Island, CA, May 31, 1950. Actors Studio.
Harrison, Noel London, England, Jan. 29, 1936.
Harrold, Kathryn Tazewell, VA, Aug. 2, 1950. Mills College.
Harry, Deborah Miami, IL, July 1, 1945.
Hart, Ian Liverpool, England, Oct. 8, 1964.
Hart, Roxanne Trenton, NJ, July 27, 1952. Princeton.
Hartley, Mariette NYC, June 21, 1941.
Hartman, David Pawtucket, RI, May 19, 1935. Duke U.
Hartnett, Josh San Francisco, July 21, 1978.
Hassett, Marilyn Los Angeles, CA, Dec. 17, 1947.
Hatcher, Teri Sunnyvale, CA, Dec. 8, 1964.
Hathaway, Anne Brooklyn, Nov. 12, 1982.
Hatosy, Shawn Fredrick, MD, Dec. 29, 1975.

Anne Hathaway

Katie Holmes

Djimon Hounsou

Scarlett Johansson

Hauer, Rutger Amsterdam, Holland, Jan. 23, 1944.
Hauser, Cole Santa Barbara, CA, Mar. 22, 1975.
Hasuer, Wings (Gerald Dwight Hauser) Hollywood, CA, Dec. 12, 1947.
Havoc, June (Hovick) Seattle, WA, Nov. 8, 1916.
Hawke, Ethan Austin, TX, Nov. 6, 1970.
Hawn, Goldie Washington, DC, Nov. 21, 1945.
Hayek, Salma Coatzacoalcos, Veracruz, Mexico, Sept. 2, 1968.
Hayes, Isaac Covington, TN, Aug. 20, 1942.
Hays, Robert Bethesda, MD, July 24, 1947. South Dakota State College.
Haysbert, Dennis San Mateo, CA, June 2, 1954.
Headly, Glenne New London, CT, Mar. 13, 1955. AmCollege.
Heald, Anthony New Rochelle, NY, Aug. 25, 1944. Michigan State U.
Heard, John Washington, DC, Mar. 7, 1946. Clark U.
Heatherton, Joey NYC, Sept. 14, 1944.
Heche, Anne Aurora, OH, May 25, 1969.
Hedaya, Dan Brooklyn, NY, July 24, 1940.
Heder, Jon Fort Collins, CO, Oct. 26, 1977.
Hedison, David Providence, RI, May 20, 1929. Brown U.
Hedren, Tippi (Natalie) Lafayette, MN, Jan. 19, 1931.
Hegyes, Robert Metuchen, NJ, May 7, 1951.
Helmond, Katherine Galveston, TX, July 5, 1934.
Hemingway, Mariel Ketchum, ID, Nov. 22, 1961.
Hemsley, Sherman Philadelphia, PA, Feb. 1, 1938.
Henderson, Florence Dale, IN, Feb. 14, 1934.
Hendry, Gloria Winter Have, FL, Mar. 3, 1949.
Henner, Marilu Chicago, IL, Apr. 6, 1952.
Henriksen, Lance NYC, May 5, 1940.
Henry, Buck (Henry Zuckerman) NYC, Dec. 9, 1930. Dartmouth.
Henry, Justin Rye, NY, May 25, 1971.
Henstridge, Natasha Springdale, Newfoundland, Canada, Aug. 15, 1974.
Hernandez, Jay (Javier Hernandez, Jr.) Montebello, CA, Feb. 20, 1978.
Herrmann, Edward Washington, DC, July 21, 1943. Bucknell, LAMDA.
Hershey, Barbara (Herzstein) Hollywood, CA, Feb. 5, 1948.
Hesseman, Howard Lebanon, OR, Feb. 27, 1940.
Heston, Charlton Evanston, IL, Oct. 4, 1922. Northwestern.
Hewitt, Jennifer Love Waco, TX, Feb. 21, 1979.
Hewitt, Martin Claremont, CA, Feb. 19, 1958. AADA.

Heywood, Anne (Violet Pretty) Birmingham, England, Dec. 11, 1932.
Hickman, Darryl Hollywood, CA, July 28, 1933. Loyola U.
Hickman, Dwayne Los Angeles, CA, May 18, 1934. Loyola U.
Hicks, Catherine NYC, Aug. 6, 1951. Notre Dame.
Higgins, Anthony (Corlan) Cork City, Ireland, May 9, 1947. Birmingham Dramatic Arts.
Higgins, Michael Brooklyn, NY, Jan. 20, 1921. AmThWing.
Highmore, Freddie London, Feb. 14, 1992.
Hill, Arthur Saskatchewan, Canada, Aug. 1, 1922. U Brit. College.
Hill, Bernard Manchester, England, Dec. 17, 1944.
Hill, Steven Seattle, WA, Feb. 24, 1922. U Wash.
Hill, Terrence (Mario Girotti) Venice, Italy, Mar. 29, 1941. U Rome.
Hillerman, John Denison, TX, Dec. 20, 1932.
Hinds, Ciaran Belfast, Northern Ireland, Feb. 9, 1953.
Hingle, Pat Denver, CO, July 19, 1923. Texas U.
Hirsch, Emile Topanga Canyon, CA, Mar. 13, 1985.
Hirsch, Judd NYC, Mar. 15, 1935. AADA.
Hobel, Mara NYC, June 18, 1971.
Hodge, Patricia Lincolnshire, England, Sept. 29, 1946. LAMDA.
Hoffman, Dustin Los Angeles, CA, Aug. 8, 1937. Pasadena Playhouse.
Hoffman, Philip Seymour Fairport, NY, July 23, 1967. NYU.
Hogan, Jonathan Chicago, IL, June 13, 1951.
Hogan, Paul Lightning Ridge, Australia, Oct. 8, 1939.
Holbrook, Hal (Harold) Cleveland, OH, Feb. 17, 1925. Denison.
Holliman, Earl Tennass Swamp, Delhi, LA, Sept. 11, 1928. UCLA.
Holm, Celeste NYC, Apr. 29, 1919.
Holm, Ian Ilford, Essex, England, Sept. 12, 1931. RADA.
Holmes, Katie Toledo, OH, Dec. 18, 1978.
Homeier, Skip (George Vincent Homeier) Chicago, IL, Oct. 5, 1930. UCLA.
Hooks, Robert Washington, DC, Apr. 18, 1937. Temple.
Hopkins, Anthony Port Talbot, So. Wales, Dec. 31, 1937. RADA.
Hopper, Dennis Dodge City, KS, May 17, 1936.
Horne, Lena Brooklyn, NY, June 30, 1917.
Horrocks, Jane Rossendale Valley, England, Jan. 18, 1964.
Horsley, Lee Muleshoe, TX, May 15, 1955.
Horton, Robert Los Angeles, CA, July 29, 1924. UCLA.
Hoskins, Bob Bury St. Edmunds, England, Oct. 26, 1942.

Houghton, Katharine Hartford, CT, Mar. 10, 1945. Sarah Lawrence.
Hounsou, Djimon Benin, West Africa, Apr. 24, 1964.
Houser, Jerry Los Angeles, CA, July 14, 1952. Valley, Jr. College.
Howard, Arliss Independence, MO, 1955. Columbia College.
Howard, Ken El Centro, CA, Mar. 28, 1944. Yale.
Howard, Ron Duncan, OK, Mar. 1, 1954. USC.
Howard, Terrence Chicago, Mar. 11, 1969. Pratt Inst.
Howell, C. Thomas Los Angeles, CA, Dec. 7, 1966.
Howes, Sally Ann London, England, July 20, 1930.
Howland, Beth Boston, MA, May 28, 1941.
Hubley, Season NYC, May 14, 1951.
Huddleston, David Vinton, VA, Sept. 17, 1930.
Hudson, Ernie Benton Harbor, MI, Dec. 17, 1945.
Hudson, Kate Los Angeles, CA, Apr. 19, 1979.
Huffman, Felicity Bedford, NY, Dec. 9, 1962. NYU.
Hughes, Barnard Bedford Hills, NY, July 16, 1915. Manhattan College.
Hughes, Kathleen (Betty von Gerkan) Hollywood, CA, Nov. 14, 1928. UCLA.
Hulce, Tom Plymouth, MI, Dec. 6, 1953. North Carolina School of Arts.
Hunnicut, Gayle Ft. Worth, TX, Feb. 6, 1943. UCLA.
Hunt, Helen Los Angeles, CA, June 15, 1963.
Hunt, Linda Morristown, NJ, Apr. 1945. Goodman Theatre.
Hunt, Marsha Chicago, IL, Oct. 17, 1917.
Hunter, Holly Atlanta, GA, Mar. 20, 1958. Carnegie-Mellon.
Hunter, Tab (Arthur Gelien) NYC, July 11, 1931.
Huppert, Isabelle Paris, France, Mar. 16, 1955.
Hurley, Elizabeth Hampshire, England, June 10, 1965.
Hurt, John Lincolnshire, England, Jan. 22, 1940.
Hurt, Mary Beth (Supinger) Marshalltown, IA, Sept. 26, 1948. NYU.
Hurt, William Washington, DC, Mar. 20, 1950. Tufts, Juilliard.
Huston, Anjelica Santa Monica, CA, July 9, 1951.
Huston, Danny Rome, May 14, 1962.
Hutton, Betty (Betty Thornberg) Battle Creek, MI, Feb. 26, 1921.
Hutton, Lauren (Mary) Charleston, SC, Nov. 17, 1943. Newcomb College.
Hutton, Timothy Malibu, CA, Aug. 16, 1960.
Hyer, Martha Fort Worth, TX, Aug. 10, 1924. Northwestern.

Ice Cube (O'Shea Jackson) Los Angeles, CA, June 15, 1969.
Idle, Eric South Shields, Durham, England, Mar. 29, 1943. Cambridge.
Ifans, Rhys Ruthin, Wales, July 22, 1968.
Ingels, Marty Brooklyn, NY, Mar. 9, 1936.
Ireland, Kathy Santa Barbara, CA, Mar. 8, 1963.
Irons, Jeremy Cowes, England, Sept. 19, 1948. Old Vic.
Ironside, Michael Toronto, Canada, Feb. 12, 1950.
Irving, Amy Palo Alto, CA, Sept. 10, 1953. LADA.
Irwin, Bill Santa Monica, CA, Apr. 11, 1950.
Isaak, Chris Stockton, CA, June 26, 1956. U of Pacific.
Ivanek, Zeljko Lujubljana, Yugoslavia, Aug. 15, 1957. Yale, LAMDA.
Ivey, Judith El Paso, TX, Sept. 4, 1951.
Izzard, Eddie Aden, Yemen, Feb. 7, 1962.

Jackson, Anne Alleghany, PA, Sept. 3, 1926. Neighborhood Playhouse.
Jackson, Glenda Hoylake, Cheshire, England, May 9, 1936. RADA.
Jackson, Janet Gary, IN, May 16, 1966.
Jackson, Kate Birmingham, AL, Oct. 29, 1948. AADA.

Jackson, Michael Gary, IN, Aug. 29, 1958.
Jackson, Samuel L. Atlanta, Dec. 21, 1948.
Jackson, Victoria Miami, FL, Aug. 2, 1958.
Jacobi, Derek Leytonstone, London, England, Oct. 22, 1938. Cambridge.
Jacobi, Lou Toronto, Canada, Dec. 28, 1913.
Jacobs, Lawrence-Hilton Virgin Islands, Sept. 14, 1953.
Jacoby, Scott Chicago, IL, Nov. 19, 1956.
Jagger, Mick Dartford, Kent, England, July 26, 1943.
James, Clifton NYC, May 29, 1921. Oregon U.
Jane, Thomas Baltimore, MD, Jan. 29, 1969.
Janney, Allison Dayton, OH, Nov. 20, 1960. RADA.
Jarman, Claude, Jr. Nashville, TN, Sept. 27, 1934.
Jean, Gloria (Gloria Jean Schoonover) Buffalo, NY, Apr. 14, 1927.
Jeffreys, Anne (Carmichael) Goldsboro, NC, Jan. 26, 1923. Anderson College.
Jeffries, Lionel London, England, June 10, 1926. RADA.
Jillian, Ann (Nauseda) Cambridge, MA, Jan. 29, 1951.
Johansen, David Staten Island, NY, Jan. 9, 1950.
Johansson, Scarlett NYC, Nov. 22, 1984.
John, Elton (Reginald Dwight) Middlesex, England, Mar. 25, 1947. RAM.
Johns, Glynis Durban, S. Africa, Oct. 5, 1923.
Johnson, Don Galena, MO, Dec. 15, 1950. U Kansas.
Johnson, Page Welch, WV, Aug. 25, 1930. Ithaca.
Johnson, Rafer Hillsboro, TX, Aug. 18, 1935. UCLA.
Johnson, Richard Essex, England, July 30, 1927. RADA.
Johnson, Robin Brooklyn, NY, May 29, 1964.
Johnson, Van Newport, RI, Aug. 28, 1916.
Jolie, Angelina (Angelina Jolie Voight) Los Angeles, CA, June 4, 1975.
Jones, Cherry Paris, TN, Nov. 21, 1956.
Jones, Christopher Jackson, TN, Aug. 18, 1941. Actors Studio.
Jones, Dean Decatur, AL, Jan. 25, 1931. Actors Studio.
Jones, Grace Spanishtown, Jamaica, May 19, 1952.
Jones, Jack Bel-Air, CA, Jan. 14, 1938.
Jones, James Earl Arkabutla, MS, Jan. 17, 1931. U Michigan
Jones, Jeffrey Buffalo, NY, Sept. 28, 1947. LAMDA.
Jones, Jennifer (Phyllis Isley) Tulsa, OK, Mar. 2, 1919. AADA.
Jones, L.Q. (Justice Ellis McQueen) Aug 19, 1927.
Jones, Orlando Mobile, AL, Apr. 10, 1968.
Jones, Sam J. Chicago, IL, Aug. 12, 1954.
Jones, Shirley Smithton, PA, March 31, 1934.
Jones, Terry Colwyn Bay, Wales, Feb. 1, 1942.
Jones, Tommy Lee San Saba, TX, Sept. 15, 1946. Harvard.
Jourdan, Louis Marseilles, France, June 19, 1920.
Jovovich, Milla Kiev, Ukraine, Dec. 17, 1975.
Joy, Robert Montreal, Canada, Aug. 17, 1951. Oxford.
Judd, Ashley Los Angeles, CA, Apr. 19, 1968.

Kaczmarek, Jane Milwaukee, WI, Dec. 21, 1955.
Kane, Carol Cleveland, OH, June 18, 1952.
Kaplan, Marvin Brooklyn, NY, Jan. 24, 1924.
Kapoor, Shashi Calcutta, India, Mar. 18, 1938.
Kaprisky, Valerie (Cheres) Paris, France, Aug. 19, 1962.
Karras, Alex Gary, IN, July 15, 1935.
Kartheiser, Vincent Minneapolis, MN, May 5, 1979.

Karyo, Tcheky Istanbul, Oct. 4, 1953.
Kassovitz, Mathieu Paris, France Aug. 3, 1967.
Katt, William Los Angeles, CA, Feb. 16, 1955.
Kattan, Chris Mt. Baldy, CA, Oct. 19, 1970.
Kaufmann, Christine Lansdorf, Graz, Austria, Jan. 11, 1945.
Kavner, Julie Burbank, CA, Sept. 7, 1951. UCLA.
Kazan, Lainie (Levine) Brooklyn, NY, May 15, 1942.
Kazurinsky, Tim Johnstown, PA, March 3, 1950.
Keach, Stacy Savannah, GA, June 2, 1941. U California, Yale.
Keaton, Diane (Hall) Los Angeles, CA, Jan. 5, 1946. Neighborhood Playhouse.
Keaton, Michael Coraopolis, PA, Sept. 9, 1951. Kent State U.
Keegan, Andrew Los Angeles, CA, Jan. 29, 1979.
Keener, Catherine Miami, FL, Mar. 26, 1960. Wheaton College.
Keeslar, Matt Grand Rapids, MI, Oct. 15, 1972.
Keitel, Harvey Brooklyn, NY, May 13, 1939.
Keith, David Knoxville, TN, May 8, 1954. U Tennessee.
Keller, Marthe Basel, Switzerland, 1945. Munich Stanislavsky School.
Kellerman, Sally Long Beach, CA, June 2, 1936. Actors Studio West.
Kelly, Moira Queens, NY, Mar. 6, 1968.
Kemp, Jeremy (Wacker) Chesterfield, England, Feb. 3, 1935. Central School.
Kennedy, George NYC, Feb. 18, 1925.
Kennedy, Jamie Upper Darby, PA, May 25, 1970.
Kennedy, Leon Isaac Cleveland, OH, 1949.
Kensit, Patsy London, England, Mar. 4, 1968.
Kerr, Deborah Helensburg, Scotland, Sept. 30, 1921. Smale Ballet School.
Kerr, John NYC, Nov. 15, 1931. Harvard, Columbia.
Kerwin, Brian Chicago, IL, Oct. 25, 1949.
Keyes, Evelyn Port Arthur, TX, Nov. 20, 1919.
Kidder, Margot Yellow Knife, Canada, Oct. 17, 1948. U British Columbia.
Kidman, Nicole Hawaii, June 20, 1967.
Kiel, Richard Detroit, MI, Sept. 13, 1939.
Kier, Udo Koeln, Germany, Oct. 14, 1944.
Kilmer, Val Los Angeles, CA, Dec. 31, 1959. Juilliard.
Kincaid, Aron (Norman Neale Williams, III) Los Angeles, CA, June 15, 1943. UCLA.
King, Perry Alliance, OH, Apr. 30, 1948. Yale.
Kingsley, Ben (Krishna Bhanji) Snaiton, Yorkshire, England, Dec. 31, 1943.
Kinnear, Greg Logansport, IN, June 17, 1963.
Kinski, Nastassja Berlin, Germany, Jan. 24, 1960.
Kirby, Bruno NYC, Apr. 28, 1949.
Kirk, Tommy Louisville, KY, Dec. 10 1941.
Kirkland, Sally NYC, Oct. 31, 1944. Actors Studio.
Kitt, Eartha North, SC, Jan. 26, 1928.
Klein, Chris Hinsdale, IL, March 14, 1979.
Klein, Robert NYC, Feb. 8, 1942. Alfred U.
Kline, Kevin St. Louis, MO, Oct. 24, 1947. Juilliard.
Klugman, Jack Philadelphia, PA, Apr. 27, 1922. Carnegie Tech.
Knight, Michael E. Princeton, NJ, May 7, 1959.
Knight, Shirley Goessel, KS, July 5, 1937. Wichita U.
Knightley, Keira Teddington, England, Mar. 26, 1985.
Knox, Elyse Hartford, CT, Dec. 14, 1917. Traphagen School.
Knoxville, Johnny (Phillip John Clapp) Knoxville, TN, March 11, 1971.
Koenig, Walter Chicago, IL, Sept. 14, 1936. UCLA.

Kohner, Susan Los Angeles, CA, Nov. 11, 1936. U California.
Korman, Harvey Chicago, IL, Feb. 15, 1927. Goodman.
Korsmo, Charlie Minneapolis, MN, July, 20, 1978.
Koteas, Elias Montreal, Quebec, Canada, 1961. AADA.
Kotto, Yaphet NYC, Nov. 15, 1937.
Kozak, Harley Jane Wilkes-Barre, PA, Jan. 28, 1957. NYU.
Krabbe, Jeroen Amsterdam, The Netherlands, Dec. 5, 1944.
Kretschmann, Thomas Dessau, East Germany, Sept. 8, 1962.
Kreuger, Kurt St. Moritz, Switzerland, July 23, 1917. U London.
Krige, Alice Upington, South Africa, June 28, 1955.
Kristel, Sylvia Amsterdam, The Netherlands, Sept. 28, 1952.
Kristofferson, Kris Brownsville, TX, June 22, 1936. Pomona College.
Kruger, Hardy Berlin, Germany, April 12, 1928.
Krumholtz, David NYC, May 15, 1978.
Kudrow, Lisa Encino, CA, July 30, 1963.
Kurtz, Swoosie Omaha, NE, Sept. 6, 1944.
Kutcher, Ashton (Christopher Ashton Kutcher) Cedar Rapids, IA, Feb. 7, 1978.
Kwan, Nancy Hong Kong, May 19, 1939. Royal Ballet.

LaBelle, Patti Philadelphia, PA, May 24, 1944.
LaBeouf, Shia Los Angeles, CA, June 11, 1986.
Lacy, Jerry Sioux City, IA, Mar. 27, 1936. LACC.
Ladd, Cheryl (Stoppelmoor) Huron, SD. July 12, 1951.
Ladd, Diane (Ladner) Meridian, MS, Nov. 29, 1932. Tulane U.
Lahti, Christine Detroit, MI, Apr. 4, 1950. U Michigan.
Lake, Ricki NYC, Sept. 21, 1968.
Lamas, Lorenzo Los Angeles, CA, Jan. 28, 1958.
Lambert, Christopher NYC, Mar. 29, 1958.
Landau, Martin Brooklyn, NY, June 20, 1931. Actors Studio.
Lane, Abbe Brooklyn, NY, Dec. 14, 1935.
Lane, Diane NYC, Jan. 22, 1963.
Lane, Nathan Jersey City, NJ, Feb. 3, 1956.
Lang, Stephen NYC, July 11, 1952. Swarthmore College.
Lange, Jessica Cloquet, MN, Apr. 20, 1949. U Minnesota
Langella, Frank Bayonne, NJ, Jan. 1, 1940. Syracuse U.
Lansbury, Angela London, England, Oct. 16, 1925. London Academy of Music.
LaPaglia, Anthony Adelaide, Australia. Jan 31, 1959.
Larroquette, John New Orleans, LA, Nov. 25, 1947.
Lasser, Louise NYC, Apr. 11, 1939. Brandeis U.
Lathan, Sanaa NYC, Sept. 19, 1971.
Latifah, Queen (Dana Owens) East Orange, NJ, Mar. 18, 1970.
Laughlin, John Memphis, TN, Apr. 3.
Laughlin, Tom Minneapolis, MN, 1938.
Lauper, Cyndi Astoria, Queens, NYC, June 20, 1953.
Laure, Carole Montreal, Canada, Aug. 5, 1951.
Laurie, Hugh Oxford, England, June 11, 1959.
Laurie, Piper (Rosetta Jacobs) Detroit, MI, Jan. 22, 1932.
Lauter, Ed Long Beach, NY, Oct. 30, 1940.
Lavin, Linda Portland, ME, Oct. 15 1939.
Law, John Phillip Hollywood, CA, Sept. 7, 1937. Neighborhood Playhouse, U Hawaii.
Law, Jude Lewisham, England, Dec. 29, 1972.

Lawrence, Barbara Carnegie, OK, Feb. 24, 1928. UCLA.
Lawrence, Carol (Laraia) Melrose Park, IL, Sept. 5, 1935.
Lawrence, Martin Frankfurt, Germany, Apr. 16, 1965.
Lawrence, Vicki Inglewood, CA, Mar. 26, 1949.
Lawson, Leigh Atherston, England, July 21, 1945. RADA.
Leachman, Cloris Des Moines, IA, Apr. 30, 1930. Northwestern.
Leary, Denis Boston, MA, Aug. 18, 1957.
Léaud, Jean-Pierre Paris, France, May 5, 1944.
LeBlanc, Matt Newton, MA, July 25, 1967.
Ledger, Heath Perth, Australia, Apr. 4, 1979.
Lee, Christopher London, England, May 27, 1922. Wellington College.
Lee, Jason Huntington Beach, CA, Apr. 25, 1970.
Lee, Mark Sydney, Australia, 1958.
Lee, Michele (Dusiak) Los Angeles, CA, June 24, 1942. LACC.
Lee, Sheryl Augsburg, Germany, Arp. 22, 1967.
Lee, Spike (Shelton Lee) Atlanta, GA, Mar. 20, 1957.
Legge, Michael Newry, Northern Ireland, 1978.
Legros, James Minneapolis, MN, Apr. 27, 1962.
Leguizamo, John Columbia, July 22, 1965. NYU.
Leibman, Ron NYC, Oct. 11, 1937. Ohio Wesleyan.
Leigh, Jennifer Jason Los Angeles, CA, Feb. 5, 1962.
Le Mat, Paul Rahway, NJ, Sept. 22, 1945.
Lemmon, Chris Los Angeles, CA, Jan. 22, 1954.
Leno, Jay New Rochelle, NY, Apr. 28, 1950. Emerson College.
Lenz, Kay Los Angeles, CA, Mar. 4, 1953.
Lenz, Rick Springfield, IL, Nov. 21, 1939. U Michigan.
Leonard, Robert Sean Westwood, NJ, Feb. 28, 1969.
Leoni, Téa (Elizabeth Téa Pantaleoni) NYC, Feb. 25, 1966.
Lerner, Michael Brooklyn, NY, June 22, 1941.
Leslie, Joan (Joan Brodell) Detroit, MI, Jan. 26, 1925. St. Benedict's.
Lester, Mark Oxford, England, July 11, 1958.
Leto, Jared Bossier City, LA, Dec. 26, 1971.
Levels, Calvin Cleveland. OH, Sept. 30, 1954. CCC.
Levin, Rachel (Rachel Chagall) NYC, Nov. 24, 1954. Goddard College.
Levine, Jerry New Brunswick, NJ, Mar. 12, 1957, Boston U.
Levy, Eugene Hamilton, Canada, Dec. 17, 1946. McMaster U.
Lewis, Charlotte London, England, Aug. 7, 1967.
Lewis, Damian London, Feb. 11, 1971. Guildhall.
Lewis, Geoffrey San Diego, CA, Jan. 1, 1935.
Lewis, Jerry (Joseph Levitch) Newark, NJ, Mar. 16, 1926.
Lewis, Juliette Los Angeles CA, June 21, 1973.
Li, Jet Beijing, China, Apr. 26, 1963.
Ligon, Tom New Orleans, LA, Sept. 10, 1945.
Lillard, Matthew Lansing, MI, Jan. 24, 1970.
Lincoln, Abbey (Anna Marie Woolridge) Chicago, IL, Aug. 6, 1930.
Linden, Hal Bronx, NY, Mar. 20, 1931. City College of NY.
Lindo, Delroy London, England, Nov. 18, 1952.
Lindsay, Robert Ilketson, Derbyshire, England, Dec. 13, 1951, RADA.
Linn-Baker, Mark St. Louis, MO, June 17, 1954, Yale.
Linney, Laura New York, NY, Feb. 5, 1964.
Liotta, Ray Newark, NJ, Dec. 18, 1955. U Miami.
Lisi, Virna Rome, Italy, Nov. 8, 1937.
Lithgow, John Rochester, NY, Oct. 19, 1945. Harvard.
Liu, Lucy Queens, NY, Dec. 2, 1967.

Livingston, Ron Cedar Rapids, IA, June 5, 1968.
LL Cool J (James Todd Smith) Queens, NY, Jan. 14, 1968.
Lloyd, Christopher Stamford, CT, Oct. 22, 1938.
Lloyd, Emily London, England, Sept. 29, 1970.
Locke, Sondra Shelbyville, TN, May, 28, 1947.
Lockhart, June NYC, June 25, 1925. Westlake School.
Lockwood, Gary Van Nuys, CA, Feb. 21, 1937.
Loggia, Robert Staten Island, NY, Jan. 3, 1930. U Missouri.
Lohan, Lindsay NYC, July 2, 1986.
Lohman, Alison Palm Springs, CA, Sept. 18, 1979.
Lollobrigida, Gina Subiaco, Italy, July 4, 1927. Rome Academy of Fine Arts.
Lom, Herbert Prague, Czechoslovakia, Jan. 9, 1917. Prague U.
Lomez, Celine Montreal, Canada, May 11, 1953.
Lone, John Hong Kong, Oct 13, 1952. AADA.
Long, Justin Fairfield, CT, June 2, 1978.
Long, Nia Brooklyn, NY, Oct. 30, 1970.
Long, Shelley Ft. Wayne, IN, Aug. 23, 1949. Northwestern.
Lopez, Jennifer Bronx, NY, July 24, 1970.
Lopez, Perry NYC, July 22, 1931. NYU.
Lords, Tracy (Nora Louise Kuzma) Steubenville, OH, May 7, 1968.
Loren, Sophia (Sophia Scicolone) Rome, Italy, Sept. 20, 1934.
Louis-Dreyfus, Julia NYC, Jan. 13, 1961.
Louise, Tina (Blacker) NYC, Feb. 11, 1934, Miami U.
Love, Courtney (Love Michelle Harrison) San Francisco, CA, July 9, 1965.
Lovett, Lyle Klein, TX, Nov. 1, 1957.
Lovitz, Jon Tarzana, CA, July 21, 1957.
Lowe, Chad Dayton, OH, Jan. 15, 1968.
Lowe, Rob Charlottesville, VA, Mar. 17, 1964.
Lucas, Josh Little Rock, AR, June 20, 1971.
Lucas, Lisa Arizona, 1961.
Luckinbill, Laurence Fort Smith, AK, Nov. 21, 1934.
Luft, Lorna Los Angeles, CA, Nov. 21, 1952.
Luke, Derek Jersey City, NJ, Apr. 24, 1974.
Lulu (Marie Lawrie) Glasgow, Scotland, Nov. 3, 1948.
Luna, Barbara NYC, Mar. 2, 1939.
Luna, Diego Mexico City, Dec. 29, 1979.
Lundgren, Dolph Stockolm, Sweden, Nov. 3, 1959. Royal Institute.
LuPone, Patti Northport, NY, Apr. 21, 1949, Juilliard.
Lydon, James Harrington Park, NJ, May 30, 1923.
Lynch, Kelly Minneapolis, MN, Jan. 31, 1959.
Lynley, Carol (Jones) NYC, Feb. 13, 1942.
Lyon, Sue Davenport, IA, July 10, 1946.
Lyonne, Natasha (Braunstein) NYC, Apr. 4, 1979.

Mac, Bernie (Bernard Jeffrey McCollough) Chicago, IL, Oct. 5, 1958.
MacArthur, James Los Angeles, CA, Dec. 8, 1937. Harvard.
Macchio, Ralph Huntington, NY, Nov. 4, 1961.
MacCorkindale, Simon Cambridge, England, Feb. 12, 1953.
Macdonald, Kelly Glasgow, Scotland, Feb. 23, 1976.
MacDowell, Andie (Rose Anderson MacDowell) Gaffney, SC, Apr. 21, 1958.
MacFadyen, Angus Scotland, Oct. 21, 1963.
MacGraw, Ali NYC, Apr. 1, 1938. Wellesley.
MacLachlan, Kyle Yakima, WA, Feb. 22, 1959. U Washington.
MacLaine, Shirley (Beaty) Richmond, VA, Apr. 24, 1934.

Queen Latifah   Jennifer Lopez   Steve Martin   Ewan McGregor

MacLeod, Gavin Mt. Kisco, NY, Feb. 28, 1931.
MacNaughton, Robert NYC, Dec. 19, 1966.
Macnee, Patrick London, England, Feb. 1922.
MacNicol, Peter Dallas, TX, Apr. 10, 1954. U Minnesota.
MacPherson, Elle Sydney, Australia, Mar. 29, 1963.
MacVittie, Bruce Providence, RI, Oct. 14, 1956. Boston U.
Macy, William H. Miami, FL, Mar. 13, 1950. Goddard College.
Madigan, Amy Chicago, IL, Sept. 11, 1950. Marquette U.
Madonna (Madonna Louise Veronica Cicone) Bay City, MI, Aug. 16, 1958. U Michigan.
Madsen, Michael Chicago, IL, Sept. 25, 1958.
Madsen, Virginia Winnetka, IL, Sept. 11, 1963.
Magnuson, Ann Charleston, WV, Jan. 4, 1956.
Maguire, Tobey Santa Monica, CA, June 27, 1975.
Maharis, George Astoria, NY, Sept. 1, 1928. Actors Studio.
Mahoney, John Manchester, England, June 20, 1940. Western Illinois U.
Mailer, Stephen NYC, Mar. 10, 1966. NYU.
Majors, Lee Wyandotte, MI, Apr. 23, 1940. Eastern Kentucky State College.
Makepeace, Chris Toronto, Canada, Apr. 22, 1964.
Mako (Mako Iwamatsu) Kobe, Japan, Dec. 10, 1933. Pratt.
Malden, Karl (Mladen Sekulovich) Gary, IN, Mar. 22, 1914.
Malkovich, John Christopher, IL, Dec. 9, 1953, Illinois State U.
Malone, Dorothy Chicago, IL, Jan. 30, 1925.
Malone, Jena Lake Tahoe, NV, Nov. 21, 1984.
Mann, Terrence KY, July 1, 1951. NC School Arts.
Manoff, Dinah NYC, Jan. 25, 1958. Cal Arts.
Mantegna, Joe Chicago, IL, Nov. 13, 1947. Goodman Theatre.
Manz, Linda NYC, 1961.
Marceau, Sophie (Maupu) Paris, France, Nov. 17, 1966.
Marcovicci, Andrea NYC, Nov. 18, 1948.
Margulies, Julianna Spring Valley, NY, June 8, 1966.
Marin, Cheech (Richard) Los Angeles, CA, July 13, 1946.
Marinaro, Ed NYC, Mar. 31, 1950. Cornell.
Mars, Kenneth Chicago, IL, Apr. 14, 1936.
Marsden, James Stillwater, OK, Sept. 18, 1973.
Marsh, Jean London, England, July 1, 1934.
Marshall, Ken NYC, June 27, 1950. Juilliard.

Marshall, Penny Bronx, NY, Oct. 15, 1942. UN. Mex.
Martin, Andrea Portland, ME, Jan. 15, 1947.
Martin, Dick Battle Creek, MI Jan. 30, 1923.
Martin, George N. NYC, Aug. 15, 1929.
Martin, Millicent Romford, England, June 8, 1934.
Martin, Pamela Sue Westport, CT, Jan. 15, 1953.
Martin, Steve Waco, TX, Aug. 14, 1945. UCLA.
Martin, Tony (Alfred Norris) Oakland, CA, Dec. 25, 1913. St. Mary's College.
Martinez, Olivier Paris, France, Jan. 12, 1966.
Mason, Marsha St. Louis, MO, Apr. 3, 1942. Webster College.
Massen, Osa Copenhagen, Denmark, Jan. 13, 1916.
Masters, Ben Corvallis, OR, May 6, 1947. U Oregon.
Masterson, Mary Stuart Los Angeles, CA, June 28, 1966, NYU.
Masterson, Peter Angleton, TX, June 1, 1934. Rice U.
Mastrantonio, Mary Elizabeth Chicago, IL, Nov. 17, 1958. U Illinois.
Masur, Richard NYC, Nov. 20, 1948.
Matheson, Tim Glendale, CA, Dec. 31, 1947. Cal State.
Mathis, Samantha NYC, May 12, 1970.
Matlin, Marlee Morton Grove, IL, Aug. 24, 1965.
Matthews, Brian Philadelphia, PA, Jan. 24. 1953. St. Olaf.
May, Elaine (Berlin) Philadelphia, PA, Apr. 21, 1932.
Mayron, Melanie Philadelphia, PA, Oct. 20, 1952. AADA.
Mazursky, Paul Brooklyn, NY, Apr. 25, 1930. Brooklyn College.
Mazzello, Joseph Rhinebeck, NY, Sept. 21, 1983.
McAdams, Rachel London, Ontario, Oct. 7, 1976.
McAvoy, James Glasgow, Scotland, Jan. 1, 1979.
McCallum, David Scotland, Sept. 19, 1933. Chapman College.
McCarthy, Andrew NYC, Nov. 29, 1962, NYU.
McCarthy, Kevin Seattle, WA, Feb. 15, 1914. Minnesota U.
McCartney, Paul Liverpool, England, June 18, 1942.
McClanahan, Rue Healdton, OK, Feb. 21, 1934.
McClure, Marc San Mateo, CA, Mar. 31, 1957.
McClurg, Edie Kansas City, MO, July 23, 1950.
McCormack, Catherine Alton, Hampshire, England, Jan. 1, 1972.
McCowen, Alec Tunbridge Wells, England, May 26, 1925. RADA.
McCrane, Paul Philadelphia, PA, Jan. 19. 1961.
McCrary, Darius Walnut, CA, May 1, 1976.

McDermott, Dylan Waterbury, CT, Oct. 26, 1962. Neighborhood Playhouse.
McDonald, Christopher NYC, Feb. 15, 1955.
McDonnell, Mary Wilkes Barre, PA, Apr. 28, 1952.
McDonough, Neal Dorchester, MA, Feb. 13, 1966.
McDormand, Frances Illinois, June 23, 1957. Yale.
McDowell, Malcolm (Taylor) Leeds, England, June 19, 1943. LAMDA.
McElhone, Natascha (Natasha Taylor) London, England, Mar. 23, 1971.
McEnery, Peter Walsall, England, Feb. 21, 1940.
McEntire, Reba McAlester, OK, Mar. 28, 1955. Southeastern St. U.
McGavin, Darren Spokane, WA, May 7, 1922. College of Pacific.
McGill, Everett Miami Beach, FL, Oct. 21, 1945.
McGillis, Kelly Newport Beach, CA, July 9, 1957. Juilliard.
McGinley, John C. NYC, Aug. 3, 1959. NYU.
McGoohan, Patrick NYC, Mar. 19, 1928.
McGovern, Elizabeth Evanston, IL. July 18, 1961. Juilliard.
McGovern, Maureen Youngstown, OH, July 27, 1949.
McGregor, Ewan Perth, Scotland, March 31, 1971.
McGuire, Biff New Haven, CT, Oct. 25. 1926. Mass. State College.
McHattie, Stephen Antigonish, NS, Feb. 3, 1947. Acadia U AADA.
McKean, Michael NYC, Oct. 17, 1947.
McKee, Lonette Detroit, MI, July 22, 1955.
McKellen, Ian Burnley, England, May 25, 1939.
McKenna, Virginia London, England, June 7, 1931.
McKenzie, Ben (Benjamin Schenkkan) Austin, TX, Sept. 12, 1978. U Virginia.
McKeon, Doug Pompton Plains, NJ, June 10, 1966.
McLerie, Allyn Ann Grand Mere, Canada, Dec. 1, 1926.
McMahon, Ed Detroit, MI, Mar. 6, 1923.
McNair, Barbara Chicago, IL, Mar. 4, 1939. UCLA.
McNamara, William Dallas, TX, Mar. 31, 1965.
McNichol, Kristy Los Angeles, CA, Sept. 11, 1962.
McQueen, Armelia North Carolina, Jan. 6, 1952. Bklyn Consv.
McQueen, Chad Los Angeles, CA, Dec. 28, 1960. Actors Studio.
McRaney, Gerald Collins, MS, Aug. 19, 1948.
McShane, Ian Blackburn, England, Sept. 29, 1942. RADA.
McTeer, Janet York, England, May 8, 1961.
Meadows, Jayne (formerly Jayne Cotter) Wuchang, China, Sept. 27, 1924. St. Margaret's.
Meaney, Colm Dublin, May 30, 1953.
Meara, Anne Brooklyn, NY, Sept. 20, 1929.
Meat Loaf (Marvin Lee Aday) Dallas, TX, Sept. 27, 1947.
Medwin, Michael London, England, July 18, 1923. Instut Fischer.
Mekka, Eddie Worcester, MA, June 14, 1952. Boston Cons.
Melato, Mariangela Milan, Italy, Sept. 18, 1941. Milan Theatre Acad.
Menzel, Idina Syosset, NY, May 30, 1971. NYU.
Meredith, Lee (Judi Lee Sauls) Oct. 22, 1947. AADA.
Merkerson, S. Epatha Saganaw, MI, Nov. 28, 1952. Wayne St. Univ.
Merrill, Dina (Nedinia Hutton) NYC, Dec. 29, 1925. AADA.
Messing, Debra Brooklyn, NY, Aug. 15, 1968.
Metcalf, Laurie Edwardsville, IL, June 16, 1955. Illinois State U.
Metzler, Jim Oneonda, NY, June 23, 1955. Dartmouth.
Meyer, Breckin Minneapolis, May 7, 1974.
Michell, Keith Adelaide, Australia, Dec. 1, 1926.
Midler, Bette Honolulu, HI, Dec. 1, 1945.
Milano, Alyssa Brooklyn, NY, Dec. 19, 1972.

Miles, Joanna Nice, France, Mar. 6, 1940.
Miles, Sarah Ingatestone, England, Dec. 31, 1941. RADA.
Miles, Sylvia NYC, Sept. 9, 1934. Actors Studio.
Miles, Vera (Ralston) Boise City, OK, Aug. 23, 1929. UCLA.
Miller, Barry Los Angeles, CA, Feb. 6, 1958.
Miller, Dick NYC, Dec. 25, 1928.
Miller, Jonny Lee Surrey, England, Nov. 15, 1972.
Miller, Linda NYC, Sept. 16, 1942. Catholic U.
Miller, Penelope Ann Santa Monica, CA, Jan. 13, 1964.
Miller, Rebecca Roxbury, CT, Sept. 15, 1962. Yale.
Mills, Donna Chicago, IL, Dec. 11, 1945. U Illinois.
Mills, Hayley London, England, Apr. 18, 1946. Elmhurst School.
Mills, Juliet London, England, Nov. 21, 1941.
Milner, Martin Detroit, MI, Dec. 28, 1931.
Mimieux, Yvette Los Angeles, CA, Jan. 8, 1941. Hollywood High.
Minnelli, Liza Los Angeles, CA, Mar. 19, 1946.
Miou-Miou (Sylvette Henry) Paris, France, Feb. 22, 1950.
Mirren, Helen (Ilynea Mironoff) London, England, July 26, 1946.
Mistry, Jimi Scarborough, England, 1973.
Mitchell, James Sacramento, CA, Feb. 29, 1920. LACC.
Mitchell, John Cameron El Paso, TX, Apr. 21, 1963. Northwestern.
Mitchell, Rhada Melbourne, Australia, Nov. 12, 1973.
Mitchum, James Los Angeles, CA, May 8, 1941.
Modine, Matthew Loma Linda, CA, Mar. 22, 1959.
Moffat, Donald Plymouth, England, Dec. 26, 1930. RADA.
Moffett, D. W. Highland Park, IL, Oct. 26, 1954. Stanford U.
Mohr, Jay New Jersey, Aug. 23, 1971.
Mokae, Zakes Johannesburg, So. Africa, Aug. 5, 1935. RADA.
Molina, Alfred London, England, May 24, 1953. Guildhall.
Moll, Richard Pasadena, CA, Jan. 13, 1943.
Monaghan, Dominic Berlin, Dec. 8, 1976.
Monk, Debra Middletown, OH, Feb. 27, 1949.
Montalban, Ricardo Mexico City, Nov. 25, 1920.
Montenegro, Fernanda (Arlete Pinheiro) Rio de Janiero, Brazil, 1929.
Montgomery, Belinda Winnipeg, Canada, July 23, 1950.
Moody, Ron London, England, Jan. 8, 1924. London U.
Moor, Bill Toledo, OH, July 13, 1931. Northwestern.
Moore, Demi (Guines) Roswell, NM, Nov. 11, 1962.
Moore, Dick Los Angeles, CA, Sept. 12, 1925.
Moore, Julianne (Julie Anne Smith) Fayetteville, NC, Dec. 30, 1960.
Moore, Kieron County Cork, Ireland, Oct. 5, 1924. St. Mary's College.
Moore, Mandy Nashua, NH, Apr. 10, 1984.
Moore, Mary Tyler Brooklyn, NY, Dec. 29, 1936.
Moore, Roger London, England, Oct. 14, 1927. RADA.
Moore, Terry (Helen Koford) Los Angeles, CA, Jan. 7, 1929.
Morales, Esai Brooklyn, NY, Oct. 1, 1962.
Moranis, Rick Toronto, Canada, Apr. 18, 1954.
Moreau, Jeanne Paris, France, Jan. 23, 1928.
Moreno, Catalina Sandino Bogota, Colombia, Apr. 19, 1981.
Moreno, Rita (Rosita Alverio) Humacao, P.R., Dec. 11, 1931.
Morgan, Harry (Henry) (Harry Bratsburg) Detroit, Apr. 10, 1915. U Chicago.
Morgan, Michele (Simone Roussel) Paris, France, Feb. 29, 1920. Paris Dramatic School.
Moriarty, Cathy Bronx, NY, Nov. 29, 1960.

Moriarty, Michael Detroit, MI, Apr. 5, 1941. Dartmouth.
Morison, Patricia NYC, Mar. 19, 1915.
Morris, Garrett New Orleans, LA, Feb. 1, 1937.
Morrow, Rob New Rochelle, NY, Sept. 21, 1962.
Morse, David Hamilton, MA, Oct. 11, 1953.
Morse, Robert Newton, MA, May 18, 1931.
Mortensen, Viggo New York, NY, Oct. 20, 1958.
Mortimer, Emily London, Dec. 1, 1971.
Morton, Joe NYC, Oct. 18, 1947. Hofstra U.
Morton, Samantha Nottingham, England, May 13, 1977.
Mos Def (Dante Beze) Brooklyn, Dec. 11, 1973.
Moses, William Los Angeles, CA, Nov. 17, 1959.
Moss, Carrie-Anne Vancouver, BC, Canada, Aug. 21, 1967.
Mostel, Josh NYC, Dec. 21, 1946. Brandeis U.
Mouchet, Catherine Paris, France, 1959. Ntl. Consv.
Moynahan, Bridget Binghamton, NY, Sept. 21, 1972.
Mueller-Stahl, Armin Tilsit, East Prussia, Dec. 17, 1930.
Muldaur, Diana NYC, Aug. 19, 1938. Sweet Briar College.
Mulgrew, Kate Dubuque, IA, Apr. 29, 1955. NYU.
Mulhern, Matt Philadelphia, PA, July 21, 1960. Rutgers U.
Mull, Martin N. Ridgefield, OH, Aug. 18, 1941. RI School of Design.
Mulroney, Dermot Alexandria, VA, Oct. 31, 1963. Northwestern.
Mumy, Bill (Charles William Mumy, Jr.) San Gabriel, CA, Feb. 1, 1954.
Muniz, Frankie Ridgewood, NJ, Dec. 5, 1985.
Murphy, Brittany Atlanta, GA, Nov. 10, 1977.
Murphy, Cillian Douglas, Ireland, March 13, 1974.
Murphy, Donna Queens, NY, March 7, 1958.
Murphy, Eddie Brooklyn, NY, Apr. 3, 1961.
Murphy, Michael Los Angeles, CA, May 5, 1938. U Arizona.
Murray, Bill Wilmette, IL, Sept. 21, 1950. Regis College.
Murray, Don Hollywood, CA, July 31, 1929.
Musante, Tony Bridgeport, CT, June 30, 1936. Oberlin College.
Myers, Mike Scarborough, Canada, May 25, 1963.

Nabors, Jim Sylacauga, GA, June 12, 1932.
Nader, Michael Los Angeles, CA, 1945.
Namath, Joe Beaver Falls, PA, May 31, 1943. U Alabama.
Naughton, David Hartford, CT, Feb. 13, 1951.
Naughton, James Middletown, CT, Dec. 6, 1945.
Neal, Patricia Packard, KY, Jan. 20, 1926. Northwestern.
Neeson, Liam Ballymena, Northern Ireland, June 7, 1952.
Neill, Sam No. Ireland, Sept. 14, 1947. U Canterbury.
Nelligan, Kate London, Ontario, Mar. 16, 1951. U Toronto.
Nelson, Barry (Robert Nielsen) Oakland, CA, Apr. 16, 1920.
Nelson, Craig T. Spokane, WA, Apr. 4, 1946.
Nelson, David NYC, Oct. 24, 1936. USC.
Nelson, Judd Portland, ME, Nov. 28, 1959, Haverford College.
Nelson, Lori (Dixie Kay Nelson) Santa Fe, NM, Aug. 15, 1933.
Nelson, Tim Blake Tulsa, OK, Nov. 5, 1964.
Nelson, Tracy Santa Monica, CA, Oct. 25, 1963.
Nelson, Willie Abbott, TX, Apr. 30, 1933.
Nemec, Corin Little Rock, AK, Nov. 5, 1971.
Nero, Franco (Francisco Spartanero) Parma, Italy, Nov. 23, 1941.
Nesmith, Michael Houston, TX, Dec. 30, 1942.

Nettleton, Lois Oak Park, IL, 1931. Actors Studio.
Neuwirth, Bebe Princeton, NJ, Dec. 31, 1958.
Newhart, Bob Chicago, IL, Sept. 5, 1929. Loyola U.
Newman, Barry Boston, MA, Nov. 7, 1938. Brandeis U.
Newman, Laraine Los Angeles, CA, Mar. 2, 1952.
Newman, Nanette Northampton, England, May 29, 1934.
Newman, Paul Cleveland, OH, Jan. 26, 1925. Yale.
Newmar, Julie (Newmeyer) Los Angeles, CA, Aug. 16, 1933.
Newton, Thandie Zambia, Nov. 16, 1972.
Newton-John, Olivia Cambridge, England, Sept. 26, 1948.
Nguyen, Dustin Saigon, Vietnam, Sept. 17, 1962.
Nicholas, Denise Detroit, MI, July 12, 1945.
Nicholas, Paul Peterborough, Cambridge, England, Dec. 3, 1945.
Nichols, Nichelle Robbins, IL, Dec. 28, 1933.
Nicholson, Jack Neptune, NJ, Apr. 22, 1937.
Nickerson, Denise NYC, Apr. 1, 1959.
Nielsen, Brigitte Denmark, July 15, 1963.
Nielsen, Connie Elling, Denmark, July 3, 1965.
Nielsen, Leslie Regina, Saskatchewan, Canada, Feb. 11, 1926. Neighborhood Playhouse.
Nighy, Bill Caterham, England, Dec. 12, 1949. Guildford.
Nimoy, Leonard Boston, MA, Mar. 26, 1931. Boston College, Antioch College.
Nivola, Alessandro Boston, MA, June 28, 1972. Yale.
Nixon, Cynthia NYC, Apr. 9, 1966. Columbia U.
Noble, James Dallas, TX, Mar. 5, 1922, SMU.
Noiret, Philippe Lille, France, Oct. 1, 1930.
Nolan, Kathleen St. Louis, MO, Sept. 27, 1933. Neighborhood Playhouse.
Nolte, Nick Omaha, NE, Feb. 8, 1940. Pasadena City College.
Norris, Bruce Houston, TX, May 16, 1960. Northwestern.
Norris, Christopher NYC, Oct. 7, 1943. Lincoln Square Acad.
Norris, Chuck (Carlos Ray) Ryan, OK, Mar. 10, 1940.
North, Heather Pasadena, CA, Dec. 13, 1950. Actors Workshop.
Northam, Jeremy Cambridge, Eng., Dec. 1, 1961.
Norton, Edward Boston, MA, Aug. 18, 1969.
Norton, Ken Jacksonville, Il, Aug. 9, 1945.
Noseworthy, Jack Lynn, MA, Dec. 21, 1969.
Nouri, Michael Washington, DC, Dec. 9, 1945.
Novak, Kim (Marilyn Novak) Chicago, IL, Feb. 13, 1933. LACC.
Novello, Don Ashtabula, OH, Jan. 1, 1943. U Dayton.
Nuyen, France (Vannga) Marseilles, France, July 31, 1939. Beaux Arts School.

O'Brian, Hugh (Hugh J. Krampe) Rochester, NY. Apr. 19, 1928. Cincinnati U.
O'Brien, Clay Ray, AZ, May 6, 1961.
O'Brien, Margaret (Angela Maxine O'Brien) Los Angeles, CA, Jan. 15, 1937.
O'Connell, Jerry (Jeremiah O'Connell) New York, NY, Feb. 17, 1974.
O'Connor, Glynnis NYC, Nov. 19, 1955. NYSU.
O'Donnell, Chris Winetka, IL, June 27, 1970.
O'Donnell, Rosie Commack, NY, March 21, 1961.
Oh, Sandra Nepean, Ontario, Nov. 30, 1970.
O'Hara, Catherine Toronto, Canada, Mar. 4, 1954.
O'Hara, Maureen (Maureen Fitzsimons) Dublin, Ireland, Aug. 17, 1920.
O'Keefe, Michael Larchmont, NY, Apr. 24, 1955. NYU, AADA.

Okonedo, Sophie London, England, Jan. 1, 1969.
Oldman, Gary New Cross, South London, England, Mar. 21, 1958.
Olin, Ken Chicago, IL, July 30, 1954. U Pa.
Olin, Lena Stockholm, Sweden, Mar. 22, 1955.
Olmos, Edward James Los Angeles, CA, Feb. 24, 1947. CSLA.
O'Loughlin, Gerald S. NYC, Dec. 23, 1921. U Rochester.
Olson, James Evanston, IL, Oct. 8, 1930.
Olson, Nancy Milwaukee, WI, July 14, 1928. UCLA.
Olyphant, Timothy HI, May 20, 1968.
O'Neal, Griffin Los Angeles, CA, 1965.
O'Neal, Ryan Los Angeles, CA, Apr. 20, 1941.
O'Neal, Tatum Los Angeles, CA, Nov. 5, 1963.
O'Neil, Tricia Shreveport, LA, Mar. 11, 1945. Baylor U.
O'Neill, Ed Youngstown, OH, Apr. 12, 1946.
O'Neill, Jennifer Rio de Janeiro, Feb. 20, 1949. Neighborhood Playhouse.
Ontkean, Michael Vancouver, B.C., Canada, Jan. 24, 1946.
O'Quinn, Terry Newbury, MI, July 15, 1952.
Ormond, Julia Epsom, England, Jan. 4, 1965.
O'Shea, Milo Dublin, Ireland, June 2, 1926.
Osment, Haley Joel Los Angeles, CA, Apr. 10, 1988.
O'Toole, Annette (Toole) Houston, TX, Apr. 1, 1953. UCLA.
O'Toole, Peter Connemara, Ireland, Aug. 2, 1932. RADA.
Overall, Park Nashville, TN, Mar. 15, 1957. Tusculum College.
Owen, Clive Keresley, England, Oct. 3, 1964.
Oz, Frank (Oznowicz) Hereford, England, May 25, 1944.

Pacino, Al NYC, Apr. 25, 1940.
Pacula, Joanna Tamaszow Lubelski, Poland, Jan. 2, 1957. Polish Natl. Theatre Sch.
Paget, Debra (Debralee Griffin) Denver, Aug. 19, 1933.
Paige, Janis (Donna Mae Jaden) Tacoma, WA, Sept. 16, 1922.
Palance, Jack (Walter Palanuik) Lattimer, PA, Feb. 18, 1920. UNC.
Palin, Michael Sheffield, Yorkshire, England, May 5, 1943, Oxford.
Palmer, Betsy East Chicago, IN, Nov. 1, 1926. DePaul U.
Palmer, Gregg (Palmer Lee) San Francisco, Jan. 25, 1927. U Utah.
Palminteri, Chazz (Calogero Lorenzo Palminteri) New York, NY, May 15, 1952.
Paltrow, Gwyneth Los Angeles, CA, Sept. 28, 1973.
Pampanini, Silvana Rome, Sept. 25, 1925.
Panebianco, Richard NYC, 1971.
Pankin, Stuart Philadelphia, Apr. 8, 1946.
Pantoliano, Joe Jersey City, NJ, Sept. 12, 1954.
Papas, Irene Chiliomodion, Greece, Mar. 9, 1929.
Paquin, Anna Winnipeg, Manitoba, Canada, July, 24, 1982.
Pardue, Kip (Kevin Ian Pardue) Atlanta, GA, Sept. 23, 1976. Yale.
Pare, Michael Brooklyn, NY, Oct. 9, 1959.
Parker, Corey NYC, July 8, 1965. NYU.
Parker, Eleanor Cedarville, OH, June 26, 1922. Pasadena Playhouse.
Parker, Fess Fort Worth, TX, Aug. 16, 1925. USC.
Parker, Jameson Baltimore, MD, Nov. 18, 1947. Beloit College.
Parker, Mary-Louise Ft. Jackson, SC, Aug. 2, 1964. Bard College.
Parker, Nathaniel London, England, May 18, 1962.
Parker, Sarah Jessica Nelsonville, OH, Mar. 25, 1965.
Parker, Trey Auburn, AL, May 30, 1972.

Parkins, Barbara Vancouver, Canada, May 22, 1943.
Parks, Michael Corona, CA, Apr. 4, 1938.
Parsons, Estelle Lynn, MA, Nov. 20, 1927. Boston U.
Parton, Dolly Sevierville, TN, Jan. 19, 1946.
Pascal, Adam Bronx, NY, Oct. 25, 1970.
Patinkin, Mandy Chicago, IL, Nov. 30, 1952. Juilliard.
Patric, Jason NYC, June 17, 1966.
Patrick, Robert Marietta, GA, Nov. 5, 1958.
Patterson, Lee Vancouver, Canada, Mar. 31, 1929. Ontario College.
Patton, Will Charleston, SC, June 14, 1954.
Paulik, Johan Prague, Czech., Mar. 14, 1975.
Paulson, Sarah Tampa, FL, Dec. 17, 1975.
Pavan, Marisa (Marisa Pierangeli) Cagliari, Sardinia, June 19, 1932. Torquado Tasso College.
Paxton, Bill Fort Worth, TX, May. 17, 1955.
Paymer, David Long Island, NY, Aug. 30, 1954.
Pays, Amanda Berkshire, England, June 6, 1959.
Peach, Mary Durban, South Africa, Oct. 20, 1934.
Pearce, Guy Ely, England, Oct. 5, 1967.
Pearson, Beatrice Dennison, TX, July 27, 1920.
Peet, Amanda NYC, Jan. 11, 1972.
Peña, Elizabeth Cuba, Sept. 23, 1961.
Pendleton, Austin Warren, OH, Mar. 27, 1940. Yale.
Penhall, Bruce Balboa, CA, Aug. 17, 1960.
Penn, Chris Los Angeles, CA, June 10, 1962.
Penn, Kal Montclair, NJ, Apr. 23, 1977.
Penn, Sean Burbank, CA, Aug. 17, 1960.
Pepper, Barry Campbell River, BC, Canada, Apr. 4, 1970.
Perabo, Piper Toms River, NJ, Oct. 31, 1976.
Perez, Jose NYC, 1940.
Perez, Rosie Brooklyn, NY, Sept. 6, 1964.
Perkins, Elizabeth Queens, NY, Nov. 18, 1960. Goodman School.
Perkins, Millie Passaic, NJ, May 12, 1938.
Perlman, Rhea Brooklyn, NY, Mar. 31, 1948.
Perlman, Ron NYC, Apr. 13, 1950. U Mn.
Perreau, Gigi (Ghislaine) Los Angeles, CA, Feb. 6, 1941.
Perrine, Valerie Galveston, TX, Sept. 3, 1943. U Ariz.
Perry, Luke (Coy Luther Perry, III) Fredricktown, OH, Oct. 11, 1966.
Pesci, Joe Newark, NJ. Feb. 9, 1943.
Pescow, Donna Brooklyn, NY, Mar. 24, 1954.
Peters, Bernadette (Lazzara) Jamaica, NY, Feb. 28, 1948.
Petersen, Paul Glendale, CA, Sept. 23, 1945. Valley College.
Petersen, William Chicago, IL, Feb. 21, 1953.
Peterson, Cassandra Colorado Springs, CO, Sept. 17, 1951.
Pettet, Joanna London, England, Nov. 16, 1944. Neighborhood Playhouse.
Petty, Lori Chattanooga, TN, Mar. 23, 1963.
Pfeiffer, Michelle Santa Ana, CA, Apr. 29, 1958.
Phifer, Mekhi NYC, Dec. 12, 1975.
Phillippe, Ryan (Matthew Phillippe) New Castle, DE, Sept. 10, 1975.
Phillips, Lou Diamond Phillipines, Feb. 17, 1962, U Tx.
Phillips, MacKenzie Alexandria, VA, Nov. 10, 1959.
Phillips, Michelle (Holly Gilliam) Long Beach, CA, June 4, 1944.
Phillips, Sian Bettws, Wales, May 14, 1934. U Wales.
Phoenix, Joaquin Puerto Rico, Oct. 28, 1974.

Picardo, Robert Philadelphia, PA, Oct. 27, 1953. Yale.
Picerni, Paul NYC, Dec. 1, 1922. Loyola U.
Pidgeon, Rebecca Cambridge, MA, Oct. 10, 1965.
Pierce, David Hyde Saratoga Springs, NY, Apr. 3, 1959.
Pigott-Smith, Tim Rugby, England, May 13, 1946.
Pinchot, Bronson NYC, May 20, 1959. Yale.
Pine, Phillip Hanford, CA, July 16, 1920. Actors' Lab.
Piscopo, Joe Passaic, NJ, June 17, 1951.
Pisier, Marie-France Vietnam, May 10, 1944. U Paris.
Pitillo, Maria Elmira, NY, Jan. 8, 1965.
Pitt, Brad (William Bradley Pitt) Shawnee, OK, Dec. 18, 1963.
Pitt, Michael West Orange, NJ, Apr. 10, 1981.
Piven, Jeremy NYC, July 26, 1965.
Place, Mary Kay Tulsa OK, Sept. 23, 1947. U Tulsa.
Platt, Oliver Windsor, Ontario, Can., Oct. 10, 1960.
Playten, Alice NYC, Aug. 28, 1947. NYU.
Pleshette, Suzanne NYC, Jan. 31, 1937. Syracuse U.
Plimpton, Martha NYC, Nov. 16, 1970.
Plowright, Joan Scunthorpe, Brigg, Lincolnshire, England, Oct. 28, 1929. Old Vic.
Plumb, Eve Burbank, CA, Apr. 29, 1958.
Plummer, Amanda NYC, Mar. 23, 1957. Middlebury College.
Plummer, Christopher Toronto, Canada, Dec. 13, 1927.
Podesta, Rossana Tripoli, June 20, 1934.
Poitier, Sidney Miami, FL, Feb. 27, 1927.
Polanski, Roman Paris, France, Aug. 18, 1933.
Polito, Jon Philadelphia, PA, Dec. 29, 1950. Villanova U.
Polito, Lina Naples, Italy, Aug. 11, 1954.
Pollack, Sydney South Bend, IN, July 1, 1934.
Pollak, Kevin San Francisco, CA, Oct. 30, 1958.
Pollan, Tracy NYC, June 22, 1960.
Pollard, Michael J. Passaic, NJ, May 30, 1939.
Polley, Sarah Toronto, Ontario, Canada, Jan. 8, 1979.
Portman, Natalie Jerusalem, June 9, 1981.
Posey, Parker Baltimore, MD, Nov. 8, 1968.
Postlethwaite, Pete London, England, Feb. 7, 1945.
Potente, Franka Dulmen, Germany, July 22, 1974.
Potter, Monica Cleveland, OH, June 30, 1971.
Potts, Annie Nashville, TN, Oct. 28, 1952. Stephens College.
Powell, Jane (Suzanne Burce) Portland, OR, Apr. 1, 1928.
Powell, Robert Salford, England, June 1, 1944. Manchester U.
Power, Taryn Los Angeles, CA, Sept. 13, 1953.
Power, Tyrone, IV Los Angeles, CA, Jan. 22, 1959.
Powers, Mala (Mary Ellen) San Francisco, CA, Dec. 29, 1921. UCLA.
Powers, Stefanie (Federkiewicz) Hollywood, CA, Oct. 12, 1942.
Prentiss, Paula (Paula Ragusa) San Antonio, TX, Mar. 4, 1939. Northwestern.
Presle, Micheline (Micheline Chassagne) Paris, France, Aug. 22, 1922. Rouleau Drama School.
Presley, Priscilla Brooklyn, NY, May 24, 1945.
Presnell, Harve Modesto, CA, Sept. 14, 1933. USC.
Preston, Kelly Honolulu, HI, Oct. 13, 1962. USC.
Preston, William Columbia, PA, Aug. 26, 1921. Pennsylvania State U.
Price, Lonny NYC, Mar. 9, 1959. Juilliard.

Priestley, Jason Vancouver, Canada, Aug, 28, 1969.
Primus, Barry NYC, Feb. 16, 1938. CCNY.
Prince (P. Rogers Nelson) Minneapolis, MN, June 7, 1958.
Principal, Victoria Fukuoka, Japan, Jan. 3, 1945. Dade, Jr. College.
Prinze, Freddie, Jr., Los Angeles, CA, March 8, 1976.
Prochnow, Jurgen Berlin, June 10, 1941.
Prosky, Robert Philadelphia, PA, Dec. 13, 1930.
Proval, David Brooklyn, NY, May 20, 1942.
Provine, Dorothy Deadwood, SD, Jan. 20, 1937. U Washington.
Pryce, Jonathan Wales, UK, June 1, 1947. RADA.
Pucci, Lou Taylor Seaside Heights, NJ, July 27, 1985.
Pullman, Bill Delphi, NY, Dec. 17, 1954. SUNY/Oneonta, U Mass.
Purcell, Lee Cherry Point, NC, June 15, 1947. Stephens.
Purdom, Edmund Welwyn Garden City, England, Dec. 19, 1924. St. Ignatius College.

Quaid, Dennis Houston, TX, Apr. 9, 1954.
Quaid, Randy Houston, TX, Oct. 1, 1950. U Houston.
Qualls, DJ (Donald Joseph) Nashville, TN, June 12, 1978.
Quinlan, Kathleen Mill Valley, CA, Nov. 19, 1954.
Quinn, Aidan Chicago, IL, Mar. 8, 1959.

Radcliffe, Daniel London, England, July 23, 1989.
Raffin, Deborah Los Angeles, CA, Mar. 13, 1953. Valley College.
Ragsdale, William El Dorado, AK, Jan. 19, 1961. Hendrix College.
Railsback, Steve Dallas, TX, Nov. 16, 1948.
Rainer, Luise Vienna, Austria, Jan. 12, 1910.
Ramis, Harold Chicago, IL, Nov. 21, 1944. Washington U.
Rampling, Charlotte Surmer, England, Feb. 5, 1946. U Madrid.
Rapaport, Michael March 20, 1970.
Rapp, Anthony Chicago, Oct. 26, 1971.
Rasche, David St. Louis, MO, Aug. 7, 1944.
Rea, Stephen Belfast, Northern Ireland, Oct. 31, 1949.
Reason, Rex Berlin, Germany, Nov. 30, 1928. Pasadena Playhouse.
Reddy, Helen Melbourne, Australia, Oct. 25, 1942.
Redford, Robert Santa Monica, CA, Aug. 18, 1937. AADA.
Redgrave, Corin London, England, July 16, 1939.
Redgrave, Lynn London, England, Mar. 8, 1943.
Redgrave, Vanessa London, England, Jan. 30, 1937.
Redman, Joyce County Mayo, Ireland, Dec. 9, 1918. RADA.
Reed, Pamela Tacoma, WA, Apr. 2, 1949.
Rees, Roger Aberystwyth, Wales, May 5, 1944.
Reese, Della Detroit, MI, July 6, 1932.
Reeves, Keanu Beiruit, Lebanon, Sept. 2, 1964.
Regehr, Duncan Lethbridge, Canada, Oct. 5, 1952.
Reid, Elliott NYC, Jan. 16, 1920.
Reid, Tara Wyckoff, NJ, Nov. 8, 1975.
Reid, Tim Norfolk, VA, Dec, 19, 1944.
Reilly, Charles Nelson NYC, Jan. 13, 1931. U Ct.
Reilly, John C. Chicago, IL, May 24, 1965.
Reiner, Carl NYC, Mar. 20, 1922. Georgetown.
Reiner, Rob NYC, Mar. 6, 1947. UCLA.
Reinhold, Judge (Edward Ernest, Jr.) Wilmington, DE, May 21, 1957. NC
Reinking, Ann Seattle, WA, Nov. 10, 1949.

Cillian Murphy

Clive Owen

Keanu Reeves

Chris Rock

Reiser, Paul NYC, Mar. 30, 1957.

Remar, James Boston, MA, Dec. 31, 1953. Neighborhood Playhouse.

Renfro, Brad Knoxville, TN, July 25, 1982.

Reno, Jean (Juan Moreno) Casablanca, Morocco, July 30, 1948.

Reubens, Paul (Paul Reubenfeld) Peekskill, NY, Aug. 27, 1952.

Revill, Clive Wellington, NZ, Apr. 18, 1930.

Rey, Antonia Havana, Cuba, Oct. 12, 1927.

Reynolds, Burt Waycross, GA, Feb. 11, 1935. Florida State U.

Reynolds, Debbie (Mary Frances Reynolds) El Paso, TX, Apr. 1, 1932.

Reynolds, Ryan Vancouver, BC, Can, Oct. 23, 1976.

Rhames, Ving (Irving Rhames) NYC, May 12, 1959.

Rhoades, Barbara Poughkeepsie, NY, Mar. 23, 1947.

Rhodes, Cynthia Nashville, TN, Nov. 21, 1956.

Rhys, Paul Neath, Wales, Dec. 19, 1963.

Rhys-Davies, John Salisbury, England, May 5, 1944.

Rhys-Meyers, Jonathan Cork, Ireland, July 27, 1977.

Ribisi, Giovanni Los Angeles, CA, Dec. 17, 1974.

Ricci, Christina Santa Monica, CA, Feb. 12, 1980.

Richard, Cliff (Harry Webb) India, Oct. 14, 1940.

Richards, Denise Downers Grove, IL, Feb. 17, 1972.

Richards, Michael Culver City, CA, July 14, 1949.

Richardson, Joely London, England, Jan. 9, 1965.

Richardson, Miranda Southport, England, Mar. 3, 1958.

Richardson, Natasha London, England, May 11, 1963.

Rickles, Don NYC, May 8, 1926. AADA.

Rickman, Alan Hammersmith, England, Feb. 21, 1946.

Riegert, Peter NYC, Apr. 11, 1947. U Buffalo.

Rifkin, Ron NYC, Oct. 31, 1939.

Rigg, Diana Doncaster, England, July 20, 1938. RADA.

Ringwald, Molly Rosewood, CA, Feb. 16, 1968.

Rivers, Joan (Molinsky) Brooklyn, NY, NY, June 8, 1933.

Roache, Linus Manchester, England, Feb. 1, 1964.

Robards, Sam NYC, Dec. 16, 1963.

Robbins, Tim NYC, Oct. 16, 1958. UCLA.

Roberts, Eric Biloxi, MS, Apr. 18, 1956. RADA.

Roberts, Julia Atlanta, GA, Oct. 28, 1967.

Roberts, Tanya (Leigh) Bronx, NY, Oct. 15, 1954.

Roberts, Tony NYC, Oct. 22, 1939. Northwestern.

Robertson, Cliff La Jolla, CA, Sept. 9, 1925. Antioch College.

Robertson, Dale Oklahoma City, July 14, 1923.

Robinson, Chris West Palm Beach, FL, Nov. 5, 1938. LACC.

Robinson, Jay NYC, Apr. 14, 1930.

Robinson, Roger Seattle, WA, May 2, 1940. USC.

Rochefort, Jean Paris, France, Apr. 29, 1930.

Rock, The (Dwayne Johnson) Hayward, CA, May 2, 1972.

Rock, Chris Brooklyn, NY, Feb. 7, 1966.

Rockwell, Sam Daly City, CA, Nov. 5, 1968.

Rodriguez, Michelle Bexar County, TX, July 12, 1978.

Rogers, Mimi Coral Gables, FL, Jan. 27, 1956.

Rogers, Wayne Birmingham, AL, Apr. 7, 1933. Princeton.

Romijn, Rebecca Berkeley, CA, Nov. 6, 1972.

Ronstadt, Linda Tucson, AZ, July 15, 1946.

Rooker, Michael Jasper, AL, Apr. 6, 1955.

Rooney, Mickey (Joe Yule, Jr.) Brooklyn, NY, Sept. 23, 1920.

Rose, Reva Chicago, IL, July 30, 1940. Goodman.

Roseanne (Barr) Salt Lake City, UT, Nov. 3, 1952.

Ross, Diana Detroit, MI, Mar. 26, 1944.

Ross, Justin Brooklyn, NY, Dec. 15, 1954.

Ross, Katharine Hollywood, Jan. 29, 1943. Santa Rosa College.

Rossellini, Isabella Rome, June 18, 1952.

Rossovich, Rick Palo Alto, CA, Aug. 28, 1957.

Rossum, Emmy NYC, Sept. 12, 1986.

Roth, Tim London, England, May 14, 1961.

Roundtree, Richard New Rochelle, NY, Sept. 7, 1942. Southern Il.

Rourke, Mickey (Philip Andre Rourke, Jr.) Schenectady, NY, Sept. 16, 1956.

Rowe, Nicholas London, England, Nov. 22, 1966, Eton.

Rowlands, Gena Cambria, WI, June 19, 1934.

Rubin, Andrew New Bedford, MA, June 22, 1946. AADA.

Rubinek, Saul Fohrenwold, Germany, July 2, 1948.

Rubinstein, John Los Angeles, CA, Dec. 8, 1946. UCLA.

Ruck, Alan Cleveland, OH, July 1, 1960.

Rucker, Bo Tampa, FL, Aug. 17, 1948.

Rudd, Paul Boston, MA, May 15, 1940.

Rudd, Paul Passaic, NJ, Apr. 6, 1969.

Rudner, Rita Miami, FL, Sept. 17, 1955.
Ruehl, Mercedes Queens, NY, Feb. 28, 1948.
Ruffalo, Mark Kenosha, WI, Nov. 22, 1967.
Rule, Janice Cincinnati, OH, Aug. 15, 1931.
Rupert, Michael Denver, CO, Oct. 23, 1951. Pasadena Playhouse.
Rush, Barbara Denver, CO, Jan. 4, 1927. U California.
Rush, Geoffrey Toowoomba, Queensland, Australia, July 6, 1951. U Queensland.
Russell, Jane Bemidji, MI, June 21, 1921. Max Reinhardt School.
Russell, Kurt Springfield, MA, Mar. 17, 1951.
Russell, Theresa (Paup) San Diego, CA, Mar. 20, 1957.
Russo, James NYC, Apr. 23, 1953.
Russo, Rene Burbank, CA, Feb. 17, 1954.
Rutherford, Ann Toronto, Canada, Nov. 2, 1920.
Ryan, John P. NYC, July 30, 1936. CCNY.
Ryan, Meg Fairfield, CT, Nov. 19, 1961. NYU.
Ryder, Winona (Horowitz) Winona, MN, Oct. 29, 1971.

Sacchi, Robert Bronx, NY, 1941. NYU.
Sägebrecht, Marianne Starnberg, Bavaria, Aug. 27, 1945.
Saint, Eva Marie Newark, NJ, July 4, 1924. Bowling Green State U.
Saint James, Susan (Suzie Jane Miller) Los Angeles, CA, Aug. 14, 1946. Conn. College.
St. John, Betta Hawthorne, CA, Nov. 26, 1929.
St. John, Jill (Jill Oppenheim) Los Angeles, CA, Aug. 19, 1940.
Sala, John Los Angeles, CA, Oct. 5, 1962.
Saldana, Theresa Brooklyn, NY, Aug. 20, 1954.
Salinger, Matt Windsor, VT, Feb. 13, 1960. Princeton, Columbia.
Salt, Jennifer Los Angeles, CA, Sept. 4, 1944. Sarah Lawrence College.
Samms, Emma London, England, Aug. 28, 1960.
San Giacomo, Laura Orange, NJ, Nov. 14, 1961.
Sanders, Jay O. Austin, TX, Apr. 16, 1953.
Sandler, Adam Bronx, NY, Sept. 9, 1966. NYU.
Sands, Julian Yorkshire, England, Jan 15, 1958.
Sands, Tommy Chicago, IL, Aug. 27, 1937.
San Juan, Olga NYC, Mar. 16, 1927.
Sara, Mia (Sarapocciello) Brooklyn, NY, June 19, 1967.
Sarandon, Chris Beckley, WV, July 24, 1942. U West Virginia., Catholic U.
Sarandon, Susan (Tomalin) NYC, Oct. 4, 1946. Catholic U.
Sarrazin, Michael Quebec City, Canada, May 22, 1940.
Sarsgaard, Peter Scott Air Force Base, Illinois, Mar. 7, 1971. Washington U St. Louis
Savage, Fred Highland Park, IL, July 9, 1976.
Savage, John (Youngs) Long Island, NY, Aug. 25, 1949. AADA.
Saviola, Camille Bronx, NY, July 16, 1950.
Savoy, Teresa Ann London, England, July 18, 1955.
Sawa, Devon Vancouver, BC, Canada, Sept. 7, 1978.
Saxon, John (Carmen Orrico) Brooklyn, NY, Aug. 5, 1935.
Sbarge, Raphael NYC, Feb. 12, 1964.
Scacchi, Greta Milan, Italy, Feb. 18, 1960.
Scalia, Jack Brooklyn, NY, Nov. 10, 1951.
Scarwid, Diana Savannah, GA, Aug. 27, 1955, AADA. Pace U.
Scheider, Roy Orange, NJ, Nov. 10, 1932. Franklin-Marshall.
Schell, Maximilian Vienna, Dec. 8, 1930.

Schlatter, Charlie Englewood, NJ, May 1, 1966. Ithaca College.
Schneider, John Mt. Kisco, NY, Apr. 8, 1960.
Schneider, Maria Paris, France, Mar. 27, 1952.
Schreiber, Liev San Francisco, CA, Oct. 4, 1967.
Schroder, Rick Staten Island, NY, Apr. 13, 1970.
Schuck, John Boston, MA, Feb. 4, 1940.
Schultz, Dwight Baltimore, MD, Nov. 24, 1947.
Schwartzman, Jason Los Angeles, CA, June 26, 1980.
Schwarzenegger, Arnold Austria, July 30, 1947.
Schwimmer, David Queens, NY, Nov. 12, 1966.
Schygulla, Hanna Katlowitz, Germany, Dec. 25, 1943.
Sciorra, Annabella NYC, Mar. 24, 1964.
Scofield, Paul Hurstpierpoint, England, Jan. 21, 1922. London Mask Theatre School.
Scoggins, Tracy Galveston, TX, Nov. 13, 1959.
Scolari, Peter Scarsdale, NY, Sept. 12, 1956. NYCC.
Scott, Campbell South Salem, NY, July 19, 1962. Lawrence.
Scott, Debralee Elizabeth, NJ, Apr. 2, 1953.
Scott, Gordon (Gordon M. Werschkul) Portland, OR, Aug. 3, 1927. Oregon U.
Scott, Lizabeth (Emma Matso) Scranton, PA, Sept. 29, 1922.
Scott, Seann William Cottage Grove, MN, Oct. 3, 1976.
Scott Thomas, Kristin Redruth, Cornwall, Eng., May 24, 1960.
Seagal, Steven Detroit, MI, Apr. 10, 1951.
Sears, Heather London, England, Sept. 28, 1935.
Sedgwick, Kyra NYC, Aug. 19, 1965. USC.
Segal, George NYC, Feb. 13, 1934. Columbia U.
Selby, David Morganstown, WV, Feb. 5, 1941. U West Virginia.
Sellars, Elizabeth Glasgow, Scotland, May 6, 1923.
Selleck, Tom Detroit, MI, Jan. 29, 1945. USC.
Sernas, Jacques Lithuania, July 30, 1925.
Serrault, Michel Brunoy, France. Jan. 24, 1928. Paris Consv.
Seth, Roshan New Delhi, India. Aug. 17, 1942.
Sevigny, Chloë Springfield, MA, Nov. 18, 1974.
Sewell, Rufus Twickenham, England, Oct. 29, 1967.
Seymour, Jane (Joyce Frankenberg) Hillingdon, England, Feb. 15, 1952.
Shalhoub, Tony Green Bay, WI, Oct. 9, 1953.
Shandling, Garry Chicago, IL, Nov. 29, 1949.
Sharif, Omar (Michel Shalhoub) Alexandria, Egypt, Apr. 10, 1932. Victoria College.
Shatner, William Montreal, Canada, Mar. 22, 1931. McGill U.
Shaver, Helen St. Thomas, Ontario, Canada, Feb. 24, 1951.
Shaw, Fiona Cork, Ireland, July 10, 1955. RADA.
Shaw, Stan Chicago, IL, July 14, 1952.
Shawn, Wallace NYC, Nov. 12, 1943. Harvard.
Shea, John North Conway, NH, Apr. 14, 1949. Bates, Yale.
Shearer, Harry Los Angeles, CA, Dec. 23, 1943. UCLA.
Shearer, Moira Dunfermline, Scotland, Jan. 17, 1926. London Theatre School.
Sheedy, Ally NYC, June 13, 1962. USC.
Sheen, Charlie (Carlos Irwin Estevez) Santa Monica, CA, Sept. 3, 1965.
Sheen, Martin (Ramon Estevez) Dayton, OH, Aug. 3, 1940.
Sheffer, Craig York, PA, Apr. 23, 1960. E. Stroudsberg U.
Sheffield, John Pasadena, CA, Apr. 11, 1931. UCLA.
Shelley, Carol London, England, England, Aug. 16, 1939.

Mark Ruffalo

Jason Schwartzman

Chloë Sevigny

Alicia Silverstone

Shepard, Sam (Rogers) Ft. Sheridan, IL, Nov. 5, 1943.
Shepherd, Cybill Memphis, TN, Feb. 18, 1950. Hunter, NYU.
Sher, Antony England, June 14, 1949.
Sherbedgia, Rade Korenica, Croatia, July 27, 1946.
Sheridan, Jamey Pasadena, CA, July 12, 1951.
Shields, Brooke NYC, May 31, 1965.
Shire, Talia Lake Success, NY, Apr. 25, 1946. Yale.
Short, Martin Toronto, Canada, Mar. 26, 1950. McMaster U.
Shue, Elisabeth S. Orange, NJ, Oct. 6, 1963. Harvard.
Siemaszko, Casey Chicago, IL, March 17, 1961.
Sikking, James B. Los Angeles, CA, Mar. 5, 1934.
Silva, Henry Brooklyn, NY, 1928.
Silver, Ron NYC, July 2, 1946. SUNY.
Silverman, Jonathan Los Angeles, CA, Aug. 5, 1966. USC.
Silverstone, Alicia San Francisco, CA, Oct. 4, 1976.
Silverstone, Ben London, England, Apr. 9, 1979.
Simmons, Jean London, England, Jan. 31, 1929. Aida Foster School.
Simon, Paul Newark. NJ, Nov. 5, 1942.
Simpson, O. J. (Orenthal James) San Francisco, CA, July 9, 1947. UCLA.
Sinbad (David Adkins) Benton Harbor, MI, Nov. 10, 1956.
Sinden, Donald Plymouth, England, Oct. 9, 1923. Webber-Douglas.
Singer, Lori Corpus Christi, TX, May 6, 1962. Juilliard.
Sinise, Gary Chicago, Mar. 17. 1955.
Sizemore, Tom Detroit, MI, Sept. 29, 1964.
Skarsgård, Stellan Gothenburg, Vastergotland, Sweden, June 13, 1951.
Skerritt, Tom Detroit, MI, Aug. 25, 1933. Wayne State U.
Skye, Ione (Leitch) London, England, Sept. 4, 1971.
Slater, Christian NYC, Aug. 18, 1969.
Slater, Helen NYC, Dec. 15, 1965.
Smart, Amy Topanga Canyon, CA, Mar. 26, 1976.
Smith, Charles Martin Los Angeles, CA, Oct. 30, 1953. Cal State U.
Smith, Jaclyn Houston, TX, Oct. 26, 1947.
Smith, Jada Pinkett Baltimore, MD, Sept. 18, 1971.
Smith, Kerr Exton, PA, Mar. 9, 1972.
Smith, Kevin Red Bank, NJ, Aug. 2, 1970.
Smith, Kurtwood New Lisbon, WI, Jul. 3, 1942.
Smith, Lewis Chattanooga, TN, 1958. Actors Studio.

Smith, Lois Topeka, KS, Nov. 3, 1930. U Washington.
Smith, Maggie Ilford, England, Dec. 28, 1934.
Smith, Roger South Gate, CA, Dec. 18, 1932. U Arizona.
Smith, Will Philadelphia, PA, Sept. 25, 1968.
Smithers, William Richmond, VA, July 10, 1927. Catholic U.
Smits, Jimmy Brooklyn, NY, July 9, 1955. Cornell U.
Snipes, Wesley NYC, July 31, 1963. SUNY/Purchase.
Snoop Dogg (Calvin Broadus) Long Beach, CA, Oct. 20, 1971.
Sobieksi, Leelee (Liliane Sobieski) NYC, June 10, 1982.
Solomon, Bruce NYC, Aug. 12, 1944. U Miami, Wayne State U.
Somers, Suzanne (Mahoney) San Bruno, CA, Oct. 16, 1946. Lone Mt. College.
Sommer, Elke (Schletz) Berlin, Germany, Nov. 5, 1940.
Sommer, Josef Greifswald, Germany, June 26, 1934.
Sorvino, Mira Tenafly, NJ, Sept. 28, 1967.
Sorvino, Paul NYC, Apr. 13, 1939. AMDA.
Soto, Talisa (Miriam Soto) Brooklyn, NY, Mar. 27, 1967.
Soul, David Chicago, IL, Aug. 28, 1943.
Spacek, Sissy Quitman, TX, Dec. 25, 1949. Actors Studio.
Spacey, Kevin So. Orange, NJ, July 26, 1959. Juilliard.
Spade, David Birmingham, MS, July 22, 1964.
Spader, James Buzzards Bay, MA, Feb. 7, 1960.
Spall, Timothy London, England, Feb. 27, 1957.
Spano, Vincent Brooklyn, NY, Oct. 18, 1962.
Spenser, Jeremy London, England, July 16, 1937.
Spinella, Stephen Naples, Italy, Oct. 11, 1956. NYU.
Springfield, Rick (Richard Spring Thorpe) Sydney, Australia, Aug. 23, 1949.
Stadlen, Lewis J. Brooklyn, NY, Mar. 7, 1947. Neighborhood Playhouse.
Stahl, Nick Dallas, TX, Dec. 5, 1979.
Stallone, Frank NYC, July 30, 1950.
Stallone, Sylvester NYC, July 6, 1946. U Miami.
Stamp, Terence London, England, July 23, 1939.
Stanford, Aaron Westford, MA, Dec. 18, 1977.
Stang, Arnold Chelsea, MA, Sept. 28, 1925.
Stanton, Harry Dean Lexington, KY, July 14, 1926.
Stapleton, Jean NYC, Jan. 19, 1923.
Stapleton, Maureen Troy, NY, June 21, 1925.

Starr, Ringo (Richard Starkey) Liverpool, England, July 7, 1940.

Staunton, Imelda London, Jan. 9, 1956.

Steele, Barbara England, Dec. 29, 1937.

Steele, Tommy London, England, Dec. 17, 1936.

Steenburgen, Mary Newport, AR, Feb. 8, 1953. Neighborhood Playhouse.

Sterling, Robert (William Sterling Hart) Newcastle, PA, Nov. 13, 1917. U Pittsburgh.

Stern, Daniel Bethesda, MD, Aug. 28, 1957.

Sternhagen, Frances Washington, DC, Jan. 13, 1932.

Stevens, Andrew Memphis, TN, June 10, 1955.

Stevens, Connie (Concetta Ann Ingolia) Brooklyn, NY, Aug. 8, 1938. Hollywood Professional School.

Stevens, Fisher Chicago, IL, Nov. 27, 1963. NYU.

Stevens, Stella (Estelle Eggleston) Hot Coffee, MS, Oct. 1, 1936.

Stevenson, Juliet Essex, England, Oct. 30, 1956.

Stevenson, Parker Philadelphia, PA, June 4, 1953. Princeton.

Stewart, Alexandra Montreal, Canada, June 10, 1939. Louvre.

Stewart, Elaine (Elsy Steinberg) Montclair, NJ, May 31, 1929.

Stewart, French (Milton French Stewart) Albuquerque, NM, Feb. 20, 1964.

Stewart, Jon (Jonathan Stewart Liebowitz) Trenton, NJ, Nov. 28, 1962.

Stewart, Martha (Martha Haworth) Bardwell, KY, Oct. 7, 1922.

Stewart, Patrick Mirfield, England, July 13, 1940.

Stiers, David Ogden Peoria, IL, Oct. 31, 1942.

Stiles, Julia NYC, Mar. 28, 1981.

Stiller, Ben NYC, Nov. 30, 1965.

Stiller, Jerry NYC, June 8, 1931.

Sting (Gordon Matthew Sumner) Wallsend, England, Oct. 2, 1951.

Stockwell, Dean Hollywood, Mar. 5, 1935.

Stockwell, John (John Samuels, IV) Galveston, TX, Mar. 25, 1961. Harvard.

Stoltz, Eric Whittier, CA, Sept. 30, 1961. USC.

Stone, Dee Wallace (Deanna Bowers) Kansas City, MO, Dec. 14, 1948. UKS.

Storm, Gale (Josephine Cottle) Bloomington, TX, Apr. 5, 1922.

Stowe, Madeleine Eagle Rock, CA, Aug. 18, 1958.

Strassman, Marcia New Jersey, Apr. 28, 1948.

Strathairn, David San Francisco, Jan. 26, 1949.Williams Col.

Strauss, Peter NYC, Feb. 20, 1947.

Streep, Meryl (Mary Louise) Summit, NJ, June 22, 1949 Vassar, Yale.

Streisand, Barbra Brooklyn, NY, Apr. 24, 1942.

Stritch, Elaine Detroit, MI, Feb. 2, 1925. Drama Workshop.

Stroud, Don Honolulu, HI, Sept. 1, 1937.

Struthers, Sally Portland, OR, July 28, 1948. Pasadena Playhouse.

Studi, Wes (Wesley Studie) Nofire Hollow, OK, Dec. 17, 1947.

Summer, Donna (LaDonna Gaines) Boston, MA, Dec. 31, 1948.

Sutherland, Donald St. John, New Brunswick, Canada, July 17, 1935. U Toronto.

Sutherland, Kiefer Los Angeles, CA, Dec. 18, 1966.

Suvari, Mena Newport, RI, Feb. 9, 1979.

Svenson, Bo Goreborg, Sweden, Feb. 13, 1941. UCLA.

Swank, Hilary Bellingham, WA, July 30, 1974.

Swayze, Patrick Houston, TX, Aug. 18, 1952.

Sweeney, D. B. (Daniel Bernard Sweeney) Shoreham, NY, Nov. 14, 1961.

Swinton, Tilda London, England, Nov. 5, 1960.

Swit, Loretta Passaic, NJ, Nov. 4, 1937, AADA.

Symonds, Robert Bistow, AK, Dec. 1, 1926. Texas U.

Syms, Sylvia London, England, June 1, 1934. Convent School.

Szarabajka, Keith Oak Park, IL, Dec. 2, 1952. U Chicago.

T, Mr. (Lawrence Tero) Chicago, IL, May 21, 1952.

Tabori, Kristoffer (Siegel) Los Angeles, CA, Aug. 4, 1952.

Takei, George Los Angeles, CA, Apr. 20, 1939. UCLA.

Talbot, Nita NYC, Aug. 8, 1930. Irvine Studio School.

Tamblyn, Amber Santa Monica, CA, May 14, 1983.

Tamblyn, Russ Los Angeles, CA, Dec. 30, 1934.

Tambor, Jeffrey San Francisco, CA, July 8, 1944.

Tarantino, Quentin Knoxville, TN, Mar. 27, 1963.

Tate, Larenz Chicago, IL, Sept. 8, 1975.

Tautou, Audrey Beaumont, France, Aug. 9, 1978.

Taylor, Elizabeth London, England, Feb. 27, 1932. Byron House School.

Taylor, Lili Glencoe, IL, Feb. 20, 1967.

Taylor, Noah London, England, Sept. 4, 1969.

Taylor, Renée NYC, Mar. 19, 1935.

Taylor, Rod (Robert) Sydney, Australia, Jan. 11, 1929.

Taylor-Young, Leigh Washington, DC, Jan. 25, 1945. Northwestern.

Teefy, Maureen Minneapolis, MN, Oct. 26, 1953, Juilliard.

Temple, Shirley Santa Monica, CA, Apr. 23, 1927.

Tennant, Victoria London, England, Sept. 30, 1950.

Tenney, Jon Princeton, NJ, Dec. 16, 1961.

Terzieff, Laurent Paris, France, June 25, 1935.

Tewes, Lauren Braddock, PA, Oct. 26, 1954.

Thacker, Russ Washington, DC, June 23, 1946. Montgomery College.

Thaxter, Phyllis Portland, ME, Nov. 20, 1921. St. Genevieve.

Thelen, Jodi St. Cloud, MN, June 12, 1962.

Theron, Charlize Benoni, So. Africa, Aug. 7, 1975.

Thewlis, David Blackpool, Eng., Mar. 20, 1963.

Thomas, Henry San Antonio, TX, Sept. 8, 1971.

Thomas, Jay New Orleans, July 12, 1948.

Thomas, Jonathan Taylor (Weiss) Bethlehem, PA, Sept. 8, 1981.

Thomas, Marlo (Margaret) Detroit, Nov. 21, 1937. USC.

Thomas, Philip Michael Columbus, OH, May 26, 1949. Oakwood College.

Thomas, Richard NYC, June 13, 1951. Columbia.

Thompson, Emma London, England, Apr. 15, 1959. Cambridge.

Thompson, Fred Dalton Sheffield, AL, Aug. 19, 1942.

Thompson, Jack (John Payne) Sydney, Australia, Aug. 31, 1940.

Thompson, Lea Rochester, MN, May 31, 1961.

Thompson, Rex NYC, Dec. 14, 1942.

Thompson, Sada Des Moines, IA, Sept. 27, 1929. Carnegie Tech.

Thornton, Billy Bob Hot Spring, AR, Aug. 4, 1955.

Thorson, Linda Toronto, Canada, June 18, 1947. RADA.

Thurman, Uma Boston, MA, Apr. 29, 1970.

Ticotin, Rachel Bronx, NY, Nov. 1, 1958.

Tiffin, Pamela (Wonso) Oklahoma City, OK, Oct. 13, 1942.

Tighe, Kevin Los Angeles, CA, Aug. 13, 1944.

Tilly, Jennifer Los Angeles, CA, Sept. 16, 1958.

Tilly, Meg Texada, Canada, Feb. 14, 1960.

Tobolowsky, Stephen Dallas, TX, May 30, 1951. Southern Methodist U.

Todd, Beverly Chicago, IL, July 1, 1946.

Todd, Richard Dublin, Ireland, June 11, 1919. Shrewsbury School.

Mena Suvari

Uma Thurman

Michelle Trachtenberg

Michael Vartan

Tolkan, James Calumet, MI, June 20, 1931.
Tomei, Marisa Brooklyn, NY, Dec. 4, 1964. NYU.
Tomlin, Lily Detroit, MI, Sept. 1, 1939. Wayne State U.
Topol (Chaim Topol) Tel-Aviv, Israel, Sept. 9, 1935.
Torn, Rip Temple, TX, Feb. 6, 1931. U Texas.
Torres, Liz NYC, Sept. 27, 1947. NYU.
Totter, Audrey Joliet, IL, Dec. 20, 1918.
Towsend, Robert Chicago, IL, Feb. 6, 1957.
Townsend, Stuart Dublin, Ireland, Dec. 15, 1972.
Trachtenberg, Michelle NYC, Oct. 11, 1985.
Travanti, Daniel J. Kenosha, WI, Mar. 7, 1940.
Travis, Nancy Astoria, NY, Sept. 21, 1961.
Travolta, Joey Englewood, NJ, Oct. 14, 1950.
Travolta, John Englewood, NJ, Feb. 18, 1954.
Trintignant, Jean-Louis Pont-St. Esprit, France, Dec. 11, 1930. DullinBalachova Drama School.
Tripplehorn, Jeanne Tulsa, OK, June 10, 1963.
Tsopei, Corinna Athens, Greece, June 21, 1944.
Tubb, Barry Snyder, TX, 1963. Am Consv Th.
Tucci, Stanley Katonah, NY, Jan. 11, 1960.
Tucker, Chris Decatur, GA, Aug. 31, 1972.
Tucker, Jonathan Boston, May 31, 1982.
Tucker, Michael Baltimore, MD, Feb. 6, 1944.
Tune, Tommy Wichita Falls, TX, Feb. 28, 1939.
Tunney, Robin Chicago, June 19, 1972.
Turner, Janine (Gauntt) Lincoln, NE, Dec. 6, 1963.
Turner, Kathleen Springfield, MO, June 19, 1954. U Maryland.
Turner, Tina (Anna Mae Bullock) Nutbush, TN, Nov. 26, 1938.
Turturro, John Brooklyn, NY, Feb. 28, 1957. Yale.
Tushingham, Rita Liverpool, England, Mar. 14, 1940.
Twiggy (Lesley Hornby) London, England, Sept. 19, 1949.
Twomey, Anne Boston, MA, June 7, 1951. Temple U.
Tyler, Liv Portland, ME, July 1, 1977.
Tyrrell, Susan San Francisco, Mar. 18, 1945.
Tyson, Cathy Liverpool, England, June 12, 1965. Royal Shake. Co.
Tyson, Cicely NYC, Dec. 19, 1933. NYU.

Uggams, Leslie NYC, May 25, 1943. Juilliard.
Ullman, Tracey Slough, England, Dec. 30, 1959.
Ullmann, Liv Tokyo, Dec. 10, 1938. Webber-Douglas Acad.
Ulrich, Skeet (Bryan Ray Ulrich) North Carolina, Jan. 20, 1969.
Umeki, Miyoshi Otaru, Hokaido, Japan, Apr. 3, 1929.
Underwood, Blair Tacoma, WA, Aug. 25, 1964. Carnegie-Mellon U.
Unger, Deborah Kara Victoria, British Columbia, May 12, 1966.
Union, Gabrielle Omaha, NE, Oct. 29, 1973.

Vaccaro, Brenda Brooklyn, NY, Nov. 18, 1939. Neighborhood Playhouse.
Valli, Alida Pola, Italy, May 31, 1921. Academy of Drama.
Van Ark, Joan NYC, June 16, 1943. Yale.
Van Damme, Jean-Claude (J-C Vorenberg) Brussels, Belgium, Apr. 1, 1960.
Van De Ven, Monique Zeeland, Netherlands, July 28, 1952.
Van Der Beek, James Chesire, CT, March 8, 1977.
Van Devere, Trish (Patricia Dressel) Englewood Cliffs, NJ, Mar. 9, 1945. Ohio Wesleyan.
Van Dien, Casper Ridgefield, NJ, Dec. 18, 1968.
Van Doren, Mamie (Joan Lucile Olander) Rowena SD, Feb. 6, 1933.
Van Dyke, Dick West Plains, MO, Dec. 13, 1925.
Vanity (Denise Katrina Smith) Niagara, Ont., Can, Jan. 4, 1959.
Van Pallandt, Nina Copenhagen, Denmark, July 15, 1932.
Van Patten, Dick NYC, Dec. 9, 1928.
Van Patten, Joyce NYC, Mar. 9, 1934.
Van Peebles, Mario NYC, Jan. 15, 1958. Columbia U.
Van Peebles, Melvin Chicago, IL, Aug. 21, 1932.
Vance, Courtney B. Detroit, MI, Mar. 12, 1960.
Vardalos, Nia Winnipeg, Manitoba, Can., Sept. 24, 1962.
Vartan, Michael Boulogne-Billancourt, France, Nov. 27, 1968.
Vaughn, Robert NYC, Nov. 22, 1932. USC.
Vaughn, Vince Minneapolis, MN, Mar. 28, 1970.
Vega, Isela Hermosillo, Mexico, Nov. 5, 1940.
Veljohnson, Reginald NYC, Aug. 16, 1952.
Vennera, Chick Herkimer, NY, Mar. 27, 1952. Pasadena Playhouse.
Venora, Diane Hartford, CT, Aug. 10, 1952. Juilliard.
Vereen, Ben Miami, FL, Oct. 10, 1946.

Victor, James (Lincoln Rafael Peralta Diaz) Santiago, D.R., July 27, 1939. Haaren HS/NYC.

Vincent, Jan-Michael Denver, CO, July 15, 1944. Ventura.

Violet, Ultra (Isabelle Collin-Dufresne) Grenoble, France, Sept. 6, 1935.

Visnjic, Goran Sibenik, Yugoslavia, Sept. 9, 1972.

Vitale, Milly Rome, Italy, May 6, 1932. Lycee Chateaubriand.

Voight, Jon Yonkers, NY, Dec. 29, 1938. Catholic U.

Von Bargen, Daniel Cincinnati, OH, June 5, 1950. Purdue.

Von Dohlen, Lenny Augusta, GA, Dec. 22, 1958. U Texas.

Von Sydow, Max Lund, Sweden, July 10, 1929. Royal Drama Theatre.

Wagner, Lindsay Los Angeles, CA, June 22. 1949.

Wagner, Natasha Gregson Los Angeles, CA, Sept. 29, 1970.

Wagner, Robert Detroit, Feb. 10, 1930.

Wahl, Ken Chicago, IL, Feb. 14, 1953.

Waite, Genevieve Cape Town, South Africa, Feb. 19, 1948.

Waite, Ralph White Plains, NY, June 22, 1929. Yale.

Waits, Tom Pomona, CA, Dec. 7, 1949.

Walken, Christopher Astoria, NY, Mar. 31, 1943. Hofstra.

Walker, Clint Hartfold, IL, May 30, 1927. USC.

Walker, Paul Glendale, CA, Sept. 12, 1973.

Wallach, Eli Brooklyn, NY, Dec. 7, 1915. CCNY, U Texas.

Wallach, Roberta NYC, Aug. 2, 1955.

Wallis, Shani London, England, Apr. 5, 1941.

Walsh, M. Emmet Ogdensburg, NY, Mar. 22, 1935. Clarkson College, AADA.

Walter, Jessica Brooklyn, NY, Jan. 31, 1944 Neighborhood Playhouse.

Walter, Tracey Jersey City, NJ, Nov. 25, 1942.

Walters, Julie London, England, Feb. 22, 1950.

Walton, Emma London, England, Nov. 1962. Brown U.

Wanamaker, Zoë NYC, May 13, 1949.

Ward, Burt (Gervis) Los Angeles, CA, July 6, 1945.

Ward, Fred San Diego, CA, Dec. 30, 1942.

Ward, Rachel London, England, Sept. 12, 1957.

Ward, Sela Meridian, MS, July 11, 1956.

Ward, Simon London, England, Oct. 19, 1941.

Warden, Jack (Lebzelter) Newark, NJ, Sept. 18, 1920.

Warner, David Manchester, England, July 29, 1941. RADA.

Warner, Malcolm-Jamal Jersey City, NJ, Aug. 18, 1970.

Warren, Jennifer NYC, Aug. 12, 1941. U Wisc.

Warren, Lesley Ann NYC, Aug. 16, 1946.

Warren, Michael South Bend, IN, Mar. 5, 1946. UCLA.

Washington, Denzel Mt. Vernon, NY, Dec. 28, 1954. Fordham.

Washington, Kerry Bronx, Jan. 31, 1977.

Wasson, Craig Ontario, OR, Mar. 15, 1954. U Oregon.

Watanabe, Ken Koide, Japan, Oct. 21, 1959.

Waterston, Sam Cambridge, MA, Nov. 15, 1940. Yale.

Watson, Emily London, England, Jan. 14, 1967.

Watson, Emma Oxford, England, Apr. 15, 1990.

Watts, Naomi Shoreham, England, Sept. 28, 1968.

Wayans, Damon NYC, Sept. 4, 1960.

Wayans, Keenen Ivory NYC, June 8, 1958. Tuskegee Inst.

Wayans, Marlon NYC, July 23, 1972.

Wayans, Shawn NYC, Jan. 19, 1971.

Wayne, Patrick Los Angeles, CA, July 15, 1939. Loyola.

Weathers, Carl New Orleans, LA, Jan. 14, 1948. Long Beach CC.

Weaver, Dennis Joplin, MO, June 4, 1924. U Oklahoma.

Weaver, Fritz Pittsburgh, PA, Jan. 19, 1926.

Weaver, Sigourney (Susan) NYC, Oct. 8, 1949. Stanford, Yale.

Weaving, Hugo Nigeria, Apr. 4, 1960. NIDA.

Weber, Steven Queens, NY, March 4, 1961.

Wedgeworth, Ann Abilene, TX, Jan. 21, 1935. U Texas.

Weisz, Rachel London, England, Mar. 7, 1971. Cambridge.

Welch, Raquel (Tejada) Chicago, IL, Sept. 5, 1940.

Weld, Tuesday (Susan) NYC, Aug. 27, 1943. Hollywood Professional School.

Weldon, Joan San Francisco, Aug. 5, 1933. San Francisco Conservatory.

Weller, Peter Stevens Point, WI, June 24, 1947. Am. Th. Wing.

Welling, Tom NYC, Apr. 26, 1977.

Wendt, George Chicago, IL, Oct. 17, 1948.

West, Adam (William Anderson) Walla Walla, WA, Sept. 19, 1929.

West, Dominic Sheffield, England, Oct. 15, 1969.

West, Shane Baton Rouge, LA, June 10, 1978.

Westfeldt, Jennifer Guilford, CT, Feb. 2, 1971.

Wettig, Patricia Cincinatti, OH, Dec. 4, 1951. Temple U.

Whaley, Frank Syracuse, NY, July 20, 1963. SUNY/Albany.

Whalley-Kilmer, Joanne Manchester, England, Aug. 25, 1964.

Wheaton, Wil Burbank, CA, July 29, 1972.

Whitaker, Forest Longview, TX, July 15, 1961.

Whitaker, Johnny Van Nuys, CA, Dec. 13, 1959.

White, Betty Oak Park, IL, Jan. 17, 1922.

White, Charles Perth Amboy, NJ, Aug. 29, 1920. Rutgers U.

Whitelaw, Billie Coventry, England, June 6, 1932.

Whitman, Stuart San Francisco, Feb. 1, 1929. CCLA.

Whitmore, James White Plains, NY, Oct. 1, 1921. Yale.

Whitney, Grace Lee Detroit, MI, Apr. 1, 1930.

Whitton, Margaret Philadelphia, PA, Nov, 30, 1950.

Widdoes, Kathleen Wilmington, DE, Mar. 21, 1939.

Widmark, Richard Sunrise, MN, Dec. 26, 1914. Lake Forest.

Wiest, Dianne Kansas City, MO, Mar. 28, 1948. U Maryland.

Wilby, James Burma, Feb. 20, 1958.

Wilcox, Colin Highlands, NC, Feb. 4, 1937. U Tennessee.

Wilder, Gene (Jerome Silberman) Milwaukee, WI, June 11, 1935. U Iowa.

Wilkinson, Tom Leeds, England, Dec. 12, 1948. U Kentucky.

Willard, Fred Shaker Heights, OH, Sept. 18, 1939.

Williams, Billy Dee NYC, Apr. 6, 1937.

Williams, Cara (Bernice Kamiat) Brooklyn, NY, June 29, 1925.

Williams, Cindy Van Nuys, CA, Aug. 22, 1947. KACC.

Williams, Clarence, III NYC, Aug. 21, 1939.

Williams, Esther Los Angeles, CA, Aug. 8, 1921.

Williams, Jobeth Houston, TX, Dec 6, 1948. Brown U.

Williams, Michelle Kalispell, MT, Sept. 9, 1980.

Williams, Olivia London, England, Jan. 1, 1968.

Williams, Paul Omaha, NE, Sept. 19, 1940.

Williams, Robin Chicago, IL, July 21, 1951. Juilliard.

Williams, Treat (Richard) Rowayton, CT, Dec. 1, 1951.

Williams, Vanessa L. Tarrytown, NY, Mar. 18, 1963.

Williamson, Fred Gary, IN, Mar. 5, 1938. Northwestern.

Williamson, Nicol Hamilton, Scotland, Sept. 14, 1938.

Willis, Bruce Penns Grove, NJ, Mar. 19, 1955.

Paul Walker   Ken Watanabe   Reese Witherspoon   Evan Rachel Wood

Willison, Walter Monterey Park, CA, June 24, 1947.
Wilson, Demond NYC, Oct. 13, 1946. Hunter College.
Wilson, Elizabeth Grand Rapids, MI, Apr. 4, 1925.
Wilson, Lambert Neuilly-sur-Seine, France, Aug. 3, 1958.
Wilson, Luke Dallas, TX, Sept. 21, 1971.
Wilson, Owen Dallas, TX, Nov. 18, 1968.
Wilson, Patrick Norfolk, VA, July 3, 1973.
Wilson, Scott Atlanta, GA, Mar. 29, 1942.
Wincott, Jeff Toronto, Canada, May 8, 1957.
Wincott, Michael Toronto, Canada, Jan. 6, 1959. Juilliard.
Windom, William NYC, Sept. 28, 1923. Williams College.
Winfrey, Oprah Kosciusko, MS, Jan. 29, 1954. Tennessee State U.
Winger, Debra Cleveland, OH, May 17, 1955. Cal State.
Winkler, Henry NYC, Oct. 30, 1945. Yale.
Winn, Kitty Washington, D.C., Feb, 21, 1944. Boston U.
Winningham, Mare Phoenix, AZ, May 6, 1959.
Winslet, Kate Reading, England, Oct. 5, 1975.
Winslow, Michael Spokane, WA, Sept. 6, 1960.
Winter, Alex London, England, July 17, 1965. NYU.
Winters, Jonathan Dayton, OH, Nov. 11, 1925. Kenyon College.
Winters, Shelley (Shirley Schrift) St. Louis, Aug. 18, 1922. Wayne U.
Withers, Googie Karachi, India, Mar. 12, 1917. Italia Conti.
Withers, Jane Atlanta, GA, Apr. 12, 1926.
Witherspoon, Reese (Laura Jean Reese Witherspoon) Nashville, TN, Mar. 22, 1976.
Wolf, Scott Newton, MA, June 4, 1968.
Wong, B.D. San Francisco, Oct. 24,1962.
Wong, Russell Troy, NY, Mar. 1, 1963. Santa Monica College.
Wood, Elijah Cedar Rapids, IA, Jan 28, 1981.
Wood, Evan Rachel Raleigh, NC, Sept. 7, 1987.
Woodard, Alfre Tulsa, OK, Nov. 2, 1953. Boston U.
Woodlawn, Holly (Harold Ajzenberg) Juana Diaz, PR, 1947.
Woods, James Vernal, UT, Apr. 18, 1947. MIT.
Woodward, Edward Croyden, Surrey, England, June 1, 1930.
Woodward, Joanne Thomasville, GA, Feb. 27, 1930. Neighborhood Playhouse.
Woronov, Mary Brooklyn, NY, Dec. 8, 1946. Cornell.

Wright, Amy Chicago, IL, Apr. 15, 1950.
Wright, Jeffrey Washington, DC, Dec. 7, 1965. Amherst Col.
Wright, Max Detroit, MI, Aug. 2, 1943. Wayne State U.
Wright, Robin Dallas, TX, Apr. 8, 1966.
Wuhl, Robert Union City, NJ, Oct. 9, 1951. U Houston.
Wyatt, Jane NYC, Aug. 10, 1910. Barnard College.
Wyle, Noah Los Angeles, CA, June 2, 1971.
Wyman, Jane (Sarah Jane Fulks) St. Joseph, MO, Jan. 4, 1914.
Wymore, Patrice Miltonvale, KS, Dec. 17, 1926.
Wynn, May (Donna Lee Hickey) NYC, Jan. 8, 1930.
Wynter, Dana (Dagmar) London, England, June 8. 1927. Rhodes U.

York, Michael Fulmer, England, Mar. 27, 1942. Oxford.
York, Susannah London, England, Jan. 9, 1941. RADA.
Young, Alan (Angus) North Shield, England, Nov. 19, 1919.
Young, Burt Queens, NY, Apr. 30, 1940.
Young, Chris Chambersburg, PA, Apr. 28, 1971.
Young, Sean Louisville, KY, Nov. 20, 1959. Interlochen.
Yulin, Harris Los Angeles, CA, Nov. 5, 1937.
Yun-Fat, Chow Lamma Island, Hong Kong, May 18, 1955.

Zacharias, Ann Stockholm, Sweden, Sept. 19, 1956.
Zadora, Pia Hoboken, NJ, May 4, 1954.
Zahn, Steve Marshall, MN, Nov. 13, 1968.
Zegers, Kevin Woodstock, Ontario, Can., Sept. 19, 1984.
Zellweger, Renée Katy, TX, Apr. 25, 1969.
Zerbe, Anthony Long Beach, CA, May 20, 1939.
Zeta-Jones, Catherine Swansea, Wales, Sept. 25, 1969.
Zimbalist, Efrem, Jr. NYC, Nov. 30, 1918. Yale.
Zuniga, Daphne Berkeley, CA, Oct. 28, 1963. UCLA

OBITUARIES
2005

Don Adams (Donald James Yarmy), 82, New York City-born comedian-actor, best known for his Emmy Award-winning role as bumbling Secret Agent Maxwell Smart in the series *Get Smart*, died in Los Angeles on Sept. 25, 2005 of a lung infection. His handful of theatrical film credits are *The Nude Bomb* (also playing Maxwell Smart), *Jimmy the Kid*, *Back to the Beach*, and *Inspector Gadget* (voice). Survived by six children, a sister, five grandchildren, and three great-grandchildren.

Mason Adams, 86, Brooklyn-born screen, stage and television character actor, perhaps best known for his role as Charlie Hume on the series *Lou Grant*, died on Apr. 26, 2005 in New York of natural causes. Among his movies are *The Happy Hooker*, *God Told Me To*, *The Final Conflict*, *F/X*, *Toy Soldiers* (1991), *Son in Law*, *Houseguest*, and *Touch*. He is survived by his wife, a daughter, a son, and a brother.

Tony Adams, 52, Dublin-born film producer, who worked for 18 years in collaboration with director Blake Edwards, died of a stroke in Manhattan on Oct. 22, 2005. His credits include *The Return of the Pink Panther*, *10*, *S.O.B.*, *Victor/Victoria*, *The Man Who Loved Women* (1983), *Micki +Maude*, *The Man Who Loved Women*, *That's Life!*, *Skin Deep*, and *Switch*. Survivors include his third wife and four children.

Eddie Albert (Edward Albert Heimberger), 99, Illinois-born screen, stage, and television actor, who received Oscar nominations for his performances in *Roman Holiday* and *The Heartbreak Kid*, died on May 26, 2005 of pneumonia in Pacific Palisades, CA. Following his 1938 debut in *Brother Rat*, he appeared in such other movies as *On Your Toes*, *Four Wives*, *A Dispatch from Reuters*, *The Wagons Roll at Night*, *Thieves Fall Out*, *Out of the Fog*, *Eagle Squadron*, *Strange Voyage*, *Smash Up: The Story of a Woman*, *Every Girl Should Be Married*, *Carrie* (1952), *Actors and Sin*, *The Girl Rush*, *Oklahoma!*, *I'll Cry Tomorrow*, *Attack*, *The Teahouse of the August Moon*, *The Sun Also Rises*, *The Joker is Wild*, *The Roots of Heaven*, *The Young Doctors*, *The Longest Day*, *Captain Newman M.D.*, *Miracle of the White Stallions*, *The Longest Yard* (1974), *Escape to Witch Mountain*, and *Yes, Giorgio*. On television he was best remembered for the sitcom *Green Acres*. He was married for 40 years to actress Margo, who died in 1985. He is survived by his son, actor Edward Albert, a daughter, and two granddaughters.

Keith Andes (John Charles Andes), 85, New Jersey-born screen, stage, and television actor was found dead at his home in Santa Clarita, CA, on Nov. 11, 2005 having committed suicide by asphyxiation. He had been suffering from bladder cancer and other ailments. Among his movies were *The Farmer's Daughter* (1947), *Clash by Night*, *Blackbeard the Pirate*, *Away All Boats*, *Tora! Tora! Tora!* (as Gen. George C. Marshall), and *...And Justice for All*. Survived by his two sons and three grandchildren.

Avril Angers, 86, British comedienne and actress died on Nov. 9, 2005 in London of pneumonia. She was seen in such pictures as *Don't Blame the Stork*, *The Family Way*, *Three Bites of the Apple*, *The Best House in London*, *Staircase*, *There's a Girl in My Soup*, and *Cry of the Penguins* (Mr. Forbush and the Penguins). Survived by two brothers.

Leon Askin, 97, Vienna-born character player died on June 3, 2005 in Vienna of natural causes. He was seen in such movies as *Road to Bali*, *South Sea Woman*, *The Robe*, *Knock on Wood*, *Valley of the Kings*, *One, Two, Three*, *John Goldfarb Please Come Home*, *What Did You Do in the War Daddy?*, *The Maltese Bippy*, *The World's Greatest Athlete*, and *Young Frankenstein*.

Anne Bancroft (Anna Maria Italiano), 73, Bronx-born screen, stage, and television actress, who won an Academy Award for playing Annie Sullivan in *The Miracle Worker* and became one of the iconic figures of the '60s with her Oscar-nominated performance as the predatory seductress Mrs. Robinson in *The Graduate*, died of uterine cancer on June 6, 2005 in Manhattan. Following her 1952 debut in *Don't Bother to Knock*, she was seen in such films as *The Kid from Left Field*, *Demetrius and the Gladiators*, *Gorilla at Large*, *A Life in the Balance*, *Walk the Proud Land*, *The Girl in Black Stockings*, *The Pumpkin Eater* (Oscar nomination), *The Slender Thread*, *7 Women*, *Young Winston*, *The Prisoner of Second Avenue*, *The Hindenburg*, *The Turning Point* (Oscar nomination), *Fatso* (which she also wrote and directed), *The Elephant Man*, *To Be or Not to Be* (1983), *Garbo Talks*, *Agnes of God* (Oscar nomination), *'night, Mother*, *84 Charing Cross Road*, *Torch Song Trilogy*, *Honeymoon in Vegas*, *Point of No Return*, *Malice*, *How to Make an American Quilt*, *G.I. Jane*, *Great Expectations* (1998), *Keeping the Faith*, and *Up at the Villa*. She is survived by her husband, director-writer Mel Brooks, a son, her mother, and two sisters.

Barbara Bel Geddes, 82, New York City-born screen, stage, and television actress, who earned an Oscar nomination for playing Katrin Hanson in the 1948 film *I Remember Mama*, died of lung cancer on Aug. 8, 2005 in Northeast Harbor, ME. Following her 1947 debut in *The Long Night*, she was seen in such other pictures as *Blood on the Moon*, *Panic in the Streets*, *Fourteen Hours*, *Vertigo*, *The Five Pennies*, *5 Branded Women*, and *Summertree*. She won an Emmy Award for the series *Dallas*.

Adrian Biddle, 54, British cinematographer, who earned an Oscar nomination for his work on *Thelma & Louise*, died of a heart attack on Dec. 7, 2005 in London. Among his other credits are *Aliens*, *The Princess Bride*, *Willow*, *The Tall Guy*, *1492: Conquest of Paradise*, *Fierce Creatures*, *The Butcher Boy*, *The Mummy* (1989), *The World is Not Enough*, *Reign of Fire*, and *Laws of Attraction*. Survived by his wife and three children.

Norman Bird, 80, British character actor from television and film died of cancer on Apr. 22, 2005 in Wolverhampton, England. His many movies include *The League of Gentleman*, *The Angry Silence*, *Whistle Down the Wind*, *Victim*, *The Mind Benders*, *The Hill*, *The Wrong Box*, *A Dandy in Aspic*, *The Virgin and the Gypsy*, *Young Winston*, and *Shadowlands*.

Lloyd Bochner, 81, Ontario-born character actor died of cancer on Oct. 29, 2005 at his home in Santa Monica. His film credits include *The Night Walker*, *Sylvia* (1965), *Point Blank*, *Tony Rome*, *The Detective*, *Ulzana's Raid*, *The Man in the Glass Booth*, and *The Lonely Lady*. Survivors include his wife; two sons, one of whom is actor Hart Bochner; and a daughter.

Tommy Bond, 79, former child actor, who played tough guy "Butch" in the *Our Gang/Little Rascals* series of shorts, died of complications from heart disease on Sept. 24, 2005 in Northridge, CA. In addition to his work in the series, he played Jimmy Olsen in the 1948 *Superman* serial.

James Booth, 77, British screen, television, and stage actor who starred in such films as *Zulu* and *The Bliss of Mrs. Blossom*, died on Aug. 11, 2005 in Hadleigh, England. His other movies include *The Trials of Oscar Wilde*, *Jazz Boat*, *The Secret of My Success* (1965), *Fraulein Doktor*, *Macho Callahan*, *Darker Than Amber*, *Brannigan*, *Airport '77*, *The Jazz Singer* (1980), and *Zorro the Gay Blade*.

Eddie Albert

Anne Bancroft

Barbara Bel Geddes

Constance Cummings

John Brabourne, 80, London-born film producer, who received Oscar nominations for *Romeo and Juliet* and *A Passage to India*, died on Sept. 22, 2005 in Kent, England. His other credits include *Sink the Bismarck!*, *Damn the Defiant* (*H.M.S. Defiant*), *Othello* (1965), *The Dance of Death*, *Murder on the Orient Express*, *Death on the Nile*, *The Mirror Crack'd*, *Evil Under the Sun*, and *Little Dorrit*. He is survived by his wife, four sons, and two daughters.

Jocelyn Brando, 86, San Francisco-born actress, the older sister of screen legend Marlon Brando, died of natural causes on Nov. 27, 2005 in Santa Monica, CA. Her films include *The Big Heat*, *Ten Wanted Men*, *The Explosive Generation*, *Bus Riley's Back in Town*, *Movie Movie*, *Mommie Dearest*, and two in support of her brother, *The Ugly American* and *The Chase*. Survivors include her son.

John Bromfield (Farron McClain Brumfield), 83, Indiana-born screen and television actor of the '50s died of kidney failure on Sept. 18, 2005 in Palm Desert, CA. Among his film credits are *Sorry Wrong Number*, *Rope of Sand* (featuring his first wife, Corinne Calvet), *The Furies*, *The Cimarron Kid*, *Easy to Love*, *Revenge of the Creature*, *Frontier Gambler*, and *Curucu: Beast of the Amazon*. He retired from acting in the early 1960s to become a commercial fisherman. Survived by his third wife.

Hamilton Camp, 70, London-born character player died of a heart attack in Los Angeles on Oct. 2, 2005. He appeared in such movies as *My Cousin Rachel*, *Nickelodeon*, *American Hot Wax*, *Heaven Can Wait* (1978), *S.O.B.*, *Eating Raoul*, *No Small Affair*, and *Dick Tracy*.

J.D. Cannon (John Donovan Cannon), 83, Idaho-born screen, stage, and television character actor died on May 20, 2005 at his home in upstate New York. He appeared in such movies as *An American Dream*, *Cool Hand Luke*, *Krakatoa East of Java*, *Cotton Comes to Harlem*, *Scorpio*, and *Raise the Titanic*. On television he was best known for playing the police chief on *McCloud*. Survivors include his wife and two brothers.

Jean Carson, 82, West Virginia-born screen, stage, and television actress died of complications from a stroke on Nov. 2, 2005 in Palm Springs, CA. Among her movie credits are *The Phenix City Story*, *I Married a Monster from Outer Space*, *The Sound and the Fury*, *Gunn*, *The Party*, and *Fun with Dick and Jane* (1977). Survived by two sons.

Johnny Carson, 79, Iowa-born talk show host and comedian, who ruled late night television for thirty years as the host of *The Tonight Show*, died in Los Angeles on Jan. 23, 2005 of emphysema. He made cameo appearances playing himself in two feature films, *Looking for Love* and *Cancel My Reservation*. He is survived by his fourth wife, two sons, his brother, and his sister.

George P. Cosmatos, 64, Italy-born director died on Apr. 19, 2005 in Victoria, Canada, from lung cancer. His films include *The Cassandra Crossing* (for which he also wrote the screenplay), *Rambo: First Blood Part II*, *Cobra*, *Leviathan*, *Tombstone*, and *Shadow Conspiracy*. His earlier credits include serving as assistant director and appearing in *Zorba the Greek*. Survived by a son, a brother, and a nephew.

Constance Cummings (Constance Halverstadt), 95, Seattle-born Hollywood screen actress who later moved to London and became one of England's prominent stage performers, died on Nov. 23, 2005 in Oxfordshire. Her motion pictures include *The Criminal Code*, *The Guilty Generation*, *Behind the Mask*, *Movie Crazy*, *Washington Merry-Go-Round*, *Night After Night*, *The Mind Reader*, *Haunted Honeymoon* (*Busman's Honeymoon*), *Blithe Spirit*, *John and Julie*, *The Battle of the Sexes*, and *A Boy Ten Feet Tall* (*Sammy Going South*). On Broadway she won a Tony Award for *Wings*. Her forty-year marriage to playwright Benn Levy ended with his death in 1973. She is survived by her son and daughter.

Ossie Davis (Raiford Chattman Davis), 87, Georgia-born screen, stage and television actor-director-writer-producer, one of the pioneering black performers who often teamed with his wife, actress Ruby Dee, was found dead of natural causes at a Miami Beach motel room on Feb. 4, 2005 while on location for a film. His motion picture credits include *No Way Out* (his debut in 1950), *Fourteen Hours*, *The Joe Louis Story*, *Gone Are the Days* (also screenplay), *The Cardinal*, *The Hill*, *The Scalphunters*, *Slaves*, *Let's Do It Again*, *Countdown at Kusini* (also director, producer), *Harry and Son*, *School Daze*, *Do the Right Thing*, *Jungle Fever*, *Grumpy Old Men*, *The Client*, and *I'm Not Rappaport*. In addition to Dee, he is survived by three children and seven grandchildren.

Ossie Davis

Sandra Dee

Geraldine Fitzgerald

June Haver

Sandra Dee (Alexandra Zuck), 62, New Jersey-born actress, an iconic teen star of the late '50s and early '60s of such pictures as *Gidget* and *A Summer Place*, died of kidney disease on Feb. 20, 2005 in Thousand Oaks, CA. Her other films include *Until They Sail*, *The Reluctant Debutante*, *The Restless Years*, *Imitation of Life* (1959), *Portrait in Black*, *Romanoff and Juliet*, *Tammy Tell Me True*, *Come September* (appearing opposite Bobby Darin whom she would marry), *Tammy and the Doctor*, *Take Her She's Mine*, *I'd Rather Be Rich*, *That Funny Feeling*, *Doctor You've Got to Be Kidding*, *Rosie!*, and *The Dunwich Horror*. Survived by her son.

Bob Denver, 70, New Rochelle-born actor, best known for his roles on the series *Gilligan's Island* and *The Many Loves of Dobie Gillis*, died on Sept. 2, 2005 in Winston-Salem, NC of complications following surgery for throat cancer. His movies include *Take Her She's Mine*, *For Those You Think Young*, *Who's Minding the Mint?*, *Did You Hear the One About the Traveling Saleslady?*, *The Sweet Ride*, and *Back to the Beach*. Survived by his wife and four children.

Stanley DeSantis, 52, screen and television character actor died of a heart attack on Aug. 9, 2005 in Los Angeles. He could be seen in such pictures as *Black Moon Rising*, *Candyman*, *Ed Wood*, *The Birdcage*, *Clockwatchers*, *Boogie Nights*, *Bulworth*, *Rush Hour*, *I Am Sam*, and *The Aviator*. Survivors include three sisters.

Beach Dickerson, 81, Georgia-born actor died on Dec. 7, 2005 in Los Angeles. Appearing mostly in drive-in fare his credits included *Attack of the Crab Monsters*, *Teenage Caveman*, *The Savage Seven*, *Angels Die Hard*, and *Crazy Mama*. Survived by his son.

Badja Djola, 56, born screen, stage and theatre actor died of a heart attack in Los Angeles on Jan. 8, 2005. He could be seen in such movies as *Penitentiary*, *Mississippi Burning*, *A Rage in Harlem*, *Player's Club*, *Rosewood*, and *An Innocent Man*. Survived by his mother.

James Doohan, 85, Vancouver-born actor, best known for his role as Engineer Montgomery Scott in the series *Star Trek* and seven of its motion picture spin-offs, died on July 20, 2005 of pneumonia and Alzheimer's disease at his home in Redmond, WA. His other movies include *The Wheeler Dealers*, *Bus Riley's Back in Town*, *Pretty Maids All in a Row*, *Man in the Wilderness*, and *National Lampoon's Loaded Weapon 1*. Survivors include his third wife and nine children.

Dana Elcar, 77, Michigan-born character actor died of complications from pneumonia on June 6, 2005 in Ventura, CA. Among his movie credits were *Fail-Safe*, *The Fool Killer*, *A Lovely Way to Die*, *The Boston Strangler*, *The Maltese Bippy*, *Adam at 6 A.M.*, *The Sting*, *W.C. Fields and Me*, *The Nude Bomb*, *Buddy Buddy*, and *All of Me*.

Stephen Elliott, 86, New York City-born screen, stage, and television character actor, perhaps best known for playing Jill Eikenberry's dad in the 1981 comedy hit *Arthur*, died of congestive heart failure on May 21, 2005 in Los Angeles. Among his other movies are *Three Hours to Kill*, *The Hospital*, *Death Wish*, *The Hindenburg*, *Cutter and Bone*, *Kiss Me Goodbye*, and *Beverly Hills Cop*. Survived by his wife, a daughter, a son, two stepsons, and three grandchildren.

John Fiedler, 80, Wisconsin-born character player, who supplied the voice of Piglet in the Winnie-the-Pooh cartoons, died of cancer on June 25, 2005 in Englewood, NJ. His on-screen movie roles include *Twelve Angry Men*, *Stage Struck*, *A Raisin in the Sun* (repeating his Broadway role), *That Touch of Mink*, *The World of Henry Orient*, *Kiss Me Stupid*, *A Fine Madness*, *The Odd Couple* (repeating his Broadway role), *True Grit*, and *Sharky's Machine*. Survivors include his brother and sister.

Geraldine Fitzgerald, 91, Dublin-born screen, stage, and theatre actress, who earned an Oscar nomination for playing Isabella Linton in the 1939 film *Wuthering Heights*, died on July 17, 2005 at her home in Manhattan following a long battle with Alzheimer's disease. Her other movies include *Dark Victory*, *Watch on the Rhine*, *The Pawnbroker*, *Rachel Rachel*, *Harry and Tonto*, *Arthur*, and *Easy Money*. She is survived by her son, director Michael Lindsay-Hogg; her daughter; two grandchildren; and one step-grandchild.

Suzanne Flon, 86, French actress, perhaps best known to American audiences for her role as Myriamme Hyam in the 1952 Toulouse-Lautrec bio *Moulin Rouge*, died in Paris on June 15, 2005, of gastroenteritis. Her other films include *Mr. Arkadin* (*Confidential Report*), *The Trial*, *The Train*, *Mr. Klein*, and *Quartet*.

Ruth Hussey   Frances Langford   Virginia Mayo   Lon McCallister

Elizabeth Fraser, 85, Brooklyn-born screen, stage, and television character actress, died of congestive heart failure on May 5, 2005 in Woodland Hills, CA. Among her films were *One Foot in Heaven*, *The Man Who Came to Dinner*, *Commandos Strike a Dawn*, *Death of a Salesman*, *Young at Heart*, *Ask Any Girl*, *Two for the Seesaw*, *A Patch of Blue*, *The Glass Bottom Boat*, *Seconds*, *Tony Rome*, and *The Graduate*. She is survived by three daughters, two from her first marriage to dancer-actor Ray McDonald.

Christopher Fry (Christopher Fry Harris), 97, British playwright and screenwriter, died on June 30, 2005 in Chichester, England of natural causes. Best known for the play *The Lady's Not for Burning*, he also worked on the screenplays for *The Beggar's Opera*, *Ben-Hur* (uncredited), *Barabbas*, and *The Bible*. Survivors include his son.

Frank Gorshin, 72, Pittsburgh-born actor and impressionist, perhaps best known for his portrayal of The Riddler on the '60s TV series *Batman* (and its 1966 movie spin-off), died on May 17, 2005 in Burbank, CA, of pneumonia. He appeared in such motion pictures as *Hot Rod Girl*, *Dragstrip Girl*, *Invasion of the Saucer Men*, *Warlock*, *Bells Are Ringing*, *Where the Boys Are* (1960), *The George Raft Story*, *That Darn Cat!* (1965), *Skidoo*, *The Meteor Man*, *Twelve Monkeys*, and *Man of the Century*. Survived by his wife of 48 years, his son, and a sister.

Joe Grant, 96, New York City-born Disney animator-writer died of a heart attack on May 6, 2005 in Glendale, CA. He had worked on the studio's pioneering first animated feature, *Snow White and the Seven Dwarfs* and also had credits on such other films as *Fantasia*, *Pinocchio*, *The Reluctant Dragon*, *Beauty and the Beast*, *Pocahontas*, and *Mulan*. Survived by his two daughters and his grandchildren.

Guy Green, 91, British cinematographer-turned-director died at his Beverly Hills home of heart and kidney failure on Sept. 15, 2005. He received the Academy Award for photographing the 1947 version of *Great Expectations*, and then went on to direct such pictures as *Sea of Sand* (*Desert Patrol*), *The Angry Silence*, *The Mark*, *Light in the Piazza*, *Diamond Head*, *A Patch of Blue* (which he also wrote and produced), *A Matter of Innocence* (*Pretty Polly*), *A Walk in the Spring Rain*, *Luther*, and *Once is Not Enough*. Survived by his wife of 57 years, a son, a daughter, and two grandchildren.

Kevin Hagen, 77, Chicago-born character player, best known for his role as Dr. Hiram Baker on the NBC series *Little House on the Prairie*, died of esophageal cancer on July 9, 2005 in Grants Pass, OR. He could also been seen in such movies as *Pork Chop Hill*, *Rio Conchos*, *Shenandoah*, *The Learning Tree*, and *Power*. He is survived by his fourth wife and his son.

June Haver (June Stovenour), 79, Illinois-born actress, star of several 1940s musicals including *The Dolly Sisters* and *Look for the Silver Lining*, died on July 4, 2005. Her other movies include *The Gang's All Here* (debut, 1943), *Home in Indiana*, *Irish Eyes Are Smiling*, *Where Do We Go from Here?*, *Three Little Girls in Blue*, *I Wonder Who's Kissing Her Now*, *Scudda Hoo! Scudda Hay!*, *The Daughter of Rosie O'Grady*, and her last, *The Girl Next Door*, in 1953. After briefly entering a convent she ended up marrying actor Fred MacMurray in 1955. They remained wed until his death in 1991. She is survived by her two daughters, two stepchildren, seven grandchildren, and four great-grandchildren.

Debra Hill, 54, New Jersey-born film producer and writer, best known for co-writing and producing the horror hit *Halloween* with John Carpenter, died on March 7, 2005 in Los Angeles, of cancer. Her other credits include *The Fog*, *Escape from New York*, *Clue*, *Adventures in Babysitting*, *The Fisher King*, and *Crazy in Alabama*. Survived by her parents and her brother.

Joel Hirschhorn, 67, songwriter who won Oscars for "The Morning After" from *The Poseidon Adventure* and "We May Never Love Like This Again" from *The Towering Inferno*, died of a heart attack on Sept. 18, 2005 in Thousand Oaks, CA. He and collaborator Al Kasha were also nominated for the song "Candle on the Water" from *Pete's Dragon*. He is survived by his wife, two stepsons, a sister, his mother, and a grandson.

Evan Hunter, 78, New York City-born writer, best known for his series of *87th Precinct* novels which he wrote under the pseudonym "Ed McBain," died of larynx cancer on July 6, 2005. He adapted two of his novels, *Strangers When We Meet* and *Fuzz*, to the screen and wrote the scripts for *The Birds* and *Walk Proud*. Among his other books adapted into films by others were *Blackboard Jungle* and *Last Summer*. He is survived by his wife and three sons.

Ruth Hussey (Ruth Carol O'Rourke), 93, Providence-born screen, stage, and television actress, who earned an Oscar nomination for playing wisecracking reporter Liz Imbrie in the classic comedy *The Philadelphia Story*, died on Apr. 19, 2005 in Newbury Park, CA, from complications of an appendectomy. Following her 1937 debut in *The Big City*, she was seen in such other pictures as *Marie Antoinette, Honolulu, Maisie, The Women, Northwest Passage, Susan and God, H.M. Pulham Esq.; Tennessee Johnson, Tender Comrade, The Uninvited, I, Jane Doe, The Great Gatsby* (1949), *Mr. Music, That's My Boy, Stars and Stripes Forever*, and *The Facts of Life*. She is survived by two sons, a daughter, four grandchildren, and a great-grandchild.

Agenore Incrocci, 86, one of Italy's most prolific screen writers, who (billed simply as "Age") earned Oscar nominations for his collaborations with Furio Scarpelli and Mario Monicelli for *The Organizer* and *Casanova '70*, died on Nov. 15, 2005 in Rome of a heart attack. His other films include *At Sword's Edge, The Bigamist, Big Deal on Madonna Street, The Passionate Thief, Seduced and Abandoned, The Good, the Bad and the Ugly, The Pizza Triangle, We All Loved Each Other So Much, A Joke of Destiny*, and several *Toto* comedies.

Mary Jackson, 95, Michigan-born screen, stage and television character actress, best known for playing Miss Emily Baldwin on the series *The Waltons*, died on Dec. 10, 2005 in Los Angeles of complications from Parkinson's disease. Among her films are *Targets, Airport, Blume in Love, Fun with Dick and Jane* (1977), *Coming Home, Big Top Pee-wee, Leap of Faith*, and *A Family Thing*. She is survived by her husband of 68 years.

Jerry Juhl, 67, St. Paul-born head-writer for the Muppets for many years, died from complications of cancer on September 26, 2005. He wrote the films *The Muppet Movie, The Great Muppet Caper, The Muppet Christmas Carol, Muppet Treasure Island*, and *Muppets from Space*. He is survived by his wife and his brother.

Gavin Lambert, 80, British writer, who received Oscar nominations for his screenplays of *Sons and Lovers* and *I Never Promised You a Rose Garden*, died of pulmonary thrombosis on July 17, 2005 in Los Angeles. His other scripts include *Bitter Victory, The Roman Spring of Mrs. Stone*, and *Inside Daisy Clover*, which he adapted from his own novel. He is survived by his brother.

Frances Langford, 91, Florida-born singer-actress, who introduced the classic song "I'm in the Mood for Love" in the 1935 musical *Every Night at Eight*, died of congestive heart failure on July 11, 2005 at her home in Jensen Beach, FL. She was also seen in such other pictures as *Broadway Melody of 1936, Collegiate, Born to Dance, Hollywood Hotel, Too Many Girls, Yankee Doodle Dandy, Cowboy in Manhattan, This is the Army, The Girl Rush*, and *The Glenn Miller Story*. She was also well known on radio for the series *The Bickersons*. Survived by her husband.

Alberto Lattuada, 91, Italian film director-writer died on July 3, 2005 in Rome. His credits include *Variety Lights* (co-directed with Federico Fellini), *Tempest* (1959), *Mandragola, Matchless, Fraulein Doktor*, and *Stay as You Are*. Survived by his wife, actress Carla Del Poggio.

Marc Lawrence, 95, New York City-born character actor, who specialized in villains and gangster roles over a seventy-year period, died on Nov. 26, 2005 in Palm Springs, CA, of heart failure. Among his many films are *G Men, San Quentin, Murder in Greenwich Village, Invisible Stripes, Johnny Apollo, The Monster and the Girl, Blossoms in the Dust, Hold That Ghost, This Gun for Hire,*

The Ox-Bow Incident, Dillinger (1945), *Key Largo, The Asphalt Jungle, My Favorite Spy, Helen of Troy, Krakatoa East of Java, The Man with the Golden Gun, Marathon Man, Foul Play, The Big Easy, Newsies, The Shipping News*, and *Looney Tunes: Back in Action*. Survived by his wife, a daughter, and a son.

Ernest Lehman, 89, Long Island-born screenwriter-producer died on July 2, 2005 at UCLA Medical Center following a long illness. He received Oscar nominations for the screenplays of *Sabrina* (1954), *North by Northwest, West Side Story*, and *Who's Afraid of Virginia Woolf?*, and additional nominations as producer of *Virginia Woolf* and *Hello, Dolly!* His other scripts include *Executive Suite, The King and I, Somebody Up There Likes Me, Sweet Smell of Success* (adapted from his own story), *From the Terrace, The Sound of Music, Portnoy's Complaint* (which he also directed), *Family Plot*, and *Black Sunday*. In 2001 he was awarded a special Academy Award. Survived by his second wife and his three sons.

Sid Luft, 89, New York City-born producer, best known for the 1954 remake of *A Star is Born*, starring his then-wife Judy Garland, died of a heart attack on Sept. 15, 2005 in Santa Monica, CA. His other credits were *Kilroy Was Here* and *French Leave*. Survivors include his third wife, and his two children with Garland, one of which is singer-actress Lorna Luft.

Bruce Malmuth, 71, Brooklyn-born film director died in Los Angeles on June 29, 2005 of esophageal cancer. His feature credits include *Fore Play, Nighthawks* (1981), *The Man Who Wasn't There* (1983), and *Hard to Kill*. He is survived by his wife, a son, a sister, and two brothers.

Barney Martin, 82, Queens-born character actor, who played Liza Minnelli's grubby dad in the 1981 hit comedy *Arthur*, died of cancer on March 21, 2005 at his home in Studio City, CA. Best known on television for playing Jerry Seinfeld's father in *Seinfeld* and on stage for introducing the song "Mr. Cellophane" in the original Broadway production for *Chicago*, his other movies include *The Producers, Charly, Movie Movie*, and *Hot Stuff*. He is survived by his wife, a son, two grandsons, and two great-grandsons.

Virginia Mayo (Virginia Clara Jones), 84, St. Louis-born actress who appeared in such notable '40s films as *The Best Years of Our Lives* and *The Secret Life of Walter Mitty*, died on Jan. 17, 2005 in Thousand Oaks, CA, of pneumonia and heart failure. Her other movies include *Jack London* (starring Michael O'Shea, whom she married in 1947), *Up in Arms, The Princess and the Pirate, Wonder Man, The Kid from Brooklyn, A Song is Born, Flaxy Martin, The Girl from Jones Beach, Colorado Territory, White Heat, Always Leave Them Laughing, The Flame and the Arrow, The West Point Story, Captain Horatio Hornblower, She's Working Her Way Through College, King Richard and the Crusaders, The Silver Chalice, Great Day in the Morning, The Story of Mankind, Fort Dobbs, Fort Utah, Won Ton Ton the Dog Who Saved Hollywood*, and *Evil Spirits*. She is survived by a daughter from her marriage to O'Shea (who died in 1973) and three grandchildren.

Lon McCallister (Herbert Alonzo McCallister, Jr.), 82, Los Angeles-born screen actor, best known for her roles in such '40s films as *Winged Victory* and *Home in Indiana*, died of heart failure at his home in Lake Tahoe, CA, on June 11, 2005. Following bit roles in such pictures as *Romeo and Juliet* (1936) and *The Adventures of Tom Sawyer*, he moved up to leads in such movies as *Stage Door Canteen, The Red House, Thunder in the Valley, The Big Cat, The Story of Seabiscuit, The Boy from Indiana*, and his last, *Combat Squad*, in 1953, after which he retired from show business. He is survived by his brother and sister.

Pat McCormick, 78, Ohio-born comedy writer and performer, perhaps best known for his work on *The Tonight Show*, died on July 29, 2005 in Woodland Hills, CA, following the effects of a massive stroke. He appeared in such motion pictures as *The Phynx*, *Buffalo Bill and the Indians* (as Grover Cleveland), *The Shaggy D.A.*, *Smokey and the Bandit*, *A Wedding*, *Hot Stuff*, *History of the World Part 1*, *Under the Rainbow*, and *Ted and Venus*. He is survived by a son and a grandson.

Ismail Merchant, 68, Bombay-born producer, known for his collaborations with James Ivory, which brought him Oscar nominations for *A Room with a View*, *Howards End*, and *The Remains of the Day*, died on May 25, 2005 in London after surgery for abdominal ulcers. His other credits as producer include *The Wild Party*, *Heat and Dust*, *Maurice*, *Slaves of New York*, and *Mr. & Mrs. Bridge*. He is survived by Ivory and four sisters.

Arthur Miller, 89, New York City-born playwright, who created such seminal works of the American theatre as *Death of a Salesman* and *The Crucible*, died on Feb. 10, 2005 in Roxbury, CT, of congestive heart failure. While such Miller works as *Salesman*, *All My Sons*, *Enemy of the People* (which he had adapted from Ibsen), and *Focus* were translated into movies by others, Miller himself was credited on two original screenplays, *The Misfits*, which featured his second wife, actress Marilyn Monroe, and *Everybody Wins*. He also did the 1996 screen adaptation of *The Crucible,* which brought him an Oscar nomination. He is survived by his three children, one of whom is actress-writer Rebecca Miller.

John Mills, 97, British actor, whose long and distinguished 60-year-plus career on screen included an Academy Award for the film *Ryan's Daughter*, died at his home in Denham, England on April 23, 2005 after a brief illness. Following his 1932 debut in *The Midshipman*, he appeared in such motion pictures as *Nine Days a Queen (Tudor Rose)*, *Goodbye Mr. Chips* (1939), *In Which We Serve*, *Young Mr. Pitt*, *This Happy Breed*, *Waterloo Road*, *The Way to the Stars*, *Great Expectations* (in one of his best known roles, as Pip), *So Well Remembered*, *Scott of the Antarctic*, *The Rocking Horse Winner*, *Mr. Denning Drives North*, *Hobson's Choice*, *The End of the Affair* (1955), *War and Peace* (1956), *Around the World in Eighty Days*, *I Was Monty's Double*, *Season of Passion* (*Summer of the Seventeenth Doll*), *Tiger Bay*, *Swiss Family Robinson*, *Tunes of Glory*, *The Singer Not the Song*, *The Truth About Spring*, *The Chalk Garden*, *Operation Crossbow*, *King Rat*, *The Wrong Box*, *The Family Way*, *Oh! What a Lovely War*, *Young Winston*, *Oklahoma Crude*, *Zulu Dawn*, *Gandhi*, *Who's That Girl*, *Gentlemen Don't Eat Poets*, *Hamlet* (1996), and *Bright Young Things*. Survived by his wife of 64 years, writer Mary Hayley Bell, who would die later that year on Dec. 1st; his two daughters, actresses Hayley Mills and Juliet Mills; his son; and his grandchildren.

Constance Moore, 84, Sioux City-born film and television actress died on Sept. 16, 2005 in Los Angeles of heart failure. Her movie credits include *Prison Break*, *Mutiny on the Blackhawk*, *You Can't Cheat an Honest Man*, *Charlie McCarthy—Detective*, *Argentine Nights*, *Las Vegas Nights*, *I Wanted Wings*, *Atlantic City* (1944), *Show Business*, *In Old Sacramento*, and the serial *Buck Rogers*, in which she appeared as Wilma Deering. She is survived by a son, a daughter, two sisters, two grandchildren, and one great-grandchild.

Pat Morita, 73, California-born comedian-turned-actor, best known for his Oscar nominated role of the mentor Mr. Miyagi in the 1984 film *The Karate Kid*, died of natural causes on Nov. 24, 2005 in Los Angeles. His motion pictures include *Thoroughly Modern Millie*, *Honeymoon in Vegas*, *Spy Hard*, *Even Cowgirls Get the Blues*, *Mulan* (voice), *The Center of the World*, and three *Karate Kid* sequels. Survived by his wife and three daughters.

Howard Morris, 85, actor, director, and voice-over performer, best known for appearing on the classic variety series *Your Show of Shows*, died on May 21, 2005 of a heart ailment. He acted in such movies as *Boys' Night Out*, *The Nutty Professor* (1963), *Fluffy*, *High Anxiety*, *History of the World Part 1*, *Splash*, and *Life Stinks*. His credits as a director include episodes of such programs as *The Andy Griffith Show* (on which he also played the recurring role of Ernest T. Bass), *The Dick Van Dyke Show*, and *Hogan's Heroes*, as well as the features *Who's Minding the Mint?*, *With Six You Get Eggroll*, *Don't Drink the Water*, and *Goin' Coconuts*. Survived by his son.

Robert Newmyer, 49, Washington DC-born motion picture producer died on Dec. 12, 2005 in Toronto of a heart attack brought on by an asthma attack. His credits include *Sex, Lies and Videotape*, *Indian Summer*, *The Santa Clause*, *Addicted to Love*, *Ready to Rumble*, and *Training Day*. He is survived by his wife, four children, his parents, and two sisters.

Sheree North (Dawn Bethel), 72, Los Angeles-born screen, stage and television actress, who starred in such 20th Century Fox films of the '50s as *How to Be Very, Very Popular* and *The Lieutenant Wore Skirts*, died on Nov. 4, 2005 in LA of complications from cancer surgery. Her other movies include *Living It Up*, *The Best Things in Life Are Free*, *No Down Payment*, *In Love and War*, *Mardi Gras*, *Madigan*, *The Gypsy Moths*, *Lawman*, *Charley Varrick*, *The Shootist*, and *Defenseless*. She is survived by her husband, two daughters, and a grandchild.

Louis Nye, 92, Connecticut-born comedian-actor, best known for his appearances on *The Steve Allen Show*, died on October 9, 2005 at his Los Angeles, following a long battle with lung cancer. He was seen in such movies as *The Facts of Life*, *Sex Kittens Go to College*, *The Wheeler Dealers*, *Good Neighbor Sam*, *A Guide for the Married Man*, *Won Ton Ton the Dog Who Saved Hollywood*, and *Harper Valley PTA*. Survivors include his son.

Dan O'Herlihy, 85, Irish screen, stage, and television actor, who earned an Oscar nomination for his performance in the 1954 film *The Adventures of Robinson Crusoe*, died of natural causes at his home in Malibu on Feb. 17, 2005. After his 1947 debut in *Odd Man Out*, he appeared in such movies as *Macbeth* (1948, as Macduff), *Kidnapped* (1948), *Soldiers Three*, *The Highwayman*, *The Blue Veil*, *At Sword's Point*, *The Black Shield of Falworth*, *The Virgin Queen*, *Imitation of Life* (1959), *The Night Fighters* (*A Terrible Beauty*), *King of the Roaring '20s: The Story of Arnold Rothstein*, *Fail-Safe*, *100 Rifles*, *Waterloo*, *The Tamarind Seed*, *MacArthur* (as FDR), *The Last Starfighter*, *RoboCop*, and *The Dead*. He is survived by his wife, five children, 10 grandchildren, and one great-grandchild.

John Mills

Sheree North

Dan O'Herlihy

Brock Peters

Jean Parker, 90, Montana-born screen actress, best known for playing Beth in the 1933 version of *Little Women*, died of a stroke on Nov. 30, 2005 in Woodland Hills, CA. She appeared in such other pictures as *Gabriel Over the White House*, *Lady for a Day*, *Operator 13*, *A Wicked Woman*, *Murder in the Fleet*, *The Ghost Goes West*, *The Texas Rangers*, *Penitentiary*, *The Flying Deuces*, *No Hands on the Clock*, *Minesweeper*, *One Body Too Many*, *Those Redheads from Seattle*, and *Apache Uprising*. Survived by her son and two granddaughters.

Brock Peters (George Fisher), 78, New York City-born actor, perhaps best known for portraying Tom Robinson in the 1962 classic *To Kill a Mockingbird*, died of pancreatic cancer in Los Angeles on Aug. 23, 2005. His other films include *Carmen Jones*, *Porgy and Bess*, *Heavens Above!*, *The L-Shaped Room*, *Major Dundee*, *The Pawnbroker*, *The Incident*, *Ace High*, *Black Girl*, *Soylent Green*, *Lost in the Stars* (repeating his stage role), *Two Minute Warning*, and *Star Trek IV: The Voyage Home*. He is survived by his companion and a daughter.

Otto Plaschkes, 75, Vienna-born producer, best known for the 1966 film *Georgy Girl*, died of heart failure on Feb. 14, 2005 in London. His other credits include *The Bofors Gun*, *The Homecoming*, *Butley*, *In Celebration*, and *The Holcroft Covenant*. He is survived by his wife, a daughter, and a sister.

Richard Pryor, 65, Illinois-born comedian and film actor, considered one of the most influential of all standup comics, died of a heart attack on Dec. 10, 2005 in Encino, CA. He could seen in such movies as *The Busy Body* (debut, 1967), *The Phynx*, *Lady Sings the Blues*, *Uptown Saturday Night*, *The Bingo Long Traveling All-Stars and Motor Kings*, *Silver Streak*, *Greased Lightning*, *Blue Collar*, *The Wiz*, *California Suite*, *The Muppet Movie*, *Stir Crazy*, *Bustin' Loose* (also producer, story), *Some Kind of Hero*, *The Toy*, *Brewster's Millions* (1985), *Jo Jo Dancer Your Life is Calling* (also director, writer, producer), *Critical Condition*, *See No Evil Hear No Evil*, *Harlem Nights*, *Another You*, *Lost Highway*, and the concert films *Richard Pryor: Live in Concert*, *Richard Pryor: Live on the Sunset Strip* (also producer), and *Richard Pryor: Here and Now* (also director). He was also one of the writers on the Mel Brooks' comedy *Blazing Saddles*. He is survived by his sixth wife and several children.

Ford Rainey, 96, Idaho-born character actor died on July 25, 2005 in Santa Monica, CA, following a series of strokes. He could be seen in such pictures as *White Heat*, *3:10 to Yuma*, *John Paul Jones*, *Flaming Star*, *Parrish*, *Two Rode Together*, *Kings of the Sun*, *The Sand Pebbles*, and *The Traveling Executioner*. He is survived by his wife, two sons, a daughter, and five grandchildren.

John Raitt, 88, California-born singer-actor, best known for creating the role of Billy Bigelow in the original 1945 Broadway production of *Carousel*, died of complications from pneumonia on Feb. 20, 2005 in Pacific Palisades, CA. Although he had bits in such movies as *Billy the Kid* and *Sunday Punch*, his only movie lead was recreating his stage role in the 1957 film of *The Pajama Game*. Survived by his wife and three children, one of whom is singer Bonnie Raitt.

Ron Randell, 86, Sydney-born screen, stage, and television actor, died of stroke complications on June 11, 2005 in Los Angeles. His movies include *Bulldog Drummond Strikes Back* (as Drummond), *The Sign of the Ram*, *The Loves of Carmen*, *China Corsair*, *The Mississippi Gambler*, *Kiss Me Kate* (as Cole Porter), *I Am a Camera*, *The She-Creature*, *The Story of Esther Costello*, *Davy*, *King of Kings*, *The Longest Day*, and *The Seven Minutes*. He is survived by his wife of 48 years, actress Laya Raki.

Thurl Ravenscroft, 91, Nebraska-born voice-over performer and singer, whose distinctive deep tones were used for Kellogg's "Tony the Tiger" commercials and the holiday perennial *How the Grinch Stole Christmas*, died on May 22, 2005 in Santa Ana, CA, of prostate cancer. He could be seen on screen in such movies as *Lost Canyon*, *The Glenn Miller Story*, *Rose Marie* (1954), *The Five Pennies*, and *It Happened at the World's Fair*, and heard in such pictures as *Cinderella* (1950), *Alice in Wonderland* (1951), *Daddy Long Legs* (1955), *101 Dalmatians* (1961), *Gay Purr-ee*, and *Snoopy Come Home*, and also provided his voice for many Disney Theme Park attractions. He is survived by two children.

Charles Rocket (Charles Claverie), 56, Maine-born comedian-actor, a one-time member of TV's *Saturday Night Live*, committed suicide by cutting his throat near his home in Canterbury, CT, on Oct. 7, 2005. His movie credits include *Fraternity Vacation*, *Earth Girls are Easy*, *How I Got Into College*, *Dances with Wolves*, *Hocus Pocus*, *Short Cuts*, *It's Pat*, *Dumb and Dumber*, *Tom and Huck*, and *Fathers' Day*. Survived by his wife and a son.

Richard Pryor

Maria Schell

Robert Wise

Teresa Wright

Nipsey Russell, 81, Atlanta-born comedian-actor, known for his humorous poetry, died of cancer on Oct. 2, 2005 in New York City. His few movies include *The Wiz* (as the Tin Man), *Wildcats*, *Posse*, and *Car 54, Where are You?* (repeating his role from the early '60s TV series). Survived by his cousins.

Maria Schell, 79, Vienna-born screen and television actress, known for such English-language features as *The Brothers Karamazov* and *The Mark*, died on Apr. 26, 2005 in Kaernten, Austria of unspecified causes. The older sister of actor Maximilian Schell, she made her motion picture debut in 1941 in the Swiss film *Streinbruch* (*Quarry*). Her other credits include *The Magic Box*, *The Heart of the Matter*, *The Hanging Tree*, *As the Sea Rages*, *Cimarron* (1960), *99 Women*, *The Odessa File* (which also featured her brother), *Voyage of the Damned*, *Superman*, and *Just a Gigolo*. In addition to her brother, she is survived by a son and a daughter.

Vincent Schiavelli, 57, Brooklyn-born character actor, best known for playing the "Subway Ghost" in the 1990 hit *Ghost*, died of lung cancer on Dec. 26, 2005 at his home in Sicily. His many other films include *Taking Off*, *One Flew Over the Cuckoo's Nest*, *Fast Times at Ridgemont High*, *Amadeus*, *Better Off Dead*, *Valmont*, *Waiting for the Light*, *Batman Returns*, *A Little Princess*, *Tomorrow Never Dies*, *Man on the Moon*, and *Death to Smoochy*. He is survived by his wife and two children.

Debralee Scott, 52, New Jersey-born actress, best known for her role of "Cathy Shumway" on the cult series *Mary Hartman, Mary Hartman*, died on Apr. 5, 2005 in Amelia Island, FL of natural causes. She also appeared in such motion pictures as *Dirty Harry*, *American Graffiti*, *Our Time*, *The Reincarnation of Peter Proud*, *Police Academy*, and *Misplaced*.

Simone Simon, 93, French actress, best known in America for her starring role in the 1943 horror film *The Cat People*, died on Feb. 22, 2005 in Paris of natural causes. Her other pictures include *Girls' Dormitory*, *Seventh Heaven* (1937), *The Devil and Daniel Webster* (*All That Money Can Buy*), *Mademoiselle Fifi*, *The Curse of the Cat People*, *Women Without Names*, and *The Extra Day*. No reported survivors.

Lane Smith, 69, Memphis-born screen, stage, and television character actor, died in Northridge, CA, on June 13, 2005 of Lou Gehrig's disease. His films include *Man on a Swing*, *Network*, *Between the Lines*, *Over the Edge*, *Resurrection*, *Prince of the City*, *Frances*, *Places in the Heart*, *Weeds*, *Air America*, *My Cousin Vinny*, *The Mighty Ducks*, *The Distinguished Gentleman*, *Son in Law*, *The Scout*, *Why Do Fools Fall in Love*, and *The Legend of Bagger Vance*. On television he was best known for playing President Richard M. Nixon on the mini-series *The Final Days* and Perry White on the series *Lois & Clark: The New Adventures of Superman*. Survived by his wife, his son, and a stepson.

John Spencer, 58, New York City-born screen and television character actor died of a heart attack on Dec. 16, 2005 in Los Angeles. At the time of his death he was still continuing his Emmy-winning role of chief of staff Leo McGary on the NBC series *The West Wing*. His movies include *WarGames*, *Sea of Love*, *Black Rain*, *Presumed Innocent*, *Forget Paris*, *Cop Land*, and *Twilight*.

Wendy Jo Sperber, 43, Los Angeles actress died on Nov. 29, 2005 in Sherman Oaks, CA, after a long battle with breast cancer. She appeared in such pictures as *I Wanna Hold Your Hand*, *1941*, *Bachelor Party*, *Back to the Future*, and *Moving Violations*. She is survived by a son, a daughter, her parents, two sisters, and a brother.

Harold Stone, 92, New York City-born screen, stage and television character actor died of natural causes on Nov. 18, 2005 in Woodland Hills, CA. He could be seen in such motion pictures as *The Harder They Fall*, *Somebody Up There Likes Me*, *The Wrong Man*, *The Garment Jungle*, *The Invisible Boy*, *Spartacus*, *The Chapman Report*, *X: The Man with the X-Ray Eyes*, *The Greatest Story Ever Told*, *The St. Valentine's Day Massacre*, *The Big Mouth*, *The Seven Minutes*, and *Mitchell*. Survived by two sons, a daughter, and four grandchildren.

Herbert I. Strock, 87, Boston-born filmmaker of such "B" pictures as *I Was a Teenage Frankenstein* and *How to Make a Monster* died of heart failure in Moreno Valley, CA, on Nov. 30, 2005. His other directorial credits include *Gog*, *Battle Taxi*, and *The Crawling Hand*. He is survived by his wife, three daughters, and two grandsons.

Lorna Thayer, 86, Boston-born character actress, best known as the waitress who confronted Jack Nicholson over a chicken-salad sandwich in the film *Five Easy Pieces*, died in Woodland Hills, CA, on June 4, 2005. She was also seen in such movies as *The Lusty Men*, *The Women of Pitcairn Island*, *Cisco Pike*, *Skyjacked*, *Buddy Buddy*, and *Nothing in Common*. Survived by two daughters and ten grandchildren.

Beverly Tyler (Beverly Jean Saul), 78, Scranton-born film actress died of a pulmonary embolism on Nov. 23, 2005 in Reno, NV. She could be seen in such pictures as *The Green Years*, *My Brother Talks to Horses*, *The Fireball*, *The Cimarron Kid*, *Voodoo Island*, and *Toughest Gun in Tombstone*. Survived by her son and three stepdaughters.

John Vernon, 72, Saskatchewan-born character player, best known for playing Dean Wormer in the 1978 hit comedy *National Lampoon's Animal House*, died in his sleep at his home in Los Angeles on Feb. 1, 2005, following complications from heart surgery. Among his other motion picture credits are *1984* (1956, as the voice of Big Brother), *Nobody Waved Goodbye*, *Point Blank*, *Justine*, *Topaz*, *Tell Them Willie Boy is Here*, *Dirty Harry*, *Charley Varrick*, *The Outlaw Josey Wales*, *Chained Heat*, *Fraternity Vacation*, and *I'm Gonna Git You Sucka*.

Coley Wallace, 77, boxer-turned-actor, best known for starring in the 1953 bio-pic *The Joe Louis Story*, died of heart failure on Jan. 30, 2005 in Manhattan. His three other films were *Carib Gold*, *Raging Bull* (once again appearing as Joe Louis), and *Rooftops*. He is survived by his wife and a daughter.

George D. Wallace, 88, New York City-born screen, stage and television actor died on July 22, 2005 in Los Angeles of complications from injuries he sustained earlier in the year after falling. His films include *The Big Sky*, *Arena*, *Man Without a Star*, *The Night of the Hunter*, *Forbidden Planet*, *Texas Across the River*, *The Towering Inferno*, *Lifeguard*, *Protocol*, *Punchline*, *Postcards from the Edge*, *Defending Your Life*, and *Minority Report*. Survived by his wife.

Kay Walsh, 93 British actress, perhaps best known for playing Nancy in her then-husband David Lean's 1948 film of *Oliver Twist*, died in London on Apr.16, 2005. Among her other movies are *In Which We Served*, *This Happy Breed*, *Vice Versa* (1948), *Stage Fright*, *Last Holiday*, *Young Bess*, *The Horse's Mouth*, *Tunes of Glory*, *Greyfriars Bobby*, *Circus World*, *A Study in Terror*, *Scrooge*, *The Ruling Class*, and *Night Crossing*. No reported survivors.

Herta Ware, 88, Delaware-born actress-singer died on Aug. 15, 2005 in Topanga, CA. Her films include *The Black Marble*, *2010*, *Cocoon*, *Slam Dance*, *Soapdish*, *Species*, *Practical Magic*, and *Cruel Intentions*. With her former husband Will Geer she founded Theatricum Botanicum. She is survived by three daughters and a son, nine grandchildren, and one great-grandson.

Ruth Warrick, 89, Missouri-born screen, stage and television actress, best known for her thirty-year stint as Phoebe Tyler on the daytime serial *All My Children*, died of complications from pneumonia on Jan. 15, 2005 in Manhattan. She made her motion picture debut playing the first wife of the title character in the 1941 classic *Citizen Kane*. Her other films include *The Corsican Brothers* (1941), *Obliging Young Lady*, *Forever and a Day*, *Journey Into Fear* (1943), *Mr. Winkle Goes to War*, *Daisy Kenyon*, *Arch of Triumph*, *Let's Dance*, *Roogie's Bump*, and *The Great Bank Robbery*. Survived by three children, one grandson, and six great-grandchildren.

Mel Welles, 81, New York City-born character actor, best known for playing the owner of *The Little Shop of Horrors* in the 1960 cult movie of the same name, died in Norfolk, VA, on Aug. 19, 2005, of heart failure. Among his other movies are *The Silver Chalice*, *Soldiers of Fortune*, *Abbott and Costello Meet the Mummy*, *Attack of the Crab Monsters*, *The Undead*, *The Brothers Karamazov*, *Dr. Heckyl and Mr. Hype*, and *Rented Lips*.

Onna White, 83, Nova Scotia-born choreographer, who received a special Academy Award for her work on the Oscar-winning musical *Oliver!*, died on Apr. 8, 2005 in West Hollywood. Her other movie credits were *The Music Man*, *Bye Bye Birdie*, *The Great Waltz* (1972), *1776*, *Mame*, and *Pete's Dragon*.

Paul Winchell, 82, New York City-born entertainer, best known for his work as a ventriloquist with his dummy Jerry Mahoney, died in his sleep at his home in Moorpark, CA, on June 24, 2005. He appeared in the features *Stop! Look! and Laugh!* and *Which Way to the Front?* and could be heard in countless animated films and television programs, notably in the *Winnie-the-Pooh* shorts as the voice of Tigger. He is survived by his wife, five children, and three grandchildren.

Robert Wise, 91, Indiana-born filmmaker, who won Academy Awards for directing and producing two of the most popular musicals of all time, *West Side Story* and *The Sound of Music*, died of heart failure in Los Angeles on Sept. 14, 2005, four days after his 91st birthday. Starting as an editor, he earned his first Oscar nomination for his work on *Citizen Kane*, and made his leap to director with *The Curse of the Cat People* in 1944. He would go on to direct such other pictures as *The Body Snatcher*, *Born to Kill*, *Blood on the Moon*, *The Set-Up*, *The House on Telegraph Hill*, *The Day the Earth Stood Still*, *Executive Suite*, *Helen of Troy*, *Somebody Up There Likes Me*, *Until They Sail*, *Run Silent Run Deep*, *I Want to Live!* (Oscar nomination as director), *Odds Against Tomorrow* (also producer), *Two for the Seesaw*, *The Haunting* (1963; also producer), *The Sand Pebbles* (Oscar nomination as producer), *Star!*, *The Andromeda Strain* (also producer), *The Hindenburg* (also producer), *Audrey Rose*, *Star Trek: The Motion Picture*, and *Rooftops*. He received an Irving G. Thalberg Award and the D.W. Griffith Award from the Directors Guild. He is survived by his wife, a son, a stepdaughter, and a granddaughter.

Robert Wright, 90, best known for his stage collaborations with his partner George Forrest (who died in 1999) on such musicals as *Song of Norway*, *Kismet*, and *Grand Hotel*, died on July 27, 2005 in Miami, FL, of natural causes. His work could be heard in such motion pictures as *Maytime*, *The Firefly*, *Dance Girl Dance*, and *I Married an Angel*.

Teresa Wright, 86, New York City-born screen, stage, and television actress, who won an Academy Award for playing Greer Garson's daughter-in-law in the 1942 film *Mrs. Miniver*, died of a heart attack on March 6, 2005 in New Haven, CT. She received additional Oscar nominations for her 1941 motion picture debut, in *The Little Foxes*, and for *The Pride of the Yankees*, the same year she would win for *Mrs. Miniver*. Her other films include *Shadow of a Doubt*, *Casanova Brown*, *The Best Years of Our Lives*, *Pursued*, *The Trouble with Women*, *Enchantment*, *The Men*, *Something to Live For*, *The Steel Trap*, *The Actress*, *The Search for Bridey Murphy*, *Escapade in Japan*, *The Restless Years*, *Hail Hero!*, *The Happy Ending*, *Roseland*, *Somewhere in Time*, *The Good Mother*, and *John Grisham's The Rainmaker*. She is survived by a son, a daughter, and two grandchildren.

INDEX

A